Personal Insolvency Law in Practice

CELEBRATING 150 YEARS
JORDANS

Personal Insolvency Law in Practice

Susan Morgan
Senior Manager, KPMG LLP

Neil Smyth
Partner, Taylor Wessing LLP

John Tribe
KPMG Lecturer in Restructuring
Kingston Law School, Kingston University

JORDANS

Published by
Jordan Publishing Limited
21 St Thomas Street
Bristol BS1 6JS

British Library Cataloguing-in-Publication Data

A catalogue record for this book is available from the British Library.

ISBN 978 1 84661 135 3

Typeset by Letterpart Ltd, Reigate, Surrey

Printed in Great Britain by CPI Antony Rowe, Chippenham and Eastbourne

INTRODUCTION

> 'Insolvency is not a very thrilling or amusing subject.'
> (Lord Mishcon, Hansard, 15 January 1985)

Personal insolvency and over-indebtedness is by its nature a pervasive subject that touches on many complex and difficult areas of life. The tentacles of the personal insolvency law that has been developed to address these difficulties stretch into many disparate areas of law. This makes this book a composite of, inter alia, property law, equity, finance law, securities law, and family law. To address this all encompassing quality of the subject thoroughly this personal insolvency law practitioners' text is a collaborative effort between three authors writing from three different perspectives. The author team comprises a practicing solicitor who specialises in insolvency law; an accountant technical and compliance manager at one of the big four accountancy firms; and finally, an academic who specialises in personal insolvency law (hereinafter collectively referred to as the 'author team'). We hope that this combined inter-disciplinary approach has made for a book that is more insightful and practically relevant than would otherwise be possible. We have tried to bring our respective experiences and perceptions to the project during the drafting of the entire text so that each chapter has been imbued with practical and scholarly elements. In the interests of our main audience, namely, insolvency lawyers and insolvency practitioners (hereinafter referred to collectively as 'the profession'), we have decided to include a question format throughout the text (where appropriate) and have attempted to answer these common questions in a practical manner. We have done this because we hope it will make the book easier to use in terms of navigation and practical relevance. Overall we also hope that this book goes some way to disprove Lord Mishcon's contention as cited above!

The book is divided into 27 chapters. This treatment provides guidance on the various personal insolvency procedures that are currently in force in England, Wales and Northern Ireland. The first five chapters examine the topic of personal debt together with the solutions that are available to debtors. In particular we examine the nature of personal debt, the key players who are involved in the personal insolvency landscape, the formal solutions that are available and, finally, we examine the assets that may be available to satisfy creditors.

This broad discussion is followed by more detailed procedural chapters relating to bankruptcy proceedings, Individual Voluntary Arrangements (IVAs) and low income solutions. A glossary and appendix of pertinent materials is also included.

This book includes a signposting system which begins in the first two chapters. The first chapter sets out the main solutions that are available to the users of the personal insolvency regime, namely, debtors and creditors and also includes a section on the best advice process as this is particularly important as part of the current personal insolvency zeitgeist. The key stakeholders, along with some other parties are looked at in detail in Chapter 2. An exposition of the different types of debt and assets then follows to complete this section of the book. These chapters should be read as background and a general introduction that serves as a signposting mechanism to a more thorough treatment elsewhere in the text.

We then move to the beginning of our thorough procedural treatment. In the second section of the book we have attempted to provide an exposition of the current personal insolvency procedures in England, Wales and Northern Ireland. This treatment encompasses a critical discussion of bankruptcy, individual voluntary arrangements, debt relief orders, county court administration orders, and deeds of arrangement. The majority of our treatment is spent on the bankruptcy jurisdiction (Chapters 6 to 20). We have included chapters on current vogue subjects, ie cross-border insolvency in the personal context (Chapter 20), and bankruptcy and the matrimonial home (Chapter 18), as well as more traditional discussions, such as deeds of arrangements and their successor individual voluntary arrangements (Chapters 23 to 27). We have also attempted to provide an examination of some of the newer low-income procedures, ie debt relief orders (Chapter 27).

Our treatment of procedures has been divided along chronological lines in terms of the timeline of the process, ie pre-petition, creditor's and debtor's petition, creditor communications, discharge, and such like. We hope that this flow aids the practical utility of the book.

We cannot of course refer to previous editions of this practitioners' text and the volume of case-law and legislation that has appeared in-between editions as this is the first edition. We can however highlight some of the key cases that have been of interest to the profession over the last couple of years or so and which have been discussed in our treatment. We have dedicated an entire chapter (18) to bankruptcy and the matrimonial home to reflect the importance of the House of Lord's opinion in *Stack v Dowden* [2007] UKHL17, 2 AC 432 and the Court of Appeal's recent decision in *Hill v Haines* [2007] EWCA (Civ) 1284; [2008] 2 WLR 1250 and *Jones v Kernott* [2011] UKSC 53. Chapter 20 contains a critical examination of the vexed issue of cross-border bankruptcy and the effect of the judgment in *Re HIH Casualty and General Insurance Ltd* [2008] UKHL 21, as it applies to personal insolvency law. Similarly, we have included a discussion of the new low-income personal insolvency procedures in Chapter 27, and the reform documents that led to these innovative new procedures. In so doing we hope that we have addressed some of the issues that are of interest to the profession at the current time. We hope we have also gone some way to address Mr Basil Montagu QC's contention that:

> 'Our professional duties consist, not merely in activity and in publication upon some practical part of professional knowledge, which repay themselves; but in availing ourselves of every opportunity to visit and strengthen the route and foundation of the science itself.'
>
> (Montagu, B. *Some Observations upon the Bill for the Improvement of the Bankrupt Laws* (1822) Butterworths, London, at page 73)

We must now turn to those whom we as the author team owe a debt. We would like to thank Sally Drever and Mary Kenny of Jordan Publishing Ltd, our publishers, for their immense patience and help in bringing this book to fruition. They have been tireless in their support and encouragement and for that we are very grateful indeed. A particular debt of gratitude is owed to Barbara McKenzie, Deborah Manzoori and Sarah Harmsworth who have painstakingly read and commented on various draft chapters of this book. We are grateful for their comments. We also have a number of individual acknowledgements. Sue Morgan (SM) would like to thank her friends and family for all their support. John Tribe (JT) would like to thank his colleagues at Kingston Law School for providing a vibrant research and teaching environment and Professors Graham, Fletcher, Walters, Finch, Rajak, Keay and Milman for their continued encouragement and support. John is also grateful to KPMG LLP and the partners of the firm, particularly John Milsom, for the continued support for the *KPMG Lectureship in Restructuring*.

Although recent anecdotal evidence suggests that increasing numbers of women are using formal insolvency solutions in this book for consistency the masculine includes the feminine and the singular includes the plural. The law that is contained in this book is correct up to and including the 31 December 2012 and covers in detail the 2010 amendment rules which came into force on 6 April 2010. Where possible we will provide materials that go some way to update the text via the www.jordansinsolvencylaw.co.uk website, pending any future editions. The author team would be grateful for any feedback on the form and contents of the book. The usual caveats apply in terms of the contents of the book. Any defects, shortcomings, errors or omissions are the collective responsibility of the author team.

SM, NS and JT
February 2013
Salisbury Square, London

CONTENTS

TABLE OF CASES

References are to paragraph numbers.

TABLE OF STATUTES

References are to paragraph numbers.

TABLE OF STATUTORY INSTRUMENTS

References are to paragraph numbers.

Chapter 1

PERSONAL DEBT

'Know, there are found, on whose dilated breasts
The heav'n-descended dove of pity rests,
Souls that delight with fostering smiles to cheer
The broken heart, and dry affliction's tear;
Pluck the wan debtor from his noisome den,
And launch him on the cheerful walks of men.'[1]

INTRODUCTION

1.1 This chapter looks briefly at the problem of personal debt in modern society and the options that an individual has, both formal and informal, that are available to alleviate the burden of personal over indebtedness. In order to assist the understanding of these options there is a summary of the various parties who may be encountered in each process. For formal solutions this chapter sets out briefly the statutory framework which governs each procedure. The specific provisions are covered in more detail in chapters 2 and 3.[2]

What options does an individual in debt have?

1.2 There are both formal and informal solutions available to alleviate debt problems. The following informal options are available to an individual in debt:

- consolidation loans and /or moving debt to the cheapest options available;
- conversion of short term unsecured debt to long term secured debt;
- debt management arrangements[3] (these are informal in England, Wales and Northern Ireland but are also available under a regulated scheme in Scotland);
- other *ad hoc* arrangements which can be made with individual creditors or groups of creditors depending on circumstances.

---

1 Epilogue written by R Cumberland Esq, published in *The Annual Register 1773*, by Edmund Burke.

2 The statutory framework is covered in chapter 3 and a detailed explanation of the various key players and their roles in the various procedures is covered in chapter 2.

3 The Insolvency Practices Council (IPC) in their annual report for 2010 have noted at p 4 that there were some 350,000 in existence at the time the report was written. This solution is also sometimes referred to as debt management plan.

A lot of different agencies including the Insolvency Service, the Citizens Advice Bureau (CAB)[4] and several money advice charities,[5] issue guidance on the options available to people in debt.[6]

1.3 There are also a number of different statutory regimes available in different parts of the United Kingdom including some recent additions to the options for relief. The following are the formal options that are available and the jurisdiction in which they can be used:

- Bankruptcy (England and Wales and Northern Ireland, this is called sequestration in Scotland).
- Debt relief orders (England and Wales) which is effectively a new route into bankruptcy for low income individuals and has also recently been introduced into Northern Ireland.
- Low income low assets (Scotland) which is a new route into sequestration for low income individuals.
- Individual voluntary arrangements (England and Wales and Northern Ireland).
- Voluntary trust deeds (Scotland).
- County court administration orders (England and Wales).
- Debt management schemes (Scotland).
- Deeds of arrangement (England and Wales and Northern Ireland).
- Enforcement restriction orders (pending introduction in England and Wales)[7].

THE 'BEST ADVICE' PROCESS

1.4 In order to determine which solutions are appropriate for an individual a number of factors need to be considered. The first factor is the cause or causes of the liquidity problems that the debtor is facing, and in particular whether they are short term or long term issues. In most circumstances there will almost certainly be a combination of causes and they all need to be identified in order

---

4 See www.citizensadvice.org.uk.

5 See the Consumer Credit Counselling Service (CCCS) at www.cccs.co.uk; Money Advice Trust at www.moneyadvicetrust.org.

6 See the Insolvency Service Guidance leaflet on alternatives to bankruptcy available at www.insolvency.gov.uk.

7 See further Consultation paper CP01/08 *Administration and Enforcement Restriction Orders: Setting the Parameters* (Ministry of Justice and Her Majesty's Court Service, January 2008).

to determine the best solution for each individual. The second and third factors are the level of debt and the available assets and income of the debtor. Finally, any other ongoing procedural ramifications on the debtor such as bankruptcy restrictions or occupational considerations, social or otherwise, need to be taken into account. These factors are considered in more detail below.[8]

What are the causes of an individual's debt problem?

1.5 The causes of unsustainable debts can be split into long term and short term problems and those that can be remedied and those that require a modification of behaviour. Any solution must address all these issues otherwise the debtor will simply find themselves back in the same situation again. Debtors will often be unaware of the real underlying causes and it is up to any adviser to identify these underlying issues rather than focussing on the 'straw which broke the camel's back' which is often blamed as the cause of the insolvency.[9] The key to identifying the causes is in determining the level of the deficiency (shortfall of assets over liabilities) and the period over which it has accrued. The makeup of the shortfall is also key as it may consist mainly of bank charges and interest or it could help to identify overspending and areas in which a change of behaviour may be required.

Does the level and type of debt matter?

1.6 The types of debt and creditors are dealt with in more detail in chapter 4 but for the purpose of determining the options available an overview of the level and type of debt is required. In addition to the legally recognised types of debt, individuals also need to consider how they manage 'priority' creditors, those creditors who must be paid to avoid more serious consequences but who have no formal preferential status or security. Some examples are listed below with the type of sanction that these creditors can exercise.

The total level of debt will also directly affect which debt solutions are available especially formal solutions some of which have statutory limits. These are set out in the table below.[10]

Priority Debts	**Potential Creditor Action**
TV Licence	Fine, distraint, imprisonment
Mortgage	Repossession, eviction
Secured Loan	Repossession, eviction
Rent	Eviction
Council Tax	Distraint, wage or benefit deductions, bankruptcy, fine or imprisonment

8 See **1.15–1.18.**

9 On the causes of personal insolvency and procedure use see J Tribe *Bankruptcy Courts Survey 2005: A Pilot Study* (2006).

10 Guidance on what to pay first can be found on various debt charity websites see the Consumer Credit Counselling Service (CCCS) at www.cccs.co.uk or Money Advice Trust at www.moneyadvicetrust.org.

Gas and Electricity	Supply disconnected
Water Rates	Supply disconnected
Magistrates' Court Fines	Distraint, wage / benefit deductions
Maintenance	Distraint, wage / benefit deductions
Hire Purchase or Conditional Sale	Repossession
Income Tax; National Insurance; VAT	Distraint or bankruptcy

Does the level of available assets and income matter?

1.7 Similarly the level of assets and available income will also directly affect the options available to the debtor as some processes require a minimum return to be paid to creditors. The reference to assets in this question includes all assets owned by the individual. The various types of assets and how they are treated are looked at in more detail in chapter 5. The term 'income' for these purposes refers to net income received from whatever source. Whether or not it is a sustainable source is very important in the decision process; for instance, overtime and other payments received which are variable should be left out of any long term calculations unless they are guaranteed as part of the payment package.

What other circumstances need to be taken into consideration during the advice process?

1.8 In addition to the financial circumstances of the debtor, any physical or mental incapacity or disability[11] needs to be considered pursuant to the Human Rights Act 1998. An example of this is the case of *Hunt and Fylde Borough Council*[12] which concerned a bankruptcy order where the debtor had Huntington's disease. The condition caused the debtor to become a recluse. Consequentially he fell into arrears with his council tax[13] and a bankruptcy order was made. District Judge Ashton annulled[14] the bankruptcy order and held that at the time the bankruptcy order was made the debtor was an incapacitated person pursuant to IR86.[15] Similarly, in *Haworth v Cartmel and Her Majesty's Revenue and Customs*[16] a bankruptcy order on a revenue petition was annulled because of the debtor's lack of capacity under the Mental Capacity Act 2005.[17] It was also found that HMRC should not have brought the petition because it was in breach of its obligations under the Disability Discrimination Act 1995.

There are also some occupational restrictions which may affect available solutions and these are discussed further below.

---

11 On incapacity in relation to bankruptcy see chapter 16.
12 [2008] BPIR 1368.
13 See chapter 4 for detailed information on the treatment of council tax arrears.
14 See chapter 10 for the treatment of council tax arrears in bankruptcy.
15 IR86, r 7.43.
16 [2011] EWHC 36 (Ch), [2011] BPIR 428.
17 Mental Capacity Act 2005, s 2.

What are the key principles of the Human Rights Act 1998 and when did they come into force?

1.9 The key principles of the Human Rights Act 1998 (HRA98)[18] are:

- the compatibility of existing legislation;
- the compatibility of new legislation;
- the compatibility of acts by public authorities.

1.10 The following sections all came into force when HRA98 received Royal Assent on 9 November 1998: s 18 (appointment of judges from the UK to the European Court of Human Rights), s 20 (powers of Ministers to make orders under the Act) and s 21(5) (substitution of other sentences for the death penalty). Section 19 (the duty of Ministers to produce a statement of compatibility in relation to new Acts) came into force on 24 November 1998. The rest of the HRA98 came into force on 2 October 2000.

What does compatibility with 'existing legislation' mean?

1.11 The HRA98[19] requires that all legislation – Acts of Parliament, regulations, rules and orders – so far as is possible, be read and given effect to in a way which is compatible with the rights enshrined in the HRA98. Every effort must be made to interpret legislation in accordance with those rights. Where there are two possible interpretations of a provision – one which is compatible with the Convention rights and one which is not – the one which is compatible must be adopted. The fact that a court may have interpreted legislation in a certain way before does not mean that, after the coming into force of the HRA98, it will continue to interpret the provision in that same way. Nor can that earlier interpretation be relied upon by a public authority.[20]

What does compatibility with 'new legislation' mean?

1.12 All new Bills passing through Parliament must carry a statement from a Minister that its provisions are compatible with the Convention rights.[21] If he cannot make such a statement, he must say so and ask Parliament to proceed with the Bill, which is then likely to be examined by the Human Rights Committee.

---

18 HRA98, s 3.

19 HRA98, s 3.

20 See D Moeckli, S Shah and S Sivakumaran (eds) *International Human Rights Law* (Oxford University Press, 2010). See also C Tomuschat *Human Rights between Idealism and Realism* (2nd edn, Oxford University Press, 2008).

21 HRA98, s 19.

What does compatibility of 'acts by public authorities' mean?

1.13 The HRA98 makes it unlawful for a public authority to act (or fail to act) in a way which is incompatible with a Convention right.[22] In the context of insolvency the HRA98 is likely to cover government bodies including HM Revenue and Customs, the Insolvency Service and local authorities. The courts must also act in a way which is compatible. Staff in public authorities should ensure that respect for human rights is at the core of their day to day work and that they act in a way which positively reinforces the principles of the Act. If a public authority's existing procedures are not compatible, it will need to implement new policies and procedures which are consistent with Convention rights. All aspects of the public authority's activities are covered, including:

- drafting rules and regulations;
- internal staff and personnel issues;
- administrative procedures;
- decision making;
- policy implementation;
- interaction with members of the public.

Which occupations have restrictions on available options for debt relief?

1.14 A number of professional bodies have restrictions on the type of solution available to individuals in financial difficulty.[23] In some cases the professional body has to be advised and agree to the terms of any proposed individual voluntary arrangement (IVA). Bankruptcy can result in any practising certificate being revoked.[24] A sample of some of the professional bodies is set out below. For other professions reference should be made to the relevant professional regulations.

- *The Institute of Chartered Accountants (England and Wales, Scotland or Northern Ireland)*: bankruptcy leads to mandatory expulsion. But expulsion is discretionary for IVAs. Re-admission after expulsion is possible but difficult. There are no funds available for member assistance.

---

22 HRA98, s 6.

23 In addition MI6 on their website (www.sis.gov.uk) note that aspirant spies who are subject to a bankruptcy order or IVA should not apply. See further http://bankruptcyandinsolvency.blospot.com/2009/11/bankrupt-bond-no-miss-moneypenny.html.

24 For more detailed guidance see R Wilmot 'Personal Insolvency of Professionals' (1994) *Insolvency Intelligence*, 7(2) pp 9–14; L Katz and S Tate 'Personal Insolvency and the Professional: Part 1' (2002) *Insolvency Intelligence*, No 15(8) pp 57–60, September and October 2002; and L Katz and S Tate Personal Insolvency and the Professional: Part 1' (2002) *Insolvency Intelligence*, No 15(9) pp 65–68, September and October 2002.

- *The Chartered Association of Certified Accountants*: the Council has an absolute discretion over expulsion which is therefore not mandatory and depends on the severity of the member's behaviour. Suspension is often ordered during the period of the bankruptcy or the IVA.

- *The Law Society (England and Wales, and Scotland)*: bankruptcy leads to mandatory suspension but this is discretionary for IVAs. The suspension is normally lifted after the bankruptcy order has been made to allow the debtor to continue to work but restricts his ability to handle client funds. There is also some financial assistance available from the Solicitors' Benevolent Association.

- *The Bar Council of England and Wales*: the Bar Standards Board has issued a guidance statement for barristers explaining what they should do if they are subject to bankruptcy proceedings or an IVA. All barristers, whether in practice or not, are required to report to the Bar Standards Board any bankruptcy or IVA proceedings.[25]

What are the main differences between formal and informal options?

1.15 The advantages and disadvantages between formal and informal options can be compared by looking at the following issues:

- the process of debt forgiveness and discharge from liability;

- the effect of a moratorium (a statutory breathing space during which further legal action cannot be taken without court consent);

- the accruing of interest on some debts;

- the effect on an individual's credit rating and the ability to obtain finance in the future;

- the restrictions imposed by the statutory regimes;

- the stigma of some options.

What is debt forgiveness?

1.16 Debt forgiveness describes a range of solutions which allow part or all of a debt to be written off in exchange for certain restrictions being imposed on the debtor. The restrictions vary depending on the option chosen. These are looked at in detail later. For instance, bankruptcy discharge releases the bankrupt from the majority of debts.[26] After discharge the debtor cannot be pursued for debts included in the bankruptcy proceedings. It is therefore

---

[25] The Bar Standards Board, Code of Conduct of the Bar of England and Wales (8th edn, 2004), para 905(c).

[26] IA86, s 281(1). See further chapter 11.

important to ensure that all debts are correctly listed. In informal proceedings the extent to which debts will be written off will have to be agreed with each creditor.

What is a moratorium?

1.17 A moratorium is a period during which all legal actions are suspended. This allows time for a permanent solution to be considered or implemented. In formal solutions a moratorium can be obtained at various stages. For instance, if an IVA is being proposed then the debtor has the opportunity to apply for an interim order[27] which provides this breathing space and once the IVA is in place none of the creditors can take further legal action.[28] Similarly in bankruptcy once the order has been made creditors cannot continue or commence any legal actions without court permission.[29] In addition the court has the power to suspend or stay proceedings once a bankruptcy petition has been filed in court.[30] In bankruptcy the moratorium relates to all of a bankrupt's property and not just the assets that are comprised in the estate.[31] Any moratorium does not generally affect the rights of a secured creditor[32] except where goods are held by way of pledge and such items may not be sold until permission is given in bankruptcy.[33]

In what circumstances can interest be frozen?

1.18 Interest is frozen in all formal options except for creditors with security. But there may be circumstances when even secured creditors are prepared to freeze interest payments for a period. Even for informal arrangements agreement can often be reached whereby interest charges are frozen while payments are made.

INFORMAL OPTIONS

What is debt consolidation?

1.19 Debt consolidation usually includes the process during which several loans or credit card balances are paid off and replaced with one loan. This can be unsecured but is likely to extend over a much longer period and can sometimes also include some additional element of security.

What does conversion of unsecured to secured loans include?

1.20 This includes any agreement or loan which relies on releasing equity in a property and is likely to extend the period over which repayments are made and

---

27 IA86, ss 252–254 or INO89, arts 226–228.
28 IA86, s 260 or 263D or INO89, art 236 or 237.
29 IA86, s 285(3) or INO89, art 258(3).
30 IA86, s 285(1) and (2) or INO89, art 258(1) and (2).
31 IA86, s 285(6) or INO89, art 258(6).
32 IA86, s 285(4) or INO89, art 258(4).
33 IA86, s 285(5) or INO89, art 258(5).

may be as long as 25 years depending on the age of the individual. The main sources of information on these products are media advertising and promotional material in newspapers, magazines, and the internet.

What is a debt management plan?

1.21 A debt management plan (DMP) in England and Wales is currently an informal agreement with creditors. A DMP can be proposed by the debtor but is usually proposed through the agency of a professional accountant or other advisors from organisations such as the CAB. No moratorium is available to stop any non-assenting creditor from pursuing the debt. The agreements can last for any period of time but are usually of quite short duration, they can last up to 10 years. The main providers of this solution are the CAB, PayPlan[34] and the National Debtline[35] which are funded by the government, charitable organisations or by the credit industry. In addition, there are profit-making organisations which advertise their services extensively. DMPs include arrangements both where payment is made in full and those where some debt relief is granted.

1.22 The Tribunals, Courts and Enforcement Act 2007 (TCEA 2007) empowers the Lord Chancellor (or his delegate) to approve a body of persons to operate 'approved schemes' in England and Wales which will allow creditor participation to be compelled and to allow a partial write-off of the debts (non-business debts only). These provisions have not yet been implemented but are in place ready for commencement once the consultation process has been completed.[36]

What are the advantages and disadvantages of informal options for debt relief?

1.23 Informal options often include co-operation between all of the following parties:

- The debtor.
- Any advisor (CAB or other debt advice service).
- The creditors.

1.24 Informal arrangements are generally more suitable for individuals:

- who are having debt problems but are expected to be able to make the normal repayments again in a few months; or
- who cannot afford the full monthly repayments but are expected to be able to afford a smaller regular amount each month.

---

34 See www.payplan.com.

35 See www.nationaldebtline.co.uk.

36 For more detail see chapter 27.

The first step in an informal arrangement is to work out how much the individual can afford to pay to creditors each month after essential living costs have been met. Once the available funds are known then each creditor must be contacted and the situation explained. Each creditor will need to agree to accept a lower payment until the financial situation improves when full repayments will be recommenced.[37]

1.25 The advantages of an informal arrangement are:

- they can often be set up quickly and for free by either the individual debtor, a CAB or other free advice agency;
- they can offer an effective solution for short term problems;
- they can offer an effective solution if the creditors are prepared to accept lower payments until normal repayments can be made again.

The disadvantages of an informal arrangement are:

- they are not enforceable and a creditor is not obliged to accept reduced payments and they can change their mind at any time;
- that creditors may accept reduced payments as a short-term measure and where it is clear that the debtor's situation is unlikely to change they are likely to want to consider alternative options.

1.26 In February 2013, the debt management protocol was launched which will assist debtors who pay for services in respect of managing their debt. Providers who sign up to the protocol will be required to provide consumers with information about other debt solutions and the availability of free debt advisory services. Those who sign up have also agreed to spread the cost of their services over the first 6 month period of any debt management plan agreed and a standing committee headed by the IS will report on the outcome of this protocol towards the end of the first 12 months of its operation.

FORMAL OPTIONS: ENGLAND AND WALES

Bankruptcy

What is a bankruptcy order?

1.27 Bankruptcy is a legal condition imposed on or sought by an individual who cannot pay their debts. In English and Welsh law bankruptcy is a legal state to which only individuals are susceptible. It can be imposed on an unwilling debtor by his creditors or upon unwilling creditors by a debtor

---

37 See generally the Insolvency Service Guidance leaflet on alternatives to bankruptcy available at http://www.bis.gov.uk/insolvency/publications.

seeking protection, without the need for agreement. Unlike informal options bankruptcy is governed by a statutory framework with the associated delegated legislation.

1.28 Bankruptcy is the most well known option for an individual with debt problems and the process in England and Wales is governed by the IA86 together with ancillary rules and regulations (see chapter 7). Similar legislation covers the process in Northern Ireland.

Bankruptcy is a court process with a moratorium on creditors being able to take or continue other recovery action. All of the bankrupt's assets vest in the trustee in bankruptcy and in most cases,[38] the Official Receiver (OR) or Scottish equivalent, the accountant in bankruptcy (AiB), initially act as trustee in bankruptcy.

If there are sufficient assets for distribution by way of dividend to be paid to creditors, then a licensed insolvency practitioner (IP) may be appointed to act as trustee instead. The trustee can be appointed either by a meeting of creditors[39] or by the Secretary of State,[40] or directly by the court.[41]

How does the bankruptcy process work?

1.29 Formal bankruptcy proceedings are commenced by 'petition' and the bankruptcy process can be broadly divided into five 'phases'.[42] First, before the petition is presented, secondly, after the petition has been presented but before the bankruptcy order is made, thirdly, after the making of the bankruptcy order but before the appointment of a trustee (whether this is an IP or the OR) in bankruptcy, fourthly after the appointment of the trustee and before the bankrupt's discharge, and fifthly the period after discharge.

1.30 Provided that the minimum conditions are met, namely, that the debtor is subject to the jurisdiction of the relevant courts (England and Wales, Northern Ireland[43] and Scotland),[44] that he has debts which exceed the current

---

38 On vesting see chapter 16.

39 IA86, s 292(1)(a).

40 IA86, s 292(1)(b).

41 IA86, s 292(1)(c).

42 On this chronological approach to bankruptcy see: S Baister 'Bankruptcy Basics – Statutory Demands' (2006) *Insolvency Law and Practice* No 55; S Baister 'Bankruptcy basics – applying to set aside bankruptcy statutory demands' (2006) *Insolvency Law and Practice* No 166; S Baister 'Bankruptcy Basics – Preparing the Bankruptcy Petition' (2006) *Insolvency Law and Practice* No 6; S Baister 'Bankruptcy basics – filing and issuing the petition' (2007) *Insolvency Law and Practice* No 23 p 5; S Baister 'Bankruptcy Basics – Before the Petition Is Heard' (2007) *Insolvency Law and Practice* No 23 p 45; S Baister 'Bankruptcy Basics – The Hearing of the Petition' (2007) *Insolvency Law and Practice* No 23 p 80; S Baister 'Who can apply for an annulment and on what grounds?' (2007) *Insolvency Law and Practice* No 23 p 115.

43 IR86, r 6.9 or IRNI91, r 6.09.

44 Bankruptcy (Scotland) Act 1985, s 9.

statutory minimum (for England and Wales this is £750,[45] for Scotland this is £1,500[46] for a debtor's petition and £3,000 for a creditor's petition) and that the petition is in order,[47] a bankruptcy order may be made.[48] The court has a wide discretion in deciding how to dispose of a bankruptcy petition, but once the petition is filed it cannot be withdrawn by the petitioner, whether creditor or debtor, without the permission of the court.[49]

What is the effect of the bankruptcy order?

1.31 As well as the appointment of a trustee and the 'vesting' of the bankrupt's property in the trustee, the bankruptcy order has a number of other effects. Restrictions are imposed on the bankrupt during the proceedings and creditors have limited remedies against the bankrupt and his property. The discharge from bankruptcy has the effect of releasing the bankrupt from the vast majority of his debts.

1.32 The principal effect of a bankruptcy order being made is that all property which the bankrupt owns at the commencement of the bankruptcy (called his 'estate')[50] is divested from him.

Initially, the OR acts as receiver and manager of the bankrupt's estate.

The estate later vests in the trustee in bankruptcy who is appointed to get in the property and distribute the proceeds among the debtor's creditors in accordance with the statutory priorities.[51]

The trustee may also claim after-acquired property. This is property acquired by the bankrupt after the commencement of the bankruptcy but before discharge.[52] This area is discussed in detail in chapter 17.

1.33 Before discharge the bankrupt is subject to a number of restrictions. There are limitations on a bankrupt's ability to obtain credit. The bankrupt cannot act as a director or be involved in the promotion, formation or management of a company without the leave of the court. A bankruptcy order

---

45 IA86, s 267(2)(a), (4) or INO89, art 241(2)(a) but this amount is currently subject to consultation.

46 Substituted by Bankruptcy (Scotland) Act 1993, s 36.

47 See chapters 7 to 9 for England and Wales and chapter 29 for Scotland.

48 The remedy is discretionary (see IA86, s 271 and IR86, r 6.25). However, a creditor with an unimpugned debt which the debtor is unable or unwilling to pay will generally be entitled to a bankruptcy order as a matter of right (*ex debito justitiae*). See for example *John Lewis v Pearson Burton* [2004] BPIR 70, *Nottingham City Council v Pennant* [2009] EWHC 2437 (Ch), *Harrison v Segger* [2005] EWHC 411 (Ch), [2005] BPIR 583, ChD.

49 IA86, s 266(2), IR86, r 6.32.

50 IA86, s 283.

51 IA86, s 305(2) or INO89, art 278(2).

52 IA86, s 307 or INO89, art 280.

disqualifies the bankrupt from holding some public offices although a number of restrictions have been relaxed in recent years.[53] This area is covered in detail in chapter 10.

1.34 Bankruptcy is a statutory contract between a debtor and his creditors which releases the bankrupt from the majority of the debts upon discharge from the proceedings.[54] After discharge the debtor is free once again to acquire and to own property in his own name. However, the property subject to the bankruptcy order remains vested in the trustee for distribution among the creditors.[55] Any property remaining after the creditors have been paid and the costs and expenses of the bankruptcy have been covered will revert to the debtor.[56]

1.35 Provided the debtor co-operates with his trustee he will be discharged from bankruptcy automatically at the end of one year from the date of the order being made, or earlier if the OR agrees.[57] His estate, however, remains vested in the trustee.[58] In addition a discharged bankrupt continues to owe a duty to his trustee. Prior to 1 April 2004 in England and Wales, discharge was usually granted automatically after 3 years, but in the post Enterprise Act 2002 regime, discharge is now granted after one year, or less in some circumstances. If the debtor fails to co-operate, or comply with his statutory obligation, the court can suspend the automatic discharge period,[59] and also has power to impose a number of restrictions on the debtor which will last for a period of between 2 and 15 years and will survive discharge.[60] This area is covered in detail in chapter 9.

1.36 The statutory framework for bankruptcy is set out in chapter 3. The key players are covered in detail in chapter 2. For bankruptcy proceedings they include the following:

- The bankrupt (ie the debtor).
- The creditors.
- The petitioning creditor (creditor's petitions only).
- The OR (England and Wales) or accountant in bankruptcy (Scotland).
- The trustee or trustee in bankruptcy.

---

53 CDDA86, s 11(1).
54 IA86, s 281(1) or INO89, art 255(1).
55 IA86, s 306 or INO89, art 279.
56 IA86, s 330(5) or INO89, art 303(5).
57 IA86, ss 278–280 or INO89, arts 252–254.
58 IA86, s 306; note, however, the exception created by s 283A which provides for re-vesting of his home in the bankrupt at the end of 3 years beginning with the date of the bankruptcy. See chapter 19.
59 Bankruptcy restrictions orders and undertakings are dealt with in IA86, Sch 4A, para 3.
60 Bankruptcy restrictions orders and undertakings are dealt with in IA86, Sch 4A, para 4.

- The relevant court: High Court, county court or sheriff court (Scotland).
- The registrars (High Court).
- The district judges (county court).
- The High Court judges (Appeal proceedings).
- The sheriff.

What are the advantages and disadvantages of bankruptcy?

1.37 The advantages of bankruptcy for debtors are:

- Creditors can no longer continue collection processes or undertake individual execution. Once the bankruptcy order is made, there is a moratorium in place and creditors cannot take any further legal action without leave of the court.
- The majority of debts are written off on discharge.
- Any contributions from income are based on the ability to pay.

1.38 The disadvantages of bankruptcy for debtors are:

- Bankruptcy orders are registered and until discharge there are restrictions on obtaining credit and the type of bank account that can be held.
- Post discharge an individual's credit rating will be affected for up to 6 years, and sometimes longer, making it more difficult to obtain loans, credit or a mortgage.
- An inability to continue certain types of professional activity.
- Loss of property and costs of administering the bankruptcy process.
- The stigma of the procedure.[61]

---

61 On the problem of stigma and bankruptcy: Insolvency Service Report (2008) *Attitudes to Bankruptcy revisited: A report produced by the Insolvency Service*. Available on the IS website at www.insolvency.gov.uk.

Debt relief orders

What is a debt relief order?

1.39 A debt relief order (DRO) is a relatively new process[62] introduced by the TCEA 2007.[63] It is administered by the OR[64] and is the equivalent of a bankruptcy order for individuals with low levels of debts,[65] few assets[66] and a low level of income.[67] The DRO procedure could almost be called '*bankruptcy-lite*'. The DRO is made on the application of the debtor[68] and the moratorium usually stays in force for a period of one year.[69] The creditors are notified of the order and have the opportunity to object to the order being made. The DRO 'stays' the enforcement of all debts and at the end of the moratorium, the debts are discharged.[70] Similar restrictions to those that apply to an adjudged bankrupt apply, including restriction orders and undertakings.[71]

1.40 The debt, assets and surplus income levels are a maximum of £15,000 (excluding unliquidated debts), £300 (excluding motor vehicles up to £1,000) and a maximum £50 per month. There is a fee of £90 which is substantially less than the cost of a bankruptcy petition and, to keep costs low, an application can only be made online via authorised intermediaries such as the CAB. A DRO cannot be made if one has been made in the previous 6 years, or the individual is already subject to an IVA or bankruptcy order. Chapter 27 covers the low income options in more detail.

1.41 The statutory framework for a DRO is set out in detail in chapter 3. The key players are dealt with in chapter 2 and for DROs they are:

- The debtor.
- The OR.
- The authorised intermediaries.
- The competent authorities.

---

62 See further D Milman 'Debt Relief Orders: A new option for the distressed individual debtor' (2009) Insolv.int. 22(10, 153-155).
63 TCEA 2007, s 108 introduces into IA86 Part 7A (ss 251A onwards) and Schs 4ZA and 4ZB.
64 IA86, s 251C.
65 IA86, Sch 4ZA, para 6.
66 IA86, Sch 4ZA, para 8.
67 IA86, Sch 4ZA, para 7.
68 IA86, s 251A(1).
69 IA86, s 251H.
70 IA86, s 251I.
71 IA86, s 251V, Sch 4ZB.

What are the advantages and disadvantages of a debt relief order?

1.42 The advantages for the debtor are:

- The cost of entry is lower than bankruptcy.
- Contributions from income are based on the ability to pay and are paid to the OR and not individual creditors.
- Once the DRO is in place, there is a moratorium and creditors cannot take any further legal action without leave of the court.
- Can be used if an IVA has failed as long as other criteria are met.
- The individual is designated a debtor and not a bankrupt so avoiding the stigma associated with bankruptcy.

1.43 The disadvantages for the debtor are:

- The maximum level of debt owed must be less than £15,000.
- Assets must not exceed £500 (excluding any motor vehicle valued at less than £1,000).
- Surplus income must be less than £50 per month.
- A DRO is the equivalent of a bankruptcy order. As DROs are included on the register of personal insolvency this will affect an individual's ability to get credit both before and after discharge. When the debtor is discharged the entry will be removed from the register (see chapter 10 for more details on the Individual Insolvency Register). A certificate can be requested as proof of discharge.

Individual voluntary arrangements

What is an IVA?

1.44 An IVA is a binding agreement between a debtor and their creditors[72] introduced as a statutory regime in the IA86. It is largely a court process. The arrangement has to be supervised by a licensed IP[73] with a majority of 75% in value of the creditors[74] (with exclusion of votes of 'connected' creditors in certain circumstances)[75] having approved the arrangement. A moratorium on the enforcement rights of dissenting creditors[76] comes into operation on

---

72 IA86, s 260(2)(b).
73 IA86, s 388(2)(c).
74 IR86, r 5.23(1).
75 IR86, r 5.23(4).
76 IA86, s 260(2)(b).

approval of the proposal. The proposal sets out the assets to be included in the arrangement together with the period and in what proportion the debts of the creditors are to be paid in full satisfaction of the debts.[77] The length of the arrangement can vary subject to creditor agreement but is usually 5 years.[78] The proposal should also set out the circumstances in which the IVA is deemed to have failed together with the consequences for the debtor.[79]

1.45 That statutory framework is set out in detail in chapter 3. The parties involved in an IVA are dealt with in detail in chapter 2 and for an IVA they are:

- The debtor.
- The adviser.
- The nominee.
- The supervisor.
- The court.

What options are available for switching between bankruptcy and an IVA?

1.46 There are two types of IVAs, a normal IVA and a fast track IVA. A fast track IVA can be proposed by an undischarged bankrupt under s 263B IA86. The OR must act as the nominee. The bankrupt is required to submit a proposal to the official receiver who will have 28 days to consider the contents. See chapter 23 for details on this procedure.

What are the advantages and disadvantages of an IVA?

1.47 The advantages of an IVA for a debtor are:

- It avoids the stigma of bankruptcy.
- The cost of the procedure should be cheaper than bankruptcy.
- The procedure can provide less harsh consequences for members of some professions (see **1.14**).

1.48 The disadvantages of an IVA for a debtor are:

- The procedure will often last longer than a bankruptcy.
- Some creditors insist on minimum returns (these are sometimes called 'hurdle rates') which are often higher than might otherwise be offered.

---

77 IR86, r 5.3.

78 IR86, r 5.3(2)(e).

79 Paragraphs 5.3 and 9.2 of SIP3, version 4 published April 2007.

- All IVAs are registered on the Personal Insolvency Register which is available to the general public.
- Credit reference status will be affected for up to 6 years.

County court administration order

What is a county court administration order?

1.49 This option is only available in England and Wales. Currently it can only be obtained if one or more creditors have obtained a county court judgment[80] against an individual.[81] A county court administration order (CCAO) is a court-based procedure which requires regular payments to whichever court has made the order. The total debts owed must not be more than £5,000[82] and the individual needs to be in receipt of enough regular income to make weekly or monthly repayments.

There is no fee for the order. Instead the court takes a small percentage towards its costs[83] from the money paid in. If regular payments are not made the court may cancel the order and the creditors will be allowed to resume normal collection procedures. If the individual's circumstances change an application can be made to the court to change the order.

The TCEA 2007 introduced a new regime by adding ss 112A–112AH[84] into the County Courts Act 1984 (CCA84). These new provision drastically change how the procedure will work but they have not yet been enabled. These changes are discussed in chapter 27 and the rest of this section refers to the existing legislation that remains in force.[85]

How does a current county court administration order work?

1.50 The debtor needs to apply to the court[86] who will make an order based on what the individual can afford. The order sets out how much has to be paid each month and how long the arrangement is to last. The court can require payments to continue until all the debts are paid in full, although some orders may only ask for part of the total debt to be paid. The order can also require the payments schedule to be reviewed at specified intervals. When the funds held by the court are distributed to the creditors a fee of up to 10% of the total debt can be charged by taking a percentage from each payment made to the creditors.

---

80 CCA84, s 112(1)(b).

81 CCA84, s 112(1)(b).

82 CCA84, s 112(1)(b), (4)(b) refers to the county court limit and limits s 112(4)(b); s 112(7) allows the Secretary of State to vary the limits set in s 112(4)(b).

83 CCA84, s 117(1)(a) sets the maximum court costs at 10p in £.

84 Tribunals, Courts and Enforcement Act 2007, Part 5.

85 CCA84, s 28 without any amendments.

86 Using form N270 which can be found under 'forms and guidance' on the Court Service website at www.hmcourts-service.gov.uk.

1.51 The statutory framework for a county court administration order as it currently stands is set out in detail in chapter 4. The role of each of these parties is discussed further in chapter 2:

- The debtor.
- The court.
- The district judge.

What are the advantages and disadvantages of a current county court administration order?

1.52 The advantages of a current CCAO for the debtor are:

- Only one monthly payment has to be made to the court and contributions from income are based on the ability to pay.
- If the debt limit is exceeded the court may set aside the order but it is not automatically invalidated.[87]
- Once the order is made, the debtor is protected by a moratorium and creditors cannot take any further legal action without leave of the court. However if creditors are not notified then they may not be bound and can appeal to the court.[88] There is no requirement that a county court administration order should stay any pending bankruptcy proceedings.[89]

1.53 The disadvantages of a current CCAO for the debtor are:

- If a payment is missed the arrangement is likely to fail.
- The individual must have at least one county court judgment and the total amount owed must be less than £5,000.[90]
- There is no definition or clarity in respect of the nature of a debt[91] that can be included in a CCAO. Consequently problems arise with the types of debts included or excluded from such orders. This becomes important in relation to mortgages, other secured debts, consumer credit debts, maintenance payments and community charges.[92] There are also differing views in respect of the inclusion of arrears and whether in some cases the entire sum is the debt or just the arrears (see chapter 28 for a more detailed explanation).

---

87 CCA84, s 112(5).
88 CCA84, s 114(1).
89 CCA84, s 114(3).
90 CCA84, s 112.
91 CCA84, s 112.
92 See further *Re Preston Borough Council v Riley and another* (1995) *The Times,* 19 April, CA.

- Usually payment in full is expected unless a composition order is made (see chapter 27 for a fuller explanation).
- The registration of administration orders is likely to affect an individual's ability to get credit as they are registered in the Register of County Court Judgments. The register is updated when the order is paid in full and will be marked as 'satisfied'. A request can be made for a certificate to prove the payments have been made.
- A landlord retains the right to distrain for rent.[93]

Deeds of arrangement

What is a deed of arrangement?

1.54 A deed of arrangement (DoA) is a court process and the provisions are set out in the Deeds of Arrangement Act 1914 (DAA 1914) and Deeds of Arrangement Rules 1925.[94] It is usually only recommended when the liabilities are less than £5,000, as the court fees increase with the level of debt. Only a simple majority in number and value is needed to approve the arrangement but a dissenting creditor is not bound and can continue to pursue their debt. Under the Deed, usually all or most of the assets of the debtor will have been assigned to the trustee of the arrangement for the benefit of the creditors generally, and the only practical remedy for a dissenting creditor would be to petition for the debtor's bankruptcy.

There have been no Deeds registered since 1999.[95]

How does a deed of arrangement work?

1.55 A DoA is void unless it is registered with the Registrar of Bills of Sale within 7 days of execution.[96] A copy also needs to be sent to the Registrar of the local county court of the district in which the debtor resides.[97] The trustee of the arrangement is required to obtain and maintain security to the value of the assets available for distribution.[98]

What are the advantages and disadvantages of a deed of arrangement?

1.56 The advantages of a DoA are:

- Avoids the stigma of bankruptcy.

---

93 CCA84.
94 SR & O 1925/795.
95 See the Insolvency Service website at http://www.insolvency.gov.uk/.
96 DAA 1914, s 2.
97 DAA 1914, s 10.
98 DAA 1914, s 11.

- A DoA only requires the approval of a simple majority of creditors in number and value.
- In some circumstances they can be a cheaper and simpler solution because no report to court is required and it is not necessary to call a meeting of creditors.
- The act of entering into a deed of arrangement is no longer allowed as the basis of a bankruptcy petition. This reduces the threat of a dissenting creditor petitioning for bankruptcy in circumstances where they were previously unable to do so.

1.57 The disadvantages of a DoA are:

- The maximum level of debt owed must be less than £5,000.
- A dissenting creditor retains the right to take action against the debtor.
- DoAs can sometimes be relatively expensive.

Enforcement restriction orders

1.58 Enforcement restriction orders (ERO) have not yet been implemented. The ERO scheme was enacted in Chapter 2 of Part 5 of the TCEA 2007 which inserts new sections after Part 6 on administration orders into the County Courts Act 1984. There was extensive consultation with both the financial advice and credit sectors during the development of this new scheme. The scheme is aimed specifically at debtors with unexpected short-term financial problems who are expected to see improvements within a year. Other options exist for those with more long-term problems. These would include options such as the reformed CCAO, which is contained in Chapter 1 of Part 5 of the TCEA 2007.

What is an enforcement restriction order?

1.59 The ERO will impose certain requirements on the relevant creditors and the debtor as the court considers fair and equitable. These orders are not meant to last for more than 6 months but can last a maximum of a year[99] with the court having flexibility on shortening or extending the period as required. The ERO provides a moratorium on interest charges and collection, and if the debtor is already subject to another debt management procedure then this will automatically cease.[100] The TCEA 2007[101] sets out the need to ensure that a debtor is only subject to one procedure at a time. The criteria for obtaining an ERO are at least two qualifying debts with the debtor unable to pay at least one of them. The concept of 'qualifying debts' is introduced which excludes

---

99 TCEA 2007, s 107 inserts a new s 117H into the CCA84.

100 TCEA 2007, s 107 inserts a new s 117I into the CCA84.

101 TCEA 2007, Part 5, Chapter 2.

business debt,[102] secured debt and other amounts not provable in bankruptcy proceedings, such as criminal fines, student loans, and child support payments.

1.60 The parties involved in an ERO will be:

- The debtor.
- The creditors.
- The intermediary.

Each of these parties is discussed in detail in chapter 2.

What are the advantages and disadvantages of an ERO?

1.61 The advantages for the debtor are foreseen as:

- Contributions from income are based on the ability to pay and are paid to the court.
- Once the order is in place, there is a moratorium and creditors cannot take any further legal action without leave of the court.

1.62 The disadvantages for the debtor will depend largely on the entry levels into the process. These have not yet been published.

FORMAL OPTIONS: NORTHERN IRELAND

Deeds of arrangement

How is a deed of arrangement different in Northern Ireland?

1.63 As in England and Wales a deed of arrangement (DoA) is a court process but for Northern Ireland the provisions are currently set out in the Insolvency (Northern Ireland) Order 1989 and the Insolvency (Northern Ireland) Rules 1991. As in England and Wales the provisions are seldom used.[103]

Other personal insolvency procedures in Northern Ireland

1.64 Bankruptcy, debt relief orders and IVAs are almost identical in Northern Ireland however the basis of the legislation is slightly different. The statutory framework for each is set out in chapter 3.

---

102 Clause 89 of the Bill inserts a new s 117B into CCA84.

103 See the NI statistics at www.insolvency.gov.uk/otherinformation/statistics/201102/table6.pdf.

FORMAL OPTIONS: SCOTLAND

1.65 The provisions for formal insolvency procedures have historically always differed in Scotland with the use of different legal terminology.[104] This section examines sequestration and the new low asset, low income route (LILA) into the process together with the other formal alternatives which are a protected trust deed or a managed debt arrangement scheme (DAS). Each of these options is looked at in turn.

Sequestration

How is sequestration different from bankruptcy?

1.66 Sequestration is the Scottish equivalent of bankruptcy and is a court procedure administered by a trustee. The process allows the appointment of an interim trustee whose function is to preserve the debtor's estate until the appointment of a trustee. The role of the trustee is to collect in and sell the assets of the debtor and to distribute the proceeds among the creditors in the prescribed order of priority.

In sequestration the equivalent of a bankruptcy order is an award of sequestration which is similarly made by the court on petition by either a creditor or the debtor. The petition can nominate an interim trustee, who may subsequently be confirmed as trustee at the statutory meeting of creditors. This meeting must be held within 60 days of the date of the award.

The sheriff formalises the appointment by the issue of an Act and Warrant. Both the interim trustee and the trustee must be a licensed IP.

1.67 In cases where no trustee is nominated the AiB automatically becomes the interim trustee and trustee. The role of the AiB is explained in detail in chapter 3. The AiB is normally required to notify creditors of the decision as to the need for a statutory meeting of creditors within 60 days of the date of the award.

The AiB also outsources the administration of these cases under agency agreements. The key players are similar to bankruptcy but include the following and they are each covered in more detail in chapter 3:

- The bankrupt.
- The AiB.

---

[104] On Scottish personal insolvency generally see D McKenzie Skene (1999) *Insolvency Law in Scotland*, pp 423 and xlii, T&T Clark; D Mackenzie Skene 'Forgiving our debtors: a Scottish perspective on a fresh start for debtors (2005) *International Insolvency Review*, 14(1), pp 1–26; D McKenzie Skene 'Morally bankrupt? Apportioning blame in bankruptcy' (2004) *Journal of Business Law*, pp 171–218.

- The trustee.
- The court.
- The creditors.

What are the advantages and disadvantages of a sequestration?

1.68 The advantages are:

- Contributions from income, if any, are based on the ability to pay.
- Once the order is in place, there is a moratorium in place and creditors cannot take any further legal action without leave of the court.

1.69 The disadvantages are:

- The award of sequestration is registered and until discharge there are restrictions on obtaining credit.
- Post discharge an individual's credit rating will be affected for up to 6 years making it more difficult to obtain loans, credit or a mortgage.

Low income low asset (LILA)

What is a LILA?

1.70 A LILA is a relatively new route into bankruptcy in Scotland which is administered by the AiB. It is specifically designed for individuals located in Scotland with low levels of debts and few assets in Scotland. The order is made on the application of the debtor and stays in force for a period of one year.

1.71 The statutory framework for a LILA is set out in detail in chapter 3. The key players in a LILA are the same as for sequestration and they are covered in chapter 2.

What are the advantages and disadvantages of a LILA?

1.72 The advantages are:

- Low cost.
- All the other advantages of sequestration.

1.73 The disadvantages are:

- Assets must not exceed £10,000 and no single asset should be worth more than £1,000 and any asset that does not vest in the trustee should be disregarded.

- All the disadvantages of sequestrations.

Voluntary trust deed

1.74 In Scotland another alternative solution is a trust deed. A trust deed[105] is a voluntary agreement between a debtor and his creditors to repay part of what they are owed. As with bankruptcy and sequestration, a trust deed transfers the debtor's rights to the assets that he owns to a trustee. Similarly the role of the trustee is to dispose of them and pay the proceeds to the creditors. A trust deed usually also includes a contribution from income for a specified period. This is normally 3 years but does vary and is not usually longer than 5 years. The trustee must also be a licensed insolvency practitioner (see chapter 3 for more detail). An ordinary trust deed is not binding on creditors unless they agree to its terms including the level of fees to be charged but a trust deed can become protected and this process is explained below.

What is a 'protected trust deed'?

1.75 A protected trust deed is a trust deed that is binding on all creditors. This status is obtained by giving the creditors an opportunity to object and provided the debtor subsequently complies with the terms of the arrangement the trust deed remains protected and the creditors can take no further action against the debtor. A protected trust deed also prevents a debtor from petitioning for their own bankruptcy or for a debt payment programme under the DAS. If a debtor acquires any new debts after signing a trust deed, there is no protection from the new creditors who can take enforcement action to collect their debt.

1.76 The current statutory framework is set out in the Protected Trust Deeds (Scotland) Regulations 2008.[106] Prior to the introduction of these regulations the framework for administering a trust deed was based on the requirements for a sequestration and was therefore more akin to an English bankruptcy than an IVA. The key players are covered in detail in chapter 2 and for trust deeds include the following:

- The debtor.
- The AiB.
- The trustee.
- The creditors.

What are the consequences of signing a trust deed?

1.77 A debtor must be given independent advice before signing a trust deed and any advisor must ensure that the debtor fully understands the

---

[105] BSA85, s 72, Sch 5.
[106] SSI 2008/143.

consequences of signing a trust deed. Any proposed trustee must also ensure that debtor has been given advice on all the available options before allowing the debtor to sign. The various alternatives explained to the debtor must include a debt management plan and a debt payment plan under DAS. The trustee must also provide every debtor with a copy of the Scottish Government's debt advice and information package.[107]

1.78 The consequences of entering a trust deed are very similar to bankruptcy and include potential long term problems with their credit rating and some occupations have restrictions. If a trust deed fails to become protected the creditors can make the debtor bankrupt. As regards costs the trustee is entitled to charge for their work and the trustee must give the debtor an indication of the quantum that will be charged before the trust deed is signed. Every debtor can choose a trustee and will usually take into account the amount of fees expected to be charged.

What are the advantages and disadvantages of a trust deed?

1.79 The advantages are:

- There is a moratorium.
- Contributions are calculated on ability to pay.
- Avoids the stigma of sequestration.

1.80 The disadvantages are:

- The trust deed is registered which will affect the individual's credit rating.

The debt arrangement scheme (DAS)

1.81 The DAS is a statutory scheme[108] administered by the Scottish Executive. The scheme was designed to give debtors time to pay by reducing the threat of court action. The scheme is delivered by approved money advisers[109] at local authority money advice units or Citizens Advice Scotland[110] and is free of charge. The scheme can protect a debtor's assets, including their home (as long as any mortgage payments are kept up to date).

What advantages does a Debt Arrangement Scheme offer?

1.82 DAS offers the following advantages:

- Free debt advice including how to manage their finances.

---

107 Available at: www.aib.gov.uk/guidance/debt-advice-and-information-package.

108 Debt Arrangement and Attachment (Scotland) Act 2002, s 1 and Debt Arrangement Scheme (Scotland) Regulations 2004, SSI 2004/468.

109 SSI 2004/468, regs 7–11.

110 See www.cas.org.uk.

- Protection from court enforcement, bankruptcy and loss of the matrimonial home (provided mortgage or rent payments are kept up to date).

- The opportunity to freeze interest, fees and charges on the debt, if the DAS debt payment plan is approved.

- The provision of a breathing space and extra time to pay.

- Continued support throughout the process especially if the individual's circumstances change.

- The scheme is often free for people paying debts under an approved debt payment programme (DPP). However, this needs to be confirmed with the chosen money adviser, prior to entering into any agreement.

- For the purposes of DAS, the individual must have more than one debt which they want to pay off.

- DAS is not sequestration and so can avoid any associated stigma.

Under a DAS, a single regular payment is made to an approved payments distributor.[111] If the payments are made in accordance with the agreed plan the creditors cannot take enforcement action on the debt. Similar protection is afforded to an individual who has intimated an intention to apply for a debt payment programme or has an application awaiting approval. DAS also freezes interest, fees and charges on the debt from the date the DAS debt payment plan is approved.

What was the purpose of introducing debt arrangement schemes?

1.83 The Scottish Government (then the Scottish Executive) introduced the procedure because of the increasing levels of personal over indebtedness in Scotland.

The Debtors (Scotland) Act 1987 had already introduced two forms of 'diligence stoppers' (prevention of court action). These are time to pay directions and time to pay orders; however, these were only available from the courts and only applied to single debts so were of little use to people with multiple debts.

As a result this third 'diligence stopper' was introduced, a scheme whereby those with more than two debts could get help but didn't have to go through the courts. As a result the debt arrangement scheme was introduced.

---

[111] SSI 2004/468, reg 13(3), Sch 5.

How does a debt arrangement scheme work?

1.84 The initial requirement is to locate a money adviser using the search facilities on one of the money advice agencies.[112] Their advice is often free, but some money advisers may charge for their service. The money adviser will talk through the individual's problems and suggest the options available for dealing with the debt. DAS should always be one of the options considered by an over indebted Scottish debtor.

1.85 If the DAS is the preferred option the money adviser will suggest a DAS approved money adviser[113] who will apply for a debt payment programme (DPP). Under DAS, a single regular payment is made to an approved payments distributor.[114] If the agreed payments are made the creditors cannot carry out any further enforcement action.[115] A similar moratorium applies when an individual has intimated an intention to apply for a debt payment programme or has an application awaiting approval. DAS also freezes interest, fees and charges from the date the DAS payment plan is approved.

Eligibility for the scheme

1.86 Eligibility for a DPP under DAS has the following conditions:

- The individual in debt must live in Scotland (it does not matter where the creditors are based).[116]
- The individual must have more than one debt[117] (If there are two or more debts to a single creditor, such as 2 years' arrears of council tax, which counts as a multiple debt).
- The individual must not already be in a trust deed or protected trust deed[118] or be sequestrated,[119] bankrupt[120] or subject to a bankruptcy restrictions order[121] or undertaking.

Who are the key players involved in a DAS?

1.87 The following parties are involved in a DAS and more detailed explanations can be found in chapter 3:

---

112 For example Money Advice Scotland (www.moneyadvicescotland.or.uk).
113 SSI 2004/468, reg 7.
114 SSI 2004/468, reg 13(3), Sch 5.
115 SSI 2004/468, reg 35.
116 SSI 2004/468, reg 20(1).
117 SSI 2004/468, reg 21(1).
118 SSI 2004/468, reg 21(2)(b).
119 SSI 2004/468, reg 21(2)(c).
120 SSI 2004/468, reg 21(2)(d).
121 SSI 2004/468, reg 21(2)(e).

- The debtor in a DAS is someone who has personal debts and has agreed to a debt payment programme (DPP) with a DAS approved money adviser.

- The DAS approved money adviser[122] provides debt management advice to the debtor. Unlike other money advisers they must have completed additional training and hold a certificate issued by MATRICS (a Scottish Executive funded partnership between Money Advice Scotland and Citizens Advice Scotland).

- The creditor in a DAS is someone who is owed money and has agreed or is obliged to accept payments under a DPP.

- The DAS administrator is responsible for maintaining the DAS register which contains details of debt payment programmes, the approval of money advisers and payments distributors, and the approval of a DPP.

- The AiB is currently the DAS administrator on behalf of the Scottish Ministers.[123]

- The payments distributor is required to assist the money adviser on payment distributions by distributing the available sums, collecting voluntary contributions and reporting on progress to the money adviser and creditors in accordance with the DPP.[124]

---

[122] SSI 2004/468, reg 8.
[123] SSI 2004/468 reg 2(1).
[124] SSI 2004/468 reg 15(1).

Chapter 2

KEY PLAYERS

'One must have some sort of occupation nowadays.
If I hadn't my debts I shouldn't have anything to think about.'[1]

INTRODUCTION

2.1 This chapter examines each of the key players involved in the personal insolvency solutions. First we examine those players that are generic followed by those that are specific to the different jurisdictions ie England, Wales, Northern Ireland and Scotland. This chapter also describes each of the offices that an IP can hold separately, together with details of the relevant court officials that play a role in each of the jurisdictions in the UK. There is also a brief explanation of associates and connected parties for the purposes of formal personal insolvency proceedings at the end of the chapter.

GENERIC TERMS

Who and what is a 'debtor'?

2.2 Debtor is the term used for any individual who owes money to a creditor. They may or may not also be a bankrupt or be subject to some other formal or informal procedure.

Who and what is a 'bankrupt'?

2.3 A bankrupt is any individual who has been made bankrupt as a result of either a debtor's or creditor's petition being made by the court. This term also applies to individuals subject to sequestrations in Scotland. A bankrupt is either discharged or undischarged which indicates their current status and whether restrictions still apply to them.

What is a creditor?

2.4 A creditor is the term used to describe a person or entity, to whom a debt is owed; this can include *inter alia*, the government, banks, hire purchase companies, corporations, small businesses, individuals, and partnerships. In fact anyone who can prove that they are owed a sum of money by the debtor, whether or not they have security for that debt can be termed a creditor. The role of the creditor as a potential member of a creditors' committee is covered

---

1 Oscar Wilde (1893) *A Woman of No Importance* (Penguin Books, London, 1996).

in more detail later in this chapter. The various types of creditor and the effect of any security they might hold on their status is also considered.

What is a 'partnership'?

2.5 For the purposes of insolvency legislation a partnership is treated as a separate entity from the individuals or other entities subject to any partnership agreement although the legal status of partnerships varies between Scotland, and England and Wales. There are a number of types of partnership including unlimited, limited, and the more recent limited liability partnerships. The remedies and processes available to partnerships are dealt with in chapter 22.

INSOLVENCY PRACTITIONER

Who and what is an insolvency practitioner ('IP')?

2.6 The term IP is used in the IA86 to denote a person 'qualified to act' under s 390 IA86 in relation to a debtor's affairs. Section 388 IA86 sets out the meaning of 'act as insolvency practitioner' and the offices which must be held by an IP. An IP is not required to have previous qualifications as an accountant or lawyer but this is usually the case. All IPs must be licensed under Part XIII of IA86 and the Insolvency Practitioners Regulations 2005.[2] A 'person' is only qualified to act if he or she is an individual.[3] This means that a firm or organisation cannot be qualified: only individuals who are licensed and hold the necessary enabling bond[4] can accept appointments.

What authorisations are required for an insolvency practitioner?

2.7 In 1986 the initial qualification was appropriate experience and membership of one of the recognised professional bodies (RPB) which are discussed in more detail below. This process became known as 'grandfathering'. However, from 1 April 1990, reg 6 and Sch 1 of the IPR90[5] introduced a minimum level of academic qualifications and a new examination set by the Joint Insolvency Examination Board (JIEB). These requirements have changed over time and the current requirements are now set out in Part 2 IPR05.[6] These are summarised below. The requirements are split between those individuals who have not previously been authorised and those who have and are making a re-application. In summary the requirements are:

- To demonstrate that the individual is a 'fit and proper' person.[7]

---

2 SI 2005/524 or INO89, art 349.

3 Corporate or firm appointments have been mooted at different times but have been rejected because of the potential lack of accountability for example see further The Insolvency Practices Council (IPC) in their annual report for 2010 have noted at p 8, para 1.

4 IPR05, Part 3 or IPRN06, Part 3.

5 SI 1990/439 now replaced by the IPR05.

6 SI 2005/524.

7 IPR05, reg 6 or IPRN06.

- To have appropriate education, training and experience.[8]

Can someone from another EU country qualify to act as an Insolvency Practitioner in the UK?

2.8 Applications can be made by suitably qualified people to the Secretary of State for permission to act as an IP under the EU Directive 2005/36. In the context of IP the Directive provides that practitioners who have acquired professional qualifications in one relevant state (members of EEA and Switzerland) must have access to that profession in the other relevant states. In practical terms an applicant from a relevant state, who wishes to become established in another state (the host state), will be able to apply for authorisation to a competent authority and that authority will be required to recognise equivalent professional qualifications obtained in the applicant's home state or other relevant state where he is authorised to act in that state.[9]

What offices can an Insolvency Practitioner hold in personal insolvency proceedings?

2.9 An IP can hold the following offices in relation to personal insolvents and each of these are covered briefly in this chapter in the following order:

- Interim receiver.
- Receiver and manager.
- Trustee.
- Special manager.
- Nominee.
- Supervisor.

INTERIM RECEIVER

Who can appoint an interim receiver and for what period?

2.10 The court can appoint the OR,[10] an IP[11] or any other suitable person[12] as an interim receiver at any time after a bankruptcy petition has been presented if it is felt that the debtor's property is at risk from dispersal.[13] The interim

---

[8] IPR05, regs 7 and 8 or IPRN06.
[9] European Communities (Recognition of Professional Qualifications) Regulations 2007, SI 2007/2781 implement in part the EC Directive 2005/36.
[10] IA86, s 286(1).
[11] IA86, s 286(2).
[12] IA86, s 286(3).
[13] *Gibson Dunn and Crutcher v Rio Properties Inc* [2004] EWCA Civ 1043, [2004] BPIR 1203.

receiver only remains in office for the period between the filing of the petition and either the dismissal of the petition or the making of the bankruptcy order.[14]

What is the role and function of an interim receiver?

2.11 The role of the interim receiver is to take immediate possession of the debtor's estate or that part of the estate to which the court order applies.[15] The debtor is required to provide the interim receiver with an inventory of his property and provide any other information as required by the interim receiver. The interim receiver may also require the debtor to attend on him for the purposes of carrying out his duties.[16] These requests must be reasonable.[17] References to the debtor's property include all of the debtor's property whether or not it would be comprised in the debtor's estate if he were adjudged bankrupt.[18]

RECEIVER AND MANAGER

Who can act as a receiver and manager, and for what period?

2.12 Between the making of the bankruptcy order and the appointment of the trustee the OR is automatically the receiver and manager of the estate[19] unless a special manager is appointed.[20]

What is the role and function of a receiver and manager?

2.13 The main purpose of this role is to protect the estate pending the appointment of the trustee in bankruptcy. The receiver and manager has the same powers as if appointed by the High Court (England and Wales)[21] and has the power to sell or otherwise dispose of any perishable goods which are likely to diminish in value.[22]

2.14 The OR is not liable to any person in respect of any loss or damage resulting from the seizure or disposal except in so far as that loss or damage is caused by his negligence. The receiver and manager also has a lien on the property, or the proceeds of its sale for any expenses incurred in connection with the seizure or sale.[23]

---

14 IA86, s 286(6).

15 IA86, s 286(4). See generally *Re Baars* [2002] EWHC 2159 (Ch), [2003] BPIR 523.

16 IA86, s 366. Also s 367 IA86, sets out the court's enforcement powers and s 368 extends these two sections to any interim receiver.

17 IA86, s 286(5).

18 IA86, s 286(8).

19 IA86, s 287(1).

20 IA86, s 370.

21 IA86, s 286(3).

22 IA86, s 287(2)(b).

23 IA86, s 287(4)(b).

TRUSTEE

What is the role and function of a trustee?

2.15 The role of trustee is the term used for the office holder in a number of formal procedures relating to individuals. These include bankruptcy,[24] sequestration,[25] DROs, and trust deeds.[26] The role of interim trustee[27] is also available in some sequestrations when assets need to be safeguarded between petition and sequestration[28] in much the same way as an interim receiver can also be appointed by the court in England and Wales.

2.16 The role of trustee is essentially the same in each of these proceedings, namely, to collect in and distribute the assets of the debtor or bankrupt. In each of these proceedings the assets belonging to the debtor vest in the trustee[29] at the date of appointment.

SPECIAL MANAGER

Who can appoint a special manager?

2.17 The court may, on an application appoint any person to be the special manager[30] over:

- a bankrupt's estate; or
- the business of an undischarged bankrupt; or
- the property or business of a debtor in whose case the OR has been appointed interim receiver under s 286 IA86.

2.18 An application can be made by the OR or the trustee of the bankrupt's estate in any case where it appears that either of these office holders requires another person to manage the estate, property or business. Someone appointed under this provision is required to provide security to the court[31] and prepare and keep accounts of all transactions as prescribed.[32]

---

24 IA86, s 292.
25 BSA85, s 2(1).
26 Protected Trust Deeds (Scotland) Regulations 2008, SSI 2008/143, reg 5.
27 BSA85, s 2(6A).
28 See chapter 29 for a fuller explanation.
29 For bankruptcy see IA86, s 306 or NIO89, art 279. See further chapter 18.
30 IA86, s 370.
31 IA86, s 37(5)(a).
32 IA86, s 37(5)(b)

What is the role and function of a special manager?

2.19 The role of special manager is to assist the OR or trustee with dealing with the bankrupt's estate normally because the nature of the property or business, or the interests of creditors generally require someone to manage it on a day to day basis.

NOMINEE AND SUPERVISOR

Who can nominate or appoint a nominee or supervisor?

2.20 A nominee is the title given to the IP who is nominated by the debtor to be the supervisor of an IVA.[33] The nominee may or may not become the appointed supervisor depending on the wishes of the creditors.

2.21 A supervisor is the title given to the IP who is appointed by the creditors to implement and supervise an approved IVA.[34] It is useful but not necessary for the supervisor to be the same IP as the nominee.

What is the role and function of a nominee?

2.22 The nominee's primary role is to report to the court on the viability of the proposed IVA.[35] His duty is to advise the court on whether a meeting of creditors should be convened and the likelihood of whether the arrangement being proposed will be first approved and then successfully implemented.[36] The OR performs a similar role as the nominee in a Fastrack IVA (which is a type IVA implemented by an undischarged bankrupt post bankruptcy).[37]

What is the role and function of a supervisor?

2.23 The supervisor's main duty is to ensure that the IVA proceeds in accordance with the terms of the agreed proposal which includes collecting in and distributing the assets and ensuring the debtor complies with his obligations. This will require maintaining regular contact with the debtor and providing creditors with regular updates in accordance with the IR86.[38]

RECOGNISED PROFESSIONAL BODY (RPB)

What is a recognised professional body and who are they?

2.24 An RPB is an organisation that is allowed to issue licences to its members to practice as IPs. These organisations were existing professional

---

33 IA86, s 253(2).
34 IA86, s 263(2).
35 IA86, s 256.
36 IR86, r 5.11(3).
37 IR86, r 5.38(1). See chapter 23 for more detail.
38 See chapters 23 to 26 for more detail.

bodies prior to the IA86 and satisfied the Secretary of State in respect of their procedures. They are themselves monitored regularly by the IS.[39] The Secretary of State can additionally licence IPs.[40]

2.25 The seven RPBs authorised by the 1986 Order[41] are as follows:

- The Chartered Association of Certified Accountants (ACCA).[42]
- The Insolvency Practitioners Association (IPA).[43]
- The Institute of Chartered Accountants in England and Wales (ICAEW).[44]
- The Institute of Chartered Accountants in Ireland (ICAI).[45]
- The Institute of Chartered Accountants of Scotland (ICAS).[46]
- The Solicitors Regulation Authority (Law Society).[47]
- The Law Society of Scotland (LSS).[48]

OFFICES HELD IN SPECIFIC JURISDICTIONS

England and Wales and Northern Ireland

Approved Intermediaries (AI)

What is an AI and what is their role?

2.26 The TCEA 2007[49] created the role of approved intermediary for debt advisers able to assist with processing the new DROs. They are members of the debt advice sector who have been approved by a competent authority to act as DRO advisers. AIs will advise and help complete the online application for a DRO. Only an approved AI can submit an application online.

---

39 IA86, s 391 and Insolvency Practitioners (Recognised Professional Bodies) Order 1986, SI 1986/1764.

40 Although the Office for Trading called for the abolition of this function in its report The Market for Corporate Insolvency Practitioners: a market study, June 2010 Office of Fair Trading (OFT1245). See further: Consultation on reforms to the regulation of insolvency practitioners, February 2011, Insolvency Service.

41 Insolvency Practitioners (Recognised Professional Bodies) Order 1986, SI 1986/1764.

42 See www.acca.org.uk.

43 See www.ipa.uk.com.

44 See www.icaew.co.uk.

45 See www.charteredaccountants.ie.

46 See www.icas.org.uk/icas/.

47 See www.lawsociety.org.uk.

48 See www.lawscot.org.uk.

49 TCE07, s 108 introduces Part 7A (ss 251A onwards) and Schs 4ZA and 4ZB into the IA86.

What are the approval criteria for an AI?

2.27 AIs must be approved by a competent authority (see below) and meet all the pertinent criteria, ie clear demonstration of experience and expertise in provision of debt advice as well as more specific criteria. The criteria include the following:

- the AI must have no criminal convictions;
- the AI cannot be an insolvent or be subject to any insolvency restrictions (such as bankruptcy restriction orders);
- the AI must exhibit independence and integrity;
- the AI must have a consumer credit licence and indemnity insurance.

Competent Authorities

2.28 The TCEA 2007 also created the role of competent authority to authorise individuals to act as AIs for the DRO process. They are debt and financial advice organisations that have been appointed to the position of competent authority by the Secretary of State and can therefore authorise a member of the debt advice sector to act as an AI. These organisations currently include the following:

- The National Association of Citizens Advice Bureau.
- The Foundation of Credit Counselling (Consumer Credit Counselling Service).
- Institute of Money Advisers.
- National Debtline.
- Payplan Ltd.
- IPA.
- Advice (UK).
- Shelter.

Official Receiver (OR)

What is an OR?

2.29 The OR is an officer of the court[50] and is employed by the IS which is an executive agency of the Department of Business Innovation and Skills (BIS). Each court exercising a bankruptcy jurisdiction in England and Wales must have an OR attached to it.[51] Some ORs cover more than one court and the busier courts can have more than one OR attached to it. The bankruptcy jurisdiction of courts is explained below and the list of courts and ORs offices are included in Appendix 2. The OR acts as trustee in bankruptcy at first instance and liquidator for compulsory liquidations in addition to other functions.

What is the role of an Official Receiver?

2.30 The OR has a wide range of roles. In relation to bankrupts their key functions are the investigation and administration of a bankrupt's affairs. In addition in the period between the making of the bankruptcy order and the vesting of the bankrupt's estate in a trustee, the OR is the receiver[52] and, unless a special manager has been appointed, under s 370 IA86, manager of the bankrupt's estate. His principal function is to protect the estate, including arranging insurance where appropriate. This can also include continuing a business.

What is the investigation role?

2.31 Under s 289(1) IA86, the OR is under a statutory obligation to investigate the conduct and affairs of every bankrupt and make a report to the court if appropriate. This is rarely done in practice. However, the EA02 introduced s 289(2) IA86 which makes s 289(1) IA86 inoperable when the OR decides that an investigation is unnecessary.

What is the administration role?

2.32 The OR has an administrative role in relation to fast track IVAs and DROs. These varied duties include the following for bankruptcy proceedings:

- Completion of the case assessment record.
- Meeting of creditors.[53]
- Statement of affairs.[54]

---

50 IA86, s 400(2).
51 IA86, s 399(5).
52 See **2.18–2.20**.
53 IR86, r 6.79(1).
54 IR86, rr 6.62, 6.76.

- Report to creditors.[55]
- Case files.
- Continued duty to investigate.[56]
- Consolidation of petitions.

Insolvency Service

2.33 The Insolvency Service (IS) is an executive agency of BIS.[57] The Service's costs are met from a mixture of funding provided by BIS from general taxation, HM Revenue and Customs (HMRC) and income from fees that are charged directly for services that it delivers. The IS delivers a range of complex services and fulfils a range of equally complex statutory functions including:

- The development and maintenance of the regulatory framework.
- Investigation and enforcement.
- Public delivery of bankruptcy services.
- Policy formation.

Other government departments involved in personal insolvency matters

Office of Fair Trading

2.34 The OFT is a non-ministerial government department established by statute in 1973. The OFT is the UK's consumer and competition authority and has recently launched an investigation into the UK corporate insolvency Market. Its purpose is to ensure markets work well for consumers and their stated goals are to:

- encourage businesses to comply with competition and consumer law and to improve their trading practices through self-regulation;
- act decisively to stop hardcore or flagrant offenders;
- study markets and recommending action where required;

---

55 IR86, rr 6.73(1), 6.77.

56 IA86, s 289(1).

57 The Department for Business Innovation and Skills (BIS) was created on 5 June 2009 by merging the Department for Enterprise and Regulatory Reform (BERR) and the Department for Innovation, Universities and Skills (DIUS).

- empower consumers with the knowledge and skills to make informed choices and get the best value from markets, and helping them resolve problems with suppliers through Consumer Direct.

Financial Services Authority

2.35 From 1 April 2013 the Financial Services Authority (FSA) will no longer exist as one body and will be split into two regulators, the Prudential Regulatory Authority (PRA) and the Financial Conduct Authority (FCA). The key change is the way that firms are supervised. The two bodies will work to different objectives (with separate risk mitigation programmes) with the PRA dedicating its resources to the continuing supervision of businesses while the FCA will focus separately on the bigger risk issues and policies. As a result some organisations will be monitored by both organisations which may appear to be duplicating a similar role but will be looking at the results of their separate monitoring with different objectives in mind.

Scotland

Accountant in bankruptcy

2.36 The accountant in bankruptcy (AiB) is appointed by Scottish Ministers and is an officer of the court.[58] A Deputy (sic) accountant in bankruptcy can also be appointed when the AiB is unable to act.

What is the role of the accountant in bankruptcy?

2.37 In Scotland all personal insolvency is administered by the AiB which includes the responsibility to maintain the register of personal insolvency for Scotland. Unlike the Insolvency Service the AiB employs agents to deliver most of their services through government contracts. For instance most sequestrations are dealt with by agent IPs.

2.38 The AiB has the following general functions in the administration of personal insolvency proceedings in Scotland including sequestrations and Trust Deeds:

- The supervision of the performance of interim trustees, all trustees and commissioners.[59] The AiB is required to report any failures by these officers to the relevant sheriff[60] and the Lord Advocate.[61]

- The determination of debtor applications.[62]

---

58 BSA85, s 1(1A).
59 BSA85, s 1A(1)(a).
60 BSA85, s 1A(2).
61 BSA85, s 1A(3).
62 BSA85, s 1A(1)(aa).

- The maintenance of the 'register of insolvencies'.[63]
- The preparation of an annual report for the Secretary of State and the Court of Session and any other functions conferred by them.[64]

Money advisers

2.39 There are two types of money advisers in relation to debt management in Scotland. There are routine money advisers who are trained to offer advice on debt and can help negotiate informal repayment plans. These should be differentiated from DAS approved money advisers. These are money advisers who have received additional training and can negotiate a formal debt payment programme between a debtor and their creditors. These advisers have to be approved by the DAS administrator who is currently the AiB.

What is the process for becoming a DAS money adviser?

2.40 The approval process is set out in reg 8 of the Debt Arrangement Scheme Regulations 2004.[65] The adviser must be a fit and proper person[66] and have undergone and successfully completed the designated training.[67]

What are the functions and duties of a DAS money adviser?

2.41 The functions are set out in reg 11 of the Debt Arrangement Scheme Regulations and include:

- providing money advice to a debtor;[68]
- liaising with creditors on behalf of a debtor;[69]
- assisting a debtor with, and advising on the implementation or variation of a debt payment programme;[70]
- the preparation and submission of an application on behalf of a debtor;[71]
- reviewing each debt payment programme every 6 months;[72]
- accepting instructions from a debtor to act as a lay representative in court;[73]

---

63 BSA85, s 1A(1)(b).
64 BSA85, s 1A(1)(c) and (d).
65 SI 2004/468.
66 SI 2004/468, reg 10.
67 SI 2004/468, reg 8(3).
68 SI 2004/468, reg 11(1)(a).
69 SI 2004/468, reg 11(1)(b).
70 SI 2004/468, reg 11(1)(c).
71 SI 2004/468, reg 11(1)(d).
72 SI 2004/468, reg 11(1)(e).
73 SI 2004/468, reg 11(1)(f).

- providing any information required by the DAS administrator in respect of a debtors participation in a debt payment programme.[74]

A fee can only be charged by a money adviser if the adviser has informed the debtor that the same advise can be obtained free of charge and has provided details of advisers in the same locality.[75] The debtor must agree to any fee in writing.[76]

Associates and connected parties

Who are associates for the purposes of personal insolvency proceedings and why does it matter?

2.42 The significance of being an associate means that transactions made by the bankrupt with this group of people are subject to greater scrutiny over longer periods of time than those with bona fide third parties. For the purposes of the IA 1986 whether a person is an associate of another person is determined by their relationship as set out below.[77] Any person with any one of the following relationships is deemed to be an associate of that individual:

- the individual's husband, wife or civil partner;[78]
- a relative of the individual[79] (see definition of relative at **2.43** which is very wide);
- a relative of the individual's husband, wife or civil partner;[80]
- the husband, wife or civil partner of a relative of the individual including their husband, wife or civil partner;[81]
- any person with whom the individual is in partnership;
- a trustee of any trust of whom the individual or any relative or associates are beneficiaries excluding a trustee in any insolvency proceedings or a trustee of any pension fund or employee's share scheme;[82]
- the husband, wife or civil partner or any person with whom the individual is in partnership;

---

74 SI 2004/468, reg 11(1)(h).
75 10 kilometre radius; SI 2004/468, reg 11(2)(b).
76 SI 2004/468, reg 11(2).
77 IA86, s 435.
78 IA86, s 435(2)(b)(ii).
79 IA86, s 435(2)(b)(i).
80 IA86, s 435(2)(c)(i).
81 IA86, s 435(2)(c)(ii).
82 IA86, s 435(5).

- any employer or employee and for these purpose any officer of a company is treated as an employee;[83]
- any company of any type (add explanation below) that is controlled by the individual;[84]
- any company of any type that is controlled by an associate or associates;[85]
- any company that is controlled by any person or persons with whom the individual is in partnership.[86]

Also, an individual voluntary arrangement has to be approved not only by 75% of the debtor's creditors but also by 50% of his unassociated creditors.[87]

What is the definition of a relative?

2.43 The definition of a relative is very wide and includes brother, sister, uncle, aunt, nephew, niece, lineal ancestor or lineal descendent of the individual or any husband, wife, civil partner or former husband, wife or civil partner.[88]

Lineal ancestor or lineal descendent include:

- any relationship of the half blood as a relationship of the whole blood and the stepchild or adopted child of any person as his child,[89] and
- an illegitimate child as a legitimate child of his mother and any reputed father.[90]

THE COURTS AND JUDICIARY

England and Wales

Which courts can deal with personal insolvency proceedings in England and Wales?

2.44 The court refers to the High Court or county court where the proceedings are being heard. 'The court' is represented by the individual judge hearing the application and making the decision. Not all county courts have

83 IA86, s 435(4); see further *Smurthwaite v Simpson-Smith* [2005] All ER (D) 275, [2006] BPIR 1504, CA.
84 IA86, s 435(7).
85 IA86, s 435(7).
86 IA86, s 435(9).
87 See IR86, r 5.23 and *National Westminster Bank plc v Kapoor* [2011] EWHC 255 (Ch), involving a post-proposal assignment of a debt from an associated creditor to an unassociated one, with a view to avoiding the effect of these provisions.
88 IA86, s 435(8).
89 IA86, s 435(8)(a).
90 IA86, s 435(8)(b).

jurisdiction and only those designated as bankruptcy courts can deal with bankruptcy petitions or applications for interim orders. There are 132 county courts with insolvency jurisdiction and these are listed in Appendix 2 together with the relevant ORs offices that cover each court. Note that jurisdiction is geographical rather than by value.

2.45 The bankruptcy court in the High Court is part of the Chancery Division and covers proceedings relating to insolvent individuals arising under Parts VIII to XI IA86 and related legislation. These include applications for interim orders to support an individual voluntary arrangement, applications to set aside statutory demands, bankruptcy petitions and various applications concerned with the realisation and distribution of the assets of bankrupts, as well as proceedings concerning the administration in bankruptcy of the insolvent estate of a deceased person.

Registrar

2.46 A registrar is the judge who deals with bankruptcy cases at first instance in the High Court. A bankruptcy registrar is a specialist in insolvency matters. See chapters 6 and 7 in relation to bankruptcy jurisdiction.

District judge

2.47 A district judge deals with bankruptcy cases at first instance in the county court. Appendix 2 lists the county courts with bankruptcy jurisdiction as not all county courts deal with bankruptcy proceedings. A district judge is not a specialist in personal insolvency matters. See chapters 6 and 7 in relation to bankruptcy jurisdiction.

Bailiffs and enforcement officers

2.48 Bailiffs and enforcement officers are people authorised to remove and sell a debtor's possessions in order to pay the money owed by them to another person or an organisation. They also conduct evictions, and arrest people. There are a variety of different types of bailiffs some of which are explained in detail below.

What is a county court bailiff?

2.49 County court bailiffs are employed by Her Majesty's Courts Service (HMCS), and are responsible for enforcing orders by recovering money owed under a county court judgment. They can seize and sell a debtor's goods to recover the amount of the debt. They can also effect and supervise the possession of the property and the return of goods under hire purchase agreements, and serve court documents.

What is a civilian enforcement officer?

2.50 Civilian enforcement officers (CEO) are employed by HMCS and are responsible for enforcing magistrates' court orders. They can seize and sell a debtor's goods to recover the amount owed under a fine and community penalty notice. They can also execute warrants of arrest, committal, detention and distress issued by a magistrates' court under any one of a range of statutes, including those covering the enforcement of fines and community penalties. A CEO can execute such a warrant anywhere within England and Wales.

What is an enforcement officer?

2.51 Enforcement officers (High Court) are appointed on behalf of the Lord Chancellor and are responsible for enforcing court orders by recovering money owed under a High Court judgment, or a county court judgment transferred to the High Court. They can seize and sell a debtor's goods to cover the amount of the debt. They can also enforce and supervise the possession of property and the return of goods. The Directory of High Court Enforcement Officers contains names of enforcement officers in England and Wales who have been authorised to execute High court writs under the provision contained in s 99 and Sch 7 of the Courts Act 2003.

What is a certificated bailiff?

2.52 Certificated bailiffs can enforce a variety of debts on behalf of organisations such as local authorities and landlords. They can seize and sell a debtor's goods to cover the amount of the debt owed. They also hold a certificate, which enables them, and them alone, to levy distress for rent, road traffic debts, council tax and non-domestic rates. They cannot enforce the collection of money due under High Court or county court orders.

Northern Ireland

Which courts can deal with personal insolvency proceedings in Northern Ireland?

2.53 All bankruptcy petitions are dealt with in the High Court in Belfast. Only disputes regarding claims of less than £15,000 can be dealt with in the county courts in Northern Ireland.

What is the court structure in Northern Ireland?

2.54 In Northern Ireland the court structure consists of the Court of Appeal and the High Court of Justice both of which are situated in the Royal Courts of Justice in central Belfast.

2.55 The Court of Appeal hears appeals in civil cases from the High Court, on matters of fact or law in cases (mainly personal injury claims) which originated in the High Court. It also hears appeals by way of case stated on a point of law only from the High Court (in cases brought to that court on appeal from lower courts), from the county courts and magistrates' court, and from various tribunals. The Lord Chief Justice and three Lord Justices of Appeal are appointed to sit in the Court and when hearing cases there will normally be two or three judges present. Appeals from the decisions of the Court of Appeal in most civil cases lie to the Supreme Court in London.

2.56 The High Court of Justice has three divisions:

- The Queen's Bench Division deals principally with actions in contract and tort (primarily personal injury actions) in which the amount in issue is £15,000 or more, defamation, public law cases (mainly applications for judicial review) and a variety of other cases for which special provision has been made by statute. It is to this Division that most appeals from the county courts are taken.

- The Chancery Division deals mainly with land and property matters, cases arising from the declaration or execution of trusts, company law, bankruptcy and winding-up proceedings and the dissolution of partnerships.

- The Family Division deals with matrimonial cases such as divorce and matters relating to the dissolution of a marriage (especially the custody of the children and the allocation of financial resources), the adoption of children, the guardianship and wardship of children and the affairs of mental patients and probate matters

In addition to the Lord Chief Justice (who is the President of the High Court), cases may be heard by any of the three Lord Justices of Appeal or by one of the ten High Court judges. The work of the Court is supported by seven Masters and the bankruptcy registrars of the Supreme Court.

2.57 The main work of the county courts is the resolution of disputes in contract and tort in which less than £15,000 is at stake (or less than £45,000 in equity matters). Many of these cases in which £2,000 or less is at stake are dealt with more quickly and informally by the small claims procedure. The county courts also have jurisdiction in equity matters (such as trusts) and disputes relating to the recovery of, or title to, land and the probate of wills. These courts may also hear uncontested petitions for divorce, applications for adoption, and applications for the granting of intoxicating liquor licences and certificates of registration for clubs. Contested cases involving £5,000 or more are normally heard by a county court judge (or deputy county court judge); contested cases involving less than £5,000 and uncontested cases involving up to £15,000 are heard by district judges (or deputy district judges). Cases dealt with using the small claims procedure are usually simple consumer disputes and may either be dealt with in default of a court hearing or will be heard by a district judge or deputy district judge. Parties are encouraged to represent themselves rather than engaging solicitors and legal aid is not available for representation in small claims cases.

Chancery master

2.58 All bankruptcy matters are dealt with in the High Court in Belfast by a chancery master. Other small debt matters can be dealt with in the county courts but none have bankruptcy jurisdiction.

Scotland

Which courts deal with debtor's bankruptcy petitions in Scotland?

2.59 In Scotland debtor's petitions are dealt with direct by the AiB however if a creditor wants to petition this is done through the sheriff court.[91] On presenting a petition the debtor will receive a 'warrant to cite' ordering them to appear at the court for the bankruptcy hearing. If the debtor appears in person or is represented then they may be given up to 6 weeks to pay off the debt or enter an alternative collection process such as a debt arrangement scheme or trust deed. If an award is subsequently made against an individual by the sheriff court then an 'award notice' will be issued and sent to the AiB who will then issue a 'certificate of award' of bankruptcy. Both the award notice issued by the sheriff court and the certificate of award of bankruptcy issued by the AiB will name the trustee appointed to administer the bankruptcy. The trustee will either be appointed and paid direct from the estate funds or will be appointed on an agency basis by the AiB who will fund the cost of administering the estate.

Which courts can deal with creditor's bankruptcy petitions in Scotland?

2.60 Bankruptcy and debt enforcement matters are dealt with by the sheriff courts along with other civil matters such as claims for compensation, contract disputes, family matters such as divorce, eviction, anti-social behaviour and matters such as licensing. There are 49 sheriff courts across Scotland.

2.61 The Court of Session is the supreme civil court in Scotland. It is based in Edinburgh. The Court of Session is both a court at first instance for initial consideration of cases and the court of appeal for most civil matters, although sheriff's principal can also hear appeals at a local level as an alternative.

2.62 The jurisdiction of the Court of Session (ie the civil matters it deals with) as a court of first instance is broadly the same as the jurisdiction of the sheriff court although there are some matters that can be raised only in the Court of Session: judicial review of decisions by administrative authorities is an example. Decisions of the Court of Session in appeals are subject to ultimate appeal to the Supreme Court.

---

[91] See chapter 29 for background information on sheriff courts.

Sheriff officers and messengers-at-arms

2.63 Sheriff officers and messengers-at-arms both work for the Scottish courts. They enforce court orders, serving legal documents and collecting debts. They do similar work to county court bailiffs in England and Wales. Sheriff officers hold a 'commission' to work in a particular region, while messengers-at-arms can travel anywhere in Scotland to enforce orders of the Court of Session. Collectively they are known as 'officers of court'. The duties of a sheriff include:

- writing to debtors to ask for payment;
- talking to debtors and arranging for them to repay in instalments;
- serving court papers such as writs and summonses;
- offering money management advice;
- repossessing goods and property;
- arranging for recovered goods to be sold at auction;
- keeping accurate records and being responsible for any money and goods recovered.

What qualifications and experience is required for a sheriff's officer?

2.64 The normal career progression would be to start as a witness to a sheriff officer. The following experience is required:

- to be 20 years old or over;
- to have at least 3 years' training with an officer of court;
- to have a full, clean driving licence and the use of a car;
- to pass the Society of Messengers-at-Arms and Sheriff Officers exam.

The office of sheriff

What is the office of sheriff?

2.65 The sheriff usually acts as judge in the first instance, but can also exercise some appellate functions and a large number of administrative and quasi-judicial functions. There are 49 sheriff courts situated throughout Scotland. Each sheriff has the same powers and responsibilities within his or her sheriff court district. In the cities and larger towns there will be more than one sheriff and in some remote areas, particularly those in the islands, the resident sheriff may sit in more than one court during the course of a week. More recently there have been appointments of sheriffs who are directed to sit where there is a need from time to time: such sheriffs are known as all-Scotland floating sheriffs. The sheriff court has exclusive jurisdiction for all claims under £1,500. Beyond that limit, and subject to a small number of exceptions, the jurisdiction of the sheriff court and of the Court of Session is the same. Because solicitors as well as advocates have a right of audience in the sheriff court, solicitors can choose to raise the most complicated and important cases in the sheriff court. There is no pecuniary limit. Important and complex cases, which might otherwise have been taken in the Court of Session, are taken in the sheriff court for reasons of finance or geographical convenience.

What qualifications are required for the office of sheriff?

2.66 To qualify for appointment as sheriff a person must be and have been an advocate or solicitor for at least 10 years. Because of the nature of the office, those appointed must be practitioners of standing, whether Queen's Counsel, advocates or solicitors with considerable court experience. Before appointment, the person would in many cases have had some experience of the 'shrieval' bench as a temporary or part-time sheriff. Initially, before sitting alone, a sheriff will normally undergo 5 days of specific training plus 5 days sitting alongside an experienced sheriff. As the jurisdiction of the sheriff is vast, he or she must have a grasp of every aspect of law, both civil and criminal, as well as mastery of the rules of evidence. Each sheriff is required to devote considerable time to maintaining an up-to-date knowledge and awareness of the relevant law, rules of evidence and procedure. Sheriffs are required to be aware of the legislation of the UK and Scottish Parliaments as well as the decided case law and jurisprudence of the Scottish courts and the European Court of Human Rights.

Chapter 3

FORMAL SOLUTIONS: STATUTORY FRAMEWORKS AND OTHER GUIDANCE

'Where you find the laws most numerous, there you will find also the greatest injustice.'[1]

INTRODUCTION

3.1 This chapter sets out in more detail the statutory framework for each formal solution listed in chapter 1. Subsequent chapters will look at these procedures in depth. The purpose of this chapter is to provide an overview of the relevant legislation for each process and these have been set out by jurisdiction. The key players and the enforcement processes in place in each jurisdiction are covered in chapter 2.

ENGLAND AND WALES

3.2 The law and procedure governing personal insolvency procedures are laid down by statute.[2] The modern process for England and Wales is set out principally in the Insolvency Act 1986 (IA86) and the Insolvency Rules 1986 (IR86).[3] These have both been amended on numerous occasions since 1986 including a complete rewrite planned for implementation in 2014.

Bankruptcy

What is the statutory framework for bankruptcy?

3.3 The main provisions which currently apply to bankruptcy are found in the Insolvency Act 1986, Part IX, ss 264–371. This act has principally been amended by the Insolvency Act 2000; the Enterprise Act 2002 and the Legislative Reform (Insolvency) (Miscellaneous Provisions) Order 2010.[4] All of these changes are governed by additional commencement and transitional provision orders.[5]

---

1 Arcesilaus.

2 On the statutory material see: D Milman and L Sealy, *Sealy and Milman: Annotated Guide to the Insolvency Legislation* (Sweet and Maxwell Ltd, 14th edn, 2011). See also: A Keay and L Doyle, *Insolvency Legislation: Annotations and* Commentary (Jordan Publishing, 3rd edn, 2009).

3 Both have been subject to amendments.

4 Legislative Reform (Insolvency) (Miscellaneous Provisions) Order 2010, SI 2010/18.

5 SI 2001/766; SI 2002/2711; SI 2003/2093.

In addition the main statutory instrument governing bankruptcy is the Insolvency Rules 1986,[6] Part VI, rr 6.1–6.251. These have been amended on multiple occasions between 2003 and 2012.[7]

What statutory provisions apply to pre-1986 bankruptcies?

3.4 Bankruptcies made before 29 December 1986 are governed by the Bankruptcy Act 1914.[8] Extensive case law applying and interpreting the IA86[9] and IR86[10] must also be referred to.[11] In the case of debtors with international connections, or assets in foreign jurisdictions and particularly in the case of foreign creditors the EC Council Regulation on Insolvency Proceedings[12] came into force on 31 May 2002 and the Cross-Border Insolvency Regulations 2006[13] giving effect to the UNCITRAL Model Law (came into force in England and Wales with effect from 1 April 2006) will also apply. These are covered in more detail in chapter 20.

What additional statutory provisions relate to bankruptcy and other formal processes?

3.5 There are a number of other regulations that have general applicability to personal insolvency as well as other ancillary statutory provisions which must be borne in mind when approaching any personal insolvency. For bankruptcy in England and Wales these can be divided into general provisions applicable across a wide range of proceedings and those that are very specific.

3.6 The general provisions include Insolvency Proceedings (Monetary Limits) Order 1986;[14] Insolvency Fees Order 1986;[15] Insolvency Regulations 1994;[16] Insolvency Act 1986 Section 72A (Appointed Date) Order 2003;[17] Insolvency Proceedings (Fees) Order 2004.[18] A further set of these general rules and regulations relate specifically to the regulation of Insolvency Practitioners and include the Insolvency Practitioners

---

6 SI 1986/1925.
7 Insolvency (Amendment) Rules 2003, SI 2003/1730; Insolvency (Amendment) Rules 2004, SI 2004/584; Insolvency (Amendment) Rules 2005, SI 2005/527; Insolvency (Amendment) Rules 2006, SI 2006/1272; Insolvency (Amendment) Rules 2008, SI 2008/737; Insolvency (Amendment) Rules 2009, SI 2009/642; Insolvency (Amendment) Rules 2010, SI 2010/686; Insolvency (Amendment) (No 2) Rules 2010, SI 2010/734; Insolvency (Amendment) Rules 2011, SI 2011/785 ; Insolvency (Amendment) Rules 2012, SI 2012/465.
8 On the provisions in this act see Williams and Muir Hunter *The Law and Practice in Bankruptcy* (1979).
9 Insolvency Act 1986 (as amended).
10 Insolvency Rules 1986, SI 1986/1925.
11 See for example Jordans Bankruptcy and Personal Insolvency Reports.
12 EC 2000/1346.
13 SI 2006/1030.
14 SI 1986/1996.
15 SI 1986/2030.
16 SI 1994/2507.
17 SI 2003/2095.
18 SI 2004/593.

Regulations 2005;[19] the Insolvency Practitioners Regulations 1990[20] (these only remain in force for appointments commenced before 1 April 2005 under the transitional provision rules); the Insolvency Practitioners (Recognised Professional Bodies) Order 1986;[21] and the Insolvency Practitioners Tribunal (Conduct of Investigations) Rules 1986.[22] Those that are very specific include the Administration of Insolvent Estates of Deceased Persons Order 1986.[23] This is covered in more detail in chapter 21.

What are prescribed forms for bankruptcy?

3.7 The prescribed forms for bankruptcy are set out in Sch 4, Part 6 IR86. These forms are referred to throughout the IR86 and set out the format for the various official documents required by specific rules. They are published as part of the statutory instrument and ensure that the relevant information and evidence is supplied to the court or other parties as required. Details of the forms and their purpose are set out in Appendix 4. The information required on these prescribed forms has been embodied in the text during the 2010 rule amendment process to aid the introduction of electronic communication.

What other guidance is available for bankruptcy proceedings?

3.8 Other materials include best practice guidance, Civil Procedure Rules and Practice Directions. The Association of Business Recovery Professionals (R3) which is the trade body for insolvency practitioners issues on behalf of the Joint Insolvency Committee (JIC) best practice statements. They set out standards which IPs must adhere to in administering cases.

3.9 A full version of the Civil Procedure Rules and Practice Directions are available on the Ministry of Justice website.[24] The following are some of the most relevant practice directions that have been issued in relation to insolvency matters specifically:

- *Practice Direction: Insolvency Proceedings.*
- *Practice Direction: The Fixing and Approval of the Remuneration of Appointees.*
- *Practice Direction: The Hearing of Insolvency Proceedings.*
- *Practice Direction: Validation Orders.*

All of these documents are due to be consolidated once the modernised Insolvency Rules are implemented in 2014.

---

19 SI 2005/524.
20 SI 1990/439.
21 SI 1986/1764.
22 SI 1986/952.
23 SI 1986/1999.
24 http://www.justice.gov.uk/civil/procrules_fin/index.htm.

3.10 The Insolvency Service issues periodic guidance in 'Dear IP' newsletters which are available on their website[25] and can be viewed chronologically or by topic in relevant chapters. The following chapters are most directly relevant to individuals in bankruptcy proceedings:

- Chapter 3: Authorisation and appointment of insolvency practitioners
- Chapter 8: Crown departments
  1. Use of proxy holders at Section 98 Creditors Meeting (Aug-93)
  2. Notification: Form VAT 769 and Procedures (Mar-93)
  3. Notification to H.M Customs and Excise Jan-93 (Second Publication) (Mar-93)
  4. VAT 100 Returns for Insolvent Firms (Aug-93)
  5. Relocation of VAT Insolvency Branch (Aug-93)
  6. Notification of petition of costs to IPs, trustees and liquidators (Jul-99)
  7. Guidance for trustees and Liquidators in Dealing with IR (Aug-93)
  8. S98 Notices to the Inland Revenue (Nov-91)
  9. New Voluntary Arrangement Service May Edition (June-01)
  10. Further Guidance for trustees and Liquidators in Dealing with the Inland Revenue July 2002 Edition
  11. Improving the time taken to lodge the Inland Revenue's claim:how IPs can help (Sep-03)
  12. Enterprise Act 2002 and Finance Act 2003; Tax Changes (Dec-03)
  13. New Administrations – Information to the Inland Revenue (Dec-03)
  14. Date of Budget Resolution (Dec-03)
  15. New Administrations:Information to the Inland Revenue
  16. Insolvency Claims: HM Revenue and Customs
  17. The House of Lords judgment on 4 March 2004 in the case of 'Leyland DAF Limited'
  18. The House of Lords judgment in the Spectrum Plus case
  19. Enquiries addressed to DVLA (June-07)
  20. Book debt proceeds subject to floating charge security being paid to and retained by banks (March-08)
- Chapter 9: Discharge from Bankruptcy
  1. Application to Suspend the running of a Bankrupts Discharge Period (Oct-98)
  2. Suspension of a Discharge Period in bankruptcy Jul-91 (Second publication) (Aug 94)
  3. Suspension of a Discharge Under Section 279(3) (Oct-95)
  4. Changes to Discharge from Bankruptcy (Feb-04)
  5. Bankruptcy Restrictions Orders/Undertakings (Feb-04)
  6. Rule 6.214A – notice under section 279 (2)
  7. Early Discharge Process (Dec-05)
  8. Application for suspension of discharge (Dec-05)
  9. The Enterprise Act 2002 (Disqualification from Office: General) Order 2006:S.I. 2006 No.1722 (Nov-06)
  10. Application for suspension of discharge
- Chapter 10: Disqualification
  1. Company Directors Disqualification Act Compliance (May-97)
  2. IP's costs (Feb-01)

[25] See http://www.bis.gov.uk/insolvency/insolvency-profession/dear-ip.

3 Guidance Visits (Feb-01)
4 Insolvency Act 2000 (IA 2000) and the Company Directors Disqualification Act 1986 (CDDA) March Edition (Apr-01)
5 Extension of time for lodging reports May Edition (June-01)
6 D Return Reminder Letters (June-03)
7 Company Director Disqualification Act 1986:"D" Forms (Sep-03)
8 Update on the Procedure on Disclosure of the D Report or Decision (Dec-03)
9 Extensions for submission of D Reports / Returns (Mar-04)
10 New Reminder Letters (Mar-04)
11 Disqualification Undertakings In Northern Ireland (Oct-04)
12 Changes to the procedure for filing D returns/reports in respect of Scottish registered companies
13 Submission of Conduct Reports under the Company Director Disqualification Act 1986 (April-06)
14 Targeting D1 Conduct Reports for Investigation (Jan-07)
15 Creation of the Initial Investigation Team (Jan-07)
16 Changes in procedure affecting Scottish cases (March-08)

- Chapter 13: General
- Chapter 17: Legislation

1 The Judgements Act 1838 (Mar-93)
2 Schedule 4(1) of the Insolvency Act 1986 Preferential claims Oct-97 (Second Publication) (Mar-98)
3 Environment Act 1995 (Apr-96)
4 Criminal Procedure and Investigation Act 1996 (Sep-98)
5 Civil Procedure Rules 1998 (Apr-99)
6 The Late Payment of Commercial Debts (Interest) Act 1998 (Sep-98)
7 Education (Student Loan) Act 1990 (Jan-99)
8 Data Protection Act 1998 (Mar-00)
9 Welfare Reform Act 1999 (Jun-00)
10 EC Regulation on Insolvency Proceedings (Mar-02)
11 Welfare Reform and Pensions Act 1999 April-02 Edition
12 Occupational and Personal Pensions Scheme (Bankruptcy) Regulations 2002 April-02 Edition
13 The Occupational Pension Schemes (Winding up Notices and Reports etc) April-02 Edition
14 Secure Register for Home Addresses April-02 Edition
15 Secure Register for Usual Residential Addresses July-02 Edition
16 Financial Services and Markets Act 2000 July-02 Edition
17 Late Payment of Commercial Debt:New Provisions (Nov-02)
18 Insolvency Act 2000 – Voluntary Arrangement Provisions and other Amendments (Nov-02)
19 Education (Student Loans) Act 1990 Teaching and Higher Education Act 1998 (Dec-02)
20 Enterprise Act 2002:Insolvency Provisions (Dec-02)
21 The Insurers (Reorganisation and Winding Up) Regulations 2003 (2003 No 1102) (June-03)
22 Revision of Court Fees (Jun-03)
23 Enterprise Act 2002 (Sep-03)
24 Stamp Duty Land Tax (Mar-04)
25 The Financial Collateral Arrangements (Mar-04)
26 Money Laundering Regulations (Mar-04)
27 The Insurers Regulations (Mar-04)

28 Courts Act 2003 (May-04)
29 Higher Education Act 2004:Student Loans (July-04)
30 Section 176A of the Insolvency Act 1986 (Share of Assets for unsecured creditors) (July-04)
31 The Commonhold and Leasehold Reform Act 2002 (July-04)
32 The Higher Education Act 2004 and its further effect on the status of student loan debts in bankruptcy (Oct-04)
33 Evaluation of Insolvency Act 2000 and Enterprise Act 2002 (Dec-04)
34 Revision of Court Fees
35 Pensions Act 2004
36 Transsexual People:The Gender Recognition Act 2004
37 Amendments to the EC Regulation on Insolvency Proceedings
38 Pensions Act 2004
39 EC Regulation No 1348/2000 on the service in the Member States of judicial and extra judicial documents in civil or commercial matters
40 Community Interest Companies
41 Courts Act 2003 – Periodical Payments For Damages For Personal Injury
42 Civil Partnership Act 2004
43 Pensions Act 2004, new responsibilities for insolvency practitioners (April-06)
44 Licensing Act 2003 (April-06)
45 Civil Proceedings Rules (Jan-07)
46 Amendment to Section 188 The Insolvency Act 1986 (March-07)
47 The Tribunals Court and Enforcement Bill: Debt Relief Orders (March-07)
48 EU Directive 2005/36 (Sept-07)
49 Money Laundering Regulations 2007 (Sept-07)
50 Pensions Act 2004 (Sept-07)
51 The "Trident Fashions" case and The Non-Domestic Rating (Unoccupied Property) Regulations 1989
52 EU Directive 2006/123: Services in the Internal Market
53 Non-Domestic Rates in administration (March-08)

- Chapter 18: Matrimonial Homes
- Chapter 23: Remuneration and fees

3.11 The Insolvency Service also publishes a lot of guides which are available to download free of charge.[26] These include the following with the publications with their most recent publication date:

A Guide for Creditors	URN 10/943	1 April 2010
A Guide to Bankruptcy	URN 12/1262	19 November 2012
A Guide to Debt Relief Orders	URN 12/1259	4 November 2012
Alternatives to Bankruptcy	URN 11/1313	11 October 2011
Bankruptcy Restriction Orders	URN 12/849	25 May 2012
Can my bankruptcy be cancelled?	URN 11/837	1 April 2011

[26] See http://www.bis.gov.uk/insolvency/Publications.

Dealing with debt: how to make someone bankrupt	URN 11/1004	1 June 2011
Debt Relief Restriction Orders	URN 12/850	25 May 2012
How to petition for your own bankruptcy	URN 12/1182	3 October 2012
Income Payments Orders and Agreements	URN 10/1302	1 November 2010
In Debt – Dealing with creditors	URN 12/694	22 May 2012
Statutory Demands	URN 12/10B	3 August 2012
The Individual Insolvency register	URN 12/1187	4 October 2012
Trustees in Bankruptcy	URN 11/1406	22 November 2011
What is a Fastrack IVA?	URN 12/1317	22 November 2012
What happens when you are interviewed by the OR?	URN 12/578	31 January 2012
What will happen to my bank account?	URN 11/1455	23 December 2011
What will happen to my home?	URN 11/1445	19 December 2011
What will happen to my pension?	URN 10/832	1 April 2010
What will happen to my motor vehicle?	URN 12/589	8 February 2012
When will my bankruptcy end?	URN 11/906	1 May 2011

Debt relief order

What are the statutory provisions for a debt relief order?

3.12 The Tribunals, Courts and Enforcement Act 2007,[27] introduced a number of reforms to existing personal insolvency regimes and some new additions to the personal insolvency procedure menu. In particular Sch 17 introduced a new Part 7A into the IA86 (inserting ss 251A–251S) and Sch 18 introduced a new Sch 4ZA (conditions for making a DRO). These provisions amend the IA86 bringing about a new debt relief order (DRO) procedure.[28]

---

27 In respect of this statute see: R McKee The Tribunals Bill (2007) JIANL (2007) 21(1), 14-20; S Barc 'Tribunals, Courts and Enforcement Act 2007' (2007) CSR, 31(18), 142-143; and M van Rooyen 'The Tribunals, Courts and Enforcement Act 2007' (2008) Adviser, 128, 55-57; J Chuah 'Implications of the Tribunals, Courts and Enforcement Act 2007' (2008) F. and C.L, Apr, 1-4. See also The Tribunals, Courts and Enforcement Bill [HL] Bill 65 of 2006-07, House of Commons Library Research Paper, 07/22, 1 March 2007.

28 DROs have attracted a fair amount of article comment. See for example: Debt relief orders (England and Wales) T.B. 2009, 86(Apr) 86.3; R Woolley 'The Debt Relief Order Unit' (2009) Adviser, 132, 47-49,56; M Gallagher 'Debt Relief Orders' (2009) Adviser, 132, 34-46; S O'Sullivan 'Debt relief orders: a new debt solution' (2009) Q.A, 12 (Spring), 10-12; A Crossley 'Debt relief orders and money advisers' (2008) Q.A. 2008, 8 (Spring), 12-13; S Stanhope

The detailed provisions were inserted in the IR86 by the 2009 amendment rules which inserted a new Part 5A (rr 5A.1–5A.27) and these came into effect on 6 July 2009.

The DRO procedure is covered in more detail in chapter 27 but should be generally considered as a 'cheap' bankruptcy option. As Joyce has observed, the DRO is for individuals 'with unsecured debts not exceeding £15,000, surplus income of less than £50 a month and gross assets worth less than £300 (excluding, for example, home-owners even in negative equity)'.[29] The full details of these changes are discussed in more detail in chapter 28. It should be noted that debt relief orders were additionally introduced in Northern Ireland in 2011.

Individual voluntary arrangement

What are the current statutory provisions for an IVA?

3.13 The current provisions which relate to IVAs are principally covered in the Insolvency Act 1986 (IA86), Part VIII, ss 252–263. These provisions have been amended by the Insolvency Act 2000 and the Enterprise Act 2002. Both of these are also governed by various commencement and transitional provisions orders.[30] The detailed provisions for IVAs are covered in the Insolvency Rules 1986[31] (IR86), Part 5, rr 5.1–5.30. These have also been amended on numerous occasions between 2003 and 2012.[32] A complete rewrite of these rules are expected in 2014.

What are the prescribed forms?

3.14 The prescribed forms for IVAs are set out in Sch 4, Part 5, IR86. These forms are referred to throughout the IR86 and set out the format for the various official documents required by specific rules. They are published as part of the statutory instrument and ensure that the relevant information and evidence is supplied to the court or other parties as required. Details of the forms and their purpose are set out in Appendix 4. The information required

---

'Insolvency law:proposed changes' (2006) Adviser, 117, 52-54; S Quinn 'Painting the Forth Bridge' (2006) Adviser, 117, 66-67; G Player 'Personal finance survey' (2006) Recovery, Autumn, 29: A Crossley 'A new kind of debt relief?' (2005) Adviser, 107, 41-43; Ed. (2005) Proposals for new debt relief scheme published by the Insolvency Service, Comp. Law, 26(7), 215.

29 P Joyce 'A simple solution to debt? Cork revisited' (2009) *Insolvency Intelligence* No 22(5), 71-73.

30 SI 2001/766; SI 2002/2711; SI 2003/2093.

31 SI 1986/1925.

32 Insolvency (Amendment) Rules 2003, SI 2003/1730; Insolvency (Amendment) Rules 2004, SI 2004/584; Insolvency (Amendment) Rules 2005, SI 2005/527; Insolvency (Amendment) Rules 2006, SI 2006/1272; Insolvency (Amendment) Rules 2008, SI 2008/737; Insolvency (Amendment) Rules 2009, SI 2009/642; Insolvency (Amendment) Rules 2010, SI 2010/686; Insolvency (Amendment) Rules 2011, SI 2011/785; Insolvency (Amendment) Rules 2012, SI 2012/465.

on these prescribed forms has generally now been embodied in the text during the 2010 rule amendment process to aid the introduction of electronic communication.

What other guidance is available?

3.15 R3 issues a wide range of best practice statements but there is specifically a practice statement covering guidance for voluntary arrangements. The latest version published is shown as version 3 but is in fact version 4 which was issued 1 April 2007.

3.16 The Insolvency Service also issues periodic guidance in 'Dear IP' newsletters which are available on their website[33] and chapter 24[34] covers all the guidance issued on voluntary arrangements. Reference to this guidance is included in chapters 23–26 of this book.[35]

County court administration order

What are the main current statutory provisions?

3.17 A county court administration order empowers the court to take over administration of a defendant's debts, whilst an agreed regular amount is repaid. These are currently covered by the County Courts Act 1984 Part VI, ss 112–117.

New sections have been added by the Tribunals, Courts and Enforcement Act 2007 but these have not yet taken effect. The details of the changes are discussed in more detail in chapter 27. The current key elements of a county court administration order (CCAO) remain that:

- Any debtor, against whom at least one county court judgment is registered, can make application to the court for an administration order.
- If granted, this provides protection from further action by creditors in respect of any debts listed under the order.
- Creditors not included in the order cannot pursue their debts separately through the courts – if they try, these debts are automatically added to the administration order.

The register of judgments, orders and fines replaced the old register of county court judgments.[36]

---

33 http://www.insolvency.gov.uk/insolvencyprofessionandlegislation/dearip/dearipindex.htm.

34 Chapter 24, Dear IP: http://www.insolvency.gov.uk/insolvencyprofessionandlegislation/dearip/dearipindex.htm.

35 Chapter 24, at **24.20**.

36 Register of Judgments, Orders and Fines Regulations 2005, SI 2005/3595.

What information is included on the register of county court orders?

3.18 All courts are required to provide details of administration orders against individuals for inclusion in the public register, which is kept by Registry Trust Ltd (RTL) on behalf of the Ministry of Justice. The information on the register includes the following data:[37]

- Court name and order number.
- Name and address of defendant.
- Total amount payable.
- Date of order.
- Date of varied order, satisfaction or revocation.
- Any orders registered after 6 April 2006 will, where known, include date of birth and the address will include as mandatory the debtor's postcode.

The information on the register is updated when RTL are advised of any changes by the court including any variation of the order. A variation can occur when the amount of the debt agreed under the original order has been changed by the addition of new creditors or when a composition order (debt reduced to % of £ owed) is made. The courts must notify RTL and the varied order replaces the original one.

Deed of arrangement

What is a deed of arrangement?

3.19 A deed of arrangement (DoA) is a court process and the provisions are set out in the Deeds of Arrangement Act 1914 for England and Wales and Northern Ireland. A brief outline was provided in chapter 1 but there have been no Deeds registered in England and Wales since 1999.[38] One of the main disadvantages of the process is that any dissenting creditor can continue to pursue their debt[39] however often the only practical remedy for a dissenting creditor would be to petition for the debtor's bankruptcy.

---

37 SI 2005/3595, reg 10.

38 See the Insolvency Service website http://www.insolvency.gov.uk.

39 Deeds of Arrangement Act 1914, s 3.

NORTHERN IRELAND

Bankruptcy and debt relief orders

What are the main current statutory provisions for bankruptcy in Northern Ireland?

3.20 In Northern Ireland bankruptcy provisions are very similarly dealt with as in England and Wales. The principle legislation is the Insolvency (Northern Ireland) Order 1989[40] (INO89), Part VI, Arts 238–345. This order like the IA86 has been amended on many occasions between 1994 and 2012.[41] The detailed provisions for bankruptcy can be found in The Insolvency Rules (Northern Ireland) 1991[42] (IRN91), Part VI, rr 6.001–6.260. These rules have also been amended on multiple occasions during the same period.[43]

3.21 In Northern Ireland both the initial Order[44] and Rules[45] came into effect on 1 October 1991 nearly 5 years later than in England and Wales. For debt relief orders these have recently been introduced by the 2011 amendment rules which inserted a new Part 5A including rr 5A.1–5A.30 into the IRN91 duplicating closely the amendments made to IR86[46] for England and Wales.[47]

Individual voluntary arrangements

What are the main current statutory provisions for an IVA in Northern Ireland?

3.22 The current principal provisions which relate to IVAs are the Insolvency (Northern Ireland) Order 1989,[48] Part VIII, arts 226–237 as amended by the Insolvency Act 1994; the Insolvency (No 2) Act 1994; the Insolvency (Northern Ireland) Order 2002; and the Insolvency (Northern Ireland) Order 2005. These amendments have additionally been governed by various commencement and transitional provisions.[49]

---

40 SI 1989/2405 (NI 19).

41 Insolvency Act 1994; Insolvency (No 2) Act 1994; Insolvency (Northern Ireland) Order 2002, SI 2002/3152 (NI 6); Insolvency (Northern Ireland) Order 2005, SI 2005/1455 (NI 10).

42 SR 1991/364.

43 Insolvency (Amendment) Rules (Northern Ireland) 2000, SR 2000/247; Insolvency (Amendment) Rules (Northern Ireland) 2002, SR 2002/261; Insolvency (Amendment) Rules (Northern Ireland) 2003, SR 2003/549; Insolvency (Amendment) Rules (Northern Ireland) 2006, SR 2006/47; Insolvency (Amendment) Rules (Northern Ireland) 2008, SR 2008/118; Insolvency (Amendment) Rules (Northern Ireland) 2009, SR 2009/404.

44 Insolvency (Northern Ireland) Order 1989, SI 1989/2405 (NI 19).

45 Insolvency (Amendment) Rules (Northern Ireland) 2011, SR 2011/151.

46 DRO's came into force in England Wales on 6 July 2009 and in Northern Ireland on 30 June 2011.

47 Insolvency (Amendment) Rules (Northern Ireland) 2011, SR 2011/151.

48 Insolvency (Northern Ireland) Order 1989, SI 1989/2405 (NI 19).

49 SI 2001/766; SI 2002/2711; SI 2003/2093.

The detailed provisions are set out in the Insolvency Rules (Northern Ireland) 1991[50] (IRN91), Part VI, rr 5.01–5.30, which have also been updated by numerous amendment rules issued between 2000 and 2012.[51]

High Court administration order

What are the current statutory provisions for High Court administration orders in Northern Ireland?

3.23 In Northern Ireland, as in England and Wales, if a debtor has one or more creditors who have obtained a judgment, the Enforcement of Judgments Office (EJO) can make an administration order against the individual. The EJO administers the process and are located at the following address: Enforcement of Judgements Office, Bedford House, Bedford Street, Belfast, BT2 7FD.

Exactly the same rules apply as in England and Wales in that total debts must not exceed £5,000 and the administration of the order is covered by the EJO taking a small percentage of the funds received. If payments are missed the order can be cancelled and bankruptcy proceedings may be instigated.

SCOTLAND

Sequestrations and LILAs

What is the statutory and regulatory framework for bankruptcy proceedings in Scotland?

3.24 Sequestration is the Scottish equivalent of bankruptcy and Low Income Low Asset (LILA) is an additional, cheaper route into sequestration for individuals with few assets on low income in a similar manner to debt relief orders. For Scotland the bankruptcy process is governed by the Bankruptcy (Scotland) Act 1985 (BSA85); The Insolvency (Scotland) Rules 1986[52] (ISR86); and The Bankruptcy (Scotland) Act 1985 (Low Income, Low Asset Debtors etc) Regulations 2008[53] (LILA08), which introduced the new low cost route into bankruptcy in Scotland.

The schedules to the Bankruptcy (Scotland) Act 1985 cover the following topics:

---

50 SR 1991/364.

51 Insolvency (Amendment) Rules (Northern Ireland) 2000, SR 2000/247; Insolvency (Amendment) Rules (Northern Ireland) 2002, SR 2002/261; Insolvency (Amendment) Rules (Northern Ireland) 2003, SR 2003/549; Insolvency (Amendment) Rules (Northern Ireland) 2006, SR 2006/47; Insolvency (Amendment) Rules (Northern Ireland) 2008, SR 2008/118; Insolvency (Amendment) Rules (Northern Ireland) 2009, SR 2009/404; Insolvency (Amendment) Rules (Northern Ireland) 20011, SR 2011/151.

52 SI 1986/1915 (as amended).

53 SSI 2008/81.

- Adaptation of procedure where permanent trustee not elected (Sch 2).
- Consequential amendments and re-enactments (Sch 7).
- Determination of amount of creditor's claim (Sch 1).
- Discharge on composition (Sch 4).
- Meetings of creditors and commissioners (Sch 6).
- Preferred Debts (Sch 3).
- Repeals (Sch 8).

The detailed provisions as they relate to personal insolvency are set out in Appendix 3.

3.25 Other regulations govern the actions of IPs and court procedures in Scotland including the Bankruptcy (Scotland) Regulations 2008[54] (BSR08) and the Act of Sederunt (Sheriff Court Bankruptcy Rules) 2008[55] (SCR08). The most recent court procedures are dealt with in the Act of Sederunt (Sheriff Court Bankruptcy Rules) 2008[56] for sequestrations post 1 April 2008. This act has the effect of providing rules in the sheriff court for the purpose of the Bankruptcy (Scotland) Act 1985. It includes a schedule of Sheriff Court Bankruptcy Rules covering the following areas:

- Appeals to the sheriff (Sch 7).
- Appeals to the sheriff principal and the Court of Session (Sch 8).
- Application to determine amount for ailment and obligation (Sch 6).
- Applications (Sch 5).
- Approved debt payment programmes (Sch 12).
- Expenses (Sch 16).
- Forms and register of insolvencies (Sch 9).
- Forms of petitions (Sch 2).
- Holding of sederunt book by accountant in bankruptcy (Sch 11).
- Intimation of appointment of trustee (Sch 4).

---

54 SSI 2008/82.
55 SSI 2008/119.
56 SSI 2008/119.

- Petitions for sequestration (Sch 3).
- Reports (Sch 10).
- Representation (Sch 15).
- UNCITRAL Model Law on Cross-Border Insolvency (Sch 13).
- Vulnerable witnesses (Sch 14).

In addition Appendix 1 of the Act of Sederunt (Sheriff Court Bankruptcy Rules) 2008[57] lists the forms and Appendix 2 lists the information to be contained in the register of insolvencies for sequestrations, Protected Trust Deeds and Bankruptcy Restriction Orders and Undertakings (including interim orders).

- Petition by a qualified creditor (Form 1) (s 5(2)(b)(iv) BSA 1985).[58]
- Trustee for failed trust deed (Form 3).
- Undertaking (Form 4).

3.26 In addition to the above the Bankruptcy Scotland Regulations 2008[59] covers the following matters for sequestrations:

- Abandonment of heritable property (Forms 21 and 22) (reg 19).
- Apparent insolvency/creditor debt threshold £1,500 (reg 13).
- Application to limited partnership (reg 8).
- Bond premium as an expense (reg 7).
- Claims in foreign currency (reg 5).
- Debt advice and information pack (reg 12).
- Debtor applications: low income low assets (reg 15).
- Debtor applications (reg 14).
- Debtors SoA (Form 23) (reg 20).
- Income payment agreements (Form 20) (reg 18).

---

57 SSI 2008/119.

58 Bankruptcy Scotland Act 1985.

59 SSI 2008/82.

- Interest on claims (reg 6).
- Notice of sequestration in *Edinburgh Gazette* (reg 11).
- Preference for employee's remuneration (reg 10).
- Report of no meeting to AiB (Form 18) (reg 16).
- Saving Regulations for 1985 Regulations (retains reg 18 re trust deeds) (reg 20).
- Trustee resignation (Form 19) (reg 17).

Trust Deeds

What are the main current statutory provisions for trust deeds?

3.27 The statutory framework for trust deeds is set out in the Bankruptcy (Scotland) Act 1985, s 59 and Sch 5 with amendments made by the Bankruptcy and Diligence etc (Scotland) Act 2007. There are a series of complicated commencement orders which are not separately listed here.[60] However the changes made to the trust deed framework are supported by the detailed provisions of The Protected Trust Deeds (Scotland) Regulations 2008[61] (for deeds signed after 1 April 2008). These detailed provisions as they relate to trust deeds are set out in Appendix 3.

Debt arrangement schemes

What are the main current statutory provisions for debt arrangement schemes?

3.28 The statutory framework for debt arrangement schemes (DAS) is set out in the Debt Arrangement Scheme (Scotland) Regulations 2004.[62] Subsequent amendments have been made by The Debt Arrangement Scheme (Scotland) Amendment Regulations 2007[63] which came into force on 30 June 2007.

---

60 The Bankruptcy and Diligence etc. (Scotland) Act 2007 (Commencement No 3, Savings and Transitionals) Order 2008 (SSI 2008/115); the Bankruptcy and Diligence etc. (Scotland) Act 2007 (Commencement No 7 and Transitionals) Order 2011 (SSI 2011/31).

61 SSI 2008/143.

62 SSI 2004/468.

63 SSI 2007/262.

Chapter 4

TYPES OF DEBT AND METHODS OF ENFORCEMENT

'A debt is just as hard for a Government to pay as it is for an individual.
No debt ever comes due at a good time.
Borrowing is the only thing that seems handy all the time.'[1]

INTRODUCTION

4.1 Personal debts and liabilities may arise in many different ways between individuals or between individuals and commercial or statutory entities. This chapter will examine the different types of debt that can be incurred by an individual and the legislation which governs them. Although the policy underlying formal insolvency remedies is that each unsecured creditor should be treated equally and the debtor should be able to divest himself of all debt through entry into an insolvency remedy. In practice there are exceptions to this principle and certain types of debt will survive bankruptcy or entry into an IVA or other formal debt solutions. In other cases certain types of debt can be given priority.

4.2 This chapter will also examine the different types of security available to an individual's creditors and how the treatment of debts under various types of procedure will vary according to the security held by the creditor. All types of debt will be looked at together with the sanctions that each type of creditor can use to enforce payment or to obtain the return of their goods. This chapter will go on to consider the effect on employees of the insolvency of their employer when the employer is an individual or a sole trader. Finally the different enforcement procedures in each jurisdiction are covered at the end of the chapter.

What is debt?

4.3 In the simplest terms a debt is a sum of money which one person (the creditor) has the right to claim from another person (the debtor) who has an obligation to pay the creditor either immediately or at a specified future date. The IA86[2] contemplates that a debt or liability may be present or future, certain

---

1 Will Rogers, March 1, 1931.
2 IA86, ss 385(1) and 382(3).

or contingent for an amount which may be fixed or liquidated or capable of being ascertained by fixed rules or as a matter of opinion. Other statutory instruments vary this definition.[3]

4.4 There are many definitions for liability and can include all of the following: an obligation to pay money or money's worth, any liability for breach of trust, any liability in contract, tort or bailment and any liability arising out of an obligation to make restitution.

4.5 In the context of bankruptcy r 12.3(1) IR86 provides that all claims by creditors are provable as debts against the bankrupt whether they are present or future, certain or contingent. The same rule also lists debts that are not provable, such as Child Support Agency (CSA) assessments, fines, maintenance and student loans, and these are covered later.

4.6 A debt can arise in the following circumstances:

- when a creditor has given the debtor the right to use a sum of money for a period of time subject to the debtor promising to return the sum at a future date (loan); or
- when a creditor has provided goods or services for which he levies a charge at a later date (account); or
- when the debtor has failed to pay sums due by way of tax or other statutory obligation or under a contract (arrears); or
- when one of the parties to a contract defaults on an obligation to pay money under a statute or as the result of a judgment or order against the debtor results.

What is credit?

4.7 The Consumer Credit Act 1974 defines the meaning of 'credit'[4] as including a cash loan and any other form of financial accommodation. The Consumer Credit Act 2006[5] (which was fully implemented on 1 October 2008) amended the 1974 act. Its purpose was to establish a fairer, clearer and more competitive market for consumer credit by updating the existing consumer credit legislation.

---

3 See chapter 27, at **27.6**.
4 Consumer Credit Act 1974, s 9.
5 Consumer Credit Act 2006.

What is a 'contingent liability'?

4.8 In bankruptcy for a contingent liability to arise in the context of s 382 IA86 there must be an existing legal obligation at the date of the bankruptcy order even if the obligation does not have to be fulfilled until the happening of some future event.

TYPES OF DEBT

What are the different types of debt?

4.9 Debt can be split initially into those creditors who have security and those who do not ie secured and unsecured debt. The types of security available are extensive and these are covered in more detail below, however holding security allows a creditor's debt to be paid first from the asset against which the security is held. Security can be formal or informal and this concept is discussed in more detail below. Some creditors who don't have any security have their status improved by legislation and these are known as preferential creditors ie they receive payment of any dividend ahead of the rest of the ordinary unsecured creditors. They also receive payment ahead of any security held over a general pool of assets ie a floating charge. In insolvency proceedings this status is created by s 386 IA86 and the creditors are listed in detail in Sch 6 IA86. In the debt advice sector other types of unsecured debt are treated as having priority because of the sanctions that they can impose for non-payment. These 'priority' unsecured creditors are looked at in more detail later in this chapter[6] but have no legal priority in a formal insolvency procedure.

TYPES OF SECURITY

What are the types of security available to creditors?

4.10 Security can be formal or informal. Fully secured creditors are prevented from proving in the bankruptcy because they are able to realise their debt from the property against which it is secured. Partially secured creditors must value their security and may only prove in the bankruptcy for the unsecured balance of their debt.

What is the definition of security?

4.11 For the purposes of insolvency in England and Wales 'security' is interpreted to mean,[7] any mortgage, charge, lien or other security and in respect

---

6 See **4.37**.

7 IA86, s 383(2).

of Scotland, any security (whether heritable or moveable) and any right of lien or preference and any right of retention (other than a right of compensation or set off).[8]

4.12 Some creditor's rights will be stronger than others depending on the date when the security was granted and the type of security held eg a legal mortgage is stronger than an equitable mortgage and will take priority over a charging order if the charging order is obtained after the legal mortgage was granted. The various different types of security are listed below with a brief explanation.

4.13 The status of the security can be affected by the type of procedure chosen. In *Re a Debtor No 10 of 1992*[9] the debtors proposed an IVA and obtained an interim order. The applicant, Mr Peck, had obtained a judgment against them and a writ of *fi. fa.*[10] had been executed in that the bailiff had taken walking possession of the debtor's chattels. He objected to the IVAs on the grounds that it prejudiced his interests in having the chattels sold. The court had to decide whether a writ of *fi. fa.* which had already been executed by walking possession constituted 'security' within the terms of s 383(4) IA86. Deciding that it did the judge then held that the IVA was not properly constituted because it had prejudiced Mr Peck's interests.

What is walking possession?

4.14 The judge interpreted the walking possession as being equivalent to a lien as contemplated by s 383(2) IA86 and distinguished the position under bankruptcy in which s 346(1) IA86 prevents a judgment creditor from retaining the benefit of the execution unless the execution has been completed before the commencement of the bankruptcy (the date of the bankruptcy order and not the petition), which would have meant removal of the assets covered by the walking possession agreement, not just the entering into of the agreement.

What is a legal mortgage?

4.15 A legal mortgage is one of the most secure and comprehensive forms of security. It transfers legal title to the mortgagee and prevents the mortgagor from dealing with the mortgaged asset while it is subject to the mortgage. Modern mortgages are now granted as legal charges which are described below.

What is an equitable mortgage?

4.16 An equitable mortgage arises where the formalities to create a legal mortgage have not been completed or where the asset being mortgaged is only an equitable interest. An equitable mortgage only transfers a beneficial interest in the asset to the mortgagee with legal title remaining with the mortgagor.

---

8 For further reading on this area see RM Goode *Legal Problems of Credit and Security* (Sweet and Maxwell).

9 *Peck v Craighead and Others* [1995] BCC 525.

10 As to writ of *fi. fa*, see **4.57**.

What is a legal charge?

4.17 The word 'charge' in legal charge is used to mean charged with the care of something, and that the lender who loaned the money has been put in legal charge of the property owned by the individual. This does not mean that they are physically in control of the property but that any default can result in the lender repossessing and selling it since their right to legal charge of the property has been lodged with the Land Registry.

What is a charging order?

4.18 A charging order is a means of enforcing a judgment by which a judgment creditor applies to the court for an order securing the amount awarded under the judgment against property held by the debtor (land, shares or funds in court). Charging orders are governed by the Charging Orders Act 1979 and by Part 73 of the Civil Procedure Rules. A charging order over land is usually protected by registration either at HM Land Registry

4.19 A charging order is obtained in two stages. The first stage is an interim order which is usually granted without a court hearing, where the judgment creditor satisfies the court of the fact of the judgment debt and the judgment debtor's probable interest in the property. The second stage is the hearing at which the court makes the decision resulting in the granting of the final order where the court considers all the circumstances of the case (eg the value of the property, the value of the judgment debt and the 'judgment debtor's' other creditors) in order to determine if it is appropriate to make the final order. The debtor will have notice of the final hearing and he will be able to apply for the interim charging order to be discharged.

What is a third party debt order?

4.20 A third party debt order (previously known as a garnishee order) is a court order requiring a third party who owes money to the judgment debtor to pay the debt to the judgment creditor in satisfaction of the judgment debt. It is obtained in two stages. The first stage is an interim order which is usually granted without a court hearing, where the judgment creditor satisfies the court of the fact of the judgment debt and the 'judgment debtor's' probable interest in the property. The second stage is the hearing at which the court considers all the circumstances of the case (eg the value of the debt owed, the value of the judgment debt and the judgment debtor's other creditors) in order to determine if it is appropriate to make the final order. Third party debt orders are governed by Civil Procedure Rules Part 72.

What is a pledge?

4.21 A pledge or 'pawn' is usually an object of value given or held as security to guarantee payment of a debt or fulfilment of an obligation. Most contracts of this type are now governed by the Consumer Credit Act 1974.[11]

---

[11] CCA 1974, ss 114–122.

What is 'distress' and 'distraint'?

4.22 Distress is a common law remedy. The process can be described as the taking of an asset or personal chattel, without legal process, from the possession of the debtor by the creditor as a pledge for the repayment of the debt. For the purposes of this book we are looking at a due debt. The process depends on the type of debt and more detail is provided under the relevant types of debt that allow distraint as a remedy.

4.23 Distraint is a similar process used by HMRC to recover revenue debts. There are three stages to this process: taking away the property, selling the property and completion of the process by paying the funds to the creditor.

What is 'illegal distress'?

4.24 This is one of the main offences seen by the courts. This includes situations where the bailiff has levied on goods that do not belong to the individual, where goods are listed that should be exempt or most importantly, illegal distress is where the bailiff is found not to be a certificated bailiff, as required by law. See chapter 2[12] for more information on bailiffs and enforcement officers.

4.25 For council tax, business rates, road traffic debts, magistrate court fines etc, the bailiff must, by law, be 'certificated' if he levies (seizes) goods. This can be either goods within the house that he lists on a walking possession, or a vehicle or other items outside. If it is found that the bailiff has acted illegally then the levy itself is void and therefore must be cancelled. In seeking damages for illegal distress, the owner of the goods could make a claim for trespass, and as such, any claim would be against the bailiff who levied, and any creditor authorising the illegal act. Action to sue to recover some compensation, which typically will be for trespass to land, or trespass to goods, should be made on the relevant county court form. In claims in respect of trespass to goods, it may be possible to also ask the court for an order for the recovery of the goods. In relation to parking penalties, it is important to note s 78(7) of the Road Traffic Act 1991, which states that:

> 'Any person who is not a certificated bailiff but who purports to levy a distress as such a bailiff, and any person authorising him to levy it, shall be deemed to have committed a trespass.'

What is 'irregular distress'?

4.26 This includes anything done in the wrong manner or without the proper formalities. This offence occurs when the levy was correct, but the events following it were not and could include any of the following:

- The bailiff has used the wrong forms.

---

[12] See **2.63–2.67**.

- Goods that have been taken were sold far too cheaply.

- The bailiff failed to give proper notice of the forthcoming sale of the goods to the debtor.

The courts generally see this offence as one of a technical offence in contrast to illegal distress. As a result the remedy is only the actual damage suffered by the claimant, which can prove difficult to calculate and is therefore not very often pursued.

What is excessive distress?

4.27 This offence occurs where more goods have been taken than are 'reasonably required' to clear both the debt and the bailiff's costs'. The following issues need to be considered before making such a claim:

- The goods have to actually be removed and not just threatened with removal.

- The value of any goods removed are not the original purchase price even if they are relatively new, but the second hand value which in many cases is only a fraction of any price paid.

- If one expensive item is removed to satisfy a very small debt this in itself is not considered excessive if that item was the only asset available to settle the debt. This is a particular problem when a debtor refuses entry to a bailiff and the only visible asset is often a motor vehicle. Note that a bailiff cannot levy on a motor vehicle if it is kept in a locked garage, parked elsewhere, or is not registered in the debtor's name.

What charges can a bailiff levy?

4.28 The fees that a bailiff can charge are set by the Government under statutory regulations.[13] However, incorporated into the fee scale is the provision for the bailiff to charge what is described as 'reasonable costs' for attendance fees, etc, and it is the interpretation of what is 'reasonable' that is the cause of most disputes in respect of charges levied. The most common area of dispute and usually concerns charges for the following:

- alleged visits, that did not actually take place;

- levy fees, where no levy was made etc;

- walking possession fee, where no walking possession has been signed;

---

[13] Council Tax (Administration and Enforcement) Regulations 1992, SI 1992/613, reg 8, Sch 5.

- attendance to remove fees, and/or van fees.[14]

Preferential creditors

Who are preferential creditors in insolvency proceedings?

4.29 Section 386 and Sch 6 IA86 makes provision for certain types of unsecured debt to be paid in priority to the unsecured debts of other creditors. It is an exception to the broad *pari passu* principle of equality.[15] Prior to the passing of the Enterprise Act 2002 (EA02) there were two main categories of preferential creditors who benefited from the section: employees of the debtor and the Crown. Section 251 EA02 abolished the Crown's right to recover unpaid taxes as a preferential debt, so the section is now in practice applicable only to the debtor's employees and to levies on the production of coal and steel. Neither category is commonly present in individual insolvency as a general rule. It should be noted that any money paid to employees in lieu of giving notice is not a preferential debt.

Preferential creditors for formal insolvency procedures are set out in Sch 6 IA86. The following types of debt which must be paid first out of assets realised for the bankrupt's estate, before the other unsecured creditors:

- Contributions to occupational pension schemes.[16]
- Arrears of salary,[17] holiday pay[18] and sick pay owed to employees.[19]
- Maternity pay.[20]
- Redundancy pay.[21]
- Levies on coal and steel production.[22]

Non-statutory 'priority' debts

4.30 It is important to distinguish between debts which are paid as a priority out of the bankrupt's estate within s 386 IA86 to preferential creditors

---

14 For guidance on the reasonableness of fees charged for different types of debt, see the following website at: http://bailiffadviceonline.com/bailifffeecomplaints_examplect.htm.

15 V Finch and S Worthington 'The Pari Passu Principle and Ranking Restitutionary Claims' in F Rose (ed) (2000) *Restitution and Insolvency* (Lloyd's of London Press, London) and also RJ Mokal 'Priority as Pathology: The Pari Passu Myth' (2001) *The Cambridge Law Journal* 60:3:581-621.

16 IA86, Sch 6, Category 4 (8).

17 IA86, Sch 6, Category 5 (9).

18 IA86, Sch 6, Category 5 (10) and (15).

19 IA86, Sch 6, Category 5 (13(2)(c).

20 IA86, Sch 6, Category 5 (13(2)(c).

21 IA86, Sch 6, Category 5 (14).

22 IA86, Sch 6, Category 6.

(principally debts to employees). The former debts are sometimes referred to as 'priority debts' by advice agencies because the consequences of default are more serious for the debtor than the general run of unsecured debts. They should therefore be regarded as a priority by the non-bankrupt debtor even though they are not formally statutory priority debts.

What are priority debts?

4.31 Some unsecured creditors have the ability to use alternative methods of obtaining payment which gives them a different type of importance. There are varying legal rules that allow certain creditors to get back what is owed to them in different ways. These include repossession, eviction, disconnection, distraint (removal of possessions by bailiffs) and in extreme cases, imprisonment. Some creditors can take action without a court order although a warning will always be given before any action is taken. Creditors who have these rights are known as priority creditors because this ability may influence the decision on which creditors are paid when funds are limited. These 'priority debts' include the following:

Priority Debt	**Potential Creditor Action**
TV Licence	Fine, distraint, imprisonment
Mortgage	Repossession
Secured Loan	Repossession
Rent	Eviction
Council Tax[23]	Distraint, wage or benefit deductions, imprisonment
Gas and Electricity[24]	Disconnection
Water Rates	Disconnection
Magistrates' Court Fines	Distraint, wage or benefit deductions, imprisonment
Maintenance	Distraint, wage or benefit deductions
Hire Purchase or Conditional Sale	Repossession
Income Tax and National Insurance	Distraint
VAT	Distraint
Car tax	Fine, imprisonment, impounding
Car insurance	Fine, imprisonment

4.32 These priority debts need to be distinguished from other debts where the creditors do not have additional recovery procedures and they therefore need to be paid in priority to other debts such as:

- Credit cards.

---

[23] Local Government Finance Act 1992 and Council Tax (Administration and Enforcement) Regulations 1992, SI 1992/613.

[24] Gas Act 1986 and Electricity Act 1989.

- Personal loans with finance companies.
- Bank or building society loans.
- Bank or building society overdrafts.
- Charge cards.
- Mail order catalogue debts.
- Personal debts to friends and family.
- Doorstep-collected loans.
- Credit sale agreements.
- Trading cheques or vouchers.

Council Tax

What is council tax and how are arrears collected?

4.33 Council tax is payable by all residents of all dwellings under the Local Government Finance Act 1992 (LGFA92). There are some limited exceptions as set out in Sch 1 of the LGFA92 and in the Council Tax (Exempt Dwellings) Order 1992 but the presumption is that all dwellings will be subject to council tax. The tax is payable by the resident of the property, defined in s 6 LGFA92 as an individual who has attained the age of 18 and has his sole or main residence in the dwelling who has the greatest interest in the property moving down through the sub-sections of the subsections and stopping at the first one to apply. So a resident in the property who owns the freehold of the property will be liable in advance of a resident in the same property who owns a leasehold interest in the same property or a resident who has a contractual licence to occupy part of the property.

4.34 There is a distinction for the purpose of the statute between a 'resident' and an 'occupier'. If no-one occupying the dwelling qualifies as a resident then the person liable for the council tax is the owner of the dwelling. The tax is payable on a daily basis, assessed once a year in March and billed in advance for each financial year which runs from 1 April to 31 March. Payment may be made in one lump sum but is more usually made in 10 monthly instalments.

4.35 In recent years it has been the policy of many local authorities to use bankruptcy as a remedy against defaulting debtors. The procedure for appealing against a council tax bill is not widely publicised[25] and there have been a number of recent cases where bankruptcy orders have been made, and

---

25 As seems to have been the case in *R (Kinsley) v Barnet Magistrates Court, London Borough of Barnet* [2009] EWHC 464 (Admin) which provides a useful analysis of the procedure.

applications to annul dismissed,[26] even where the debtor has had a valid challenge to the sum claimed. The enforcement process is therefore described in some detail. Reference should be made however to the text of the Local Government Finance Act 1992 and the Council Tax (Administration and Enforcement) Regulations 1992 for the specific provisions.[27]

4.36 The LGFA92 provides for the assessment and collection of council tax. Enforcement of unpaid council tax liabilities is governed by the Council Tax (Administration and Enforcement) Regulations 1992 (CTAER92). A number of enforcement methods are authorised by the LGFA92. Each of them requires the local authority to have assessed the sum due and unpaid.

4.37 It is a requirement of the LGFA92 and the enforcement regulations that the local authority should estimate the amount of council tax due by the resident of a dwelling in advance in the financial year before the tax is payable.[28] The estimate of the amount of council tax due is based on a number of assumptions that the conditions applicable to the property and the resident that apply on the first day of the council tax period (being a financial year running from 1 April to 31 March) will continue to apply on each day of the period of the estimate.

4.38 The local authority serves a demand notice[29] at the start of the council tax period requiring the resident to pay the amount estimated by instalments.[30] If an instalment is missed during the course of the council tax period the local authority is required to serve a reminder notice[31] in respect of that instalment. However, no reminder notice is required in the following circumstances:

- Where all the instalments have fallen due (at the end of the council tax period).[32]
- Where an instalment is missed within 7 days of a reminder notice having been issued.[33]
- Where an instalment is missed after two reminder notices have been issued within the same council tax period.[34]

---

26 See for example: *Watts v London Borough of Newham* [2009] EWHC 377 (Ch).

27 For the relevant time for enforcement of the council tax debt (6 years from due date) and recovery by presentation of a petition on a liability order (no limit), see *(1) Bolsover District Council (2) Mansfield District Council v (1) Ashfield Nominees Ltd (2) Dennis Rye Ltd (3) East Midlands Developments Ltd (4) Hardwick Nominees Ltd* [2010] EWCA Civ 1129, [2011] BPIR 7.

28 SI 1992/613, reg 20.

29 SI 1992/613, reg 18.

30 SI 1992/613, Sch 1.

31 SI 1992/613, reg 23.

32 SI 1992/613, reg 23(2).

33 SI 1992/613, reg 23(3).

34 SI 1992/613, reg 23(4).

What is a 'liability order'?

4.39 Liability orders are dealt with at para 3 of Sch 4 to LGFA92 and reg 34 CTAER92. A local authority may apply to a magistrates' court and the court must make an order if it is satisfied that the sum claimed is payable and has not been paid. Once the liability order has been made the local authority has a variety of options as to how it enforces the liability order.

What enforcement methods can be used for council tax arrears?

4.40 The following enforcement methods are available and are looked at in more detail below:

- Attachment of earnings.
- Deductions from income support.
- Distress.
- Commitment to prison.
- Bankruptcy and winding-up.
- Charging order.

What is the process for an attachment of earnings for council tax arrears?

4.41 The attachment of earnings order is made in the magistrates' court and the debtor has a right of appeal to the magistrates' court against any action taken by the local authority in relation to the attachment of earning order under para 5 of Sch 4 to LGFA92.

What is the process for deductions from income support for council tax arrears?

4.42 Paragraph 6 of Sch 4 to LGFA92 provides for deductions to be made directly from income support paid in accordance with Social Security Contributions and Benefits Act 1992. Deductions cannot be made from payments of non means-tested benefits including disability living allowance.

How is 'distress' levied for council tax arrears?

4.43 Paragraph 7 of Sch 4 to LGFA92 empowers a local authority to exercise distress over the goods of a person subject to a liability order. The distress is not rendered unlawful by reason of formal defects in the liability order and any person who has suffered damage as a result of an irregularly exercised distress may recover a sum in compensation for the damage suffered. The sum claimable is limited to the amount of special damage suffered and the principles embodied in the Distress for Rent Act 1689, whereby damages for wrongful distress can in certain circumstances be assessed at double or treble the value of the special damage suffered, are expressly disapplied.

What is the process for commitment to prison for council tax arrears?

4.44 Where the local authority has attempted and failed to levy distress under para 8 of Sch 4 to LGFA92, it may apply to the magistrates' court for an order of commitment to prison. The warrant for commitment must state the amount outstanding and the length of the period of commitment. Commitment to prison is only available if the court is satisfied that the failure to pay is due to wilful refusal to pay or culpable neglect. The maximum period of commitment to prison is 3 months.

What is the process for bankruptcy proceedings to be commenced in respect of council tax arrears?

4.45 Paragraph 9 of Sch 4 to LGFA 92 provides that the amount due under a liability order is deemed to be a debt for the purposes of s 267 IA86 and can therefore form the grounds of a creditor's petition for bankruptcy where the debtor is an individual. Unless some other type of execution such as distress or attachment of earnings has been returned unsatisfied the local authority can serve a statutory demand in respect of the liability order. This statutory power was confirmed by the Court of Appeal in *Lonergan v Gedling Borough Council*,[35] which also confirmed the statutory power of the local authority to delegate the power to bring proceedings to a subordinate council official under s 151 of the Local Government Act 1972. Recently, there has been much debate about the extent to which it is appropriate for a local authority to seek a bankruptcy order against a council tax defaulter, especially one who may have mental difficulties, and the effect of the local authority not following the proper procedures. On a number of occasions, the Ombudsman has held that the local authority has acted inappropriately to such an extent so as to justify a finding of maladministration.[36] However, the courts have tended to adopt a harsher view, namely that a local authority owed money is entitled to collect it, by bankruptcy if necessary.[37] These issues are considered in greater detail in chapter 7.[38]

What is the process for a charging order for council tax arrears?

4.46 Charging orders are governed by para 11 of Sch 4 to LGFA92. Charging orders against an interest in property owned by the debtor can be obtained

---

35 [2009] EWCA Civ 1569, [2010] BPIR 911.

36 See for example, *Ford v Wolverhampton City Council (Local Government Ombudsman's Report)* [2008] BPIR 1304, *Report of an Investigation into Complaint No 07/A/12661 against the London Borough of Camden* [2008] BPIR 1572, *Report of an Investigation into Complaint No 07B10432 against Manchester CC* [2010] BPIR 476, *Report of an Investigation into Complaint No 08 014 087 against Brighton and Hove Council* [2010] BPIR 1407 and *Report of an Investigation into Complaint No 09 006 694 against Thurrock Council* [2010] BPIR 1420.

37 See for example *Parveen v Manchester CC and Hellard* [2010] BPIR 152, *Nottingham CC v Pennant* [2009] EWHC 2437 (Ch), [2010] BPIR 430, *R (Mohammed) v The London Borough of Southwark* [2009] EWHC 311 (Admin), [2009] BPIR 882, *London Borough of Redbridge v Mustafa* [2010] EWHC 1105 (Ch), [2010] BPIR 893, *Lonergan v Gedling Borough Council* [2009] EWCA Civ 745, [2009] EWCA Civ 696, [2009] EWCA Civ 1569, [2010] BPIR 911, *Banfield v Harrow LBC* [2010] EWHC 2707 (Ch) [2011] BPIR 4.

38 See **7.55**ff.

under s 1 of the Charging Orders Act 1979 or reg 50 of the Council Tax (Administration and Enforcement) Regulations 1992. Procedure is governed by CPR Part 73. A charging order is obtained in two stages: an interim order, dealt with by a judge without a hearing and a final order.

Other types of debt

What other types of debt are there?

4.47 The most common other debts are those covered by the Consumer Credit Act 1974 which include:

- Credit cards.
- Bank overdrafts.
- Hire purchase.
- Credit hire eg mobile telephones, motor cars, satellite television services, the use of other large electrical goods and household items.

4.48 Other debts for trading individuals include:

- Income tax.
- VAT.
- Other trade debts.

4.49 Other common debts are:

- Student loans.
- Payments for utilities.
- Fines and court fees.
- Payments under matrimonial court orders.

A small number of specific types of debt will not be released through bankruptcy or other insolvency procedure. These 'non-provable' debts include maintenance payments in family proceedings, student loans, gambling debts.[39] In each case the debt will survive the bankruptcy and the debtor will remain liable for it. Equally the creditor will not participate in the distribution of the debtor's assets and will be required to continue to levy enforcement against the debtor.

---

39 For bankruptcy non-provable debts are set out in IR86, r 12.3.

How are student loans dealt with?

4.50 A student or former student may have a liability to repay a loan taken out under various legislative rules in England and Wales or Northern Ireland and in general these student loans can no longer be written off in bankruptcy proceedings and the following rules apply depending on the type and date of the loan and the jurisdiction.

4.51 Since 1 July 2004 student loan debts incurred in England and Wales under the Education (Student Loans) Act 1990 (ESLA90) (mortgage style loans) and from 1 September 2004 student loan debts incurred under the Teaching and Higher Education Act 1998 (THEA98) (income contingent loans) are no longer provable in bankruptcy.

4.52 Any person whose bankruptcy commenced[40] on or after 1 September 2004 and who had a liability to repay a loan under THEA98, that loan is no longer a provable debt in any bankruptcy proceedings.[41] Additionally, any student who becomes bankrupt after 1 September 2004 and who has not completed their education is able to receive further student loans, these loans do not become acquired property. Consequently they should not be taken into account when calculating whether or not to obtain an income payments order/agreement.

4.53 Similarly in Northern Ireland but with effect from 15 January 2005, in the case of bankruptcies which commenced[42] on or after 15 January 2005, any liability to repay a loan[43] is no longer a provable debt in bankruptcy and will no longer be written off on the bankrupt's discharge.

4.54 In Scotland student loans can no longer be written off in bankruptcy with effect from 1 April 2008[44] and was one of the main changes introduced by the Bankruptcy and Diligence etc. (Scotland) Act 2007.

Which other debts require specialist advice?

4.55 The following debts require specialist advice:

- Rent and utilities from a previous property.
- Hire-purchase or conditional sale where goods have gone back to the company.
- Debts with cheque-cashing services.

---

40 As defined by IA86, s 278.
41 Education (Student Support) (No 2) Regulations 2002 (Amendment) (No 3) Regulations 2004.
42 As defined by INO89, art 252.
43 Loans repayable under the Education (Student Support) (Northern Ireland) Order 1998.
44 Bankruptcy and Diligence etc. (Scotland) Act 2007 received Royal Assent on 15 January 2007.

- Gambling and spread betting debts.[45]
- Business debts.
- Professional fees (solicitors, vets etc).
- Statute barred debts are covered in detail in chapter 19.

ENFORCEMENT PROCEDURES IN ENGLAND AND WALES

Writs and orders in aid of execution of judgments

What are the enforcement procedures in England and Wales?

4.56 A creditor who has obtained a judgment against a debtor will not be a secured creditor unless he has executed the judgment or obtained a charging order over the debtor's property. Execution can be levied against real property (land), moveable property (goods), bank accounts or salary. There are a number of enforcement methods open to a judgment creditor against a non-bankrupt debtor. The Tribunals Courts and Enforcement Act 2007 (TCEA 2007) will make some changes to these procedures but at the time of writing it is not yet fully in force.

4.57 Once a creditor has obtained judgment against a debtor if the debtor does not voluntarily satisfy the judgment it will be necessary for the creditor to levy execution against the debtor's property by taking possession of the property and selling it. One way of doing this is by a writ of *fieri facias* which is a procedure by which a bailiff or enforcement officer takes 'walking possession' of the debtor's goods. Henceforth the goods are held by the debtor subject to the right of the judgment creditor to take and to sell the goods.

Procedure	**Effect**	**Process**	**TCEA 2007**
Writ of *fieri facias* (except writs of *fieri facias de bonis ecclesiasticis*) High Court for debts exceeding £5,000	The debtor's movable property is charged in the creditor's favour	A bailiff (enforcement agent) takes 'walking possession' of the goods which may then be sold on the creditor's behalf at a later date[46]	Writ of control Part 3 Sections 62–70

---

[45] See, for example, *Feldman v Nissim* [2010] EWHC 1353 (Ch), [2010] BPIR 815.

[46] High Court and County Courts Jurisdiction Order 1991, SI 1991/724; also RSC Order 46.

Procedure	**Effect**	**Process**	**TCEA 2007**
Warrant of execution county court	The debtor's movable property is charged in the creditor's favour	A bailiff (enforcement agent) takes 'walking possession' of the goods which may then be sold on the creditor's behalf at a later date[47]	Warrant of control Part 3 Sections 62–70
3rd party debt order (previously a Garnishee Order)	The debtor's property in the hands of a 3rd party including a bank is charged in the creditor's favour	An initial order is made without a hearing (interim order) followed by a final order made at a hearing[48]	N/A
Attachment of Earnings	Debtor's employer directed to pay a specific sum to the creditor	Orders can be made without a hearing[49]	Part 4 Section 91

Charging orders and IVAs

4.58 In *Clarke v Coutts and Co*[50] the Court of Appeal dealt with the question of what effect an interim order under s 252(2) IA86 would have when a charging order nisi was made absolute without the leave of the Court during the period when the moratorium was in force. The Court of Appeal discharged the charging order, holding that the moratorium meant that it should not have been made final.

Charging orders and bankruptcy

4.59 In *Nationwide Building Society v Wright*[51] the Court of Appeal considered the effect of a final charging order which was made after the bankruptcy petition was issued but before the bankruptcy order was made. It considered that the 'commencement' of the bankruptcy for the purposes of s 284 IA86 was the date of the bankruptcy order as specified in s 278 IA86. Since the charging order had been completed before the bankruptcy order the charging order meant that the judgment creditor was a secured creditor. Somewhat exceptionally, in *Tagore Investments SA v Official Receiver*[52] an interim charging order was final after a bankruptcy order had been made against the debtor. The debtor's conduct had the effect of misleading the court prior to judgment, his petition for bankruptcy was a pre-planned act of

47 High Court and County Courts Jurisdiction Order 1991, SI 1991/724; also CCR Order 26.
48 CPR, Part 72.
49 CCR Order 27.
50 [2002] EWCA Civ 943.
51 [2009] EWCA Civ 811.
52 [2008] EWHC 3495 (Ch), [2009] BPIR 392. The court recognised that this was a very unusual case and that care should be taken in deriving too much from it; normally the *pari passu* rule would prevail.

manipulation and the creditor had not delayed in enforcing the judgment. There were few unsecured creditors in the bankruptcy apart from the creditor and the balance of justice was in its favour.

4.60 These decisions contrast with *Roberts Petroleum Ltd v Bernard Kenny Ltd*[53] in which the House of Lords held that a final charging order should not have been made against a debtor company which had passed a resolution for voluntary winding up at a date between the date of the interim order and the final order. In corporate winding up proceedings the statutory scheme for protection and distribution of the debtor's assets is triggered by the filing of the winding up petition or the resolution of the board to wind the company up. In bankruptcy by contrast the statutory scheme does not commence until the bankruptcy order is made.

4.61 The types of enforcement procedures available to a creditor in England and Wales will depend on the type of debt. The table above lists some of the key types of debt and the sort of enforcement procedures that can be used. Other creditors will usually require a judgment to be obtained from the court and if the judgment remains unpaid the debt can then be enforced by a number of different routes. These are set out below:

- a warrant of execution – sending a court bailiff to collect the money;
- an attachment of earnings order – stopping the money from the defendant's wages;
- a third party debt order – freezing the defendant's money that is held, for example, in a bank account; or
- a charging order – the money is paid on the sale of the defendant's house.

What is a warrant of execution?

4.62 Before the court can issue a warrant, the debtor must be in arrears by having:

- failed to pay the amount he or she has been ordered to pay by the court; or
- fallen behind with at least one payment.

A warrant of execution will only help if the debtor has:

- enough goods at their known address that can be sold at auction to raise money to cover the debt; or
- have sufficient money to meet the claim listed on the warrant in full.

---

53 [1983] AC 192.

What is an attachment of earnings order?

4.63 Before the court can issue an attachment of earnings the debtor must have:

- failed to pay the amount he or she has been ordered to pay by the court; or
- fallen behind with at least one payment; and
- the amount outstanding must be £50 or more.

An attachment of earnings order is only of use if the debtor is in paid employment.

Who are bailiffs and enforcement officers?

4.64 Bailiffs and enforcement officers are authorised to remove and sell an individual's assets in order to pay the money owed. In some cases they may also have authority to conduct evictions and arrest people. Bailiffs and enforcement officers have differing roles. These roles are covered in detail in chapter 2.

When can goods be repossessed under the Consumer Credit Acts?

4.65 The Consumer Credit Act 1974 provides some protection against repossession and goods can only be removed in the following circumstances:

- a written default notice must be served on the debtor covering the following issues;
- it must give the debtor at least 7 days notice of any action intended;
- the notice should say how much must be paid to bring payments up to date;
- when those payments must be made;
- what will happen if payments are not made ie what action is intended;
- how the agreement will be brought to an end; and that if payments are made the agreement will not be brought to an end;
- if less than one third of the total price of the goods has been paid under a HP agreement then the creditor can take the goods back if more than one third has been paid then a court order must be obtained first. Even if a court order has been obtained the debtor can ask the court to suspend the 'return order' and accept an offer to pay the outstanding amounts by instalments.

ENFORCEMENT PROCEDURES IN NORTHERN IRELAND

What are the enforcement procedures in Northern Ireland?

4.66 The Judgments and Enforcements (Northern Ireland) Order 1981 is the principle legislation for enforcement in Northern Ireland. The Enforcement of Judgements Office which is an agency of the Department of Justice controls the enforcement processes including debt recovery. They do not have a bailiff system as in England and Wales. Any judgment obtained anywhere in the UK can be enforced by this single office.[54] The office has a wide range of remedies and can issue one or more of the following orders after investigating the circumstances of the individual.

What types of order are available?

4.67 The enforcement officer has complete discretion over the type of order chosen and it cannot be stipulated by either the creditor or the debtor:[55]

- an instalment order;
- a seizure of goods order;
- an order charging land;
- a delivery of possession of land order;
- a delivery of goods order;
- a charging order on funds, stocks or shares;
- an attachment of debts order;
- an order for payment by garnishee;
- an attachment of earnings order;
- the appointment of a receiver;

If the enforcement is successful the office will issue a certificate of satisfaction however if it is not enforceable the office will issue a certificate of unenforceability. This certificate is sufficient grounds for a creditor to present a bankruptcy petition[56]. The office will also stay any further proceedings for a period of six weeks during which the debtor has an opportunity to enter into an arrangement with creditors either formal or informal.

---

54 Art 5, Judgments and Enforcements (Northern Ireland) Order 1981, SI 1981/226 (NI 6).
55 Art 4, Judgments and Enforcements (Northern Ireland) Order 1981, SI 1981/226 (NI 6).
56 Article 242(1)(b) IO89.

ENFORCEMENT PROCEDURES IN SCOTLAND

What are the enforcement procedures in Scotland?

4.68 The enforcement procedures in Scotland were overhauled by the Bankruptcy and Diligence etc (Scotland) Act 2007 (BAD07) which came into force in April 2008. In Scotland, there are a number of ways that people can be made to pay by the courts. The most common forms of enforcement (otherwise known as diligence) are:

- Arrestment.[57]
- Earnings arrestment.
- Attachment.
- Other forms of diligence.

What is arrestment?

4.69 This means that money or goods held by a third party are 'frozen'. The most common example is arrestment of funds in a bank account but 'arrestable' funds or goods can include:

- Funds held in bank or building society accounts.
- Goods owned by a debtor but in the hands of a third party, for example, goods in a warehouse or in storage.
- 'Incorporeal' property such as rights under a trust, for damages or due under life assurance policies.

The third party holding funds or assets caught by the arrestment, has a duty to disclose to the creditor precisely what has been caught by the arrestment. Unless objection is lodged with the court, funds or assets caught must be automatically released to a creditor after a period of fourteen weeks. So far as the balance in the bank account of an individual is concerned, a protected minimum amount is exempt from the arrestment. Finally, rather than secure all funds due to the debtor by the third party or all assets held by the third party, the arrestment will be limited to the balance due to the creditor. Approval of a DAS programme will cancel an arrestment.

What is an earnings arrestment?

4.70 For individuals who are working, money can be taken from their wage or salary by their employer under an earnings arrestment. An ordinary arrestment is a 'once-only' freeze of property. But earnings arrestment doesn't freeze

---

[57] Bankruptcy and Diligence etc (Scotland) Act 2007, Part 10.

anything. An employer is required to continue to make regular payments until the sum due is paid. There are three different types of earnings arrestment: earnings arrestment, continuous maintenance arrestment, and conjoined arrestment. They all follow the same basic principle. Approval of a debt arrangement scheme programme will cancel an earnings arrestment.

What is an attachment?

4.71 Attachment freezes property held by the person in debt. Anything that has been 'attached' can be sold at auction. The money raised is then handed over to the creditor. Attachment replaces the old system of poinding ('pinding').[58] The main difference between attachment and poinding is that the courts have to give permission first before a person can enter a house to 'attach' goods. Approval of a DAS programme or other formal insolvency proceedings will cancel an attachment unless notice of an auction has been given, or the attached property is about to be, or has been, removed for auction.

What is a money attachment and when can it be used?

4.72 From the 23 November 2009 a new form of diligence was introduced in Scotland which allows a creditor to seize money belonging to a debtor in satisfaction of a debt. In principle, all assets owned by a debtor are at risk. But prior to this enactment, creditors were unable to take diligence against cash owned by a debtor. To rectify this anomaly, a special category of diligence called money attachment was introduced by Part 8 BAD07.[59] A money attachment can be used after a creditor has first obtained a decree (ie judgment) or other document of debt and the charge for payment has expired (usually after 14 days).

What is included in a money attachment?

4.73 For these purposes money includes cash (sterling and other currencies), cheques, negotiable instruments, promissory notes, money orders and postal orders, all of which can be physically removed. However, sheriff officers have no power to enter a debtor's house, so in practice the attachment is usually confined to a debtor's business premises. A money attachment cannot be carried out on Sundays or public holidays, or between 8pm and 8am unless the court specifically approves it.

How is the money attached and how are objections raised?

4.74 It is assumed that money found on a debtor's business premises belongs to him, although sheriff officers must make reasonable enquiries at the time the money is removed. The sheriff's officer must also submit a report to the court which sets out a description and value of the money removed. The creditor

---

58 Repealed by Debt Arrangement and Attachment (Scotland) Act 2002, s 58.

59 Bankruptcy and Diligence etc (Scotland) Act 2007.

then has 14 days to apply to the court for a payment order authorising the sheriff officer to release the money to them (after deduction of the sheriff officer's own fees).

4.75 This application can be made by the debtor or a third party. The sheriff will then have a hearing to allow both parties to make representations. The onus of proof is on the applicant to show that the money removed does not belong to the debtor. The debtor can also apply to court for an order to return the money if there are extenuating circumstances.

4.76 If there have been any procedural irregularities during the attachment process, the sheriff can also order the return of the money. In those circumstances all of the money must be returned to the debtor. The new rules are not complex, but to protect the debtor they must be followed explicitly: if not, the money attachment is invalidated.

4.77 Another practical difficulty is actually determining the ownership of the money. Under the new rules, arguments over who owns the money attached must be resolved in court but this may be difficult in practice as few people retain large amounts of cash especially when they are in debt. The real usefulness will probably be in enforcing debts against cash businesses such as shops, bars, clubs or restaurants, where there is likely to be cash on the premises. In these cases, a well-timed and properly executed money arrestment is a useful enforcement tool.

What other forms of 'diligence' are used in Scotland?

4.78 The less common ways to enforce court orders include adjudication and admiralty arrestment. DAS and other forms of formal insolvency proceedings will stop both these forms of diligence, but as they are specialised technical legal advice should be taken.

4.79 This new regime for obtaining permission for (and recalling) diligence on the dependence of a court action (ie arrestment and inhibition) requires the court to be satisfied that:

- there is a good, arguable case on the merits;
- there is a real and substantial risk that enforcement of any decree would be defeated by the debtor being insolvent, or likely to dispose of his assets; and
- that it is reasonable in the circumstances for diligence to be granted;

before granting or recalling a warrant for diligence. This test has recently been considered in the appeal case of *McCormack v Hamilton Academical Football Club*[60] when the court decided that the warrant for arrestment should not have

60 [2009] CSIH 16.

been recalled but instead restricted to a reasonable sum and that both the current and future financial positions needed to be considered. The judgment helpfully clarified the 'real and substantial risk' test.

What is 'an inhibition' and what changes have been made to the process in Scotland?

4.80 An inhibition is an order granted by the court against an individual or legal person preventing them from voluntarily selling or granting security over land owned by them. An inhibition also previously conferred a preference over non-inhibiting creditors in the event of bankruptcy. Inhibition is available either pre-judgment ('on the dependence') or after judgment ('in execution').

4.81 Until April 2009 a creditor's authority to inhibit a debtor was obtained by application to the Court of Session in Edinburgh with the Inhibition itself being recorded in the Register of Inhibitions and Adjudications. The procedure was previously governed by common law but with effect from 22 April 2009 the former procedure for obtaining an inhibition was abolished. Warrant or authority to inhibit an execution (after judgment) is now contained in an extract of the court decree or a document of debt containing 'a consent to registration for preservation and execution'.

4.82 Warrant to inhibit on the dependence (prior to judgment) will also be obtainable from the sheriff court as well as the Court of Session. Previously it had only been available in the Court of Session. For the avoidance of doubt an inhibition is confirmed as taking effect on the date of recording of the letters of inhibition in the Register of Inhibitions. More importantly an inhibition will no longer confer any preference in a bankruptcy.

Chapter 5

ASSETS: REALISING THEIR VALUE

'At last it is all gone. Nothing is left about the house
but scattered leaves of catalogues,'[1]

INTRODUCTION

5.1 This chapter briefly examines the range of assets that may be owned by an individual and briefly compares how those assets are treated in DMPs, IVAs, bankruptcy and DROs. Any assets that can potentially be excluded from formal insolvency proceedings are briefly discussed within each section. Chapter 17 deals with other assets that may fall into a bankrupt's estate and how these are dealt with specifically in bankruptcy. Further discussion is provided specifically on the matrimonial home in bankruptcy proceedings in chapter 18. For any individual that is in financial difficulty the option to sell assets and realise their potential will often be the first step to trying to solve any financial difficulty.

LAND AND BUILDINGS

How are land and buildings treated?

5.2 Land and buildings can be the most valuable asset in a personal insolvency and therefore the most important asset. Conversely any loans secured on the property may also be substantial. The following paragraphs will examine land, before going on to discuss buildings on that land and the different forms of ownership that can exist in relation to both domestic and commercial property, ie sole and joint ownership; freehold and leasehold interests and equitable interests. The type of insolvency process together with details of ownership will dictate how land and buildings are dealt with in each case.

5.3 Land, or realty, is intrinsically valuable even without buildings. For this reason it is of interest to any relevant office holder for the purposes of realisation but also for the purposes of an office holder's ongoing obligations to safeguard the assets that form part of the estate.[2] In terms of the nature of land

---

1 Charles Dickens, Chapter 59, *Dombey and Son*.

2 Issues such as waste management licences and previous commercial use (eg toxic waste residue resulting from previous use) may make land a burden.

this can be wide and disparate in value, extent and type.[3] Bare land can of course be made more valuable when developed and this brings us to the first type of ownership.

5.4 Freehold property is the most valuable species of proprietary interest in land. The owner of the freehold is absolutely entitled to use the land in any way he so chooses without interference except for local planning rules and other consent requirements. It is because of this that freehold property is of the utmost interest to relevant office holders and it is usually this species of property that makes up a large percentage of an individual's personal realisable assets in bankruptcy. The most common example of this type of interest is the matrimonial home; this subject is dealt with in-depth in chapter 18.

5.5 In terms of DMPs, IVAs and DROs there are a number of nuances in relation to the other formal personal insolvency procedures as regards freehold property and in particular the matrimonial home. DROs by their nature, ie the asset restriction[4] of £300, preclude individuals with freehold property. In relation to IVAs there can be more creative solutions than just selling the property especially where family and friends can provide funds in lieu of any equity held.

Is the type of ownership important?

5.6 Freehold property can be owned either jointly or solely. Caution must be exercised as legal title is not necessarily indicative of actual ownership. For example there are cases in which legal title did not ultimately reflect the true beneficial interest in the property.[5]

5.7 The issues raised above in relation to solely owned property do invariably of course arise in relation to jointly owned property. This the most common type of property ownership in use today. Joint ownership can either be as tenants in common or joint tenants.[6]

How is the matrimonial or residential home treated?

5.8 The matrimonial or residential home is potentially very difficult to deal with as even if there is equity in the property, which can be released, this may not be possible if the debtor or his family have insufficient income to service any additional borrowing. Alternatively selling the property and renting instead may also not be an option if suitable rented accommodation is not available at an affordable cost. Other issues such as location of schools, work, etc may also need to be taken into consideration.

---

3 For example agricultural, brown field sites etc.

4 See chapter 27 at **27.5**.

5 See the recasting of the law by the Court of Appeal in *Oxley v Hiscock* [2004] EWCA Civ 546, [2005] Fam 211 and the House of Lords in *Stack v Dowden* [2007] UKHL 17, [2007] 2 AC 432, [2007] BPIR 913 and the long line of cases subsequently considering them.

6 On this further see, Gray & Gray, *Land Law* (OUP, 2007).

How are second or investment homes treated?

5.9 Second homes or investment properties which are often the cause of financial problems will be treated in the same way as any other asset. However, issues often arise when they have been purchased abroad or as a timeshare and specialist advice will be required depending on the circumstances of each case.

How is leasehold property treated?

5.10 A leasehold interest is a proprietary interest which is carved out of a freehold interest. This species of proprietary interest can be for short or long periods of time. It is from this time span that we get the 99-year leasehold period on a significant number of London properties. Leasehold interests can however, be agreed for various periods of time, some much shorter. A leasehold interest, particularly a long lease, can be of interest to the office holder for its potential realisable value. Leasehold interests usually have annual payment conditions such as ground rent in respect of the land and maintenance requirements in respect of any buildings. The longer the period remaining on the lease the more valuable it is as an asset. By comparison shorter leasehold interests such as assured shorthold tenancies are not as easily realisable.

How is solely owned leasehold property treated?

5.11 As with freehold interests in land, leasehold interests can also be in the nature of sole legal ownership.

How is jointly owned leasehold property treated?

5.12 Similarly as with freehold proprietary interests in land, leasehold interests can also be in the nature of joint legal ownership.

How is commercial leasehold property treated?

5.13 One of the main species of use for leasehold property is commercial. Complications can arise in cases where the insolvent individual is trading or has been in business. Most commercial leases are of a short duration and as a consequence unless the site is in a sought after location there is often little value in the lease. The other issue that needs to be considered is the potential liability from the use of the building, eg covenants to repair, and in formal insolvency situations there is the ability to disclaim onerous property. Specialist advice will be required depending on the circumstances of each case.

What is an equitable charge?

5.14 A secured loan can take effect as an equitable charge instead of a legal charge. This can be done for several reasons:

- an existing secured lender has refused to give permission for a further loan to be secured against the property;

- the charge documentation is defective;

– the borrower only has an equitable interest such as an interest under a trust.

This will still give the lender rights in respect of the property and may be registered against the property on the Land Register. A registration entry for an equitable charge will look slightly different to the entry relating to a legal charge.

What is an equitable interest?

5.15 An equitable interest is different from a lien and although recognizable by a court of law it is enforceable only in limited circumstances as opposed to a contractual obligation which is strictly enforceable regardless of the parties involved. An equitable interest usually carries with it an element of fairness whereas contractual interests are strictly enforceable. An equitable interest in land may not be registered and can drop away if a later purchaser of the property was not aware of the equitable interest before entering the contract. To avoid this happening anyone with an equitable interest in a property should consult a solicitor about having the matter registered as a covenant to maintain its long-term validity.

MOTOR VEHICLES

How are motor vehicles treated?

5.16 Motor vehicles can be an asset but can also be the cause of financial problems. The repossession of a car may often result in further charges accruing and just handing back the keys will often not be the simple option it seemed to clear the debt. If a car is owned outright and not an absolute necessity then selling it may be an option to raise funds. In bankruptcy a car that is needed for work and is not particularly valuable can be retained by the bankrupt under the exempt property rule.[7] Similar considerations will be allowed in other formal insolvency procedures.[8] Caravans and motor homes will be treated in the same way unless they are the main residential home. Cherished registration numbers may also have a value.[9]

CASH AT BANK

How are bank accounts treated?

5.17 Bank accounts are usually 'frozen' by most banks when they become aware of a bankruptcy order or debt relief order. Most advisers will usually tell debtors to go to a different bank or building society and open a basic account

---

7 IA86, s 283(2)(a).

8 Eg IVAs where the comparison to the outcome in bankruptcy allows creditors to see the financial difference.

9 See *Pick (Trustee in Bankruptcy of Virdi) v Goel* [2006] EWHC 833 (Ch), [2006] BPIR 827.

immediately after any bankruptcy order has been made so that any wages can be paid as normal. Some banks may allow an existing account to be continued. But even if the bank agrees to this, they will freeze the account when they first hear about the bankruptcy order and any money in the account at the date of the bankruptcy order will become an asset in the bankruptcy estate. The funds will be claimed by the official receiver or the trustee (if an insolvency practitioner has been appointed in place of the official receiver).[10] However, the official receiver or trustee may release some money for any necessary domestic expenses or if the funds relate to a student loan which falls outside the scope of the bankruptcy. If the account is overdrawn the money owed to the bank is a debt in the bankruptcy. The debtor must be advised not to make any payments direct to the bank, unless it has a charge[11] on the debtor's home.

How are joint bank accounts treated?

5.18 If the bank account is in joint names, the official receiver or trustee will decide how much of the money to release to the joint account holder based on information provided. If your bank account is in joint names and the account is overdrawn, the bank can ask the joint account holder to pay all the money owed.

What is the position re bank accounts post BO?

5.19 After the bankruptcy order, the debtor can open a new bank or building society account, but they must be told about the bankruptcy proceedings. It is for the bank or building society to decide the terms on which the account can be operated. Overdraft or credit facilities should not be requested without informing the bank or building society of the bankruptcy proceedings. Some banks also operate restrictions on the use of cheques in case of misuse.

INSURANCE AND INVESTMENTS

How is any life insurance policy treated?

5.20 Life insurance policies fall into a number of categories either Term life or Whole life. Neither type of policy will usually have a surrender value and are therefore of no value however some policies may also be linked to an endowment insurance policy which will in most circumstances have a surrender value and will be treated as an asset. Endowment policies may be secured as part of a mortgage package and depending on how this has been done will determine if there is a surplus that can be realised.[12]

---

10 The Insolvency Service issues a booklet explaining the situation and this can be obtained at http://www.bis.gov.uk/assets/insolvency/docs/publication-pdfs/11-1455-what-will-happen-to-my-bank-account.pdf.

11 See explanations in chapter 18.

12 See chapter 21 for what happens to a policy in the event of a deceased insolvent.

What happens to other insurance policies?

5.21 Other insurance policies may or may not have some form of residual value and each type of policy should be reviewed even if that policy has lapsed. In recent years payment protection insurance was often sold attached to a wide variety of financial products, sometimes even without the informed consent of the purchaser. Many of these policies are currently subject to ongoing complaints with either the provider or the ombudsman.

What happens to any investments?

5.22 These are relatively easy assets to sell and should be one of the first assets to be sold to settle any outstanding debts. The timing of any sale may need to be considered in the event that there are penalties for early disposal. The same will apply to any stocks and shares or premium bonds held.

PENSIONS

How are pensions dealt with?

5.23 Only formal solutions are likely to affect a pension. In bankruptcy the following series of questions sets out how the different types of pensions and how they are dealt with.

What types of pensions are there?

5.24 There are four types of pension available:

- **State Pension**

- **Occupational Pension**
  An occupational pension is where an employer has set up a pension scheme. The employer may make all, none, or part of the pension contributions.

- **Personal Pension**
  A personal pension is a pension policy taken out by an individual with a pension provider, usually a life insurance company;

- **Group Personal Pension**
  Payments are made to a pension provider, often on favourable terms negotiated by an employer/trade association or union. In bankruptcy these are treated in the same way as other personal pensions.

If the bankrupt is actually receiving the pension payments, the trustee in bankruptcy will include such income in assessing whether the bankrupt can afford to make contributions towards his bankruptcy debts (under an income payments agreement or order). If the bankrupt is not due to receive the pension until sometime in the future, the trustee needs to establish whether the pension is a bankruptcy asset.

When is a pension an asset that can be realised?

5.25 A state pension does not form part of a bankrupt's estate.[13] Both personal and occupational pension schemes can potentially form part of the bankrupt's estate. If a pension policy does form part of a bankrupt's estate, the trustee in bankruptcy can claim the lump sum as well as the regular payments. However, it is possible for the bankrupt to 'buy back' his interest in the pension policy from the trustee in bankruptcy, and the bankrupt should contact his trustee to negotiate.

5.26 For all bankruptcy petitions presented after 29 May 2000, as long as the scheme has been approved by HM Revenue and Customs (HMRC), generally speaking it cannot be claimed in any bankruptcy proceedings.

5.27 Where a bankrupt holds an interest in a pension, this does not form part of the bankrupt's estate if the scheme has been approved by HMRC.[14] Most occupational and personal pension schemes will have been approved by HMRC, and will not form part of the bankruptcy estate. However, if the pension comes into payment during the period of the bankruptcy, the trustee can claim the lump sum under a one-off income payments order (IPO).[15] Also, the regular payments received can be used in any calculation of the bankrupt's ability to make payments under an IPO.

5.28 If the pension scheme has not been approved by HMRC (which may arise where the pension scheme is run by a small business, for example) the rules[16] for petitions presented before 29 May 2000 still apply and these are set out below.

How are personal pensions treated?

5.29 On the making of a bankruptcy order, all rights and benefits under a paid-up personal pension policy vests in the bankruptcy estate, except any State Earnings Related Pension Scheme (SERPS) related part (known as protected rights). The nature of a pension is such that the trustee in bankruptcy can have no better title to the policy than the bankrupt did. As a consequence, the trustee in bankruptcy cannot take the pension benefits until the bankrupt reaches the earliest retirement age under the terms of the policy (eg 50th birthday).

---

13 Pensions in bankruptcy are dealt with in more detail in chapter 17.

14 Welfare Reform and Pensions Act 1999.

15 See High Court case re Williamson which is covered in more detail in chapter 17.

16 See chapter 17 for details on pensions in bankruptcy.

How are occupational pensions treated?

5.30 Some occupational pension schemes have 'forfeiture clauses', which means that in the event of bankruptcy, the bankrupt automatically loses his pension rights, and therefore, there is no asset for the bankruptcy estate. The trustee needs to inspect the pension scheme rules to establish whether the pension scheme has a valid forfeiture clause.

5.31 There are also provisions which allow excessive premiums paid into otherwise exempt funds to be recovered. Recovery provisions in bankruptcy are dealt with in chapter 17. Similar rules will apply to IVAs.

PERSONAL ITEMS

What are 'unreasonable' personal assets?

5.32 This is not an easy question to answer but will cover any item that would otherwise be exempt but is of a high value and can be substituted for a similar or identical item at a lower cost. Items that would fall into this category are expensive electrical items, including televisions, computers etc. Motor vehicles are dealt with separately at **5.16**. In addition any valuable non-essential item, such as jewellery, or any item that will require additional sums to maintain, such as a horse are considered unreasonable assets. Similar rules apply to collectibles, antiques, artwork etc.

ASSETS THAT MAY HAVE A FUTURE VALUE

How are assets with a potential future value treated?

5.33 Assets with a potential future value include such things as:

- Intellectual property.
- Royalties: books/television appearances, etc.
- Rights to commission payments.

This type of asset is more difficult to deal with but may still be saleable depending on the reliability of the expected income stream. Alternatively they could be dealt with as income and additional voluntary contributions requested based on the funds received.

What are Liens?

5.34 A lien is the right to hold another person's property as security for the performance of an obligation but does not give a right of ownership. This property right attaches to the property until full payment has been made. A lien can also involve the possession of the property until the debt is paid in full or it may just involve registration such as in the case of land. In this case the lien is enforced by legal action resulting in the sale of the property to which it attaches with the debt being paid from the proceeds of the sale.

5.35 A possessory lien allows the creditor to retain possession of his debtor's property until the debt has been paid in full. This can be differentiated from a common law lien which only lasts so long as possession is retained, but while it lasts it can be asserted against the whole world.

5.36 A charging lien is the right to charge property in another person's possession with the payment of a debt or the performance of a duty.

5.37 A vendor's lien is the right of a seller to retain the property until payment of the purchase price is made.

5.38 A particular lien exists only as a security for the particular debt incurred, while a general lien is available as a security for all debts arising out of similar transactions between the parties.

5.39 An equitable lien does not require possession and can attach to property not in possession at the time the debt or obligation was incurred. However it cannot be enforced against any purchaser of such property for value, who did not have notice of the lien.

What assets are exempt in bankruptcy?

5.40 Assets that are treated as exempt are dealt with in more detail in chapter 17 but for the purposes of this chapter they are the following:

- Household items essential for basic domestic needs e g clothes, furniture, television and other domestic items etc.
- A vehicle, depending on circumstances and value.
- A residential tenancy.
- Items needed for trade or employment, such as tools and computing equipment.
- Money held in pension funds, see later for a more detailed explanation.
- Money obtained from a student loan, if a balance of the loan remains payable.
- Residential property can in some circumstances be exempt, see chapter 18.

When can an individual dispose of assets to settle outstanding debts?

5.41 If bankruptcy is potentially looming and may be unavoidable, most people will consider selling some or all of their assets that would otherwise be taken and sold by a trustee in bankruptcy, especially expensive items such as a motor vehicle. The trustee may sell the items at public auction with the intention of getting a reasonable price in the quickest time and therefore if a better or similar price can be obtained and used to pay the debts then this is likely to be a better option. This may even prevent ultimate bankruptcy if enough cash is raised to offer creditors a full and final settlement.

What is selling at an 'undervalue'?

5.42 Generally any asset must not be given away or sold knowingly at less than its true value. If this happens then it is called a 'transaction at under value'.[17] This may result in a bankruptcy restriction order being made in any subsequent bankruptcy,[18] or recovery proceedings being brought by the trustee in bankruptcy against the recipient.[19] This is covered in detail in chapter 16.

CAUSES OF ACTION

What is a cause of action?

5.43 This is when there are a set of circumstances that has arisen that allow an individual a right to seek a legal remedy against another person or entity. This right is an asset and should be included in any consideration of an individual's assets. In bankruptcy any cause of action forms part of the estate of the individual and title to that action vests in the trustee.[20] In addition, in bankruptcy the trustee accrues additional rights to challenge prior transactions to determine that full value has been obtained and that preferences have accrued from the transaction. These are looked at in more detail in chapter 16.

---

17 For bankruptcy see IA86, s 339.

18 IA86, Sch 4A, para 2(2)(c).

19 See IA86, s 339.

20 IA86, s 306.

Chapter 6

PRE-BANKRUPTCY PETITION CONSIDERATIONS

'Those who have made the laws, have apparently supposed, that every deficiency of payment is the crime of the debtor. But the truth is that the creditor always shares the act, and often more than not shares the guilt of improper trust.'[1]

INTRODUCTION

6.1 This chapter looks at what bankruptcy is and the pre-petition requirements including a detailed review of statutory demands and how they can be challenged. This chapter also looks at bankruptcy jurisdiction generally including the impact of EU regulations on personal insolvency proceedings. Subsequent chapters deal with the specific requirements for different types of bankruptcy petitions.[2]

What is bankruptcy?

6.2 Bankruptcy is a legal condition imposed upon or sought by a debtor who is unable to pay his debts. In English law bankruptcy is a legal state to which only individuals are susceptible.[3] Unlike a voluntary arrangement[4] it can be imposed on an unwilling debtor by his creditors or upon unwilling creditors by a debtor seeking protection through the procedure, without the need for an agreement. The law and procedure governing bankruptcy are laid down by statute. The modern scheme for England and Wales is set out in the Insolvency Act and Insolvency Rules 1986[5] together with the case law interpreting that legislation. Bankruptcies made before 1986 are still governed by the Bankruptcy Act 1914.[6]

6.3 Each bankruptcy order is based on a petition presented to the court and the court has a wide discretion in deciding how to dispose of any bankruptcy petition. However once a petition is filed it cannot be withdrawn by the

---

1 'Imprisonment of Debtors', published in *The Idler* (1758–1760), Dr Samual Johnson; cited in B Montagu *Enquiries Respecting the Insolvent Debtors Bill* (London, 1815), at p 520.

2 See chapter 7 for creditors' petitions and chapter 8 for debtors' petitions.

3 In Scotland slightly different rules apply to sequestration.

4 See chapter 23.

5 Insolvency Act 1986; Insolvency Rules 1986, SI 1986/1925; in Northern Ireland the equivalent are Insolvency (Northern Ireland) Order 1989, SI 1989/2405 (NI 19) (INO89) and Insolvency Rules (Northern Ireland) 1991, SR 1991/364 (IRN91).

6 On the provisions in this act see IF Fletcher *The Law of Bankruptcy*, (MacDonald and Evans, Plymouth, 1978).

petitioner without the permission of the court as bankruptcy is a class action on behalf of all creditors, not just the petitioner.

BEFORE THE PETITION

6.4 A bankruptcy petition may only be presented against a debtor who is unable to pay his debts. Inability to pay is most commonly established by serving on the debtor a statutory demand, although failed execution of a judgment or order may also suffice. These are the only gateways into the bankruptcy regime, contrasting with corporate insolvency where it is not uncommon for a creditor with an (allegedly) undisputed debt due on, say, an invoice, proceeding straight to the petition stage without prior recourse to a statutory demand.

How is 'inability to pay' demonstrated by a petitioning creditor?

6.5 Section 268, IA86 defines inability to pay by reference to a statutory demand or unsatisfied execution. The debtor appears to be unable to pay a debt within the meaning of s 268 in the following circumstances:

- if the debt is payable immediately inability to pay under s 267(2)(c), IA86 is demonstrated as follows:
  - where the petitioning creditor to whom the debt is owed has served on the debtor a demand in the prescribed form requiring him to pay the debt or to secure or compound for it to the satisfaction of the creditor, at least 3 weeks have elapsed since the demand was served and the demand has been neither complied with nor set aside in accordance with the rules;[7] or
  - execution or other process issued in respect of the debt on a judgment or order of any court in favour of the petitioning creditor, or one or more of the petitioning creditors to whom the debt is owed, has been returned unsatisfied in whole or in part.[8]

- if the debt is payable at a future date inability to pay under s 267(2)(c)[9] is demonstrated as follows:
  - the petitioning creditor to whom it is owed has served on the debtor a demand (also known as 'the statutory demand') in the prescribed form requiring him to establish to the satisfaction of the creditor that there is a reasonable prospect that the debtor will be able to pay the debt when it falls due;[10]

---

7 IA86, s 268(1)(a) or INO89, art 242(1)(a).

8 IA86, s 268(1)(b) or INO89, art 242(1)(b). As to which see r 7.55 IR86 and *Re a debtor* (No 340 of 1992) [1996] 2 All ER 211.

9 IA86, s 268(2) or INO89, art 242(2).

10 IA86, s 268(2)(a) or INO89, art 242(2)(a).

— at least 3 weeks have elapsed since the demand was served;[11] and
— the demand has been neither complied with nor set aside in accordance with the rules.[12]

THE STATUTORY DEMAND

What is a statutory demand?

6.6 A statutory demand is a formal demand for payment of a debt. It is not issued at court, but served on a debtor giving him an opportunity to make payment or to indicate why the debt has not been paid before bankruptcy proceedings are commenced. The form, content and procedure of a statutory demand are governed by s 268, IA86, the rules set out in rr 6.1–6.5 IR86 and the forms set out in Sch 4 to the IR86. It is an extra-judicial step, and is not the equivalent of commencing proceedings by a claim form.

6.7 The importance of a statutory demand in bankruptcy is illustrated by the judgment of the Court of Appeal in *TSB Bank v Platts*:[13]

> 'It is accordingly quite different from a statutory demand in the field of company law which merely provides one means of establishing a company's inability to pay its debts, the usual ground on which a company is wound up compulsorily. In contrast in bankruptcy, it is not the debtor's general inability to pay his debts that is crucial but the apparent inability to pay the debt in the statutory demand, and at the hearing of the bankruptcy petition the failure to pay or secure or compound for that debt.'

Thus, the statutory demand is the only gateway into the bankruptcy regime. A creditor cannot proceed directly to the petition stage, even with an undisputed or admitted debt, or the benefit of a judgment.

What information is included in a statutory demand?

6.8 A statutory demand will be in one of the forms prescribed[14] and must contain the following information:

- an explanation of the purpose of the demand;[15]

- confirmation that failure to pay or to apply to have the demand set aside may result in bankruptcy proceedings being commenced;[16]

---

11 IA86, s 268(2)(b) or INO89, art 242(2)(b).
12 IA86, s 268(2)(c) or INO89, art 242(2)(c).
13 Peter Gibson LJ, Otton LJ, Sir John Balcombe [1998] 2 BCLC 1 at 6–7.
14 IR86, Sch 4, Part 6, Forms 6.1, 6.2, 6.3.
15 IR86, r 6.2(1)(a) or IRN91, r 6.002(1)(a).
16 IR86, r 6.2(1)(a) or IRN91, r 6.002(1)(a).

- the time within which the demand must be complied with;[17]
- the way in which the debtor can comply with the demand;[18]
- the debtor's right to apply to court to have the demand set aside;[19]
- the address and telephone number of one or more individuals the debtor can contact to obtain information about the debt with a view to securing or compounding it to the satisfaction of the creditor.[20]

6.9 In addition the statutory demand must:

- be signed and dated by the creditor or a person authorised to do so on his behalf;[21]
- specify whether the debt is payable immediately[22] or at some future date;[23]
- specify the amount of the debt;[24]
- specify the consideration provided, or if none, the way in which the debt arose;[25]
- if the debt is payable immediately it must specify if the debt is founded on a judgment or order of court, and if so provide details;[26]
- if the debt is payable at some future date it must specify the grounds on which the debtor appears to have no prospect of making payment;[27]
- specify the amount of any interest included in the claim;[28]
- specify the amount of any charges included in the claim;[29]
- specify the nature and detail of any security held and the creditor's value of that security at the date of the demand.[30]

---

17 IR86, r 6.2(1)(b) or IRN91, r 6.002(1)(b).
18 IR86, r 6.2(1)(c) or IRN91, r 6.002(1)(c).
19 IR86, r 6.2(1)(d) or IRN91, r 6.002(1)(d).
20 IR86, r 6.2(2) or IRN91, r 6.002(2).
21 IR86, r 6.1(1) or IRN91, r 6.001(1).
22 IA86, s 268(1) or INO89, art 242(1).
23 IA86, s 268(2) or INO89, art 242(2). Also see IR86, r 6.1(2) or IRN91, r 6.001(2).
24 IR86, r 6.1(3) or IRN91, r 6.001(3).
25 IR86, r 6.1(3) or IRN91, r 6.001(3).
26 IR86, r 6.1(3)(a) or IRN91, r 6.001(3)(a).
27 IR86, r 6.1(3)(b) or IRN91, r 6.001(3)(b).
28 IR86, r 6.1(4)(a) or IRN91, r 6.001(4)(a).
29 IR86, r 6.1(4)(b) or IRN91, r 6.001(4)(b).
30 IR86, r 6.1(5) or IRN91, r 6.001(5).

What are the consequences of irregularities in the statutory demand or inaccurate statements of debt?

6.10 A statutory demand which is defective or which overstates the debt will not necessarily be set aside.[31]

How do you serve a statutory demand?

6.11 A creditor is obliged to do all that is reasonably possible to bring a statutory demand to a debtor's attention, and, if practicable, to cause personal service to be effected.[32] The *Practice Statement: Insolvency Proceedings*[33] provides that where it is not possible to effect prompt personal service, service may be effected by other means such as first class post or by insertion through a letter box.[34] Normally the following steps will justify service other than personal service:

(1) One personal call at the residence and place of business of the debtor where both are known or at either of such places as is known. Where it is known that the debtor has more than one residential or business address, personal calls should be made at all the addresses.

(2) Should the creditor fail to effect service, a first class prepaid letter should be written to the debtor referring to the call(s), the purpose of the same and the failure to meet with the debtor, adding that a further call will be made for the same purpose at a specified date, time and place. At least two business days' notice must be given of the appointment and copies of the letter sent to all known addresses of the debtor. The appointment letter should also state the following:

   - in the event of the time and place not being convenient, the debtor is to name some other time and place reasonably convenient for the purpose;
   - if the debtor fails to keep the appointment the creditor proposes to serve the debtor by one of the following: advertisement; post; by insertion through a letter box and that, in the event of a bankruptcy petition being presented, the court will be asked to treat such service as service of the demand on the debtor.

(3) In attending any appointment made by letter, inquiry should be made as to whether the debtor has received all letters left for him. If the debtor is away, inquiry should also be made as to whether or not letters are being forwarded to an address within the jurisdiction (England and Wales) or elsewhere.

---

31 After some debate, this issue was settled in *Re a Debtor (No 1 of 1987, Lancaster)* [1989] 1 WLR 271 CA and *Re a Debtor (490-SD-91)* [1992] 1 WLR 507. See also *Coulter v Chief of Dorset Police* and *Interframe Ltd v Brown* [2005] EWHC 3527 (Ch), [2008] BPIR 49.

32 IR86, r 6.3(2) or IRN91, r 6.003(2).

33 Can be found at http://www.justice.gov.uk.

34 Practice Direction: Insolvency Proceedings, para 11.1.

(4) If the debtor is represented by a solicitor, an attempt should be made to arrange an appointment for personal service through that solicitor. The Insolvency Rules enable a properly instructed solicitor to accept service of a statutory demand on behalf of his client but there is no similar provision in respect of service of a bankruptcy petition.[35]

The written evidence filed pursuant to r 6.11 IR86 should deal with all the above matters including all relevant facts as to the debtor's whereabouts and whether the appointment letter(s) have been returned.

6.12 In cases where a judgment or order has been obtained and the creditor has reasonable grounds for suspecting that the debtor is avoiding service,[36] and there is no real prospect of recovery of the debt by execution or other process, then the demand may be advertised in one or more newspapers *in lieu* of personal service.[37] The time limit on the statutory demand will then run from the date of the advertisement's first publication.[38] As there is no statutory form of advertisement, the court will accept an advertisement in the form below.[39]

STATUTORY DEMAND

(Debt for liquidated sum payable immediately following a judgment or order of the court)

To (Block letters)

of

TAKE NOTICE that a statutory demand has been issued by:

Name of Creditor:

Address:

The creditor demands payment of £ the amount now due on a judgment or order of the (High Court of Justice Division) (...........County Court) dated the day of 201X.

The statutory demand is an important document and it is deemed to have been served on you on the date of the first appearance of this advertisement. You must deal with this demand within 21 days of the service upon you or you could be made bankrupt and your property and goods taken away from you. If you are in any doubt as to your position, you should seek advice immediately from a solicitor or your nearest Citizens' Advice Bureau. The statutory demand can be obtained or is available for inspection and collection from:

---

35 Practice Direction: Insolvency Proceedings, para 11.4.

36 IR86, r 6.3(3)(a) or IRN91, r 6.003(3)(a).

37 IR86, r 6.3(3)(b) or IRN91, r 6.003(3)(b).

38 IR86, r 6.3(3)(b) or IRN91, r 6.003(3)(b).

39 Practice Direction: Insolvency Proceedings, para 11.2.

Name:

Address:

(Solicitor for) the Creditor

Tel No:

Reference:

You have only 21 days from the date of the first appearance of this advertisement before the creditor may present a Bankruptcy Petition. You have only 18 days from that date within which to apply to the Court to set aside the demand

It is possible to serve a statutory demand on solicitors representing a debtor provided they consent to accept service.[40] If they do not consent, service is not effective.

What proof does the court require of service of a statutory demand?

6.13 If a statutory demand is being relied on as the basis of a bankruptcy petition then when the petition is filed in court it must be accompanied by a witness statement of service (formerly an affidavit) of the statutory demand exhibiting a copy of the demand that was served on the debtor.[41]

Who has to complete the evidence of service?

6.14 If the demand has been served personally on the debtor, the person who effected that service must authenticate the certificate with a statement of truth.[42] If the demand has not been served personally similarly the certificate must be authenticated by a person or persons with direct personal knowledge of the means adopted to serve the demand.[43] Previously similar rules applied in respect of affidavits or the witness statements required. Where the debtor denies receipt of the statutory demand the court has power within its inherent jurisdiction to order the deponent of the affidavit of service to attend for cross-examination.

What is the requirement if the demand was served by advertisement?

6.15 If the demand was served by advertisement[44] the certificate of service or previously the affidavit in Form 6.12 must be made by the creditor or by the person with direct knowledge of the circumstances.[45] It must include:

---

40 *Re a Debtor (No 234 and 236 of 1991)* (1992) *The Independent*, 29 June.

41 IR86, r 6.11(1) and (2) or IRN91, r 6.010-CP(1) and (2).

42 IR86, r 6 11(3) or IRN91, r 6.010-CP(3).

43 IR86, r 6 11(4) or IRN91, r 6.010-CP(4).

44 IR86, r 6.3(3) or IRN91, r 6.003(3).

45 IR86, r 6.11(8) or IRN91, r 6.010-CP(8).

- the means of the creditor's knowledge or (as the case may be) belief required for the purposes of that rule; and
- the date or dates on which, and the newspaper in which, the statutory demand was advertised under that rule; a copy of the advertisement must be exhibited.

The court may decline to file the petition if not satisfied that the creditor has discharged the obligation imposed on him by r 6.3(2) IR86[46] which is to do everything that is reasonable to bring the statutory demand to the debtor's attention.

How do you set aside a statutory demand?

6.16 An application must be made to the court on Form 6.4 within 18 days from the date of service of the demand on the debtor. Where the demand was advertised the application must be made within 18 days of the publication date of the advertisement.[47] The time limit for compliance with the statutory demand ceases to run as soon as an application is filed in court.[48] The debtor's application to set aside the statutory demand must be supported by an affidavit on Form 6.5 which states:

- the date on which the statutory demand came into his hands;[49] and
- the grounds on which he claims that it should be set aside.[50]

A copy of the statutory demand must be exhibited to the affidavit.[51]

Which court do you make the application to set aside in?

6.17 In most cases the application to set aside should be made to the county court with insolvency jurisdiction nearest to the debtor's home.[52]

Where the statutory demand is issued by a Government Department or Minister of Crown, is based on a judgment or order exceeding £750[53] and indicates that the creditor intends to present the petition in the High Court, the application to set aside should also be made to the High Court. From 6 April 2011, creditor petitions for less than £50,000 and debtor petitions for less than £100,000 in the London Insolvency District should be presented in the Central London County Court.

---

46 IR86, r 6.11(9) or IRN91, r 6.010-CP(9).
47 IR86, r 6.4(1) or IRN91, r 6.004(1).
48 IR86, r 6.4(3) or IRN91, r 6.004(3).
49 IR86, r 6.4(1)(a) or IRN91, r 6.004(1)(a).
50 IR86, r 6.4(1)(b) or IRN91, r 6.004(1)(b).
51 IR86, r 6.4(1)(b) or IRN91, r 6.004(1)(b).
52 Being the court where the debtor would file his own petition under r 6.40 IR86 or r 6.040 IRN91.
53 IA86, s 267(4) or INO89, art 241(4).

On what grounds may the court set aside a statutory demand?

6.18 The court may set aside a statutory demand on one or more of the following grounds:

- the debtor appears to have a counterclaim, set-off or cross demand which equals or exceeds the amount of the debt or debts specified in the demand;[54] or
- the debt is disputed on grounds which appear to be substantial;[55] or
- it appears that the creditor holds some security in respect of the debt claimed in the demand and either r 6.1(5) has not been complied with or the court is satisfied that the value of the security equals or exceeds the full amount of the debt;[56] or
- the court is satisfied on other grounds that the demand ought to be set aside.[57]

6.19 The making of an order setting aside a statutory demand is a matter of discretion (as the court emphasised in *Re a Debtor No 106 of 1992*[58]). However, the discretion is exercised in accordance with well established principles. The burden is on the applicant (the debtor) to demonstrate that there is 'genuine triable issue' on substantial grounds.[59] It is not necessarily the case that the issue has to be litigated or raised prior to the statutory demand.

What options does the court have on receiving an application to set aside a statutory demand?

6.20 An application to set aside a statutory demand is initially considered by a Registrar or district judge without a hearing. If satisfied that the application is based upon insufficient grounds then, without further notice to the creditor, the court can dismiss the application.[60] Where a debt or part of the debt in the demand is admitted the court will generally dismiss the application. It will also do so where the demand is based on a judgment or order and the debtor does not assert a counterclaim, set off or cross-demand equal to or in excess of the debt claimed.[61] If the application to set aside the statutory demand is not so dismissed, then the court will proceed to fix a venue for the hearing.[62]

---

54 IR86, r 6.5(4)(a) or IRN91, r 6.005(4)(a).
55 IR86, r 6.5(4)(b) or IRN91, r 6.005(4)(b).
56 IR86, r 6.5(4)(c) or IRN91, r 6.005(4)(c).
57 IR86, r 6.5(4)(d) or IRN91, r 6.005(4)(d).
58 (1992) *The Independent*, 20 April.
59 Practice Statement: Insolvency Proceedings, para 12.4. As to the nature of that test see *Ashworth v Newnote Ltd* [2007] EWCA Civ 793, [2007] BPIR 1012.
60 IR86, r 6.5(1) or IRN91, r 6.005(1).
61 *Practice Direction: Insolvency Proceedings*, paras 12.3 and 12.4.
62 IR86, r 6.5(2) or IRN91, r 6.005(2).

What is the procedure to be followed and what orders can the court decide to hear an application to set aside a statutory demand?

6.21 The court is required to give the applicant for the hearing (the debtor or his solicitor) and the creditor (and any person named in the statutory demand for communication purposes) who served the statutory demand at least 7 days notice of the venue.[63]

6.22 The court on hearing an application to set aside a statutory demand can do one of the following:

- summarily determine the application on Form 6.6;[64]
- adjourn it, giving such directions as it thinks appropriate;[65] or
- if the court dismisses the application, it will make an order authorising the creditor to present a bankruptcy petition either forthwith, or on or after a date specified in the order.[66] A copy of the order must be sent immediately by the court to the creditor.[67]

How are procedural defects in a statutory demand dealt with?

6.23 Whilst care should be taken in the drafting and formulation of a statutory demand, minor defects will not generally suffice to set one aside. In *Re a Debtor (Lancaster No 1 of 1987)*[68] the court rejected the debtor's argument that the demand was 'perplexing' holding that old technical arguments about defects in bankruptcy notices under the Bankruptcy Act 1914 could no longer be relied on in the new regime. By the same token mere overstatement of the debt would not necessarily suffice to warrant setting aside the demand. In *Coulter v Chief Constable of Dorset*[69] the court took a similar approach to an argument as to whether the identity (but not the office) of the creditor had changed. In *Oben v Blackman*[70] the court held that failure to comply with r 6.8 IR86 by failing to state the consideration for the debt in the statutory demand was of itself insufficient to warrant dismissing a petition. In short, the defect would, it seems, have to be of a nature such as to warrant setting aside on a ground other than the ground specified in r 6.5(4)(d) IR86.[71]

6.24 In *Re a Debtor (No 1 of 1987)*[72] Nichols LJ, with whom Glidewell LJ and Sir Stephen Brown agreed, expressed the view that the IA86 and IR86

---

63 IR86, r 6.5(2) or IRN91, r 6.005(2).
64 IR86, r 6.5(3) and (4) or IRN91, r 6.005(3) and (4).
65 IR86, r 6.5(3) or IRN91, r 6.005(3).
66 IR86, r 6.5(6) or IRN91, r 6.005(6).
67 IR86, r 6.5(6) or IRN91, r 6.005(6).
68 [1988] 1 WLR 419.
69 [2005] 1 WLR 130.
70 [1999] BCC 446, [2000] BPIR 302.
71 IR86 or IRN91, r 6.005(4)(d).
72 [1989] 1 WLR 271.

introduced a new code governing statutory demands which must be construed unfettered by the technicalities of the old bankruptcy law. Furthermore:[73]

> 'The new statutory code affords the court a desirable degree of flexibility when confronted with an application to set aside a statutory demand containing one or more defects. This is not to be taken by banks or others as a charter for the slipshod preparation of statutory demands. The making of a bankruptcy order remains a serious step so far as the debtor is concerned, and the prescribed preliminaries are intended to afford protection to him. If a statutory demand is served in an excessive amount or is otherwise defective, the court will be alert to see whether those mistakes have caused or will cause any prejudice to the debtor. In the present case no prejudice has resulted, or will result, and hence it is right that the statutory demand should be allowed to stand. But if there had been prejudice, the bank would only have itself to blame if the court had set aside the statutory demand.'

As a result r 7.55 IR86 cannot be used to cure any procedural defects.[74]

What evidence is required by the court for a counterclaim?

6.25 The amount of the counterclaim under r 6.5(4)(a) IR86 must be large enough to exceed the amount of the petitioner's debt and there must be mutuality between the debts ie the same legal character as is required for set-off.

6.26 The court will take a broader approach in the insolvency jurisdiction than it might in others. Thus it will not assist a creditor to seek to exclude a counterclaim, set-off or cross demand on the basis of law or a contractual provision (*McAllister v The Society of Lloyd's*[75] and *Garrow v Society of Lloyd's*[76]). Similarly a debtor may rely on a cross-claim even in the face of a demand based on a dishonoured cheque (*Hofer v Strawson*[77]).

What evidence is required by the court that the debt is disputed on 'substantial grounds'?

6.27 When disputing a claim on substantial grounds under r 6.5(4)(b) IR86 the debtor must show that there is a genuine triable issue. The test allows for a range of possibilities best illustrated by reference to two corporate authorities. In *Re A Company*[78] Hoffmann J, (as he then was) reminded creditors that service of a statutory demand was a 'high risk strategy'. On the other hand the bare assertion of a dispute is not enough:[79] a debtor must do more than raise what Chadwick J called a 'cloud of objections'. An application to set aside a

---

73 At 280C–280E.

74 See *Re A Debtor (No 190 of 1987)* (1988) *The Times*, 21 May.

75 [1999] BPIR 548.

76 [1999] BPIR 885, CA

77 [1999] BPIR 501, contrasting with the position where an application for summary judgment on a dishonoured cheque will generally be successful.

78 *No 0012209 of 1991* [1992] 1 WLR 351, [1992] BCLC 865.

79 *Re a Company (No 006685 of 1996)* [1997] BCC 830.

statutory demand does not allow the court to take the course of ordering payment into court where it is confronted with a shadowy defence. The jurisdiction is all or nothing and there is no 'grey area'.[80]

What happens when the creditor holds some form of security and there is a dispute over the value being deducted from the debt due?

6.28 Rule 6.1(5) IR86[81] requires the creditor to set out the security in respect of his debt, and where the court is satisfied that the security is under-valued in the statutory demand, the creditor may be required to amend the demand accordingly (but without prejudice to his right to present a bankruptcy petition by reference to the original demand).[82]

6.29 Rule 6.5(4)(c) IR86[83] allows the debtor to challenge a fully secured creditor. The form of statutory demand allows a creditor to identify both any security held by it and the value of that security. The term 'security' is defined in s 383(2), IA86 as being a mortgage, charge, lien or other security over any property owned by the debtor.[84]

6.30 Where the valuation of security is in dispute, the appropriate method of valuation is on a forced sale basis, the burden of proof in establishing that the creditor is fully secured resting on the debtor: *Platts v Western Trust and Savings Ltd.*[85] For r 6.5(4)(c) IR86 purposes the value of security should not include any estimated value for the associated costs of enforcing the security, even if such costs are provided for under the terms of the security itself: *Owo-Samson v Barclays Bank.*[86]

What evidence is required by the court that the debt is disputed on 'other grounds'?

6.31 The scope and nature of the 'other grounds' under r 6.5(4)(d) IR86 was identified in the judgment of Nicholls LJ in *Re a Debtor (No 1 of 1987)*[87] as follows:

> 'When therefore the rules provide, as does rule 6.5(4)(d), for the court to have a residual discretion to set aside a statutory demand, the circumstances which normally will be required before a court can be satisfied that the demand 'ought' to be set aside, are circumstances which would make it unjust for the statutory demand to give rise to those consequences in the particular case. The court's intervention is called for to prevent that injustice. This approach to subpara (d) is in line with the particular ground specified in subparas (a) to (c) of rule 6.5(4).

---

80 *Re A Debtor (490-SD-1991)* [1992] 1 WLR 507.

81 Or for Northern Ireland IRN91, r 6.001(5).

82 IR86, r 6.5(5) or IRN91, r 6.005(5).

83 Or for Northern Ireland IRN91, r 6.005(4)(c).

84 See *Re a Debtor (No 310 of 1988)* [1989] 1 WLR 452. See also chapter 4 at **4.10** et seq which looks at different types of security.

85 [1996] BPIR 339.

86 [2003] EWCA Civ 714, [2003] BPIR 1373.

87 [1989] 1 WLR 271 at 271D-271F.

Normally it would be unjust that an individual should be regarded as unable to pay a debt if the debt is disputed on substantial grounds: subpara (b). Likewise, if the debtor has a counterclaim, set-off or cross-demand which equals or exceeds the amount of the debt: subpara (a). Again, if the creditor is fully secured: subpara (c).'

6.32 There are a number of grounds which may be sufficient to oppose the making of a bankruptcy order at the petition stage which the court will not consider on the hearing of an application to set aside a statutory demand. The issue at the statutory demand stage is whether the debt claimed in the demand is owing. Thus, the court will not set aside a statutory demand on a jurisdictional basis since the jurisdiction of the court to make an order arises only after the presentation of a petition. Similarly issues such as the reasonableness of an offer to secure or compound for the petition debt fall to be considered on the hearing of the petition not in relation to the statutory demand.[88]

6.33 It would appear that the court should not set aside a statutory demand only on the basis that the debt claimed is less than £750 since it would be possible for the creditor to aggregate his debt with those of other creditors and petition with them.[89]

What is a 'petitionable' debt?

6.34 A petitionable debt must be unsecured, exceed the bankruptcy level[90] and be for a liquidated sum payable either immediately or at some certain future time.[91] Historically the petitioning creditor's debt must be for a liquidated sum.[92] Thus, a claim for damages cannot be a petitionable debt.[93] Recently, there has been much debate as to whether solicitors' invoices for legal services provided, which were unassessed under the Solicitors Act 1974, could amount to a liquidated debt for the purposes of a petition. In *Truex v Toll*[94] Proudman J held that a claim for solicitors' fees not yet judicially assessed or determined

88 *Re a Debtor (No 451-SD-1993)* [1994] 2 All ER 168.

89 IA86, s 264(1)(a) or INO89, art 238(1)(a).

90 IA86, s 267(4) or INO89, art 241(4).

91 IA86, s 267(2)(b) or INO89, art 241(2)(b).

92 *Ex p Charles* [1811] 14 East 197. As to what constitutes a liquidated debt see *Ex p Broadhurst* [1852] 22 LJ Bank 21; *Walker v Broadhurst* [1853] 23 LJ Ex 71; *Owen v Routh* [1854] 23 LJCP 105; *Johnson v Diamond* [1855] 24 LJ Ex 217; *Hope v Premierpace (Europe) Ltd* [1999] BPIR 695.

93 However, Briggs J recently commented that there was some doubt as to whether a person having merely an unliquidated claim in damages should or should not be able to use the statutory demand/bankruptcy petition procedure. Further, he observed that, the distinctions that were said to operate in either the purpose behind s 267(2)(b) IA86 or that area where the precise amount of the claim was clear and undisputed were illogical and did not serve the interests of good case management; see *McGuinness v Norwich and Peterborough Building Society* [2010] EWHC 2989 (Ch), [2011] BPIR 213.

94 [2009] BPIR 692. It was held that a claim in a solicitor's bill could be converted to a liquidated debt by an admission or acknowledgement on behalf of the client, but none had been given in that case. See also *Wallace LLP v Yates* [2010] EWHC 1098 (Ch) [2010] BPIR 1041 and *Moseley v Else Solicitors LLP* [2010] BPIR 1192.

could not amount to a claim for a liquidated debt that could be the subject of a bankruptcy petition under s 267 of IA86, even if the period for challenge under the Solicitors Act 1974 had passed.

What is the effect of the EC Regulation on personal insolvency proceedings?

6.35 The Council of the European Union Regulation on Insolvency Proceedings[95] came into force on 31 May 2002 and has direct application as domestic law. It applies in all EU member states except Denmark. It applies to 'collective insolvency proceedings which entail the partial or total divestment of a debtor and the appointment of a liquidator'.[96] In this Regulation the term 'liquidator' includes a trustee in bankruptcy.[97] The Regulation does not apply to insurance and certain other financial undertakings,[98] but this consideration rarely has to be taken into account in bankruptcy.

6.36 The Regulation provides for insolvency proceedings to be main proceedings or secondary (or territorial) proceedings.[99] Jurisdiction is founded primarily by reference to the debtor's centre of main interests, unhelpfully defined in para 3 of the preamble as the place which 'should correspond to the place where the debtor conducts the administration of his interests on a regular basis and is therefore ascertainable by third parties'. In the case of an individual living and/or carrying on business only in the UK this presents no problem since it will be the place of the debtor's business or his place of ordinary residence (in the absence of evidence to the contrary). Main proceedings are proceedings brought in the place of the debtor's centre of main interests and are universal in scope.

6.37 Secondary or territorial proceedings may be brought in a country in which the debtor has an establishment, again unhelpfully defined as the 'place of operations where the debtor carries out a non-transitory economic activity with human means and goods'.[100] Such proceedings are limited to assets within the territory. A petitioner is therefore obliged to consider whether the court will have jurisdiction to hear the petition and make a bankruptcy order. If the court makes a bankruptcy order it is obliged to state whether the Regulation applies and if so whether the proceedings are main or secondary.

---

95 No 1346/2000 (OJ L 160, 30.6.2000). See generally on this complex topic I F Fletcher *Insolvency in Private International Law* (Oxford, 1999) and Gabriel Moss, I F Fletcher and Stuart Isaacs (eds) *The EC Regulation on Insolvency Proceedings* (Oxford, 2002).

96 Art 1(1) (which includes bankruptcy), Art 2(a) and Ann A EC Regulation No 1346/2000 on Insolvency Proceedings (OJ L 160, 30.6.2000).

97 Art 2(b) and Ann C EC Regulation No 1346/2000 on Insolvency Proceedings (OJ L 160, 30.6.2000).

98 Art 1(2) EC Regulation No 1346/2000 on Insolvency Proceedings (OJ L 160, 30.6.2000).

99 Art 3(1) and (2) EC Regulation No 1346/2000 on Insolvency Proceedings (OJ L 160, 30.6.2000).

100 Arts 2(h) and 3(2) EC Regulation No 1346/2000 on Insolvency Proceedings (OJ L 160, 30.6.2000).

What rulings have there been in respect of jurisdiction and 'Centre of Main Interest' in personal insolvency proceedings?

6.38 There have been some significant decisions in the field of individual insolvency. In *Skjevesland v Geveran Trading Co Ltd*[101] the debtor was found by Mr Registrar Jacques to have had a residence in London thus founding jurisdiction. But after trial and before judgment was handed down the EC Regulation 1346/2000 came into force. The debtor decided to make a second application, contending that his centre of main interests (which the court was then obliged to consider) was either in Spain or Switzerland. The registrar decided that a debtor's centre of main interest would generally be the place where he could be contacted. In the case of a professional person, that would be his professional domicile, and in the case of a non-professional person the place where he habitually resided. In the circumstances of the case the registrar concluded that the Regulation had no impact in the light of his decision about London (which had become Mr Skjevesland's centre of main interest); Switzerland could have no effect as it was not a member state for the purpose of the Regulation. The registrar's decision was upheld on appeal.

6.39 *Shierson v Vlieland-Boddy*[102] concerned a debtor who had moved to Spain. In 2004 he returned to England to propose an individual voluntary arrangement to his creditors. The debtor satisfied the court that his centre of main interests was in the United Kingdom for the purpose of obtaining an interim order. His proposal was not validly approved. A creditor issued bankruptcy proceedings. The debtor then contended that his centre of main interests was in Spain so that no bankruptcy order could be made. At first instance Mr Registrar Rawson decided against him on the facts and made a bankruptcy order, relying in part on the debtor's earlier representation to the court that his centre of main interests was in the UK. The registrar's decision was overturned on appeal by the judge. There was a further appeal to the Court of Appeal.

6.40 The Court of Appeal allowed the appeal in part holding that the debtor's centre of main interests had to be established at the point when proceedings were opened and did not fall to be determined by relation to the place where the debts were incurred; a debtor could move his centre of main interests but it had to be fixed as an objective exercise. On the facts of the case, however, business interests of the debtor (including a business controlling a property in Dorset and the existence of a London flat) were sufficient to establish that the debtor had an establishment in the UK making him susceptible to a bankruptcy order.

6.41 *Re Staubitz-Schreiber*[103] is the only authority on the subject (at least in individual insolvency) so far decided by the European Court. The debtor operated a business as a sole trader in Germany until 2001. In April 2002 she

---

[101] [2003] BPIR 73 and 924.
[102] [2005] BPIR 1170.
[103] Case C-1/04, [2006] BPIR 510.

moved to Spain to live and work there. She applied for a bankruptcy order in Wuppertal but the Amtsgericht refused to open the proceedings on the ground that there were no assets. The Landgericht dismissed her appeal against that order. She appealed to the Bundesgerichtshof which made a reference to the Grand Chamber of the European Court which decided that the court of the member state in the territory of which the debtor's centre of main interests is situated at the time when the debtor lodges a request to open insolvency proceedings retains jurisdiction to open those proceedings if the debtor moves his centre of main interests to the territory of another member state after lodging the request but before the proceedings are opened. The decision sits oddly alongside Art 2(f) of the Regulation which provides that the time of opening of proceedings means the time at which the judgment opening proceedings becomes effective.

6.42 In *Official Receiver v Eichler*[104] Mr Registrar Baister, following *Shierson v Vlieland-Boddy* and *Re Staubitz-Schreiber*, declined to direct the Official Receiver to apply to annul a bankruptcy order made on the debtor's own petition in spite of the fact that the debtor was a German national all of whose debts were in Germany, holding on the facts that the debtor appeared to have moved his centre of main interests from Germany to the United Kingdom.

6.43 Contrast this case, however, with *Stojevic v Official Receiver*[105] where bankruptcy orders were made in both England and Austria, but in which the English order was annulled on the basis that the debtor's centre of main interests was in Austria.

JURISDICTION

What are the jurisdictional requirements for presenting a bankruptcy petition where the EC Regulation does not apply?

6.44 A bankruptcy petition may only be presented if the debtor is domiciled in England or Wales, or is present in England or Wales on the day the petition is presented, or has been ordinarily resident, or has had a place of residence or has carried on business in England or Wales during the 3 years ending with the day of presentation of the petition.[106]

---

104 [2007] BPIR 1636. After the Enterprise Act 2002 relaxed the bankruptcy regime in England and Wales, there has been a surge in 'bankruptcy tourists', ie debtors seeking to make themselves bankrupt in England and Wales rather than in a more rigorous European bankruptcy regime. Consequently, the Official Receiver or foreign creditors have launched cases seeking the annulment or rescission of bankruptcy orders inappropriately made against foreign nationals. See also *Official Receiver v Mitterfellner* [2009] BPIR 1075 and *Re Hagemeister (a bankrupt) and others* [2010] BPIR 1093. The issues are almost entirely factual, arising out of the personal circumstances of the particular debtor.

105 [2007] BPIR 141.

106 IA86, s 265(1)(a) (b) and (c) (as amended) or INO89, art 239(1)(a) (b) and (c).

What does 'domicile' mean?

6.45 Every individual has a domicile of origin acquired at birth. The domicile of origin can be changed by selecting a domicile of choice. If the domicile of choice is abandoned the domicile of origin revives. A person will generally be taken to be domiciled in the country where he is permanently resident, although this is not always necessarily the case. Establishing a person's domicile is a mixed question of law and fact. The concept of domicile was most recently considered in the context of personal insolvency in *Barlow Clowes International Limited and others v Henwood.*[107]

What does 'ordinarily resident' mean?

6.46 The concepts of residence and ordinarily resident are not defined in the legislation. The question whether a person is ordinarily resident or has a place of residence in the country is one to be determined on the facts. In *Re Brauch*[108] the Court of Appeal held that it was not necessary to establish residence at a particular address or addresses merely that residence is within the jurisdiction.[109]

6.47 An individual who has not appealed tax assessments made against him by the Inland Revenue may dispute his residence within the jurisdiction based on the fact of those assessments alone.[110]

What constitutes carrying on business?

6.48 Any reference to an individual carrying on business includes the following:[111]

- the carrying on of business by a firm or partnership of which the individual is a member;[112] and

- the carrying on of business by an agent or manager for the individual or for such a firm or partnership.[113]

Again this is a question of fact and was considered in *Re Brauch*[114] where the Court of Appeal held that running a company was not carrying on business.

6.49 A debtor who has left the jurisdiction continues to carry on business in the jurisdiction until the debts of any business have been paid.[115]

---

[107] [2008] EWCA Civ 577, [2008] BPIR 778.
[108] [1978] Ch 316.
[109] See also *Re Norris* (1885) 5 Morr 111; *Re Hecquard* (1889) 24 CEBD 71; and *Re Nordenfelt* (1894) ICEB 151.
[110] *Wilkinson v IRC* [1998] BPIR 418.
[111] IA86, s 265(2) or INO89, art 239(2).
[112] IA86, s 265(2)(a) or INO89, art 239(2)(a).
[113] IA86, s 265(2)(b) or INO89, art 239(2)(b).
[114] [1978] Ch 316.
[115] *Re a Debtor* (No 784 of 1991) [1992] Ch 554 and *Theophile v Solicitor General* [1950] AC 186.

What constitutes personal presence?

6.50 The expression has its natural meaning and is a question of fact. See *Re Thulin*[116] where the debtor was a non-resident Swede living in Belgium.

116 [1995] 1 WLR 165.

Chapter 7

A CREDITOR'S BANKRUPTCY PETITION

'Our commercial code, so far as bankruptcy administration is concerned, is a national disgrace, and we are compelled to exclaim, with Hamlet, "Reform it altogether"'.[1]

INTRODUCTION

7.1 This chapter examines the process of completing, presenting and dealing with a creditor's petition generally together with the safeguards that can be put in place by a petitioning creditor to protect the assets of the bankrupt's estate. The effect of the filing of a bankruptcy petition is to prevent a bankrupt from continuing to manage his affairs.[2] This chapter also covers the safeguards in place to ensure that the bankrupt's estate does not suffer any loss during this period.[3] The topics are covered in the following order for ease of reference:

- Bankruptcy jurisdiction.
- Bankruptcy petition requirements.
- Presenting a bankruptcy petition.
- Service of a bankruptcy petition.
- The petition hearing.
- Challenging a petition.
- Registration of a bankruptcy petition.
- Post-petition dispositions and validation orders.
- Protection of assets and the role of the interim receiver.

---

1 'Anomalies of the Bankruptcy System' The Bankers' Magazine and Journal of the Money Market. Vol 13, September, 1853, pp 609–615, at p 615.

2 IA86, s 284 or INO89, art 257.

3 Usually 14 days: see IR86, r 6.18 or IRN91, r 6.018.

BANKRUPTCY JURISDICTION

Which court should bankruptcy proceedings be commenced in?

7.2 The provisions as to the court in which the bankruptcy petition is to be presented are set out in r 6.9A, IR86. If the debtor is resident in England and Wales, the petition must, be presented to the High Court if the petition is presented by a Minister of the Crown or a Government department, and either:

- in any statutory demand on which the petition is based the creditor has indicated the intention to present a bankruptcy petition to that Court,[4] or
- the petition is presented under s 268(1)(b), IA86; (ie the petition is based on an unsatisfied execution of a judgment debt or other court order).[5]

If the debtor is resident in England and Wales, the petition must, be presented to the High Court if for the greater part of the 6 months immediately preceding the presentation of the petition, the debtor either:

- has carried on a business in the London insolvency district;[6] or
- has not carried on a business in England and Wales but has resided in the London insolvency district.[7]

If the debtor is resident in England and Wales, the petition must, be presented to the High Court if the petitioner is unable to ascertain the debtor's residence or place of business within England and Wales.[8] The London insolvency district comprises the areas situated within the districts of the following county courts: Barnet, Bow, Brentford, Central London, Clerkenwell and Shoreditch, Edmonton, Lambeth, Mayor's and City of London, Wandsworth, West London and Willesden.[9]

7.3 Where the debtor is resident in England and Wales and s 264(1), IA86 does not apply, the petition must be presented to the debtor's own county court if the debtor either

- has carried on a business in England and Wales other than in the London insolvency district;[10] or
- has not carried on a business in England and Wales and has resided outside the London insolvency district.[11]

---

4 IR86, r 6.9A(1)(a)(i).
5 IR86, r 6.9(1)(a)(ii).
6 IR86, r 6.9A(1)(b)(i).
7 IR86, r 6.9A(1)(b)(ii).
8 IR86, r 6.9A(1)(c).
9 London Insolvency District (Central London County Court) Order 2011, SI 2011/761, art 2.
10 IR86, r 6.9A(2)(a).
11 IR86, r 6.9A(2)(b).

7.4 If the debtor is not resident in England and Wales but was resident or carried on business in England and Wales within the 6 months immediately preceding the presentation of the petition, the petition must be presented to the High Court if the debtor:

- carried on a business in the London insolvency district for a longer period in those 6 months than in any other insolvency district;[12] or
- did not carry on a business in England and Wales but resided in the London insolvency district for a longer period in those 6 months than in any other insolvency district.[13]

In any other case the petition may be presented either to the debtor's own county court or to the High Court.[14]

7.5 The petition must be presented to the High Court if the debtor is not resident in England and Wales and

- has not resided or carried on business in England and Wales within the 6 months immediately preceding the presentation of the petition;[15] or
- the petitioner is unable to ascertain the debtor's residence or place of business.[16]

7.6 Notwithstanding any other provision of r 6.9A, IR86, where a voluntary arrangement under Part 8 of the Act is in force for the debtor, the petition must be presented to the court to which the nominee's report under s 256 was submitted.[17]

7.7 For the purposes of r 6.9A, IR86, the debtor's own county court is either:

- where the debtor has carried on a business within the 6 months immediately preceding the presentation of the petition, the county court for the insolvency district where for the greater part of that period of 6 months
  - the debtor carried on the business;[18] or

---

[12] IR86, r 6.9A(4)(a)(i).

[13] IR86, r 6.9A(4)(a)(ii).

[14] IR86, r 6.9A(4)(b).

[15] IR86, r 6.9A(5)(a).

[16] IR86, r 6.9A(5)(b).

[17] This covers the position where an interim order is in force. It is not clear what the position is where there was no interim order, for in those circumstances the nominees' report does not have to be filed with the court.

[18] IR86, r 6.9A(3)(a)(i).

– the principal place of business was located, if the business was carried on in more than one insolvency district;[19] or

where the debtor has not carried on a business in the 6 months immediately preceding the presentation of the petition, the county court for the insolvency district where the debtor resided for the greater part of that 6 month period.[20]

In summary, the jurisdiction is based on the location of the debtor's business rather than his residence and the petition must contain sufficient information to establish that it is being filed in the appropriate court.[21]

7.8 The provisions are now slightly different as regards the London insolvency district as a result of amendments to the Insolvency Rules in 2011. Chief Registrar Baister summarised the changes in a note in the following terms:

'Changes to bankruptcy jurisdiction in the London Insolvency District

(1) The Insolvency (Amendment) Rules 2011[22] and the London Insolvency District (Central London County Court) Order[23] came into force on 6 April 2011. The principal changes are set out below.

Creditors' petitions

(2) New r 6.9A Insolvency Rules 1986 provides that with effect from 6 April 2011 where the petition debt is £50,000 or more, the debtor has not resided or had a place of business in England or Wales for 6 months preceding the date of presentation of the petition, the debtor's residence or place of business cannot be ascertained or the petition is presented against a member of a partnership that is being wound up by the High Court, the petition should be presented to the High Court.

(3) Where the petition debt is less than £50,000, subject to the exceptions mentioned, the petition should be presented to the Central London county court.

Debtors' petitions

(4) New r 6.40A makes similar provision in respect of debtor's petitions save that the amount of the indebtedness is £100,000 instead of £50,000.

(5) Practitioners are advised to read the amendments thoroughly to ensure that they are familiar with the detail of the changes.

---

19 IR86, r 6.9A(3)(a)(ii).
20 IR86, r 6.9A(3)(b).
21 IR86, r 6.9(5).
22 SI 2011/785.
23 SI 2011/761.

Central London County Court

(6) The district judges assigned to bankruptcy work in the Central London County Court will sit in the Thomas More Building of the Royal Courts of Justice.

(7) For the time being users should notice little change in the administration of the bankruptcy work. Petitions will continue to be issued on the second floor of the Thomas More Building. The Registry will continue on the third floor, and litigants and their advisers should continue to report to TM 110 on the first floor where they will be directed to the registrars or district judges for their hearings.

(8) The registrars have already transferred a number of low value bankruptcy hearings to the county court and will continue to do so where appropriate.

(9) The registrars are now in the Rolls Building in Fetter Lane.

(10) Bankruptcy cases assigned to the Central London County Court will continue thereafter to be heard in the Thomas More Building of the Royal Courts of Justice.

(11) Companies Court cases dealt with by the registrars will be unaffected by the changes.'

BANKRUPTCY PETITION REQUIREMENTS

What is the cost of filing a bankruptcy petition in court?

7.9 Under the Insolvency Proceedings (Fees) Order 2004[24] the deposit payable for a creditor's petition under s 264(1)(a), (ba), (bb), (c) and (d), IA86 is £700 from 1 June 2011 (previously £600).

In addition to paying the deposit a court fee is also payable[25] by the petitioning creditor. Both these amounts plus any solicitor's costs are recoverable from the estate of the bankrupt if there are funds available.

Who can present a creditor's bankruptcy petition?

7.10 A bankruptcy petition can be presented by the following,[26]

- one or more creditors[27] (who may petition jointly);

---

24 Reg 6 of SI 2004/593 amended by SI 2011/1167: The Insolvency Proceedings (Fees) (Amendment) Order 2011: art 6 amended for increases in deposits: (b) in sub-para (b), for '£450' substitute '£525'; and (c) in sub-para (c), for '£600' substitute '£700'.

25 See chapter 13 for details of other fees and costs.

26 IA86, s 264(1)(a) or INO89, art 238(1)(a).

27 IA86, s 264(1)(a) or INO89, art 238(1)(a).

- a temporary administrator within the meaning of Art 38 of the EC Regulation on Insolvency Proceedings;[28]
- a liquidator within the meaning of Art 2(b) of the EC Regulation appointed in proceedings by virtue of Regulation EC No 1346/2000 Art 3(1) of the EC Regulation;[29]
- the supervisor of or any person bound by an individual voluntary arrangement (other than the individual who proposes it);[30]
- the Financial Services Authority.[31]

7.11 The petitioner must use the form appropriate to the grounds of the petition. The prescribed forms for a creditor's petition are set out in Sch 4, IR86 and are as follows:

Form 6.7 — Liquidated sum payable immediately.

Form 6.8 — Liquidated sum payable at a future date.

Form 6.9 — Execution of judgment debt returned.

Form 6.10 — Failed IVA.

When can a creditor present a bankruptcy petition?

7.12 A creditor can file a bankruptcy petition if the following circumstances apply:

- the petitioning creditor is owed at least one debt by the debtor;[32]
- the aggregate petition debt including interest but excluding costs of the petition is £750 or more;[33]
- the amount owed is a liquidated sum and payable either immediately or at a certain future date;[34]
- the amount is unsecured;[35]

---

28 IA86, s 264(1)(ba) or INO89, art 238(1)(ba).
29 IA86, s 264(1)(bb) or INO89, art 238(1)(bb).
30 IA86, s 264(1)(c) or INO89, art 238(1)(c).
31 Financial Services and Markets Act 2000, s 372.
32 IA86, s 267(1) or INO89, art 241(1).
33 IA86, s 267(2)(a) and (4) or INO89, art 241(2)(a). The figure has remained at £750 since the Insolvency Act 1986 came into force, and is likely to be reviewed upwards in the near future.
34 IA86, s 267(2)(b) or INO89, art 241(2)(b); as to liquidated sums see *Hope v Premierpace (Europe) Ltd* [1999] BPIR 695.
35 IA86, s 267(2)(b) or INO89, art 241(2)(b).

- the debtor appears unable to pay the debt or to have no reasonable prospect of being able to pay by the due date;[36]

- the debt or part of it, equivalent to £750 or more, is not disputed and if based on a statutory demand there is no outstanding application to set the statutory demand aside;[37]

- the debtor is indebted on a judgment or order and execution or other process has been returned unsatisfied.[38] As to which see r 7.55, IR86 and *Re a Debtor (No 340 of 1992)*.[39]

When can a group of creditors present a bankruptcy petition?

7.13 Creditors who individually are owed less than the minimum debt can group together to present a bankruptcy petition as long as the combined level of debt exceeds the minimum bankruptcy level.[40]

When can a supervisor present a bankruptcy petition?

7.14 The court may only make a bankruptcy order on the basis of a failed IVA when one or more of the following conditions set out in s 276(1), IA86[41] have been demonstrated by the supervisor in relation to an arrangement that is a valid and subsisting one:[42]

- that the debtor has failed to comply with his obligations under the voluntary arrangement;[43] or

- that information which was false or misleading in any material particular or which contained material omissions;[44] or

- was contained in any statement of affairs or other document supplied by the debtor under Part VIII, IA86 to any person;[45] or

- was otherwise made available by the debtor to his creditors at or in connection with a meeting summoned under Part VIII, IA86;[46] or

- that the debtor has failed to do all such things as may for the purposes of the voluntary arrangement have been reasonably required of him by the

---

36 IA86, s 267(2)(c) or INO89, art 241(2)(c).
37 IA86, s 267(2)(d) or INO89, art 241(2)(d).
38 IA86, s 268(1)(b) or INO89, art 242(1)(b).
39 [1996] 2 All ER 211.
40 See *Re Allen, Re a Debtor (No 367 of 1992)* [1998] BPIR 319 at 320F–320G (Ferris J).
41 Or INO89, art 250(1).
42 IA86, s 264(1)(c) or INO89, art 238(1)(c).
43 IA86, s 276(1)(a) or INO89, art 250(1)(a).
44 IA86, s 276(1)(b) or INO89, art 250(1)(b).
45 IA86, s 276(1)(b)(i) or INO89, art 250(1)(b)(i).
46 IA86, s 276(1)(b)(ii) or INO89, art 250(1)(b)(ii).

supervisor of the arrangement.[47] The voluntary arrangement must be valid and subsisting at the date of the petition.[48]

Whilst the court retains a discretion whether or not to make a bankruptcy order, the court does not generally look kindly upon the failure of a debtor to comply with his obligations under the terms of an approved individual voluntary arrangement. A bankruptcy order can be made even where the non-compliance was through no fault of the debtor,[49] where the non-compliance has been remedied[50] or where the majority of creditors do not wish for a bankruptcy order to be made.[51] Similarly, the court does not look kindly upon failures to provide creditors with full information for the purposes of the creditors' meeting.[52]

Can a supervisor present a bankruptcy petition even after the approved IVA period has expired?

7.15 In *Harris v Gross*[53] His Honour Judge Maddocks, sitting as a High Court judge, held that a supervisor may present a default petition even after the expiration of any fixed term for which the arrangement subsists, although such petition must be presented within a reasonable period following expiration.

How does a creditor identify the debtor in a bankruptcy petition?

7.16 A bankruptcy petition must identify the debtor by including all of the following information:

- the debtor's full name;[54]
- a statement by the petitioner confirming any other names by which the debtor is or has been known;[55]

---

47 IA86, s 276(1)(c) or INO89, art 250(1)(c).

48 For examples of cases where a petition was defeated on the grounds that the IVA was not valid see *Re Plummer* [2004] BPIR 767.

49 See *Re Keenan* [1998] BPIR 205, where the debtor had promised to sell some shares in a US company and make available the proceeds to their respective IVAs. Through no fault of the debtors, the shares were not sold. Despite the lack of culpability, a bankruptcy order was made on a supervisor's petition, supported by all the creditors. See also *Stanley v Phillips* [2003] EWHC 720 (Ch), [2004] BPIR 632.

50 See *Vadher v Weisgard* [1998] BPIR 295, where instalments ie under the agreed individual voluntary arrangements were not maintained. Despite there being offers to clear the arrears, a bankruptcy order was made and upheld on appeal. In *Carter Knight v Peat* [2000] BPIR 968, it was held that the court could make a bankruptcy order even if the default had been remedied by the time of the hearing of the petition. See also *Clarke v Birkin* [2006] EWHC 340 (Ch), [2006] BPIR 632.

51 See *Harris v Gross* [2001] BPIR 586.

52 See *Bradburn v Kaye* [2006] BPIR 605, where a potential tax liability had been understated.

53 [2001] BPIR 586 at 589D-589H. See also *Re Arthur Rathbone Kitchens Ltd* [1998] BPIR 1 (where the same conclusion was reached in respect of a winding up petition presented by the supervisor of a company voluntary arrangement) and *Stanley v Phillips* [2003] EWHC 720 (Ch), [2004] BPIR 632.

54 IR86, r 6.7(1)(a) or IRN91, r 6.007(1)(a).

55 IR86, r 6.7(3) or IRN91, r 6.007(3).

- the debtor's residential address;[56]
- the debtor's occupation;[57]
- the name or names of any business which the debtor uses or has used during the period in which the debt has been incurred;[58]
- whether or not any of these businesses are carried on solely or jointly with others;[59]
- the address of each business;[60]
- the nature of each business;[61]
- confirmation of the debtor's centre of main interests.[62]

How does a creditor specify the debt due in a bankruptcy petition?

7.17 The petitioning creditor must identify the debt due in the bankruptcy petition as follows:

- the amount of the debt;[63]
- the consideration for it or the way the debt has arisen;[64]
- when the debt was incurred or became due;[65]
- any interest that has accrued that has not already been notified to the debtor;[66]
- any other charge that has accrued or is accruing together with an explanation of the basis on which it is being charged.[67]

---

56 IR86, r 6.7(1)(a) or IRN91, r 6.007(1)(a). See *Tetteh and Another v London Borough of Lam*beth [2008] BPIR 241 in which an annulment was granted based on the fact that the Tettehs did not reside at the address at which both the statutory demands and petitions were served on by substituted service.

57 IR86, r 6.7(1)(a) or IRN91, r 6.007(1)(a).

58 IR86, r 6.7(1)(b) or IRN91, r 6.007(1)(b).

59 IR86, r 6.7(1)(d) or IRN91, r 6.007(1)(d).

60 IR86, r 6.7(1)(e) or IRN91, r 6.007(1)(e).

61 IR86, r 6.7(1)(c) or IRN91, r 6.007(1)(c).

62 IR86, r 6.7(1)(f) or IRN91, r 6.007(1)(f).

63 IR86, r 6.8(1)(a) or IRN91, r 6.008(1)(a).

64 IR86, r 6.8(1)(a) or IRN91, r 6.008(1)(a).

65 IR86, r 6.8(1)(b) or IRN91, r 6.008(1)(b).

66 IR86, r 6.8(1)(c)(i) or IRN91, r 6.008(1)(c)(i).

67 IR86, r 6.8(1)(c)(ii) or IRN91, r 6.008(1)(c)(ii).

7.18 The debt must be:

- a liquidated sum payable immediately which the debtor appears unable to pay;[68]
- a liquidated sum payable at a certain future date and the debtor appears to have no reasonable prospect of paying it;[69]
- based on a statutory demand which is not being challenged;[70] or
- based on a judgment or order of court with execution returned unsatisfied whose particulars must be specified.[71]

How is a creditor with security dealt with in a bankruptcy petition?

7.19 The creditor may only petition for the unsecured element of the debt owed and therefore under s 269(1), IA86 either has to give up the security held completely,[72] or, value the security and only claim for the remaining unsecured element.[73] The two elements of the debt are treated as two separate debts.[74] A failure to comply with the requirements of s 269, IA86 may not be sufficiently serious to prevent the making of the bankruptcy order if the debtor has not been misled and has suffered no prejudice.[75]

In *1st Credit (Finance) Ltd v Bartram*[76] the statutory demand related to a debt of £18,879 secured by a final charging order, but the creditor stated in the demand that it was prepared to give up its security if a bankruptcy order could be obtained. Roth J held that the deputy district judge erred in setting aside the statutory demand on the basis that the creditor was secured, because IA86, s 269 recognised that a secured creditor could petition for a bankruptcy order provided it was prepared to give up its security.

What distinction is made between 'provable' and 'non-provable' debts for the purpose of a bankruptcy petition?

7.20 In *Levy v Legal Services Commission*[77] the Court of Appeal held that, given that no distinction is made between provable and non-provable debts in ss 264 and 383(1), IA86, the court had jurisdiction to make a bankruptcy order on a petition based on a non-provable debt, although it would only do so in very exceptional circumstances.

---

[68] IR86, r 6.8(1)(d)(i) or IRN91, r 6.008(1)(d)(i).
[69] IR86, r 6.8(1)(d)(ii) or IRN91, r 6.008(1)(d)(ii).
[70] IR86, r 6.8(2) or IRN91, r 6.008(2).
[71] IR86, r 6.8(3) or IRN91, r 6.008(3).
[72] See *Zandfarid v Bank of Credit and Commerce International SA (in liquidation)* [1996] 1 WLR 1420 and IA86, s 269(1)(a).
[73] IA86, s 269(1)(b).
[74] IA86, s 269 or INO89, art 243.
[75] See *Barclays Bank plc v Mogg* [2003] EWHC 2645 (Ch), [2004] BPIR 259.
[76] [2010] EWHC 2910 (Ch), [2011] BPIR 1.
[77] [2000] BPIR 1065 at 1075A–1075F.

7.21 A creditor may only 'prove' (ie claim in the bankruptcy) for a bankruptcy debt. A bankruptcy debt is any debt or liability to which the bankrupt is subject at the commencement of the bankruptcy or to which he may become subject after the commencement of the bankruptcy by reason of an obligation incurred before commencement of the bankruptcy including interest as mentioned in s 382(2), IA86.[78] This may include a liability in tort.[79] It is immaterial whether the debt or liability is present, future, certain or contingent, fixed or liquidated.[80]

7.22 Liability means a liability to pay money or money's worth, including a liability for breach of trust, in contract, tort, and bailment or arising out of an obligation to make restitution.[81] A costs order in legal proceedings existing as at the date of the bankruptcy order, but not made against a debtor until after the making of a bankruptcy order, is not a debt contingently due at the date of the bankruptcy order, since no obligation to pay the costs exists until the making of the costs order,[82] unless the liability was pursuant to a pre-bankruptcy contractual liability.[83]

7.23 A secured creditor may not prove for a secured debt. A creditor who has valued his security for the purpose of obtaining a bankruptcy order is deemed to have waived security to the extent that he has relied on the unsecured part of the debt[84] ie the amount proved for is unsecured.

7.24 Provable debts are defined, and thus further restricted, by r 12.3, IR86. The consequences of certain types of debt being non-provable is that the bankrupt remains personally liable for them during the course of the bankruptcy and after discharge. These non-provable debts include the following:

- certain fines;[85]
- obligations arising under an order made in family proceedings[86] other than an obligation to pay a lump sum order or costs;[87]

---

78 IA86, s 382(1).
79 IA86, s 382(2).
80 IA86, s 382(3).
81 IA86, s 382(4).
82 See *Glenister v Rowe* [2000] Ch 76, [1999] BPIR 674, CA.
83 See *Cornelius v Casson* [2008] BPIR 504.
84 IA86, s 383.
85 Fine has the meaning given by s 281(8), IA86 which applies the definition given by s 150, Magistrates Courts Act 1980, 'fine', except for the purposes of any enactment imposing a limit on the amount of any fine, includes any pecuniary penalty or pecuniary forfeiture or pecuniary compensation payable under a conviction. See also IR86, r 12.3(2).
86 As defined by the Matrimonial Proceedings Act 1984. Periodical payments are provable. As to family obligations arising as a result of foreign proceedings see *Wehmeyer v Wehmeyer* [2001] BPIR 548 and *Cartwright v Cartwright* [2002] EWCA Civ 931, [2002] BPIR 895.
87 IR86, r 12.3(2).

- obligations to pay child maintenance under the Child Support Act 1991;[88]
- certain foreign tax debts;[89]
- claims arising under criminal compensation and confiscation orders;[90]
- some student loans are no longer provable.[91]

It should be noted that a tax penalty is not a fine and is therefore provable.[92] Also a fine imposed by a professional body is contractual and not a fine as defined by the IA86.[93] In addition debts which are time barred cannot be enforced.[94]

How does a creditor withdraw a petition?

7.25 A bankruptcy petition may be withdrawn, but only with permission of the court.[95] Where the petitioner seeks permission to withdraw he must, unless the court otherwise orders, file an affidavit (or witness statement) specifying the grounds and circumstances of the application.[96] In fact the court generally dispenses with such evidence on the basis that the petitioner rarely knows the details of the grounds and circumstances where the debt has been paid.

7.26 Note that permission to withdraw may not be given before the hearing.[97] An order will not therefore be made on paper. A petitioner wishing to withdraw before the date fixed should apply to abridge time for the hearing.[98]

What is substitution and change of carriage?

7.27 Bankruptcy is a class remedy. Even where a petition has been presented by one creditor, other creditors are entitled to appear and be heard, whether to support or oppose the making of a bankruptcy order.

Where a creditor:

---

88 See section 281(5)(b), IA 86, applied in *Child Maintenance and Enforcement Commission v Beesley and Whyman* [2010] EWHC 485 (Ch), [2010] BPIR 552 and [2010] EWCA Civ 1344.

89 *Government of India v Taylor* [1955] AC 491. Note, however, that foreign tax debts are now provable where the EC Regulation on Insolvency Proceedings applies.

90 *R v Barnett JJ ex parte Phillippou*; cf IR86, r 6.223.

91 See full detail in chapter 5.

92 *Re Hurren* [1993] 1 WLR 183.

93 *Marcus v Institute of Chartered Accountants* [2004] EWHC 3010 Ch, [2005] BPIR 413. In *Casson and Wales v The Law Society* [2009] EWHC 1943 (Admin), [2010] BPIR 49 it was held that a fine levied by the Legal Complaints Service on a solicitor post-bankruptcy in respect of pre-bankruptcy conduct was a post-bankruptcy liability, applying the principles in *Glenister v Rowe*.

94 *Cotterell v Price* [1960] 1 WLR 1097.

95 IA86, s 266(2) or INO89, art 240(2).

96 IR86, r 6.32 or IRN91, r 6.029; see in particular the requirements of sub-rule (2).

97 IR86, r 6.32(3) IRN91, r 6.029(3).

98 IR86, r 12.9(2).

- is found not to be entitled to petition; or
- consents to withdraw his petition; or
- consents to allow it to be dismissed; or
- consents to adjourn; or
- fails to appear; or
- appears but does not apply for an order in terms of the prayer of his petition (ie a bankruptcy order);

the court may, on such terms as it thinks fit, order substitution in place of the petitioner of any creditor who has given notice of intention to appear at the hearing under r 6.23, IR86. The petitioner who wishes to prosecute the petition must, at the date of the petition, himself be in a position to present a bankruptcy petition.[99] The last requirement is sometimes misunderstood: it is not sufficient to be a creditor; the creditor must have served his own demand in respect of his debt and 3 weeks must have elapsed since service, alternatively the creditor must be able to rely on failed execution on a judgment or order in his favour.

7.28 As a general rule, if the court orders substitution it will order the petition to be amended, re-verified and re-served. It will also require filing of evidence of service of the statutory demand and inspection of any unsatisfied return in respect of an unsatisfied judgment.

The court may also order change of carriage, that is to say that carriage of the petition be given to another creditor in place of the petitioner.[100] The court may order change of carriage on such terms as it thinks fit if:

- the creditor seeking the order has given notice of intention to appear under r 6.23, IR86;
- the petitioner intends to secure the postponement, adjournment or withdrawal of the petition; or
- does not intend to prosecute the petition diligently or at all; and
- the applicant for the order is an unpaid and unsecured creditor of the debtor.[101]

7.29 Whilst a creditor seeking change of carriage must be a creditor, amendment of the petition is unnecessary since the creditor obtaining carriage

---

99 IR86, r 6.30 or IRN91, r 6.027.
100 IR86, r 6.31 or IRN91, r 6.028.
101 IR86, r 6.31(2) or IRN91, r 6.028(2).

prosecutes the petition based on the original petitioner's debt rather than his own. Thus, the petition debt must be properly due. The court may not make an order giving carriage to another creditor where the petition debt has been paid, secured or compounded for by means of a disposition of property made by a person other than the debtor or by a disposition of the debtor's own property made with the approval of or ratified by the court.[102]

7.30 The rationale for this is that the debtor is entitled to have the petition dismissed if there is no longer a debt. However, if he has paid the debt out of his own assets without that disposition having been approved or ratified, the effect of s 284, IA86 is that the petitioner is bound to hold what he has received on trust for the general body of creditors and account to the trustee if a bankruptcy order has been made. The provisions of s 284, IA86 cannot, however, bite on assets not belonging to the debtor.

7.31 If a change of carriage order is made the creditor with carriage of the petition is entitled to rely on all the evidence adduced in the proceedings.[103] As to the operation of change of carriage orders and the difficulties to which they can give rise see *Re Purvis and another*[104] and *Smith v Ian Simpson and Co.*[105]

What is an expedited petition?

7.32 In the case of a creditor's petition presented wholly or partly in respect of a debt which is the subject of a statutory demand under s 268, IA86, the petition may be presented before the end of the 3-week period otherwise required if there is a serious possibility that the debtor's property or the value of any of his property will be significantly diminished during that period. The petition must contain a statement to that effect.[106]

An expedited petition may still be presented even though there is an extant application to set aside the statutory demand.[107] It is still necessary for the statutory demand to be served first.[108]

The court may dismiss the petition if the claim for expedition is not made out.[109]

A bankruptcy order on an expedited petition cannot be made until at least three weeks have elapsed since the service of the statutory demand.[110]

---

102 IR86, r 6.31(2) IRN91, r 6.028(2). As to which see IA86, s 284 or INO89, art 257.
103 IR86, r 6.32(5) or IRN91, r 6.029(5).
104 [1997] 3 All ER 663.
105 [2001] Ch 239, [2000] 3 All ER 434, [2000] BPIR 667.
106 IA86, s 270 or INO89, art 244.
107 *Re a Debtor (No 22 of 1993)* [1994] 1 WLR 46.
108 *Wehmeyer v Wehmeyer* [2001] BPIR 548.
109 *Re a Debtor (No 22 of 1993)* [1994] 1 WLR 46.
110 IA86, s 271(2).

When can security for costs be applied for?

7.33 When a petition is presented in respect of a future debt and the creditor claims there is no reasonable prospect of payment then the debtor may request the petitioning creditor to provide security for his costs.[111] The nature and amount of the security is at the court's discretion.[112] If an order is made the petition must not be heard until the security has been provided.[113]

PRESENTING A PETITION

What is the procedure for presenting a creditor's bankruptcy petition to court?

7.34 Once the bankruptcy petition has been completed and the court in which it needs to be filed is determined, the following procedures need to be followed:

- The petition must be verified by affidavit or witness statement on Form 6.13.[114] The affidavit is *prima facie* evidence of the truth of the statements in the petition.
- The petition must be exhibited to the affidavit.[115]
- If the petition includes debts of more than one creditor each debt must be separately verified by each creditor.[116]
- The person swearing the affidavit may be either the petitioner or someone authorised to sign on his behalf and their capacity, authority and knowledge of the debt needs to be stated.[117]
- If the petition is based on a statutory demand and more than 4 months have elapsed since service of the demand, an explanation for the delay must be provided.[118]

7.35 Three copies of the petition must be provided to the court as follows:

- one exhibited to the affidavit;[119]

---

[111] IR86, r 6.17(1) and (2) or IRN91, r 6.016(1) and (2).
[112] IR86, r 6.17(3) or IRN91, r 6.016(3).
[113] IR86, r 6.17(4) or IRN91, r 6.016(4).
[114] IR86, rr 6.10(1) and 6.12(1) or IRN91, rr 6.009(1) and 6.011(1).
[115] IR86, r 6.12(3) or IRN91, r 6.011(3).
[116] IR86, r 6.12(2) or IRN91, r 6.011(2).
[117] IR86, r 6.12(4) and (5) or IRN91, r 6.011(4) and (5).
[118] IR86, r 6.12(7) or IRN91, r 6.011(7).
[119] IR86, r 6.10(3)(b) or IRN91, r 6.009(3)(b).

- one for service on the debtor[120] plus an additional copy for proof of personal service;[121]

- one for the supervisor of any IVA (if the supervisor is not the petitioner);[122]

It will also be necessary to file the original evidence of service of the statutory demand or the return in respect of any unsatisfied execution. A receipt must be attached to the petition confirming payment of the court fee and the deposit[123] or confirmation that alternative arrangements for the deposit have been agreed.[124] The date and time of filing in the court will be marked on each copy.[125] The court will fix a time and date for the hearing of the petition (generally about 6 to 8 weeks from the date of presentation) and will also add this to each copy.[126] The detailed procedure for serving the petition on the debtor is dealt with below.

The court is then required to notify the presentation of the bankruptcy petition to the Chief Land Registrar.[127] However, it does not always do so, although the failure of the Court Service to notify of the fact of such a petition, with the effect that a debtor is able to dispose of a property between petition and bankruptcy order, does not give rise to an actionable claim in damages for negligence or breach of statutory duty against the Ministry of Justice.[128]

What is the procedure when the bankruptcy petition is in respect of a failed IVA and requests the appointment of a former supervisor as trustee?

7.36 Where a petition contains a request for the appointment of a person as trustee in accordance with s 297(5), IA86 (appointment of former supervisor as trustee) the person whose appointment is sought, must file in court a report containing the following information at least 2 days before the petition hearing:[129]

- Confirmation of the date on which written notice was given, to all the creditors bound by the arrangement, of the intention to seek his appointment as trustee. This date being at least 10 days before the day on which the report is filed in court.[130]

---

120 IR86, r 6.10(3)(a) or IRN91, r 6.009(3)(a).
121 IR86, r 6.15(2)(a) or IRN91, r 6.014(2)(a).
122 IR86, r 6.10(3)(c) or IRN91, r 6.009(3)(c).
123 IR86, r 6.10(2) or IRN91, r 6.009(2).
124 IR86, r 6.10(2A) or IRN91, r 6.009(2A).
125 IR86, r 6.10(4) or IRN91, r 6.009(4).
126 IR86, r 6.10(5) or IRN91, r 6.009(5).
127 IR86, rr 6.13 and 6.43 and Form 6.14 or IRN91, rr 6.012 and 6.036. See also **7.61**.
128 See *Trustee in Bankruptcy of Louise St John Poulton v Ministry of Justice* [2010] EWCA Civ 392, [2010] BPIR 775.
129 IR86, r 6.09(6).
130 IR86, r 6.10(6)(a) or IRN91, r 6.009(6)(a).

- Details of any response from creditors to that notice, including any objections to his appointment.[131]

While the court has discretion as to who should be appointed trustee on a petition presented by a supervisor, the exercise of that discretion by the court can, however, be challenged if not judiciously exercised. If there are no reasonable grounds for complaint against the supervisor it would not be a proper exercise of that discretion to refuse to appoint the supervisor as trustee in bankruptcy.[132]

SERVICE OF A PETITION

What is the procedure for serving a sealed copy of a creditor's bankruptcy petition on the debtor?

7.37 The bankruptcy petition will have been filed in court and a sealed copy obtained for serving on the debtor. Service should be effected as follows:

- If possible the sealed copy of the petition should be served personally on the debtor by one of the following:[133]
  - an officer of the court;
  - the petitioning creditor or his agent;
  - the petitioning creditor's solicitor or his agent.
- If the court is satisfied by affidavit or witness statement that prompt personal service cannot be effected because the debtor is keeping out of the way to avoid service of the petition or other legal process, or for any other cause, it may order substituted service to be effected in such manner as it thinks fit. The usual form of order will provide for service by first class post and recorded delivery, effective on the seventh day after posting. Orders for substituted service by advertisement are rare. Forms 6.15 (advertisement) and 6.16 (notice in *Gazette*) should be used as appropriate.[134] The steps to be taken are the same as in relation to substituted service of a statutory demand. This order should be in Form 6.15. If the order is advertised, the advertisement should follow Form 6.16.
- If the debtor dies before service of the petition, the court may order service to be effected on his personal representatives, or on such other persons as it thinks fit.[135]

---

131 IR86, r 6.10(6)(b) or IRN91, r 6.009(6)(b).

132 See *Landsman v De Concilio* [2005] EWHC 267 (Ch), [2005] BPIR 829.

133 IR86, r 6.14(1) or IRN91, r 6.013(1).

134 IR86, r 6.14(2) or IRN91, r 6.013(2).

135 IR86, r 6.16 or IRN91, r 6.015.

- If, to the petitioner's knowledge, there is an IVA in force for the debtor and the petitioner is not the supervisor then a copy of the petition must be sent to the supervisor.[136]
- If, to the petitioner's knowledge, there is a member state liquidator appointed in main proceedings in relation to the bankrupt, a copy of the petition must also be sent by him to the member state liquidator.[137]

Can the bankruptcy petition be amended?

7.38 After a petition has been filed in court it may only be amended with the permission of the court.[138] As to the general power of the court to allow amendments, see *Aspinalls Club Ltd v Halabi*.[139]

THE PETITION HEARING

When is the bankruptcy petition heard?

7.39 Generally a petition may not be heard until at least 14 days have elapsed since the petition was served on the debtor.[140] However an expedited petition may be heard earlier.[141] Also the debtor can consent to an earlier hearing.[142]

What proof is required by the court that the petition has been served on the debtor?

7.40 Service of a bankruptcy petition must be proved by affidavit or witness statement in Form 6.17 or 6.18[143] which should be filed in court immediately after service has been effected.[144] The affidavit must exhibit a sealed copy of the ordered petition[145] and if substituted service has been used (Form 6.18) a sealed copy of the order.[146]

7.41 A bankruptcy order should never be made without an affidavit of service and r 7.55, IR86 cannot be used to remedy this formal defect regardless of any injustice.[147]

The court has discretion to order the deponent of the affidavit of service for cross-examination if service is denied as a defence.

---

136 IR86, r 6.14(4) or IRN91, r 6.013(4).
137 IR86, r 6.14(5) or IRN91, r 6.013(5).
138 IR86, r 6.22 or IRN91, r 6.019.
139 [1998] BPIR 322.
140 IR86, r 6.18(1) or IRN91, r 6.017(1).
141 IR86, r 6.18(2) or IRN91, r 6.017(2).
142 IR86, r 6.18(2) or IRN91, r 6.017(2).
143 IR86, r 6.15(1) or IRN91, r 6.014(1).
144 IR86, r 6.15(2) or IRN91, r 6.014(2).
145 IR86, r 6.15(2)(a) or IRN91, r 6.014(2)(a).
146 IR86, r 6.15(2)(b) or IRN91, r 6.014(2)(b).
147 See *Re Awan* [2000] BPIR 241.

Who may attend the hearing?

7.42 The following people may attend and be heard at the hearing of a bankruptcy petition:[148]

- The petitioning creditor.
- The debtor.
- The supervisor of any IVA.
- Any creditor who has given notice under r 6.23(1), IR86 (see Form 6.20) of his intention to appear.[149] Such notice must be in Form 6.20, specifying:
  - — the name, address, telephone number and reference of the person making it, or any person authorised to speak or act on his behalf;[150]
  - — whether he intends to support or oppose the petition;[151] and
  - — the amount and nature of his debt.[152]

This notice must be given to the petitioning creditor by 1600 hours on the business day before the hearing,[153] although the court may give permission to appear if r 6.23, IR86[154] has not been complied with.[155]

What orders can the court make on the hearing of a creditor's petition?

7.43 The court may do any of the following:[156]

- dismiss the petition (Form 6.22);
- give permission to withdraw;
- adjourn it (Form 6.23);[157]
- make a bankruptcy order (Form 6.25); or
- extend the hearing date.

---

148 IR86, r 6.18(3) or IRN91, r 6.017(3).
149 IR86, r 6.23(1).
150 IR86, r 6.23(2)(a).
151 IR86, r 6.23(2)(b).
152 IR86, r 6.23(2(c) IR86 or IRN91, r 6.020(2).
153 IR86, r 6.23(3) IR86 or IRN91, r 6.020(3).
154 Or for Northern Ireland IRN91, r 6.020.
155 IR86, r 6.23(4) IR86 or IRN91, r 6.020(4).
156 IR86, r 6.25 IR86 or IRN91, r 6.022.
157 IR86, r 6.29 IR86 or IRN91, r 6.026.

What happens if a creditor's petition is dismissed or withdrawn?

7.44 If the petition is dismissed or withdrawn by permission of the court, an order will be made at the same time permitting vacation of the registration of the petition as a pending action; and the court will send two sealed copies of the order on Form 6.22 to the debtor.[158]

What happens if a creditor's petition is adjourned?

7.45 The court will not generally issue an adjournment order on Form 6.23: as a general rule it is for the petitioning creditor to give notice of adjournment in accordance with r 6.29(2), IR86, which the petitioning creditor must submit on Form 6.24 to:

- the debtor;[159] and
- any other creditor who served notice of attendance but who failed to attend.[160]

What happens if the creditor's petition has not been served before the date of the hearing?

7.46 There can be no hearing of the petition until it has been served. The petitioning creditor can apply to the court for an extension of the hearing date if the petition has not been served[161] but must state the reasons why the petition has not been served.[162] Notice of the new venue must be served by the petitioning creditor.[163] Any costs of the delay will only be allowed with the permission of the court and provided the application to extend the hearing date is made at least 2 days before the date fixed for the hearing.[164]

What are the requirements for the petitioning creditor to attend the petition hearing?

7.47 The petitioning creditor or his representative must appear at the hearing. If he fails to appear and the petition is dismissed he cannot present a further petition against the same debtor without the permission of the court.[165] As to the principles to be followed when exercising discretion in the absence of the petitioning creditor see *Omgate Ltd v Gordon*.[166]

---

158 IR86, r 6.27 or IRN91, r 6.024.
159 IR86, r 6.23(2)(a) or IRN91, r 6.020(2)(a).
160 IR86, r 6.29(2)(b) or IRN91, r 6.026(2)(b).
161 IR86, r 6.28(1) or IRN91, r 6.025(1).
162 IR86, r 6.28(2) or IRN91, r 6.025(2).
163 IR86, r 6.28(4) or IRN91, r 6.025(4).
164 IR86, r 6.28(3) or IRN91, r 6.025(3).
165 IR86, r 6.26 or IRN91, r 6.023-CP.
166 [2001] BPIR 909 at [10].

Which other creditors can attend the hearing of the bankruptcy petition?

7.48 The petitioning creditor is required to hand to the court before the commencement of the hearing a list of all creditors who have given notice of intention to appear.[167] The list should be on Form 6.21[168] and against the name of each creditor should be stated whether they intend to support or oppose the petition.[169] If any creditor has been given permission of the court to be added as an additional petitioning creditor, that information must be given to the originating petitioning creditor so that the new creditor can be added to the list.[170]

7.49 The only creditors who can attend the petition hearing are those who have given notice on Form 6.20 to the petitioning creditor or his solicitor.[171] Any creditor who fails to give notice may only appear on the hearing of the petition with permission of the court.[172]

How does a creditor give notice of intention to attend the hearing to the petitioning creditor?

7.50 Any notice must be sent to the petitioning creditor or his solicitor no later than 16.00 hours on the business day before that which is appointed for the hearing (or, where the hearing has been adjourned, for the adjourned hearing).[173] The notice should be on Form 6.20 specifying:

- the name, address, telephone number and reference of the person making it, or any person authorised to speak or act on his behalf;[174]
- whether he intends to support or oppose the petition;[175] and
- the amount and nature of his debt.[176]

The court may give permission to appear if r 6.23, IR86[177] has not been complied with.[178]

---

167 IR86, r 6.24(3) or IRN91, r 6.021(3).
168 IR86, r 6.24(1) or IRN91, r 6.021(1).
169 IR86, r 6.24(2) or IRN91, r 6.021(2).
170 IR86, r 6.24(4) or IRN91, r 6.021(4).
171 IR86, r 6.23(1) or IRN91, r 6.020(1).
172 IR86, r 6.23(4) or IRN91, r 6.020(4).
173 IR86, r 6.23(3) or IRN91, r 6.020(3).
174 IR86, r 6.23(2)(a).
175 IR86, r 6.23(2)(b).
176 IR86, r 6.23(2(c) or IRN91, r 6.020(2).
177 Or IRN91, r 6.020.
178 IR86, r 6.23(4) or IRN91, r 6.020(4).

What issues does the court need to consider before making a bankruptcy order on a creditor's petition?

7.51 The court needs to be satisfied of the following:

- that the petition debt, having been payable at the date of the petition or having since become payable, has been neither paid,[179] secured nor compounded for;[180] or
- the debtor has no reasonable prospect of being able to pay the debt when it falls due;[181]
- in the case of an expedited petition, that at least 3 weeks have elapsed since the service of any statutory demand under s 268, IA86.[182]

A creditor has a *prima facie* right to obtain a bankruptcy order as long as there is evidence that the petition has been properly served and is for a valid debt.[183]

For a discussion on the scope of r 6.25, IR86 see *Legal Services Commission v Leonard.*[184]

The meaning of 'compounded for' includes the debt being settled or secured in some other manner.

When can the court dismiss or adjourn a creditor's petition?

7.52 The court may dismiss the petition if it is satisfied that the debtor is able to pay all his debts[185] or is satisfied[186] that:

- the debtor has made an offer to secure or compound for a debt in respect of which the petition is presented;
- the acceptance of that offer would have required the dismissal of the petition; and
- the offer has been unreasonably refused.

---

179 This is a reference to unconditional payment. If the payment has been made from the debtor's funds, such that the payment may be liable to be set aside under s 284, IA 86, the court retains discretion to make a bankruptcy order. See *Smith v Ian Simpson and Co* [2001] Ch 239, [2000] 3 All ER 434, [2000] BPIR 667,

180 IA86, s 271(1)(a) and IR86, r 6.25(1) or for Northern Ireland see INO89, art 241(1)(a) and IRN91, r 6.022(1).

181 IA86, s 271(1)(a) or INO89, art 241(1)(a).

182 IA86, s 271(2) or INO89, art 241(2).

183 IR86, r 6.25(1) or IRN91, r 6.022(1).

184 [2000] EWCA Civ 744, [2002] BPIR 994 at [38]–[44].

185 IA86, s 271(3) or INO89, art 245(3).

186 IA86, s 271(3) or INO89, art 245(3).

The court will also take into account all of the debtor's debts including contingent and prospective liabilities. In determining the meaning of 'a reasonable prospect' the court should take into account any facts and other matters known to the creditor at the time he originally entered into the transaction with the debtor.[187]

7.53 In practice it is difficult to run a defence to a petition based on an unreasonable refusal of an offer to secure or compound for the debt. In *Re a Debtor (No 32 of 1993)*[188] the court held that the debtor must demonstrate that no reasonable hypothetical creditor would have refused the offer. In *Inland Revenue Commissioners v A Debtor*[189] the court held that it was not unreasonable to refuse security instead of payment.[190] As far as collection of taxes and council tax are concerned, the courts have made it clear that there is no obligation on the creditor to accept security for the full debt, In *Ross and another v Commissioners for HM Revenue and Customs*[191] the evidence suggested that the prospects of receiving payment in full from a trustee were good, when the debtor was making an offer of security (including second and third charges over a portfolio of properties that required planning consent) subject to conditions, including that marketing should not begin for 6 months or earlier if the planning consents were obtained. Henderson J specifically observed that, if accepted, HMRC would have been involved in planning and marketing as well as negotiations with prior encumbrancers when they did not have resources for such activities and that if such offers were routinely accepted HMRC could find themselves as the biggest property owner in the country. Those views were echoed in *Nottingham City Council v Pennant*,[192] where it was held that the local authority had not been unreasonable in rejecting the debtor's offer of the grant of a charging order over the relevant property, as a charging order would involve the council in further expense should it require enforcement.

A proposal of an IVA does not constitute an offer within the meaning of s 271(3), IA86 since it is made to all the creditors rather than one.[193]

7.54 The courts do not consider that proportionality is a relevant issue when making a bankruptcy order.[194]

---

[187] IA86, s 271(4) or INO89, art 245(4).

[188] [1994] 1 WLR 899, [1994] BCC 438.

[189] [1995] BCC 971.

[190] See also *HM Customs and Excise v Dougall* [2001] BPIR 269 where it was held that HM Customs and Excise did not act unreasonably in refusing to accept full security from the mother-in-law of a debtor who had been convicted of VAT evasion.

[191] [2010] EWHC 13 (Ch), [2010] BPIR 652.

[192] [2009] EWHC 2437 (Ch), [2010] BPIR 430.

[193] *Re. a Debtor (No 2389 of 1989)* [1991] Ch 326.

[194] See *John Lewis plc v Pearson Burton* [2004] BPIR 70.

7.55 The court may adjourn if it thinks there is a reasonable prospect of the debt being paid in full within a reasonable time.[195] Whilst many bankruptcy petitions are routinely adjourned at the first hearing for discussions and negotiations to take place regarding payment by instalments, when called upon to decide the issue, the court is usually quite harsh as to the expected period of time. Whilst an adjournment to allow instalments to be made over 7 years[196] or 4 years[197] would be clearly inappropriate, in *Nottingham City Council v Pennant*[198] it was held not to be appropriate to adjourn the bankruptcy petition for 3 months just to see if the debtor would keep to his promise to pay off his debts by instalments. In *Ross and another v Commissioners for HM Revenue and Customs*[199] the Court ruled, on appeal, that a reasonable time for payment in full could have been no more than a further 2 or 3 months at the most and there was no credible prospect of payment being received in that timescale. In *Raguz v Scottish and Newcastle Ltd*[200] a district judge's decision not to adjourn the petition for 3 months was upheld as being legitimately within the scope of his discretion.

What issues does the court need to consider before making a bankruptcy order on the petition of a supervisor for a failed IVA?

7.56 The court can only make a bankruptcy order on the petition of a supervisor or creditor bound by a failed IVA when the following is demonstrated:

- that the debtor has failed to comply with his obligations under the voluntary arrangement;[201] or
- that information which was false or misleading in any material particular or which contained material omissions;[202]
- was contained in any statement of affairs or other document supplied by the debtor under Part VIII to any person;[203] or
- was otherwise made available by the debtor to his creditors at or in connection with a meeting summoned under that Part;[204] or

---

195 *Re Gilmartin (a Bankrupt)* [1989] 1 WLR 513 and *Harrison v Seggar* [2005] EWHC 411 (Ch), [2005] BPIR 583.
196 See *John Lewis plc v Pearson Burton* [2004] BPIR 70.
197 See *Harrison v Seggar* [2005] EWHC 411 (Ch), [2005] BPIR 583.
198 [2009] EWHC 2437 (Ch), [2010] BPIR 430.
199 [2010] EWHC 13 (Ch), [2010] BPIR 652.
200 [2010] EWHC 1384 (Ch), [2010] BPIR 945.
201 IA86, s 276(1)(a) or INO89, art 250(1)(a).
202 IA86, s 276(1)(b) or INO89, art 250(1)(b).
203 IA86, s 276(1)(b)(i) or INO89, art 250(1)(b)(i).
204 IA86, s 276(1)(b)(ii) or INO89, art 250(1)(b)(ii).

- that the debtor has failed to do all such things as may for the purposes of the voluntary arrangement have been reasonably required of him by the supervisor of the arrangement.[205]

Whilst the court retains a discretion whether or not to make a bankruptcy order, it does not generally look kindly upon the failure of a debtor to comply with his obligations under the terms of an approved individual voluntary arrangement. A bankruptcy order can be made even where the non-compliance was through no fault of the debtor,[206] where the non-compliance has been remedied[207] or where the majority of creditors do not wish for a bankruptcy order to be made.[208] Similarly, the court does not look kindly upon failures to provide creditors with full information for the purposes of the creditors' meeting.[209]

CHALLENGING A PETITION

What does a debtor need to do if he intends to oppose a creditor's petition?

7.57 The IR86 stipulates that that at least 7 days before the hearing of the bankruptcy petition the debtor must:

- file in court a notice specifying the grounds on which he will object to the making of a bankruptcy order in Form 6.19;[210] and

- send a copy of the notice to the petitioning creditor or his solicitor.[211]

7.58 In practice, this is a requirement that is rarely insisted on by the court. Having regard to the draconian nature of bankruptcy the court will almost invariably accept late service of a notice of opposition, and in practice will often dispense with one, ordering the debtor to file and serve evidence in opposition and giving the petitioner an opportunity to file and serve evidence in reply.

---

205 IA86, s 276(1)(c) or INO89, art 250(1)(c).

206 See *Re Keenan* [1998] BPIR 205, where the debtor had promise to sell some shares in a US company and make available the proceeds to their respective IVAs. Through no fault of the debtors, the shares were not sold. Despite the lack of culpability, a bankruptcy order was made on a supervisor's petition, supported by all the creditors. See also *Stanley v Phillips* [2003] EWHC 720 (Ch), [2004] BPIR 632.

207 See *Vadher v Weisgard* [1998] BPIR 295, where instalments ie under the agreed individual voluntary arrangements were not maintained. Despite there being offers to clear the arrears, a bankruptcy order was made and upheld on appeal. In *Carter Knight v Peat* [2000] BPIR 968, it was held that the court could make a bankruptcy order even if the default had been remedied by the time of the hearing of the petition. See also *Clarke v Birkin* [2006] EWHC 340 (Ch), [2006] BPIR 632.

208 See *Harris v Gross* [2001] BPIR 586.

209 See *Bradburn v Kaye* [2006] BPIR 605, where a potential tax liability had been understated.

210 IR86, r 6.21(a) or IRN91, r 6.018(a).

211 IR86, r 6.21(a) or IRN91, r 6.018(a).

What grounds can be used to challenge a bankruptcy petition?

7.59 A petition can be challenged on a number of grounds:

- The court has no jurisdiction over the debtor (either by reason of the provisions of the EC Regulation 1346/2000 on Insolvency Proceedings or by reason of the provisions of s 265, IA86).

- The petitioner has failed in his obligation to do all that is reasonable to bring the statutory demand to his attention. Note that it is not sufficient simply to show that the demand did not come to his attention: that is a higher obligation than that imposed by r 6.3(2), IR86.

- The petitioner has failed to take proper steps to serve the petition on him (although in practice this is hard to run if the debtor has actually appeared so that it is plain that he knows about the petition).

- The debt is secured. However, the court will accept a forced sale value for the purposes of valuing the security and will proceed to determine the extent to which the debt may or may not be secured.

- The debt is disputed on substantial grounds or a ground sufficient to have enabled him to set aside the statutory demand.[212] As a general rule a debtor may not raise at the petition stage an argument that has already been decided and disposed of on an application to set aside the statutory demand.[213]

- The petitioner has unreasonably refused an offer to secure or compound for the petition debt.

The court will not as a general rule go behind the judgment or order of another court save in exceptional circumstances (as to which see, for example, *Royal Bank of Scotland v Farley*[214] and *Hunter v Lex Vehicle Finance Ltd*[215]). The general practice is to adjourn the petition to allow an appeal or an application to set aside the judgment provided such appeal or application appears to be bona fide (*Royal Bank of Scotland v Farley*; *Society of Lloyd's v Beaumont*.[216])

---

212 See for example *HMRC v Potter* [2008] BPIR 1033 and *Dean and Dean v Angel Airlines SA* [2009] EWHC 447 (Ch), [2009] BPIR 409 where, in each case, it was not clear that the debtor was actually indebted to the petitioning creditor.

213 *Brillouet v Hachette Magazines Ltd* [1996] BPIR 518 and *Turner v Royal Bank of Scotland* [2000] BPIR 683, referred to in para 7.53.

214 [1996] BPIR 638.

215 [2005] EWHC 223 (Ch), [2005] BPIR 586.

216 [2006] BPIR 1021.

It is open to the court to make a bankruptcy order even in circumstances in which the petition debt has been reduced below £750 as a result of payment made by the debtor as opposed to a third party.[217]

Can a debtor challenge a bankruptcy petition using the same arguments used unsuccessfully to set aside an earlier statutory demand?

7.60 It is not open to a debtor to use the same argument to challenge a bankruptcy petition as those used unsuccessfully to challenge an earlier statutory demand.

7.61 In *Turner v Royal Bank of Scotland*[218] Chadwick LJ confirmed authoritatively the view expressed by Vinelott J in *Re a Debtor (No 27 of 1990), Brillouet v Hachette Magazines Ltd*:[219]

> 'Rule 6.25 of the 1986 Rules provides that on the hearing of the petition, the court may make a bankruptcy order if satisfied that the statements in the petition are true and that the debt on which it is founded has not been paid or secured or compounded for. So the court is not bound to make a bankruptcy order; there is a residual discretion in the court to decide on the hearing of the petition whether or not to make the bankruptcy order. But it cannot have been intended, as it seems to me, that when exercising the discretion (which it undoubtedly has under r 6.25), whether or not to make a bankruptcy order at the hearing of the petition, the court is required to revisit the arguments which have already been advanced on the hearing of the application to set aside the statutory demand, and which have already been rejected at that hearing. As Vinelott J pointed out in the Brillouet case, the debtor cannot go back and reargue the very grounds on which he unsuccessfully sought to have the statutory demand set aside. It will require some change of circumstances between the unsuccessful attempt to set aside the statutory demand and the hearing of the petition before the court (on the hearing of the petition) can be asked to go into the question which has already been determined at the hearing of the statutory demand. To hold otherwise would be to encourage a waste of the court time, and a waste of the parties' money, and would defeat the obvious purpose of the statutory scheme.'

7.62 For an example of the court's refusal to allow re-argument see *Coulter v Chief of Dorset Police*.[220] It is submitted that a change of circumstance will not include a change of emphasis in the debtor's argument, or any attempt to introduce material which the debtor could reasonably be expected to have produced to the court at the set-aside stage. Conversely, change of circumstance would include evidence which could not reasonably have been produced or which was not available at the earlier hearing or, it is submitted, at least arguably and subject to confirmatory evidence given the draconian nature of a bankruptcy order, the advancing of an entirely new line of argument which was

---

217 *Re Patel (A Debtor)* [1996] 1 WLR 221 and *Smith v Ian Simpson and Co* [2001] Ch 239, [2000] 3 All ER 434, [2000] BPIR 667.

218 [2000] BPIR 683 at 694A–694AD.

219 [1996] BPIR 518 at 520B–694AD.

220 [2005] BPIR 76.

not touched upon at the earlier hearing and of which the debtor only becomes aware following a change of legal representation.

7.63 Certainly it has been held that if there had not been a hearing at the statutory demand stage, either because an application to set aside was not actually made or because the application was dismissed for procedural reasons without determination of the issues, the court's discretion under s 271, IA86 would almost invariably result in the non-application of the principle in *Brillouet and Turner*: see *Adams v Mason Bullock*.[221] In addition to a review of the post-Turner authorities the deputy judge indicated at [29] that the taking of a point at the petition stage which was not advanced at the set-aside stage would depend on whether allowing the point would be in the interests of justice, given the explanation presented to the court. If there is no reasonable determination at the earlier stage and an application is struck out on the ground of a formal defect then the principle in Turner is not engaged: *Commissioners of Inland Revenue v Lee-Phipps*.[222]

REGISTRATION

What are the requirements for and effects of the registration of a bankruptcy petition?

7.64 Details of every bankruptcy petition filed in court are recorded at the Land Charges Department of the Land Registry on the pending actions register.[223] This register is separate and distinct from the 16 district Land Registries which record proprietorship and charges as detailed below. This record is also in addition to the individual insolvency register maintained by the Secretary of State which includes details of bankruptcy orders and IVAs.

Land Charges Department Plymouth	District Registries (16 offices)
	Register of Title *Title No* *(in 3 parts)*
1. Pending Actions Petitions registered by courts 2. Record of actions affecting unregistered land Caution against first registration by the wrong person.	1. Property Register Freehold/Leasehold Address and Description 2. Proprietorship Register: Owner/Quality of title (Absolute title) Bankruptcy Inhibition (BO) will be registered here.

221 [2004] EWHC 2910 (Ch), [2005] BPIR 241 at [28] (Bernard Livesey QC sitting as a Deputy High Court Judge).

222 [2003] BPIR 803 (Lancelot Henderson QC, sitting as a Deputy High Court Judge).

223 IR86, rr 6.13 and 6.43 and Form 6.14 or IRN91, rr 6.013 and 6.039.

3. Registration of writs and orders A name based register, which results in the first caution at (1) above being withdrawn once an order is made. There is no protection at petition stage for jointly owned properties.	3. Charges Register: Financial Charges Restrictive Covenants Notice of intended deposit of the land / charge certificate Bankruptcy Inhibition (Bankruptcy Order) Will NOT contain details of any land held in trust. Caution against dealings

POST-PETITION DISPOSITIONS AND VALIDATION ORDERS

How is a bankrupt prevented from selling land and property?

7.65 When a petition is presented a notice is sent to the Chief Land Registrar registering the petition as a pending action.[224] The purpose of registration is to prevent disposition of the debtor's property.

7.66 Section 284, IA86 restricts dispositions of the debtor's property during the period following presentation of a petition and ending with the date on which a bankrupt's property vests in his trustee (s 284(1) and (3), IA86). Any such disposition (or payment)[225] is void unless made with the consent of the court or subsequently ratified by the court. Note that subsection (4) provides protection to a *bona fide* purchaser for value without notice that the petition had been presented. The purpose of the statutory provisions is to ensure that the debtor's estate is not dissipated and that creditors are dealt with on a *pari passu* basis and in accordance with the statutory priorities. The debtor need not have effected the disposition voluntarily, as the section is effective as against court orders made against the debtor.[226]

What is a 'validation order' and what is the procedure for obtaining one?

7.67 A debtor or creditor may apply for relief from the effects of s 284, IA86 by means of an application for what is commonly called a 'validation order' (if applied for while the petition is pending) or a ratification order (if applied for after a bankruptcy order has been made).

7.68 Guidance as to the practice and procedure relating to such applications is given in the *Practice Direction: Insolvency Proceedings* which came into effect

---

[224] IR86, r 6.13 or IRN91, r 6.012.

[225] As to what constitutes a payment see *Pettit v Novakovic* [2007] BCC 462.

[226] See *Re Flint* [1993] Ch 319, approved in *Moutney v Treharne* [2002] EWCA Civ 1174, [2002] BPIR 1126 and applied in *Treharne and Sands v Forrester* [2004] EWHC 2784 (Ch), [2004] BPIR 338.

on 23 February 2012 and replaces all earlier Practice Directions, Practice Statements and Practice Notes. Guidance on applications in individual cases is as follows:

> 'A person against whom a bankruptcy petition has been presented may apply to the court after presentation of the petition for relief from the effects of Section 284(1)–(3), IA86 by seeking an order that any disposition of his assets or payment made out of his funds, including any bank account (whether it is in credit or overdrawn), shall not be void in the event of a bankruptcy order being made on the petition (a validation order).[227]

In accordance with the *Practice Direction: Insolvency Proceedings*,[228] an application for a validation order should be made to the registrar or district judge.

Save in exceptional circumstances, notice of the making of the application should be given to: (a) the petitioning creditor(s) or other petitioner; (b) any creditor who has given notice to the petitioner of his intention to appear on the hearing of the petition pursuant to r 6.23, IR86; (c) any creditor who has been substituted as petitioner pursuant to r 6.30, IR86; and (d) any creditor who has carriage of the petition pursuant to r 6.31, IR86.[229]

The application should be supported by a witness statement which, save in exceptional circumstances, should be made by the debtor. If appropriate, supporting evidence in the form of a witness statement from the debtor's accountant should also be produced.[230]

The extent and contents of the evidence should include the following information:

(a) when and to whom notice has been given;

(b) brief details of the circumstances leading to presentation of the petition;

(c) how the debtor became aware of the presentation of the petition;

(d) whether the petition debt is admitted or disputed and, if the latter, brief details of the basis on which the debt is disputed;

(e) full details of the debtor's financial position including details of his assets (including details of any security and the amount(s) secured) and liabilities, which should be supported, as far as possible, by documentary evidence, eg accounts, draft accounts, management accounts or estimated statement of affairs;

---

227 Practice Direction: Insolvency Proceedings, 23 February 2012, para 14.8.1.
228 Practice Direction: Insolvency Proceedings, 23 February 2012, para 15.
229 Practice Direction: Insolvency Proceedings, 23 February 2012, para 14.8.2.
230 Practice Direction: Insolvency Proceedings, 23 February 2012, para 14.8.3.

(f) a cash flow forecast and profit and loss projection for the period for which the order is sought;

(g) details of the dispositions or payments in respect of which an order is sought;

(h) the reasons relied on in support of the need for such dispositions or payments to be made;

(i) any other information relevant to the exercise of the court's discretion;

(j) details of any consents obtained from the petitioning and/or supporting creditors.

Where an application is made urgently to enable payments to be made which are essential to continued trading (eg wages) and it is not possible to assemble all the evidence listed above, the court may consider granting limited relief for a short period, but there should be sufficient evidence to satisfy the court that the interests of creditors are unlikely to be prejudiced.[231]

Where the debtor is not trading or carrying on business and the application relates only to a proposed sale, mortgage or re-mortgage of the debtor's home evidence of the following will generally suffice:

(a) when and to whom notice has been given;

(b) whether the petition debt is admitted or disputed and, if the latter, brief details of the basis on which the debt is disputed;

(c) details of the property to be sold, mortgaged or re-mortgaged (including its title number);

(d) the value of the property and the proposed sale price, or details of the mortgage or re-mortgage;

(e) details of any existing mortgages or charges on the property and redemption figures;

(f) the costs of sale (eg solicitors' or agents' costs);

(g) how and by whom any net proceeds of sale (or sums coming into the debtor's hands as a result of any mortgage or re-mortgage) are to be held pending the final hearing of the petition;

(h) any other information relevant to the exercise of the court's discretion;

---

231 Practice Direction: Insolvency Proceedings, 23 February 2012, para 14.8.5.

(i) details of any consents obtained from the petitioning and/or supporting creditors.

Whether or not the debtor is trading or carrying on business, where the application involves a disposition of property the court will need to be satisfied that any proposed disposal will be at a proper value. Accordingly, an independent valuation should be obtained and exhibited to the evidence.[232]

The court will need to be satisfied by credible evidence that the debtor is solvent and able to pay his debts as they fall due or that a particular transaction or series of transactions in respect of which the order is sought will be beneficial to or will not prejudice the interests of all the unsecured creditors as a class.[233]

A draft of the order sought should be attached to the application.[234]

Similar considerations to those set out above are likely to apply to applications seeking ratification of a transaction or payment after the making of a winding up order or bankruptcy order.'[235]

It is exceedingly rare for validation or ratification to be ordered unless it can be shown that the transaction will be for the benefit of the general body of creditors.[236]

PROTECTION OF ASSETS AND ROLE OF INTERIM RECEIVER

What safeguards can be put in place to protect assets?

7.69 If the petitioning creditor has concerns about potential disposition of the assets between the date of the filing of the petition and the making of the bankruptcy order then the official receiver may be appointed as interim receiver to safeguard and manage the estate until the bankruptcy petition can be heard.[237] This also includes dealing with perishable stock.

7.70 In *Gibson Dunn and Crutcher v Rio Properties Inc*[238] the Court of Appeal held that although s 286(1), IA86 refers to the appointment of the official receiver this does not exclude the appointment of an insolvency practitioner as well as the official receiver. The circumstances of the case must be sufficiently

---

232 Practice Direction: Insolvency Proceedings, 23 February 2012, para 14.8.6.

233 Denney v John Hudson and Co Ltd [1992] BCLC 901, [1992] BCC 503, CA; Re Fairway Graphics Ltd [1991] BCLC 468. Practice Direction: Insolvency Proceedings, 23 February 2012, para 14.8.7.

234 The order requires a recital endorsed on it. Practice Direction: Insolvency Proceedings, 23 February 2012, para 14.8.8.

235 Practice Direction: Insolvency Proceedings, 23 February 2012, para 14.8.9.

236 Practice Direction: Insolvency Proceedings, 23 February 2012, para 14.8.10.

237 IA86, s 370 or INO89, art 341.

238 [2004] EWCA Civ 1043, [2004] BPIR 1203.

exceptional to lead to the conclusion that it would be just and convenient to make such an appointment.[239] In general it was said that there should not be two receivers of the bankrupt's property acting concurrently.

Who may apply for the appointment of an interim receiver?

7.71 An application for the appointment of an interim receiver under s 286, IA86 may be made by any of the following:[240]

- a creditor;[241]
- the debtor;[242]
- an insolvency practitioner appointed under s 273(2), IA86[243] by the court to report on whether an IVA would be a preferable solution;
- a temporary administrator;[244] or
- a member state liquidator appointed in main proceedings.[245]

How is the application made?

7.72 The application must be supported by a witness statement[246] stating the following:

- the grounds on which it is proposed that the interim receiver should be appointed;[247]
- whether or not the official receiver has been informed of the application and, if so, has been given a copy;[248]
- whether to the applicant's knowledge there has been proposed or is in force a voluntary arrangement under Part VIII of the IA86;[249] and
- the applicant's estimate of the value of the property or business in respect of which the interim receiver is to be appointed.[250]

---

239 Per Jonathan Parker LJ at 52.
240 IR86, r 6.51(1) or IRN91, r 6.049(1).
241 IR86, r 6.51(1)(a) or IRN91, r 6.049(1)(a).
242 IR86, r 6.51(1)(b) or IRN91, r 6.049(1)(b).
243 IR86, r 6.51(1)(c) or IRN91, r 6.049(1)(c).
244 IR86, r 6.51(1)(d) or IRN91, r 6.049(1)(d).
245 IR86, r 6.51(1)(e) or IRN91, r 6.049(1)(e).
246 With effect from 6 April 2010 affidavit was replaced with a witness statement. See change to r 6.51 made by r 307 Insolvency (Amendment) (No 3) Rules 2009, SI 2009/642.
247 IR86, r 6.51(2)(a) or IRN91, r 6.049(2)(a).
248 IR86, r 6.51(2)(b) or IRN91, r 6.049(2)(b).
249 IR86, r 6.51(2)(c) or IRN91, r 6.049(2)(c).
250 IR86, r 6.51(2)(d) or IRN91, r 6.049(2)(d).

7.73 If an insolvency practitioner has been appointed by the court under s 273, IA86 to report to the court on whether an IVA would be a more suitable solution, and it is proposed that he (and not the official receiver) should be appointed interim receiver, and it is not the insolvency practitioner himself who is the applicant under r 6.51, IR86, the affidavit under para (2) must state that he has consented to act.[251]

7.74 The official receiver and the insolvency practitioner (if appointed) may attend the hearing and make representations.[252]

7.75 The applicant must deposit with the interim receiver or otherwise secure a sum sufficient to cover the remuneration and expenses of the interim receiver.[253] This sum may be increased by the court on the application of the official receiver. Any order made by the court must be complied with within 2 days after service on the person to whom the order is directed. If the order is not complied with then the court may discharge the order appointing the interim receiver.[254]

7.76 If a bankruptcy order is made after an interim receiver has been appointed, any money deposited under r 6.53, IR86 must (unless it is required by reason of insufficiency of assets for payment of remuneration and expenses of the interim receiver, or the deposit was made by the debtor out of his own property) be repaid to the person depositing it. If the money deposited is required for the payment of the interim receiver's remuneration or expenses, or the deposit was paid by the debtor out of his own property then these funds will not be repaid.[255]

7.77 Where an insolvency practitioner is appointed as interim receiver he must provide security[256] (in practice he will usually seek an indemnity from the person appointing him). If he fails to give or keep up such security the court may remove him from office.[257]

If an order is made under r 6.55, IR86, the court must give directions as to whether any, and if so what, steps should be taken for the appointment of another person in his place.[258]

What does the order appointing an interim receiver contain?

7.78 The following provisions apply to the order for an appointment of an interim receiver:[259]

---

251 IR86, r 6.51(3) or IRN91, r 6.049(3).
252 IR86, r 6.51(4) or IRN91, r 6.049(4).
253 IR86, r 6.53(1) or IRN91, r 6.051(1).
254 IR86, r 6.53(2) or IRN91, r 6.051(2).
255 IR86, r 6.63(3) or IRN91, r 6.061(3).
256 IR86, r 6.54(2) or IRN91, r 6.052(2).
257 IR86, r 6.55 or IRN91, r 6.053.
258 IR86, r 6.55(1) or IRN91, r 6.053(1).
259 Form 6.32.

- the court may make an appointment on any terms deemed appropriate;[260]

- the order must state the nature and a short description of the property of which the person appointed is to take possession;[261]

- the duties to be performed by him in relation to the debtor's affairs.[262]

Immediately after making the order the court must send 2 sealed copies to the person appointed interim receiver (one of which he must send forthwith to the debtor).[263]

How is the appointment of an interim receiver terminated, and what directions can the court make?

7.79 The appointment of an interim receiver can be terminated as follows:

- by the court on the interim receivers' application, or

- on that of the official receiver,

- by the debtor, or

- by any creditor;[264]

on the dismissal of the bankruptcy petition, the court may give such directions as it thinks fit with respect to the accounts of his administration and any other matters which it thinks appropriate.[265]

How are the interim receiver's fees fixed?

7.80 The interim receiver is required to apply to the court for his remuneration to be fixed.[266] There is no fixed timing for this to happen but will usually be towards the end of the process to avoid multiple hearings. The court is required to take the following into account:

- the time properly given by him (as interim receiver) and his staff in attending to the debtor's affairs;[267]

- the complexity (or otherwise) of the case;[268]

---

260 IR86, r 6.51(5) or IRN91, r 6.049(5).
261 IR86, r 6.52(1) or IRN91, r 6.050(1).
262 IR86, r 6.52(1) or IRN91, r 6.050(1).
263 IR86, r 6.52(2) or IRN91, r 6.050(2).
264 IR86, r 6.57(1) or IRN91, r 6.055(1).
265 IR86, r 6.57(2) or IRN91, r 6.055(2).
266 IR86, r 6.56(1) or IRN91, r 6.054(1).
267 IR86, r 6.56(2)(a) or IRN91, r 6.054(2)(a).
268 IR86, r 6.56(2)(b) or IRN91, r 6.054(2)(b).

- any responsibility of an exceptional kind or degree[269] taken on in connection with dealing with the debtor's affairs;
- the effectiveness with which the interim receiver appears to be carrying out, or to have carried out, his duties as such;[270] and
- the value and nature of the property with which he has to deal.[271]

7.81 As to remuneration generally see the *Practice Statement: The Fixing and Approval of the Remuneration of Appointees* (2004) which is dealt with in detail in chapter 13.

How are the interim receiver's fees paid?

7.82 Without prejudice to any order the court may make as to costs, remuneration of the interim receiver (whether the official receiver or another) must be paid to him, and the amount of any expenses incurred by him reimbursed (including the remuneration and expenses of any special manager appointed under s 370, IA86).[272]

7.83 If a bankruptcy order is not made he is paid out of the property of the debtor.[273] If a bankruptcy order is made he is paid out of the estate in the prescribed order of priority, or, where funds are insufficient, out of the deposit.[274]

Unless the court otherwise directs, in a case where no bankruptcy order is made the interim receiver may retain out of the debtor's property such sums or property as are or may be required for meeting his remuneration and expenses.[275]

What functions can the OR perform while acting as receiver or manager?

7.84 The function of the official receiver while acting as receiver or manager of the bankrupt's estate under s 287, IA86 is to protect the estate. For this purpose he has the following powers:[276]

- the same powers as if he were a receiver or manager appointed by the High Court; and

---

269 IR86, r 6.56(2)(c) or IRN91, r 6.054(2)(c).
270 IR86, r 6.56(2)(d) or IRN91, r 6.054(2)(d).
271 IR86, r 6.56(2)(e) or IRN91, r 6.054(2)(e).
272 IR86, r 6.56(3) or IRN91, r 6.054(3).
273 IR86, r 6.56(3)(a) or IRN91, r 6.054(3)(a).
274 IR86, r 6.56(3)(b) or IRN91, r 6.054(3)(b).
275 IR86, r 6.56(4) or IRN91, r 6.054(4).
276 IA86, s 287(2) or INO89, art 260(2).

- the power to sell or otherwise dispose of any perishable goods comprised in the estate and any other goods in the estate the value of which is likely to diminish if they are not disposed of.

7.85 The official receiver while acting as receiver or manager of the estate under s 287 IA86 has the following duties:[277]

- to take all steps necessary to protect any property which may be claimed for the estate by the trustee of that estate;

- is not, except in pursuance of directions given by the Secretary of State, required to do anything that involves incurring expenditure;

- may, if he thinks fit (and must, if so directed by the court), at any time summon a general meeting of the bankrupt's creditors.

Where:

- the official receiver acting as receiver or manager of the estate seizes or disposes of any property which is not comprised in the estate;[278] and

- at the time of the seizure or disposal he believes, or has reasonable grounds for believing, that he is entitled (whether in pursuance of an order of the court or otherwise) to seize or dispose of that property;

- he is not to be liable to any person for any loss or damage resulting from the seizure or disposal except in so far as it is caused by his negligence; and he has a lien on the property, or the proceeds of its sale, for the expenses of the bankruptcy incurred in connection with the seizure or disposal.[279]

What is the role and function of a special manager?

7.86 The role of special manager is to assist the Official Receiver or trustee with dealing with the bankrupt's estate normally because the nature of the property or business, or the interests of creditors generally require someone to manage it on a day to day basis.

How and when is a special manager appointed?

7.87 The court may, on an application appoint any person to be the special manager[280] over:

- a bankrupt's estate, or

---

277 IA86, s 287(3) or INO89, art 260(3).
278 IA86, s 287(4)(a) or INO89, art 260(4)(a).
279 IA86, s 287(4)(b) or INO89, art 260(4)(b).
280 IA86, s 370.

- the business of an undischarged bankrupt, or

- the property or business of a debtor in whose case the OR has been appointed interim receiver under s 286, IA86.

7.88 An application can be made by the OR or the trustee of the bankrupt's estate in any case where it appears that either of these office holders requires another person to manage the estate, property or business. Someone appointed under this provision is required to provide security to the court[281] and prepare and keep accounts of all transactions as prescribed.[282]

281 IA86, s 370(5)(a).
282 IA86, s 370(5)(b).

Chapter 8

A DEBTOR'S BANKRUPTCY PETITION

'Neither a borrower nor a lender be.'[1]

INTRODUCTION

8.1 This chapter looks at bankruptcy from a debtor's perspective and covers the procedure that should be followed by a debtor who wants to file their own bankruptcy petition. Before considering filing a bankruptcy petition a debtor should have already received advice on all the other options available including informal and formal processes. All the available solutions are covered in chapter 1 and a debtor should be actively encouraged to consider all these options prior to commencing down the bankruptcy route.

PREPARING A DEBTOR'S PETITION

What information does a debtor's bankruptcy petition include?

8.2 A debtor's petition must be on Form 6.27 and include the following information:

- the debtor's full name;[2]
- the debtor's residential address;[3]
- the debtor's occupation;[4]
- the name or names of any business which the debtor uses or has used during the period in which debts have been incurred;[5]
- whether or not any of these businesses are carried on solely or jointly with others;[6]
- the address of each business;[7]

---

1 Shakespeare, *Hamlet*, Act I, Scene III.
2 IR86, r 6.38(1)(a) or IRN91, r 6.035(1)(a).
3 IR86, r 6.38(1)(a) or IRN91, r 6.035(1)(a).
4 IR86, r 6.38(1)(a) or IRN91, r 6.035(1)(a).
5 IR86, r 6.38(1)(d) or IRN91, r 6.035(1)(d).
6 IR86, r 6.38(1)(d) or IRN91, r 6.035(1)(d).
7 IR86, r 6.38(1)(c) or IRN91, r 6.035(1)(c).

- the nature of each business;[8]
- confirmation of the debtor's centre of main interests or establishment within the meaning of the EC Regulation on Insolvency Proceedings 2000;[9]
- any other names by which the debtor has ever been known;[10]
- details of any previous bankruptcy, composition of debts, scheme or voluntary arrangement entered into during the previous 5 years;[11]
- details of any voluntary arrangement in force at the date of the petition;[12]
- the statement that the petitioner is unable to pay his debts and a request that a bankruptcy order be made.[13]

What documents need to be filed in court for a debtor's bankruptcy petition?

8.3 The following documents need to be filed in court together with payment of the court fee and the official receiver's deposit.[14] These are set out below under costs and publication:

- the original petition plus 3 copies;[15] and
- a statement of affairs.[16]

What is a debtor's statement of affairs?

8.4 A statement of affairs is a document listing the assets and liabilities of the debtor and is completed on Form 6.28 for a debtor's petition. Currently the statement of affairs consists of a detailed booklet with thirteen sections covering the following information (references below are internal references to the booklet provided):

> '(1) Personal details including name, address, date and place of birth, status, NI number, and benefit claim details etc. It also requires full details of any pending or previous legal actions, previous bankruptcy, IVA or other financial arrangements.
>
> (2) Business details including company or partnership details, trading dates, aliases or other business names, trading addresses, names of employees

---

8 IR86, r 6.38(1)(a) or IRN91, r 6.035(1)(a).

9 This information is not prescribed by r 6.38 but is included as part of the prescribed Form 6.27; see IR86, r 6.7(1)(f) applicable to a creditor's petition.

10 IR86, r 6.38(3) or IRN91, r 6.035(3).

11 IR86, r 6.39(2) or IRN91, r 6.036(2).

12 IR86, r 6.39(3) or IRN91, r 6.036(3).

13 IR86, r 6.39(1) or IRN91, r 6.036(1).

14 IR86, r 6.42(1) or IRN91, r 6.038(1).

15 IR86, r 6.42(1) or IRN91, r 6.038(1).

16 IR86, rr 6.41 and 6.42(1) or IRN91, rr 6.037 and 6.038(1).

(anyone employed during the previous two years), accountant, tax or other advisers etc. Also required are copies of any business accounts and all the business records.

(3) Assets including all assets both business and personal. The list of business assets should include stock, equipment, motor vehicles, other property etc. The personal assets must include everything you own including potentially exempt assets. See chapters 5 and 16–18. Also any assets that have been sold or given away in the previous 5 years should be listed and the details provided to the official receiver. See chapter 16. The official receiver also needs to be provided with the details of any assets that were seized or taken by creditors in the previous twelve months.

(4) Creditors including full details of all creditors:names and addresses, account numbers etc together with details of any security that they might hold. A best estimate of the amount outstanding should be entered. Also include any sums received for work not yet completed and any amounts not yet due but which the debtor is aware of together with the date the amounts are due for payment.

(5) Bank accounts and credit card details including account numbers, sort codes, other account holders, addresses. Any amounts outstanding must be listed in item (4) above. If any of the accounts are in funds the balance will usually be claimed as an asset of the estate. The Official Receiver may release some money for necessary domestic expenses. If the account is in joint names, the Official Receiver will decide how much of the money should be released to the joint account holder.

(6) Employment and present income details including employment status, employer address, company directorships. Also details of all members of the household are required together with any contributions they make to the household budget. This section of the form together with section 7 is used to determine whether the bankrupt has sufficient income to contribute regular payments under either and Income Payments order or Income Payments Agreement. The figures provided in this section will be used to assess whether an Income Payments Order/Income Payments Agreement is appropriate. The Official Receiver will not, except in exceptional circumstances, contact any employer.

(7) Outgoings of the household: as above full details are required and documentary evidence is likely to be requested to substantiate amounts listed.

(8) Current property details are required including whether the property is owned or rented together with full details of any mortgage or other financial arrangements connected to it.

(9) Property disposed of in the last 5 years. The list should include all property sold or given away together with full details of the transaction i e payments received and name and details of the purchaser.

(10) Members of the household and other dependents together with details of contributions or services provided.

(11) The causes of the bankruptcy: this section provides an opportunity for the debtor to explain the background and set out the causes of the financial difficulty. Any contributory factors need to be added here e g health issues, alcohol or drug addiction, gambling etc.

(12) Declaration:this is conformation that all the information provided is true to the best of the debtor's knowledge and belief.

(13) Extra information: this section provides additional space for answers from any of the preceding sections.'

What happens to a debtor's petition and statement of affairs after they have been filed in court?

8.5 The court clerk delivers the copies of the petition as listed below and the statement of affairs is sent to the official receiver with the petition:[17]

- one is returned to the petitioner, endorsed with the time and date of the hearing for the bankruptcy order;[18]
- the second is endorsed with the hearing date and sent to the official receiver;[19]
- the remaining copy is retained by the court, to be sent to an insolvency practitioner (if one is appointed under s 273(2), IA86);[20]

If the court hears the petition on the same day that it is received then the documents will be delivered by the bankrupt to the official receiver.[21] Historically, it was unusual for a debtor's petition not to be heard on the same day as its presentation. However, given the recent rise in debtor's petitions, some courts have been unable to cope with the volume with the effect that the debtor's petition is often heard on a subsequent date. In this respect, s 284, IA86 as regards avoiding post-petition dispositions applies equally.

PETITION COSTS AND PUBLICATION

What is the cost of filing a bankruptcy petition in court?

8.6 Under the Insolvency Proceedings (Fees) Order 2004[22] the deposit payable on a debtor's petition[23] filed on or after 1 June 2011 is £525 up from £450. The official receiver's deposit is to cover his costs in administering the estate and this is in addition to the court fee of £175 (currently £115 in Northern Ireland which can be paid in cash, cheque or postal order made payable to 'Supreme Court Fees Account'). The court fee is means tested and may not be required if the debtor is in receipt of certain benefits.

8.7 In *R v Lord Chancellor ex parte Lightfoot*[24] the debtor failed in her challenge to the debtor's petition deposit on the grounds that the requirement to pay denied her access to justice on the grounds that she was too poor to pay the fee. The court held that the mandatory deposit required under arts 8(1) and

---

17 IR86, r 6.42(4) or IRN91, r 6.038(4).
18 IR86, r 6.42(3)(a) or IRN91, r 6.038(3)(a).
19 IR86, r 6.42(3)(b) or IRN91, r 6.038(3)(b).
20 IR86, r 6.42(3)(c) or IRN91, r 6.038(3)(c).
21 IR86, r 6.42(6) or IRN91, r 6.038(6).
22 SI 2004/593 as amended by the Insolvency Proceedings (Fees) (Amendment) Order 2011 (SI 2011/1167).
23 IA86, s 264(1)(b) or INO89, art 238(1)(b).
24 [2000] 2 WLR 318.

9(b) of the Insolvency Fees Order 1986 that is paid to the official receiver for the performance of his duties on the making of the bankruptcy order was not for access to the court, but towards the costs of services provided by others for the benefit of the petitioning debtor; that a debtor did not have a constitutional right to be rehabilitated under a scheme for the relief of debtors irrespective of the ability to contribute to the costs of administering the scheme; that it was for Parliament to decide whether or not to provide any such scheme, and whether or not a requirement for the debtor to contribute to the administrative costs of the scheme should be mandatory; and that, accordingly, arts 8(1) and 9(b) of the Insolvency Fees Order 1986 infringed no constitutional right and was not unlawful.

8.8 The court is required to notify the presentation of every bankruptcy petition to the Chief Land Registrar.[25] This was covered in chapter 7.

What issues does the court consider before making a bankruptcy order on a debtor's petition?

8.9 The court will consider whether the debtor is unable to pay his debts[26] taking into account each of the following:

- whether it has jurisdiction to make the order;
- whether the aggregate amount of the bankruptcy debts, so far as unsecured, would be less than the small bankruptcies level (currently £4,000) then an order should not be made;[27]
- whether the value of the bankrupt's estate would be equal to or more than the minimum amount then an order should not be made (currently £4,000);[28]
- whether within the period of 5 years ending with the presentation of the petition the debtor has neither been adjudged bankrupt nor made a composition with his creditors in satisfaction of his debts or a scheme of arrangement of his affairs,[29] and that it would be appropriate to appoint a person to prepare a report under s 274, IA86;
- whether notice should be given to the supervisor of any individual voluntary arrangement in force.[30]

---

25 IR86, rr 6.13 and 6.43 and Form 6.14 or IRN91, rr 6.012 and 6.039.

26 IA86, s 272(1) or INO89, art 246(1).

27 IA86, s 273(1)(a) or INO89, art 246(1)(a).

28 IA86, s 273(1)(b) or INO89, art 246(1)(b).

29 IA86, s 273(1)(c) or INO89, art 246(1)(c).

30 IR86, r 6.42(4A) or IRN91, r 6.038(4A). The court may waive this requirement if the supervisor consents to the making of a bankruptcy order or confirms that the voluntary arrangement has failed.

Note that 'the minimum amount' and 'the small bankruptcies level' mean such amounts as may for the time being be prescribed for the purposes of this section.[31]

What orders can the court make on the hearing of a debtor's petition?

8.10 The court may:

- where the bankruptcy debts are less than the small bankruptcies level and the value of the estate would be equal to no more than the minimum amount (£40,000 and £4,000 respectively), appoint an insolvency practitioner to report on the circumstances of the debtor as to whether an individual voluntary arrangement would be preferable (see Form 6.29);[32]

- adjourn the petition (see Form 6.23); or

- make a bankruptcy order (see Form 6.30).

What does the court do when an insolvency practitioner is appointed?

8.11 Use of this procedure is extremely rare but when used the court must send a notice to the appointed insolvency practitioner and the debtor.[33] The notice must include a time and date for consideration of the report[34] together with the following:

- a sealed copy of the order of appointment;[35] and

- copies of the petition and statement of affairs.[36]

When and to whom does the insolvency practitioner have to report?

8.12 At least 3 days before the appointed hearing date the insolvency practitioner must file a copy of his report in court and send copies to the debtor and the official receiver.[37]

8.13 The report should indicate if the debtor is suitable for and prepared to enter into an IVA. The report must specifically state the following:[38]

- whether, in the opinion of the person making the report, a meeting of the debtor's creditors should be summoned to consider the proposal;[39] and

---

31 IA86, s 273(1)(d) or INO89, art 246(1)(d).
32 IA86, s 273(2) or INO89, art 246(2).
33 IR86, r 6.44(1)(c) or IRN91, r 6.041(1)(c).
34 IR86, r 6.44(1)(b) or IRN91, r 6.041(1)(b).
35 IR86, r 6.44(1)(a)(i) or IRN91, r 6.041(1)(a)(i).
36 IR86, r 6.44(1)(a)(ii) or IRN91, r 6.041(1)(a)(ii).
37 IR86, r 6.44(2) or IRN91, r 6.041(2).
38 IA86, s 274 or INO89, art 248.
39 IA86, s 274(2)(a) or INO89, art 248(2)(a).

- if in that person's opinion such a meeting should be summoned, the date on which, and time and place at which, he proposes the meeting should be held.[40]

8.14 The debtor is entitled to attend the hearing at which the insolvency practitioner's report is considered and may be ordered to attend and answer any questions put by the court.[41]

After considering the report the court may make either of the following orders:

- without any application, make an interim order under s 252, IA86, if it thinks that it is appropriate to do so for the purpose of facilitating the consideration and implementation of the debtor's proposal;[42] or

- if it thinks it would be inappropriate to make such an order, make a bankruptcy order.[43]

THE FUTURE

8.15 The Insolvency Service has consulted widely on the issue of debtor's petitions, especially since their astronomical growth in numbers after the introduction of the new bankruptcy regime by the Enterprise Act 2002.[44] It was clear that interested parties see benefits in removing the court from the process in circumstances where it is unnecessary for a court to take a decision. Accordingly, the Insolvency Service is exploring with the Ministry of Justice and HM Courts and Tribunals Service how best to realise those benefits to produce a bankruptcy system that is suitably accessible and affordable, as well as providing an efficient service for all those who need to use it. The strong likelihood is that the court will be taken out of the debtor's petition process completely.

---

40 IA86, s 274(2)(b) or INO89, art 248(2)(b).

41 IR86, r 6.44(3) or IRN91, r 6.041(3).

42 IA86, s 274(3)(a) or INO89, art 248(3)(a).

43 IA86, s 274(3)(b) or INO89, art 248(3)(b).

44 Reforming Debtor Petition Bankruptcy and Early Discharge from Bankruptcy (November 2009) and the Ministerial Statement on the Insolvency Service Consultation on Debtor Petition Reform and Early Discharge (28 October 2010).

Chapter 9

THE EFFECT OF A BANKRUPTCY ORDER

'A few words must be said about the uninteresting but important subject of bankruptcy jurisdiction ...'[1]

INTRODUCTION

9.1 This chapter looks at what happens after a bankruptcy order has been made both procedurally and in practical terms. It also describes the rights and duties of the bankrupt as well as the restrictions of being bankrupt. It also considers the different procedures in respect of debtor's and creditor's petitions.

THE MAKING OF A BANKRUPTCY ORDER

What information is included in a bankruptcy order made on a debtor's petition?

9.2 A bankruptcy order made on a debtor's petition is in Form 6.30 and contains the following information:

- the full description of the debtor as it appears in the petition;
- the date of the presentation of the petition on which the order is made;[2]
- the date and time of the making of the order;[3]
- a notice requiring the bankrupt, forthwith after the service of the order on him, to attend on the OR, at the place stated in the order,[4] and
- where the bankrupt is represented by a solicitor, the solicitor's name, address, telephone number and reference.[5]
- it may also include a provision to stay any action or proceedings.[6]

---

1 E Jenks *A Short History of English Law: From the Earliest Times to the End of the Year 1911* (Methuen and Co, 1912).
2 IR86, r 6.54(2)(a) or IRN91, r 6.052(2)(a).
3 IR86, r 6.54(2)(a) or IRN91, r 6.052(2)(a).
4 IR86, r 6.54(2)(b) or IRN91, r 6.052(2)(b).
5 IR86, r 6.54(4) or IRN91, r 6.052(4).
6 IA86, s 346 and IR86, r 6.54(3) or IRN91, r 6.052(3).

What information is included in a bankruptcy order made on a creditor's petition?

9.3 A bankruptcy order made on a creditor's petition is in Form 6.25 and contains the following:

- The full description of the debtor as included in the petition.
- The date of the presentation of the petition on which the order is made.[7]
- The date and time of the making of the order.[8]
- A notice requiring the bankrupt, forthwith after the service of the order on him, to attend on the OR, at the place stated in the order.[9]
- It may also include a provision to stay any action or proceedings.[10]
- Where the petitioning creditor is represented by a solicitor, the solicitor's name, address, telephone number and reference.[11]

What happens immediately after a bankruptcy order is made on a debtor's petition?

9.4 The court must send two sealed copies of the bankruptcy order to the OR.[12] The OR must then:

- send notice on Form 6.26 to the Chief Land Registrar, for registration in the register of writs and orders affecting land;[13]
- advertise the bankruptcy order in an appropriate newspaper;[14] and
- gazette the making of the bankruptcy order.[15]

Any of these actions can be suspended by the court on application of a creditor.[16] Any application made to the court must be supported by a witness statement and copied to the OR.

---

7 IR86, r 6.33(2)(a) or IRN91, r 6.030(2)(a).
8 IR86, r 6.33(2)(a) or IRN91, r 6.030(2)(a).
9 IR86, r 6.54(2)(b) or IRN91, r 6.052(2)(b).
10 IA86, s 346 and IR86, r 6.33(3) or IRN91, r 6.030(3).
11 IR86, r 6.33(4) or IRN91, r 6.030(4).
12 IR86, r 6.46(1) or IRN91, r 6.043(1).
13 IR86, r 6.46(2)(a) or IRN91, r 6.043(2)(a).
14 IR86, r 6.46(2)(b) or IRN91, r 6.043(2)(b).
15 IR86, r 6.46(2)(c) or IRN91, r 6.043(2)(c).
16 IR86, r 6.46(2)(d) or IRN91, r 6.043(2)(d).

What happens immediately after a bankruptcy order is made on a creditor's petition?

9.5 The court must send two sealed copies of the bankruptcy order to the OR.[17] The OR must then notify the making of the order by:

- sending a notice of the making of the order to the Chief Land Registrar, for registration in the register of writs and orders affecting land;[18]
- advertising the order in an appropriate newspaper;[19] and
- publishing the order in the *London Gazette*.[20]

Any of these actions can be suspended by the court on application of the bankrupt or a creditor.[21] Any application made to the court must be supported by a witness statement and copied to the OR. This is called a 'stay of advertising'.

When can the description on the bankruptcy order be amended?

9.6 The description on the bankruptcy order can be amended at any time after the order has been made and should be amended when any missing information is confirmed[22] by the OR. Any changes must also be notified to the Chief Land Registrar for corresponding amendment of the register; and, if the court so directs, he shall also cause notice of the amended order gazetted, and to be advertised in any newspaper previously used or any newspaper as the OR thinks fit.

CONSEQUENCES OF A BANKRUPTCY ORDER

What are the normal restrictions on a bankrupt?

9.7 Restrictions imposed on an undischarged bankrupt fall under the following headings:

- Obtaining credit.
- Use of a trading style.
- Ability to hold office in a limited liability company.
- Post discharge restrictions.

---

17 IR86, r 6.34(1) or IRN91, r 6.031(1).
18 IR86, Form 6.26 and r 6.34(2)(a) or IRN91, r 6.031(2)(a).
19 IR86, r 6.34(2)(b) or IRN91, r 6.031(2)(b).
20 IR86, r 6.34(2)(c) or IRN91, r 6.031(2)(c).
21 IR86, r 6.34(3) or IRN91, r 6.031(3).
22 IR86, r 6.35(1) or IRN91, r 6.032(1).

What are the circumstances in which an undischarged bankrupt can obtain credit?

9.8 A bankrupt may only obtain credit (either alone or jointly) of £500 or more if he discloses his status as an undischarged bankrupt.[23] For these purposes, the definition of obtaining credit includes purchasing assets on hire purchase or conditional sale agreement and requesting a deposit in advance for the supply of goods or services.[24] Failure to comply is a criminal offence.[25]

The restriction similarly applies to any person who has been sequestrated in Scotland or made bankrupt in Northern Ireland[26] and any person who is discharged but still subject to a bankruptcy restriction order.[27]

What offences can be committed by a debtor before a bankruptcy order is made?

9.9 A bankrupt commits the criminal offence of fraudulent dealing in property if:

- in the 12 months before a petition, or in the period between presentation of the petition and the commencement of bankruptcy, any property is disposed that was obtained on credit and at the time it was disposed of, it had not been paid for.[28]

Any person commits the criminal offence of fraudulent dealing in property if:

- in the 12 months before a petition, or in the initial period, acquires or receives property from a bankrupt knowing or believing:

  (a) that the bankrupt owed money in respect of the property, and
  (b) that the bankrupt did not intend, or was unlikely to be able, to pay the money he so owed.[29]

Disposing of property includes pawning or pledging it.[30] A person is not guilty of an offence under these provisions if the disposal, acquisition or receipt of the property was in the ordinary course of a business carried on by the bankrupt at the time of the disposal, acquisition or receipt.[31]

---

23 IA86, s 360(1)(a) and (2)(a) or INO89, art 331(1)(a).
24 IA86, s 360(2)(a) and (b) or INO89, art 331(2)(a) and (b).
25 IA86, s 360(1) or INO89, art 331(1).
26 IA86, s 360(3) or INO89, art 331(3).
27 IA86, s 360(5) or INO89, art 331(5).
28 IA86, ss 359(1) and 351(b) or INO89, arts 330(1) and 322(b).
29 IA86, ss 359(2) and 351(b) or INO89, arts 330(2) and 322(b).
30 See also chapter 4, at **4.30**.
31 IA86, s 359(3) or INO89, art 330(3).

Trading style

What are the circumstances in which an undischarged bankrupt can continue to trade or set up in business?

9.10 An undischarged bankrupt may continue to trade, either directly or indirectly, or set up in business as long as the individual uses the same name in which they were adjudged bankrupt, or discloses such name to anyone with whom a business transaction is entered into.[32] Breach of this provision is a criminal offence.[33]

Involvement in the management of a limited liability company

Can an undischarged bankrupt remain a director of a limited liability company?

9.11 An undischarged bankrupt commits a criminal offence if he takes part in, or is concerned in the promotion, formation or management of a company, without the permission of the court in which he was made bankrupt.[34]

Can a person who is subject to a bankruptcy restriction order remain a director of a limited liability company?

9.12 An individual who is subject to a bankruptcy restrictions order is subject to virtually the same disabilities as an undischarged bankrupt.[35] Any person who is subject to a bankruptcy restriction order[36] may only remain or become a director of a limited liability company with the permission of the court in which he was made bankrupt.[37] An application for permission to act is made as an application in the bankruptcy and should be supported by evidence as to the grounds being relied on.

What is the procedure for an application to court for leave to continue to act as a director of a limited liability company?

9.13 The following procedure needs to be followed:

- Notice of intention to apply must be served on the OR[38] as it is the OR's duty to attend and oppose the application if it is felt the application is not in the public interest.

- After the bankrupt's application is filed in court a venue will be fixed for the hearing and the court will give notice to the applicant.[39] The bankrupt must give at least 28 days notice of the hearing to the OR and any trustee.

---

32 IA86, s 360(1)(b) or INO89, art 331(1)(b).
33 IA86, s 360(1) or INO89, art 331(1).
34 Company Directors Disqualification Act 1986, s 11(1)(a) and IR86, r 6.203.
35 Company Directors Disqualification Act 1986, s 11(1)(b).
36 IR86, r 6.202A or IRN91, r 6.199A.
37 Company Directors Disqualification Act 1986, s 11(2) and IR86, r 6.200.
38 Company Directors Disqualification Act 1986, s 11(3).
39 IR86, r 6.203(5) or IRN91, r 6.200(5).

The notice must be accompanied by copies of the application and the witness statement under r 6.203, IR86.

- At least 14 days before the hearing the OR must file in court a report of any matters which he considers ought to be drawn to the court's attention. A copy of the report must be sent by him (immediately after he has filed it in court) to the bankrupt and to any trustee.[40]

- At least 7 days before the hearing the bankrupt can file a notice specifying any statements in the OR's report which he intends to deny or dispute. If he gives notice under this paragraph, he shall send copies of it, not less than 4 days before the date of the hearing, to the OR and to any trustee.

What should be included in the bankrupt's witness statement and what happens at the hearing?

9.14 The applicant must prepare a witness statement to be filed in court which should include the following information:[41]

- the nature of the business or intended business, and the place or places where that business is, or is to be, carried on;[42]

- whether it is, or is to be, a private or a public company;[43]

- the persons who are, or are to be, principally responsible for the conduct of its affairs (whether as directors, shadow directors, managers or otherwise);[44]

- the manner and capacity in which the applicant proposes to take part or be concerned in the promotion or formation of the company or, as the case may be, its management;[45]

- the emoluments and other benefits to be obtained from the directorship;[46]

- if the company is already in existence, the witness statement must specify the date of its incorporation and the amount of its nominal and issued share capital;[47]

---

40 IR86, r 6.204(2) or IRN91, r 6.201(2).
41 IR86, r 6.203(2) or IRN91, r 6.200(2).
42 IR86, r 6.203(2)(a) or IRN91, r 6.200(2)(a).
43 IR86, r 6.203(2)(b) or IRN91, r 6.200(2)(b).
44 IR86, r 6.203(2)(c) or IRN91, r 6.200(2)(c).
45 IR86, r 6.203(2)(d) or IRN91, r 6.200(2)(d).
46 IR86, r 6.203(2)(e) or IRN91, r 6.203(2)(e).
47 IR86, r 6.203(3) or IRN91, r 6.200(3).

- if not, it must specify the amount, or approximate amount, of its proposed commencing share capital, and the sources from which that capital is to be obtained;[48]

- where the bankrupt intends to take part or be concerned in the promotion or formation of a company, the witness statement must contain an undertaking by him that he will, within not less than 7 days of the company being incorporated, file in court a copy of its memorandum of association and certificate of incorporation.[49]

9.15 The OR and the trustee may appear on the hearing of the application, and may make representations to the court and question the bankrupt.[50] If the court grants the bankrupt's application, the order may include any of the following terms:

- The order must specify the role that the bankrupt has permission to play.[51] For instance he may be allowed to have a sales role but not a finance position.

- The order may vary an income payments order or an income payments agreement already in force in respect of the bankrupt,[52] or if no income payments order is in force, make one.[53]

- Permission may be granted for a limited period and/or subject to conditions.

Copies of the order must be sent by the court to the bankrupt, any trustee and the OR.[54]

THE BANKRUPT'S OBLIGATIONS

What are a bankrupt's obligations?

9.16 The bankrupt must:

- provide the trustee with any information requested about his affairs,[55] even after his discharge;[56] and

---

48 IR86, r 6.203(3) or IRN91, r 6.200(3).
49 IR86, r 6.203(4) or IRN91, r 6.200(4).
50 IR86, r 6.204(4) or IRN91, r 6.201(4).
51 IR86, r 6.205(1) or IRN91, r 6.202(1).
52 IR86, r 6.205(2)(a) or IRN91, r 6.202(2)(a).
53 IR86, r 6.205(2)(b) or IRN91, r 6.202(2)(b).
54 IR86, r 6.205(3) or IRN91, r 6.202(3).
55 IA86, s 333(1)(a) or INO89, art 304(1)(a).
56 IA86, s 333(3) or INO89, art 304(3).

- attend on the trustee at any reasonable time,[57] even after his discharge;[58] and
- comply with any other reasonable request made by the trustee which he may require for the purposes of carrying out his functions as trustee,[59] even after the debtor has been discharged;[60]
- where at any time after the commencement of the bankruptcy any property is acquired by, or devolves upon, the bankrupt or there is an increase of the bankrupt's income, the bankrupt must, within the prescribed period,[61] give the trustee notice.[62]

Failure to comply with any of these obligations without reasonable excuse constitutes contempt of court. A bankrupt is liable to be punished accordingly (in addition to any other punishment to which he may be subject).[63]

The information a bankrupt needs to provide

What are the duties of the bankrupt to the OR?

9.17 Where a bankruptcy order has been made, the bankrupt is under a duty:

- to deliver possession of his estate to the OR;[64] and
- to deliver up to the OR all books, papers and other records of which he has possession or control and which relate to his estate and affairs (including any which would be privileged from disclosure in any proceedings).[65]

9.18 In the case of any assets that belong to the bankrupt's estate that cannot be physically delivered to the trustee, and in the case of any property that may be claimed for the bankrupt's estate by the trustee, it is the bankrupt's duty to ensure that the property is safeguarded and to comply with any request from the OR in respect of the protection of that property.[66]

9.19 The bankrupt must provide the OR with a list of all of his assets and such other information as requested, and must attend on the OR at such times as reasonably required:[67]

---

57 IA86, s 333(1)(b) and (2) or INO89, art 304(1)(b) and (2).
58 IA86, s 333(3) or INO89, art 304(3).
59 IA86, s 333(1)(c) and (2) or INO89, art 304(1)(c) and (2).
60 IA86, s 333(3) or INO89, art 304(3).
61 The prescribed period is 21 days, see IR86, r 6.200.
62 IA86, s 333(2) or INO89, art 304(2).
63 IA86, s 333(4) or INO89, art 304(4).
64 IA86, s 291(1)(a) or INO89, art 264(1)(a), see also s 312(1), IA86.
65 IA86, s 291(1)(b) or INO89, art 264(1)(b).
66 IA86, s 291(2) or INO89, art 264(2).
67 IA86, s 291(4) or INO89, art 264(4).

- for a purpose of securing his assets;[68] or
- in connection with the making of a bankruptcy restrictions order.[69]

9.20 If the bankrupt, without reasonable excuse, fails to comply with any obligation imposed by s 291, IA86, he is guilty of a contempt of court and liable to be punished accordingly (in addition to any other punishment to which he may be subject).[70]

9.21 Section 333, IA86 sets out the further obligations of the bankrupt. He must give the trustee such information as he might require; he must attend on the trustee; and he must do 'all ... other things as the trustee may ... reasonably require' for the purpose of carrying out his functions.[71] These obligations continue after discharge.[72] The bankrupt is also under an obligation to give notice to the trustee of after-acquired property.[73] Again it is a contempt of court if the bankrupt fails to comply with these obligations.[74]

9.22 Further, s 363(2), IA86 provides:

> 'Without prejudice to any other provision in this Group of Parts, an undischarged bankrupt or a discharged bankrupt whose estate is being administered under Chapter IV of this Part shall do all such things as he may be directed to do by the court for the purposes of his bankruptcy, or, as the case may be, the administration of that estate.'

9.23 For examples of the effective use of the provisions compelling a bankrupt to cooperate with his trustee see *Hardy v Buchler*[75] (the bankrupt was ordered by the court on its own motion to pay money the court held was vested in the estate) and *Official Receiver v Cummings-John*[76] (where the bankrupt was sent to prison for contempt for failing to answer questions in the course of a public examination).

9.24 It is worth bearing in mind that the IA86 contains criminal as well as civil sanctions:

- it is an offence for a bankrupt to fail to disclose the property comprised in his estate, or to fail to inform the OR or trustee of any disposal of property which would otherwise be comprised in the estate (save in the ordinary course of business or ordinary expenses);[77]

---

68 IA86, s 291(4)(a) or INO89, art 264(4)(a).
69 IA86, s 291(4)(b) or INO89, art 264(4)(b).
70 IA86, s 291(6) or INO89, art 264(6)
71 IA86, s 333(1)(a)–(c) or INO89, art 306(1)(a)–(c).
72 IA86, s 333(3) or INO89, art 306(3).
73 IA86, s 333(2)or INO89, art 306(2).
74 IA86, s 333(4) or INO89, art 306(4).
75 [1997] BPIR 643.
76 [2000] BPIR 320.
77 IA86, s 353 or INO89, art 324.

- it is an offence not to deliver up property or to conceal a debt or property;[78]
- it is an offence to remove property which ought to be delivered up to the trustee;[79]
- it is an offence not to deliver up, or to conceal or falsify, books or records;[80]
- it is an offence to make certain false statements (this includes any statements made in respect of any meeting of creditors held within 12 months prior to the petition such as required in an IVA);[81]
- it is an offence to fraudulently dispose of property in the period of 5 years before commencement of the bankruptcy;[82]
- it is an offence to abscond.[83]

Statement of affairs

What is a statement of affairs?

9.25 A statement of affairs is a document setting out a full list of all the bankrupts' assets, debts and other liabilities.[84] It is required to be produced on the following forms:

- In the case of a debtor's petition it must be on Form 6.28 and filed in court with the petition.[85]
- In the case of a creditor's petition it will be on Form 6.33[86] and will be filed in court by the OR.[87]

Both forms must be verified by a witness statement,[88] and for a creditor's petition the forms may be verified by the OR or a duly authorised officer of the Department or court.[89]

---

78 IA86, s 354 or INO89, art 325.
79 IA86, s 354 or INO89, art 325.
80 IA86, ss 355 and 356 or INO89, arts 326 and 327.
81 IA86, s 356 or INO89, art 327.
82 IA86, s 357 or INO89, art 328.
83 IA86, s 358 or INO89, art 329.
84 IA86, s 288(1) or INO89, art 261(1).
85 IR86, r 6.68 or IRN91, r 6.066.
86 IR86, r 6.59 or IRN91, r 6.057.
87 IR86, r 6.058(3) or IRN91, r 6.60(3).
88 IR86, rr 6.41(1) and 6.60(4) or IRN91, rr 6.037(1) and 6.060(4).
89 IR86, r 6.60(2) and (4) or IRN91, r 6.058(2) and (4).

When is a bankrupt required to complete a statement of affairs?

9.26 When a debtor has filed his own bankruptcy petition he should have completed a statement of affairs and filed it in court with his petition.[90] Debtors who have been made bankrupt on a creditor's petition will be required to complete and file a statement of affairs on Form 6.33 with the OR.[91]

9.27 A statement of affairs must be submitted within 21 days of commencement of the proceedings[92] unless an extension or release is obtained.[93] Failure to submit the statement of affairs without a reasonable excuse is an offence and the bankrupt will be guilty of contempt of court.[94] However, where the contents or part of the contents could prejudice the conduct of the bankruptcy, limited disclosure can be agreed by the court with those parts restricted only being available with the leave of the court.[95]

When can a bankrupt obtain an extension or release from producing a statement of affairs?

9.28 An extension or release can be applied for under s 288(3), IA86 to either the OR or the court. The OR can exercise his discretion as to the circumstances in which either an extension or release is granted.[96] If a bankrupt's request for either is denied by the OR then an application can be made to the court.[97] The court may:

- dismiss the application but only after the bankrupt has been given the opportunity to attend court for an *ex parte* hearing with at least 7 days' notice to the bankrupt;[98] or
- arrange to hear the application. In this case the court must give the bankrupt sufficient notice of the hearing to allow him time to serve notice on the OR. On receipt of that notice the bankrupt is required to send a copy of his application to the OR together with any evidence that he intends to rely on, at least 14 days before the hearing.[99]

9.29 The OR may appear in person at the hearing or may file a written report of any matters which he considers ought to be drawn to the court's attention. If a written report is filed then a copy must be sent to the bankrupt at least 5 days before the hearing.[100]

---

90 IR86, r 6.68 and Form 6.28 or IRN91, r 6.068.
91 IR86, r 6.60(1) or IRN91, r 6.058(1).
92 IA86, s 288(1) or INO89, art 261(1).
93 IA86, s 288(3) or INO89, art 261(3).
94 IA86, s 288(4) or INO89, art 261(4).
95 IR86, r 6.61 or IRN91, r 6.059.
96 IR86, r 6.62(1) or IRN91, r 6.060(1).
97 IR86, r 6.62(2) or IRN91, r 6.060(2).
98 IR86, r 6.62(3) or IRN91, r 6.060(3).
99 IR86, r 6.62(4) or IRN91, r 6.060(4).
100 IR86, r 6.62(5) or IRN91, r 6.060(5).

Sealed copies of any order made must be served on both the OR and the bankrupt.[101]

The bankrupt's costs of any application must be met by him unless ordered to be paid as an expense of the estate.[102]

When can the expenses of preparing a statement of affairs be met as an expense of the estate?

9.30 The OR may decide that the bankrupt is unable to complete the statement of affairs himself[103] or the bankrupt may apply to the OR for an allowance to employ someone to assist with its preparation.[104] Any request by the bankrupt should be accompanied by an estimate and it will be the OR who authorises the employment.[105] The OR can impose any conditions he deems necessary in respect of access to the bankrupt's books and records.[106] Despite receiving assistance the bankrupt still remains responsible for the completion and content of his statement of affairs.[107]

Creditor's petition

When does a bankrupt have to submit accounts to the OR?

9.31 The OR may request accounts from the bankrupt for any period up to a date beginning 3 years preceding the presentation of the bankruptcy petition[108] and the court, on the OR's application, may order accounts to be produced for any earlier period.[109]

9.32 If considered necessary, the OR may insist that any accounts provided be verified by witness statement. In these circumstances a period of 21 days, or other period specified by the OR, is allowed for the accounts to be produced.[110] Two copies of the accounts are required, one set to be delivered to the OR and the second set attached to the witness statement and filed in court.[111]

9.33 The OR may require further information to be provided to amplify, modify or explain previous information provided.[112] As with the accounts the

---

[101] IR86, r 6.62(6) or IRN91, r 6.060(6).
[102] IR86, r 6.62(7) or IRN91, r 6.060(7).
[103] IR86, r 6.63(1) or IRN91, r 6.061(1).
[104] IR86, r 6.63(2) or IRN91, r 6.061(2).
[105] IR86, r 6.63(3) or IRN91, r 6.061(3).
[106] IR86, r 6.63(4) or IRN91, r 6.061(4).
[107] IR86, r 6.63(5) or IRN91, r 6.061(5).
[108] IR86, r 6.64(2) and (3) or IRN91, r 6.062(2) and (3).
[109] IR86, r 6.64(4) or IRN91, r 6.064(4).
[110] IR86, r 6.65(1) or IRN91, r 6.063(1).
[111] IR86, r 6.65(2) or IRN91, r 6.063(2).
[112] IR86, r 6.66(1) or IRN91, r 6.064(1).

OR may insist the documents are verified by a witness statement in which case two copies are required, one copy being filed in court. Expenses may be claimed for assistance with this requirement.[113]

Debtor's petition

When does a bankrupt have to submit accounts to the OR?

9.34 The OR may request accounts from the bankrupt for any period up to a date beginning 3 years preceding the presentation of the bankruptcy petition[114] and the court on the OR's application may order accounts to be produced for any earlier period.[115]

9.35 If considered necessary the OR may insist that any accounts provided be verified by witness statement. In these circumstances a period of 21 days or other period specified is allowed for the accounts to be produced.[116] Two copies of the accounts are required, one set to be delivered to the OR and the second set attached to the witness statement and filed in court.[117]

9.36 The OR can at any time require further information to be provided to amplify, modify or explain previous information provided.[118] As with the accounts the OR can insist the documents are verified by witness statement[119] in which case two copies are required, one copy being filed in court. Expenses may be claimed for assistance with this requirement.[120]

NON-COOPERATION BY THE BANKRUPT

What powers does the OR have to compel a bankrupt to provide information about his affairs?

9.37 The OR has wide-ranging powers to assist him with the investigation of the bankrupt's affairs. These include applying:

- for public examination of the bankrupt;[121]

---

113 IR86, r 6.63 or IRN91, r 6.061.
114 IR86, r 6.69(1), (2) or IRN91, r 6.067(1), (2).
115 IR86, r 6.69(3) or IRN91, r 6.067(3).
116 IR86, r 6.70(1) or IRN91, r 6.068(1).
117 IR86, r 6.70(2) or IRN91, r 6.068(2).
118 IR86, r 6.72(1) or IRN91, r 6.070(1).
119 IR86, r 6.72(2) or IRN91, r 6.070(2).
120 IR86, r 6.71 or IRN91, r 6.069.
121 IA86, s 290 or INO89, art 263.

- for private examination of the bankrupt, any spouse, former spouse or any other person believed to have information relating to the bankrupt's property or affairs (s 366, IA86), including orders for the production of any documents or other records;[122]
- under the general power of the court to make orders;[123]
- for the bankrupt's arrest;[124]
- for an order for the production of documents from HMRC;[125]
- for an order redirecting the bankrupt's mail.[126]

PUBLIC EXAMINATION

What is a 'public examination'?

9.38 A public examination is a public hearing at which the OR, trustee and creditors may question an undischarged bankrupt about his affairs.[127] The process is only usually invoked when the OR or trustee has been unable to obtain the cooperation of the bankrupt, or the bankrupt has been evasive in answering questions about his affairs before the public examination.[128]

When can a public examination be convened?

9.39 A public examination may be convened by the OR at any time before the discharge of the bankrupt.[129] The bankrupt's trustee or at least half of the bankrupt's creditors (calculated by value) can also request the OR to convene a public examination.[130]

What is the procedure for the OR to apply for a public examination?

9.40 To apply for a public examination the OR sends an application to the court under s 290, IA86.[131] It will normally be accompanied by a short report giving details of the bankrupt's failure to cooperate. The court will then fix a venue for the hearing.[132] Note that, in contrast to the procedure relating to a

---

122 IA86, s 366(3)(b) or INO89, art 337(3)(b).
123 IA86, s 363 or INO89, art 334.
124 IA86, s 364 or INO89, art 335.
125 IA86, s 368 or INO89, art 339.
126 IA86, s 371 or INO89, art 342.
127 IR86, r 6.175(1) or IRN91, r 6.172(1).
128 On public examinations generally see further J Tribe (forthcoming) *The Poulson Affair: Corruption and the Role of Public Examinations in the Bankruptcy Law of the early 1970s.*
129 IA86, s 290(1) or INO89, art 263(1).
130 IA86, s 290(2) or INO89, art 263(2).
131 IR86, r 6.172(1) or IRN91, r 6.169.
132 IA86, s 290(3) or INO89, art 263(3) and IR86, r 6.172(2).

private examination, the court has no discretion whether to make the order. The OR must then give at least 14 days' notice to the following people:

- any trustee who has been nominated or appointed;[133]
- any special manager who has been appointed;[134] and
- subject to any contrary direction of the court, to every creditor of the bankrupt who is known to the OR or is identified in the bankrupt's statement of affairs.[135]

The OR may, if he thinks fit, cause notice of the order to be given by public advertisement.[136] The bankrupt will be sent notice in writing of the time and date of the examination. Form 6.56 will be attached[137] to the notice.

What is the procedure for the trustee to apply for a public examination?

9.41 There is no specific procedure prescribed for the trustee to make an application but the trustee can request the OR to convene a public examination at any time. The trustee must justify this request and provide sufficient information for the OR to make the application to court. If the request is denied by the OR then the trustee may enlist the help of the creditors in requesting an examination.

What is the procedure for creditors to apply for a public examination?

9.42 Any creditor who wants a public examination to be held must apply to the OR in writing accompanied by Form 6.56.[138] The requisitioning creditor must have support of at least half of the creditors (calculated by value and including the creditor making the application).[139]

The application needs to contain the following information:

- a list of the creditors concurring with the request and the amount of their respective claims in the bankruptcy;[140]
- from each creditor concurring, written confirmation of his concurrence;[141] and
- a statement of the reasons why the examination is requested.

---

133 IR86, r 6.172(3)(a) or IRN91, r 6.169(3)(a).
134 IR86, r 6.172(3)(b) or IRN91, r 6.169(3)(b).
135 IR86, r 6.172(3)(c) or IRN91, r 6.169(3)(c).
136 IR86, r 6.172(4) or IRN91, r 6.169(4).
137 IR86, r 6.173 or IRN91, r 6.170.
138 IR86, r 6.173(1) or IRN91, r 6.170(1).
139 IA86, s 290(2) or INO89, art 263(2).
140 IR86, r 6.173(1)(a) or IRN91, r 6.170(1)(a).
141 IR86, r 6.173(1)(b) or IRN91, r 6.170(1)(b).

The application does not need this information[142] if the requisitioning creditor's debt is alone more than half the total value, without the concurrence of others.[143]

9.43 The following process needs to be observed:

- The application must be accompanied by the appropriate deposit as agreed with the OR, by way of security for the expenses of the hearing.[144]
- The OR must make the application to court within 28 days of receiving the request and funds.[145]
- If the OR is of the opinion that the request is an unreasonable one in the circumstances, he may apply to the court for an order relieving him from the obligation to make the application.[146]
- The OR must immediately notify the requisitionist of any order made without notice to any other party.[147] If the application is dismissed by the court, the OR's application under s 290(2), IA86 must be made immediately after the hearing.[148]

Who can take part in a public examination?

9.44 The following people can take part[149] in the public examination:

- the OR and, in the case of an individual adjudged bankrupt on a petition under s 264(1)(d), IA86, the official petitioner;
- the trustee of the bankrupt's estate, if his appointment has taken effect;
- any person who has been appointed as special manager of the bankrupt's estate or business;
- any creditor of the bankrupt who has submitted a proof of debt in the bankruptcy proceedings.

What happens at a public examination and what records are retained?

9.45 The bankrupt may be asked questions about his affairs, dealings and property[150] by any of the persons listed as attending[151] and will be required to

142 IR86, r 6.173(1)(a) and (b) do not apply.
143 IR86, r 6.173(1)(c) or IRN91, r 6.170(1)(c).
144 IR86, r 6.173(2) or IRN91, r 6.170(2).
145 IR86, r 6.173(3) or IRN91, r 6.170(3).
146 IR86, r 6.173(4) or IRN91, r 6.170(4).
147 'Without notice to any other party' replaced *Ex parte* from 6 April 2010.
148 IR86, r 6.173(5) or IRN91, r 6.170(5).
149 IA86, s 290(4) or INO89, art 263(4).
150 IA86, s 290(4) or INO89, art 263(4).
151 IA86, s 290(4) or INO89, art 263(4) and IR86, r 6.175(2).

answer under oath. The bankrupt may employ a solicitor, with or without counsel, at his own expense to help him explain or qualify any answers that he may give.[152] A record will be produced of the proceedings and should be read and signed by the bankrupt and verified by witness statement at a venue fixed by the court.[153]

Can the records of the public examination be used in criminal proceedings?

9.46 This written record can be used as evidence against the bankrupt in any future proceedings.[154] If criminal proceedings have already been instituted against the bankrupt and the court is of the opinion that continuing would prejudice a fair trial, the public examination may be adjourned.[155]

What if the bankrupt is ill or fails to attend his public examination?

9.47 If the bankrupt fails to attend the court may issue a warrant for his arrest.[156] He is also guilty of a contempt of court and may be punished accordingly.[157] If the bankrupt is unfit to attend an application should be made to the court on Form 6.57 for the court to either stay the order or conduct the examination in such manner or place as may be considered suitable.[158]

9.48 The application should be made:[159]

- by a person who has been appointed by a court in the United Kingdom or elsewhere to manage the affairs of, or to represent, the bankrupt; or
- by a relative or friend of the bankrupt whom the court considers to be a proper person to make the application; or
- by the OR.

9.49 If the application is made by the OR then it can be heard *ex parte*; otherwise the following procedure must be followed:

- unless the bankrupt is a patient within the meaning of the Mental Health Act 1983, it must be supported by the witness statement of a registered medical practitioner as to the bankrupt's mental and physical condition;
- at least 7 days' notice of the application must be given to the OR and the trustee (if any); and

---

152 IR86, r 6.175(3) or IRN91, r 6.172(3).
153 IR86, r 6.175(4) or IRN91, r 6.172(4).
154 IR86, r 6.175(5) or IRN91, r 6.172(5).
155 IR86, r 6.175(6) or IRN91, r 6.172(6).
156 IA86, s 364(2)(e) or INO89, art 335(2)(e).
157 IA86, s 290(5) or INO89, art 263(5).
158 IR86, r 6.174(1) or IRN91, r 6.171(1).
159 IR86, r 6.174(2) or IRN91, r 6.171(2).

- before any order is made on the application, the applicant must deposit with the OR such sum as he requires for the additional expenses of any examination that may be ordered. Any order made on the application may provide that the expenses of the examination be paid out of the deposit rather than out of the estate.

Can a public examination be adjourned and what are the consequences?

9.50 A public examination can be adjourned by the court, either to a fixed date or generally.[160] Where the examination is adjourned generally, the OR may, there and then, apply for the suspension of the bankrupt's discharge under s 279(3), IA86.[161]

What is the procedure when a public examination is adjourned?

9.51 Where the examination has been adjourned generally, the court may at any time on the application of the OR or of the bankrupt:[162]

- fix a venue for the resumption of the examination;[163]
- give directions as to the manner in which, and the time within which, notice of the resumed public examination is to be given to persons entitled to take part in it.

9.52 Where the bankrupt applies for the adjournment, the court may grant it on terms that the expenses of giving the required notices be paid by him and that, before the resumed public examination is fixed, he deposit with the OR such sum as may be necessary to cover those expenses.[164]

If the court makes an order suspending the bankrupt's discharge, copies of the order must be sent by the court to the OR, the trustee and the bankrupt.[165]

Who pays the costs and expenses of a public examination?

9.53 The costs and expenses are usually paid out of the estate, but where a public examination of the bankrupt has been ordered by the court on a creditor's requisition under r 6.173, IR86, the court may order that the expenses of the examination be paid out of the deposit required by r 6.173(2), IR86, instead of out of the estate.[166] In no case do the costs and expenses of a public examination fall on the OR personally.[167]

---

160 See IR86, Form 6.59 and r 6.176(1).
161 IR86, r 6.176(4) or IRN91, r 6.173.
162 IR86, r 6.176(2) or IRN91, r 6.173(2).
163 Form 6.60.
164 IR86, r 6.176(3) or IRN91, r 6.173(3).
165 IR86, r 6.176(5) or IRN91 (r 6.173(5).
166 IR86, r 6.177(1) or IRN91, r 6.174(1).
167 IR86, r 6.177(2) or IRN91, r 6.174(2).

PRIVATE EXAMINATION

What is a private examination and who can be summoned to attend?

9.54 The court, on the application of the OR or the trustee of the bankrupt's estate, may summon to appear before it:[168]

(a) the bankrupt or the bankrupt's spouse or former spouse or civil partner or former civil partner;

(b) any person known or believed to have any property comprised in the bankrupt's estate in his possession or to be indebted to the bankrupt;

(c) any person appearing to the court to be able to give information concerning the bankrupt or the bankrupt's dealings, affairs or property.

The court can require the persons in (b) or (c) above to submit a witness statement to the court containing an account of his dealings with the bankrupt or to produce any documents in his possession or under his control relating to the bankrupt, his dealings, affairs or property.[169]

9.55 Note that the persons mentioned in category (b) must be persons 'known or believed' to have property comprised in the estate; persons in category (c) must be persons 'appearing' to be able to give information concerning the bankrupt's dealings affairs or property. The definition of affairs in this section includes business.[170]

9.56 The use of private examinations has been the subject of considerable judicial scrutiny. The making of an order is a matter of discretion. The case-law suggests a balancing act is required, taking into account on the one hand the reasonable requirements of the office holder to carry out its tasks whilst on the other hand avoiding making an order which is unreasonable, unnecessary or oppressive to the person concerned.[171] Particular care must be taken where the object of the order for private examination (whether the bankrupt or a third party) is a potential respondent to recovery proceedings, such as the recipient of a potential transaction at an undervalue or preference.

In *Shierson v Rastogi*[172] the provisional liquidators of a company had commenced proceedings against four individuals including R and J, (directors of the company) alleging fraud and claiming damages and/or compensation in excess of US$400 million. R and J were not willing to cooperate with the liquidators in respect of questions concerning the issues raised in the

---

168 IA86, s 366.
169 IA86, s 336(1) or INO89, art 309(1).
170 IA86, s 385(2).
171 *British and Commonwealth Holdings plc v Spicer and Oppenheim* [1993] AC 426, HL; *Joint Liquidators of Sasea Finance Ltd v KPMG* [1998] BCC 216.
172 [2002] EWCA Civ 1624, [2003] 1 WLR 586, [2003] BPIR 148.

proceedings. The liquidators issued applications for their examination.[173] The Court of Appeal held that even though R and J were directors and subject to a statutory obligation to cooperate[174] it was oppressive to require them, when accused of serious wrongdoing in the proceedings, to provide what amounted to pre-trial depositions. And to prove the case against themselves on oath but such oppression could be outweighed by the legitimate requirements of the liquidators. On the facts of the case, the legitimate requirements of the liquidators in reconstituting, investigating and understanding the Company's affairs and realising all its assets outweighed the oppression to R and J and little weight should be given to the fact that the information obtained on the private examination might come into the hands of, and be used by, regulatory or prosecuting authorities.

What must be included in the application?

9.57 The application must state whether the applicant is seeking an order for the respondents to appear before the court or to submit a witness statement, and if the latter, it must give them particulars of the matters to which the respondent is required to swear or of the documents to be produced.[175] It must be accompanied by 'a brief statement of the grounds on which it is made'.[176]

9.58 The applicant must generally give at least 14 days notice of the application to the respondent.[177] As to making an application without notice see *Re Murjani (a Bankrupt)*[178] and *Hickling v Baker.*[179]

When can privilege be invoked?

9.59 The general rule is that the bankrupt may not assert privilege against his trustee. The Law Society has given guidance to solicitors as to how they should approach applications for information about a bankrupt's affairs in the chapter entitled 'Insolvency of the Client' in 'The Guide to the Professional Conduct of Solicitors'. In respect of the rights of the bankrupt in relation to professional privilege see *Barclays Bank v Eustice*.[180]

9.60 However, complicated issues may arise regarding the identity of the particular client in respect of whom privilege may be invoked. In *Long v Farrer and Co and Farrer*[181] the trustee in bankruptcy was investigating a potential transaction at an undervalue between the bankrupt and the trustees of a family trust. He asked the settlement trustees to provide documents and information. The settlement trustees asserted privilege, but the trustee argued that as the

---

173 Under IA 86, s 236, the corporate equivalent of IA 86, s 366.
174 Under IA 86, s 235.
175 IR86, r 9.2 or IRN91, r 9.002
176 IR86, r 9.2(1) or IRN91, r 9.002(1).
177 IR86, r 9.3(2) or IRN91, r 9.003(2).
178 [1996] 1 WLR 1498, [1996] 1 All ER 65.
179 [2007] EWCA Civ 287, [2007] BPIR 346.
180 [1995] 1 WLR 1238, [1996] BPIR 1.
181 [2004] EWHC 1774 (Ch), [2004] BPIR 1218.

bankrupt had been a client, it could not be invoked. The solicitors for the settlement trustees responded that their clients were the settlement trustees, not the settlement trustees and the bankrupt. Rimer J held that the issue of the identity of the client, and thus whether privilege could be invoked, was not one that could be determined on the assessment of witness statement evidence in the absence of cross-examination.

9.61 Occasionally, privileged material may come into the hands of the trustee in bankruptcy pursuant to the use (or threatened use) of his statutory powers, and issues may arise as to how that material, might be used. In *Re Ouvaroff (a Bankrupt)*[182] the trustee in bankruptcy was investigating the bankrupt's transfer of his interest in their former matrimonial home to his wife pursuant to a consent order made in divorce proceedings. The trustee sought the wife's solicitors' files, threatening an application under IA86, s 366 if they did not comply. New solicitors first asserted privilege, but, after further pressure from the trustee's solicitors, later disclosed the whole file. The trustee used some of the privileged material in support of his application to set aside the transfer as a transaction at an undervalue. The wife applied to strike out the evidence on the footing that the trustee should be given leave to re-swear the evidence without exhibiting or referring to the privileged material and for an injunction restraining the trustee from using the privileged material. The application was dismissed.

Whilst the powers of a trustee do not override the right of a third party to assert legal professional privilege and refuse to deliver up documents, in this case there was no evidence that the trustee or his solicitor had known that there demand was unjustified. They had believed and been entitled to believe that the wife had consented to the production of the privileged material. The court confirmed that neither the trustee nor his solicitor had acted in way as to justify the court's exercise of its jurisdiction to restrain its use. The privileged material had not been obtained by a trick or a mistake of which the trustee or his solicitors had been aware such that the court had a discretion whether to grant the injunction sought. The trustee and his solicitors had been entitled to use the privileged material in that the wife's solicitors had had ostensible authority to waive privilege and had done so on her behalf.

When can the privilege against self-incrimination be invoked?

9.62 A bankrupt may not invoke the privilege against self-incrimination to avoid his obligations to his trustee. However, the court may decline to compel a bankrupt to answer a question it considers oppressive. See generally on this area *Bishopsgate Investment Management Ltd v Maxwell*[183] and *Re London United Investments plc*.[184]

---

182 [1997] BPIR 712.
183 [1993] Ch 1, CA.
184 [1992] Ch 578, CA.

The bankrupt's obligation to provide information continues even after discharge such that an order for private examination may be made.[185]

9.63 At any examination the applicant may attend in person or be represented by a solicitor with or without counsel.[186] Any other person who could have applied for an order under s 336, IA86 may also attend and put questions to the respondent, but only through the applicant. Where a creditor has provided information, that creditor may, with the permission of the court, and provided the applicant does not object, attend and put questions, but again only through the applicant. The respondent may employ a solicitor and counsel 'who may put to him such questions as the court may allow for the purpose of enabling him to explain or qualify any answers given by him and may make representations on his behalf'.[187]

9.64

What records are retained of an examination and what penalties can the court impose?

A written record of the examination must be made and read over by the respondent and signed by him.[188] That record may be used in evidence against the respondent.[189]

The court may issue for a warrant for the arrest of any person or for the seizure of any books, papers, records, money or goods in that person's possession.[190] The power is generally exercised only if the person to be examined fails without good reason to appear to be examined or to comply with any order made. As to other enforcement powers of the court see s 367, IA86 which gives the court power to order delivery up of property and payment to be made of any sum due to the estate.

9.65 As to the power of the court to order the committal of the bankrupt for any failure to cooperate with his trustee and the interplay between ss 236, 333, 364 and 366, IA86 and the provisions of the Human Rights Act 1998, see *Hickling v Baker*.[191] In that case, the Court of Appeal summarised the principles as follows:

- In principle, arrest under an order made under IA 86, s 364 could be justified under Art 5(1)(b) of the European Convention on Human Rights.

---

185 *Oakes v Simms* [1997] BPIR 499.
186 IR86, r 9.4(1).
187 IR86, r 9.4(5) or IRN91, r 9.004(5).
188 IR86, r 9.4(6) or IRN91, r 9.004(6).
189 IR86, r 9.4(7) or IRN91, r 9.004(7).
190 IA86, s 366(3) or INO89, art 337(3).
191 [2007] EWCA Civ 287, [2007] BPIR 346, CA.

- Article 5 did not require that notice of an application for a committal order under s 364 of the Act be given to the person to be arrested in all cases.

- However, were the application to be made without notice, the evidence in support of the application must make it clear why this is said to be justified as an exception to the normal rule.

- If the order was made on an application without notice, it was necessary that the order should provide that, once the arrest has been effected, the person arrested be brought before the court at an early opportunity.

- The order did not have to specify any particular obligation whose fulfillment was intended to be secured, in terms of Art 5(1)(b).

- There were serious doubts as to whether the withholding of evidence could ever be justified on an application under s 364.

9.66 Sections 336 and 337, IA86 may also be used where an interim receiver has been appointed. Rule 9.6, IR86 provide that the court may order the costs of any examination to be paid by the respondent, but unless the court orders otherwise they will generally come out of the estate. The rule was interpreted in *Miller v Bain*[192] to mean that a liquidator (as the office holder was in that case) should be entitled to his costs where he was 'reasonably entitled to conclude that there was a risk that [the respondent] would not cooperate with him and attend for an interview otherwise than under the compulsion of a court order'.

When can search and seizure warrants be used?

9.67 A trustee in bankruptcy or the OR may apply for a warrant for the arrest of a debtor or undischarged bankrupt or for the seizure of his books, papers, records, money or goods if it appears to the court that:

(a) there are reasonable grounds for believing that he has absconded, or is about to abscond, with a view to avoiding or delaying the payment of any of his 'debts', or his appearance to a bankruptcy petition or to avoiding, delaying or disrupting any proceedings in bankruptcy against him or any examination of his affairs;

(b) that he is about to remove his goods with a view to preventing or delaying possession being taken of them by the OR or the trustee;

(c) that there are reasonable grounds for believing that he has concealed or destroyed, or is about to conceal or destroy, any of his goods or any books, papers or records which might be of use to his creditors in the course of his bankruptcy or in connection with the illustration of his estate;

---

192 [2003] BPIR 959.

(d) that he has, without the permission of the OR or his trustee, removed any goods in his possession the value of which exceeds £1,000;

(e) that he has failed without reasonable excuse to attend any examination ordered by the court.[193]

9.68 Furthermore, the OR or trustee may apply for a warrant to seize any property comprised in the bankrupt estate, or any books, papers or records relating to the bankrupt, his estate or his affairs which are in the possession or under the control of the bankrupt or of any other person liable to hand them over to the trustee or the OR.[194] Any person executing the warrant may break into any premises where the bankrupt is believed to be and any receptacle of the bankrupt's which contains or is believed to contain anything may be seized under the warrant.[195] The power may extend to premises not belonging to the bankrupt.[196] There is little authority on these provisions.[197]

THIRD PARTY INFORMATION ABOUT A BANKRUPT'S BUSINESS AFFAIRS

What is the process for enquiries to be made with parties other than the bankrupt?

9.69 The OR may make enquiries about the bankrupt's affairs of any person who may have information that may assist in the location and realisation of the bankrupt's assets. If any person refuses to cooperate, the OR or trustee may apply to court for assistance in obtaining the information or records as follows. Commonly the OR or trustee in bankruptcy will make enquiries of the bankrupt's former (or existing) accountants or lawyers with a view to building up information as regards the bankrupt's dealings, in particular in respect of any suspect antecedent transactions.

Who can be examined by the OR about a bankrupt's acts and dealings?

9.70 The OR can apply for the following persons to be examined:

- the bankrupt or the bankrupt's spouse or former spouse, civil partner or former civil partner;[198]

- any person known or believed to have any property comprised in the bankrupt's estate in his possession or to be indebted to the bankrupt;[199]

---

[193] IA86, s 364(2) or INO89, art 335(2).
[194] IA86, s 365(1) or INO89, art 336(1).
[195] IA86, s 365(2) or INO89, art 336(2).
[196] IA86, s 365(3) or INO89, art 336(3.
[197] Generally see *Hickling v Baker* [2007] EWCA Civ 287, [2007] BPIR 346, CA.
[198] IA86, s 366(1)(a) or INO89, art 337(1)(a).
[199] IA86, s 366(1)(b) or INO89, art 337(1)(b).

- any person appearing to the court to be able to give information concerning the bankrupt or the bankrupt's dealings, affairs or property.

The court may require a person to submit a witness statement to the court containing an account of his dealings with the bankrupt or to produce any documents in his possession or under his control relating to the bankrupt or the bankrupt's dealings, affairs or property.[200]

What sanctions are available for continued non-cooperation?

9.71 If any person fails to appear before the court when summoned without reasonable excuse,[201] or there are reasonable grounds for believing that a person has absconded,[202] or is about to abscond, with a view to avoiding his appearance before the court,[203] the court may issue a warrant:[204]

- for the arrest of that person;[205] and

- for the seizure of any books, papers, records, money or goods in that person's possession.[206]

The court may authorise a person arrested under such a warrant to be kept in custody, and anything seized under such a warrant to be held, in accordance with the rules, until that person is brought before the court under the warrant or until such other time as the court may order.[207]

Does a bankrupt commit an offence if he leaves or attempts to leave the country with any of his assets?

9.72 A bankrupt commits an offence if he leaves, or attempts or makes preparation to leave, England and Wales with any property which he is required to deliver up and which has a value greater than the prescribed amount (currently £1,000).[208] The period may extend to 6 months prior to the petition being filed.[209]

---

[200] IA86, s 366(1)(c) or INO89, art 337(1)(c).
[201] IA86, s 366(2)(a) or INO89, art 337(2)(a).
[202] IA86, s 366(2)(b) or INO89, art 337(2)(b).
[203] IA86, s 366(2)(b) or INO89, art 337(2)(b).
[204] IA86, s 366(3) or INO89, art 337(3).
[205] IA86, s 366(3)(a) or INO89, art 337(3)(a).
[206] IA86, s 366(3)(a) or INO89, art 337(3)(a).
[207] IA86, s 366(4) or INO89, art 337(4).
[208] Insolvency Proceedings (Monetary Limits) Order 1986, SI 1986/1996; IA86, s 358(a) or INO89, art 329(a).
[209] IA86, s 358(b) or INO89, art 329(b). For an example of a recent suspended prison sentence http://bankruptcyandinsolvency.blogspot.com/2009/12/time-called-on-bankrupts-according-to.html.

Redirection of a bankrupt's mail

When can a bankrupt's mail be redirected to the official receiver or trustee?

9.73 The OR or trustee may apply to the court for a redirection of the bankrupt's mail for a maximum period of 3 months.[210]

In *Foxley v United Kingdom*[211] the European Court of Human Rights held that the provision was not a breach of Art 8 of the European Convention on Human Rights provided that the time limit as to the duration of the order was observed. A similar point was made in *Narinen v Finland*.[212]

In *Singh v Official Receiver*[213] Sir Richard Scott V-C gave guidance as to the procedural considerations the court should take into account. Since then, the Insolvency Rules have been amended and more detailed procedural provisions are provided by r 6.235A, IR86. The practice of the courts has also developed such that in certain cases any order may provide for redirected post to go first to an independent lawyer with the task of ensuring that privileged or embarrassing material does not find its way into the hands of the trustee.

How is a mail redirection application made?

9.74 The following procedure should be followed:

- The application will normally be made without giving notice to the bankrupt or any other person, unless the court directs otherwise.[214]
- The application must be accompanied by a report setting out the reasons why the order is being requested.[215]
- The court will fix a venue for the hearing and if considered necessary will give the applicant notice.[216]
- The court can make any order it considers appropriate in the circumstances of the case.[217]
- The order will identify the person(s) on which it needs to be served depending on the content of the order.[218]

---

210 IA86, s 371(1) or INO89, art 342(1).
211 [2000] BPIR 1009.
212 [2004] BPIR 914.
213 [1997] BPIR 530.
214 IR86, r 6.235A(2).
215 IR86, r 6.235A(3).
216 IR86, r 6.235A(4).
217 IR86, r 6.235A(5).
218 IR86, r 6.235A(6).

Chapter 10

DISCHARGE FROM BANKRUPTCY AND ASSOCIATED ORDERS AND RESTRICTIONS

'It has been said that insolvency and bankruptcy laws are the poor-laws of the middle classes … that unless the insolvency laws be reformed, the vices of idleness, extravagance, and dishonesty encouraged by them, will destroy the middle classes.'[1]

INTRODUCTION

10.1 This chapter looks at discharge from bankruptcy, together with the other orders and agreements that can be obtained from a bankrupt after the commencement of the bankruptcy. The procedures will be covered in the following order:

- Discharge from bankruptcy.
- Suspension from discharge.
- Restrictions on discharge that can be obtained:
  - — Bankruptcy restrictions orders (BRO);
  - — Bankruptcy restrictions undertakings (BRU).
- Other orders including:
  - — Income payments orders (IPO);
  - — Income payments agreements (IPA).

This chapter also covers the personal insolvency register which includes, *inter alia;* the registration of the original bankruptcy order and any subsequent restriction orders, undertakings or agreements obtained against the bankrupt. Finally at the end of the chapter is a brief summary of restrictions imposed on an undischarged bankrupt by other legislation.

---

1 J Houston Browne and WW Ogbourne, The Bankrupt Law Consolidation Act 1849 [12 and 13 Vic c 106]; with a popular explanation of the Powers, Duties, Obligations, and Responsibilities of Debtors and Creditors; the facilities for avoiding Bankruptcy, and the Provisions for punishing Fraud (1849, London).

DISCHARGE

What is discharge?

10.2 Discharge is the formal release from the state of bankruptcy. Under previous statutes[2] a bankrupt had to apply for discharge, but post the IA86 discharge has been granted automatically.[3] The current period was brought in by s 256(1), Enterprise Act 2002 (EA02) and transitional provisions were introduced for existing bankruptcy orders. From 1976 and prior to the IA86 the discharge period was 5 years and this was reduced to 3 years and further reduced to one year by the EA02 which came into effect on 1 April 2004. Where the bankrupt has failed to cooperate with the trustee or has acted inappropriately, an application can be made to suspend the automatic discharge period from running for periods between 2 and 15 years.[4]

What is the effect of discharge?

10.3 Discharge releases a bankrupt from all his bankruptcy debts, but has no effect on the following:

- the functions of the trustee (so far as they remain to be carried out);[5] or
- the operation of Part IX of the IA86;
- discharge does not affect the right of any creditor of the bankrupt to prove in the bankruptcy for any debt from which the bankrupt has been released;[6] or
- the right of any secured creditor of the bankrupt to enforce his security for the payment of a debt from which the bankrupt is released.[7]

In addition discharge does not release the bankrupt from:

- any bankruptcy debt which he incurred in respect of, or forbearance in respect of which was secured by means of, any fraud or fraudulent breach of trust to which he was a party.[8]

---

2 Insolvency Act 1976.
3 IA86, s 279.
4 IA86, s 281(1)(b) or INO89, art 255(1)(b).
5 IA86, s 281(1)(a) or INO89, art 255(1)(a).
6 IA86, s 281(1)(b) or INO89, art 255(1)(b).
7 IA86, s 281(2).
8 IA86, s 281(3). As to the application of these provisions, see *Masters and others v Leaver* [2000] BPIR 284, *Woodland-Ferrari v UCL Group Retirement Benefits Scheme* [2002] BPIR 1270 and *Soutzos v (1) Asombang (2) Dawkins (3) Fox* [2010] EWHC 842 (Ch), [2010] BPIR 960. Further, in *Mander v Evans* [2001] BPIR 902 it was held that the use of the word 'fraud' must be taken to mean fraud in the sense of deceit as defined in *Derry v Peek* (1889) 14 App Cas 337 and not what might be viewed as the wider equitable notion of constructive fraud.

- any liability in respect of any fine or liability imposed as a result of any offence or similar penalty.

- except to such extent and on such conditions as the court may direct, any bankruptcy debt which consists in a liability to pay damages for negligence, nuisance or breach of a statutory, contractual or other duty, or to pay damages by virtue of Part I of the Consumer Protection Act 1987, being in either case damages in respect of personal injuries to any person.[9] For these purposes, 'personal injuries' includes death and any disease or other impairment of a person's physical or mental condition.[10]

- except to such extent and on such conditions as the court may direct, any bankruptcy debt which arises under any order made in family proceedings or under a maintenance calculation made under the Child Support Act 1991.[11] For these purposes, 'family proceedings' means:

  — family proceedings within the meaning of the Magistrates Courts Act 1980 and any proceedings which would be such proceedings but for s 65(1)(ii) of that Act (proceedings for variation of order for periodical payments). For these purposes, 'personal injuries' includes death and any disease or other impairment of a person's physical or mental condition;[12] and
  — family proceedings within the meaning of Part V of the Matrimonial and Family Proceedings Act 1984. For these purposes, 'personal injuries' includes death and any disease or other impairment of a person's physical or mental condition.[13]

10.4 In summary discharge does not release the bankrupt from any debts not provable in his bankruptcy.[14]

Also, for the avoidance of doubt, discharge does not release any person other than the bankrupt from any liability (whether as partner or co-trustee of the bankrupt or otherwise) from which the bankrupt is released by the discharge, or from any liability as surety for the bankrupt or as a person in the nature of such a surety.[15]

What are post discharge restrictions?

10.5 Section 281A and Sch 4A, IA86 give the court power to impose a BRO if it thinks it appropriate to do so having regard to the conduct of the bankrupt.

---

9 IA86, s 281(5)(a).
10 IA86, s 281(8).
11 IA86, s 281(5)(b).
12 IA86, s 281(8)(a).
13 IA86, s 281(8)(b).
14 IA86, s 281(6).
15 IA86, s 281(7).

A BRO effectively extends the normal restrictions on an undischarged bankrupt for a period of 2 to 15 years.[16]

What are the grounds considered for discharge suspension?

10.6 In *Randhawa v Official Receiver*[17] Mr Launcelot Henderson QC (sitting as a Deputy High Court judge) considered the BRO jurisdiction in some detail. The following four principles arose:

(1) The first was centred on the protection of the public:

- keeping bankrupts whose conduct warrants a bankruptcy restrictions order 'off the road';
- deterring such bankrupts from repeating such conduct (individual deterrence);
- deterring others (general deterrence).[18]

(2) The second compared the jurisdiction with that under the Company Directors Disqualification Act 1986 and the need to determine if the alleged conduct has been established. If so, determine whether the matters of conduct viewed individually and cumulatively, and taking account of any extenuating circumstances, failed to meet the proper standards of probity and competence as the standard required of individuals conducting their financial affairs.

(3) Thirdly, although the court will consider the grounds set out in Sch 4A, IA86 (see below for a full list) and any prior bankruptcy, such conduct of itself will not necessarily warrant the making of an order.

(4) Fourthly, the period of an order should be fixed by reference to the principles set out in *Re Sevenoaks Stationers (Retail) Ltd.*[19] In *Re Sevenoaks Stationers (Retail) Ltd*, Dillon LJ in the Court of Appeal divided the potential maximum 15 year period of disqualification into three distinct brackets:

- more than 10 years for particularly serious cases (for example, where a director has been disqualified previously);
- between 2 and 5 years for 'relatively not very serious' cases;
- a middle bracket of between 6 and 10 years for serious cases not meriting the top bracket.

What are the grounds listed in Sch 4A IA86?

10.7 The following conduct is listed in Sch 4A IA86 and needs to be taken into consideration:

---

16 IA86, Sch 4A, para 4(2).

17 [2006] EWHC 2946 (Ch), [2006] BPIR 1435, [2007] 1 WLR 170.

18 See also *Jenkins v Official Receiver* [2007] EWHC 1402 (Ch), [2007] BPIR 740.

19 [1991] Ch 164 at 174E-G.

- Failing to keep records which account for loss of property by the bankrupt or by any business carried on by him, where the loss occurred in the period beginning 2 years before the petition and ending with the date of the application.[20]

- Failing to produce any records requested by the OR or trustee.[21]

- Entering into a transaction at an undervalue.[22]

- Giving a preference.[23]

- Making an excessive pension contribution.[24]

- Failing to supply goods and services which were wholly or partly paid for and which gave rise to a claim provable in the bankruptcy.[25]

- Trading at a time before the commencement of the bankruptcy when the bankrupt knew or ought to have known that he was unable to pay his debts.[26]

- Incurring, before the commencement of the bankruptcy, any debt which he had no reasonable expectation of being able to pay.[27]

- Failing to account satisfactorily to the court, the OR or the trustee for a loss of property or for an insufficiency of property to meet bankruptcy debts.[28]

- Carrying on any gambling, rash or hazardous speculation or unreasonable extravagance which may have materially contributed to or increased the extent of the bankruptcy debts or which took place between the presentation of the petition and commencement of the bankruptcy.[29]

- Neglect of business affairs of a kind which may have materially contributed to or increased the extent of the bankruptcy debts.[30]

- Fraud or fraudulent breach of trust.[31]

---

20 IA86, Sch 4A, para 2(2)(a).
21 IA86, Sch 4A, para 2(2)(b).
22 IA86, Sch 4A, para 2(2)(c); see also chapter 17.
23 IA86, Sch 4A, para 2(2)(d); see also chapter 17.
24 IA86, Sch 4A, para 2(2)(e); see also chapter 17.
25 IA86, Sch 4A, para 2(2)(f).
26 IA86, Sch 4A, para 2(2)(g).
27 IA86, Sch 4A, para 2(2)(h).
28 IA86, Sch 4A, para 2(2)(i).
29 IA86, Sch 4A, para 2(2)(j).
30 IA86, Sch 4A, para 2(2)(k).
31 IA86, Sch 4A, para 2(2)(l).

- Failing to cooperate with the OR or the trustee.[32]
- Any previous bankruptcy proceedings in which the individual remained an undischarged bankrupt in the previous 6 years.[33]

How is the discharge period calculated?

10.8 The bankruptcy of an individual commences with the day on which the bankruptcy order is made,[34] and continues until the individual is discharged.[35]

A bankrupt is automatically discharged from bankruptcy at the end of the period of one year beginning with the date on which the bankruptcy commences[36] or earlier if the OR files a notice with the court stating that his investigations are complete.[37]

Where discharge takes effect automatically there is no need to return to court.

There were complicated arrangements in the transitional provisions as a consequence of the amendments introduced by the EA02. Essentially, neither the previously prevailing regime under the IA86, nor the new regime as introduced by the EA02 applied to existing bankrupts as at 1 April 2004, the date of implementation of the EA02. In the absence of suspension of automatic discharge, such bankrupts would be discharged on 1 April 2005 (the one-year anniversary of the introduction of the EA02) or, if earlier, the three-year anniversary of the making of the bankruptcy orders. There were further exceptions as regards second-time bankrupts. Any person who was an undischarged bankrupt as at 1 April 2004, and whom had had a bankruptcy order made against him in the 15 years before, would, in the absence of a suspension of discharge, be discharged on 1 April 2009 (the five-year anniversary of the introduction of the EA02).[38]

Can the discharge period be suspended?

10.9 An application can be made, by the OR or the trustee, to the court to suspend the discharge period from running either to a specified date[39] or until specified conditions have been fulfilled.[40] The court may only make such an order if satisfied that the bankrupt has failed to comply with his obligations.[41]

---

32 IA86, Sch 4A, para 2(2)(m).
33 IA86, Sch 4A, para 2(3).
34 IA86, s 278(a) or INO89, art 252(a).
35 IA86, s 278(b) or INO89, art 252(b).
36 IA86, s 279(1) or INO89, art 253(1).
37 IA86, s 279(2) or INO89, art 253(2).
38 The transitional provisions are set out in Sch 19 to the EA02.
39 IA86, s 279(3)(a) or INO89, art 253(3)(a).
40 IA86, s 279(3)(b) or INO89, art 253(3)(b).
41 IA86, s 279(5) or INO89, art 253(5).

What is the procedure for an application to suspend an automatic discharge from running?

10.10 The process is as follows:

- The OR or trustee must file evidence in support of the application setting out the reasons why the order should be made.[42]

- On receipt of the application to suspend discharge the court will fix a venue for the hearing[43] which must be notified to the OR, any trustee and the bankrupt.

- Copies of the evidence provided in support of the application must also be sent by the applicant to each of the other parties[44] at least 21 days before the hearing.[45]

- The bankrupt may file a notice in court specifying any statements or evidence that he intends to dispute. This notice must be filed in court at least 7 days before the hearing[46] with copies being sent to the OR and any trustee at least 4 days before the hearing.[47]

- In cases where a public examination is adjourned, generally because of non-cooperation or non-attendance of the bankrupt, the OR may also make an application for suspension from discharge.[48]

Can the official receiver apply for an interim order suspending discharge without notifying the bankrupt?

10.11 An OR or trustee making a late application without good reason risks the application being dismissed. However, in *Bagnall v Official Receiver*[49] it was held that r 7.4(6) IR86 allowed the court to make an immediate order on short or no notice, in certain circumstances, provided the bankrupt had not been discharged.[50]

How does the court approach the decision?

10.12 Usually the court has two fundamental issues to determine. First, whether the bankrupt is in breach of any of his obligations and secondly, if so, what is the effect of such failure on the administration of the bankruptcy estate. It is not uncommon for such hearings to become tied up with the fine detail of what the bankrupt may have said to the trustee when, and whether

---

42 IR86, r 6.215(2) or IRN91, r 6.213(2).
43 IR86, r 6.215(3) or IRN91, r 6.213(3).
44 IR86, r 6.215(4) or IRN91, r 6.213(4).
45 IR86, r 6.215(5) or IRN91, r 6.213(5).
46 IR86, r 6.215(6) orIRN91, r 6.213(6).
47 IR86, r 6.215(7) or IRN91, r 6.213(7).
48 IR86, r 6.176(4) or IRN91, r 6.173(4).
49 [2003] EWCA Civ 1925, [2004] BPIR 445.
50 *Re Jacobs (a Bankrupt)* [1999] 1 WLR 619.

such conduct was compliant, or the statements true. In *Shierson and Birch v Rastogi (a Bankrupt)*[51] a bankruptcy order was made against a director who had been found responsible for a fraudulent extraction of some $300 million from the company. The trustees in bankruptcy contended that the bankrupt had failed and was continuing to fail to comply with his obligations, specifically ss 291, 311, 312 and 333 of the IA86, in three respects, namely: (1) failure to explain or account for the disparity between the amount of the judgment and the value of the assets disclosed by him; (2) failure to disclose or account for the proceeds of sale of some shares and (3) failure to disclose a beneficial interest in some trusts. Morritt C stated that the issue before the registrar was whether it had been established that the bankrupt had failed to perform his obligations under Part IX of the IA86, including the provision to the trustees of documents, information and explanations relating not only to the estate of the bankrupt but also his 'affairs' under ss 291(1)(b), 311(1) and 333(1)(a), IA86. It was clear that the bankrupt had failed to comply with the obligations imposed on him in all respects.

Morritt C further stated that it was clear from the terms of s 279, IA86 that postponement of discharge was linked to a failure to comply with the obligations imposed on a bankrupt by Part IX. It was not necessary to reach a final conclusion as to whether the purpose of the power was to provide an incentive to full compliance or that the disabilities arising from being an undischarged bankrupt should, in the public interest, continue until there had been full compliance. But the purpose of the power was probably the latter, even though its effect might be to achieve the former. Were it otherwise, Parliament would have made discharge conditional on full compliance. In these circumstances, it was essential that the bankrupt was not freed from the disabilities to which an undischarged bankrupt was subject until they had been clarified.

What happens after the hearing?

10.13 If the court makes an order suspending the bankrupt's discharge, copies of the order must be sent by the court to:

- the OR;
- any trustee who is not the OR; and
- the bankrupt.[52]

---

51 [2007] EWHC 1266 (Ch), [2007] BPIR 891.
52 IR86, r 6.215(8) or IRN91, r 6.213(8).

How does a bankrupt apply to have a suspension lifted?

10.14 A bankrupt can make an application to the court for any suspension to be lifted.[53] On receipt the court must fix a venue for the hearing giving the OR and any trustee at least 28 days' notice,[54] together with a copy of the application.

10.15 The OR and the trustee may appear and be heard on the bankrupt's application; and, whether or not they appear, the OR and trustee may file in court evidence in support of any matters which either of them considers ought to be drawn to the court's attention.[55]

What matters does the court consider before lifting the suspension?

10.16 The court may request a report from the OR or the trustee as to whether the conditions specified in the earlier order (if any) have or have not been complied with.[56] Any report or evidence provided to the court by the OR or trustee must be sent to the other party and the bankrupt at least 14 days before the hearing.[57]

10.17 The bankrupt is entitled to answer this evidence by filing in court, at least 7 days before the date of the hearing, a notice specifying which statements in the OR or trustee's report he intends to deny or dispute. Copies of the notice must also be sent to the OR and trustee at least 4 days before the date of the hearing.[58]

10.18 If the court discharges the order suspending discharge, it will issue to the bankrupt a certificate that it has done so with effect from a specified date and send copies of the certificate to the OR and the trustee.[59]

Can the bankrupt apply for discharge?

10.19 Section 280, IA86 allows a bankrupt to apply for an order discharging him from bankruptcy. He must give the OR notice of the application and deposit with him such sum as the OR may require, to cover his costs of the application.[60]

---

53 IR86, r 6.216(1) or IRN91, r 6.214(1).
54 IR86, r 6.216(2) or IRN91, r 6.214(2).
55 IR86, r 6.216(3) or IRN91, r 6.214(3).
56 IR86, r 6.216(4) or IRN91, r 6.214(4).
57 IR86, r 6.216(5) or IRN91, r 6.214(5).
58 IR86, r 6.216(6) or IRN91, r 6.214(6).
59 IR86, r 6.216(7) or IRN91, r 6.214(7).
60 IR86, r 6.217(1) or IRN91, r 6.215(1).

What is the application process?

10.20 If the court is satisfied that the bankrupt has complied with the provisions set out above it will fix a venue for the hearing of the application giving at least 42 days' notice of it to the OR and the bankrupt.[61] The following process must be followed:

- The OR must give notice to the trustee and to every creditor who, to the OR's knowledge, has a claim outstanding against the estate which has not been satisfied,[62] at least 14 days before the date fixed for the hearing of the bankrupt's application.[63]

- At least 21 days before the date fixed for the hearing of the application, the OR must file in court a report[64] (see below for report contents).

- The OR must send a copy of the report to the bankrupt and the trustee, so as to reach them at least 14 days before the date of the hearing of the application.[65]

- The bankrupt may, not later than 7 days before the date of the hearing, file in court a notice specifying any statements in the OR's report which he intends to deny or dispute[66] and send copies, not less than 4 days before the date of the hearing, to the OR and the trustee.[67]

- The OR, the trustee and any creditor may appear on the hearing, and may make representations and put to the bankrupt such questions as the court may allow.[68]

What information is included in the report to court?

10.21 At least 21 days before the date fixed for the hearing of the application, the OR must file in court a report containing the following information:

- any failure by the bankrupt to comply with his obligations under Parts VIII to XI, IA86;

- the circumstances surrounding the bankruptcy, and any previous bankruptcy;

- the extent to which, in the bankruptcy and in any previous bankruptcy, the bankrupt's liabilities exceeded his assets; and

---

61 IR86, r 6.217(2) or IRN91, r 6.215(2).
62 IR86, r 6.217(3) or IRN91, r 6.215(3).
63 IR86, r 6.217(4) or IRN91, r 6.215(4).
64 IR86, r 6.218(1) or IRN91, r 6.216(1).
65 IR86, r 6.218(2) or IRN91, r 6.216(2).
66 Form 6.75.
67 IR86, r 6.218(3) or IRN91, r 6.216(3).
68 IR86, r 6.218(4) or IRN91, r 6.216(4).

- particulars of any distribution which has been, or is expected to be, made to creditors in the present bankruptcy or that there has been and is to be no distribution; and

- any other matters which, in his opinion, ought to be brought to the court's attention.[69]

What orders may the court make on a bankrupt's application for discharge?

10.22 The court may refuse discharge, grant discharge absolutely or grant discharge subject to conditions relating to any income which may become due to the bankrupt or any property which may come to him after discharge.[70] The order may have retrospective effect.[71]

10.23 Copies of the order must be sent by the court to the bankrupt, the trustee and the OR.[72] An order made by the court on an application by the bankrupt for discharge under s 280, IA 86 may not be issued or gazetted until the time allowed for appealing has expired or, if an appeal is entered, until the appeal has been determined.[73]

What evidence can be provided of discharge?

10.24 Although discharge is usually automatic, a bankrupt may apply for a certificate of discharge.[74] The certificate will only be issued on the application of the bankrupt. The discharged bankrupt may also require the SoS to give notice of the discharge:

- in the *Gazette*; or

- in any newspaper in which the bankruptcy was advertised; or

- in both.[75]

No costs or expenses arising in relation to discharge may fall on the OR personally.[76]

---

69 IR86, r 6.218(1) or IRN91, r 6.216(1)
70 IA86, s 280(2) or INO89. art 254(2) and Form 6.76.
71 IR86, r 6.219(2) or IRN91, r 6.217(2).
72 IR86, r 6.219(3) or IRN91, r 6.217(3).
73 IR86, r 6.221 or IRN91, r 6.219.
74 See Form 6.77; see also IR86, r 6.220(1) or IRN91, r 6.218(1).
75 IR86, r 6.220(2) or IRN91, r 6.218(2).
76 IR86, r 6.222 or IRN91, r 6.220.

Bankruptcy restrictions order

What is a bankruptcy restrictions order?

10.25 A BRO is designed to protect the public in three ways and can be made for a period of between 2 and 15 years. The three types of protection are:[77]

- by keeping bankrupts 'off the road' now that discharge can be obtained much earlier;
- as a deterrent for the bankrupt against repeating their own bad conduct;
- as a deterrent to others.

What is the difference between a bankruptcy restrictions order and an undertaking?

10.26 A BRU[78] is similar to a BRO but is less formal. It has the same effect as a BRO in that it extends the restrictions imposed on an undischarged bankrupt. It is less formal in that the bankrupt agrees to the restrictions voluntarily. The court is notified of the undertaking which is registered[79] in the same way as a BRO.

By whom and when can an application for a bankruptcy restrictions order be made?

10.27 An application for a BRO can only be made by the SoS[80] or the OR acting on his behalf.[81] Any application must be made:

- before the end of the period of one year beginning with the date on which the bankruptcy commences;[82] or
- thereafter only with the permission of the court.[83]

The main factors that the court will take into account in considering whether to extend time for the making of the application for a BRO are the length of the delay, the reason for the delay and the strength of the case against the bankrupt.[84]

Where there is an order suspending the bankrupt's discharge the application can be made at any time before discharge. The period of one year referred to

---

77 *Jenkins v Official Receiver* [2007] EWHC 1402 (Ch).
78 IA86, Sch 4A, para 7.
79 IA86, Sch 4A, para 12(c).
80 IR86, r 6.241, IA86, Sch 4A, para 1(2)(a) or IRN91, r 6.234.
81 IR86, r 6.240, IA86, Sch 4A, para 1(2)(b) or IRN91, r 6.233.
82 IA86, Sch 4A, para 3(1)(a).
83 IA86, Sch 4A, para 3(1)(b).
84 See *Official Receiver v Baars* [2009] BPIR 524.

above ceases to run in respect of a bankrupt while the period set for their discharge is suspended under s 279(3), IA86.[85]

What is included in the report to the court?

10.28 The report in support of the application should include the following:

- a statement of the conduct by reference to which it is alleged that it is appropriate for a BRO to be made;[86] and
- the evidence on which the SoS or OR relies in support of the application.[87]

Any evidence by a party other than the OR must be given by witness statement.[88]

What matters need to be considered by the court?

10.29 The court must take account of any of the following kinds of conduct by the bankrupt:

- failing to keep records which account for a loss of property by the bankrupt, or by a business carried on by him, where the loss occurred in the period beginning 2 years before petition and ending with the date of the application;[89]
- failing to produce records of that kind on demand by the OR or the trustee;[90]
- entering into a transaction at an undervalue;[91]
- giving a preference;[92]
- making an excessive pension contribution;[93]
- a failure to supply goods or services which were wholly or partly paid for which gave rise to a claim provable in the bankruptcy;[94]

---

85 IA86, Sch 4A, para 3(2).
86 IR86, r 6.241(2)(a) or IRN91, r 6.234(2)(a).
87 IR86, r 6.241(2)(a) or IRN91, r 6.234(2)(a).
88 IR86, r 6.241(3) or IRN91, r 6.234(3). The affidavit was replaced by a 'witness statement' with effect from 6 April 2010.
89 IA86, Sch 4A, para 2(2)(a).
90 IA86, Sch 4A, para 2(2)(b).
91 IA86, Sch 4A, para 2(2)(c).
92 IA86, Sch 4A, para 2(2)(d).
93 IA86, Sch 4A, para 2(2)(e).
94 IA86, Sch 4A, para 2(2)(f).

- trading at a time before commencement of the bankruptcy when the bankrupt knew, or ought to have known, that he was unable to pay his debts[95] ie knowledge of insolvency;

- incurring, before commencement of the bankruptcy, a debt which the bankrupt had no reasonable expectation of being able to pay;[96]

- failing to account satisfactorily to the court, the OR or the trustee for a loss of property or for an insufficiency of property to meet bankruptcy debts;[97]

- carrying on any gambling, rash and hazardous speculation or unreasonable extravagance which may have materially contributed to or increased the extent of the bankruptcy or which took place between presentation of the petition and commencement of the bankruptcy;[98]

- neglect of business affairs of a kind which may have materially contributed to or increased the extent of the bankruptcy;[99]

- fraud or fraudulent breach of trust;[100]

- failing to cooperate with the OR or the trustee.[101]

The court will also take into consideration whether the bankrupt was an undischarged bankrupt at some time during the 6 year period ending with the date of the bankruptcy to which the application relates.[102]

10.30 The list of matters set out above is not exclusive: the court may take other misconduct into account. The conduct must constitute a failure in some significant respect to live up to the proper standards of competence or probity, and should generally involve culpability or irresponsibility.[103] It is not necessary for the conduct to have been dishonest. Once it is established that conduct which fell below the appropriate standard has occurred, the court is obliged to make a BRO.[104]

---

95 IA86, Sch 4A, para 2(2)(g).
96 IA86, Sch 4A, para 2(2)(h).
97 IA86, Sch 4A, para 2(2)(i).
98 IA86, Sch 4A, para 2(2)(j).
99 IA86, Sch 4A, para 2(2)(k).
100 IA86, Sch 4A, para 2(2)(l).
101 IA86, Sch 4A, para 2(2)(m) was considered in *Official Receiver v Bathurst* [2008] EWHC 1724 (Ch), [2008] BPIR 1548 and *Official Receiver v Baars* [2009] BPIR 524.
102 IA86, Sch 4A, para 2(3).
103 *Official Receiver v Southey* [2009] BPIR 89.
104 IA86, Sch 4A, para 2(1) and *Official Receiver v May* [2008] EWHC 1778 (Ch), [2008] BPIR 1562.

How much notice is given of the hearing and how is the bankrupt informed of the application?

10.31 The date for the hearing must be no earlier than 8 weeks from the date when the court fixes the venue for the hearing.[105] The SoS must serve notice of the application and the venue fixed by the court on the bankrupt not more than 14 days after the application is made at court.[106] A copy of the application must be served, together with copies of the report by the SoS, any other evidence filed with the court in support of the application, and an acknowledgement of service.[107]

What does a bankrupt have to do on receipt of the application?

10.32 The bankrupt must file an acknowledgement of service of the application in court not more than 14 days after service on him of the application.[108] The acknowledgment must indicate whether or not he contests the application.[109]

What happens if the bankrupt fails to file an acknowledgement of service?

10.33 Where the bankrupt has failed to file an acknowledgement of service and the time period for doing so has expired, the bankrupt may attend the hearing of the application but may not take part in the hearing unless the court gives permission.[110] Under these circumstances it is virtually certain that a BRO will be made unless there is some good reason for the failure to respond.

How can a bankrupt oppose an application for a bankruptcy restrictions order?

10.34 If the bankrupt wishes to oppose the application, he must within 28 days of the service on him of the application and evidence of the SoS, file in court any evidence which he wishes the court to take into consideration, and must serve a copy of the same on the SoS within 3 days of filing it at court.[111] The SoS may file further evidence in court. This must be done within 14 days from receiving the copy of the bankrupt's evidence.[112] Copies must also be served on the debtor as soon as reasonably practicable.[113] In practice the court will often set a different timetable to accommodate the needs of the parties at the initial hearing.

What happens at the bankruptcy restrictions order hearing?

10.35 The court will consider the application provided, regardless of whether the bankrupt appears at the hearing and whether or not he has filed any

---

[105] IR86, r 6.241(4) or IRN91, r 6.234(4).
[106] IR86, r 6.242(1) or IRN91, r 6.234(1).
[107] IR86, r 6.242(1) or IRN91, r 6.234(1).
[108] IR86, r 6.242(3) or IRN91, r 6.234(3).
[109] IR86, r 6.242(3) or IRN91, r 6.234(3).
[110] IR86, r 6.242(4) or IRN91, r 6.235(4).
[111] IR86, r 6.243(1) or IRN91, r 6.236(1).
[112] IR86, r 6.243(2) or IRN91, r 6.236(2).
[113] IR86, r 6.243(2) or IRN91, r 6.236(2).

evidence in court. The court may make a BRO in the absence of the bankrupt.[114] However, in practice the court will generally give directions at the first hearing which may include an order debarring the bankrupt from adducing evidence if he fails to file and serve it by a certain date.

Can the court grant a bankruptcy restrictions order in the face of an annulment application?

10.36 The court has jurisdiction to make a BRO in circumstances where the application has been issued prior to the annulment. In *Jenkins v Official Receiver*[115] (discussed below) Rimer J considered the court's jurisdiction and/or discretion to make a BRO notwithstanding receipt of a supervening annulment application in the bankruptcy.

10.37 In *Jenkins v Official Receiver* a bankruptcy order had been made against Mr Jenkins on 26 April 2005. Approximately 11 months later just before automatic discharge kicked in, the OR applied for a BRO on the grounds that while he was an undischarged bankrupt Mr Jenkins had remained a director of a company of which he was the sole shareholder and he had not distinguished between his own money and that of the company. Subsequently the bankrupt applied to have his bankruptcy annulled on the ground that the bankruptcy debts had been paid in full and on 17 July 2006 an annulment order was made and the bankruptcy petition dismissed. At the same hearing, the court went on to make a 4 year BRO, due to expire on 16 July 2010, on the ground that the bankrupt had acted as a director whilst a bankrupt and had used the company monies as his own.

10.38 On appeal the bankrupt argued that the effect of the annulment of his bankruptcy should have been to restore him to the position he was in before his bankruptcy, and therefore he should not be restricted in his activities by a BRO. Rimer J dismissed this ground of appeal and found that the relevant provisions clearly demonstrated that the court had jurisdiction to make a BRO in circumstances where the application had been issued prior to the annulment. In dismissing further grounds of appeal (to the effect that Mr Jenkins required to act as a director to make a living and that it had not been alleged that he had done anything culpable), the judge held:

> 'The purpose of [a BRO] is to protect the public in three senses, namely by
>
> (i) keeping bankrupts whose conduct has merited such an order 'off the road';
> (ii) by deterring them from repeating such conduct; and
> (iii) by deterring others. Having regard to Mr Jenkins's defiant insistence that he should be entitled to re-write the insolvency legislation for his own personal convenience so that he could continue to run his company in his own somewhat irresponsible way, it appears to me in no manner surprising that the registrar concluded that this was a case in which an order had to be made.'

---

114 IR86, r 6.244(1) or IRN91, r 6.236(1).

115 [2007] EWHC 1402 (Ch), [2007] BPIR 740.

What happens after a bankruptcy restrictions order has been made?

10.39 Copies of the BRO must be sent to the OR and the bankrupt as follows:

- Where the court makes a BRO, it must send two sealed copies to the SoS or OR.[116]

- The SoS or OR must send a sealed copy of the order to the bankrupt[117] as soon as reasonably practicable after receipt of the sealed copy of the order from the court.

10.40 The order will come into effect as soon as it is made[118] and will cease to have effect from the date specified in the order.[119]

What is an interim bankruptcy restrictions order and what is its purpose?

10.41 An interim BRO is an order obtained from the court which applies pending the hearing of the full application for a BRO. For the court to make an interim BRO, the SoS or OR acting on his behalf, must demonstrate that it is in the public interest to make the order,[120] in addition to demonstrating that the final order is likely to be made.[121] Thus, it is not necessarily the case that an interim BRO will be made simply because the applicant considers that it has a strong case for a final BRO being made. The test contemplates a requirement to demonstrate that the public is in some immediate need of protection. In all other respects the application process is the same.

10.42 An interim BRO has exactly the same effect as a BRO.[122] It comes into force when it is made[123] and ceases to have effect in the following circumstances:

- on determination of the application for the BRO;[124]

- on the acceptance of a BRU by the bankrupt;[125]

- if the court discharges the interim BRO on the application of the applicant or the bankrupt.[126]

---

116 IR86, r 6.244(2) or IRN91, r 6.236(2).
117 IR86, r 6.244(3) or IRN91, r 6.236(3).
118 IA86, Sch 4A, para 4(1)(a).
119 IA86, Sch 4A, para 4(1)(b).
120 *Official Receiver v Merchant* [2006] BPIR 1525.
121 IA86, Sch 4A, para 5(2)(a) and (b).
122 IA86, Sch 4A, para 5(4)(a).
123 IA86, Sch 4A, para 5(4)(b).
124 IA86, Sch 4A, para 5(5)(a).
125 IA86, Sch 4A, para 5(5)(b).
126 IA86, Sch 4A, para 5(5)(c).

What are the consequences of a bankruptcy restrictions order?

10.43 Many of the limitations that apply to an undischarged bankrupt also apply to a person against whom a bankruptcy restrictions order is made (or has given a bankruptcy restrictions undertaking). The main disqualifications and effects are:

- it is an offence for a person to act as a director of a company or directly or indirectly to take part in or be concerned in the promotion, formation or management of a company, without permission of the court;[127]
- it is an offence for a person to act as a director of a company or directly or indirectly to take part in or be concerned in the promotion, formation or management of a limited liability partnership, without permission of the court;[128]
- the person is not qualified to act as an insolvency practitioner while a bankruptcy restrictions order is in force in respect of him;[129]
- it is an offence if he acts as receiver or manager of the property of a company;[130]
- it is an offence:[131]
  - — either alone or jointly with any other person, to obtain credit to the extent of the prescribed amount [ie £500[132]] or more without giving the person from whom he obtains it the relevant information about his status; or
  - — to engage (whether directly or indirectly) in any business under a name other than that in which he was adjudged bankrupt without disclosing to all persons with whom he enters into any business transaction the name in which he was so adjudged;
- the person cannot be a charity trustee[133] or the trustee of a pensions trust scheme[134] or hold various public offices.[135]

---

127 Company Directors Disqualification Act 1986, s 11(1).
128 Limited Liability Partnerships Regulations 2001, reg 4(2).
129 IA86, s 390(5). Under IA86, s 389 it is an offence to act as an insolvency practitioner when not qualified to do so.
130 IA86, s 31(1).
131 IA86, s 360.
132 See Insolvency Proceedings (Monetary Limits) (Amendment) Order 2004.
133 See Charities Act 1993, s 72.
134 See Pensions Act 1995, s 29.
135 The full details of which are set out in a comprehensive guide on the Insolvency Service website at http://www.insolvency.gov.uk/insolvencyprofessionandlegislation/ScheduleBankruptcyRestrictionsJuly2009.pdf.

In addition, various professionals, such as solicitors, barristers, accountants, surveyors and estate agents have differing regulations applicable in the event of a bankruptcy restrictions order.

Definitions

10.44 For the purposes of discharge and related orders the following definitions apply:

- The phrase 'before petition' is construed in accordance with s 351(c), IA86[136] ie the period ending with the presentation of the petition.
- Any reference to a number of months or years before petition is to that period ending with the presentation of the bankruptcy petition.
- The phrase 'the initial period' means the period between the presentation of the bankruptcy petition and the commencement of the bankruptcy ie the bankruptcy order.
- The phrase 'excessive pension contribution' is construed in accordance with s 342A, IA86.[137]
- The meaning of 'preference' is set out in s 340, IA86.[138] An individual gives a preference if 'that person is one of the individual's creditors or a surety or guarantor for any of his debts or other liabilities,[139] and the individual does anything or suffers anything to be done which (in either case) has the effect of putting that person into a position which, in the event of the individual's bankruptcy, will be better than the position he would have been in if that thing had not been done.'[140]
- The term 'undervalue' is construed in accordance with s 339, IA86.[141]

Income payments orders

What is an income payments order and when can one be made?

10.45 The bankrupt's income is susceptible to claims by the trustee in bankruptcy. Sections 310 and 310A IA86 sets out the basis on which surplus income can be claimed by a trustee for the benefit of the estate. Chapters 16 and 16A of the IR86 cover the detailed processes that must be followed. The order may only be for payment of a sum out of the surplus income of the bankrupt, ie after allowing the bankrupt what appears to be necessary to meet

---

136 IA86, Sch 4A, para 2(4).
137 IA86, Sch 4A, para 2(4).
138 IA86, Sch 4A, para 2(4). See also chapter 17 for more detail.
139 IA86, s 340(3)(a) or INO89, art 313(3)(a).
140 IA86, s 340(3)(b) or INO89, art 313(3)(b).
141 IA86, Sch 4A, para 2(4).

his reasonable domestic needs and those of this family.[142] The payments can be directed to be made either by the bankrupt or by his employer[143] and must be for a specified period of time.[144]

What is the definition of necessary and reasonable expenses?

10.46 The definition of a 'necessary' and 'reasonable' expense has been examined in a number of cases. What is clear is that what the bankrupt's reasonable domestic needs are depends upon the circumstances of each case.[145] In practice the OR applies a set of standard criteria, based on the Consumer Credit Counselling Service figures for reasonable expenditure depending upon the bankrupt's family circumstances. Those criteria are published on the Insolvency Service website and are varied regularly.

What is the definition of income and does it include pensions?

10.47 For the purposes of IA86, s 310 the income of the bankrupt comprises every payment in the nature of income which is from time to time made to him or to which he from time to time becomes entitled to, including:[146]

- any payment in respect of the carrying on of any business or in respect of any office or employment; and
- (despite anything in s 11 or 12 of the Welfare Reform and Pensions Act 1999) any payment under a pension scheme but excluding any of the following payments:
  - payments by way of guaranteed minimum pension;[147] and
  - payments giving effect to the bankrupt's protected rights as a member of a pension scheme.[148]

In this respect 'guaranteed minimum pension' and 'protected rights' have the same meaning as in the Pension Schemes Act 1993.[149]

The courts can make an income payments order to be paid from a pension as long as the bankrupt has sufficient income to meet their reasonable domestic

142 IA86, s 310(2) or INO89, art 283(2).
143 IA86, s 310(3) or INO89, art 283(3).
144 IA86, s 310 or INO89, art 283.
145 See *Re X (A Bankrupt)* [1996] BPIR 494, *Boyden v Watson* [2004] BPIR 1131 and, in particular, *Re Rayatt (a Bankrupt)* [1998] BPIR 495 and *Scott v Davis* [2003] BPIR 1009, where the issue was whether the payment of school fees for private education could amount to a reasonable domestic need of the bankrupt.
146 IA86, s 310(7).
147 IA86, s 310(8)(a).
148 IA86, s 310(8)(6).
149 IA86, s 310(9).

needs. In this respect, a lump sum payment payable pursuant to such pension entitlement is susceptible to an income payments order.[150]

What is the procedure for applying for an income payments order?

10.48 The application can only be made by the trustee (who may be the OR) and must be made before the discharge of the bankrupt.[151] Rule 6.189, IR86 sets out the process for an application for an IPO as follows:

- The trustee must send the bankrupt notice of the applications at least 28 days before the hearing.
- The notice of application must include a copy of the application and a short statement of the grounds being relied on.
- The notice must also inform the bankrupt that he must attend the hearing unless he submits a written consent confirming agreement to the order at least 7 days before the hearing.
- The notice must also state that if the bankrupt attends the hearing he will be given an opportunity to show cause why the order should not be made.
- Where the court makes an IPO, a sealed copy of the order must be sent by the trustee to the bankrupt.[152]
- If the IPO is made under s 310(3)(b), IA86 (ie by directing payment by an employer or other person) a sealed copy of the order must also be sent by the trustee to that person.

What is the procedure for varying an income payments order?

10.49 Where an IPO is in force, either the trustee or the bankrupt may apply to the court to vary the terms or discharge the order.[153] The process is as follows:

- If the application is made by the trustee r 6.189, IR86 applies as for the initial order.[154]
- If the application is made by the bankrupt then it must be accompanied by a short statement of the grounds on which the variation is being requested.[155]

---

150 See *Kilvert v Flackett* [1998] BPIR 721 and *C Brooks Thurmond, III v Rajapakse and Rajapakse* [2008] BPIR 283.
151 IA86, s 310(1A) or INO89, art 283(1A).
152 IR86, r 6.190(1) and Form 6.65 or 6.66 or IRN91, r 6.187(1).
153 IR86, r 6.193(1) or IRN91, r 6.190(1).
154 IR86, r 6.193(2) or IRN91, r 6.190(2).
155 IR86, r 6.193(3) or IRN91, r 6.190(3).

- If the court feels that no good cause has been demonstrated then the application can be dismissed[156] but not without the applicant being able to attend the court for a hearing without notice to any other party. At least 7 days' notice must be given for the hearing.

- If the application is not dismissed as above then a hearing date must be fixed, providing at least 28 days' notice to the non-applicant (bankrupt or trustee) of the venue together with a copy of the application or statement submitted to the court.[157]

- The trustee is entitled to submit a report to court of any relevant facts at least 7 days before[158] whether or not he plans to attend the hearing. This is regardless of whether the trustee is the applicant or not. A copy must be sent to the bankrupt at the same time.

- Immediately after any order is made the court must send sealed copies to the trustee, the bankrupt and the payor (if other than the bankrupt e g employer).

10.50 If an IPO is made under s 310(3)(a), IA86, i e against the bankrupt, and the bankrupt does not comply with it, the trustee may apply to the court under r 6.89, IR86 for the order to be varied, so as to take effect under s 310(3)(b), IA86, i e requiring some other person, generally the bankrupt's employer, to pay.[159] The application may be made without notice to any other party.

Income payments agreement

What is an income payments agreement?

10.51 An alternative to an IPO is an income payments agreement[160] (IPA) available under s 310A, IA86. The trustee in bankruptcy or the OR can enter into an agreement with the bankrupt to make regular payments from income into the estate without the need for an order. The same rules apply as to an IPO. The agreement must be made before discharge[161] has been granted and should be for a specific period which may end after discharge, but must not be for more than 3 years.[162] An IPA may be varied by consent or as a result of an application to the court.[163]

---

156 IR86, r 6.193(4) or IRN91, r 6.190(4).
157 IR86, r 6.193(5) or IRN91, r 6.190(5).
158 IR86, r 6.193(6) or IRN91, r 6.190(6).
159 IR86, r 6.191 and Form 6.67 or IRN91, r 6.188.
160 IA86, s 310A or INO89, art 283A.
161 IR86, r 6.193A(1) or IRN91, r 6.190A(1).
162 IA86, s 310A(5) or INO89, art 283A(5).
163 IR86, r 6.193C or IRN91, r 6.190C.

What is the agreement process?

10.52 The process for putting an agreement in place is very similar to the making of an IPO but without the intervention of the court. As to what might constitute reasonable domestic needs see the discussion above. Exactly the same rules apply as for an IPO as follows:

- An IPA may only be entered into prior to the discharge of the bankrupt.[164]
- The application may only be made by the trustee (who may be the OR) and must be made before the discharge of the bankrupt.[165]
- The agreement must be for a specific period, may end after discharge, but must not be for more than 3 years.[166]
- The OR or trustee must send the IPA to the bankrupt for his approval.[167]
- Within 14 days or any longer period specified by the OR or trustee from the date on which the income payments agreement was sent, the bankrupt must:
  - if he decides to approve the draft income payments agreement, sign the agreement and return it to the OR or trustee; or
  - if he decides not to approve it, notify the OR or trustee in writing of his decision.[168]

What is the procedure for varying an income payments agreement?

10.53 An IPA may be varied by consent or as a result of an application to the court.[169] The following process needs to be followed when an application is made to the court:

- A copy of the original IPA must be attached[170] to the application.
- Regardless of whether the bankrupt, the trustee or OR applies a copy of the application must be served on the other parties at least 28 days before the hearing.[171]
- The court will make any variation order in Form 6.81.[172]

---

164 IR86, r 6.193A(1) or IRN91, r 6.190A(1).
165 IA86, s 310(1A) or INO89, art 283(1A).
166 IA86, s 310A(5) or INO89, art 283(5).
167 IR86, r 6.193A(2) or IRN91, r 6.190A(2).
168 IR86, r 6.193A(3) or IRN91, r 6.190A(3).
169 IR86, r 6.193C or IRN91, r 6.190C.
170 IR86, r 6.193C(1) or IRN91, r 6.190C(1).
171 IR86, r 6.193C(2) and (3) IRN91, r 6.190C(2) and (3).
172 IR86, r 6.193C(4) or IRN91, r 6.190C(4).

- Where a third party such as an employer is being required to make the payments then a copy of the order must also be served on them[173] in accordance with r 6.193B(3), IR86.

- Third party costs of this process can be deducted from the specified amount to meet clerical and administration expenses. However a written statement of any costs so deducted must be given to the bankrupt.[174]

The Electronic Individual Insolvency Register

10.54 Since 1986 a searchable register has been maintained of bankruptcy orders and individual voluntary arrangements, however, until 2004 an application had to be made to the Insolvency Service for these details. These records are now available online for free in England and Wales. In Scotland and Northern Ireland a small fee is charged.

What information is recorded on the register?

10.55 The Electronic Individual Insolvency Register (EIIR) is open to the public and has been available online since 2004.[175] The EIIR contains the following details:

- all bankruptcies that are either current, or have ended in the last 3 months;

- all current, interim and final BROs and BRUs;

- all IVAs that are current (concluded arrangements are removed immediately notice is received);

- all fast track voluntary arrangements.

Historical data is not available online but can be made available to financial or other institutions on request.

What information is recorded in the register about a bankruptcy order and when can it be amended?

10.56 The following is recorded on the register:[176]

- the name of the bankrupt,[177] and any other name by which the bankrupt has been known if different to the name in which adjudged bankrupt;[178]

---

173 IR86, r 6.193C(5) or IRN91, r 6.190C(5).
174 IR86, r 6.193C(6) or IRN91, r 6.190C(6).
175 IR86, r 6A.1(4) or IRN91, r 6A.1(4).
176 IR86, r 6A.2.
177 IR86, r 6A.4(3)(a).
178 IR86, r 6A.4(3)(d).

- the name of any business carried on by the bankrupt if other than his own name;[179]
- the gender of the bankrupt;[180]
- the date of birth of the debtor;[181]
- the bankrupt's last known address[182] and the address of any business carried on by the bankrupt;[183]
- the bankrupt's occupation;[184]
- the address at which the OR can be contacted;[185]
- the name[186] and address of any IP appointed as trustee;[187]
- the date the order was made[188] and the date of any previous bankruptcy order if made in the previous 6 years;[189]
- the court reference number as stated on the order;[190]
- the automatic discharge date under s 279 IA86.[191]
- details of any suspension of discharge[192] or subsequent changes;[193]
- details of any early discharge.[194]

10.57 If the SoS becomes aware of any inaccuracy in any information contained in the register then it must be corrected as soon as reasonably practicable.[195]

---

179 IR86, r 6A.4(3)(e).
180 IR86, r 6A.4(3)(a).
181 IR86, r 6A.4(3)(a).
182 IR86, r 6A.4(3)(b).
183 IR86, r 6A.4(3)(e).
184 IR86, r 6A.4(3)(a).
185 IR86, r 6A.4(3)(g).
186 IR86, r 6A.4(3)(f).
187 IR86, r 6A.4(3)(f).
188 IR86, r 6A.4(2)(b).
189 IR86, r 6A.4(3)(c).
190 IR86, r 6A.4(2)(d).
191 IR86, r 6A.4(3)(h).
192 IR86, r 6A.4(4).
193 IR86, r 6A.4(5).
194 IR86, r 6A.4(6).
195 IR86, r 6A.8(1).

Additional restrictions on undischarged bankrupts imposed by other legislation

What changes have been made to these additional restrictions?

10.58 Prior to the enactment of the Enterprise Act 2002 (Disqualification from Office: General) Order 2006[196] these additional restrictions were numerous. This order relaxed a wide variety of additional restrictions imposed on undischarged bankrupts. However the following restrictions do still remain in force and are grouped under associated headings.

What additional restrictions are there in respect of legal offices?

10.59 Section 15 of the Solicitors Act 1974 provides that any current practising certificate held by a solicitor is immediately suspended on the making of a bankruptcy order. The Law Society, on application, may lift the suspension of a practising certificate. There is no such restriction placed on practising barristers although as a matter of courtesy the Bar Council wish to be informed of any order made against members.[197]

An undischarged bankrupt is disqualified from an appointment as chairman of a land tribunal and an existing chairmanship may be revoked upon the making of a bankruptcy order against the chairman.[198]

What additional restrictions are there in respect of financial roles?

10.60 A consumer credit licence held by an individual is terminated if that individual is the subject of a bankruptcy order. However the licence is not specifically terminated if the individual is subject to a BRU/BRO, which are often in force after discharge.[199]

Following the making of the bankruptcy order, an undischarged bankrupt is disqualified from acting as account manager of an account held under the Individual Savings Account Regulations 1998.[200] Regulation 15(1)(b) of the Personal Equity Plan Regulations 1989 disqualifies an undischarged bankrupt from acting as a personal equity plan manager.[201]

Section 72 of the Charities Act 1993 disqualifies anyone who is an undischarged bankrupt (or who has had his/her estate sequestrated) from acting as a trustee of a charity.[202]

---

196 SI 2006/1722.
197 Solicitors Act 1974, ss 12, 15 and 16.
198 Agriculture Act 1947, Sch 9, para 13(4).
199 Consumer Credit Act 1974, s 37(1)(b).
200 Individual Savings Account Regulations 1998, reg 20(1)(b); Enterprise Act 2002 (Disqualification from Office: General) Order 2006, SI 2006/1722, Sch 2(2), para 13.
201 Personal Equity Plan Regulations 1989, reg 15(1)(b).
202 Charities Act 1993, s 72.

Section 29 of the Pensions Act 1995 disqualifies an undischarged bankrupt from being a trustee of a pension scheme, unless the disqualification is waived by the Pensions Regulator on application by the bankrupt.[203]

An undischarged bankrupt is also disqualified from acting as a fiscal representative for an aircraft operator. Written notice of his/her ceasing to act must be given to the Commissioners of HM Revenue and Customs, within 7 days of the disqualifying event taking place.[204]

What additional restrictions are there in respect of registration offices?

10.61 Regulation 5(a)(i) (disqualification for appointment) of the Registration of Births, Deaths and Marriages Regulations 1968 disqualify an undischarged bankrupt from being appointed as a Registrar of Births, Deaths and Marriages.[205]

What additional restrictions are there in respect of housing roles?

10.62 An undischarged bankrupt is disqualified from engaging in estate agency work of any sort otherwise than as an employee of another person. For this purpose the employment of the bankrupt by another person does not include his employment by a body corporate of which he is a director or controller.[206]

Under s 121 of the Housing Act 1985 there is a restriction on the 'right to buy'. The right to buy cannot be exercised if the person, or one of the persons, to whom the 'right to buy' belongs has a bankruptcy petition pending against him/her, or is an undischarged bankrupt.[207]

Where a director/trustee of a registered social landlord (which is a registered charity, an industrial and provident society, or a registered company) has been made bankrupt, the relevant authority (either a local housing authority or a social services authority) may remove them as a director/trustee.[208]

The Secretary of State may remove members of any Housing Corporation if they are adjudged bankrupt (or their estate sequestrated).[209]

What additional restrictions are there in respect of environmental, utilities and transport roles?

10.63 An undischarged bankrupt is disqualified from being or becoming a member of a regional or local flood defence committee.[210]

---

203 Pensions Act 1995, s 29(1)(b).
204 Air Passenger Duty Regulations 1994, reg 7(2)(d).
205 Registration of Births, Deaths and Marriages Regulations 1968, reg 5(a)(i).
206 Estate Agents Act 1979, s 23.
207 Housing Act 1985, s 121.
208 Housing Act 1996, Sch 1, Part 2, para 4.
209 Housing Associations Act 1985, Sch 6, para 3.
210 Environment Act 1995, Sch 5(1), para 3(1)(b).

The Secretary of State may remove a member of the Coal Authority or a member of a regional development agency if that person has been made bankrupt.

A traffic commissioner who has issued an operator's licence may revoke, suspend or curtail it where an individual to whom that licence has been issued is made bankrupt. The official receiver must notify the commissioners at the local Traffic Area Office immediately the bankruptcy order is made.[211] Also a public service vehicle operators' licence or road service licence is similarly terminated if the individual holding that licence is made bankrupt.[212]

---

[211] Goods Vehicles (Licensing of Operators) Act 1995, s 26.
[212] Public Passenger Vehicles Act 1981, s 57(2)(b).

Chapter 11

RESCISSION AND ANNULMENT IN BANKRUPTCY PROCEEDINGS

'Who could believe that, in England, in the 17th century, it was reported by a committee of the House of Commons that a woman died in prison after having been confined 45 years for a debt of £19?'[1]

INTRODUCTION

11.1 This chapter looks at both the rescission and annulment of a bankruptcy order and the circumstances in which these options can be used, together with the process of agreeing the fees, costs and expenses of the trustee and the official receiver (OR).

THE RESCISSION OF A BANKRUPTCY ORDER

What is the difference between a rescission and annulment?

11.2 Section 375(1), IA86 gives the court jurisdiction to review, rescind or vary an order it has made. The jurisdiction is wide, and includes, for example, the power to rescind a bankruptcy order. Although the jurisdiction has been held to be wide,[2] it should not be used where an appeal is more appropriate or to seek to side-step the procedure governing annulment.[3] Rather, rescission is generally confined to situations where there has been a change of circumstances since the order was made.[4] In *Raguz v Scottish and Newcastle Ltd*[5] it was said that the power of review went beyond an appeal if the conditions for the application of the section were satisfied. There had to be 'something new', 'the concept that something has changed' or 'a material difference', and a review could not merely be used to present substantially the same facts or the same arguments but more forcefully and attractively. If there was no change in circumstances, the only way to challenge the order was by appeal.

---

1 B Montagu *Enquiries Respecting the Insolvent Debtors' Bill with the opinions of Dr Paley, Mr Burke, and Dr Johnson, upon Imprisonment for Debt* (1815, London), p 515.

2 See for example *Re RS&M Engineering Co Ltd* [2000] Ch 40.

3 *Inland Revenue Commissioners v Robinson* [1999] BPIR 329.

4 *Fitch v Official Receiver* [1996] 1 WLR 242.

5 [2010] EWHC 1384 (Ch), [2010] BPIR 945.

What factors need to be considered when requesting a rescission?

11.3 The factors to be considered in relation to granting relief under s 375, IA86 were considered by Laddie J in *Papanicola v Humphreys*[6] who said:

(1) The section gives the court a wide discretion to review, vary or rescind any order made in the exercise of the bankruptcy jurisdiction.

(2) The onus is on the applicant to demonstrate the existence of circumstances which justify exercise of the discretion in his favour.

(3) Those circumstances must be exceptional.

(4) The circumstances relied on must involve a material difference to what was before the court which made the original order. In other words, there must be something new to justify the overturning of the original order.

(5) There is no limit to the factors which may be taken into account. They can include, for example, changes which have occurred since the making of the original order and significant facts which, although in existence at the time of the original order, were not brought to the court's attention at that time.

(6) Where the new circumstances relied upon consist of or include new evidence which could have been made available at the original hearing, that, and any explanation by the applicant for the failure to produce it then or any lack of such explanation, are factors which could be taken into account in the exercise of the discretion.

THE ANNULMENT OF A BANKRUPTCY ORDER

When can a bankruptcy order be annulled?

11.4 A bankruptcy order can be annulled in the following circumstances:

- That it ought not to have been made, as no grounds existed at the time the order was made.[7]

- That all the debts and expenses of the bankruptcy have been paid or secured to the satisfaction of the court. This includes the circumstances in which an IVA has been approved.[8]

- Following the approval of an IVA.[9]

---

6 [2005] 2 All ER 418, [2006] BPIR 135 (at para 25).
7 IA86, s 282(1)(a) or INO89, art 256(1)(a).
8 IA86, s 282(1)(b) or INO89, art 256(1)(b).
9 IA86, s 261(2) or INO89, art 235(2).

- Following the approval of a fast-track voluntary arrangement.[10]

The court appears to have no discretion to refuse to annul where the application follows approval of an individual voluntary arrangement.[11]

11.5 A bankruptcy order may generally be annulled at any time whether or not the bankrupt has been discharged.[12] However, the later it is, the more difficult it might be to persuade a court to exercise its discretion to annul the bankruptcy order even if the appropriate grounds are made out[13]. In the case of approval of an IVA an application may not be made during the period in which a challenge can be made by an application under s 262 or 263F, IA86 or while such an application is pending or is subject to appeal.[14]

Does an annulment invalidate any previous actions taken by the official receiver or the trustee?

11.6 Where the court annuls a bankruptcy order it does not invalidate any previous actions by any trustee or the OR appointed. The court may make whatever order is considered appropriate in the circumstances.[15] Further, annulment on the payment in full basis does not deprive the court of jurisdiction subsequent to make a bankruptcy restrictions order, provided that the application for it has been made before the annulment and before the end of the year commencing with the date of the bankruptcy order.[16]

What is the procedure to get a bankruptcy order annulled?

11.7 The procedure relating to annulment applications is governed by rr 6.206–6.214, IR86.[17]

In the case of an application under s 282(1)(a), IA86 (ie a bankruptcy order ought not to have been made):

- The application must be supported by evidence of the grounds.
- Notice must be given to the OR and any trustee who has been appointed.[18]
- Notice must also be given to the petitioning creditor.[19]

---

10 IA86, s 263(D)(3) or INO89, art 237(D)(3).
11 IA86, ss 261(2) and 263D(3).
12 IA86, s 282(3) or INO89, art 256(3).
13 *Gill v Quinn* [2004] EWHC 883 (Ch), [2005] BPIR 129.
14 IA86, ss 261(3) and 263D(4) or IO89, arts 235(3) and 237D(4).
15 IA86, s 282(4) or IO89, art 256(4).
16 *Jenkins v The Official Receiver* [2007] EWHC 1402 (Ch), [2007] BPIR 740.
17 IRN91, rr 203–212.
18 IR86, r 6.206(4) or IRN91, r 6.203(4).
19 IR86, r 6.206(5) or IRN91, r 6.203(5).

- If the application is made by a person other than the bankrupt, the bankrupt must be given notice.[20]

- No period for notice is prescribed; it must be 'sufficient time to enable them to be present at the hearing'.[21]

- The court may annul at the initial hearing or it may give directions depending on the basis on which the relief is sought.

- There is no requirement for the OR or trustee to make a report to the court.

- The court will have to deal with re-listing the petition unless it decides to annul the bankruptcy order and dismiss the petition at the same hearing.

11.8 In the case of an application under s 282(1)(b), IA86 (ie payment in full):

- Again, the application must be supported by evidence.[22]

- Notice is given only to the OR and any trustee appointed[23] and to the bankrupt if it is not his application.[24]

- Notice should be not less than 28 days before the hearing.[25]

- The trustee must file a report not less than 21 days before the hearing[26] and send it to the applicant at least 14 days before the hearing.[27] The trustee must also send his report to the OR at least 21 days before the hearing.[28]

- The trustee must attend the hearing.[29] This is one of the most frequently breached rules and it may be the subject of a proposal to change.

- The OR may attend.[30]

In either case, the application should specify whether it is made under s 282(1)(a) or (b), IA86.[31]

---

20 IR86, r 6.206(6) or IRN91, r 6.203(6).
21 IR86, r 6.206(4)(b) or IRN91, r 6.203(4)(b).
22 IR86, r 6.206(2) or IRN91, r 6.203(2).
23 IR86, r 6.206(4) or IRN91, r 6.203(4).
24 IR86, r 6.206(6) or IRN91, r 6.203(6).
25 IR86, r 6.206(4)(b) or IRN91, r 6.203(4)(b).
26 IR86, r 6.207(2) or IRN91, r 6.204(2).
27 IR86, r 6.207(4) or IRN91, r 6.204(4).
28 IR86, r 6.207(5) or IRN91, r 6.204(5).
29 IR86, r 6.210(1) or IRN91, r 6.207(1).
30 IR86, r 6.210(2) or IRN91, r 6.207(2).
31 IR86, r 206(1).

When is a stay of advertising and/or proceedings needed?

11.9 An application for an annulment may be preceded or accompanied by an application for either a stay of advertising or the proceedings generally. This will avoid additional unnecessary costs from being incurred by the OR or the trustee. The application must generally be made on notice to the OR and any trustee.

What is a stay of advertising?

11.10 The advertisement of the bankruptcy may be stayed by the court on application of the bankrupt or a creditor.[32] This is usually done where the applicant intends to apply for an annulment. Any application made to the court must be supported by a witness statement and notice given to the OR and any trustee. However, one of the practical difficulties that this gives rise to is whether all creditors have been identified or provided for in respect of an application for payment in full. Under r 6.209, IR86, if the trustee reports to the court that there are known creditors of the bankrupt who have not proved, the court may direct contact with those creditors or advertisement of the fact of the application. Therefore, it is not necessarily the case that an early application for an annulment, together with a stay of advertisement, might have the desired effect of avoiding publicity.

What is the procedure for applying for a stay of advertising and/or proceedings generally?

11.11 On application, the court can make an interim order to stay the proceedings,[33] which may or may not include a stay of advertisement depending on the point in the proceedings at which the application is made. An application may be made by any party and, except for an application to stay the bankruptcy proceedings, the application may be made without notice to any other party.[34] However, copies of any application must be sent to the OR[35] or trustee in sufficient time to make representations if necessary.[36]

It should be noted that any stay of proceedings does not affect the application of the rules laid down for annulments generally.[37]

Who must the court notify of the stay?

11.12 Any order made by the court must be served on:[38]

- the applicant;

---

32 IR86, rr 6.34(3) and 6.46(3) or IRN91, rr 6.031(3) and 6.043(3).
33 IR86, r 6.208(1) or IRN91, r 6.205(1).
34 IR86, r 6.208(2) or IRN91, r 6.205(2).
35 IR86, r 6.208(3) or IRN91, r 6.205(3).
36 IR86, r 6.208(3) or IRN91, r 6.205(3).
37 IR86, r 6.208(4) or IRN91, r 6.205(4).
38 IR86, r 6.208(5) or IRN91, r 6.205(5).

- the OR; and
- the trustee (if any).

Annulment under s 282(1)(a), IA86

Who may apply?

11.13 The IA86 does not specify who may make an application to annul a bankruptcy order on the grounds that it ought not to have been made. Commonly, the application is made by the bankrupt. However, applications are frequently made by former spouses who perceive that the bankruptcy order was sought by the debtor on their own petition, as a tactical step in order to avoid an application for ancillary relief.

Who needs to be advised after the annulment hearing has been fixed by the court?

11.14 Where the application is made under s 282(1)(a), IA86, the applicant is required to give copies of the application and details of the venue to the OR and any other trustee that has been appointed,[39] in sufficient time to enable them to be present at the hearing. In addition, notice must be given to the petitioner on whose petition the bankruptcy was made,[40] and where the application is made by someone other than the bankrupt notice must also be given to the bankrupt.[41]

On what grounds can the annulment be sought?

11.15 The circumstances under which the court may annul under s 282(1)(a), IA86 are wide. It is, however, essential that the ground being used was available at the time the bankruptcy order was made and not one that arose subsequently.[42] Whilst the court can consider evidence that was not previously before the court, that evidence must to relate to the state of affairs as at the date of the order, and not matters subsequent thereto. An annulment application should not be used to re-open issues determined by the petition,[43] nor should it be used as an alternative to an appeal.

11.16 There are many grounds upon which the debtor might seek to annul the bankruptcy order, for example:

- the debtor's non attendance at the hearing of the bankruptcy petition;[44]

---

39 IR86, r 6.206(4) or IRN91, r 6.203(4).
40 IR86, r 6.206(5) or IRN91, r 6.203(5).
41 IR86, r 6.206(6) or IRN91, r 6.203(6).
42 *Re a Debtor (68 of 1992)* [1996] BPIR 478 and, on appeal, *Royal Bank of Scotland v Farley* [1996] BPIR 638.
43 *Balendran v The Law Society* [2004] EWHC 495 (Ch), [2004] BPIR 859.
44 *Hope v Premierpace (Europe) Limited* [1999] BPIR 695.

- the debt not being a petitionable debt;[45]
- the petition being an abuse of the process.

However, the court retains discretion whether to grant the annulment even if the grounds are made out. The court adopts a two stage test: first, whether at the time that the bankruptcy order was made any ground existed on the basis of which the order ought not to have been made, and secondly whether or not to annul the bankruptcy order.[46] The annulment will not be allowed simply because the petitioning creditor consents or does not argue to the contrary.[47] The bankruptcy order may stand even if it was purportedly based on a judgment against someone other than the debtor, even when it was clear that it was the debtor indebted to the creditor.[48] The bankruptcy order will not be annulled if there is strong prima facie evidence requiring investigation that the bankrupt has concealed his assets from his trustee[49] or there is a likelihood that the bankrupt would be made bankrupt again.[50] If the debtor's conduct is significantly inappropriate, then the court may not exercise its discretion in his favour on an annulment application, even if a valid new point has been raised.[51]

How in practice are the grounds made out?

11.17 If the debtor demonstrates that he failed to attend the hearing and that, had he done so, he would have established good grounds for the petition to be dismissed, then the court may annul the bankruptcy order.[52] An annulment might be obtained if it subsequently transpires that there was no petitionable debt, either because it was not a liquidated sum[53] or because the petition was an abuse of the process.[54] However, the court will not annul a bankruptcy order made on a petition based on tax assessments if it later transpires that there was no such liability.[55] The tax assessments will stand unless challenged under the statutory procedure.[56] However, it might be annulled if HMRC is later found to

---

45 *Hope v Premierpace (Europe) Limited* [1999] BPIR 695 and *Thornhill v Atherton* [2004] EWCA Civ 1858, [2005] BPIR 437.

46 *Society of Lloyds v Waters* [2001] BPIR 698.

47 *Housiaux v HM Customs and Excise* [2003] EWCA Civ 257, [2003] BPIR 858.

48 *Askew v Peter Dominic Ltd* [1997] BPIR 163.

49 *Artman v Artman, Re a Bankrupt (No 622 of 1995)* [1996] BPIR 511.

50 *Artman v Artman, Re a Bankrupt (No 622 of 1995)* [1996] BPIR 511 and *Whig v Whig* [2007] EWHC 1856 (Fam), [2007] BPIR 1418.

51 *Guinan III v Caldwell Associates* [2004] EWHC 3348 (Ch), [2004] BPIR 531.

52 *Hope v Premierpace (Europe) Limited* [1999] BPIR 695 and *Atherton v Ogunlende* [2003] BPIR 21.

53 *Hope v Premierpace (Europe) Limited* [1999] BPIR 695 and *Thornhill v Atherton* [2004] EWCA Civ 1858, [2005] BPIR 437.

54 *Ella v Ella* [2008] EWHC 3258 (Ch), [2009] BPIR 441 and *Paulin v (1) Paulin (2) Cativo Ltd (in Liquidation)* [2009] EWCA Civ 221, [2009] BPIR 572.

55 *Lam v Inland Revenue* [2005] EWHC 592 (Ch), [2009] BPIR 301, *HM Revenue and Customs v Cassells* [2008] EWHC 3180 (Ch) [2009] BPIR 284 and *Flett v Her Majesty's Revenue Customs and Daly* [2010] EWHC 2662 (Ch) [2010] BPIR 1075.

56 See also *Cullinan v Commissioners of Inland Revenue* [2000] BPIR 996 and *Owen v Her Majesty's Revenue and Customs* [2007] EWHC 395 (Ch), [2008] BPIR 164.

be in breach of its obligations to the debtor under the Disability Discrimination Act 1995[57] or because the debtor lacked mental capacity.[58]

11.18 Solvency, or lack of it, is important. In borderline cases, a critical factor can be whether the debtor can demonstrate his ability to satisfy the petition debt and meet his other liabilities.[59] A spouse will commonly seek an annulment of a bankruptcy order made against their spouse (usually on their own petition) where they perceive that the application was motivated by a desire to prejudice an ancillary relief application.[60] In *Paulin v (1) Paulin (2) Cativo Ltd (in Liquidation)*,[61] a wife's application to annul her husband's bankruptcy order on the basis that he had provided a substantially dishonest statement of affairs, the Court of Appeal held:

- The court might annul a bankruptcy order if it concluded that, on the date of that order, the bankrupt was able to pay his debts, but it thereupon had a discretion whether to annul the order. It was well-established that the enquiry, into whether (on the relevant date) the bankrupt was able to pay his debts was an enquiry not into whether his liabilities exceeded his assets (balance sheet insolvency), but into whether he could meet his liabilities when they were due (cash flow insolvency).

- A bankruptcy order could also be annulled if it amounted to an abuse of the court's process. The bankruptcy court was able to protect the integrity of its process by striking out a petition abusive of it and consequentially annulling an order wrongly granted upon it. But if the debtor was unable to pay his debts on the date of his petition, its presentation was not, save in extreme cases, an abuse of the process of the court.

- On an application to annul a bankruptcy order the onus of proof lay on the applicant, W. She had to prove, to the civil standard, that on the date of the bankruptcy order H was able to pay his debts. There was no sliding civil standard.

- Where the applicant for annulment of a bankruptcy order made on a debtor's petition established that there was no balance sheet insolvency

---

57 *Haworth v Cartmel and Revenue and Customs Commissioners* [2011] EWHC 36 (Ch), [2011] BPIR 428. See also *Hunt v Fylde Borough Council* [2008] BPIR 1368, a similar case involving a petition based on council tax arrears. However, Lewison J did observe in *Owen v Her Majesty's Revenue and Customs* [2007] EWHC 395 (Ch), [2008] BPIR 164: 'Sympathetic though one must be to Mr Owen's mental problems, the fact remains that even those with mental problems must pay their tax.'

58 *Haworth v Cartmel and Revenue and Customs Commissioners* [2011] EWHC 36 (Ch), [2011] BPIR 428.

59 *Owo-Samson v Barclays Bank plc (No.1)* [2003] EWCA Civ 714, [2003] BPIR 1373.

60 See for example *F v F (Divorce: Insolvency: Annulment of Bankruptcy Order)* [1994] 1 FLR 359, *Couvaras v Wolf* [2002] 2 FLR 107 and *Forder v Forder* [2002] EWCA Civ 1527.

61 [2009] EWCA Civ 221, [2009] BPIR 572.

(ie his assets exceeded his liabilities) the evidential onus shifted to the debtor to establish commercial insolvency (ie nevertheless he was unable to pay his debts).

- A person made bankrupt on his own petition who was shown both to have made a substantially dishonest statement of affairs and, on the date of presentation, to have held assets which substantially exceeded his liabilities would find it hard to resist annulment on the basis that he was nevertheless unable to pay his debts.

This echoed the earlier decision of Munby J in *Whig v Whig*,[62] a more common case, where it was concluded that the husband had not made substantial under declaration of his assets and there was, as at the date of the bankruptcy order, no tangible and immediate prospect of the husband being able to pay his debts. Munby J concluded:

- The burden of proving that the bankruptcy order ought not to have been made rested on the wife as the applicant, albeit on the balance of probabilities.

- In considering whether the bankruptcy order ought not to have been made, the test as to whether the husband was 'unable to pay to his debts' was not whether his assets exceeded his liabilities but whether he was unable to pay those debts at the time they were due.

- If the husband was unable to pay his debts at the date of the bankruptcy order, the fact that his motive may have been to spite the wife and frustrate her claim to ancillary relief was neither here nor there – if his motive was corrupt the court would no doubt scrutinise with some care the self-serving assertion that he was insolvent but, if it was satisfied that he was indeed insolvent in the sense set out above, the court could not annul the bankruptcy order under s 282(1)(a) of the Act.

- Even if an annulment order had been made, it was almost inevitable that the former matrimonial home would have to be sold in order to enable the husband to pay off his commercial creditors, bearing in mind that any ancillary relief order would have to make provision for the payment of the debts owing to the commercial creditors. It was difficult to see how this could be achieved without a sale of the former matrimonial home.

- A further difficulty would arise in the event of an annulment order concerning the trustee's costs. The starting point would be that the petitioner for bankruptcy (here the husband) should pay the trustee in bankruptcy's costs and even if, contrary to his powerful argument for a

---

62 [2007] EWHC 1856 (Fam), [2007] BPIR 1418.

charge on the husband's assets, the trustee in bankruptcy were not awarded such a charge, it would remain open to him to petition for the husband's bankruptcy.

11.19 Therefore the key test is one of insolvency, rather than motivation. However, in practice, the less insolvent an individual is, the more likely that the bankruptcy order on their own petition is motivated by a desire to spite their former spouse.

Annulment under s 282(1)(b), IA86

Who may apply?

11.20 The IA86 does not specify who may make an application to annul a bankruptcy order on the grounds that the bankruptcy debts and expenses have been paid in full. Commonly, the application is made by the debtor, either very shortly after the bankruptcy order or later, when some step has been taken by the trustee in bankruptcy to realise the debtor's interest in the matrimonial home. An application may be made by a third party, commonly a spouse who might use this route, if available, if the bankruptcy is perceived as an abuse of process to stymie an ancillary relief application. It is not uncommon for a trustee in bankruptcy himself to make an application at the end of the bankruptcy, where, despite the full administration of the estate and the payment of debts and expenses in full, assets still remain; it is usually cheaper than preparing assignments in respect of all the remaining assets. The OR has successfully sought an annulment in a case where there was only one proving creditor, who had withdrawn its proof.[63]

What is included in an annulment application?

11.21 The application must specify the ground on which it is being made[64] and must be supported by a witness statement setting out all the facts required by the court. r 6.211, IR86 specifies the matters which must be proved, namely:

- that all the bankruptcy debts which have been proved have been paid in full;
- that any debt which is disputed or related to a claim by a creditor who has proved, but cannot be traced, has been secured by payment into court or entering into a bond.[65]

As to the operation of and importance of r 6.211, IR86 see *Re Robertson (a Bankrupt)*,[66] to the effect that whilst debts had to be paid in accordance with

---

63 *Official Receiver v McKay* [2009] EWCA Civ 467, [2009] BPIR 1061. Strangely, this was the hearing of the debtor's appeal against the annulment having been granted.

64 IR86, r 6.206(1) or IRN91, r 6.203(1).

65 IR86, r 6.211(2) and (3) or IRN91, r 6.208(2) and (3).

66 [1989] 1 WLR 1139.

the Insolvency Rules, that did not mean payment simply of those creditors who had proved; other creditors (whether identified or not) would have to be given an opportunity to prove in the bankruptcy. Thus a bankrupt cannot achieve an annulment merely by paying identified creditors who had submitted a proof. The court will then fix a venue for the hearing.

Who needs to be advised after the annulment hearing has been fixed by the court?

11.22 The applicant is required to give copies of the application and details of the venue to the OR and any other trustee that has been appointed[67] not less than 28 days before the hearing. In addition, where the application is made by someone other than the bankrupt notice must be given to the bankrupt.[68]

What does the trustee's report contain on an application for annulment on the grounds of payment in full?

11.23 The trustee's report will contain the following:

- the circumstances leading to the bankruptcy;[69]
- a summary of the bankrupt's assets and liabilities;[70]
- details of all known creditors who may have claims but have not proved;[71]
- any other relevant matters;[72]
- the extent (if any) to which, and the manner in which, the debts and expenses of the bankruptcy have been paid or secured;[73]
- the extent to which any security is satisfactory.[74]

In practice, the trustee's report plays an important role in determining in assisting the court as to:

- the extent to which creditors have actually been identified and paid in full; and
- whether there are relevant circumstances that would prevent the court exercising its discretion to grant the annulment.

---

67 IR86, r 6.206(4) or IRN91, r 6.203(4).
68 IR86, r 6.206(6) or IRN91, r 6.203(6).
69 IR86, r 6.207(2)(a) or IRN91, r 6.204(2)(a).
70 IR86, r 6.207(2)(b) or IRN91, r 6.204(2)(b).
71 IR86, r 6.207(2)(c) or IRN91, r 6.204(2)(c).
72 IR86, r 6.207(2)(d) or IRN91, r 6.204(2)(d).
73 IR86, r 6.207(3) or IRN91, r 6.204(3).
74 IR86, r 6.207(3) or IRN91, r 6.204(3).

Who gets a copy of the trustee's report?

11.24 The OR or the trustee must file a copy of the report in court at least 21 days before the date fixed for the hearing.[75] In practice this requirement is often waived, as is the requirement for the OR or trustee to attend court under r 6.210(1), IR86, in particular if the application has been made under s 282(1)(b), IA86 and demonstrates that the debts have been paid in full.

A copy of the report must be sent to the applicant at least 14 days before the hearing. Further witness statements answering statements made in the report may be filed with copies being sent to all parties.[76] Additionally, if the OR is not also the trustee, he may file an additional report at least 7 days before the hearing. A copy must be sent to the applicant at the same time.[77]

What notice has to be given to known creditors who have not proved in the bankruptcy?

11.25 Where the application for annulment is made under s 282(1)(b), IA86 and it has been reported to the court under r 6.207(2)(c), IR86 that there are known creditors of the bankrupt who have not proved, the court may:

- direct the trustee or, if no trustee has been appointed, the OR to send notice of the application to such of those creditors as the court thinks ought to be informed of it, with a view to their proving their debts (if they so wish) within 21 days;[78] and
- direct the trustee or, if no trustee has been appointed, the OR to advertise the fact that the application has been made, so that creditors who have not proved may do so within a specified time;[79] and
- adjourn the application meanwhile, for any period not less than 35 days.[80]

Who must attend an annulment hearing?

11.26 The following people must attend:

- The trustee must attend the hearing of the application.[81]
- The OR, if he is not the trustee, may attend, but is not required to do so unless he has filed a report under r 6.207, IR86.[82]

---

75 IR86, r 6.207(1) or IRN91, r 6.204(1).
76 IR86, r 6.207(4) or IRN91, r 6.204(4).
77 IR86, r 6.207(5) or IRN91, r 6.204(5).
78 IR86, r 6.209(a) or IRN91, r 6.206(a).
79 IR86, r 6.209(b) or IRN91, r 6.206(b).
80 IR86, r 6.209(c) or IRN91, r 6.206(c).
81 IR86, r 6.210(1) or IRN91, r 6.209(1).
82 IR86, r 6.210(2) or IRN91, r 6.209(2).

What matters need to be proved at an annulment application based on the premise of payment in full?

11.27 As expressly stated in the statute, the court may annul a bankruptcy order if it at any time appears to that, to the extent required by the rules, the bankruptcy debts and the expenses of the bankruptcy have all, since the making of the order, been either paid, or secured for to the satisfaction of the court.[83]

This is expanded upon in r 6.211, IR86 which sets out the matters which must, in an application under s 282(1)(b), IA86, be proved to the satisfaction of the court.[84] Subject to r 6.211(3), IR86, all bankruptcy debts which have been proved must have been paid in full.[85] If:

- a debt is disputed, or
- a creditor who has proved can no longer be traced,

the bankrupt must have given such security (in the form of money paid into court, or a bond entered into with approved sureties) as the court considers adequate to satisfy any sum that may subsequently be proved to be due to the creditor concerned and (if the court thinks fit) costs.[86] Where security has been given in the case of an untraced creditor, the court may direct that particulars of the alleged debt, and the security, be advertised in such manner as it thinks fit.[87] If advertisement is so ordered, and no claim on the security is made within 12 months from the date of the advertisement (or the first advertisement, if more than one), the court shall, on application in that behalf, order the security to be released.[88]

11.28 In *Halabi v London Borough of Camden*[89] John Jarvis QC, sitting as a High Court judge, set out what 'payment in full' for these purposes means:

> '[13] … It seems to me that the wording of s 282 is very clear that, in order for the Court to exercise its discretion to order annulment, the bankruptcy debts and expenses of the bankruptcy must have been paid. [Counsel for the bankrupt] argued that the words 'paid' in that section were qualified by the words, 'To the satisfaction of the Court'.
>
> [14] Ingenious as that submission may be, I cannot accept it, because it seems to me that the qualification to the satisfaction of the Court governs the giving of security. A debt is either paid or not paid. It seems to me that the rules make this quite clear. Rule 6.211(2) simply states that:

---

83 IA86, s 282(1)(b).
84 IR86, r 6.211(1).
85 IR 86, r 6.211(2).
86 IR 86, r 6.211(3).
87 IR 86, r 6.211(4).
88 IR 86, r 6.211(4).
89 [2008] EWHC 322 (Ch), [2008] BPIR 370.

> "All bankruptcy debts which have been proved must be paid in full."
>
> There is no qualification to that. There is, however, a qualification in r 6.211(3) as to security being such as:
>
> > "The court considers adequate to satisfy any sum."
>
> [15] It seems to me that the word 'paid' in s 282.1(b) cannot embrace the giving of security for a debt. Even if I were to consider that the word 'paid' was qualified by the words: 'To the satisfaction of the Court' it would not, in my judgment, be sufficient to enable me to say that 'paid' could mean secured by an undertaking. The two are simply quite different concepts. There is support for this analysis in the case of *Re Keet* [1905] 2 KB 666 where Stirling LJ, at 677, said whilst referring to the Bankruptcy Act 1883, s 35:
>
> > "The language of the Act, interpreted according to its natural meaning, appears to me to require a payment in full, a payment of money, something which in an action of law could, under the old practice, have been pleaded as a payment."
>
> I am quite clear that the offering of a security by way of an undertaking would not amount to payment.'

Thus the deputy judge held that the prevailing county court practice of accepting undertakings to pay the bankruptcy debts and expenses out of sums to be borrowed on the security of property otherwise vested in the trustee in bankruptcy was inappropriate; paid meant paid. Considering *Engel v Peri*,[90] the deputy judge therefore held that it was appropriate to make a conditional annulment order, not to take effect until the trustee in bankruptcy notified the court that (1) the bankruptcy debts, (2) statutory interest thereon, (3) the trustee's legal fees, disbursements and time costs, (4) the petitioning creditor's costs and (5) the Secretary of State's fees had been paid, and that security had been provided for a disputed debt.

11.29 There has been an increasing practice of annulment applications being funded by specialist funders, loaning the money to the debtor at interest rates higher than the prevailing rates and usually secured on the matrimonial home that is preserved by the annulment application. Recently, there have been cases where the funder has then sought to enforce against the defaulting debtor. Whether those arrangements are enforceable or not is dependent upon the general law.[91]

---

90 [2002] EWHC 799 (Ch), [2002] BPIR 961.

91 See *Annulment Funding Company Ltd v (1) Cowey (2) Cowlam* [2010] EWCA Civ 711, [2010] BPIR 1304, *Consolidated Finance Ltd v Hunter* [2010] BPIR 1322 and *Cook v Consolidated Finance Ltd* [2010] EWCA Civ 369, [2010] BPIR 1331.

What happens regarding the trustee's remuneration and fees?

11.30 The trustee's remuneration has to be paid or, if disputed, secured for.[92] The expenses of the OR are a charge on the estate of the former bankrupt[93] and must also have been paid.

How is the SoS's fee dealt with on annulment?

11.31 It has been the practice of the Insolvency Service (IS) to submit that the court should, when dealing with an application for annulment where the (former) bankrupt had available assets, take into account the SoS fee when assessing the extent of the bankruptcy expenses even where the arrangements for payments of the debts has not involved payment into the insolvency services account (ISA). A number of applications were made where the arrangements for financing the application involved the (re-)mortgage of a property in which the (former) bankrupt had an interest in and which formed part of the bankruptcy estate. However, the arrangement provided that the funds were held by a solicitor and only become available if the application was successful. As a result funds were not paid into the ISA and non-payment of the SoS fee reduced the overall cost to the (former) bankrupt.

In some cases, the court had accepted this submission and ordered the payment of the SoS fee based on the value of the realisation of the asset. However following amendments to the Insolvency Fees Order 1986 and the Insolvency Proceedings (Fees) Order 2004, the SoS fee is only charged on monies paid into the ISA and if, under the relevant scheme, the creditors are paid without monies being paid into the ISA, the fee does not become chargeable.[94] In some cases matters go wrong after the order has been made and in these circumstances it must be expected that the matter will be taken back to the court not least because undertakings are usually given by the debtor's solicitor. There is also a long standing practice where the SoS fee will not be charged when monies are paid into the ISA just to meet the OR's debit balance on a case.

What happens in relation to disputed debts?

11.32 There are few, if any, reported decisions as to how the court's power under r 6.211(3) IR86 as to the security for disputed debts is to be applied. What usually happens in practice is that the court reaches a view as to how much it is appropriate for the bankrupt to have to secure for, having regard to the nature of the claim, and, as part of the annulment order, provide for a mechanism by which the creditor's claim is either determined or rejected. Obviously, at the annulment stage, the creditor is not a party to the application, and so any determination by the court for the purposes of the annulment is clearly not binding as between the creditor and the bankrupt, hence the mechanism for determining the dispute between them. Such a practice is

---

92 See further **11.32** below.

93 IR86, r 6.212(2) or IRN91, r 6.209(2).

94 Dear IP: No 47. Secretary of State fee in Annulment applications.

analogous with the historic practice adopted by the Bankruptcy Registrars in relation to disputed trustee's remuneration on an annulment application on the payment in full grounds.[95]

11.33 Once the annulment has been procured by the provision of security, the trustee in bankruptcy plays no part in the process, as, at the end of the day, the court determines effectively how the security should be divided up between the creditor and the bankrupt. What the court should not do is to conduct a mini-trial on the hearing of the annulment application to determine what debts should or should not be secured for, especially in the absence of the creditor.

How does the court exercise its discretion on a payment in full annulment application?

11.34 In *Harper v Buchler*[96] in giving directions on such an application, Deputy Registrar Barnett, provided some useful general comments as to the general principles to be applied:

- Statutory interest is not a bankruptcy debt within the meaning of s 382, IA86, so that for the purposes of an application for an annulment under s 282(1)(b), IA86, it is not necessary to show payment of statutory interest in addition to the principal debts.
- The grant of an annulment was a privilege. The court had a completely unfettered discretion in deciding whether or not to grant it.
- The court could have regard to all the circumstances of the case, and not just the conduct of the bankrupt.
- The length of time between the bankruptcy order and the annulment application could be taken into consideration. A prompt application may mean that statutory interest could be disregarded. On a delayed application, the court might consider it.
- The court might also have regard to the source of the funds to discharge the creditors, and whether the bankruptcy estate, if realised, would be sufficient to discharge both the principal debts and any statutory interest.

On the hearing of the full application,[97] Registrar Derrett held that where there was a solvent estate, with more than sufficient assets to pay all the debts, the debtor should not use the fact that third party monies were being used to fund the annulment in circumstances where (in that case, due to increase in property values substantially over time) the bankruptcy estate was in fact solvent, and more than sufficient to pay all the bankruptcy debts, costs and statutory interest. The fact that statutory interest had not been provided, in a case where

---

95 See *Barker v Bajjon* [2008] BPIR 771, referred to at **11.50**.

96 [2004] BPIR 724.

97 *Harper v Buchler (No 2)* [2005] BPIR 577.

the creditors had not received any payment for 10 years since the making of the bankruptcy order, was the ground on which the annulment was refused.[98]

11.35 These views were echoed by Deputy Registrar Schaffer in *Wilcock v Duckworth*,[99] where it was held that the fact of third party funds should not be used to deny creditors a right to statutory interest to which they were otherwise entitled. So, in giving directions as to the extent of the statutory interest that would have to be provided for when Mr Wilcock's application for annulment was determined at an adjourned hearing in the light of the directions, it was directed:

- The court might also have regard to the source of the funds to discharge the creditors, and whether the bankruptcy estate, if realised, would be sufficient to discharge both the principal debts and any statutory interest.

- The issue of whether statutory interest should be paid on annulment only arose when third party funds were being made available to finance the annulment.

- Where a bankrupt sought an annulment in circumstances where there are sufficient assets in the bankruptcy estate to pay all liabilities, costs, fees and expenses, statutory interest should be paid.

- The use of third party funds might avoid the payment of DTI fees, but that should not in principle deprive creditors of interest on their claims.

- If third party funds were linked to the assets in the estate, for example by the third party taking directly or indirectly a charge over the bankruptcy assets (e g by way of remortgage) or by securing an interest in them, then the court would normally require that statutory interest be paid.

- If that cannot be demonstrated to the satisfaction of the court, the onus being on the bankrupt, then any concession the court may consider as to statutory interest will normally be withdrawn.

- To assist the court, the trustee should normally seek the creditor's views as to whether statutory interest was sought by them, and report accordingly.

On the issue as to period, he came up with a novel approach. Whilst it was a case where statutory interest should be considered, it was not fair that the bankrupt should have to carry the burden of interest over the entire period of time since the bankruptcy order. It was equitable that the bankrupt should pay interest from the date of the bankruptcy order whilst the estate was handled by the Official Receiver until his release and then from the appointment of the

---

98 Mr Harper did eventually obtain his annulment; see *Schweppe v Harper* [2008] EWCA Civ 442, [2008] BPIR 1090, an argument about the funding of such annulment.

99 [2005] BPIR 682.

trustee until annulment.[100] However, the court must be satisfied that all creditors have been paid. If the annulment application is made so late that it is not possible to determine whether or not there has been payment in full, the court may exercise its discretion against ordering an annulment.[101]

Can the court grant a conditional annulment?

11.36 There is no power to annul a bankruptcy order conditionally, in other words to make the grant of the order subject to a condition that the debts be paid. However, the court may make an immediate order to take effect at a future time or upon the occurrence of specified events set out in the order.[102]

11.37 A practice had developed at county court level of granting annulments on the basis of undertakings from the bankrupt's solicitor to pay the debts and expenses. The practice sought to address the problem faced by a bankrupt with sufficient equity in a property to pay the bankruptcy debts and expenses who wished to remortgage rather than sell the property. While the bankruptcy order subsisted the loan could not be made. The bankrupt was thus faced with a circular conundrum in that he could not obtain the loan to secure the annulment only because of the bankruptcy which he wished to annul. The 'conditional annulment' was granted on the basis that the bankrupt's solicitor would hold funds advanced on the remortgage while giving undertakings (1) to the mortgagee not to release the funds until the annulment order had been made and (2) to the court to release those funds to pay the debts, costs and expenses of the bankruptcy in full once the order had been made.

11.38 As mentioned, the decision in *Halabi v London Borough of Camden and Another*[103] confirmed that the practice of granting an annulment on the basis of solicitors' undertakings was not available under s 282(1), IA86. Ms Halabi sought to argue that the word 'paid' as it appears in s 282(1)(b), IA86 was qualified by the phrase 'to the satisfaction of the court' which appears in the same section. The judge declined to accept this reading of the subsection, holding that the qualification 'to the satisfaction of the court' in s 282(1)(b), IA86 governs the giving of security rather than the question of whether or not the debts and expenses of the bankruptcy have been paid. Rule 6.211(2), IR86 which lists matters to be proved under s 282(1)(b), IA86 states that 'all bankruptcy debts which have been proved must have been paid in full'. The court held that the word 'paid' in s 282(1)(b), IA86 could not embrace the giving of security for a debt, and the offering of a security by way of an undertaking would not qualify as a payment.

11.39 The court recognised that there were cases in which it was not in the public interest for the bankruptcy to continue, and wished to achieve a means

---

100 This arises little in practice now, because of the impact of IA, s 283A which requires the trustee to take steps to realise the bankrupt's interest in the matrimonial home within 3 years.

101 See *Gill v Quinn* [2004] EWHC 883 (Ch), [2005] BPIR 129.

102 *Engel v Peri* [2002] EWHC 799, [2002] BPIR 961, Ch D.

103 [2008] EWHC 322 (Ch).

by which an annulment based on the remortgaging of a property could proceed. It resolved the problem by granting an order under CPR Part 40.7(1), which states that an order takes effect on the date it is made or on such other date as the court shall specify. The order provided that the annulment would take effect upon the satisfaction of the conditions set out in the order. The order was perfected as soon as it was made, sufficient to satisfy the solicitor's undertaking to the mortgagee and permit the release of funds to enable the payment of the debts and expenses. It was only the effect of the order, rather than the order itself, which was suspended until the conditions were satisfied.

11.40 An example of the type of conditions which might be required by the court is that the OR has notified the court that the bankruptcy debts, costs and expenses have been paid and that there is sufficient security in place to cover any known but unproven debts. In practice, when such orders are made, the court office may deal with them by deferring the drawing up or stamping of the annulment order until such time as satisfactory evidence of the completion of the conditions has been supplied. The precise practice of the courts across the country may well vary.

Who pays the trustee's remuneration in the event of a successful annulment application?

11.41 Whatever happens, the trustee is usually entitled to his costs and expenses. If the bankruptcy proceeds, then he is reimbursed out of realisations. If the annulment proceeds, then the trustee's costs have to be catered for somehow.

11.42 Traditionally, it has usually been the position that:[104]

- in the event of a bankruptcy order being annulled on the basis that the order ought not to have been made, the trustee's remuneration, costs and expenses are paid by the petitioning creditor; and

- in the event of a bankruptcy order being annulled on the basis that the bankruptcy debts have been paid in full, they are borne by the bankrupt.

11.43 In particular, in *Thornhill v Atherton*, the annulment was granted to the bankrupt (on the basis that the order ought not to have been made) but on terms that he had to pay the trustee's costs and expenses because of the delay in making the application. The judge therefore made the annulment order conditional upon the trustee in bankruptcy's costs and expenses being paid by the bankrupt. On appeal, the Court of Appeal held that:

- The trustee was an entirely innocent third party and was entitled to be paid his costs and expenses.

---

[104] See *Butterworth v Soutter* [2000] BPIR 582, *Thornhill v Atherton* [2004] EWCA Civ 1858, [2005] BPIR 437 and *Tetteh v Lambeth LBC* [2008] BPIR 241.

- Substantial costs and expenses had been incurred and the assets in the bankrupt's estate were sufficient to cover them. It was logical and sensible to:
  - — order the bankrupt to pay the trustee's costs and expenses; and
  - — leave the bankruptcy in place until the costs and expenses were paid so that the trustee could use his statutory powers of realisation in order to see that they were paid.
- Such an order was not unfair to the bankrupt.[105]

11.44 Thus, it has became the practice that where an annulment is granted on the basis that the order ought not to have been made, and an order in relation to the trustee in bankruptcy's remuneration, costs and expenses is made against the bankrupt (either because the court has exercised its discretion to do so or because the bankrupt was the petitioning creditor) then the annulment is granted on the basis that those costs remain charged on the bankruptcy estate.

11.45 However, recently, in *London Borough of Redbridge v Mustafa*,[106] the Chancellor applied a more flexible approach. The bankruptcy order as made on a local authority council tax petition, but it later transpired that the bankrupt's liability was nil. The application for an annulment was successful, and the local authority was ordered to pay the costs of the bankrupt, the Official Receiver and the trustee in bankruptcy following the annulment of the bankruptcy order made against her on 31 May 2007 in respect of three liability orders for council tax. The Chancellor allowed the appeal, ordering the debtor to pay the costs of the petition, the trustee in bankruptcy and of the appeal, but with no order for costs in respect of the annulment application, holding:

- The costs arising when a bankruptcy order was annulled comprised four components – the original petition, the annulment application, the Official Receiver's costs and the costs of the trustee in bankruptcy. The first and second were governed by the principles of the Civil Procedure Rules, albeit with some moulding to fit insolvency proceedings as it might not be obvious who was successful. In annulment proceedings conduct might assume a greater importance. The third and fourth were governed by a different regime. Whilst they were generally payable out of the estate, provision for them had to be made on annulment either under IA86, s 282(4) or under the court's inherent jurisdiction so that the court's discretion was not regulated by the CPR although its principles were likely to be equally applicable.

---

105 The trustee in bankruptcy subsequently enforced the payment of those costs and expenses by forcing the realisation of property vested in the bankrupt's estate; see *Thornhill v Atherton (No 2)* [2008] BPIR 691.

106 [2010] EWHC 1105 (Ch), [2010] BPIR 893. See also *Haworth v Cartmel and Revenue and Customs Commissioners* [2011] EWHC 36 (Ch), [2011] BPIR 428.

- The Council was under no duty to obtain an annulment of a bankruptcy order which had been properly made, nor was there any additional burden on it in this regard, although its conduct would be relevant on the issue of costs.

- Where a bankruptcy order was properly made there was no presumption that the petitioner should pay the costs of its annulment. The question in each case was how to exercise the court's discretion.

However, whilst saying that there was no presumption as to the incidence of costs, nothing that the Chancellor said had any impact on the practice as to how the trustee's costs and expenses should be recovered from the bankrupt when the court has determined that it is appropriate for the bankrupt to pay them, as would be the case where an annulment was sought on the basis that it ought not to have been made on the debtor's own petition. His Lordship expressly said in para 26 that the costs and expenses of the official receiver and the trustee in bankruptcy were payable out of the bankrupt's estate, in accordance with the priority laid down by r 6.224, IR86, but on annulment of a bankruptcy order provision had to be made for them, otherwise than as part of the costs of the insolvency proceedings.

11.46 In one case, the trustee was held not to be entitled to his remuneration and expenses. In *Ella v Ella*[107] it was held that a wife's bankruptcy proceedings to enforce a costs order in matrimonial proceedings were an abuse of the bankruptcy process, because the petition was presented when her only enforceable costs order was over-topped by a costs order against her. The bankruptcy proceedings had been used by the parties as a weapon in the family dispute between them and it was not a genuine case where the bankruptcy proceedings had been designed to realise the assets of an insolvent for the benefit of his creditors. The wife issued an annulment application herself under s 282(1)(a), IA86, supported by the husband. The order was annulled, with the husband and wife ordered to bear their own costs of the application. The matrimonial home, the only asset within the jurisdiction, was charged to secure the official receiver's costs, but the judge ordered that the trustees in bankruptcy's costs should not be so charged, as they should have realised these bankruptcy proceedings were highly likely to have been an abuse of the process before those costs were incurred.

How is the trustee's remuneration calculated or assessed in an annulment application?

11.47 The trustee's remuneration is governed by rr 6.138–6.142, IR86. It will normally be a matter for the creditors' committee in circumstances where there is no surplus and where annulment is not sought. However where the trustee's remuneration is not agreed by the creditors committee and requires fixing by the court, or where any party wishes to challenge the level of the trustee's remuneration, an application can be made to the court under s 363(1), IA86.

---

[107] [2008] EWHC 3258 (Ch), [2009] BPIR 441.

The court's discretion in fixing the trustee's costs and expenses is to be exercised in accordance with the guidance set out in the *Practice Statement: The Fixing and Approval of the Remuneration of Appointees.*[108]

11.48 The trustee's remuneration and expenses are frequently challenged by the debtor in a payment in full annulment application. Further, it is not uncommon for a petition creditor to challenge the trustee's costs and remuneration, in the event of it having been ordered to bear the costs after a successful application for an annulment under s 282(1)(a), IA86.

11.49 In *Engel v Peri*[109] the bankruptcy order had been annulled on the grounds that all the costs of the expenses of the bankruptcy had been paid. But the annulment was conditional upon the bankrupt paying the trustee's expenses. The bankrupt challenged the level of the trustee's fees and legal costs. His application was made under s 303, IA86 and a question arose whether he would have standing to challenge the trustee's costs in circumstances where there was no surplus. Ferris J held that where payment of the debts was being made by a third party, and the amount payable would depend on the level of the trustee's fees, then even where there was no surplus the bankrupt, who might feel a moral obligation to indemnify the third party would have standing to challenge the fees under s 303 IA86. Furthermore, the court had an inherent jurisdiction to ensure that the trustee's remuneration is reasonable and proportionate. The application could also have been made under s 363 IA86.

11.50 In *Barker v Bajjon*[110] a dispute had arisen as to the extent of the trustee's entitlement to remuneration in the context of the bankrupt's annulment application. Registrar Simmonds annulled the bankruptcy order, but only on the basis that the bankrupt's solicitors would hold a sum of £25,000 as security for the trustee's costs, and directions were given for those costs to be determined. Those costs came to be determined by the Chief Registrar in accordance with the *Practice Statement.* He upheld the position of the trustee, and ordered payment out of the sum held pursuant to Registrar Simmonds' order of the amount claimed by the trustee in respect of her remuneration together with her disbursements as claimed, a total sum less than the sum held on security.

11.51 In *Brook v Reed (Trustee in Bankruptcy of the estate of Helen Brook)*[111] the Court of Appeal had to consider the application of the *Practice Statement* to a challenge to the trustee's remuneration and expenses on an annulment

---

108 [2004] BCC 912.

109 [2002] EWHC 799 (Ch), [2002] BPIR 961. See also *Hirani v Rendle* [2003] EWHC 2358 (Ch), [2004] BPIR 274, where the trustee was ordered to file to file a witness statement containing an itemised breakdown of his remuneration, costs and expenses incurred as the trustee, such breakdown to include in respect of each item a narrative explanation which is in the reasonable opinion of the trustee sufficient to explain what that item relates to, together with details of the person and their position who carried out the work, the time spent, the relevant charge out rate and the amount claimed. Both were pre-Practice Statement cases.

110 [2008] BPIR 771.

111 [2011] EWCA Civ 331.

application. The amounts had been heavily reduced by a judge (sitting with two assessors) on a hearing without being referred to the *Practice Statement*. The bankrupt appealed further. Nonetheless, the Court of Appeal found that the judge had applied what were fundamentally the relevant criteria to the facts of this case and dismissed the appeal, after usefully setting out a full consideration of the history and development of the *Practice Statement* and guidance as to its future application.

11.52 With effect from 6 April 2010, the IR86 sets out a procedure to determine the debtor's claim that the remuneration or expenses of a trustee (other than the OR) were excessive in an application for annulment under IA86, s 282(1)(b).[112] It provides that the applicant may apply for:

- an order reducing the amount of remuneration which the trustee was entitled to charge[113]
- an order that some or all of the remuneration or expenses in question be treated as not being bankruptcy expenses[114]
- an order that the trustee or the trustee's personal representative pay to the applicant the amount of the excess of remuneration or expenses or such part of the excess as the court may specify.[115]

11.53 The application must be made no later than 5 business days before the date fixed for the hearing of the application for annulment and be accompanied by a copy of any evidence which the applicant intends to adduce in support.[116] The applicant must send a copy of the application and of any evidence accompanying it to the trustee, at the same time that the application is made.[117] If the court annuls the bankruptcy order under s 282(1)(b), IA86 and considers the application to be well-founded, it must also make one of the specified orders, and may make any other order that it thinks just.[118] In practice this will mean the court analysing the applicant's assertions and, if of the view that there is some merit to them, setting out a procedure for assessment under the *Practice Statement*. There is no set rule as to whether that assessment should take place before or after the granting of the annulment. If the debtor is seeking his annulment before finalisation of the sums due by way of remuneration or expenses, then it would appear that the remuneration and expenses will have to be secured for in the usual way.

---

112 IR86, r 6.207A(1).
113 IR86, r 6.207A(4)(a).
114 IR86, r 6.207A(4)(b).
115 IR86, r 6.207A(4)(c).
116 IR86, r 6.207A(2).
117 IR86, r 6.207A(3).
118 IR86, r 6.207(4).

Who gets a copy of the order?

11.54 Copies of the order will be sent by the court[119] to the following:

- the applicant;
- the OR;
- the trustee (if other than the OR).

If the OR has notified creditors of the bankruptcy order then he must immediately notify them of the annulment.[120]

What other notices need to be sent after the annulment has been granted?

11.55 The court must give notice of the annulment to the SoS.[121] The former bankrupt can request the SoS to give notice of the annulment as follows:

- in the *Gazette*;[122] or
- in any newspaper in which the bankruptcy order was advertised;[123] or
- in both.[124]

This application must be made by the former bankrupt in writing to the SoS[125] within 28 days of the order being made.[126]

What happens after an annulment hearing?

11.56 The trustee must submit a copy of his final account to the SoS, as soon as practicable after the court's order annulling the bankruptcy order; and also file a copy of the final account in court.[127] The final account must include a summary of the trustee's receipts and payments in the administration, and contain a statement to the effect that it has been reconciled with the account details held by the SoS in respect of the bankruptcy.[128]

How does the trustee get his release after an annulment?

11.57 The trustee is released from such time as the court may determine, having completed the following:[129]

---

119 IR86, r 6.10(3) or IRN91, r 6.209(3).
120 IR86, r 6.212(1) or IRN91, r 6.209(1).
121 IR86, r 6.213(2) or IRN91, r 6.211(2).
122 IR86, r 6.213(3)(a) or IRN91, r 6.211(3)(a).
123 IR86, r 6.213(3)(b) or IRN91, r 6.211(3)(b).
124 IR86, r 6.213(c) or IRN91, r 6.211(3)(c).
125 IR86, r 6.213(4) or IRN91, r 6.211(4).
126 IR86, r 6.213(3) or IRN91, r 6.211(3).
127 IR86, r 6.214(2) or IRN91, r 6.211(2).
128 IR86, r 6.214(3) or IRN91, r 6.211(3).
129 IR86, r 6.214(1) or IRN91, r 6.211(1).

- that the trustee has filed his final account in court in accordance with r 6.214(2), IR86;[130] and
- any security given under r 6.211(3), IR86 has been, or will be, released.[131]

The usual practice is for the court to grant the trustee his release 28 days after he has filed his final receipts and payments account.

[130] IR86, r 6.214(4)(a) or IRN91, r 6.211(4)(a).
[131] IR86, r 6.214(4)(a) or IRN91, r 6.211(4)(a).

Chapter 12

THE OFFICIAL RECEIVER AND TRUSTEE IN BANKRUPTCY

'Debt is like any other trap, easy enough to get into,
but hard enough to get out of.'[1]

INTRODUCTION

12.1 This chapter looks at the role of the OR and the circumstances and procedures for appointing a trustee other than the OR. It also covers the release of a trustee, vacation of office and the circumstances and process by which a trustee can resign or be replaced. The process by which an individual can be licensed as an IP and the role of RPBs in their regulation are covered in detail in chapter 2.

What is the role of the Official Receiver?

12.2 The OR is automatically appointed trustee on the making of every bankruptcy order except where the court orders the appointment of a trustee under either s 297(4), IA86 where there has been a reporting accountant or s 297(5), IA86 where the supervisor of a failed IVA consents to act. Any subsequently appointed trustee takes over that role from the OR but in the event of any vacancy in the office the role reverts to the OR.

What is the Official Receiver's relationship with any subsequently appointed trustee?

12.3 The general function of every trustee is to get in, realise and distribute the bankrupt's estate.[2] If the trustee is not the OR then there are further requirements to:

- provide information to the OR;[3]

- produce or permit inspection of any books, papers and other records;[4] and

- provide assistance to the OR to carry out his functions.[5]

---

1 Henry Wheeler Shaw (using the pseudonyms Josh Billings and Uncle Esek).
2 IA86, s 305(2) or INO89, art 278(2).
3 IA86, s 305(3)(a) or INO89, art 278(3)(a).
4 IA86, s 305(3)(b) or INO89, art 278(3)(b).
5 IA86, s 305(3)(c) or INO89, art 278(3)(c).

12.4 The OR is required to do all that is required to assist the trustee in taking possession of the bankrupt's estate[6] including providing all information relating to the bankrupts affairs[7] and a copy of any report prepared.[8] These requirements only apply when the trustee is appointed in succession to the OR acting as trustee.[9]

12.5 The bankrupt's estate vests in the trustee.[10] On taking possession of the estate the trustee is required to discharge any balance outstanding to the OR[11] or give an undertaking that the balance will be discharged from the first realisations.[12] The OR retains a charge over any net realisations that are paid into the estate to recoup any outstanding expenses.[13]

Is there a duty to investigate every bankruptcy?

12.6 The OR is required to investigate the conduct and affairs of each bankrupt[14] unless he files two copies of Form 6.82 in court stating that he feels it is unnecessary and advises creditors and the debtor accordingly.[15] The creditors have 28 days in which to object[16] but the OR retains the right to reject any complaint. The creditor must be informed in writing of any rejection and can appeal to the court.[17] The period allowed for the appeal will be decided by the court.[18] The trustee (if not the OR) does not specifically have a duty to investigate but is required to advise the OR of any information that he obtains during the administration of the estate, and may be requested to investigate specific matters as directed by the creditors or the creditors' committee.

Who can appoint a trustee other than the OR?

12.7 A trustee can be appointed by:

- the creditors at a creditors' meeting;[19]
- by the court under s 297;[20] or
- by the SoS[21] under s 296, 295 or 300, IA86; or

---

6 IR86, r 6.125(2) or IRN91, r 6.122(2).
7 IR86, r 6.125(7) or IRN91, r 6.122(7).
8 IR86, r 6.125(8) or IRN91, r 6.122(8).
9 IR86, r 6.125(1)(b) or IRN91, r 6.122(1)(b).
10 IA86, s 287 or INO89, art 260. See further chapter 17.
11 IR86, r 6.125(3) or IRN91, r 6.122(3).
12 IR86, r 6.125(4) or IRN91, r 6.122(4).
13 IR86, r 6.125(5) or IRN91, r 6.122(5).
14 IA86, s 289(1)(a) or INO89, art 262(1)(a).
15 IR86, r 6.214A(1).
16 IR86, r 6.214A(2).
17 IR86, r 6.214A(5)(b).
18 IR86, r 6.214A(5)(b).
19 IR86, r 6.120 or IRN91, r 6.117.
20 IR86, r 6.121 or IRN91, r 6.118.
21 IR86, r 6.122 or IRN91, r 6.119.

- in Northern Ireland by the Department under arts 269, 268 or 273, IRN89.[22]

When can and why would the creditors appoint a trustee other than the official receiver?

12.8 The creditors can appoint a trustee other than the OR at any meeting convened for that purpose.[23] The meeting can be requisitioned by creditors or may be convened by the OR. Creditors usually want a trustee other than the OR appointed when there are assets that need to be realised or other matters that they specifically want investigated.

What are the trustee's duties and the official title in any proceedings?

12.9 The functions of the trustee are to safeguard and secure the assets forming the bankrupt's estate, to realise these assets, and distribute the proceeds in accordance with the statutory provisions.[24] A bankrupt is required to deliver possession of his estate to the OR.[25]

12.10 The official name of the trustee is 'the trustee of the estate of …, a bankrupt' (inserting the name of the bankrupt); but the IP can also be referred to as 'the trustee in bankruptcy' of the particular bankrupt.[26]

What additional duties does the trustee have if he is not the official receiver?

12.11 It is the duty of the trustee to provide the OR with the following to enable the OR to carry out his functions in relation to the bankruptcy:[27]

- furnish the OR with such information;[28]

- produce to the OR, and permit inspection by the OR of, such books, papers and other records;[29] and

- give the OR such other assistance[30] as the OR may reasonably require for the purpose of enabling him to carry out his functions in relation to the bankruptcy.

22 INO89 and IRN91, r 6.119.
23 IA86, s 292(1)(a) or INO89, art 265(1)(a).
24 IA86, s 305(2) or INO89, art 278(2).
25 IA86, s 291(1)(a) or INO89, art 264(1)(a).
26 IA86, s 305(4) or INO89, art 278(4).
27 IA86, s 305(3)(c) or INO89, art 278(3)(c).
28 IA86, s 305(3)(a) or INO89, art 278(3)(a).
29 IA86, s 305(3)(b) or INO89, art 278(3)(b).
30 IA86, s 305(3)(c) or INO89, art 278(3)(c).

When can someone other than the Official Receiver be appointed as trustee?

12.12 The power to appoint a trustee other than the OR is set out in s 292(1), IA86 and stipulates the requirements for that person to be qualified to act as an IP.[31] The process is discussed below.

What powers does the trustee have?

12.13 The powers of the trustee[32] are set out in Sch 5, IA86.[33] The schedule lists both the powers that can be exercised without sanction, and those that require sanction of the creditors' committee or the court. These are identical and are reproduced below.

12.14

> **'Part I Powers exercisable with sanction**
>
> - Power to carry on any business so far as may be necessary for winding it up beneficially and so far as the trustee is able to do so without contravening any requirement imposed by or under any enactment.
> - Power to bring, institute or defend any action or legal proceedings relating to the property comprised in the bankrupt's estate.
> - Power to accept, as the consideration for the sale of any property comprised in the bankrupt's estate, a sum of money payable at a future time subject to such stipulations as to security or otherwise as the creditor's committee or the court thinks fit.
> - Power to mortgage or pledge any part of the property comprised in the bankrupt's estate for the purpose of raising money for the payment of his debts.
> - Power, where any right, option or other power forms part of the bankrupt's estate, to make payments or incur liabilities with a view to obtaining, for the benefit of the creditors, any property which is the subject of the right, option or power.
> - Power to refer to arbitration, or compromise on such terms as may be agreed on, any debts, claims or liabilities subsisting or supposed to subsist between the bankrupt and any person who may have incurred any liability to the bankrupt (this paragraph is deleted with effect from 6 April 2010).[34]
> - Power to make such compromise or other arrangement as may be thought expedient with creditors, or persons claiming to be creditors, in respect to bankruptcy debts.
> - Power to make such compromise or other arrangement as may be thought expedient with respect to any claim arising out of or incidental to the bankrupt's estate made or capable of being made, on the trustee by any person (or by the trustee on any person – these words deleted with effect from 6 April 2010).'[35]

---

[31] IA86, s 292(2) or INO89, art 265.

[32] IA86, s 314(1) or INO89, art 287.

[33] Or INO89, Sch 3.

[34] Legislative Reform (Insolvency) (Miscellaneous Provisions) Order 2009, art 11.

[35] Legislative Reform (Insolvency) (Miscellaneous Provisions) Order 2009, art 11.

Sanction is obtained usually by specific resolution from the committee, the general body of creditors or in the absence of either of these from the SoS.'

12.15

> **'Part II General Powers**
>
> - Power to sell any part of the property for the time being comprised in the bankrupt's estate, including the goodwill and book debts of any business.
> - Power to refer to arbitration, or compromise on such terms as may be agreed, any debts, claims or liabilities subsisting or supposed to subsist between the bankrupt and any person who may have incurred any liability to the bankrupt (inserted from 6 April 2010).[36]
> - Power to make such compromise, or other arrangement as may be thought expedient with respect to any claim arising out of or incidental to the bankrupt's estate or capable of being made by trustee on any person (inserted from 6 April 2010).[37]
> - Power to give receipts for any money received by him, being receipts that effectually discharge the person paying the money from all responsibility in respect of its application.
> - Power to prove, rank, claim and draw a dividend in respect of such debts due to the bankrupt as are comprised in his estate.
> - Power to exercise in relation to any property comprised in the bankrupt's estate any powers the capacity to exercise, which is vested in him under Parts VIII to XI of this Act.
> - Power to deal with any property comprised in the estate to which the bankruptcy is beneficially entitled as tenant in tail, in the same manner as the bankrupt might have dealt with it.'

These powers do not require any pre-approval.

12.16

> **'Part III Ancillary Powers**
>
> For the purposes of, or in connection with, the exercise of any of his powers under Parts VIII to XI of this Act, the trustee may, by his official name:
>
> (a) hold property of every description;
> (b) make contracts;
> (c) sue and be sued;
> (d) enter into engagements binding on himself and, in respect of the bankrupt's estate, on his successors in office;
> (e) employ an agent;
> (f) execute any power of attorney, deed or other instrument;
>
> and he may do any other act, which is necessary or expedient for the purposes of or in connection with the exercise of those powers.'

---

36 Legislative Reform (Insolvency) (Miscellaneous Provisions) Order 2009, art 11.

37 Legislative Reform (Insolvency) (Miscellaneous Provisions) Order 2009, art 11.

What is the procedure for appointing a trustee other than the OR at a creditors meeting?

12.17 The nominated IP must have provided:

- a written statement to the effect that he is a duly qualified IP, and able to act as trustee in relation to the bankrupt,[38] and
- that he consents to act in that capacity.[39]

The chairman of the meeting will certify the appointment[40] on either Form 6.40 (sole trustee) or Form 6.41 (two or more trustees appointed). A joint appointment of more than one office holder requires a declaration of the circumstances in which they may act.[41]

12.18 The appointment will become effective from the date of the certificate,[42] which may not be the same day as the meeting if the chairman of the meeting has not received the written statement and the consent to act. The chairman of the meeting (if not the OR) must also send a copy of the certificate to the OR and file another copy in court.[43]

12.19 Immediately after his certificate of appointment has been received, the trustee must advertise his appointment in such newspaper as he thinks most appropriate for ensuring that it comes to the notice of the bankrupt's creditors.[44] The trustee is entitled to be reimbursed this cost from the estate.[45]

When can the court appoint a trustee other than the official receiver and what is the procedure?

12.20 The court can appoint a trustee other than the OR in accordance with s 297, IA86:

- Where an IP's report has been submitted under s 274, IA86[46] on Form 6.42.
- Where at the time of the hearing a supervisor of a voluntary arrangement is in office[47] on Form 6.43.

---

38 IR86, r 6.120(2) or IRN91, r 6.117(2).
39 IR86, r 6.120(2) or IRN91, r 6.117(2).
40 IR86, r 6.120(2) or IRN91, r 6.117(2).
41 IA86, s 292(3) or INO89, art 265(3).
42 IR86, r 6.120(3) or IRN91, r 6.117(3).
43 IR86, r 6.120(4) and (5) or IRN91, r 6.117(4).
44 IR86, r 6.124(1) or IRN91, r 6.121(1).
45 IR86, r 6.124(2) or IRN91, r 6.121(2).
46 IA86, s 297(4) or INO89, art 270(4).
47 IA86, s 297(5) or INO89, art 270(5).

12.21 The following documents need to be filed in court:

- the person appointed must have filed in court a statement to the effect that he is an IP, duly qualified to act as trustee; and
- that he consents so to act.[48]

The court must send two copies of the order to the OR. One of the copies must be sealed, and this copy must be sent to the person appointed as trustee.[49] The trustee's appointment takes effect from the date of the order.[50]

12.22 A sealed copy of the order of appointment or (as the case may be) a copy of the certificate of his appointment can be used as proof that the named IP is duly authorised to exercise the powers and perform the duties of trustee of the bankrupt's estate.[51]

When can the Secretary of State appoint a trustee other than the OR?

12.23 The SoS[52] can appoint a trustee other than the OR in the following circumstances:

- when a meeting of creditors held under s 293 or 294 IA86 has failed to appoint a trustee;[53]
- at any time when the OR is the trustee of the estate;[54]
- at any time when there is a vacancy in the office of trustee[55] and in the interim the OR will fill the vacancy.[56]

The decision will usually be made on the basis of the level of assets available in the estate.

What is the procedure?

12.24 If the SoS makes an appointment he must send two copies of the certificate of appointment to the OR, who sends one such copy to the person appointed as trustee, and the other copy is filed in court.[57] The certificate must specify the date from which the trustee's appointment is to be effective.[58]

---

48 IR86, r 6.121(2) or IRN91, r 6.118(2).
49 IR86, r 6.121(3) or IRN91, r 6.118(3).
50 IR86, r 6.121(4) or IRN91, r 6.118(4).
51 IR86, r 6.123 (Authentication of trustee's appointment) or IRN91, r 6.120.
52 Or Department of Enterprise Trade and Investment (DETI) in Northern Ireland.
53 IA86, s 295(1) or INO89, art 268(1).
54 IA86, s 296 or INO89, art 269.
55 IA86, s 300(1) or INO89, art 273(1).
56 IA86, s 300(2) or INO89, art 273(2).
57 IR86, r 6.122(2) or IRN91, r 6.119(2).
58 IR86, r 6.122(2) or IRN91, r 6.119(2).

12.25 The person appointed must be a licensed IP[59] and should have consented to act, although this is one circumstance in which there is not a specific process for the consent to be notified to the SoS.

TRUSTEE: RESIGNATION OR REMOVAL

12.26 There are a number of different circumstances when a trustee may need to resign and also circumstances in which of loss of licence or otherwise when a trustee may need to vacate the office of trustee. Vacating the office of trustee should not be confused with release which is dealt with in detail below.

When can a trustee be removed?

12.27 A trustee can only be removed by an order of the court or a general meeting of the bankrupt's creditors summoned especially for that purpose[60] unless he was appointed by the SoS in which he can be removed in the same way.[61] The OR cannot be removed from office unless he is being replaced by another trustee.[62]

When must a trustee 'vacate his office'?

12.28 A trustee must vacate his office in the following circumstances:

- On annulment of the bankruptcy order.[63]
- After the final meeting has been held where someone other than the OR is trustee.[64]
- If the trustee ceases to be qualified to act as an IP.[65]

When can a trustee resign?

12.29 A trustee can resign at a creditors' meeting in the following circumstances:

- On the grounds of ill health.[66]
- Retirement including the cessation of qualification as an IP.[67]

---

59 IA86, s 388.
60 IA86, s 298(1) or INO89, art 271(1).
61 IA86, s 298(5) or INO89, art 271(5).
62 IA86, s 298(2) or INO89, art 271(2).
63 IA86, s 298(9) or INO89, art 271(9).
64 IA86, s 298(8) or INO89, art 271(8).
65 IA86, s 298(6) or INO89, art 271(6).
66 IR86, r 6.126(3) or IRN91, r 6.123(3).
67 IR86, r 6.126(3)(a) or IRN91, r 6.123(3)(a).

- There is some conflict of interest.[68]

- There is a change of circumstances which precludes or makes it impracticable to continue in office.[69]

- For joint office holders where at least one other trustee remains in office[70] (without prejudice to the continuation in office of the other or others) on the grounds that it is no longer expedient that there should continue to be the present number of joint trustees.[71]

In addition a trustee can apply to court for leave to resign in other circumstances eg when moving to another firm and to avoid the expense of calling multiple meetings.[72]

What is the procedure for a trustee to resign at a creditors' meeting?

12.30 The trustee can convene a creditors' meeting to accept his resignation or apply to the court. If a meeting is to be held the following procedure must be followed:

- The notice to creditors must be accompanied by an account of the trustee's administration of the bankrupt's estate, which must include:[73]

  — a summary of his receipts and payments, and
  — a statement by him that he has reconciled his account with that which is held by the SoS in respect of the bankruptcy.

- The meeting notice to creditors must include reference to the trustee's release and the ability of the creditors to resolve against the release of the trustee (see below for an explanation of the difference between vacation of office and release).[74]

- A copy of the notice shall at the same time also be sent to the OR.[75]

- Where the chairman of the meeting is other than the OR, and any of the following resolutions are passed at the meeting:[76]

  (a) that the trustee's resignation be accepted,
  (b) that a new trustee be appointed,
  (c) that the resigning trustee be not given his release,

---

68 IR86, r 6.126(3)(b) or IRN91, r 6.123(3)(b).
69 IR86, r 6.126(3)(b) or IRN91, r 6.123(3)(b).
70 IR86, r 6.126(4) or IRN91, r 6.123(4).
71 IR86, r 6.126(4) or IRN91, r 6.123(4).
72 IR86, r 6.127 or IRN91, r 6.124.
73 IR86, r 6.126(2) or IRN91, r 6.123(2).
74 IR86, r 6.127(1) or IRN91, r 6.124(1).
75 IR86, r 6.127(2) or IRN91, r 6.124(2).
76 IR86, r 6.127(3) or IRN91, r 6.124(3).

the chairman shall, within 3 days, send to the OR a copy of the resolution. If it has been resolved to accept the trustee's resignation, the chairman shall send to the OR a certificate to that effect.[77]

- If the creditors have resolved to appoint a new trustee, the certificate of the appointment must also be sent to the OR within that time, and r 6.120, IR86 must be complied with in respect of it (requirements for appointment at a creditors' meeting).[78]

- If the trustee's resignation is accepted, the notice of it required by s 298(7), IA86 shall be given by him forthwith after the meeting, and he shall send a copy of the notice to the OR. The notice shall be accompanied by a copy of the account sent to creditors under r 6.126(2), IR86.[79]

- If there is no quorum present at the meeting summoned to receive the trustee's resignation, the meeting is deemed to have been held, a resolution is deemed to have been passed that the trustee's resignation be accepted and the creditors are deemed not to have resolved against the trustee having his release.[80] The chairman of the meeting must produce a written statement stating this position.[81]

- The OR must file a copy of the notice in court.[82]

- The trustee's resignation takes effect from the date on which the OR files the copy notice in court and that date must be endorsed on the copy notice.[83]

- Where a new trustee is appointed in place of one who has resigned, the new trustee must, in the advertisement of his appointment, state that his predecessor has resigned and (if it be the case) that he has been given his release.[84]

What happens if the creditors refuse to accept a trustee's resignation at the meeting summoned for that purpose?

12.31 If the creditors resolve against the trustee's resignation the trustee can then apply to court for leave to resign using Form 6.45.[85] The court's order can include any provision it thinks appropriate with respect to matters arising in

---

77 Form 6.44.
78 IR86, r 6.127(4) or IRN91, r 6.124(4).
79 IR86, r 6.127(5) or IRN91, r 6.12545).
80 IR86, r 6.126(5) or IRN91, r 6.123(5).
81 IR86, r 6.126(6) or IRN91, r 6.123(6).
82 IR86, r 6.127(6) or IRN91, r 6.124(6).
83 IR86, r 6.127(7) or IRN91, r 6.124(7).
84 IR86, r 6.134 or IRN91, r 6.131.
85 IR86, r 6.128(1) or IRN91, r 6.125(1).

connection with the resignation, and the court must also determine the date from which the trustee's release is effective.[86]

12.32 Once the order has been made allowing the resignation the court must send two sealed copies of the order to the trustee, who must send one of the copies immediately to the OR.[87] In addition the trustee must send also send a copy of his resignation to the OR on Form 6.46.[88]

What are the procedures for the creditors to remove a trustee from office including chairing and voting procedures?

12.33 The procedure is almost identical to the process for the trustee to resign except that the meeting will usually be requisitioned by the creditors, and the meeting notice must draw the creditors' attention to the purpose of the meeting including the trustee's release.[89] As above, a copy of the meeting notice must also be sent to the OR.[90]

12.34 At the meeting, a person other than the trustee or his nominee can be elected to act as chairman; but if the trustee or his nominee is chairman and a resolution has been proposed for the trustee's removal, the chairman must not adjourn the meeting without the consent of at least one-half (in value) of the creditors present (in person or by proxy) and entitled to vote.[91]

12.35 Where the chairman of the meeting is someone other than the OR, and there is passed at the meeting any of the following resolutions:[92]

- that the trustee be removed,
- that a new trustee be appointed,
- that the removed trustee not be given his release,

the chairman must send a copy of the resolution to the OR within 3 days. If the trustee is to be removed the chairman must send a certificate to that effect to the OR.[93]

12.36 Where the creditors have resolved that the trustee be removed, the OR must file the certificate of removal in court.[94] If the creditors have resolved to appoint a new trustee, the certificate of his appointment must also be sent to

---

86 IR86, r 6.128(2) or IRN91, r 6.125(2).
87 IR86, r 6.128(3) or IRN91, r 6.125(3).
88 IR86, r 6.128(4) or IRN91, r 6.125(4).
89 Form 6.35 and IR86, r 6.129(1) or IRN91, r 6.126(1).
90 IR86, r 6.129(2) or IRN91, r 6.126(2).
91 IR86, r 6.129(3) or IRN91, r 6.126(3).
92 IR86, r 6.129(4) or IRN91, r 6.126(4).
93 Form 6.47.
94 IR86, r 6.131(1) or IRN91, r 6.129(1).

the OR within that time and r 6.120, IR86 must also be complied with.[95] The resolution for removal is effective from the date on which the OR files the certificate of removal in court, and that date must be endorsed on the certificate.[96] A copy of the certificate, so endorsed, must be sent by the OR to the trustee who has been removed and, if a new trustee has been appointed, to him as well.[97]

12.37 The OR must not file the certificate in court until the SoS has certified to him that the removed trustee has reconciled his account with that held by the SoS in respect of the bankruptcy.[98]

12.38 Where a meeting is to be held or proposed under r 6.129, IR86, the court may, on the application of any creditor give directions as to the mode of summoning it, the sending out and return of forms of proxy, the conduct of the meeting, and any other matter which appears to the court to require regulation or control.[99]

What is the procedure for the court to remove a trustee from office?

12.39 The following procedure applies:

- Form 6.48 should be used where an application is made to the court for the removal of the trustee, or for an order directing the trustee to summon a meeting of creditors for the purpose of removing him.[100]

- The court may, if it thinks that no sufficient cause is shown for the application, dismiss it; but it shall not do so unless the applicant has had an opportunity to attend the court for an ex parte hearing, of which he has been given at least 7 days' notice. If the application is not dismissed under this paragraph, the court must fix a venue for it to be heard.[101]

- The applicant must, at least 14 days before the hearing, send to the trustee and the OR notice stating the venue fixed for the hearing; and the notice must be accompanied by a copy of the application, and any evidence which the applicant intends to adduce in support of the application.[102]

- Subject to any contrary order of the court, the costs of the application do not fall on the estate.[103]

---

95 IR86, r 6.129(5) or IRN91, r 6.126(5).
96 IR86, r 6.131(2) or IRN91, r 6.129(2).
97 IR86, r 6.131(3) or IRN91, r 6.129(4).
98 IR86, r 6.131(4) or IRN91, r 6.129(5).
99 IR86, r 6.130 or IRN91, r 6.128.
100 IR86, r 6.132(1) or IRN91, r 6.129(1).
101 IR86, r 6.132(2) or IRN91, r 6.129(2).
102 IR86, r 6.132(3) or IRN91, r 6.129(4).
103 IR86, r 6.132(4) or IRN91, r 6.129(5).

- Where the court removes the trustee:[104]

  — it must send copies of the order of removal to him and to the OR;
  — the order may include such provision as the court thinks fit with respect to matters arising in connection with the removal; and
  — if the court appoints a new trustee, r 6.121, IR86 applies.

A trustee in bankruptcy should act efficiently, vigorously and in an unbiased way within the conduct of a bankruptcy. If the trustee's conduct is honest, reasonable and without misconduct, or maladministration, the court would think carefully before removing the trustee in bankruptcy, especially on an application by the bankrupt.[105] On such an application by the bankrupt, the test is a particularly high one and he has to show a very real and substantial cause, against the background of the trustee's obligation to realise assets for the benefit of creditors.[106]

What is procedure for the secretary of state to remove a trustee from office?

12.40 The procedure for removal is as follows:

- If the SoS decides to remove the trustee, before doing so he must notify the trustee and the OR of the decision and the grounds upon which it has been made, specifying the period within which the trustee can make representations against implementation of the decision.[107]

- If the SoS directs the removal of the trustee, he must immediately:[108]

  — file notice of his decision in court, and
  — send notice to the trustee and the OR.

- If the trustee is removed by direction of the SoS, the court may make any such order as it would have power to make if being removed by court.[109]

- Where a new trustee is appointed in place of one who has been removed, the new trustee must, in the advertisement of his appointment, state that his predecessor has been removed and (if it be the case) that he has been given his release.[110]

---

104 IR86, r 6.132(5) or IRN91, r 6.129(6).

105 *Smedley v Brittain* [2008] BPIR 219.

106 See *Osborn v Cole* [1999] BPIR 251, *AMP Music Box Enterprises Ltd v Hoffman* [2002] EWHC 1989 (Ch), [2003] BPIR 11, [2003] 1 BCLC 319, [2002] BCC 996, *Re Buildlead Ltd (in Liquidation) (No 2)* [2004] EWHC 2443 (Ch), [2004] BPIR 1139, [2006] 1 BCLC 9, [2005] BCC 138 and *Re Keypack Homecare Ltd* [1987] BCLC 409.

107 IR86, r 6.133(1) or IRN91, r 6.130(1).

108 IR86, r 6.133(2) or IRN91, r 6.130(2).

109 IR86, r 6.133(3) or IRN91, r 6.130(3).

110 IR86, r 6.134 or IRN91, r 6.131.

RELEASE FROM OFFICE

What is the difference between 'vacation of office' and 'release'?

12.41 An office holder can vacate office in a number of circumstances including death; loss of qualification; removal; or resignation (either during or at the conclusion of the administration of the estate). These have been dealt with in detail above.[111] Vacation of office must be differentiated from release,[112] which is not granted automatically on vacation of office and the timing of the release will depend on the circumstances in which the office has been vacated.

What is the effect of release?

12.42 Release from office terminates all liabilities in respect of any act or omission and otherwise in relation to the conduct of the office holder. Release is therefore important in respect of any subsequent claims, whereas vacation of office is not. In effect once release has been obtained no regulatory action can be taken in respect of any act or omission that took place during the administration of the case; however s 304, IA86 (misfeasance or breach of fiduciary duty by the trustee) still applies.

12.43 Release can be granted by the court,[113] the creditors,[114] or the SoS,[115] depending on the circumstances. The procedure is covered in more detail below.

What is the procedure for a trustee to vacate office?

12.44 Where the trustee intends to vacate office, whether by resignation or otherwise, he must give notice of his intention to the OR together with notice of any creditors' meeting to be held in respect of his vacation of office. This includes any meeting convened to receive a notice of resignation.[116] The notice to the OR must be given at least 21 days before any such creditors' meeting[117] is held.

12.45 Where there remains in the bankrupt's estate any property which has not been realised, applied, distributed or otherwise fully dealt with in the bankruptcy, the trustee must include in his notice to the OR:[118]

- details of the nature of that property;
- its value (or the fact that it has no value);
- its location;

---

111 See **12.28–12.41**.
112 IA86, s 299 or INO89, art 272.
113 IA86, s 299(1)(b) or INO89, art 272(1)(b).
114 IA86, s 299(1)(a) or INO89, art 272(1)(a).
115 IA86, s 299(2) or INO89, art 272(2).
116 IR86, r 6.145(1) or IRN91, r 6.142(1).
117 IR86, r 6.145(2) or IRN91, r 6.142(2).
118 IR86, r 6.145(3) or IRN91, r 6.142(3).

- any action taken by the trustee to deal with that property; or
- any reason for his not dealing with it; and
- the current position in relation to it.

How does the OR obtain his release?

12.46 The OR must give notice to the SoS under s 299(2), IA86 (that the administration of the estate is for practical purposes complete), send out notice of his intention to do so to all creditors of which he is aware and to the bankrupt.[119]

12.47 The notice must in each case be accompanied by a summary of the OR's receipts and payments as trustee.[120]

12.48 The SoS, when he has under s 299(2), IA86 determined the date from which the OR is to have his release, must give notice to the court that he has done so. The notice must be accompanied by the OR's receipts and payments as trustee.[121]

When does a trustee (not the OR) obtain his release?

12.49 A person other than the OR who has vacated office will obtain their release in the following circumstances:

- Release is automatic unless a resolution against release is proposed by a creditor. As a result removal by a general meeting of creditors means release is obtained on the date the meeting notice is filed in court.[122]
- Removal by a general meeting of creditors at which a resolution against release was obtained: release is obtained at such time as the SoS determines.[123]
- Resignation at such time as may be prescribed.[124] Resignation at a time other than the conclusion of the administration may be made either at a creditors meeting or by court application. In either case, the time of the release will be determined either by a resolution, the SoS or by court order, depending on the wishes of the creditors.

---

119 IR86, r 6.136(1) or IRN91, r 6.133(1).
120 IR86, r 6.133(2) or IRN91, r 6.136(2).
121 IR86, r 6.133(3) or IRN91, r 6.136(3).
122 IA86, s 299(3)(a) or INO89, art 272(3)(a).
123 IA86, s 299(3)(b) or INO89, art 272(3)(b).
124 IA86, s 299(3)(c) or INO89, art 272(3)(c).

- Resignation at the final meeting of creditors at which no resolution against release was obtained: release is obtained at the time of vacation of office.[125]

- Resignation at the final meeting of creditors at which a resolution against release was obtained: release is obtained at such time as the SoS determines.[126]

- Where a bankruptcy order is annulled release will be obtained at a time determined by the court[127] and this date should be included in the court order.

12.50 Where the trustee has resigned or has been removed from office he will obtain his release as follows:

- Where the trustee's resignation is accepted by a meeting of creditors which has not resolved against his release, he has his release from the date when his resignation is effective under r 6.127, IR86.[128]

- Where the trustee is removed by a meeting of creditors which has not resolved against his release, the fact of his release shall be stated in the certificate of removal.[129]

- Where the trustee resigns, and the creditors' meeting called to receive his resignation has resolved against his release, he must apply to the SoS for his release.[130]

- Where the trustee is removed by a creditor' meeting and it has also resolved against his release, he must apply to the SoS for his release.[131]

- Where the trustee is removed by court he must apply to the SoS for his release.[132]

- When an application is made to the SoS for release and he grants it, he must send a certificate verifying the date to the OR, to be filed in court[133] and a copy must be sent to the former trustee, whose release is effective from the date of the certificate.[134]

---

125 IA86, s 299(3)(d)(ii) or INO89, art 272(3)(d)(ii).
126 IA86, s 299(3)(d)(i) or INO89, art 272(3)(d)(i).
127 IA86, s 299(4) or INO89, art 272(4).
128 IR86, r 6.135(1) or IRN91, r 6.132(1).
129 IR86, r 6.135(2) or IRN91, r 6.132(2).
130 IR86, r 6.135(3)(a) or IRN91, r 6.132(3)(a).
131 IR86, r 6.135(3)(b) or IRN91, r 6.132(3)(b).
132 IR86, r 6.135(3)(b) or IRN91, r 6.132(3)(b).
133 IR86, r 6.135(4) or IRN91, r 6.132(4).
134 IR86, r 6.135(5) or IRN91 64, r 6.132(5).

How does a trustee (not the OR) obtain his release from the Secretary of State?

12.51 The trustee must apply for his release to the SoS.[135] The SoS will investigate the reasons why the creditors have resolved against release and make a decision accordingly. The SoS will issue a certificate which must be sent to the OR and filed in court,[136] with a copy also being sent to the former trustee.[137]

What are a trustee's duties on vacating office?

12.52 Once a trustee ceases to be in office he is under an obligation to deliver up to any replacement office holder the assets of the estate which have not been paid out in expenses or distributions to creditors.[138] In addition the following books and records also have to be handed over to the replacement office holder:

- the records of the bankruptcy, including correspondence, proofs and other related papers relating to the period in office;[139] and
- the bankrupt's books, papers and other records.[140]

TRUSTEE: DEATH OR LOSS OF QUALIFICATION

What happens if the trustee dies?

12.53 The OR must give notice to the court for the purpose of fixing the date of the deceased trustee's release in accordance with s 299(3)(a), IA86.[141] The OR should give notice in the following way:

- If the deceased trustee was a partner in a firm, notice may be given by a partner in the firm who is qualified to act as an IP, or is a member of any body recognised by the SoS for the authorisation of IPs.[142]
- Notice of the death may be given by any person producing to the OR the relevant death certificate or a copy of it.[143]
- In all other circumstances it is the duty of his personal representatives to give notice of the fact to the OR, specifying the date of the death.[144]

---

135 IR86, r 6.135(3) or IRN91, r 6.132(3).
136 IR86, r 6.135(4) or IRN91, r 6.132(4).
137 IR86, r 6.135(5) or IRN91, r 6.132(5).
138 IR86, r 6.149(1) or IRN91, r 6.146(1).
139 IR86, r 6.149(1)(a) or IRN91, r 6.146(1)(a).
140 IR86, r 6.149(1)(b) or IRN91, r 6.146(1)(b).
141 IR86, r 6.143(4) or IRN91, r 6.140(4).
142 IR86, r 6.143(2) or IIRN91, r 6.140(2).
143 IR86, r 6.143(3) or IRN91, r 6.140(3).
144 IR86, r 6.143(1) or IRN91, r 6.140(1).

What happens when a trustee loses their licence to practice as an insolvency practitioner?

12.54 The trustee must give notice to the OR, who will give notice to the SoS[145] and the court. The OR must give notice to the court on Form 6.51[146] for the purpose of fixing the date of the trustee's release in accordance with r 6.135, IR86.[147]

What is a block transfer order?

12.55 The 2010 Amendment Rules which came into effect on 6 April 2010 introduce new provisions[148] for the block transfer of cases between office holders. They codify a process that had become generally accepted when IPs move between firms, retire or die. A challenge as to the jurisdiction underlying such accepted practice, which had developed over a considerable number of cases, failed in *Donaldson v O'Sullivan.*[149]

12.56 Where an individual who is acting as an office holder ('the outgoing office holder') dies,[150] retires from practice,[151] or is otherwise unable or unwilling to continue in office,[152] and it is expedient to transfer some or all of the cases in which the outgoing office holder holds office to one or more office holders ('the replacement office holder') in a single transaction r 7.10B(1) IR86 applies. The court has the power to make an order ('a block transfer order'), appointing a replacement office holder in the place of the outgoing office holder to be supervisor of a voluntary arrangement under Part I or VIII of the Act.[153] Where the replacement office holder is to be appointed supervisor of a voluntary arrangement under Part I or VIII of the Act, that replacement office holder must be qualified to act as an insolvency practitioner, or a person authorised so to act.[154]

12.57 An application for a block transfer order may be made to the registrar or district judge for:[155]

(a) the transfer to the High Court of the cases specified in the schedule under r 7.10C, para (8);

(b) the transfer of the cases back to the court from which they were transferred when a replacement office holder has been appointed;

---

145 IR86, r 6.144(2) or IRN91, r 6.141(2).
146 IR86, r 6.144(2) or IRN91, r 6.141(2).
147 IR86, r 6.144(3) or IRN91, r 6.141(3).
148 New Chapter 1A, Insolvency Rules 1986 SI 1986/1925 (as amended).
149 [2008] EWHC 387 (Ch), [2008] BPIR 288, upheld on appeal at [2008] EWCA Civ 879, [2009] 1 All ER 1087.
150 See IR86, r 7.10B(1)(a).
151 See IR86, r 7.10B(1)(b).
152 See IR86, r 7.10B(1)(c).
153 IR86, r 7.10B(2)(d).
154 See IR86, r 7.10B(3)(b).
155 IR86, r 7.10C(1).

(c) the removal of the outgoing office holder by the exercise of any of the powers in r 7.10C, para (2);

(d) the appointment of a replacement office holder by the exercise of any of the powers in r 7.10C, para (3);

(e) such other order or direction as may be necessary or expedient in connection with any of the matters referred to above.

12.58 The application may be made by any of the following:[156]

- the outgoing office holder (if able and willing to do so);
- any person who holds office jointly with the outgoing office holder;
- any person who is proposed to be appointed as the replacement office holder;
- any creditor in a case subject to the application;
- the recognised professional body or recognised body by which the outgoing office holder is or was authorised; or
- the Secretary of State.

12.59 An applicant (other than the Secretary of State) must give notice of the application to the Secretary of State at least 5 business days before the hearing of the application.[157] The following must be made a respondent to the application and served with it:[158]

- the outgoing office holder (if not the applicant or deceased);
- every person who holds office jointly with the outgoing office holder; and
- such person as the registrar or district judge directs.

12.60 The application must contain a schedule setting out:[159]

- the name of each case,
- the identity of the court having jurisdiction when the application is made,
- the case number (if any), and

---

156 IR86, r 7.10C(4).
157 IR86, r 7.10C(6).
158 IR86, r 7.10C(7).
159 IR86, r 7.10C(8).

- the capacity in which the outgoing office holder was appointed.

The application must be supported by evidence setting out the circumstances that gave rise to it being expedient to appoint a replacement office holder,[160] and exhibiting the written consent to act of each person who is proposed to be appointed as replacement office holder.[161]

Where all the cases in the schedule are in a county court or more than one county court, the application may be made to a district judge of a convenient county court having insolvency jurisdiction and the rules are to apply with appropriate modifications.[162]

12.61 The registrar or district judge may in the first instance consider the application without a hearing and make such order as the registrar or district judge thinks just.[163] In the first instance, the registrar or district judge may do any of the following:[164]

- make an order directing the transfer to the High Court of those cases not already within its jurisdiction for the purpose only of the substantive application;
- if the documents are considered to be in order and that the matter is straightforward, make an order on the substantive application;
- give any directions that are considered to be necessary including (if appropriate) directions for the joinder of any additional respondents or requiring the service of the application on any person or requiring additional evidence to be provided; or
- if an order is not made on the substantive application, give directions for the further consideration of the substantive application by the registrar or district judge or a judge of the Chancery Division.

The applicant must ensure that a sealed copy of every order transferring any case to the High Court, and of every order that is made on a substantive application, is lodged with the court having jurisdiction over each case affected by such order, for filing on the court file relating to that case.[165]

12.62 Any appointment made must be notified to the Secretary of State as soon as reasonably practicable; and to the creditors, and such other persons as the court may direct. The court may direct the process to be used.[166]

---

[160] IR86, r 7.10C(9)(a).
[161] IR86, r 7.10C(9)(b).
[162] IR86, r 7.10C(10).
[163] IR86, r 7.10D(1).
[164] IR86, r 7.10D(2).
[165] IR86, r 7.10D(3).
[166] IR86, r 7.10D(6).

Where an application is made to the district judge under r 7.10C(10) ,IR86, r 7.10D, IR86 applies with appropriate modifications.[167]

Applications which are opposed on substantial grounds should be adjourned to the judge.[168]

What offences can a trustee commit and what are the penalties?

12.63 An IP is not allowed to improperly solicit creditors for support for his nomination as trustee.[169] On application the court can order that all remuneration paid out of the estate is forfeit[170] regardless of any approval being given by either the creditors or the creditors' committee.[171]

What does 'improperly solicit' mean?

12.64 Solicitation for insolvency work is covered by the Insolvency Code of Ethics (published in November 2008). Depending on the nature of the appointment the code covers the use of third party work providers and the disclosure of fees received or paid in respect of pre-appointment agreements. Office holders are also responsible for the conduct of any third parties whose services they use including the way in which they advertise and advise individuals.

---

[167] IR86, r 7.14D(7).

[168] *Practice Direction of 6 October 1988* [1988] 1 WLR 1404 per Browne-Wilkinson V-C.

[169] IR86, r 6.148 or IRN91, r 6.145.

[170] IR86, r 6.148(1) or IRN91, r 6.145(1).

[171] IR86, r 6.148(2) or IRN91, r 6.145(2).

Chapter 13

COSTS, FEES AND TRUSTEES' REMUNERATION IN BANKRUPTCY

'What power has law where only money rules.'[1]

INTRODUCTION

13.1 This chapter will look at the various costs and fees levied on a bankrupt's estate including the remuneration charged by the trustee and how this is approved. The costs levied on a bankruptcy estate are many and varied ranging from the various initial administrative costs including initial court fees and deposits to the specific costs of the official receiver and trustee for securing, insuring, realising and distributing the proceeds from the various assets. The order in which these costs and expenses are prioritised is dealt with in chapter 15 which also covers how bankruptcy funds are handled together with the impact of the regulations on banking arrangements for the trustee including the payments of dividends.

INITIAL FEES AND DEPOSITS

What court fees are payable in bankruptcy proceedings?

13.2 The current Supreme Court and county court fees were introduced with effect from 1 April 2003 by the Supreme Court Fees (Amendment) Order 2003[2] and the County Court Fees (Amendment) Order 2003.[3] Some court fees may be waived (termed remission by the court) in some circumstances[4] and the relevant forms are available on the HM Court Service website. The following are the standard fees currently payable:[5]

Description of Fees	Current Fee £	Previous Fee £
Debtor's bankruptcy petition	175	140

1 Gaius Petronius.

2 SI 2003/646.

3 SI 2003/648.

4 Remission one includes those on specific benefits and remission two covers those on low incomes.

5 Her Majesty's Court Service guides and schedules of the fees and changes are available from the Her Majesty's Court Service's website located at www.courtservice.gov.uk/using_courts/fees/index.htm.

Description of Fees	Current Fee £	Previous Fee £
Creditor's bankruptcy petition	220	190
Request for certificate of discharge	75	60
Additional copies	5	0

What other deposits are required when filing a bankruptcy petition?

13.3 On the filing of a petition a deposit for the OR must also be paid to the court and this element of the fee cannot be waived. It is paid to the OR and goes towards the cost of administering each estate. The amount of the deposit varies depending on the type of petition. For a debtor's petition the current deposit is £450 and for a creditor's petition it is £600.[6] These payments are in addition to court costs scheduled above.

OFFICIAL RECEIVERS' COSTS

What are the official receivers' costs in a bankruptcy?

13.4 The IR86 contains no provisions as to remuneration for the Official Receiver. If the OR remains as trustee of the estate his fees and charges are set out in the Insolvency Proceedings (Fees) Order 2004.[7] Regardless of whether the OR remains trustee there is, in addition to any subsequent trustee's remuneration, a one off administration fee of £1,715[8] plus a levy [called the Secretary of State's (SoS) administration fee] on chargeable receipts up to a maximum of £80,000 paid into the estate account.[9] The scale for bankruptcy orders made on or after 6 April 2010[10] is set out below. Chargeable receipts exclude funds subject to any charge. Previously this fee had been calculated at 17% on realisations again with the same maximum limit.

0%	of the first	£2,000
100%	of the next	£1,700
75%	of the next	£1,500
15%	of the next	£396,000
1%	of the remainder, subject to a maximum of £80,000	

6 See chapter 7 for creditors' petitions and chapter 8 for debtor's petitions.

7 SI 2004/593 as amended most recently by the Insolvency Proceedings (Fees) (Amendment) Order 2010, SI 2010/732.

8 Insolvency Proceedings (Fees) Order 2004 SI 2004/593, Sch 2, Fee B1.

9 Insolvency Proceedings (Fees) Order 2004 SI 2004/593, Sch 2, Fee B2.

10 Article 6, Insolvency Proceedings (Fees) (Amendment) Order 2010, SI 2010/732.

TRUSTEE'S COSTS

What remuneration is a trustee entitled to from the estate funds and how is it agreed?

13.5 The trustee is entitled to receive remuneration for his services[11] from the estate (funds realised from the sale of the bankrupt's assets). Remuneration is fixed by the following:

- Where the trustee is other than the OR, it is for the creditors' committee (if there is one) to determine whether his remuneration is to be fixed as a percentage of the value of the assets in the bankrupt's estate which are realised or distributed (singularly or in combination) or by reference to time given in attending to the bankruptcy.[12]

- This is primarily a matter for the creditors' committee, but if there is no creditors' committee, or the committee does not make the requisite determination, the trustee's remuneration may be fixed by a resolution of a meeting of creditors.[13]

- Where the trustee is not the OR and his remuneration is not fixed as above, the trustee is entitled to remuneration calculated in accordance with r 6.138A, IR86.[14]

What bases can be used to calculate a trustee's remuneration?

13.6 For bankrupts whose petitions were presented prior to 6 April 2010 the basis for the trustee's remuneration is determined as follows:

- as a percentage of the value of the assets in the bankrupt's estate which are realised or distributed, or of the one value and the other in combination,[15] or

- by reference to the time properly given by the IP.[16]

13.7 However, for bankrupts whose petitions were presented after 6 April 2010 an additional option of a 'set fee' is available plus different bases[17] and different percentages[18] can be used in respect of different things done by the trustee. For clarity the bases available are:

---

11 IR86, r 6.138(1) or IRN91, r 6.135(1).
12 IR86, r 6.138(2)(a) and (b) or IRN91, r 6.135(2)(a) and (b).
13 IR86, r 6.138(3) and (5) or IRN91, r 6.135(3) and (5).
14 IR86, r 6.138(6) or IRN91, r 6.135(6).
15 IR86, r 6.138(2)(a) or IRN91, r 6.135(2)(a).
16 IR86, r 6.138(2)(b) or IRN91, r 6.135(2)(b).
17 IR86, r 6.138(3A).
18 IR86, r 6.138(3B).

- as a percentage of the value of the assets in the bankrupt's estate which are realised or distributed, or of the one value and the other in combination,[19] or

- any responsibility of an exceptional nature or degree that results from the administration of the estate,[20] or

- as a set amount.[21]

If a time-cost basis is approved (including the rates to be charged) any subsequent challenge on quantum must be made on a period basis. If a creditor wishes to limit the trustee's fees at the outset of a case then a set fee basis must be used. The same principle applies to a percentage basis, the quantum can be challenged on a period by period basis.

13.8 The following are the matters highlighted for consideration when determining the basis and level of fees being agreed as explained above:

- the complexity (or otherwise) of the case;[22]

- in addition by applying the distribution scale set out in Sch 6, IR86 which needs to be added to the sum above. This scale is applied to the value of assets distributed to creditors of the bankrupt (including sums paid in respect of preferential debts),[23]

- the effectiveness with which the IP appears to be carrying out, or to have carried out, his duties as trustee,[24] and

- the value and nature of the assets in the estate with which the trustee has to deal.[25]

How can remuneration be calculated if there is no agreement on a basis?

13.9 Where the trustee is not the OR and his remuneration has not been fixed (for post-April 2010 cases a basis must be fixed within 18 months) in accordance with r 6.138, IR86,[26] the trustee is entitled to remuneration, calculated as follows:[27]

- by first applying the realisation scale set out in Sch 6 to the monies received by the trustee from the realisation of the assets of the bankrupt

---

19 IR86, r 6.138(2)(a) or IRN91, r 6.135(2)(a).
20 IR86, r 6.138(2)(b) or IRN91, r 6.135(2)(b).
21 IR86, r 6.138(2)(c).
22 IR86, r 6.138(4)(a) or IRN91, r 6.135(4)(a).
23 IR86, r 6.138(4)(b) or IRN91, r 6.135(4)(b).
24 IR86, r 6.138(4)(c) or IRN91, r 6.135(4)(c).
25 IR86, r 6.138(4)(d) or IRN91, r 6.135(4)(d).
26 IR86, r 6.138(6).
27 IR86, r 6.138A(1) or IRN91, r 6.135A(1).

(including any VAT thereon but after deducting any sums paid to secured creditors in respect of their securities and any sums spent out of money received in carrying on the business of the bankrupt);[28] and

- then by adding to the sum arrived at above such sum as is arrived at by applying the distribution scale set out in Sch 6, IR86 to the value of assets distributed to creditors of the bankrupt (including sums paid in respect of preferential debts).[29]

13.10 However, when applying the above, that part of the trustee's remuneration calculated by reference to the realisation scale must not exceed such sum as is arrived at by applying the realisation scale to such part of the bankrupt's assets as are required to pay some particular items,[30] namely:

- the bankruptcy debts (including any interest payable by virtue of s 328(4), IA86) to the extent required to be paid by these Rules (ignoring those debts paid otherwise than out of the proceeds of the realisation of the bankrupt's assets or which have been secured to the satisfaction of the court);[31]
- the expenses of the bankruptcy other than:
  - fees or the remuneration of the official receiver;[32] and
  - any sums spent out of money received in carrying on the business of the bankrupt;[33]
- fees payable by virtue of any order made under s 415, IA86[34] (which sets out the power to provide fees orders and by whom, and in what manner, the fees are to be collected and allocated); and
- the remuneration of the official receiver.[35]

What are the terms set out in Schedule 6, IR86?

13.11 As explained above the remuneration of trustees can be calculated using the realisation and distribution scales set out in Sch 6, IR86. The current table is reproduced below. The realisation scale should only be calculated on the funds received from assets actually realised in the estate. The distribution scale is calculated on the amount that will actually be paid to creditors.

---

28 IR86, r 6.138A(2)(a) or IRN91, r 6.135A(2)(a).
29 IR86, r 6.138A(2)(b) or IRN91, r 6.135A(2)(b).
30 IR86, r.6.138A(3).
31 IR86, r.6.138A(4)(a).
32 IR86, r.6.138A(4)(b)(i).
33 IR86, r.6.138A(4)(b)(ii).
34 IR86, r.6.138A(4)(c).
35 IR86, r.6.138A(4)(d).

Table 1

The realisation scale

(i)	on the first £5,000 or fraction thereof	20%
(ii)	on the next £5,000 or fraction thereof	15%
(iii)	on the next £90,000 or fraction thereof	10%
(iv)	on all further sums realised	5%

Table 2

The distribution scale

(i)	on the first £5,000 or fraction thereof	10%
(ii)	on the next £5,000 or fraction thereof	7.5%
(iii)	on the next £90,000 or fraction thereof	5%
(iv)	on all further sums realised	2.5%

How does the trustee in bankruptcy communicate with creditors regarding remuneration?

13.12 The first communication creditors receive after a trustee has been appointed should include the SIP9 guidance notes for creditors on remuneration[36] or details of where the information can be found. Subsequently a creditors meeting[37] will be convened to either appoint a creditors' committee or themselves (the creditors) approve a basis[38] on which the remuneration will be calculated. The different type of available bases is discussed above. Also under the post-6 April 2010 regime, creditors are subsequently provided with an annual report setting out the basis or bases approved together with details of the calculation or apportionment of costs which is included in the schedule of expenses for that period.[39] In addition SIP9[40] requires an analysis of the time charged during that period to be attached to each report and the time included in the analysis should be backed up by explanations provided in the report. There is also a requirement to include in each report details of any changes in the charge out rates being used during the period. Any challenge can look at the total quantum for the period; the hours charged; and any increases in rates being charged.

How do creditors request additional information and/or challenge the trustee's remuneration?

13.13 Creditors making up at least 10% in value will have the opportunity to request further information if requested within 21 days of receipt of each progress report.[41] In addition creditors making up at least 25% in value[42] can challenge the quantum of the trustee's fees and expenses disclosed in each

36 Para 7 SIP9 version 6 issued with effect from 1 November 2011.
37 IR86, r 6.80 (first meeting) or r 6.81 (general power to convene meetings).
38 IR86, r 6.138(3)(c) or (5).
39 IR86, r 6.78A(6) to (8).
40 Paragraphs 13–17, SIP9 version 6 issued with effect from 1 November 2011.
41 IR86, r 6.78A(1)(a).
42 IR86, r 6.142(1).

reporting period. The challenge must be made within eight weeks of receipt of each progress report[43] and the court can fix the amount to be charged in that period[44] and can also vary the basis on which fees can be charged in subsequent periods.[45] The trustee's expenses can be challenged in the same way.[46]

What other regulations apply to information about fees?

13.14 The Insolvency (Amendment) Regulations 2005[47] inserted a new Part 5A into the Insolvency Regulations 1994[48] which requires an IP[49] to supply free of charge to any creditor, director or contributory of a company, or individual where the case relates to an individual, a statement of the number of hours spent on the case by the practitioner and his staff, the average hourly rate for that work and the number of hours spent by each grade of staff. Any request must be complied with within 28 days.[50] It should not be onerous if the practitioner is keeping the records which SIP9[51] prescribes.

Can a bankrupt challenge the trustee's remuneration?

13.15 An application by a bankrupt will only be considered if there is a surplus of assets to which the bankrupt would be entitled[52] excluding any remuneration and expenses charged. This is in accordance with existing principles that, save in exceptional circumstances, the bankrupt must be able to demonstrate he has some substantial interest in (usually financial) which has been adversely affected by whatever is complained of.[53]

What is the process for agreeing the basis and quantum of remuneration?

13.16 Post-6 April 2010 the bases available for remuneration additionally includes the ability to charge a set fee[54] and explicitly states that multiple bases can be used for dealing with different assets or activities in each bankrupt's estate.[55] Equally, if a percentage basis is being used different percentages can also be used in a similar manner.[56] The creditors' committee (if there is one, if

---

43 IR86, r 6.142(1A).

44 IR86, r 6.142(4)(a).

45 IR86, r 6.142(4)(b).

46 IR86, r 6.142(4)(c).

47 SI 2005/512, reg 8.

48 SI 1994/2507.

49 Insolvency Regulations 1994, SI 1994/2507, reg 36A(7), IR86 sets out that Insolvency Practitioner must be construed in accordance with s 388, IA86.

50 Insolvency Regulations 1994, SI 1994/2507, reg 36A(6).

51 SIP 9 latest version Issue 6 wef 1 November 2011.

52 IR86, r 6.142(4A).

53 See *Port v Auger* [1994] 1 WLR 862, [1994] 3 All ER 200, *Engel v Peri* [2002] EWHC 799 (Ch), [2002] BPIR 961, *Miller (Trustee in Bankruptcy of Bayliss) v Bayliss* [2009] BPIR 1438 and *Bank of Baroda v Patel* [2008] EWHC 3390 (Ch), [2009] BPIR 255.

54 IR86, r 6.138(2)(c) or IRN91, r 6.135(2)(c).

55 IR86, r 6.138(3A).

56 IR86, r 6.138(3B).

not the creditors in general meeting) will determine the bases to be used[57] and also the quantum to be charged in each period.

13.17 A new procedure was introduced for ensuring that the quantum to be charged in each period is effectively approved but this change will only apply to cases where the debtor's petition was filed in court on or after 6 April 2010.

The existing rules will remain in place for all bankrupts with petitions filed before 6 April 2010. In these cases a challenge can still be made at any time by creditors as long as they represent at least 25% in value. They must also demonstrate that the remuneration is in all circumstances excessive.[58]

13.18 For these 'new bankruptcies' creditors should be provided with an annual report setting out the basis or bases on which the fees are to be charged and showing how these have been calculated or apportioned for the period concerned.[59] In addition the schedule of expenses attached to the report must show for each period the remuneration to be charged for that period whether taken or not. It is the figure in this schedule of expenses that creditors have the opportunity to challenge. To assist in this process creditors have the right to request additional information before deciding whether they have the necessary support to make a formal challenge. As explained above to request additional information creditors should make up at least 5% in value and this must be requested within 21 days of receipt of a progress report[60] unless a meeting has been convened to accept the trustee's resignation in which case any request must be made within 7 business days of receipt.

13.19 Any subsequent formal challenge can only be made if creditors with at least 10% in value[61] are unhappy with either the quantum being charged or the basis previously agreed. The challenge must be made within eight weeks of receipt of the progress report[62] and the court can fix the amount to be charged in that period[63] and can also vary the basis on which fees can be charged in a subsequent period.[64] Expenses can be challenged in the same way.[65]

In respect of a challenge by the bankrupt, any application to court to challenge a trustee's fees will only be considered if there is a surplus of assets to which the bankrupt would be entitled[66] ie excluding the remuneration and expenses charged to the estate.

---

57 IR86, r 6.138(3C).
58 IR86, r 6.142.
59 IR86, r 6.78A(6)–(8).
60 IR86, r 6.78C(1) and (2).
61 IR86, r 6.142(1).
62 IR86, r 6.142(1A).
63 IR86, r 6.142(4)(a).
64 IR86, r 6.142(4)(b).
65 IR86, r 6.142(4)(c).
66 IR86, r 6.142(4A).

How is a trustee paid for selling the bankrupt's secured assets?

13.20 Where the trustee is other than the OR and he realises assets on behalf of a secured creditor, he is entitled to remuneration based on the realisation scale set out in Sch 6 IR86. The amount is calculated based on the funds received including any VAT.[67] The secured creditor is entitled to agree other terms with the trustee. However, in agreeing so to act on behalf of the secured creditor, the trustee should continue to ensure that he preserves his professional independence. The trustee's duty is to exercise his powers and privileges for the benefit of the creditors for whom he was appointed trustee, and not to accept an engagement for the benefit of a secured creditor.[68]

How is the remuneration shared when two or more trustees have been appointed?

13.21 Where there are joint trustees, it is for them to agree between themselves as to how the remuneration payable should be apportioned. Any dispute between them can be referred to the court, for settlement by order,[69] or the creditors' committee or a meeting of creditors, for settlement by resolution.[70]

If the trustee is a solicitor and employs his own firm, how are any legal costs dealt with?

13.22 The creditors' committee, the creditors, or the court[71] must approve any profit costs charged to the estate for work done by any solicitor, partner or other person employed by his firm.

Can a trustee's agreed remuneration be varied?

13.23 If the trustee's remuneration has been fixed by the creditors' committee, and he considers the rates or amount to be insufficient, he may request that it be increased by resolution of the creditors.[72] Or alternatively if the trustee's remuneration has been fixed by a creditors' committee or the creditors and he considers the rates or amount to be insufficient he can apply to court.[73]

How does a trustee apply to court for approval or a variation?

13.24 A trustee may consider that the remuneration approved is insufficient or inappropriate based on either the rates being charged or the total amount due and if neither the creditors' committee nor the creditors in a general meeting agree he can make an application to the court. For pre-April 2010 cases where there is a creditors' committee the trustee must give at least 14 days' notice of his application to the committee members; and the committee may nominate

---

67 IR86, r 6.139(1) or IRNI91, r 6.136(1).

68 See *Re Ng (a Bankrupt), Trustee of the estate of Ng v Ng* [1997] BPIR 267, *Judd v Brown* [1997] BPIR 470 and on appeal at [1999] BPIR 517 and *Trustee in Bankruptcy of Syed Bukhari v Bukhari and another* [1999] BPIR 157.

69 IR86, r 6.139(2)(a) or IRN91, r 6.136(2)(a).

70 IR86, r 6.139(2)(b) or IRN91, r 6.136(2)(b).

71 IR86, r 6.139(3) or IRN91, r 6.136(3).

72 IR86, r 6.140 or IRN91, r 6.137.

73 IR86, r 6.141(1) or IRN91, r 6.138(1).

one or more members to appear or be represented, and to be heard, on the application.[74] Where there is not a creditors' committee the trustee's notice of his application must be sent to one or more of the bankrupt's creditors as the court may direct. Those creditors may nominate one or more of their number to appear or be represented at the hearing.[75]

13.25 For post-April 2010 cases the trustee can request a review of his remuneration in a similar manner as the pre-April 2010 cases but must show there has been a material and substantial change in the circumstances from those taken into account when fixing it.[76] Any change requested will only apply from the date of the request and cannot be backdated to an earlier period.[77]

What is the process for a creditor to challenge the trustee's fees in court?

13.26 For pre-April 2010 cases any creditor of the bankrupt may, with the concurrence of at least 25% in value of the creditors (including himself), apply to the court for an order that the trustee's remuneration be reduced, on the grounds that it is, in all the circumstances, excessive.[78]

13.27 The creditor can make an application to the court setting out justification for the challenge. The court may, if it thinks that no sufficient cause is shown for the application, dismiss it; but must give the applicant an opportunity to attend the court for an *ex parte* hearing (a hearing without notice to any other party). The court must give the applicant at least 5 business days notice of that hearing. If the application is not dismissed under this paragraph, the court will fix a date for the hearing.[79]

13.28 Once a hearing date has been set the applicant must give at least 14 days' notice of it by sending to the trustee a notice stating the venue and a copy of the application with any supporting evidence which will be relied on at the hearing.[80]

13.29 If the court considers the application to be well-founded, it will make an order fixing the remuneration at a reduced amount or rate[81] and unless the court orders otherwise, the costs of the application shall be paid by the applicant, and do not fall on the estate.[82] Examples of issues raised are set out below. The court may, if it appears to be an appropriate case, order the costs of the trustee's application (including the costs of any member of the creditors' committee or any creditor or any representative), to be paid out of the estate.[83]

---

74 IR86, r 6.141(2) or IRN91, r 6.138(2).
75 IR86, r 6.141(3) or IRN91, r 6.138(3).
76 IR86, r 6.142.
77 IR86, r 6.142A(3).
78 IR86, r 6.142(1) or IRN91, r 6.139(1).
79 IR86, r 6.142(2) or IRN91, r 6.139(2).
80 IR86, r 6.141.
81 IR86, r 6.142(4) or IRN91, r 6.139(4).
82 IR86, r 6.142(5) or IRN91, r 6.139(5).
83 IR86, r 6.141(4) or IRN91, r 6.138(4).

13.30 For post-April 2010 cases a similar process applies except that the creditor value required has been reduced to 10%[84] and any application must be made no later than 8 weeks after the receipt of the relevant period's progress report.[85] The basis for any challenge remains the same and must in all circumstances show the remuneration and/or expenses were excessive.[86]

What other guidance must be followed in respect of a trustee's remuneration and expenses?

13.31 Further guidance on the process of getting fees authorised is contained in *Statement of Insolvency Practice 9*[87] and Part 5 of the *Practice Direction: Insolvency Proceedings* which came into effect on 23 February 2012. SIP9 also contains guidance on reporting requirements which have been refined and take into account issues that have arisen from case law.

What fee issues have been considered by the courts?

13.32 The question of office holder's remuneration has been considered in a number of recent cases. The modern starting point is *Mirror Group Newspapers plc v Maxwell and Others (No 2)*[88] in which Ferris J undertook a detailed review of the topic making the following major points as to the exception to the rule for fiduciaries and the proper bases for consideration of charging rates and principles:

> 'Office holders are nowadays not normally expected to act gratuitously. It is salutary to remember, however, that the rule that a trustee must not profit from his trust is a rule that applies to all kinds of person who are in a fiduciary position.[89] The allowance of remuneration in particular cases represents an exception to this rule, but it inevitably involves a conflict between the interest of the fiduciary who is to receive such remuneration and the interests of those to whom the fiduciary duties are owed, who will bear whatever remuneration is allowed. A consequence of this is that it must be for the office holder who seeks to be remunerated at a particular level to justify his claim. As I see it this is simply one aspect of the obligation to account. What he retains for himself out of the property which comes into his hands as office holder is not available for those towards whom he is a fiduciary. He cannot therefore account for it by paying it over. The only other way in which he can account for it is by showing that he ought to be allowed to retain it for himself. But this is necessarily a matter for him to establish.
>
> [T]he test of whether office holders have acted properly in undertaking particular tasks at a particular cost in expenses or time spent must be whether a reasonably prudent man, faced with the same circumstances in relation to his own affairs, would lay out or hazard his own money in doing what the office holders have done. It is not sufficient, in my view, for office holders to say that what they have

---

84 IR86, r 6.142(1).

85 IR86, r 6.142(1B).

86 IR86, r 6.142(1A).

87 Latest version is No 6 issued 1 November 2011.

88 [1998] 1 BCLC 638, [1998] BCC 324, ChD in spite of the judge's concerns virtually the whole of the remuneration claimed in that case was subsequently approved on assessment.

89 See *Snell's Equity* (28th edn, 1982) pp 249–252.

done is within the scope of the duties or powers conferred upon them. They are expected to deploy commercial judgment, not to act regardless of expense. This is not to say that a transaction carried out at a high cost in relation to the benefit received, or even an expensive failure, will automatically result in the disallowance of expenses or remuneration. But it is to be expected that transactions having these characteristics will be subject to close scrutiny.

It is important not to place too great an emphasis on time spent. In 1923 in *Re Carton Ltd* PO Lawrence J, dealing with the remuneration of liquidators in the voluntary winding up of a company, said:

> "The Court as a general rule only fixes remuneration on a time-basis if there is no other method which would operate to give the liquidator fair remuneration ... Even the best accountant may spend hours over unproductive work, let alone his more or less efficient staff of clerks. Moreover, it is quite impossible to check charges based on such a system and to gauge the value of odd hours said to have been spent on the affairs of the company. The Court has long since come to the conclusion that the proper method to adopt whenever it is practicable is to assess the remuneration according to the results attained".'

13.33 Ferris J's concerns about rising levels of remuneration and over-emphasis on time cost[90] led to the establishment of a working party chaired by him which reported to the Lord Chancellor in June 1998.[91] A major outcome was the passing of the *Practice Statement (Fixing and Approval of Remuneration of Appointees 2004)* of 1 October 2004 formulated by a sub-committee of the Insolvency Courts Users' Committee. The *Practice Statement* sets out procedural matters and indicates the level and nature of the information the courts expect to see where remuneration is being applied for. It also enunciates a number of principles relevant to the assessment of remuneration: the need for the office holder to justify his remuneration; that in cases of doubt, such doubt will be resolved against the office holder; however, due regard should be paid to his professional status; remuneration should reflect value and should be fair and reasonable; the information to be provided should be proportionate to the level of remuneration sought and the remuneration itself should be proportionate to the nature, complexity and extent of the work undertaken; regard should be had to professional guidance.[92]

13.34 The majority of reported cases on remuneration relate to corporate insolvency,[93] although the principles apply equally to individual insolvency. For

---

90 Which were shared by many: see for example, (Sir) Gavin Lightman, 'Office holders' charges: cost control and transparency', *Insolvency Law and Practice* 1998, 14(3,) pp 193–198 and Mr Justice Lightman, 'The challenges ahead: address to the Insolvency Lawyers' Association', *Journal of Business Law* March 1998, pp 113–126.

91 Report of Mr Justice Ferris's *Working Party on the Remuneration of Office Holders and Certain Related Matters*; for a commentary see Michael Mulligan and John Tribe, 'The Remuneration of Office Holders in Corporate Insolvency', *Insolvency Lawyer* May 2003, Vol 3, pp 101–107.

92 See, for example, Statement of Insolvency Practice 9.

93 See **13.32**.

examples of the court's consideration of trustees' remuneration see *Engel v Peri*[94] (in which the court held that the bankrupt could challenge the remuneration of his trustee under s 363, IA86 or under the inherent jurisdiction of the court where he was applying for an annulment), *Woodbridge v Smith*[95] (where the wife of the bankrupt mounted a challenge to the basis of remuneration under s 303, IA86), *Simion v Brown*[96] (where the court reduced the trustee's remuneration) and *Barker v Bajjon*[97] (where the court increased the trustee's remuneration on her application). The decision in *Re Cabletel Installations Ltd (in Liquidation)*[98] highlighted that the ability to produce comprehensive time-sheets showing the work undertaken is not, of itself, justification for allowing an IP to draw those fees from an insolvent estate. Following this decision (and in line with the *Practice Statement* on the remuneration of insolvency office holders), there is a two fold requirement to both demonstrate that the time was correctly charged to the estate and that value was provided to the estate for the time charged.

13.35 For consideration of remuneration by the courts in other cases see also: *Re Independent Insurance Co Ltd (No 1)*;[99] *Re Independence Insurance Co Ltd (No 2)*;[100] *Mirror Group Newspapers plc v Maxwell and Others (No 2)*;[101] *Re UIC Insurance Company Ltd (In Provisional Liquidation) (No 1)*;[102] *Re UIC Insurance Company Ltd (In Provisional Liquidation) (No 2)*;[103] *Hunt v Yearwood-Grazette*[104] (in which the court refused a trustee's application for possession and sale of a bankrupt's house to pay his remuneration and expenses in line with the findings in *Re Cabletel Installations Ltd (In Liquidation)*;[105] *Freeburn v Hunt*[106] (holding that the trustee had discharged the onus of justifying the remuneration claimed by him, which was in fact about 60% of the time costs involved.)

13.36 The application of the *Practice Statement* was recently considered by the Court of Appeal in *Brook v Reed (Trustee in Bankruptcy of the estate of Helen Brook)*,[107] where the debtor had challenged the trustee's remuneration and expenses on an annulment application. The amounts had been heavily reduced by a judge (sitting with two assessors) on a hearing without being referred to the *Practice Statement*. The bankrupt appealed further. Nonetheless, the Court of Appeal found that the judge had applied what were

---

94 [2002] BPIR 961.
95 [2004] BPIR 247.
96 [2007] EWHC 511 (Ch), [2007] BPIR 412.
97 [2008] BPIR 771.
98 [2005] BPIR 28.
99 [2002] EWHC 1577 (Ch), [2003] BPIR 562, [2002] 2 BCLC 709.
100 [2003] EWHC 51 (Ch), [2003] BPIR 577, [2003] 1 BCLC 640.
101 [1998] 1 BCLC 638, [1998] BCC 324.
102 [2006] EWHC 2717 (Ch), [2007] BPIR 494.
103 [2007] BPIR 589.
104 [2009] EWHC 2112 (Ch), [2009] BPIR 810.
105 [2005] BPIR 28.
106 [2010] BPIR 325.
107 [2011] EWCA Civ 331.

fundamentally the relevant criteria to the facts of this case, and dismissed the appeal, after usefully setting out a full consideration of the history and development of the *Practice Statement* and guidance as to its future application.

What other routine costs does a trustee incur?

13.37 There are a number of routine expenses that a trustee incurs that is charged to every estate. These include items such as the cost of the required bond relating to the specific assets of the case,[108] the cost of each *Gazette* notice set out in the legislation plus variable items such as asset insurance, agent's costs in securing or safeguarding premises or assets and legal costs depending on the circumstances of each case. In cases where there are no funds available at the start of the case then these are usually paid by the trustee and reimbursed as and when funds are available but they should be shown as relevant expenses in the period in which they were incurred.

[108] Insolvency Practitioners Regulations 2005, Part 3 and Sch 2.

Chapter 14

CREDITOR COMMUNICATION INCLUDING MEETINGS AND COMMITTEE FORMALITIES IN BANKRUPTCY PROCEEDINGS

'Creditors have better memories than debtors; and creditors are a superstitious sect, great observers of set days and times.'[1]

INTRODUCTION

14.1 This chapter covers all communication with creditors including initial notifications, statutory reports and meetings. It also includes guidance on the introduction of progress reports for creditors with effect from 6 April 2010 where the trustee is someone other than the OR. The meetings section covers meeting formalities, the role of the chairman, the process of submitting claims and proxies for voting purposes and also the constitution and duties of the creditors' committee. The process of distributing the assets to creditors is dealt with in chapter 15.

Who are the creditors in a bankruptcy?

14.2 Any reference to creditors of the bankrupt includes all creditors who are known to the OR or, where the bankrupt has submitted a statement of affairs, are identified in the statement.[2] Chapter 4 looked at the different types of debt and creditors in detail.

What information is the Official Receiver required to send to the creditors?

14.3 The OR must send a report to all the creditors of a bankrupt in the following circumstances:

- At least one report must be sent advising them of the bankruptcy proceedings, and setting out the state of the bankrupt's affairs.[3]

- Where the bankrupt has submitted a statement of affairs, and it has been filed in court, the OR should send a report containing a summary of the statement with any amendments or observations in respect of the

---

1 Benjamin Franklin.
2 IR86, r 6.74 or IRN91, r 6.072.
3 IR86, r 6.73(1) or IRN91, r 6.071(1).

statement or the bankrupt's affairs generally[4] unless a report has already been sent and there are no additional matters to report.[5]

- If a bankrupt is released from the obligation of submitting a statement of affairs then the OR should send to creditors a report containing a summary of the bankrupt's affairs (so far as within his knowledge), and his observations (if any) with respect to it or the bankrupt's affairs generally[6] unless a report has already been sent and there are no additional matters to report.[7]

- A copy of any report circulated to creditors must be filed in court.[8]

- The court may, on the OR's application, relieve him of any duty imposed on him by this Chapter of the Rules, or authorise him to carry out the duty in a way other than there required.[9] The court, when considering such an application, must have regard to the cost of carrying out the duty, to the amount of the funds available in the estate, and to the extent of the interest of creditors or any particular class of them.[10]

- An application can be made to court for relief of any of these reporting duties. The court will have regard to the cost of carrying out these duties, the funds available in the estate and the interests of the creditors when considering such an application.

What information is the trustee (when not the official receiver) required to send to the creditors?

14.4 Notices of the appointment are required as follows:

- Appointment by creditors: by gazette and other advert if considered appropriate by the trustee.[11]

- Appointment by SoS: by individual notice or if the court allows by advertisement in accordance with the courts' directions.[12]

- Appointment by court: by individual notice or if the court allows by advertisement in accordance with the courts' directions.[13]

---

4 IR86, r 6.75(1) or IRN91, r 6.073(1).
5 IR86, r 6.75(2) or IRN91, r 6.073(2).
6 IR86, r 6.76(2) or IRN91, r 6.074(2).
7 IR86, r 6.76(3) or IRN91, r 6.074(3).
8 IR86, r 6.73(2) or IRN91, r 6.071(2).
9 IR86, r 6.77(1) or IRN91, r 6.075(1).
10 IR86, r 6.77(2) or IRN91, r 6.075(2).
11 IR86, r 6.124(1).
12 IA86, s 296(4) or INO89, art 269(4).
13 IA86, s 297(7) or INO89, art 270(7).

14.5 A trustee is required to convene a meeting of creditors to either constitute a committee or obtain general authorisation for the basis on which his fees are to be charged if a meeting has not already been convened by the OR. There are specific rules covering the business that can be considered at a first meeting of creditors which are discussed below.

14.6 A trustee is also required to provide any creditor on request (within 14 days) a copy of his previous year's accounts.[14] Similarly if there is a creditors' committee then they are also entitled to view the trustee's financial records[15] and report on any shortcomings to the SoS.[16]

14.7 Where a trustee other than the OR is in office[17] there is now a requirement to circulate progress reports to creditors at least annually[18] from the date of the trustee's appointment to the date he vacates office[19] except where a final report has already been issued.[20] The reports must be sent to creditors within 2 months of the end of each period of 12 months[21] except where the court has extended this period on application of the trustee.[22] The information required in each report is covered in more detail below but this only applies to cases where the bankruptcy order was made after 6 April 2010.[23]

14.8 A final meeting must be convened[24] at which the trustee lays before the creditors an account of his acts and dealings. Details of his remuneration and expenses must be provided and the creditors are given the opportunity to object to the trustee being given his release[25] after he has filed his final receipts and payments account. For cases with bankruptcy orders made after 6 April 2010 the additional requirement is that a draft of the final progress report must be sent to creditors at least 8 weeks[26] before the final meeting is held. The report will cover essentially the same information as previously required to be produced at the final creditors meeting however the new rules include additional detail on the matters that need to be covered and these are set out in detail below. The draft report must not be sent while any dividend or no dividend notice is pending[27] or there is any other matter pending preventing the

---

14 SI 1994/2507, reg 25 or SR 1996/574.
15 SI 1994/2507, reg 24(3) or SR 1996/574.
16 SI 1994/2507, reg 24(4) or SR 1996/574.
17 IR86, r 6.78A(10).
18 IR86, r 6.78A(6).
19 IR86, r 6.78A(7).
20 IR86, r 6.78A(5).
21 IR86, r 6.78A(8).
22 IR86, r 6.78A(9).
23 Draft Legislative Reform (Insolvency) (Miscellaneous Provisions) Order 2009: 'in the case of a bankruptcy, the debtor was adjudged bankrupt before 6th April 2010'. Finalised as the Legislative Reform (Insolvency) (Miscellaneous Provisions) Order 2010.
24 IA86, s 331 or INO89, art 304.
25 IR86, r 6.137(6) or IRN91, r 6.134(6).
26 IR86, r 6.138B(1) or IRN91, r 6.134(6).
27 IR86, r 6.78B(3).

final meeting from being held or concluded.[28] This new requirement gives creditors the opportunity to request additional information and if appropriate challenge the quantum of the final fees before the final meeting is held rather than having to propose a resolution against release and challenge the fees after the case is closed.

What information needs to be included in a progress report?

14.9 A progress report should contain the following information:[29]

- the bankrupt's name;[30]
- details of the court where the proceedings are and the relevant court reference number;[31]
- the title of the proceedings;[32]
- full details of the trustee's name and address and date of appointment, including any changes in office holder;[33]
- details of the basis set for the remuneration of the trustee under r 6.138, IR86 (or if not set at the date of the report, the steps taken during the period of the report to set it);[34]
- details of progress during the period of the report, including a receipts and payments account (see below for the format);[35]
- details of any assets that remain to be realised;[36] and
- any other relevant information for the creditors.[37]

14.10 The abstract receipts and payments must show the receipts and payments during the period of the report. In addition best practice guidance in SIP7 requires these abstracts to show both the period and cumulative figures together with the Statement of Affairs figures as comparatives.[38] Full details of all remuneration and expenses taken during the period or being requested for approval must also be clearly shown in the receipts and payment account and if

---

28 IR86, r 6.78B(4).
29 IR86, r 6.78A.
30 IR86, r 6.78A(1)(b).
31 IR86, r 6.78A(1)(a).
32 IR86, r 6.78A(1)(c).
33 IR86, r 6.78A(1)(d).
34 IR86, r 6.78A(1)(e).
35 IR86, r 6.78A(1)(f).
36 IR86, r 6.78A(1)(g).
37 IR86, r 6.78A(1)(h).
38 SIP 7.

these amounts cover more than one period they must be separately disclosed.[39] This does not apply where the basis of payment has not yet been agreed[40] and in the case of a fixed payment, the full amount must be shown in the period in which it is paid and not apportioned across subsequent periods.[41]

What information needs to be included in a draft final progress report?

14.11 A final progress report should contain the following information:[42]

- contain such matters and be in such terms as would comply with r 6.137, IR86 if the report were to be laid before a meeting as soon as reasonably practicably after the draft had been sent to creditors; and

- be accompanied by a statement of the creditors' right to request information under r 6.78C, IR86 and their right to challenge the trustee's remuneration and expenses under r 6.142, IR86.

What is the process for a creditor to request further information on remuneration and expenses after receipt of a progress report or draft final progress report?

14.12 Any creditor with more than 10% in value of the voting rights, or any creditor with the concurrence of at least 10% in value,[43] can within 21 days of receipt of the progress report request further information on remuneration and expenses from the trustee.[44] Where a progress report has been issued with a notice of intended resignation under r 6.126, IR86 the time allowed is only 10 days[45] instead of 21 days.

14.13 The trustee must, within 14 days of receipt of any request provide the additional information[46] except where the trustee considers any of the following apply in which case the reasons must be stated:[47]

- the time or cost of preparation of the information would be excessive; or

- disclosure of the information would be prejudicial to the conduct of the bankruptcy; or

- the trustee is subject to an obligation of confidentiality in respect of the information.

---

39 IR86, r 6.78A(4).
40 IR86, r 6.78A(3)(a).
41 IR86, r 6.78A(3)(b).
42 IR86, r 6.78A.
43 IR86, r 6.78C(1).
44 IR86, r 6.78C(1)(a).
45 IR86, r 6.78C(1)(b).
46 IR86, r 6.78C(1)(b).
47 IR86, r 6.78C(2).

14.14 If the trustee uses one of these excuses any creditor with more than 10% in value of the voting rights, or any creditor with the concurrence of at least 10% in value can apply to the court to challenge this decision and the court has the power to make any order it sees fit. The application to court must be made within 21 days of the trustee's refusal to provide the information[48] or if the trustee has failed to provide any information within 21 days of the expiry of the 14 day deadline.[49]

CREDITORS' MEETINGS

When are creditors' meetings held?

14.15 Creditors' meetings can be convened as follows:

- A first meeting: usually held to appoint a trustee other than the OR.[50]
- Creditors can requisition a meeting[51] if the OR does not convene a first meeting.
- General meeting: the OR or the trustee may at any time summon and conduct meetings of creditors for the purpose of ascertaining their wishes in all matters relating to a bankruptcy. In relation to any meeting of creditors, the person summoning it is referred to as 'the convener'.[52]
- Final meeting: if the trustee is not the OR[53] a final meeting must be held to provide creditors with a final outcome of the estate[54] and to allow creditors an opportunity to object to the trustee's release.[55]

Meeting notices

What is the procedure for convening a 'first meeting of creditors'?

14.16 The OR is usually the person who convenes the 'first meeting of creditors'.[56] The purpose of convening the meeting is to allow creditors to appoint a trustee other than himself. If a meeting is to be held it must be held within 4 months of the bankruptcy order.[57] The procedure is as follows:

---

48 IR86, r 6.78C(3)(a).
49 IR86, r 6.78C(3)(b).
50 IA86, s 293(1) or INO89, art 266(1).
51 IA86, s 294(1) or INO89, art 267(1).
52 IR86, r 6.81(1) or IRN91, r 6.079(1).
53 IA86, s 331(1)(b) or INO89, art 304(1)(b).
54 IA86, s 331(2)(a) or INO89, art 304(2)(a).
55 IA86, s 331(2)(b) or INO89, art 304(2)(b).
56 IR86, r 6.79(7) or IRN91, r 6.077(7).
57 IR86, r 6.79(1) or IRN91, r 6.077(1).

- Fix a venue.[58]
- Send a notice to court[59] as soon as the venue and date is fixed (forthwith).[60]
- Send notices to every known creditor[61] at least 21 days before the meeting date.[62]
- Advertise the meeting[63] and for bankruptcies post-5 April 2009 every meeting now must be gazetted.[64] The court may order that notice of the meeting can be given by public advertisement only rather than by individual notice to the persons concerned.[65]

What information does the meeting notice contain and when and where can a meeting be held?

14.17 The meeting notice must contain:

- The date, time and place of the meeting.
- The time and date by which proofs must be lodged (not more than 4 days before the date fixed for the meeting) and (if applicable) proxies, in order to be entitled to vote at the meeting.
- The meeting has to be located at a venue that is convenient for the creditors[66] and must be held between 10.00am and 4.00pm unless the court otherwise directs.[67]
- 'Give notice' is defined in r 13.3, IR86. It states that service must be by post unless otherwise specified in the relevant rule As a consequence a court order is required if another method of notice is going to be used.

What matters does the court consider when deciding whether notice can be given by another method?

14.18 The court will consider all the circumstances of the case including the cost of a public advertisement, the amount of the funds available in the estate, and the extent of the interest of creditors or any particular class of them.

---

58 IR86, r 6.79(2) or IRN91, r 6.077(2).
59 IR86, r 6.79(2)(a) or IRN91, r 6.077(2).
60 IR86, r 6.79(3) or IRN91, r 6.077(3).
61 IR86, r 6.79(2)(b) or IRN91, r 6.077(2)(b).
62 IR86, r 6.79(3) or IRN91, r 6.077(3).
63 IR86, r 6.79(5) or IRN91, r 6.077(5).
64 IR86, r 6.79(5) or IRN91, r 6.077(5).
65 IR86, r 6.85(1) or r 6.85(1) IRN91, r 6.85(1).
66 IR86, r 6.86(1) or IRN91, r 6.084(1).
67 IR86, r 6.86(2) or IRN91, r 6.084(2).

Who pays for the expenses of summoning a creditors' meeting?

14.19 The expenses of summoning a meeting convened by the OR or trustee are usually an expense of the estate. If someone other than the OR or trustee requisitions a meeting then the expenses are usually met by that person.[68] An appropriate sum must be deposited[69] before the meeting is convened, however once summoned the creditors can resolve that the expense of summoning and holding the meeting can be paid as an expense of the estate.[70] If this is agreed then any deposit paid must then be returned.[71]

What is the purpose of the 'first creditors' meeting'?

14.20 The creditors' meeting is held to discuss and determine the following:

- the appointment of an IP as trustee of the estate, or two or more IPs to act as joint trustees;[72]
- the establishment of creditors' committee;[73] and
- in the absence of a committee being formed resolutions in respect of the acts and dealings of the trustee including the power to act jointly or severally,[74] the basis for charging fees;[75] or
- any other resolution which the chairman allows for special reasons.[76]

What is the purpose of any subsequent creditors' meeting and what is the process for convening one?

14.21 The trustee in bankruptcy and the creditors have the power to convene a general meeting of creditors at any time and these are set out in the IR 1986. For the trustee this power is set out in r 6.81, IR86 and for creditors this power is set out in r 6.83, IR86.

14.22 The trustee or the OR will only call a meeting of creditors if there is an issue which needs to put to the creditors or other significant event which needs to be explained outside the normal reporting process. The notice for the meeting must set out this purpose clearly[77] together with the details of submitting proxies (not more than 4 days before the meeting). When the venue for the meeting has been fixed, notice for this type of meeting will be given on

---

68 IR86, r 6.87(1) or IRN91, r 6.085(1).
69 IR86, r 6.87(2) or IRN91, r 6.085(2).
70 IR86, r 6.87(3) or IRN91, r 6.085(3).
71 IR86, r 6.87(4) or IRN91, r 6.085(4)
72 IR86, r 6.80(1)(a) or IRN91, r 6.078(1)(a).
73 IR86, r 6.80(1)(b) or IRN91, r 6.078(1)(b).
74 IR86, r 6.80(1)(d) or IRN91, r 6.078(1)(d).
75 IR86, r 6.80(1)(c) or IRN91, r 6.078(1)(c).
76 IR86, r 6.80(1)(g) or IRN91, r 6.078(1)(g).
77 IR86, r 6.81(3) or IRN91, r 6.079(3).

Form 6.35 and creditors must be given at least 21 days' notice.[78] Other advertisement of the meeting will be at the trustee's discretion[79] and for appointments post-April 2009 all meetings must also be gazetted.[80]

When and why can a creditor requisition a creditors' meeting?

14.23 Section 294, IA86 allows creditors with at least one quarter in value (of the bankrupt's creditors) *to requisition* a creditors' meeting. The application needs to be made on Form 6.34 which contains the following:

- A statement of the purpose of the meeting.[81]
- A list of creditors concurring with the request including the amount of their claims.[82]
- The request can be made by a single creditor if their debt is for more than one quarter in value of the bankrupt's debts.[83] Otherwise written confirmation of agreement is required from all of the creditors listed above.[84]

14.24 Examples of a creditor's purpose are:

- To appoint a trustee in bankruptcy other than the OR where a first meeting has not been convened.[85]
- To remove or replace the trustee.[86]
- To challenge any action or inaction by the trustee in the absence of a creditors' committee.

How is a requisitioned creditors' meeting convened?

14.25 If a valid request is received then the trustee in bankruptcy (OR or IP in office) must convene a meeting as follows:

- Fix a date and place for the meeting not more than 35 days after receipt of the request.[87]

---

78 IR86, r 6.81(2) or IRN91, r 6.079(2).
79 IR86, r 6.81(4) or IRN91, r 6.079(1)(a).
80 This change was introduced by the Insolvency (Amendment) Rules 2009, SI 2009/642.
81 IR86, r 6.83(1)(c) or IRN91, r 6.081(1)(c).
82 IR86, r 6.83(1)(a) or IRN91, r 6.081(1)(a).
83 IA86, s 294(2) (as amended) or INO89, art 267(2).
84 IR86, r 6.83(1)(b) or IRN91, r 6.081(1)(b).
85 IA86, s 293(2) or INO89, art 266(2).
86 IR86, r 6.129 or IRN91, r 6.126.
87 IR86, r 6.83(2)(a) or IRN91, r 6.081(2)(a).

- Creditors must be given a minimum of 21 days' notice of the date, time and place of the meeting excluding the date of posting and the date of the meeting.[88]

- Notices have to be sent to all the known creditors[89] and the venue advertised.[90]

What should the meeting notice contain?

14.26 The meeting notice sent to creditors must include the following:

- Details of the venue[91] which includes the time, date, and place of the meeting.[92]

- Proof of debt and proxy.[93]

If a resolution is being proposed for the basis of any remuneration to be charged then the notice must also include:

- An up-to-date receipts and payments account.[94]

- An analysis of any time charged up to the date of the notice/report.[95]

- Details of the hourly rates charged by grade.[96]

- SIP9 guidance notes or where they can be found.[97]

How much notice should be given to creditors of a meeting and how are notice periods calculated?

14.27 In respect of any meeting other than a final meeting the convener must give at least 21 days' notice to the creditors.[98] For a final meeting the trustee must give at least 28 days' notice to the creditors.[99] Notice periods are always 'clear days' that is excluding the day of posting and the day of the meeting. Part 12A of the IR86 sets out all the detailed requirements for the service of documents.

---

88 IR86, r 6.83(2)(b) or IRN91, r 6.081(2)(b).
89 IR86, r 6.79(2)(b) or IRN91, r 6.077(2)(b).
90 IR86, r 6.79(5) or IRN91, r 6.077(5).
91 IR86, r 13.6.
92 If convened by the OR; IR86, r 6.79(1).
93 IR86, rr 6.93(1) and 6.97 or IRN91, rr 6.090(1) and 6.095.
94 Paragraph 3.4, SIP9 version 4.
95 Paragraph 3.4, SIP9 version 4.
96 Paragraph 3.3, SIP9 version 4.
97 Paragraph 3.1, SIP9 version 4.
98 First meeting: IR86, r 6.79(3) and General meeting: IR86, r 6.81(2) or First meeting: IRN91, r 6.077(3) and General meeting IRN91, r 6.09(2).
99 IR86, r 6.137(1) or IRN91, r 6.134(1).

What evidence is required of posting?

14.28 Office holders are required to maintain a proof of the circulation of any document circulated.[100] A certificate of posting should be completed by any relevant person including the OR, trustee, trustee's solicitor and relevant member of their staff.[101] The certificate can simply be an endorsed copy of the document sent.[102] Rules 12A.10 and 12A.11 deal with the transmission of electronic documents and the need to obtain the consent of the recipient before notices can be sent electronically rather than in hard copy.[103]

Meeting formalities

What happens at the creditors' meeting?

14.29 Before the formal business of the meeting commences the chairman of the meeting will ask all attendees to sign an attendance register[104] and identify themselves if they are attending as a proxy holder for one or more of the creditors. The formal business of a meeting may vary but will usually include the presentation of a report followed by voting on one or more resolutions proposed by the chairman. The voting process is discussed below.

Is the bankrupt required to attend a creditors' meeting?

14.30 The convener of a creditors' meeting can require a bankrupt to attend the meeting[105] but the convenor must give the bankrupt at least 21 days' notice.[106] Equally, a bankrupt may attend any creditors' meeting that has been convened if he advises the convener and obtains consent.[107] The chairman has the final decision on who may attend the meeting and any dispute should be documented in the minutes. Equally, if the bankrupt attends it is the chairman who will decide if any questions can be directed to the bankrupt.[108]

Who chairs the meeting and what are the chairman's duties?

14.31 Where the convener of a meeting is an OR then he, or a person other than an OR or his deputy can be nominated by him in writing, must chair the meeting.[109] Where the convener is someone other than an OR then the convener, or a person nominated by him in writing, must chair the meeting.[110]

---

[100] IR86, r 12A.8(1).
[101] IR86, r 12A.8(2) and (3).
[102] IR86, r 12A.8(5).
[103] IR86, r 12A.7.
[104] IR86, r 6.95(2) or IRN91, r 6.092(2).
[105] IR86, r 6.84(3) or IRN91, r 6.082(3).
[106] IR86, r 6.84(1) or IRN91, r 6.082(1).
[107] IR86, r 6.84(4) or IRN91, r 6.082(4).
[108] IR86, r 6.84(6) or IRN91, r 6.082(6).
[109] IR86, r 6.82(1) or IRN91, r 6.080(1).
[110] IR86, r 6.82(2) or IRN91, r 6.080(2).

Any person nominated by a convener must be either a qualified IP or an experienced employee of the trustee or his firm.[111]

14.32 The chairman should do the following before the meeting:

- Ensure the meeting has been validly convened by checking that notices, advertisements and gazetting have all been completed in accordance with the relevant rules.

- Inspect and adjudicate on all proxies and proofs in accordance with the detailed rules set out below.

- Take control of the proceedings and present a report on the purpose of the meeting to the creditors.

- Ensure that a register is kept of all attendees.[112]

- Conduct all voting in accordance with the rules set out below.

- Prepare minutes of the meeting.[113]

- Report the outcome to the trustee (if not being chaired by him).

- File a list of all resolutions passed in court[114] within 21 days of the meeting.

When is a creditors' meeting validly constituted and how long must a chairman wait for creditors to arrive?

14.33 A meeting is validly constituted if a quorum is present, which for these purposes is the attendance of one creditor either by person or by proxy.[115] The chairman must allow fifteen minutes for known creditors to arrive before commencing a meeting[116] or thirty minutes before declaring it inquorate.[117]

Voting procedures

How do creditors vote at a meeting?

14.34 Creditors can either attend the meeting in person or they can give a proxy to another person to vote on their behalf. With every notice summoning a creditors' meeting there must be attached a proxy form.[118]

---

[111] IR86, r 6.82(2) or IRN91, r 6.080(2).
[112] IR86, r 6.95(2) or IRN91, r 6.092(2).
[113] IR86, r 6.95 (1) or IRN91, r 6.092(1).
[114] IR86, r 6.95 (3) or IRN91, r 6.092(3).
[115] IR86, r 12.4A(2)(a).
[116] IR86, r 12.4A(4).
[117] IR86, r 6.91(2) or IRN91, r 6.089(2).
[118] Form 8.5; see IR86, r 6.86(3) or IRN91, r 6.084(3).

14.35 The person nominated on the proxy form can be any person authorised by the creditor to attend the meeting or alternatively the proxy can be given to the chairman of the meeting to vote on their behalf.

14.36 A proxy can be either 'general' or 'special'. A general proxy allows the proxy holder to vote in whatever manner they want on the creditor's behalf whereas a special proxy includes details on how the proxy holder must vote on specific resolutions. A special proxy can be used as a general proxy when voting on resolutions not specified on the proxy form.

What documentation needs to be lodged to entitle a creditor to vote?

14.37 The requirements are as follows:

- A proof of debt needs to be lodged by the time and date specified on the meeting notice.[119]

- A proxy issued specifically for that meeting needs to be lodged by the time and date specified on the meeting notice.[120] A proxy is only valid if the creditor has also submitted a claim which has been admitted for voting purposes.

- For a Member State liquidator who has claimed as a creditor in the proceedings, the claim must have been admitted under r 6.94, IR86 for the purpose of entitlement to vote.[121] if more than liquidator attempts to claim for the same debt then only the liquidator of the main proceedings can vote.[122]

14.38 The court may, in exceptional circumstances, by order declare the creditors, or any class of them, entitled to vote at creditors' meetings, without being required to prove their debts. Where a creditor is so entitled, the court may, on the application of the trustee, make such consequential orders as it thinks fit (for example, an order treating a creditor as having proved his debt for the purpose of permitting payment of dividend).[123]

How are votes counted?

14.39 A vote can only be cast as follows:

- For a liquidated sum.[124]

---

[119] IR86, r 6.93(1)(a) or IRN91, r 6.090(1)(a).
[120] IR86, r 6.93(1)(b) or IRN91, r 6.090(1)(b).
[121] IR86, r 6.93(1)(a)(ii) or IRN91, r 6.090(1)(a)(ii).
[122] IR86, r 6.93(8) or IRN91, r 6.090(8).
[123] IR86, r 6.93(2) or IRN91, r 6.090(2).
[124] IR86, r 6.93(3) or IRN91, r 6.090(3).

- For the balance outstanding after any security has been valued and deducted.[125]
- Each creditor can only use their vote once in respect of each separate resolution[126] and where a proxy has been submitted and the creditor also attends in person, only the creditors' vote will be counted.[127]
- A resolution is passed when a majority in value of those present and voting in person or by proxy, have voted in favour of the resolution.[128]
- Any dispute over the amount to be used for voting purposes must be recorded in the minutes however the chairman has the final say on the amount allowed. This process is covered in more detail below.
- The process of voting for the appointment of a trustee[129] is covered in detail in chapter 12.

What is a liquidated sum?

14.40 A liquidated sum is an amount that has been quantified or determined in some manner ie invoiced or otherwise agreed. The debtor may dispute a liquidated sum but this is a separate issue which can only be addressed after the status as a liquidated sum has been determined. Common examples of an unliquidated debt are an unassessed solicitor's bill[130] or an unquantified claim in damages.

Proof of debt and agreement of claims

14.41 This section covers the procedure for agreeing claims for voting purposes at any creditors' meeting. Chapter 15 separately covers the declaration and final admission of proofs for dividend purposes.

What is a proof of debt?

14.42 A person claiming to be a creditor of the bankrupt and wishing to recover his debt in whole or in part must (subject to any order of the court under r 6.93(2), IR86) submit his claim in writing to the OR, where acting as receiver and manager, or to the trustee.[131] The creditor is referred to as

---

125 IR86, r 6.93(4) and (5) or IRN91, r 6.090(4) and (5).
126 IR86, r 6.93(6) or IRN91, r 6.090(6).
127 IR86, r 6.93(7) or IRN91, r 6.090(7).
128 IR86, r 6.88(1) or IRN91, r 6.086(1).
129 IR86, r 6.88(1) or IRN91, r 6.086(1).
130 *Truex v Toll* [2009] EWHC 396 (Ch), [2009] BPIR 692, *Wallace LLP v Yates* [2010] EWHC 1098 (Ch), [2010] BPIR 1041 and *Moseley v Else Solicitors LLP* [2010] BPIR 1192.
131 IR86, r 6.96(1) or IRN91, r 6.094(1).

'proving' for his debt; and the document by which he seeks to establish his claim is his 'proof'.[132] The trustee or OR must send a proof of debt to each creditor for completion.[133]

What form does a proof of debt take and when can it be varied?

14.43 The proof must be in the form known as 'proof of debt' usually Form 6.37, which must be completed by or under the directions of the creditor, and signed by him or a person authorised by him.[134] A creditor's proof can be varied or withdrawn at any time with the agreement of the trustee.[135]

14.44 Alternatives may be used as follows:

- Where a debt is due to a Minister of the Crown or a Government department, the proof need not be on Form 6.37, provided that all the details required on Form 6.37 and that are relevant are provided.[136]
- Where an existing trustee proves in a later bankruptcy under s 335(5), IA86, the proof must be in Form 6.38.[137]
- A trustee can also sometimes request that the proof is in the form of an affidavit in which case Form 6.39 must be used.[138]

What information is required on a proof of debt form?

14.45 The following information is required on a proof of debt form:

- the creditor's name and address, and, if a company, its company registration number;[139]
- the total amount of the claim (including any VAT) as at the date of the bankruptcy order;[140]
- whether or not that amount includes outstanding uncapitalised interest;[141]
- particulars of how and when the debt was incurred by the debtor;[142]

---

132 IR86, r 6.96(2) or IRN91, r 6.094(2).
133 IR86, r 6.97(1) or IRN91, r 6.095(1).
134 IR86, r 6.96(3) or IRN91, r 6.094(3).
135 IR86, r 6.106 or IRN91, r 6.103.
136 IR86, r 6.96(4) or IRN91, r 6.094(4).
137 IR86, r 6.96(5) or IRN91, r 6.094(5).
138 IR86, r 6.96(6) or IRN91, r 6.094(6).
139 IR86, r 6.98(1)(a) or IRN91, r 6.096(1)(a).
140 IR86, r 6.98(1)(b) or IRN91, r 6.096(1)(b).
141 IR86, r 6.98(1)(c) or IRN91, r 6.096(1)(c).
142 IR86, r 6.98(1)(d) or) IRN91, r 6.096(1)(d).

- particulars of any security held, the date when it was given and the value which the creditor puts upon it;[143]
- details of any reservation of title in respect of goods to which the debt refers;[144] and
- the name, and address and authority of the person signing the proof (if other than the creditor himself);[145]
- the proof must specify the documents on which the claim is based and that must be provided if requested.[146]

What is uncapitalised interest?

14.46 Uncapitalised interest is interest that has accrued but is not added to the principal loan as would happen with a bank. This allows creditors who have a right to charge interest and have claimed it as due to include the amount in the debt outstanding. Only interest that has been notified as due can be claimed.

What additional information can be requested and the process for requiring an affidavit?

14.47 The proof of debt must clearly state what documentation is being relied on for the purposes of the claim and the trustee or the convenor of any creditors' meeting can request any document or other information he requires for the purpose of substantiating the claim being made.[147]

14.48 If necessary the trustee or the OR can require a claim to be verified by affidavit on Form 6.39[148] regardless of whether a proof has already been lodged by the creditor.[149] The affidavit[150] can be sworn before any of the following: the OR; a deputy OR; an officer of the Department; an officer of the court duly authorised in that behalf.[151]

14.49 Every creditor bears the cost of proving his own debt, including such as may be incurred in providing documents or evidence under r 6.98(3), IR86.[152] Any costs incurred by the trustee in estimating the value of a bankruptcy debt

---

143 IR86, r 6.98(1)(e) or IRN91, r 6.096(1)(e).
144 IR86, r 6.98(1)(f) or IRN91, r 6.096(1)(f).
145 IR86, r 6.98(1)(g) or IRN91, r 6.096(1)(g).
146 IR86, r 6.98(2) or) IRN91, r 6.096(2).
147 IR86, r 6.98(3) or) IRN91, r 6.096(3).
148 IR86, r 6.99(1) or IRN91, r 6.097(1).
149 IR86, r 6.99(2) or IRN91, r 6.097(2).
150 Form 6.39 does not appear to have been amended by the 2010 draft amendment rules to a statement of truth or witness statement.
151 IR86, r 6.99(3) or IRN91, r 6.097(3).
152 IR86, r 6.100(1) or IRN91, r 6.098(1).

under s 322(3), IA86 (debts not bearing a certain value) fall on the estate, as an expense of the bankruptcy. The court can make an order varying this if required.[153]

How are claims agreed?

14.50 The chairman of the meeting must review all proof of debt forms received before the meeting and compare the amount claimed to the statement of affairs figures and reconcile any differences with reference to the back-up documentation provided. For instance there may be small timing or other differences between the two amounts. The chairman of the meeting can then review each creditor's entitlement to vote and admit or reject their claims accordingly.[154] Any discount that would have been available to the bankrupt must be similarly deducted from the claim except for any discounts for immediate, early or cash settlements.[155]

14.51 The chairman's decision on a claim is subject to appeal[156] and if in doubt the chairman can simply mark the proof of debt 'objected to' with the validity being confirmed later.[157] This will not affect any subsequent adjudication made on the same claim for the purposes of paying a dividend. Any proof of debt lodged in bankruptcy proceedings must be made available for inspection by any creditor who has lodged a claim in the proceedings or the bankrupt or any person acting on their behalf.[158]

14.52 A creditor's proof of debt can be withdrawn or varied at any time by agreement with the trustee.[159] Formal rejection of a proof of debt for dividend purposes is dealt with in more detail in chapter 15, including the power of the court to vary or expunge a proof of debt on the application of a trustee or creditor.[160]

How are debts incurred in a foreign currency valued?

14.53 For the purpose of proving a debt incurred or payable in a currency other than sterling, the amount of the debt shall be converted into sterling at the official exchange rate prevailing on the date of the bankruptcy order.[161] 'The official exchange rate' is the middle exchange rate on the London Foreign Exchange Market at the close of business, as published for the date in question. In the absence of any such published rate, it is such rate as the court determines.[162]

---

153 IR86, r 6.100(3) or IRN91, r 6.098(3).
154 IR86, r 6.94(1) or IRN91, r 6.091(1).
155 IR86, r 6.110 or IRN91, r 6.106.
156 IR86, r 6.94(2) or IRN91, r 6.091(2).
157 IR86, r 6.94(3) or IRN91, r 6.091(3).
158 IR86, r 6.101 or IRN91, r 6.099.
159 IR86, r 6.106 or IRN91, r 6.103.
160 IR86, r 6.107 or IRN91, r 6.104.
161 IR86, r 6.111(1) or IRN91, r 6.108(1).
162 IR86, r 6.111(2) or IRN91, r 6.108(2).

How are periodical payments valued?

14.54 Periodical payments include items such as rent and a creditor may prove for any amounts due and unpaid up to the date of the bankruptcy order.[163] Where at that date any payment was accruing due, the creditor may prove for so much as would have fallen due at that date, if accruing from day to day.[164]

How is interest calculated when valuing a claim?

14.55 A creditor's claim may include interest on the debt for periods before the bankruptcy order, although not previously reserved or agreed as follows:[165]

- If the debt is due by virtue of a written instrument and payable at a certain time, interest can be claimed for the period from that time to the date of the bankruptcy order.[166]

- If the debt is due otherwise, interest can only be claimed if, before the presentation of the bankruptcy petition, a demand for payment was made in writing by or on behalf of the creditor, and notice given that interest would be payable from the date of the demand to the date of payment.[167]

- Interest can only be claimed for the period from the date of the demand to the date of the bankruptcy order.[168]

- The rate of interest used must not exceed the rate specified in s 17 of the Judgments Act 1838 on the date of the bankruptcy order.[169]

14.56 A creditor may prove for a debt of which payment was not yet due at the date of the bankruptcy order. However, any payment of a dividend on such a claim is subject to r 11.13 in Part 11, IR86 and the amount paid is reduced by calculating the net present value using the formula set out below.[170]

$$\frac{X}{1.05^{n}}$$

Where 'X' is the value of the admitted proof, and 'n' is the period beginning with the relevant date and ending with the date on which the payment of the creditor's debt would otherwise be due expressed in years and months in a decimalised form.

---

[163] IR86, r 6.112(1) or IRN91, r 6.109(1).
[164] IR86, r 6.112(2) or IRN91, r 6.109(2).
[165] IR86, r 6.113(1) or IRN91, r 6.110(1).
[166] IR86, r 6.113(2) or IRN91, r 6.110(2).
[167] IR86, r 6.113(3) or IRN91, r 6.110(3).
[168] IR86, r 6.113(4) or IRN91, r 6.110(4).
[169] IR86, r 6.113(5) or IRN91, r 6.110(5).
[170] IR86, r 6.114 or IRN91, r 6.111.

How are secured creditors' claims calculated and agreed?

14.57 A secured creditor's claim is calculated as follows:

- If a secured creditor realises their security, they may prove for the balance of the debt, after deducting the amount realised[171] as an unsecured claim.
- If a secured creditor voluntarily surrenders their security for the general benefit of creditors, they may prove for the whole debt, as if it were unsecured.[172]

14.58 The trustee must agree the value of the security[173] however if the secured creditor was also the petitioner and valued his security in the petition or has voted using on the unsecured element of the debt, then the security can only be revalued with the leave of the court.[174]

What are the consequences if a secured creditor fails to disclose or value his security?

14.59 If a secured creditor omits to disclose his security in his proof of debt, he must surrender his security for the general benefit of creditors, unless the court, on application by him, relieves him from the effect of this rule on the ground that the omission was inadvertent or the result of honest mistake.[175] If the court grants that relief, it may require or allow the creditor's proof of debt to be amended, on such terms as may be just.[176]

What powers does a trustee have over secured assets?

14.60 The trustee may at any time give notice to a creditor whose debt is secured that he proposes to redeem the security at the value put upon it in the creditor's proof after the expiration of 28 days from the date of the notice.[177] Conversely, a secured creditor may at any time, by a notice in writing, call on the trustee to elect whether he will or will not exercise his power to redeem the security at the value then placed on it; and the trustee then has 6 months in which to exercise the power or determine not to exercise it.[178]

What rights does the secured creditor have to revalue his security and can the trustee challenge the valuation?

14.61 After receiving notice from the trustee that he intends to redeem the security, the secured creditor has 21 days (or such longer period as the trustee may allow) in which, if he so wishes, to exercise his right to re-value his security

---

171 IR86, r 6.109(1) or IRN91, r 6.106(1).
172 IR86, r 6.109(2) or IRN91, r 6.106(2).
173 IR86, r 6.115(1) or IRN91, r 6.112(1).
174 IR86, r 6.115(2) or IRN91, r 6.112(2).
175 IR86, r 6.116(1) or IRN91, r 6.113(1).
176 IR86, r 6.116(2) or IRN91, r 6.113(2).
177 IR86, r 6.117(1) or IRN91, r 6.114(1).
178 IR86, r 6.117(4) or IRN91, r 6.114(4).

(with the leave of the court, where r 6.115(2), IR86 applies). If the creditor re-values his security, the trustee may only redeem at the new value.[179]

14.62 If the trustee is dissatisfied with the value which a secured creditor puts on his security (whether in his proof or by way of revaluation under r 6.117, IR86), he may require any property comprised in the security to be offered for sale.[180] The terms of sale must be agreed between the parties, or as the court may direct; and if the sale is by auction, the trustee on behalf of the estate, and the creditor on his own behalf, may appear and bid.[181] The trustee cannot challenge a previous revaluation that has been approved by the court.[182] The cost of transferring any asset is borne by the bankrupt's estate.[183]

How are claims based on negotiable instruments agreed?

14.63 Unless the trustee allows, a proof in respect of money owed on a bill of exchange, promissory note, cheque or other negotiable instrument or security cannot be admitted unless there is produced the instrument or security itself or a copy of it, certified by the creditor or his authorised representative to be a true copy.[184]

Proxies

What is a proxy and how are proxies given?

14.64 'A proxy' is an authority given by a person ('the principal') to another person ('the proxy-holder') to attend a meeting and speak and vote as his representative.[185] Proxies can be 'general' or 'specific'. General proxies can by used be the proxy holder at their discretion (except in the circumstances described below). Specific proxies must be used to vote in accordance with the instructions given but may also be used to vote generally on any matter not specified.

14.65 Only one proxy may be given by a person for any one meeting at which he desires to be represented; and it may only be given to one person, being an individual aged eighteen or over. But the principal may specify one or more other such individuals to be alternative proxy-holders, in the order in which they are named in the proxy.[186]

---

179 IR86, r 6.117(2) or IRN91, r 6.114(2).
180 IR86, r 6.118(1) or IRN91, r 6.115(1).
181 IR86, r 6.118(2) or IRN91, r 6.115(2).
182 IR86, r 6.118(3) or IRN91, r 6.115(3).
183 IR86, r 6.117(3) or IRN91, r 6.114(3).
184 IR86, r 6.108 or IRN91, r 6.105.
185 IR86, r 8.1(1).
186 IR86, r 8.1(3).

What form does a proxy take and when can they be used?

14.66 Proxies are issued with the notice of the meeting.[187] The proxy form should not be pre-completed with any name or description.[188] The proxy form must be signed by the principal, or by some person authorised by him (either generally or with reference to a particular meeting). If the form is signed by a person other than the principal, the nature of the person's authority must be stated.[189]

14.67 Proxies given for a meeting can be used at any subsequent adjournment.[190] When a proxy is given to the chairman of the meeting, the chairman cannot decline to be proxy holder[191] and it can be used by any person authorised to chair the meeting.[192] Proxies must be available for inspection at the meeting[193] and they must not be sent out pre-completed except for the title of the proceedings and the date and time of the meeting.[194] Any advice given in respect of the provision of proxies should be put in writing.

How does a company give a proxy?

14.68 A company representation must be evidenced as follows:

- Where a person is authorised under s 323, Companies Act 2006 to represent a corporation at a meeting of creditors or of the company or its contributories, he shall produce to the chairman of the meeting a copy of the resolution from which he derives his authority.[195]

- The copy resolution must be under the seal of the corporation, or certified by the secretary or a director of the corporation to be a true copy.[196]

- Nothing in this Rule requires the authority of a person to sign a proxy on behalf of a principal which is a corporation to be in the form of a resolution of that corporation.[197]

---

187 IR86, r 8.2(1).
188 IR86, r 8.2(1).
189 IR86, r 8.2(3).
190 IR86, r 8.3(1).
191 IR86, r 8.1(4) and (5).
192 IR86, r 8.3(2) and (3).
193 IR86, r 8.5(4).
194 IR86, r 8.2(1).
195 IR86, r 8.7(1).
196 IR86, r 8.7(2).
197 IR86, r 8.7(3).

What are the restrictions for a proxy holder with a financial interest?

14.69 A proxy holder must not vote in favour of any resolution which would directly or indirectly place him, or any associate of his, in a position to receive any remuneration out of the insolvent estate, unless the proxy specifically directs him to vote in that way.[198]

14.70 Where a proxy holder has signed the proxy as being authorised to do so by his principal and the proxy specifically directs him to vote in the way mentioned above, he shall nevertheless not vote in that way unless he produces to the chairman of the meeting written authorisation from his principal sufficient to show that the proxy holder was entitled so to sign the proxy.[199]

What is the meaning of 'associate' for proxy holders?

14.71 When any person who is acting as chairman of a meeting and uses proxies in that capacity under r 8.3, IR86 (where the responsible IP delegates chairmanship to some other person), the proxy holder is deemed to be an associate of the IP.[200]

What can the chairman do as proxy holder?

14.72 As proxy holder the chairman may vote as follows:

- Where the proxy requires him to vote for a particular resolution, and no other person proposes that resolution.
  - — he shall himself propose it, unless he considers that there is good reason for not doing so, and
  - — if he does not propose it, after the meeting he must notify his principal of the reason why not.
- Where the proxy gives him general discretion he may vote as he thinks fit.[201]
- A proxy holder must not vote in favour of any resolution which would directly or indirectly place him, or any associate of his, in a position to receive any remuneration out of the insolvent estate, unless the proxy specifically directs him to vote in that way.[202]
- Where a proxy holder has signed the proxy as being authorised to do so by his principal and the proxy specifically directs him to vote in the way mentioned in para (1), he shall nevertheless not vote in that way unless he

---

198 IR86, r 8.6(1).
199 IR86, r 8.6(1A).
200 IR86, r 8.6(2).
201 IR86, r 8.1(6).
202 IR86, r 8.6(1).

produces to the chairman of the meeting written authorisation from his principal sufficient to show that the proxy holder was entitled so to sign the proxy.[203]

- Rule 8.6 IR86 applies to any person acting as chairman of a meeting and using proxies in that capacity;[204] and in its application to him, the proxy holder is deemed an associate of his.[205]

What are the chairman's duties other than as proxy holder?

14.73 The chairman's duties are:

- To check that the meeting has been validly convened.

- To admit or reject every claim, in whole or in part, submitted before the deadline stated in the meeting notice.

- It is the chairman's duty to admit or reject claims submitted.

- The chairman can admit or reject a claim in whole or in part for the purposes of voting at the meeting.

- The chairman's decision is subject to appeal to the court by any creditor or by the debtor.

- If the chairman has any doubts the claim can be marked as objected to and the vote allowed subject to any subsequent declaration on invalidity if the objection is sustained.

- If on an appeal the chairman's decision is reversed or varied, or votes are declared invalid, the court may order another meeting to be summoned, or make such order as it thinks just. The court's power to make an order can only be exercised if it considers that the circumstances giving rise to the appeal are such as give rise to unfair prejudice or material irregularity.

- Any appeal must be made within 28 days beginning with the first day on which the report required by s 259, IA86 is made to the court.

- The chairman is not personally liable for any costs incurred by any person in respect of an appeal under this rule.

---

203 IR86, r 8.6(1A).
204 IR86, r 8.6.
205 IR86, r 8.6(2).

How is voting conducted for resolutions for remuneration?

14.74 There must always be a separate resolution to agree the basis of the remuneration. In addition the resolution may also include reference to type 2 disbursements and/or the timing of the payments to be made. Remuneration is dealt with in more detail in chapter 13.

What are the rules governing meeting suspensions and adjournments?

14.75 The chairman has discretion to suspend the proceedings for a period of up to an hour[206] once only during any meeting. In addition the chairman has the power to adjourn any meeting to a future time and place but not for a period of more than 21 days.[207] The meeting is not concluded until after any adjournment has taken place. Adjournments are usually invoked where a quorum is not present after thirty minutes[208] or where there is no person present who can act as chairman.[209] The reason for the adjournment should be recorded in the minutes.

How is the outcome of the meeting recorded?

14.76 The chairman of the meeting is required to document the meeting by producing minutes of the meeting.[210] Guidance on the contents of the minutes is set out in SIP 12.[211]

- The minutes should refer to the list of creditors who attended the meeting[212] and include a list of the resolutions passed.[213]

- The chairman of the meeting also needs to file in court details of each resolution passed within 21 days.[214]

Creditors also receive a report of the outcome of the meeting.

What proxy documentation needs to be retained after a meeting?

14.77 Proxies used for voting at any meeting must be retained by the chairman[215] and passed to the trustee after the meeting if he is not the trustee himself.[216] Any person attending the meeting is entitled, immediately before or in the course of the meeting, to inspect proxies and associated documents (including proofs) sent or given for the purpose of that meeting.[217] The

---

206 IR86, r 6.90 or IRN91, r 6.088.
207 IR86, r 6.91(3) or IRN91, r 6.089(3).
208 IR86, r 6.91(2) or IRN91, r 6.089(2).
209 IR86, r 6.91(4) or IRN91, r 6.099(4).
210 IR86, r 6.95(1) or IRN91, r 6.092(1).
211 Issued August 1996.
212 IR86, r 6.95(2) or IRN91, r 6.092(2).
213 IR86, r 6.95(3) or IRN91, r 6.092(3).
214 IR86, r 6.95(3) or IRN91, r 6.093(3).
215 IR86, r 8.4(1).
216 IR86, r 8.4(2).
217 IR86, r 8.5(4).

chairman must also make the proxies available for inspection by the following at all reasonable times on any business day:

- any creditor who has submitted a proof of debt[218] that has not been rejected;[219]
- for the purposes of r 8.5(1) IR86 (right of inspection of proxies) a member State liquidator appointed in main proceedings is deemed to be a creditor;[220]
- the debtor.[221]

Who can challenge the outcome of a meeting and what is the process?

14.78 Any challenge will almost certainly spring from the rejection of a claim in part or whole. The creditor whose claim has been rejected has the right make an appeal to the court.[222] The court can also order that another meeting be summoned, or make such other order as it thinks fit.[223] Also the bankrupt or any other creditor is entitled to make an application in respect of any claim submitted in the proceedings.[224]

14.79 Any application to court for review must be made within 21 days of receiving the formal rejection required by r 6.104(2), IR86. A time and place will be fixed for the hearing and the applicant must advise the trustee and the creditor (if not himself) of the venue.[225] The trustee is then required to lodge the proof of debt in court together with the statement of rejection.[226]

14.80 The costs of any application will be the responsibility of the applicant unless the court orders otherwise[227] and after the hearing the proof of debt will be returned to the trustee unless it was wholly disallowed.[228]

What constitutes unfair prejudice or material irregularity and what remedies are available?

14.81 Unfair prejudice can result from any false or misleading statement or information being provided and can result in present or future prejudice to one or more of the creditors or the bankrupt. Examples include failure to admit a proof or admit it for a materially different amount or conversely to admit a proof for a connected party that altered the outcome of the meeting.

---

218 IR86, r 8.5(1)(a).
219 IR86, r 8.5(2)(b).
220 IR86, r 8.8(2).
221 IR86, r 8.5(3)(b).
222 IR86, r 6.105(2) or IRN91, r 6.102(2).
223 IR86, r 6.105(4) or IRN91, r 6.102(4).
224 IR86, r 6.105(2) or IRN91, r 6.102(2).
225 IR86, r 6.105(3) or IRN91, r 6.102(3).
226 IR86, r 6.105(4) or IRN91, r 6.102(4).
227 IR86, r 6.105(6) or IRN91, r 6.102(6).
228 IR86, r 6.105(5) or IRN91, r 6.102(5).

Misconduct by a chairman of any meeting which prejudices creditors can also be regarded both as a 'material irregularity'.

14.82 The court has the power to make any appropriate order but this will usually be to convene another meeting and redo the vote. Depending on the circumstances of the case the chairman can be made personally responsible for the costs of such an order.[229]

Final meeting

What is the purpose of the final meeting and how is it convened?

14.83 The trustee (if not the OR) is required to present a report[230] to the creditors setting out his acts and dealings including a summary of receipts and payments[231] and statement by him that he has reconciled his account with that held by the SoS.[232] The creditors may question the trustee on any matter contained within his report and may resolve against him having his release.[233]

14.84 Where the trustee is other than the OR, he shall give at least 28 days' notice of the final meeting of creditors to be held under s 331, IA86. The notice shall be sent to all creditors, of which he is aware and to the bankrupt.[234]

Who is advised of the outcome of the final meeting and what happens if there is no quorum?

14.85 The trustee must give notice to the court that the final meeting has been held; and the notice must state whether or not he has been given his release. It should also be accompanied by a copy of the report laid before the final meeting. A copy of the notice must also be sent by the trustee to the OR.[235]

14.86 If there is no quorum present at the final meeting, the trustee shall report to the court that a final meeting was summoned in accordance with the Rules, but there was no quorum present; and the final meeting is then deemed to have been held and the creditors not to have resolved against the trustee having his release.[236]

---

229 For examples see *Ex p Bank of Ireland, Re* [1992] BCLC 137; *Re A Debtor (222 of 1990)* [1992] BCLC 137; *Ex p Bank of Ireland, Re (No 2)* [1993] BCLC 233. This construction significantly affects the jurisdiction to award costs against the Chairman: see commentary to Insolvency Act subsection (4), below.

230 IA86, s 331(2)(a).

231 IR86, r 6.137(2)(a) or IRN91, r 6.134(2)(a).

232 IR86, r 6.137(2)(b) or IRN91, r 6.134(2)(b).

233 IR86, r 6.137(3) or IRN91, r 6.134(3).

234 See Form 6.35 and IR86, r 6.135(1) or IRN91, r 6.132(1).

235 See Form 6.50 and IR86, r 6.137(4) or IRN91, r 6.134(4).

236 IR86, r 6.137(5) or IRN91, r 6.137(5).

How does a trustee get his release if the creditors have resolved against his release at the final meeting?

14.87 The trustee must file his report at court and then must obtain his release from the SoS in accordance with r 6.135, IR86.[237]

CREDITORS' COMMITTEE

What is the purpose of a creditors' committee?

14.88 The general body of creditors can resolve to establish a creditors' committee during the administration of the bankrupt's estate.[238] The purpose of the creditors' committee is two-fold:

- to protect and promote the interests of the general body of creditors; and
- to exercise control over the costs and expenses of administration.

There are also other duties that a committee fulfils if one has been constituted. Detailed guidance notes for committee members are issued by the Insolvency Service and are included with SIP 15.[239] If members of the committee are not insolvency professionals representing a creditor (these people should already have copies) then copies of the guidance notes should be provided to ensure the members are aware of their duties and responsibilities.

What reports must a trustee send to committee members?

14.89 Where the committee has come into being more than 28 days after the appointment of the trustee he must provide a summary to the members of all actions taken since the date of appointment and answer any questions on the conduct of the proceedings.[240] A person who becomes a member of the committee at any time after its first establishment can only request a summary of previous matters.[241] Nothing in r 6.152, IR86 disentitles the committee or any member of it from having access to the trustee's records of the proceedings, or from seeking an explanation of any matter within the committee's responsibility.[242]

14.90 The trustee must provide reports as and when directed by the committee (but not more than once every 2 months).[243] The reports should set out the position generally as regards the progress of the bankruptcy, and matters arising in connection with it to which the trustee considers the committee's

---

[237] IR86, r 6.137(6) or IRN91, r 6.134(6).
[238] IR86, r 6.80(1)(b).
[239] Version 3 issued 1 August 2005.
[240] IR86, r 6.152(3) or IRN91, r 6.149(3).
[241] IR86, r 6.152(4) or IRN91, r 6.149(4).
[242] IR86, r 6.152(5) or IRN91, r 6.149(5).
[243] IR86, r 6.163(1) or IRN91, r 6.160(1).

attention should be drawn. In the absence of any directions by the committee the office holder must circulate these reports every 6 months.[244] In addition, reg 24(3)[245] provides that the trustee must submit his financial records in respect of the case to the committee when required for inspection. The trustee is not required to comply with any request for information where it appears to him that the request is frivolous or unreasonable, or the cost of complying would be excessive having regard to the relative importance of the information, or there are insufficient assets or funds in the estate to enable him to comply.[246]

'SPECIAL' CREDITORS IN BANKRUPTCY PROCEEDINGS

What happens to utility creditors?

14.91 Providers of utilities (gas, water, electricity, etc) are not allowed to force repayment of outstanding bills due at the date of the bankruptcy order as a condition for obtaining continuing supplies.[247]

What happens to student loans?

14.92 Until 2004 outstanding student loans could be included in bankruptcy proceedings. The law changed in England and Wales so that from 1 September 2004 (Income Contingent Loans – post-1998) or 1 July 2004 (Mortgage Style Loans 1990–1998) student loans are no longer provable in bankruptcy. In Northern Ireland similar provisions came into effect in relation to bankruptcies commencing on or after 1 March 2005. In Scotland similar provisions came into effect from 1 April 2008.[248]

14.93 Loans received after bankruptcy proceedings have been commenced cannot be treated as either income or after-acquired property.

What happens to overpaid benefits?

14.94 In *R (on the application of Balding) v Secretary of State for Work and Pensions*[249] it was held that the liability to repay overpaid social security benefit occurring prior to a bankruptcy was a bankruptcy debt and therefore discharge from bankruptcy released the debtor from liability for recovery of the overpaid benefit. Davis J said that the claimant's liability to repay benefit arose under s 71(1) Social Security Administration Act 1992 and as such, he was liable to pay money under an enactment for the purposes of s 382(4), IA86 and the liability was therefore a bankruptcy debt.

---

244 IR86, r 6.163(2) or IRN91, r 6.160(2).
245 Insolvency Regulations 1994, SI 1994/2507.
246 IR86, r 6.152(2) or IRN91, r 6.149(2).
247 IA86, s 372.
248 Bankruptcy and Diligence etc (Scotland) Act 2007. See also chapter 4 at **4.50–4.54**.
249 [2007] BPIR 1669, [2008] 1 WLR 564.

What happens to gambling debts?

14.95 Gambling debts were historically generally regarded as unenforceable under English law, but enforceable if the debt was enforceable in a foreign jurisdiction. In *Rio Properties Inc v Al-Midani*[250] it was held that a bankruptcy petition could be based on loans made for lawful foreign gaming and His Honour Judge Maddocks, sitting as a High Court judge, allowed a $1.8 million Nevada gaming debt to justify the bankruptcy order.

14.96 However, the Gambling Act 2005 repealed the prohibition on enforcement of gaming contracts, so that in *Feldman v Nissim*,[251] the creditor was able to pursue a debt arising from spread bets that he had placed on his own account on behalf of the debtor. Similarly, in *Tradition (UK) Ltd v Ahmed*,[252] a creditor owed over £4.27 million on the basis of spread betting conducted by the debtor was able to challenge the approval of the debtor's proposal for an individual voluntary arrangement.

---

[250] [2003] BPIR 128.
[251] [2010] EWHC 1353 (Ch), [2010] BPIR 815.
[252] [2008] EWHC 2946 (Ch), [2008] EWHC 3448 (Ch).

Chapter 15

THE HANDLING OF BANKRUPTCY FUNDS (INCLUDING DISTRIBUTIONS)

'If you repay me not on such a day,
In such a place, such sum or sums as are
Express'd in the condition, let the forfeit
Be nominated for an equal pound
Of your fair flesh ...'[1]

INTRODUCTION

15.1 This chapter sets out how the funds realised from a bankrupt's estate are handled and the process which is followed to pay expenses and distributions. It also covers the requirements for completing and submitting detailed receipts and payments accounts by the trustee. The latter part of the chapter covers the agreement of claims and set-off, as well as the processes for the declaration and payment of dividends.

REALISATIONS AND BANKING

What happens to the money realised by the trustee for the bankrupt's estate?

15.2 The realisations from the sale of a bankrupt's assets must be paid into a bank account opened by the trustee for each separate estate. For bankruptcy estates these funds must be paid into the Insolvency Services Account[2] (ISA) with amounts less than £5,000 being paid in within 14 days and all larger sums immediately on receipt. The only exception to this is where the trustee intends to exercise the power to continue to carry on the business of the bankrupt and in these circumstances authorisation must be obtained from the Secretary of State (SoS) to operate such an account.[3] The SoS will usually set limits on the amount of funds that can be retained in this account[4] depending on the type of business and transactions occurring. The account must be maintained in the name of the bankrupt[5] and the trustee is required to maintain detailed records

1 Shakespeare, *Merchant of Venice*, Act I, Scene III.
2 SI 1994/2507, reg 20 or SR 1996/574, reg 20.
3 SI 1994/2507, reg 21(1) or SR 1996/574, reg 21(1).
4 SI 1994/2507, reg 21(6) or SR 1996/574, reg 21(6).
5 SI 1994/2507, reg 21(3) or SR 1996/574, reg 21(3).

of all transactions.[6] Any balance must be paid into the account on cessation of trade or vacation of office of the trustee.[7]

15.3 These regulations in respect of not mingling funds are reinforced by the best practice guidance issued in SIP11,[8] which also sets out the requirements for accounting for interest and the process for clearing cheques incorrectly made out to the trustee rather than the bankrupt's estate.[9] Any third party funds received must also be held in a separate trust account.[10]

What is the Insolvency Services Account and how is the account operated?

15.4 The ISA is operated by the Estate Accounts Directorate (EAD) who provide the banking and investment service to Insolvency Practitioners (IPs) and Official Receivers (ORs) in respect of bankruptcy estates. EAD is part of the Banking Directorate of The Insolvency Service (IS). Contact details for the relevant sections at the EAD can be found in Dear IP Chapter 5, para 63[11] located on the IS website. Updates on these contact details are published from time to time and the most recent information can be found on the IS website.

What fees and charges are levied for the use of an Insolvency Services Account?

15.5 With effect from 1 October 2012 the fees and charges for the use of the Insolvency Services Account (ISA) by Official Receivers and insolvency practitioners were increased (last increase was 2009), and the current and previous fees are set out below:

Fee Type	Previous Fee	Current Fee
Compulsory Fee	18.00	22.00
Voluntary Fee	23.00	25.00
BACS	0.15	0.15
Cheque Fee	1.00	1.10
CHAPS	10.00	10.30
Unclaimed Dividend Fee	25.00	25.75

6 SI 1994/2507, reg 21(5) or SR 1996/574, reg 21(5).
7 SI 1994/2507, reg 21 (7) or SR 1996/574, reg 21(7).
8 Paragraph 2.2, SIP 11, version 2 issued May 2007 came into effect from 1 June 2007.
9 Paragraph 2.3, SIP 11, version 2 issued May 2007 came into effect from 1 June 2007.
10 Paragraph 2.4, SIP 11, version 2 issued May 2007 came into effect from 1 June 2007.
11 http://www.insolvencydirect.bis.gov.uk/insolvencyprofessionandlegislation/dearip/dearipmill/chapter5.htm#58.

When should expenses paid by the trustee be recorded in the estate account?

15.6 In the absence of estate funds, practitioners must themselves pay any necessary disbursements on account of that estate. However these expenses should be recorded as paid by the trustee in the receipts and payments account, as upon release, it ensures that the OR is aware of any unrecovered disbursements due to them. If estate funds are received post-release, the OR (if ex-officio trustee or liquidator), or other practitioner appointed, will then reimburse the original practitioner.[12]

How often are estate accounts required to be reconciled?

15.7 ISA accounts are now available for online operation and statements are no longer routinely issued as they are available online on demand. However estate accounts should be reconciled at least quarterly[13] and preferably monthly on estates where there are large numbers of transactions. For IPs without online access 6 monthly reconciliations must be completed and additional statements requested as required. For those estates that are trading additional rules apply to local accounts set-up for trading purposes.

How do you apply for sanction to open a local bank account and what fees are payable?

15.8 A trustee's powers are set out in Sch 5, IA86. These were discussed in chapter 12 and as noted were amended in 2010.[14] The creditors' committee is required to provide approval for any powers requiring sanction and in the absence of a committee the power nominally falls to the court which is delegated to the SoS. The IS carries out this role on behalf of the SoS and forms can be found on their website to apply for sanction. There are two forms available[15] and one form is now specifically for the application to open a local bank account and to continue trading on behalf of the bankrupt. Applications can now be made online[16] using these forms. It should be noted that requests should not be made retrospectively except in genuine emergencies.

15.9 It is possible for sanction fees and any other fees payable to the DTI to be charged to the estate even though this increases the 'debit balance'. They will be treated as recoverable in the event of funds subsequently becoming available, or otherwise written off when the case is closed by the insolvency practitioner.[17]

---

12 Dear IP, Chapter 5, Para 12 Note issued April 1996.

13 ICAEW recommendation.

14 Legislative Reform (Insolvency) (Miscellaneous Provisions) Order 2009, art 11.

15 See Dear IP, Chapter 7, Para 12 Note and forms are available at: http://www.insolvencydirect.bis.gov.uk/insolvencyprofessionandlegislation/iparea/sanctionsforms/sanctionsforms.htm.

16 See Dear IP, Chapter 7, Para 10.

17 Dear IP, Chapter 5, Para 12 Note issued April 1996.

RECEIPTS AND PAYMENTS ACCOUNTS

How and when must a trustee (other than the OR) complete a receipts and payments account?

15.10 As all funds should be banked in the ISA[18] (except when sanction has been given to open a local account for trading purposes)[19] there is a statutory requirement to submit a receipts and payments account on the following events:

- if required by the SoS;[20] or
- with every progress report;[21] and
- with the draft final progress report[22] and at the final meeting of creditors;[23] or
- when a bankruptcy order is annulled.[24]

There is also best practice guidance that a receipts and payments account must be provided with every report sent to creditors.[25] Annual progress reports are mandatory for cases in which bankruptcy petitions have been filed after 5 April 2010. For these cases annual abstracts of receipts and payments accounts will be required to accompany the annual progress reports.[26] This new requirement for progress reports including a receipts and payments account (only when the trustee is not the OR) is covered in detail in chapter 14. For older cases annual progress reports do not apply but the other requirements are similar.

Distribution of assets

How are dividends calculated?

15.11 If there is surplus funds after all expenses have been paid (including the trustees remuneration) then a dividend will be payable. The amount of the dividend is calculated by dividing the available funds between all the creditors' claims that have been approved for payment. In some circumstances there may be claims that have not yet been agreed and in these cases a provision will be included to ensure sufficient funds are retained in the event the claim is subsequently agreed. If the trustee declares a dividend, and sends out the cheques, but in the meantime discovers a potential new creditor, it is

---

18 SI 1994/2507, reg 19 or SR 1996/574, reg 19.
19 SI 1994/2507, reg 21 or SR 1996/574, reg 21.
20 SI 1994/2507, reg 28 or SR 1996/574, reg 28.
21 IR 86, r 6.78A(1)(h).
22 IR 86, r 6.78B.
23 IR 86, r 6.137(2)(a).
24 IR 86, r 6.214(2) and (3).
25 Paragraph 2.2, SIP7, version 2 Issued September 1988.
26 IR86, r 6.78A.

satisfactory for the cheque to be stopped without the trustee incurring personal liability thereon.[27] It should be noted that a dividend is always expressed as payments of '*pence in the £*' which refers to the amount of the agreed claim.

What expenses are deductible and in what priority are they paid?

15.12 The costs of administering the bankrupt's estate are payable in the following priority from the funds available but do not necessarily have to be paid chronologically in this order if funds are available to meet the earlier priority items:

(1) expenses or costs which:

  (i) are properly chargeable or incurred by the OR or the trustee in preserving, realising or getting in any of the assets of the bankrupt or otherwise relating to the conduct of any legal proceedings which he has power to bring (whether the claim on which the proceedings are based forms part of the estate or otherwise) or defend;[28]
  (ii) relate to the employment of a shorthand writer, if appointed by an order of the court made at the instance of the OR in connection with an examination;[29] or
  (iii) are incurred in holding an examination under r 6.174, IR86 (examinee unfit) where the application was made by the OR;[30]

(2) any other expenses incurred or disbursements made by the OR or under his authority, including those incurred or made in carrying on the business of a debtor or bankrupt;[31]

(3) the fees payable under any order made under s 415 or s 415A, IA86, including those payable to the OR (other than the fee referred to in (4)(i) below), and any remuneration payable to him under general regulations;[32]

(4) fees and deposits incurred as follows:

  (i) the fee payable under any order made under s 415 for the performance by the OR of his general duties as OR;[33]
  (ii) any repayable deposit lodged under any such order as security for the fee mentioned in sub-para (i) (except where the deposit is applied to

---

27 *Lomax Leisure Ltd (in Liquidation) v Miller and another* [2007] EWHC 2508 (Ch), [2007] BPIR 1615. The Court of Appeal refused permission to appeal, *Lomax Leisure Ltd (in Liquidation) v Miller* [2008] EWCA Civ 525, [2008] BCC 686.

28 IR86, r 6.224(1)(a)(i) or IRNI91, r 6.222(1)(a)(i).

29 IR86, r 6.224(1)(a)(ii) or IRN91, r 6.222(1)(a)(ii).

30 Subject to the conditions specified in Insolvency (Amendment) (No 2) Rules 2002, SI 2002/2712; see also IR86, r 6.224(1)(a)(iii).

31 IR86, r 6.224(1)(b) or IRN91, r 6.222(1)(b).

32 IR86, r 6.224(1)(c) or IRN91, r 6.222(1)(c).

33 IR86, r 6.224(1)(c)(i) or IRN91, r 6.222(1)(c)(i).

the payment of the remuneration of an insolvency practitioner appointed under s 273, IA86 (debtor's petition));[34]

(5) the cost of any security provided by an interim receiver, trustee or special manager in accordance with the IA86 or the IR86;[35]

(6) the remuneration of the interim receiver (if any);[36]

(7) any deposit lodged on an application for the appointment of an interim receiver;[37]

(8) the costs of the petitioner, and of any person appearing on the petition whose costs are allowed by the court;[38]

(9) the remuneration of the special manager (if any);[39]

(10) any amount payable to a person employed or authorised, to assist in the preparation of a statement of affairs or accounts;[40]

(11) any allowance made, by order of the court, towards costs on an application for release from the obligation to submit a statement of affairs, or for an extension of time for submitting such a statement;[41]

(12) the costs of employing a shorthand writer in any case other than one appointed by an order of the court at the instance of the OR in connection with an examination;[42]

(13) any necessary disbursements by the trustee in the course of his administration (including any expenses incurred by members of the creditors' committee or their representatives and allowed by the trustee under r 6.164, IR86, but not including any payment of capital gains tax in circumstances referred to in sub-para (p) below);[43]

(14) the remuneration or emoluments of any person (including the bankrupt) who has been employed by the trustee to perform any services for the estate, as required or authorised by or under the Act or the Rules;[44]

---

34 IR86, r 6.224(1)(c)(ii) or IRN91, r 6.222(1)(c)(ii).
35 IR86, r 6.224(1)(e) or IRN91, r 6.222(1)(e).
36 IR86, r 6.224(1)(f) or IRN91, r 6.222(1)(f).
37 IR86, r 6.224(1)(g) or IRN91, r 6.222(1)(g).
38 IR86, r 6.224(1)(h) or IRN91, r 6.222(1)(h).
39 IR86, r 6.224(1)(j) or IRN91, r 6.222(1)(j).
40 IR86, r 6.224(1)(k) or IRN91, r 6.222(1)(k).
41 IR86, r 6.224(1)(l) or IRN91, r 6.222(1)(c)(l).
42 IR86, r 6.224(1)(la) or IRN91, r 6.222(1)(la).
43 IR86, r 6.224(1)(m) or IRN91, r 6.222(1)(m).
44 IR86, r 6.224(1)(n) or IRN91, r 6.222(1)(n).

(15) the remuneration of the trustee, up to any amount not exceeding that which is payable under Sch 6;[45]

(16) the amount of any capital gains tax on chargeable gains accruing on the realisation of any asset of the bankrupt (without regard to whether the realisation is effected by the trustee, a secured creditor, or a receiver or manager appointed to deal with a security);[46]

(17) the balance, after payment of any sums due under point (15) above, of any remuneration due to the trustee;[47]

(18) any other expenses properly chargeable by the trustee in carrying out his functions in the bankruptcy.[48]

How are dividends paid?

15.13 Dividends are calculated by the trustee based on the available funds divided by the total of the agreed creditors' claims. The calculation of this amount should be clearly shown in the notices to the creditors. The payment should be expressed as 'p in £' together with the detailed calculation. Payments of dividends should be made direct from the ISA. The procedure for the declaration and payment of dividends are set-out in Part 11, IR86.

What happens to unclaimed dividends or undistributed funds and how can it be reclaimed?

15.14 Unclaimed dividends[49] or funds left undistributed in a local account when trading has ceased[50] must be paid into the ISA.[51] Unclaimed dividends ie cheques or payable orders which remain uncashed after 6 months must be paid into the Unclaimed Monies Account whereas funds left undistributed must be paid into the Undistributed Funds Account. The details of each amount must be recorded for the ISA.[52] On vacation of office, the trustee must send to the Department any valid unclaimed or undelivered payment instruments for dividends after endorsing them with the word 'cancelled'.[53]

---

45 IR86, r 6.224(1)(o) or IRN91, r 6.222(1)(o).

46 IR86, r 6.224(1)(p) or IRN91, r 6.222(1)(p).

47 IR86, r 6.224(1)(q) or IRN91, r 6.222(1)(q).

48 Subject to the conditions specified in Insolvency (Amendment) (No 2) Rules 2002, SI 2002/2712: see IR86, r 6.224(1)(r) or IRN91, r 6.222(1)(r).

49 SI 1994/2507, reg 23(4) and SR 1996/574, reg 23(4).

50 SI 1994/2507, reg 21(7) and SR 1996/574, reg 21(7).

51 SI 1994/2507, reg 31 and SR 1996/574, reg 31.

52 SI 1994/2507, reg 24 and SR 1996/574, reg 24.

53 SI 1994/2507, reg 23(4) and SR 1996/574, reg 23(4).

15.15 Any person claiming to be entitled to any moneys paid into the ISA can apply to the SoS for payment. The SoS may require supporting evidence to be provided.[54] Any person dissatisfied with the decision of the SoS in respect of their claim can appeal to the court.[55]

What issues are caused by private sector tracing organisations?

15.16 Private sector tracing organisations sometimes attempt to trace the recipients of unclaimed dividends whilst the trustee is still in office. Problems arise where a dividend has been issued to a creditor in error and the IP allows it to expire after 6 months (all uncleared payments expire after this time) instead of contacting EAD to advise a cancellation. If EAD is not in receipt of a cancellation instruction to correct this error prior to the expiry of the payable order, then the tracing agent will seek to trace the creditor who may be paid in error. In such cases, EAD will refer the IP to the tracing agent to discuss recovery of these funds for the estate and negotiate the fee claimed by them.

AGREEMENT OF CLAIMS AND SET-OFF

How and when are claims agreed for dividend purposes?

15.17 The agreement of claims for voting purposes was set out in detail in chapter 14.[56] A similar process applies to agreeing claims for the purposes of dividend and in most cases the same amount will be agreed. Most claims will agree exactly or be easily reconcilable to the amounts recorded in the bankrupt's statement of affairs. The trustee will review in detail any claims that are materially different from the statement of affairs by reviewing the back-up documentation provided by the creditor or requesting additional information. The trustee is not required to deal with any claims received after the final date proving.[57]

What is the process for rejecting a claim?

15.18 Once a last date for proving claims has been advertised[58] a trustee must agree all the claims within 5 business days either admitting or rejecting the whole or part of each claim.[59] If the trustee rejects a proof in whole or part a written statement explaining the reasons must be sent to the creditor as soon as reasonably practicable.[60] The creditor with the rejected claim if dissatisfied with the reason can apply to the court within 21 days of receiving the statement for the decision to be reversed.[61]

---

54 SI 1994/2507, reg 32(1) and SR 1996/574, reg 32(1).
55 SI 1994/2507, reg 32(2) and SR 1996/574, reg 32(2).
56 See **14.41–14.63**.
57 IR86, r 11.3(2).
58 IR86, r 11.3(1).
59 IR86, r 6.104(1).
60 IR86, r 6.104(2).
61 IR86, r 6.105(2).

15.19 On receipt of the application the court will fix a venue for the hearing[62] and the trustee is required to file the relevant proof in court with a copy of the statement that he sent to the creditor.[63] The court will make a determination of the claim and then return the proof to the trustee unless the claim has been wholly disallowed.[64] The costs of any hearing will not be an expense of the estate unless ordered by the court.[65]

What is set-off and when can cross-claims be settled in this manner?

15.20 Mutual credit and set-off for bankruptcy is dealt with in s 323, IA86. Set-off is strictly limited to mutual claims existing at the relevant date; there can be no set-off in respect of claims by third parties, even with their consent, as this would be allowing parties by agreement to subvert the fundamental principle of *pari passu* distribution of an insolvent's estate. In order for set-off to be allowed there must be mutual debts arising from dealings between the same parties. For example, where a bankrupt plumber is owed money for building work by a stationary company, any debt due to the stationary company by the plumber for the supply of paper can be set off against the debt for the plumbing work done even though the transaction is of a different nature.

15.21 In calculating mutual credit and set off the trustee must not include sums due from the bankrupt to any creditor for set-off if that creditor had notice at the time the debt became due that a bankruptcy petition relating to the bankrupt was pending.[66] Only the balance (if any) of the account owed to the creditor is provable as a bankruptcy debt.[67]

What is crown set-off?

15.22 Pre-insolvency tax liabilities can be subject to the right of Crown set-off.[68] The Crown is regarded as a single entity in its dealings, even though the various departments deal with different matters.[69] Crown set-off also applies against amounts due under contracts for the supply of goods or services, for example contracts with the Ministry of Defence.

15.23 Where set-off is available to the Crown, amounts withheld from payment must be applied *pro rata* in the reduction of preferential and non-preferential liabilities. In cases where the petition was presented on or after 15 September 2003, however, it should be remembered that there will generally be no preferential status for Crown departments following the implementation of EA02. However, amounts due to the SoS for Trade in respect of payments

---

62 IR86, r 6.105(3).
63 IR86, r 6.105(4).
64 IR86, r 6.105(5).
65 IR86, r 6.105(6).
66 IA86, s 323(3).
67 IA86, s 323(3).
68 Crown Proceedings Act 1947.
69 *Re D H Curtis (Builders) Ltd* [1978] 2 WLR 28.

made to employees out of the National Insurance Fund[70] can be subject to set-off notwithstanding that the debt was not due and payable on the insolvency date. The SoS is part of the Crown with whom the insolvent has mutual dealings and the money due is a contingent claim which has become certain after the insolvency order.[71]

What is the process for declaring and paying a dividend to creditors?

15.24 Agreement of claims should not be left until the end of case. As long as there is any realistic prospect of a dividend agreement of claims should commence at the start of the administration of the case while information is still recent. The following general points need to be considered:

- Any claim not on the original Statement of Affairs should be checked back to the business records and copies of all relevant documents requested if appropriate. In particular if realisations are expected to take some time creditors should be advised to ensure that any changes of address are advised.

- Any proof that is rejected in part or whole must be sent a written statement setting out the grounds for rejection,[72] together with details of the process of appeal against the decision.[73]

- Other creditors may also apply to court to reject or vary any claim listed as being accepted in the notice to creditors.[74]

- A notice must be sent to all known creditors who have not proved of the intention to declare a dividend. These notices should highlight that a proof has not been received.[75]

- The notice when issued must state that a dividend is to be declared within 4 months of the last date for proving.[76] If more than 4 months have passed since any previously notified date for proving then a new date needs to be issued.

- If during the 4 month period any claim has been rejected, or there is an application to court for a variation or there is any other application for variation, the dividend can be postponed or cancelled.[77]

---

70 Employment Rights Act 1996, s 166.

71 *Secretary of State for Trade and Industry v Frid* (also known as *West End Networks Limited (In Liquidation)*) [2004]2 All ER 1042.

72 IR86, r 6.104 or IRN91, r 6.101.

73 IR86, r 6.105 or IRN91, r 6.102.

74 IR86, r 6.107 or IRN91, r 6.104.

75 IR86, r 11.2(1).

76 IR86, r 11.2(3).

77 IR86, r 11.4.

- If there has been no applications to court the dividend must be paid within the 4 month period.[78]

- The notice of intended dividend to be sent to all creditors who have proved their debts must include the following:[79]

  — detail of all asset realisations;
  — payments made;
  — provision for unsettled claims and amounts to be retained and the purpose of the retention;
  — the total amount to be distributed;
  — the rate of the dividend.

- In addition a schedule of agreed creditor's claims should be attached to the notice to provide evidence of the total claims and to allow creditors the opportunity to challenge any claim in accordance with the rules.[80] The dividend can be paid simultaneously with this notice.

- Notice should be given to all creditors when no further or no dividend is to be paid as follows:[81]

  — no funds have been realised; or
  — funds realised have already been distributed or used to defray expenses of the administration.

15.25 The following process should be followed for bankruptcy cases with a pre-6 April 2009 petition:

- For cases with petitions filed in court before 6 April 2009 an advertisement for claims must either be placed at the outset of the case[82] or when a dividend is due to be declared. Any advert placed must give at least 21 days[83] notice of the last date for proving.

15.26 The following process should be followed for bankruptcy cases with post 6 April 2009 petitions:

- For cases with petitions filed in court before 6 April 2009 an advertisement for claims could either be placed at the outset of the case[84]

---

78 IR86, r 11.5.

79 IR86, r 11.6.

80 IR86, r 6.107(1)(b) or IRN91, r 6.104(1)(b).

81 IR86, r 11.7.

82 If this is the usual practice then care must be taken if any claim submitted by the due date is subsequently rejected outside the 7 days in which they should be admitted or rejected under r 11.3(1), IR86.

83 IR86, r 11.2(1A).

84 See above **15.20**.

or when a dividend was due to be declared. Any advert placed had to give at least 21 days[85] notice of the last date for proving.

- For cases with petitions filed in court from 6 April 2009 no advert is required if the responsible IP has previously invited creditors to prove their debt[86] however before declaring a first dividend notice must be given in the *London Gazette*.[87]

- Once a 'last date for proving' has been declared on cases with a petition filed before 6 April 2009, all proofs must be advertised in the *London Gazette* and in whatever other publication as considered appropriate.[88]

---

85 IR86, r 11.2(1A).
86 IR86, r 11.2(1B).
87 IR86, r 11.2(1A)(a).
88 IR86, r 11.3(2).

Chapter 16

RIGHTS OF ACTION BY THE TRUSTEE IN BANKRUPTCY

'Men sooner forget the death of their father than the loss of their possessions.'[1]

INTRODUCTION

16.1 This chapter deals with the provisions which allow the trustee in bankruptcy to seek remedies for transactions made by a bankrupt in prior periods which might have prejudiced the position of the creditors in the bankruptcy proceedings or during the period of bankruptcy but prior to discharge. The following rights of actions are covered in detail in this chapter together with the significance of being an associated party to a bankrupt and the relevant periods during which these actions can be reviewed and attacked:

- Transactions defrauding creditors and antecedent:
  - preferences; and
  - transactions completed at an undervalue.
- Extortionate credit transactions.
- After-acquired property.

TRANSACTIONS DEFRAUDING CREDITORS

What are the provisions against debt avoidance?

16.2 Sections 423–425, IA86[2] contain provisions designed to avoid what used to be termed a fraudulent conveyance and are now generally referred to as transactions defrauding creditors. The provisions are designed to enable the court to set aside a transaction by a debtor at an undervalue which has been entered into for the purpose of putting assets of the debtor beyond the reach of a person who has or may make a claim against him which prejudices the interests of the person who has or may make the claim.[3] A transaction is at an undervalue for the purpose of the provision if it is a gift by the debtor or if he receives no consideration or a consideration which is significantly less valuable

1 Machiavelli (1532) *The Prince.*
2 INO89, arts 367–369.
3 IA86, s 423(1) and (3) or INO89, art 367(1) and (3).

in money or money's worth than that provided by him or if the consideration is marriage or the formation of a civil partnership.[4] The different types of transactions are discussed below.

16.3 The provisions on transactions defrauding creditors have three advantages over many of the other provisions in the IA86 relating to antecedent transactions.

- The first is that it is not subject to the time limits applicable to certain other kinds of relief such as preference or transactions at an undervalue (see, for example, *Sands v Clitheroe*,[5] but cf *Re Yates*[6] and *Re Nurkowski*[7] as to timing and limitation which will generally be 12 years from the date of the bankruptcy).

- The second is that the application may be made not only by the OR, trustee or supervisor of a voluntary arrangement but also by a 'victim of the transaction'.[8] Thus in *Re Nurkowski*, it was held that the Inland Revenue could be a victim.

- The third is that relief is not confined to circumstances in which the debtor becomes a bankrupt. Where the application is made in relation to bankruptcy it should be brought in the court sitting in bankruptcy; however, where there is no insolvency the application may be brought in any part of the High Court.[9]

What orders can the court make?

16.4 The court has a wide discretion to make such order as it thinks fit for restoring the position to what it would have been if the transaction had not been entered into and protecting the interests of the victims of the transaction.[10] In particular it may:

- require any property transferred as part of the transaction to be vested in any person, either absolutely or for the benefit of all the persons on whose behalf the application for the order is treated as made;

- require any property to be so vested if it represents, in any person's hands, the application either of the proceeds of sale of property so transferred or of money so transferred;

- release or discharge (in whole or in part) any security given by the debtor;

---

4 IA86, s 423(1) or INO89, art 367(1).
5 [2006] BPIR 1000.
6 [2005] BPIR 476.
7 [2006] EWCA Civ 542, [2006] BPIR 789.
8 IA86, s 424(1) and (2) or INO89, art 368(1) and (2).
9 IA86, s 423(4) and see *TSB Bank plc v Katz* [1997] BPIR 147 and in NI refer to INO89, art 367(4).
10 IA86, s 423(2) or INO89, art 367(2).

- require any person to pay to any other person in respect of benefits received from the debtor such sums as the court may direct;
- provide for any surety or guarantor whose obligations to any person were released or discharged (in whole or in part) under the transaction to be under such new or revived obligations as the court thinks appropriate;
- provide for security to be provided for the discharge of any obligation imposed by or arising under the order, for such an obligation to be charged on any property and for such security or charge to have the same priority as a security or charge released or discharged (in whole or in part) under the transaction.[11]

What defences are available?

16.5 There are, however, savings provisions:

An order under s 423, IA86[12] may affect the property of, or impose any obligation on, any person whether or not he is the person with whom the debtor entered into the transaction; but such an order:

- must not prejudice any interest in property which was acquired from a person other than the debtor and was acquired in good faith, for value and without notice of the relevant circumstances, or prejudice any interest deriving from such an interest; and
- must not require a person who received a benefit from the transaction in good faith, for value and without notice of the relevant circumstances to pay any sum unless he was a party to the transaction.[13]

PREFERENCES

What is a preference?

16.6 Section 340, IA86[14] allows a trustee in bankruptcy to set aside a transaction the effect of which is to give another person a preference. An individual gives a preference to a person if:

- that person is one of the individual's creditors or a surety or guarantor for any of his debts or other liabilities; and
- the individual does anything or suffers anything to be done which (in either case) has the effect of putting that person into a position which, in

---

11 IA86, s 425(1) or INO89, art 369(1).
12 INO89, art 367.
13 IA86, s 425(2) or INO89, art 369(2).
14 INO89, art 313.

the event of the individual's bankruptcy, will be better than the position he would have been in if that thing has not been done.[15]

16.7 The transaction deemed to be a preference must take place 'at a relevant time' as defined.[16] As a general rule the court will not make an order in relation to a preference unless the individual who gave the preference was influenced in deciding to give it by a desire to put that person in a better position to that of other creditors.[17] However, it will be assumed that the transaction was a preference if the person benefiting from it was an 'associate' (otherwise than by reason of being his employee).

Who are considered to be associates of a bankrupt?

16.8 Section 435, IA86 defines an associate as follows:

- A person is an associate of an individual if that person is:[18]

  - the individual's husband, wife or civil partner;
  - a relative of:

    * the individual; or
    * the individual's husband, wife or civil partner; or
  - the husband or wife or civil partner of a relative of:

    * the individual; or
    * the individual's husband, wife or civil partner.

- A person is an associate of any person with whom he is in partnership, and of the husband or wife or civil partner or a relative of any individual with whom he is in partnership; and a Scottish firm is an associate of any person who is a member of the firm.[19]

- A person is an associate of any person whom he employs or by whom he is employed.[20]

- A person in his capacity as trustee of a trust other than:[21]

  - a trust arising under any of the second Group of Parts or the Bankruptcy (Scotland) Act 1985; or
  - a pension scheme or an employees' share scheme (within the meaning of the Companies Act 2006);

---

15 IA86, s 340(3) or INO89, art 313(3).
16 IA86, s 341 or INO89, art 314.
17 IA86, s 340(4) or INO89, art 313(4).
18 IA86, s 435(2).
19 IA86, s 435(3).
20 IA86, s 435(4).
21 IA86, s 435(5).

— is an associate of another person if the beneficiaries of the trust include, or the terms of the trust confer a power that may be exercised for the benefit of, that other person or an associate of that other person.

16.9 For the purposes of s 435 IA86 a person is a relative of an individual if he is that individual's brother, sister, uncle, aunt, nephew, niece, lineal ancestor or lineal descendant, treating:[22]

- any relationship of the half blood as a relationship of the whole blood and the stepchild or adopted child of any person as his child;[23] and

- an illegitimate child as the legitimate child of his mother and reputed father;[24]

- and references in s 435 IA86 to a husband or wife include a former husband or wife and a reputed husband or wife and references to a civil partner include a former civil partner and a reputed civil partner;

- for the purposes of s 435 IA86 any director or other officer of a company is to be treated as employed by that company;[25]

- for the purposes of s 435 IA86 a person is to be taken as having control of a company if:[26]

  — the directors of the company or of another company which has control of it (or any of them) are accustomed to act in accordance with his directions or instructions; or
  — he is entitled to exercise, or control the exercise of, one third or more of the voting power at any general meeting of the company or of another company which has control of it;
  — and where two or more persons together satisfy either of the above conditions, they are to be taken as having control of the company.

How is the 'desire to prefer' identified by the courts?

16.10 The leading authority on what constitutes a preference and on the issue of 'desire to prefer' remains the corporate case, *Re M C Bacon Ltd*,[27] in which Millett, J (as he then was) considered the position where an insolvent company created a charge over its assets in favour of its bank and in particular whether the creation of the charge was influenced by a desire to prefer the bank. He held that 'desire' in the context of a preference meant 'positively wished'. In the circumstances of the case he rejected the claim that the charge amounted to a

---

[22] IA86, s 435(8).
[23] IA86, s 435(8)(a).
[24] IA86, s 435(8)(b).
[25] IA86, s 435(9).
[26] IA86, s 435(10).
[27] [1990] BCC 78.

preference because all the directors of the company had done was to pay the price dictated by the bank for its continued support. As to the application of *Re M C Bacon Ltd* to individual insolvency see *Re Ledingham-Smith*.[28] As to other cases of preference in the individual insolvency sphere see *Doyle v Saville*[29] and *Day v Coltrane*.[30]

Note that it is not necessary to prove a desire to prefer to demonstrate that the person giving the preference knew or believed himself to be insolvent or foresaw his bankruptcy.[31]

How, when and what can the court do in respect of preferences?

16.11 The making of an order is a matter of discretion as is the range of orders the court may make. Section 342(1), IA86 provides specifically that the court may:

- require any property transferred as part of the transaction, or in connection with the giving of the preference, to be vested in the trustee of the bankrupt's estate as part of that estate;[32]

- require any property to be so vested if it represents in any person's hands the application either of the proceeds of sale of property so transferred or of money so transferred;[33]

- release or discharge (in whole or in part) any security given by the individual;[34]

- require any person to pay, in respect of benefits received by him from the individual, such sums to the trustee of his estate as the court may direct;[35]

- provide for any surety or guarantor whose obligations to any person were released or discharged (in whole or in part) under the transaction or by the giving of the preference to be under such new or revived obligations to that person as the court thinks appropriate;[36]

- provide for security to be provided for the discharge of any obligation imposed by or arising under the order, for such an obligation to be charged on any property and for the security or charge to have the same

---

28 [1993] BCLC 635.
29 [2002] BPIR 947.
30 [2003] 1 WLR 1379.
31 See *Katz v McNally* [1999] BCC 291.
32 IA86, s 342(1)(a) or INO89, art 315(1)(a).
33 IA86, s 342(1)(b) or INO89, art 315(1)(b).
34 IA86, s 342(1)(c) or INO89, art 315(1)(c).
35 IA86, s 342(1)(d) or INO89, art 315(1)(d).
36 IA86, s 342(1)(e) or INO89, art 315(1)(e).

priority as a security or charge released or discharged (in whole or in part) under the transaction or by the giving of the preference;[37] and

- provide for the extent to which any person whose property is vested by the order in the trustee of the bankrupt's estate, or on whom obligations are imposed by the order, is to be able to prove in the bankruptcy for debts or other liabilities which arose from, or were released or discharged (in whole or in part) under or by, the transaction or the giving of the preference.[38]

What defences are available?

16.12 Section 342(2), IA86 provides savings provisions for persons who acquired property from the bankrupt in good faith for value and without notice. An order under s 339 or s 340, IA86 may affect the property of, or impose any obligation on, any person whether or not he is the person with whom the individual in question entered into the transaction or, as the case may be, the person to whom the preference was given; but such an order:

- shall not prejudice any interest in property which was acquired from a person other than that individual and was acquired [in good faith and for value], or prejudice any interest deriving from such an interest;[39] and

- shall not require a person who received a benefit from the transaction or preference [in good faith and for value] to pay a sum to the trustee of the bankrupt's estate, except where he was a party to the transaction or the payment is to be in respect of a preference given to that person at a time when he was a creditor of that individual.[40]

16.13 Section 339, IA86 looks at where a person has acquired an interest in property from a person other than the individual in question, or has received a benefit from the transaction or preference, and at the time of that acquisition or receipt the person:

- had notice of the relevant surrounding circumstances and of the relevant proceedings;[41] or

- was an associate of, or was connected with, either the individual in question or the person with whom that individual entered into the transaction or to whom that individual gave the preference;[42]

then, unless the contrary is shown, it shall be presumed that the interest was acquired or the benefit was not received in good faith.

---

37 IA86, s 342(1)(f) or INO89, art 315(1)(f).
38 IA86, s 342(1)(a) or INO89, art 315(1)(g).
39 IA86, s 342(2)(a) or INO89, art 315(2)(a).
40 IA86, s 342(2)(b) or INO89, art 315(2)(b).
41 IA86, s 342(2A)(a).
42 IA86, s 342(2A)(b).

TRANSACTIONS COMPLETED AT AN UNDERVALUE

What is a 'transaction at an undervalue'?

16.14 Section 339, IA86 allows the trustee in bankruptcy to apply to court to set aside a 'transaction at an undervalue' entered into by the bankrupt with another person.

A person enters into a 'transaction at an undervalue' if:

(a) he makes a gift to that person or he otherwise enters into a transaction with that person on terms that provide for him to receive no consideration;

(b) he enters into a transaction with that person in consideration of marriage or the formation of a civil partnership; or

(c) he enters into a transaction with that person for a consideration the value of which, in money or money's worth, is significantly less than the value, in money or money's worth, of the consideration provided by the individual.[43]

16.15 The nature of a transaction completed at an undervalue was considered by Millett, J (as he then was) in the corporate context in *Re M C Bacon Ltd*.[44] In relation to individual insolvency see *Re Brabon*[45] which confirms that the transaction must be one entered into by the bankrupt, and more generally *Re Share*,[46] *Simms v Oakes*[47] and *Ramlort Ltd v Reid*.[48]

16.16 Again the transaction must take place 'at a relevant time' as defined in s 341 (discussed below). The court has a wide discretion to make 'such order as it thinks fit for restoring the position to what it would have been' (including making the orders specified by s 342(1) set out above) if the transaction had not been entered into.[49] The remedy is, however, discretionary. As to which see *Singla v Brown*[50] in which the court, in exceptional circumstances, declined to exercise the discretion even where a 'transaction at an undervalue' had occurred.

What is the 'relevant time'?

16.17 Section 341, IA86 defines the relevant time for the purpose of s 339 and s 340, IA86 as follows:

---

43 IA86, s 339(3) or INO89, art 312(3).
44 [1990] BCC 78.
45 [2000] BPIR 537.
46 [2002] BPIR 194.
47 [2002] BPIR 1244.
48 [2004] EWCA Civ 800, [2004] BPIR 985.
49 IA86, s 339(2).
50 [2007] BPIR 424.

- Subject as follows, the time at which an individual enters into a transaction at an undervalue or gives a preference is a relevant time if the transaction is entered into or the preference given:

  — in the case of a transaction at an undervalue, at a time in the period of 5 years ending with the day of the presentation of the bankruptcy petition on which the individual is adjudged bankrupt;[51]
  — in the case of a preference which is not a transaction at an undervalue and is given to a person who is an associate of the individual (otherwise than by reason only of being his employee), at a time in the period of 2 years ending with that day;[52] and
  — in any other case of a preference which is not a transaction at an undervalue, at a time in the period of 6 months ending with that day.[53]

- Where an individual enters into a transaction at an undervalue or gives a preference at a time mentioned in para (a), (b) or (c) of subs (1) (not being, in the case of a transaction at an undervalue, a time less than 2 years before the end of the period mentioned in para (a)), that time is not a relevant time for the purposes of s 339 and s 340, IA86 unless the individual:

  — is insolvent at that time; or
  — becomes insolvent in consequence of the transaction or preference;

  but the requirements of this subsection are presumed to be satisfied, unless the contrary is shown, in relation to any transaction at an undervalue which is entered into by an individual with a person who is an associate of his (otherwise than by reason only of being his employee).

- For the purposes of s 341(2), IA86, an individual is insolvent if:[54]

  — he is unable to pay his debts as they fall due; or
  — the value of his assets is less than the amount of his liabilities, taking into account his contingent and prospective liabilities.

EXTORTIONATE CREDIT TRANSACTION

What is an extortionate credit transaction?

16.18 Section 343, IA86 allows the court, on the application of the trustee, to make an order setting aside, in whole or in part, an extortionate credit transaction. A transaction is extortionate if:

---

51 IA86, s 340(1)(a) or INO89, art 313(1)(a).
52 IA86, s 340(1)(b) or INO89, art 313(1)(b).
53 IA86, s 340(1)(c) or INO89, art 313(1)(c).
54 IA86, s 341(3) or INO89, art 314(3).

- the terms of it are or were such as to require grossly exorbitant payments to be made (whether unconditionally or in certain contingencies) in respect of the provision of the credit; or

- it otherwise grossly contravened ordinary principles of fair dealing.[55]

The burden of proof is reversed in that it is presumed, unless the contrary is proved, that a transaction with respect to which an application is made is or was extortionate.[56]

The transaction under attack must have been entered into within 3 years of the commencement of the bankruptcy.[57]

16.19 The granting of relief is a matter of discretion and the court may make an order containing 'one or more of the following':[58]

- provision setting aside the whole or part of any obligation created by the transaction;[59]

- provision otherwise varying the terms of the transaction or varying the terms on which any security for the purposes of the transaction is held;[60]

- provision requiring any person who is or was party to the transaction to pay to the trustee any sums paid to that person, by virtue of the transaction, by the bankrupt;[61]

- provision requiring any person to surrender to the trustee any property held by him as security for the purposes of the transaction;[62]

- provision directing accounts to be taken between any persons.[63]

Avoidance of general assignments of book debts

16.20 Section 344, IA86 renders void certain assignments of book debts by traders unless they have been registered under the Bills of Sale Act 1878. For a rare example of a case brought under this provision see *Hill v Alex Lawrie Factors*.[64]

---

55 IA86, s 343(3) or IN089, art 316(3).
56 IA86, s 343(3) or INO89, art 316(3).
57 IA86, s 343(2) or INO89, art 316(2).
58 IA86, s 343(4) or INO89, art 316(4).
59 IA86, s 343(4)(a) or INO89, art 316(4)(a).
60 IA86, s 343(4)(b) or INO89, art 316(4)(b).
61 IA86, s 343(4)(c) or INO89, art 316(4)(c).
62 IA86, s 343(4)(d) or INO89, art 316(4)(d).
63 IA86, s 343(4)(e) or INO89, art 316(4)(e).
64 [2000] BPIR 1038.

What effect does bankruptcy have on execution and other enforcement proceedings?

16.21 Where before the commencement of a bankruptcy a judgment creditor takes enforcement proceedings against a debtor's goods or property, the creditor cannot generally retain the benefit of execution or enforcement unless it was completed before the commencement of the bankruptcy.[65] As to the meaning of the 'benefit of execution' see generally *Re Caribbean Products (Yam Importers) Ltd.*[66] Section 346(5), IA86 deals with the meaning of 'completed' as follows:

- in the case of execution against goods, execution is completed by seizure and sale or by the making of a charging order;
- an execution against land is completed by seizure, by the appointment of a receiver or by the making of a charging order;
- in the case of attachment of a debt, attachment is completed on the receipt by the judgment creditor of the debt.

16.22 Where goods have been taken in execution but before execution has been completed the enforcement officer becomes aware of the making of a bankruptcy order he must deliver up the goods or money seized to the OR or trustee if requested to do so (subject to there being a first charge for his costs.[67] If the debtor's goods have been sold or money has been paid to avoid a sale and the judgment is for a debt in excess of £1,000 and within 14 days after sale the enforcement officer is given notice that a bankruptcy petition has been presented, the balance of the proceeds of execution, after deducting the costs of execution, form part of the bankrupt's estate if a bankruptcy order is made[68]

16.23 The provisions are designed to ensure that creditors' claims are dealt with in accordance with the *pari passu* principle. For the same reason the court should not generally make a final charging order or a final third party debt order where the debtor's insolvency is imminent, see *Roberts Petroleum Ltd v Bernard Kenny Ltd,*[69] *Rainbow v Moorgate Properties Ltd.*[70]

16.24 Execution within the meaning of s 346 does not include distress.[71] For more information on enforcement procedures and distress generally see chapter 4. It should be noted that enforcement procedures in Northern Ireland are different from England and Wales are different with the Judgments and

---

65 IA86, s 346.
66 [1966] Ch 331.
67 IA86, s 346(2) and IR86, rr 7.36 and 12.19.
68 IA86, s 346(3) and (4).
69 [1983] 2 AC 192.
70 [1975] 1 WLR 788.
71 *Re Modern Jet Support Ltd,* [2005] EWHC 1611 Ch, [2005] BPIR 1382.

Enforcements (Northern Ireland) Order 1981 being the principle legislation. See chapter 4 for a detailed explanation.

AFTER-ACQUIRED PROPERTY

What is 'after-acquired property'?

16.25 Section 30,7 IA86 deals with after-acquired property. After-acquired property is property which the bankrupt acquires after the bankruptcy order has been made but before the bankrupt is discharged from bankruptcy and which is not therefore included in his estate at the date of the bankruptcy order as it does not automatically vest in the trustee. After-acquired property typically may include, but is not limited to income from employment, property received under a legacy, lottery wins or any other windfall.

16.26 The bankrupt is obliged to notify his trustee of any property which he acquires or which devolves on him or of any increase in his income[72] and to do so within 21 days[73] of receipt.

16.27 If the bankrupt disposes of property before giving the notice required by r 6.200(1), IR86 or having done so disposes of the property without the written consent of the trustee within 42 days beginning with the date of the notice, he must disclose to the trustee the name and address of the disponee, and provide any other information which may be necessary to enable the trustee to trace the property and recover it for the estate.[74]

16.28 If the bankrupt carries on a business, he must, not less than every 6 months, furnish to his trustee information with respect to it, showing the total of goods bought and sold (or, as the case may be, services supplied) and the profit or loss arising from the business. The trustee may require the bankrupt to furnish fuller details (including accounts) of the business carried on by him.[75]

16.29 The trustee may claim after-acquired property for the estate but must do so by giving notice in writing.[76] He must give notice within 42 days after first becoming aware of the bankrupt's acquisition of the property or any longer period allowed by the court.[77] As to the danger of doing so late, see *Solomon v Williams*[78] and *Frances v Omerjee*.[79] The effect of service of written notice is to vest the property claimed in the trustee with effect from the date on which it was acquired.[80] However, the trustee has no claim against a person who has

---

72 IA86, s 333(2) or INO89, art 306(2).
73 IR86, r 6.200(1) or IRNI91, r 6.197(1).
74 IR86, r 6.200(3) or IRNI91, r 6.197(3).
75 IR86, r 6.200(5) or IRNI91, r 6.197(5).
76 IA86, s 307(1) or INO89, art 280(1).
77 IA86, s 309(1) or INO89, art 282(1).
78 [2001] BPIR 1123.
79 [2005] BPIR 1320.
80 IA86, s 307(3) or INO89, art 280(3).

acquired property from the bankrupt in good faith for value and without notice of the bankruptcy or against a banker who has entered into a transaction in good faith and without notice.[81]

16.30 Where property has been disposed of by the bankrupt, before or without giving the notice required by r 6.200, IR 1986, the trustee may serve notice on the disponee, claiming the property as part of the estate.[82] Such notice must be served within 28 days of the trustee becoming aware of the disponee's identity and an address at which he can be served.[83]

16.31 For examples of use of s 307, IA86 and judicial consideration of the provisions generally see *Pike v Cork Gully*;[84] *Hill v Secretary of State*;[85] and as to income see *Supperstone v Lloyd's Names Working Party*.[86]

16.32 Any assets or monies obtained from any source whilst serving bankruptcy (ie before discharge) may be claimed as part of the bankrupt's estate by the trustee. It's an offence not to disclose such information. This includes:

- Anything bequest in a will, for example a property.
- Something of little value at the time of the bankruptcy order, but rising in value before bankruptcy discharge.
- Claims made against another person through court proceedings.
- Any other windfall.
- If an individual knows or suspects they may be a benefactor of a will, it may be worthwhile to get advice on changing the benefactor to a non-serving bankrupt until after discharge.

How and when can a trustee sell a right of action?

16.33 Often the trustee will not have sufficient funds to pursue an action but can sell the right to proceed to a third party for the benefit of the estate. This is called an assignment of the action. The purchaser will stand in the shoes of the trustee for the purposes of the action. For an example see *Power v Brown and others*[87] where a bankrupt's attempt to have an assignment set aside was rejected.

---

81 IA86, s 307(4) or INO89, art 280(4).
82 IA86, s 307(3) or INO89, art 280(3).
83 IR86, r 6.201(2) or IRNI91, r 6.198(2).
84 [1997] BPIR 723.
85 [2005] EWHC 696 Ch, [2006] 1 BCLC 601.
86 [1999] BPIR 832.
87 [2009] BPIR 340.

Chapter 17

ASSETS INCLUDED IN BANKRUPTCY PROCEEDINGS (EXCLUDING THE MATRIMONIAL HOME)

'I can get no remedy against this consumption of the purse;
borrowing only lingers and lingers it out, but the disease is incurable.'[1]

INTRODUCTION

17.1 This chapter examines the different assets that form part of a bankrupt's estate and those which do not. The matrimonial home, as *prima facie*, the most valuable asset, is discussed in detail in the next chapter.[2] Income payments orders and agreements were dealt with in chapter 10. Two further sections follow. One is on the bankrupt's pension, and the other is on the vexed issue of hybrid claims. This chapter will cover a much wider range but potentially less valuable, albeit important, assets.

This examination begins with a brief tour of some pertinent statutory provisions. These sections are dispersed throughout the IA86, so some drawing together is required at an early stage to avoid confusion.[3] Following this summary is an explanation of qualifying and exempt assets. Specific examination of the status of a selection of bankrupt's assets is included in the exempt assets analysis with the relevant case law. The ORs and trustee's duty to safeguard the assets is also covered and the ways in which this duty is exercised. Finally, the chapter covers the ability of a trustee to disclaim onerous property.

17.2

Why should a bankrupt be allowed to retain certain assets?

Before we examine this area we should however first address an issue that is particularly perplexing to the layperson, namely, why should bankrupt individuals be allowed to keep certain items, or indeed, any items?[4] A partial answer can be found at para 1096 of the Cork Report. It is noted in that paragraph that the notion of debtor rehabilitation is generally useful to society

---

1 Shakespeare, *Henry IV, Part 2*, Act I, Scene II.

2 See chapter 18.

3 As with some other areas of the statute there is a certain degree of incoherency in the positioning of related sections in this area.

4 This disquiet grows all the more acute when 'high value' bankruptcies do not seem to strip the debtor of luxury goods such as large cars and houses.

at large. If the bankrupt was stripped of all their assets how would this accord with the notion of relief and rehabilitation? In relation to the assets point the Cork Report notes:

> 'in exchange for handing over virtually all that the bankrupt owns to be sold-off for the benefit of the creditors, the bankrupt will, at a later point in time, be released from all debts owing.'

This statutory compact is necessary for the placation of creditor demands. But as Cork noted, it is 'virtually all' that which the bankrupt owns. There remains some residue for their use, why? The rationale for leaving some assets with the bankrupt will hopefully become clear over the course of this chapter. Briefly stated however, bankrupts are human beings with basic human needs. These needs (and those of their family) must be recognised. Current policy also dictates that the debtor should be rehabilitated back into society as soon as possible. The debtor needs some assets to enable him to do this. The sentiment has been recognised judicially in a case involving the renewal of fishing licences where Warner J observed:

> 'Bankruptcy, putting it in its simplest terms, is a process whereby on the one hand all a debtor's property, with certain specific exceptions, is vested in his trustee in bankruptcy for realisation and distribution of the proceeds among his creditors and, on the other hand, he is forever relieved of personal liability to those creditors. The specific exceptions exist either because the property is not appropriate for distribution among the bankrupt's creditors, such as property of which he is only a trustee, or because, unlike an insolvent company, the bankrupt is a human being whose life must continue during and after insolvency. For this reason, section 283(2) excepts from the bankrupt's estate the tools and other items of equipment necessary for his personal use in his employment, business or vocation and also the clothing, bedding, furniture, household equipment and provisions necessary for the basic domestic needs of the bankrupt and his family. For the same reason the court may not make, under section 310 an income payments order reducing his income below what appears to the court to be necessary for meeting his reasonable domestic needs and those of his family.'[5]

What are the statutory provisions that relate to assets?

17.3 Before we look at the provisions on qualifying and exempt assets it is first prudent to provide a brief summary of the statutory provisions that regulate the assets that vest in the trustee. These are ss 306, 283 and 436, IA86.[6] These are set out below in edited form. The effect of s 306, IA86 is that as soon as the trustee is appointed the bankrupt's estate immediately vests in the trustee. It states:

> '306 Vesting of bankrupt's estate in trustee

---

5 *Re Rae* [1995] BCC 102, at p 111.

6 See also INO89, art 310 and 333.

(1) The bankrupt's estate shall vest in the trustee immediately on his appointment taking effect or, in the case of the official receiver, on his becoming trustee.

(2) Where any property which is, or is to be, comprised in the bankrupt's estate vests in the trustee (whether under this section or under any other provision of this Part), it shall so vest without any conveyance, assignment or transfer.'

QUALIFYING ASSETS

What is 'vesting'?

17.4 This 'vesting' concept has received judicial recognition. In *Re Oriental Inland Steam Company, ex parte Scinde Railway Company*,[7] Mellish LJ, observed, 'in bankruptcy the whole estate, both legal and beneficial, is taken out of the bankrupt, and is vested in his trustees or assignees, whereas in a winding-up the legal estate remains in the company'.[8] This essential difference between the personal side of the subject and the corporate side of the subject, ie legal title remaining vested in the company in corporate liquidation, as opposed to the vesting in the trustee is incredibly interesting,[9] not least because it speaks to the removal of the determination of the affairs of the bankrupt from the bankrupt in their entirety. Vesting as a concept therefore acknowledges that for the period of the bankruptcy, the bankrupt does not have full control of his or her own financial affairs. Indeed, it could be said that the idea of vesting acknowledges the idea that bankrupts are incapable of administering their own financial affairs. Vesting also survives the discharge of the bankrupt. This was recognised by Chadwick LJ in *Neil Owen Turner v Haworth Associates, Mrs Patricia Grieves, Alias Patricia Carter Pennington*[10] where he observed, 'But whatever property vested in the trustee under s 306 of that Act was not affected by that discharge'.[11]

What is the meaning of 'property'?

17.5 As a result of a bankruptcy order the bankrupt's estate 'vests' in the trustee. But what constitutes a bankrupt's estate? How is it determined? For an answer to the first of these questions we can focus on s 306(2), IA86 and in particular the word 'property' for it is property that comprises the bankrupt's estate. For the meaning of property we have to go to s 436, IA86. This section states that:

> '"property" includes money, goods, things in action, land and every description of property wherever situated and also obligations and every description of interest, whether present or future or vested or contingent, arising out of, or incidental to, property …'

---

7 (1873–74) LR 9 Ch App 557.

8 (1873–74) LR 9 Ch App 557, at p 560.

9 On this area see further *Cork Report* at para 1043. The company's assets may in some instance vest in the liquidator (s 145, IA86) but this is not the usual course.

10 [2001] EWCA CIV 370.

11 [2001] EWCA CIV 370 at para 2.

What do the courts say is the definition of 'property'?

17.6 This is a wide definition of property, if it is a definition at all. For some help setting the parameters of what might be considered property in the sense of s 436, IA86 we can go to the case law. Most of the judicial comment has been on the corporate side of the subject, but it is worth examining briefly, so that what property is generally can be considered, before we go on to discuss the specific discussion of the bankrupt's property later in this chapter. In *Bristol Airport Plc v Powdrill*,[12] Sir Nicolas Browne-Wilkinson V-C[13] observed in relation to s 436, IA86 that, 'It is hard to think of a wider definition of property'.[14] In a similar vein (and on the personal side of the subject) Aldous LJ pointed out in *Ord v Upton*[15] that 's 436, IA86 is not in truth a definition of the word "property". It only sets out what is included'.[16]

In another corporate judgment, Morritt LJ noted that:

> 'The word "property" is not a term of art but takes its meaning from its context: *Nokes v Doncaster Amalgamated Collieries Ltd*[17] and *Kirby (Inspector of Taxes) v Thorn EMI plc*.[18] The decided cases can only give an indication of the characteristics of "property" but as the question whether statutory exemptions or licences are property is likely to increase with increased regulation so it may be helpful to consider some of them.'[19]

On the subject of property broadly defined we will end with a statement from Lord Atkinson in which the general approach to the bankrupt's property is outlined particularly in relation to the exempt property and the reasons for allowing this exemption, as has already been touched on above.[20] In *Hollinshead v Hazleton*[21] Lord Atkinson noted that:

> 'In the context of insolvency there is 'principle of public policy, which has found expression in the provisions of the Bankruptcy Codes of … England … as estimable and as conducive to the welfare of the community as any. It is this, that in bankruptcy the entire property of the bankrupt, of whatever kind or nature it may be, whether alienable or inalienable, subject to be taken in execution, legal or equitable, or not so subject, shall, with the exception of some compassionate allowances for his maintenance, be appropriated and made available for the payment of his creditors.'

---

12 [1990] Ch 744, [1990] 2 All ER 493.
13 As he was at the time.
14 [1990] Ch 744, [1990] 2 All ER 493 at 759D.
15 [2000] Ch 352, [2000] 1 All ER 193.
16 [2000] Ch 352, [2000] 1 All ER 193 at 360.
17 [1940] 3 All ER 549 at 574, [1940] AC 1014 at 1051.
18 [1988] 2 All ER 947 at 953, [1988] 1 WLR 445 at 452
19 *Re Celtic Extraction Ltd (in liquidation); Re Bluestone Chemicals Ltd (in liquidation)* [2000] 2 WLR 991, at paras 26 and 27.
20 See **17.2.**
21 *Hollinshead v Hazleton* [1916] 1 AC 428 at 436, [1914–15] All ER Rep 1117 at 1120.

What assets are included in a bankrupt's estate?

17.7 We can now move to the section that defines the bankrupt's estate, namely, s 283, IA86.[22] It is this section that makes up the lion share of subsequent treatment within this chapter. Section 283, IA86 states:

> 'Definition of bankrupt's estate
>
> (1) Subject as follows, a bankrupt's estate for the purposes of any of this Group of Parts comprises—
> (a) all property belonging to or vested in the bankrupt at the commencement of the bankruptcy, and
> (b) any property which by virtue of any of the following provisions of this Part is comprised in that estate or is treated as falling within the preceding paragraph.
>
> (2) Subsection (1) does not apply to—
> (a) such tools, books, vehicles and other items of equipment as are necessary to the bankrupt for use personally by him in his employment, business or vocation;
> (b) such clothing, bedding, furniture, household equipment and provisions as are necessary for satisfying the basic domestic needs of the bankrupt and his family.'

Rattee J has intimated that the section must be read in the wider context of the common law. He observed in *Haig v Aitken*[23] that: 'there are some clearly established exceptions from the width of the definition of "estate", and not only those expressed by the statute itself in s 283, IA86, but others which have been established as exceptions by the common law.'[24] These additional exceptions are discussed below. The provisions have worldwide effect, so that it applies to foreign assets.[25]

What are qualifying assets?

17.8 A bankrupt's estate includes all of his assets as at the date of the commencement of his bankruptcy.[26] However, s 283(1), IA86 then goes on to list property that is exempt or is excluded, including any property held on trust for another person. These species of property are examined below. This 'catch-all' section is qualified to the extent that other persons may have rights to the assets[27] and, as noted above, to the extent that some of the bankrupt's property is deemed to be exempt property.

---

22 See also INO89, art 310.

23 [2001] Ch 110. Discussed further below.

24 [2001] Ch 110, at p 116G.

25 See for example, *Re Hayward (Deceased* [1997] Ch 45, [1996] 3 WLR 674, [1997] 1 ALL ER 32, *Pollard v Ashurst* [2001] BPIR 131, *R v R and S (Bankruptcy Jurisdiction Concerning Real Property Abroad: Setting Aside Consent Order: Estoppel)* [2007] EWHC 2589 (Fam), [2008] BPIR 647 and *Loy v O'Sullivan* [2010] EWHC 3583 (Ch), [2011] BPIR 181.

26 IA86, s 283(1).

27 IA86, s 283(5).

17.9 Tenancies are also specifically excluded as follows:

- a tenancy which is an assured tenancy or an assured agricultural occupancy, within the meaning of Part I of the Housing Act 1988, and the terms of which inhibit an assignment as mentioned in s 127(5) of the Rent Act 1977; or

- a protected tenancy, within the meaning of the Rent Act 1977, in respect of which, by virtue of any provision of Part IX of the Act, no premium can lawfully be required as a condition of assignment; or

- a tenancy of a dwelling-house by virtue of which the bankrupt is, within the meaning of the Rent (Agriculture) Act 1976, a protected occupier of the dwelling-house, and the terms of which inhibit an assignment as described in s 127(5) of the Rent Act 1977; or

- a secure tenancy, within the meaning of Part IV of the Housing Act 1985, which is not capable of being assigned, except in the cases mentioned in s 91(3) of that Act.

EXEMPT ASSETS

What are exempt assets?

17.10 Section 283(2), IA86 sets out a list of those assets excluded from a bankrupts' estate. This section bears repeating:

> '(a) such tools, books, vehicles and other items of equipment as are necessary to the bankrupt for use personally by him in his employment, business or vocation;
> (b) such clothing, bedding, furniture, household equipment and provisions as are necessary for satisfying the basic domestic needs of the bankrupt and his family. This subsection is subject to section 308 IA86 in Chapter IV (certain excluded property reclaimable by trustee).'

The question of what does and does not constitute an exempt asset has given rise to some very interesting case law. In recent years this has seen an expansion of what constitutes 'the basic domestic needs' of the bankrupt and his family.[28] We can now move to a consideration of some specific assets that have exercised the court's consideration. In so doing we also of course examine some case law authority that shows that some assets are not exempt and which are therefore qualifying assets which fall within the distributable estate. At this stage it is perhaps expedient to point out that s 283(2), IA86 is divided between what we will call the 'employment side' of a bankrupt's continued life and existence, ie subsection (a); and the 'family side' of a bankrupt's continued existence and rehabilitation, ie subsection (b). The cases can be discussed following that

---

28 The issue of school fees is discussed below.

division, although some of course traverse both areas. Where possible we will attempt to maintain the treatment of case law along the 'employment side' and 'family side' divisions.

Further, property that was the subject of a restraint order under the Proceeds of Crime Act 2002 before the bankruptcy order was made is excluded.[29]

TREATMENT BY ASSET TYPE

How are items such as fishing licences dealt with?

17.11 In *Re Rae*,[30] Warner J was asked to consider a fishing licence renewal candidacy and the question of whether or not this item should be considered as part of the bankrupt's estate. Warner J observed:

> 'There is no example, however, either in the Act or in the many authorities that were cited to me, of a bankrupt being entitled to retain for his own benefit a purely financial or commercial asset capable of realisation for the benefit of his creditors and not necessary for his personal use in his employment, business or vocation.'[31]

How is the bankrupt's correspondence dealt with?

17.12 The leading case on whether or not a bankrupt's correspondence can be used by the trustee as property to placate creditor demand is *Haig v Aitken*.[32] The case involved Mr Jonathan Aitken, a former Member of Parliament and Minister of State. He became bankrupt on 10 May 1999 following an unsuccessful IVA proposal.[33] His indebtedness arose as a result of his failed libel action and the associated litigation costs that he owed.[34] Counsel for the trustee submitted that certain letters could be realised for the benefit of creditors. This case could equally fall under **17.11** above in terms of a case involving items of commercial worth as the court had to consider, inter alia, whether particular species of correspondence could be sold, probably to a newspaper for publication that formed part of Mr Aitken's estate. The correspondence was of commercial interest as it involved correspondence with, *inter alia*, former parliamentary, ministerial and government colleagues, current and former heads of state, members of royal or ruling families and foreign statesmen. In addition to ss 306, 436 and 283 IA86, reg 30 of the Insolvency Regulations 1994[35] was also of note in the case as it states:

---

29 Proceeds of Crime Act 2002, s 417.

30 [1995] BCC 102.

31 [1995] BCC 102, at p 111.

32 [2001] Ch 110.

33 On other famous bankrupts see: http://bankruptcyandinsolvency.blogspot.com/2009/04/famous-bankrupts-throughout-history-at.html. For an example of another 'famous' bankrupt see: *Official Receiver v Southey* [2009] BPIR 89.

34 On the libel trial see further: http://www.guardian.co.uk/aitken.

35 SI 1994/2507.

> 'The trustee, on the authorisation of the official receiver, during his tenure of office or on vacating office, or the official receiver while acting as trustee, may at any time sell, destroy or otherwise dispose of the books, papers and other records of the bankrupt.'[36]

Following a review of the pertinent authorities Rattee J held:

> 'In my judgment it is inconceivable that Parliament envisaged, by passing the Act, that the effect of bankruptcy should be that a bankrupt's personal correspondence should be available for publication to the world at large at the behest of the trustee in bankruptcy. In my opinion, the concept of such a gross invasion of privacy is repugnant. I do not believe that Parliament intended it, any more than it intended creditors to have the right to damages for injury to his person or character. In my judgment, on its proper construction in the context of its apparent legislative purpose, the effect of the Act is that a bankrupt's estate does not include the bankrupt's personal correspondence which, like a right of action for damages for libel, is of a nature peculiarly personal to him and his life as a human being. That is so, in my judgment, even in the case of a famous bankrupt, whose correspondence as a result may be worth a considerable sum to the media.'[37]

Consequently it was held that Mr Aitken's personal correspondence did not form part of his estate for bankruptcy purposes.[38]

How are other personal or family assets dealt with?

17.13 Obviously, assets that are formally owned by other family members are not owned by the bankrupt and so do not vest in the bankrupt's estate. There may be issues as regards jointly owned assets, or assets owned by the bankrupt but used by the family. As noted above s 282(2)(b), IA86 lists furniture as being exempt property which does not form part of the bankrupt's estate for bankruptcy purposes. In terms of the continuance of a normal family life this is obviously a very important exemption. Although it does of course give rise to the issue of reasonable replacement, ie would a 'flat pack' table be a reasonable replacement for a Chippendale table?

How is a bankrupt's motor vehicle dealt with?

17.14 One vexing issue that arises as a consequence of the split between the employment and the social elements of s 283, IA86 hinges around the placement of the motor vehicle. Vehicles are included in subsection (a) as something that should remain exempt from the bankrupt's estate for bankruptcy purposes to help the bankrupt with their employment, business or vocation. Curiously, though the legislature (in 1986) did not consider that a vehicle was essentially for family life as vehicles are not included in subsection (b). When other exemptions that have been allowed in more recent times are considered against this anomaly, ie private school fees, the absence of a vehicle from the family exemptions seems like a yawning lacuna, and one which might

---

36 Insolvency Regulations 1994, SI 1994/2507, reg 30.

37 *Haig v Aitken* [2001] Ch 110, at p 118D–118F.

38 *Haig v Aitken* [2001] Ch 110, at p 119A.

require legislative intervention to bring this part of exempt property into line with modern expectations of family requirements. The question for policy makers is: does a motor vehicle now form part of a bankrupt family's 'basis domestic needs' If not used for business or employment.

How is work equipment dealt with?

17.15 As noted above, current bankruptcy policy is aimed at relief and rehabilitation. One way in which a bankrupt can continue to live normally is to be employed and therefore maintain some balance. Certain exemptions are therefore allowed within the 'employment side' of s 283, IA86. This work encouragement point has received judicial consideration before the Court of Appeal where Chadwick LJ (Jacobs J agreeing) examined whether the making and continuance of a bankruptcy order violates a right to work. In *Alexander v Philips Electronics (UK) Ltd,* Chadwick LJ observed:[39]

> 'In my view, there is no real prospect of persuading this court that such a right [to work] is violated by the provisions of the Bankruptcy Code now enshrined in the Insolvency Act 1986. It is noticeable that section 283(2) of the Act, re-enacting a provision which has been in bankruptcy law for (I think) at least 140 years, excludes from the bankrupt's estate tools, books, vehicles and other items of equipment necessary to the bankrupt for use personally by him in his employment, business or vocation. That provision – which, as I say, is of long standing – reflects the policy of the Bankruptcy Code that bankruptcy should not deprive an individual of his right or ability to continue in his employment, business or vocation; in particular, should not deprive him of the means of carrying on that employment, business or vocation ...'

When can exempt assets be substituted with a cheaper alternative?

17.16 The trustee can replace an exempt asset belonging to a bankrupt with a cheaper alternative.[40] The process requires the trustee to serve notice on the bankrupt that the value of the asset exceeds the cost of a reasonable replacement.[41] The trustee may then provide the replacement either before or after the asset has been realised.[42] The trustee is under no obligation to apply funds to the purchase of any replacement until he has sufficient funds in the estate for that purpose.[43]

When can third party funds be accepted to retain a specific asset?

17.17 The trustee can accept any reasonable proposal from a third party as long as the bankrupts' estate will benefit to the extent of the value of the property in question less the cost of a reasonable replacement.[44]

---

39 [2003] EWCA Civ 141.
40 IA86, s 308(3).
41 IA86, s 308(2).
42 IA86, r 6.187(1).
43 IA86, r 6.187(2).
44 IA86, r 6.188(2).

What happens to pensions?

17.18 The treatment of pensions has changed over recent years and the following sets out the various changes by looking at the different types of pensions. Sections 11 and 12, Welfare Reform and Pensions Act 1999 reverse the effect of a series of decisions[45] that personal and occupational pension fund benefits fall within the bankrupt's estate by excluding 'approved pension arrangements' as defined by s 11(11).[46] The exclusion is, however, limited to bankruptcies where the order was made on or after 29 May 2000. Pension payments may be taken into account for the purpose of an income payment order or agreement. For pre-29 May 2000 bankruptcies the old law applies allowing trustees to claim pension contributions and payments.[47] This applies to both lump sum and income entitlements. For current cases s 342A, IA86 allows a trustee to recover excessive contributions to pension schemes and s 342D, IA86 allows him to recover excessive contributions in pension-sharing cases.

17.19 Personal Occupational Pensions are covered by the Income and Corporation Taxes Act 1988, Part 8 of the Personal Pension Schemes Guidance Notes,[48] the Pension Schemes Act 1993, the Pensions Act 1995 and the Welfare and Pensions Act 1999. The net effect of these statutes is that an interest in a pension fund cannot be transferred or assigned. The only way in which the fund could be used would be to realise a lump sum and make that or the payments under an annuity available to the creditors.

17.20 By ss 634(2) and 635, Income and Corporation Taxes Act 1988 (ICT88) payment of benefits whether as a lump sum or via a purchased annuity may not commence before the beneficiary's fiftieth birthday subject only to two exceptions as set out in s 634(3), ICT88:

- the beneficiary is unable to carry on his previous occupation or any occupation of a similar nature for which he is trained or fitted by reason of infirmity of body or mind; or
- the beneficiary's normal occupation is one in which persons customarily retire before that age.

---

45 Notably *Re Landau (A Bankrupt)* [1998] Ch 223, *Krasner v Dennison* [2001] Ch 76, *Rowe v Sanders* [2002] EWCA Civ 242, [2002] BPIR 847, [2002] 2 All ER 800 and *Malcolm v Benedict Mackenzie and others* [2004] EWCA Civ 1748, [2005] BPIR 176. In *Patel v Jones* [2001] EWCA Civ 779, [2001] BPIR 919 it was held that a bankrupt's interest under an occupational pension scheme also vested in the trustee in bankruptcy.

46 Welfare Reform and Pensions Act 1999.

47 See *Malcolm v Benedict Mackenzie* [2004] EWHC 339 (Ch), [2004] BPIR 747 and on appeal at [2004] EWCA Civ 1748, [2005] BPIR 176.

48 IR 76 (2000).

What circumstances affect lump sum payments?

17.21 In *R v Cornfield*[49] the Court of Appeal held that a Confiscation Order under s 71, Criminal Justice Act 1988 could not be made in respect of future rights in a pension fund because the fund was not realisable at the date of the order (which was made before the accused's fiftieth birthday). May LJ described the pension as follows:

> 'This pension is under a scheme that is approved by the Inland Revenue under Chapter IV Part XIV of the Income and Corporation Taxes Act 1988. It is therefore not capable of assignment or surrender[50] and does not vest in a trustee in bankruptcy (see section 11(1) Welfare Reform and Pensions Act 1999). There is guidance on the administration of these schemes in an advice document entitled "Personal Pension Schemes Guidance Notes".[51] The right to an annuity cannot be surrendered or assigned, nor can the right to a lump sum. The scheme member has an unfettered right to choose whether to take a limited part of his benefit as a lump sum, but he may take it all as an annuity.'

He went on to hold that as a result of the restriction on surrender or assignment and the fact that the pension does not vest in a trustee it would not as at the date of the confiscation order have any value which could be made the subject of a confiscation order. There are various statutory provisions that provide that, on public policy grounds, certain classes of pension benefits are also exempt from enforcement, where they are derived from public duties. These apply to, in particular, Navy and Marine personnel, Army personnel, Air Force personnel, civil servants and teachers.

17.22 In contrast in *Williamson* it was held that a trustee could enforce a right to request payment under a pension scheme even when the bankrupt had not made that request and was in fact intent on retaining the fund intact until after he was discharged. At the date of the bankruptcy order the pension fund in question was valued at just short of £1 million which would yield a tax free lump sum of £248,708. The fund was available for payment on request but the bankrupt stated that he was in employment and was in receipt of sufficient income to meet his current domestic needs and had no plans to request payments while he was still bankrupt.

17.23 In historic, pre-29 May 2000 bankruptcies, the main remaining issue is whether any forfeiture clause that purport to terminate the bankrupt's interest in the pension in the event of a bankruptcy order being made against him are valid.[52] They might be void on the basis of:

---

49 [2006] EWCA Crim 2909.

50 See Income and Corporation Taxes Act 1988, s 634(6).

51 IR76 (2000).

52 For recent cases where the court has considered whether such a forfeiture clause operated to prevent enforcement against an individual's pension rights, see *Caboche v Ramsay* [1997] BPIR 377, *Re Scientific Investment Pension Plan Trusts* [1999] Ch 53, [1998] BPIR 410 and *Fisher v Harrison* [2003] EWCA Civ 1047, [2003] BPIR 1322.

- the anti-deprivation principle, namely that that there could not be a valid contract that a man's property should remain his until his bankruptcy, and on the happening of that event should go over to someone else, and be taken away from his creditors;[53] or
- the principle of bankruptcy law that prevents a person relying upon protective trusts created by his own disposition as a means of defeating the claims of his creditors.[54]

What happens to causes of action?

17.24 On the whole, causes of action are just like any other asset of the bankrupt and vest in the trustee. Causes of action relating to assets or property are treated separately from the assets themselves, Thus, where a bankrupt had, post-bankruptcy, issued proceedings in relation to a property, alleging among other things, misrepresentation against the vendors, negligence against his conveyancing solicitors and obstruction of a right of way and harassment against the neighbours and their family, all causes of action that had accrued pre-bankruptcy, it was held that that those cause of action remained vested in the trustee despite his disclaimer of the property to which the causes of action related.[55]

17.25 If the cause of action is vested in the trustee, the bankrupt cannot issue proceedings in his own name, even for protecting against the potential expiry of a limitation period, even if he expects to take an assignment of the cause of action from the trustee in due course. The proceedings will be regarded as an abuse of the process.[56]

Does the bankrupt keep any causes of action?

17.26 As noted above, there are some species of property that remain so personal to the bankrupt that they remain vested in him, despite the bankruptcy order. As a general rule, all causes of action maintainable by the bankrupt as at the date of the bankruptcy order vest in the trustee. However, where those causes of action are regarded as being purely personal to the bankrupt, they do not vest and remain with the bankrupt. These would include

---

53 *Perpetual Trustee Co Ltd and another v BNY Corporate Trustee Services Ltd and another, Butters and others v BBC Worldwide Ltd and others* [2009] EWCA Civ 1160, [2010] Ch 347, [2010] BPIR 174. See also *British Eagle International Airlines Ltd v Compagnie Nationale Air France* [1975] 1 WLR 758, *Money Markets International Stockbrokers Ltd (In Liquidation) v London Stock Exchange and Another* [2002] 1 WLR 1150, [2001] BPIR 1044, [2001] 4 All ER 223, [2001] 2 BCLC 347 and *Mayhew v King* [2010] EWHC 1121 (Ch), [2010] BPIR 1155.

54 See *Re Brewer's Settlement* [1896] 2 Ch 503, referred to at p 236D in *Landau*. This is also known as the rule in *Re Burroughs-Fowler* [1916] 2 Ch 251. See also *Krasner v Dennison* at para 48.

55 *Young v Official Receiver* [2010] EWHC 1591 (Ch) [2010] BPIR 1477. See also *Young and others v Hamilton and others* [2010] NICH 11, [2010] BPIR 1468.

56 *Pickthall v Hill Dickinson LLP* [2009] EWCA Civ 543, [2009] BPIR 1467.

claims for ancillary relief against a former spouse, or a claim against an estate under the Inheritance (Provision for Family and Dependents) Act 1975.

17.27 Thus, in *Re Rae*[57] where Warner J observed, 'the bankrupt is, within limits, allowed to keep damages awarded to him for injury to his person, such as damages for slander'[58] and in *Haig v Aitken*[59] the concept was further recognised by Rattee J who noted, 'the courts recognise that, consistently with the purpose of the Act, even valuable assets of a peculiarly personal nature, especially for instance rights of action for damages to body, mind or reputation, are not included in the wide definition of 'property' for the purposes of the definition of a bankrupt's estate in the Act'.[60] In *Heath v Tang*[61] Hoffmann LJ (as he then was[62]) noted:

> 'The property which vests in the trustee includes "things in action": see section 436. Despite the breadth of this definition, there are certain causes of action personal to the bankrupt which do not vest in his trustee. These include cases in which "the damages are to be estimated by immediate reference to pain felt by the bankrupt in respect of his body, mind or character, and without immediate reference to his rights of property": see *Beckham v Drake* (1849) 2 HL Cas 579 , 604, per Erle J and *Wilson v United Counties Bank Ltd* [1920] AC 102. Actions for defamation and assault are obvious examples. The bankruptcy does not affect his ability to litigate such claims.'[63]

17.28 But it is important to differentiate between an undetermined or unlitigated personal cause of action that the bankrupt may have had as at the date of the bankruptcy and the proceeds of a completed personal cause of action, represented by damages already paid to the bankrupt as at the date of the bankruptcy order. In *Ord v Upton*[64] Aldous LJ commenting on the general principles as follows:[65]

> 'As will appear later from the cases that have been decided over many years, actions which relate to a bankrupt's personal reputation or body have not been considered to be property and therefore they do not vest in anybody other than the bankrupt. They relate solely to his body, mind and character and any damages recovered are compensation for damage to his body, mind and character as opposed to other causes of action which have been considered to be a right of property. Thus causes of action to recover damages for pain and suffering have been held not to vest in the trustee. That has led to a number of oddities. For example, the parties agree that if at the time of the bankruptcy, the bankrupt had

57 [1995] BCC 102.

58 In *Re Rae* [1995] BCC 102, at p 111, citing *Ex p Vine; Re Wilson* (1878) 8 ChD 364.

59 *Haig v Aitken* [2001] Ch 110.

60 *Haig v Aitken* [2001] Ch 110, at 118C.

61 [1993] 1 WLR 1421.

62 In the *Haig v Aitken* [2001] Ch 110 official law report Lord Hoffmann's surname is spelt with only one 'n' (at p 116H). This misspelling accords with Rosenberg's 'much misspelled judge' comment in the article he published on the noble Lord's retirement: J Rosenberg 'How Pinochet tainted Hoffmann's brilliant career' *Law Society Gazette*, Thursday 23 April 2009.

63 [1993] 1 WLR 1421, 1423.

64 [2000] Ch 352, [2000] 2 WLR 755, [2000] 1 All ER 193, [2000] BPIR 104.

65 [2000] Ch 352, at p 360A.

in his bank a sum which included money paid as damages for a libel, that sum would vest in his trustee because the right to the money formed part of his estate and therefore was available to pay off the bankrupt's creditors. That was to be contrasted with an action personal to the bankrupt, such as a libel action, which was not settled before the end of the bankruptcy. In such circumstances the cause of action would remain with the bankrupt as would any damages awarded after discharge. If a cause of action is not personal to the bankrupt, it vests in the trustee and therefore any damages awarded whether before or after the discharge will be available to discharge the bankrupt's liabilities.'

Causes of action: both personal and general

What are 'hybrid claims'?

17.29 The decision in *Ord v Upton* is more notable for its recognition of the so-called 'hybrid claim', namely a cause of action that encompasses both personal relief that would commonly be regarded as remaining vested in the bankrupt and a cause of action that would commonly be regarded as vesting in the trustee. The Court of Appeal had to consider whether a cause of action for medical negligence vested in the trustee or remained with the bankrupt as personal property which is not available for the benefit of the creditors.

17.30 A discharged bankrupt, Ord, a labourer, alleged that he received negligent medical treatment for back pain following treatment by a doctor. Ord was adjudged bankrupt shortly after this purportedly negligent treatment. When the bankruptcy was discharged Ord brought an action against the doctor. Ord was seeking damages for loss of earnings, pain and suffering. Ord's trustee believed that he, as the office holder, was entitled to the damages for the claimant's financial loss up to the date of the discharge. Ord contended that no part of the cause in action or any subsequent damages vested in the trustee.

17.31 At first instance, it was held that the claim for loss of earnings up to the date of discharge was vested in the trustee. Ord appealed this decision. The nature of s 436, IA86 and its definition of property were considered. The definition included a cause of action. Ergo, this constituted part of the bankrupt's estate and vests in the trustee. Unless it consisted solely of a cause of action personal to the bankrupt, Aldous LJ observed:[66]

> 'I accept that Mr. **Ord**'s claim can be categorised as being one for personal injury, but that hides the true nature of the claim. The cause of action is for negligence. The result of that negligence is damage. The compensation awarded will be money and the objective will be to get at the sum which will put the injured party in the same position as he would have been in if he had not sustained the wrong. The injury is actionable at the time physical harm is done, but the court when assessing the damages looks at the position as it is at the date of the trial. Until 1970 it was the usual practice of the court to award one global sum. That practice changed after *Jefford v Gee* [1970] 2 QB 130 and since then it has been customary to place a

66 [2000] Ch 35, at p 361A.

figure on each head of relevant damage. In this case the heads of damage will include pain and suffering and loss of past and future earnings.

In modern parlance Mr. **Ord**'s claim is a single cause of action. However, I cannot accept [his Counsel's] submission that the cause of action is personal. It is a claim for damages for injury to his body and mind and also his capacity to earn and can therefore be considered as a "hybrid" claim, in part personal and in part relating to property. I have come to the conclusion that such **an** action vested in the trustee. It would only have remained with Mr. **Ord** if it fell within **an** exception established by the authorities to be excluded from the definition of property now found in section 436 of the Act of 1986. To do so it must relate *only* to a cause of action personal to the bankrupt. All causes of action which seek to recover property vest in the trustee whether or not they contain other heads of damage to which the bankrupt is entitled. The authorities to which I now turn lead to that conclusion.'

The consequences of this were observed as follows:[67]

'For my part I cannot see that there is any difference in kind between the type of action there being considered and an action for negligence for personal injury resulting in different heads of damage. That being so, any damages awarded may have to be split between a trustee in bankruptcy and the bankrupt. It follows that Mr. Ord should retain the right to the damages for pain and suffering and the right to the damages for past and future earnings vested in the trustee. That leaves the question of how those rights are to be enforced. I believe that when there is but one cause of action which includes a head of damage relating to property, then the cause of action vests in the trustee as it does not fall within an exception to the general rule. If so, the right to recover the damages which are personal and any damages recovered are held on a constructive trust for the bankrupt by the trustee.'

Aldous LJ concluded:[68]

'The authorities are only consistent with the conclusion that the trustee is entitled to the damages for past and future loss of earnings and is not entitled to the damages for pain and suffering. As there is a single cause of action, it vested in the trustee. There is in my view nothing in that conclusion which imposes practical difficulties with which the law cannot deal. The trustee as constructive trustee would have to account to the bankrupt for the property which he obtained inadvertently or by arrangement in an action which vested in him for the benefit of the creditors. The idea that the cause of action should vest in the bankrupt would not be acceptable and compulsory joinder of both could lead to difficulties when the claim for loss of earnings was small compared with the potential costs of the litigation. In such a case the trustee, if the cause of action vested in him, would have to consider carefully his duty to the bankrupt and would probably, if requested, assign the cause of action to him.'

---

67 [2000] Ch 352 at p 369H.
68 [2000] Ch 352 at p 371B.

How do 'hybrid claims' work in practice?

17.32 A typical personal injury claim (such as a road traffic accident) usually gives rise to five common heads of loss:

Head 1: expenses for medical treatment and travelling;

Head 2: damage to the vehicle and belongings;

Head 3: loss of earnings from the accident to trial;

Head 4: future loss of earnings; and

Head 5: pain and suffering and loss of amenity.

Assuming post-accident bankruptcy, it is clear that heads 1 and 2 would vest in the trustee, as they are pure money claims. Head 5, being purely personal, would remain vested in the bankrupt. The clash would be over Heads 3 and 4. Under the old law, a bankrupt was entitled to keep such post-bankruptcy income as he needed for his maintenance. But, since the law changed under the Act, a bankrupt is entitled to keep all his post-bankruptcy income, subject to an application by the trustee for an income payments order under s 310, IA86 (where the trustee will be able to recover for the benefit of the bankruptcy estate the excess income over and above that which is required for the bankrupt's reasonable domestic needs, for himself and his family). Such post-bankruptcy income is not regarded as 'after-acquired property' that can be claimed by notice (such as a post-bankruptcy inheritance or lottery win). Accordingly, there could have been some scope for arguing that claims for loss of earnings under Heads 3 and 4 would remain vested in the bankrupt, so long as they related to post-bankruptcy claims. However, the conclusion in *Ord v Upton* was very clearly that whilst the bankrupt was entitled to retain the right to the damages for pain and suffering, and the right to the damages for past and future earnings vested in the trustee.

17.33 Thus the trustee holds the cause of action on trust for himself (for the benefit of the bankrupt's estate) and the bankrupt. If the trustee settles the cause of action with the defendant, he has to ensure that the figure is appropriate, both as regards the amount of the claim to which the estate is entitled and as regards that element that is held for the bankrupt. The trustee also has to ensure that the damages are properly appropriated between the claims vested in the estate and those that remain with the bankrupt.

17.34 If the trustee refuses to litigate the claim, the bankrupt has two options. Usually, he will seek to take an assignment of the cause of action from the trustee. The trustee owes his primary duty to the general body of creditors, with a view to obtaining the best price reasonably obtainable for the assets in his hands. Accordingly, he cannot simply assign the cause of action to the bankrupt because the bankrupt was the injured party. His duty to creditors requires him to consider that bids may be made by other parties, especially the defendant. The trustee will usually enter into a closed bidding process between the bankrupt and the defendant (with no referential bids) and with no obligation to accept the highest bid. Alternatively, in his capacity as a beneficiary of the trust, technically the bankrupt can bring a derivative action on behalf of the trust, joining the trustee as a defendant.[69] That is not common.

How have the courts treated 'hybrid claims'?

17.35 In *Grady v Prison Service*[70] the matter to be determined before the Court of Appeal (Thorpe LJ; Sedley LJ; Richards J) turned on whether or not an unfair dismissal claim was a property right falling within the scope of s 436 IA86 or a personal right accruing to the bankrupt in their personal capacity and not to the trustee. If the unfair dismissal claim as property fell within the latter category it would bring the property within the distributable estate that was available to satisfy creditors. As we have already noted, this form of property question regarding types of property *prima facie* falling within the bankruptcy estate is known as a hybrid claim[71] and as Sedley LJ observed in *Grady v Prison Service*:

> 'The law has for many years distinguished … between proceedings which seek to recover money or property in which the bankrupt's creditors will have an interest and causes of action personal to the bankrupt which do not vest in the trustee.'[72]

17.36 The claimant (Sharon Marie Grady) was employed by Her Majesty's Prison Service (HMP) as an administrative officer for nearly 15 years. She brought a tripartite claim before the Leeds employment tribunal for wrongful dismissal, unfair dismissal and a disability claim following the termination of her employment in November 2000. Her claim was struck out at first instance for non-compliance with procedural directions. She gave notice to appeal to the Employment Appeal Tribunal (EAT) on the 21 November 2001. Grady was then adjudged bankrupt on the 31 January 2002. Grady's employer, HMP, posited that because all of the claimant's property vested in her trustee (by virtue of the operation of s 283(1) IA86) and that because the trustee had not assigned any property to Grady she had no *locus standi* to bring the claim.[73]

17.37 As referred to above[74] there are three sections in the IA86 that must be considered in the context of this type of property question, namely,

---

69 *Young v Official Receiver* [2010] EWHC 1591 (Ch), [2010] BPIR 1477.

70 [2003] EWCA Civ 527, [2003] 3 All ER 745, [2003] BPIR 823. See further D Preston, S Morgan and A Brown 'Grady and beyond – when is a hybrid action not a hybrid action' [2004] *Insolv Int* 17(9), 142–143.

71 See further A Walters 'Bankruptcy and hybrid claims' (2005) LQR 121(Jan), 46–48.

72 [2003] 3 All ER 745, at 748A.

73 This locus standi point was also discussed by Chadwick LJ in *In Neil Owen Turner v Haworth Associates, Mrs Patricia Grieves, Alias Patricia Carter Pennington* [2001] EWCA Civ 370, at para 13.

74 See **17.3**.

- section 306, IA86 which states that the estate of a bankrupt vests in the trustee upon the making of the bankruptcy order;
- section 283(1), IA86 which states that the bankrupt's estate is defined as property, and finally
- section 436, IA86 which defines property and it includes 'things in action' (eg a right to bring or pursue legal proceedings).

The appeal to the EAT was dismissed. Grady appealed the decision of the EAT[75] as she contended that she was entitled to the portion of her claim that related to unfair dismissal. This was because unfair dismissal was by its nature a claim for reinstatement or reengagement. This was a personal claim to Grady of which only she could benefit. This is of course different to both wrongful dismissal and disability discrimination which by their nature are both money claims. As Sedley LJ observed, 'an unfair dismissal claim, both in its nature and in its remedies, is personal to the claimant and not apt to vest in her trustee as a thing in action'.[76]

17.38 It was held by the Court of Appeal that there was a distinction between proceedings which attempted to recover money or property and proceedings which were personal to the bankrupt. This second species of property did not vest in the trustee. Sedley LJ observed, 'In our judgment the essential nature of a claim for unfair dismissal is personal, not proprietary'.[77] He went further and noted, 'In our judgment a claim for re-instatement or re-engagement consequent on an unfair dismissal, and indeed a significant element of the compensation which can be awarded *in lieu* of these, is not a thing in action of the kind which forms part of a bankrupt's estate, even though the eventual fund (if an award is made) may be'.[78]

17.39 Despite the terms of *Ord v Upton*, the Court of Appeal has considered that a bankrupt might retain entire control over the cause of action by issuing a claim in respect of which he limits the relief sought only to those heads of the claim that remain personally vested in him. In *Khan v Trident Safeguards Ltd*[79] Khan issued proceedings against his former employers on the grounds of racial discrimination. The Employment Tribunal dismissed the proceedings, on the basis that he had not been racially discriminated against and had not been victimised. The Employment Appeal Tribunal dismissed the appeal, on the basis that, by then, a bankruptcy order had been made against Khan and that the cause of action was no longer vested in him, but in his trustee, the Official Receiver. The Court of Appeal held that Khan was entitled to pursue his claim for race discrimination, even though it was a hybrid claim, provided that the relief which he sought was restricted to a declaration of discriminatory conduct

---

75 The panel consisted of His Honour Judge J McMullen QC, Mr Lambert and Mr Manners.
76 [2003] EWCA Civ 527, at para 27.
77 [2003] 3 All ER 745, at 750A.
78 [2003] 3 All ER 745, at 751f.
79 [2004] EWCA Civ 624, [2004] BPIR 881.

and compensation for injured feelings, and did not include any compensation for loss of earnings. All three judges (Buxton, Arden and Wall LJJ) concluded that Khan's claims relating to race discrimination and victimisation were 'hybrid' within *Ord v Upton* and, accordingly, vested in the Official Receiver.

17.40 Wall LJ was of the view that there was no way around this jurisdictional point, such that Khan had no standing to progress the appeal. He was reluctant as a general proposition to permit litigants who were bankrupt to select and litigate those parts of hybrid claims which had vested in their trustees, but which could be said to be 'personal', especially as such vesting of a bankrupt's cause of action in the trustee was by no means the end of the litigation road for the bankrupt. He was of the view that the law imposed a filter, and that in an appropriate case where the trustee would be unwilling to continue the litigation or to assign, a bankrupt could have recourse to the bankruptcy court to compel an assignment. Access to the court or a hearing was not being denied. However, both Buxton and Arden LJJ took a different approach.

17.41 In the critical passage at, Arden LJ said the following:[80]

> 'However, in my judgment, the critical question is not what relief Mr Khan could in theory seek but what relief he is in fact seeking. His present claim would clearly encompass a claim for a declaration and for compensation for injured feelings only. In my judgment, Mr Khan should in principle be permitted to limit his claim for relief to those items. If he does so, the claim ceases, in my judgment, to be a 'hybrid' one. As to the grant of permission to amend the claims, I do not consider it relevant that Mr Khan became bankrupt on his own petition. Moreover, if his appeals are unmeritorious, they should be disposed of on that basis and not on an issue of standing which can be resolved by amendment. The trustee is not prejudiced as he has already made it clear that he does not wish to pursue these claims and any future orders as to costs made against Mr Khan would not be provable in his present bankruptcy.'

17.42 Buxton LJ agreed with Arden LJ. He concluded that, pursuant to *Ord v Upton,* the single cause of action which constituted the hybrid cause of action vested in full, including its personal element, in the trustee. Where there was a money claim, but in the form of relief that was merely the expression in money terms of an undoubted personal claim, such as pain and suffering in assault or general damage in defamation, then the action remained a personal one. However, if a claim was added for a distinct pecuniary loss, such as the loss of past and future earnings in *Ord v Upton*, or special damage in defamation; then the whole chose became hybrid, and the whole of it passed under the control of the trustee. Then, he continued:[81]

> 'Fourthly, Mr Khan, if I understand him right, seeks to keep his actions alive by withdrawing or disclaiming any desire on his part to seek any remedy that renders his claim hybrid. In order to achieve that end he would, I think, have to limit himself to a claim for a declaration of discriminatory conduct under s 56(1)(a) and

---

[80] Paragraph 88.

[81] At para 105.

a claim for injury to feelings under s 57(4) of the RRA 1976. Both of those can be said with confidence, in the words of Erle J, not to have immediate reference to the bankrupt's rights of property. Neither of them claim, nor unlike an order under s 56(1)(c) might potentially lead to, monetary compensation of the sort that excluded the bankrupt's action in *Ord v Upton* [2000] Ch 352, [2000] BPIR 104. Nor, in circumstances where apparently the trustee is not interested in pursuing any part of Mr Khan's claim, would it be abusive for Mr Khan to abandon claims that at least in theory might enure for the benefit of his creditors. Nor can I see that it can be wrong in itself for a litigant to abandon his money claim if that frees the court to entertain a different claim which, it is agreed on all sides, would always have been open to him, bankrupt or not. Nor is that course precluded by the attitude taken to the disability discrimination claim in *Grady*,[82] even if, as a concession, that in any way bound us: because it is clear that the applicant in that case wished to maintain her full money claim.'

He too emphasised that the proper determination of discrimination claims was always essential in our pluralistic society and concluded that, to the extent that Khan wished to complain about the conduct of the hearings, it would not be right to shut him out just because he was a bankrupt whose trustee had no interest in pursuing claims that Khan did not make.

17.43 So, having commenced an application to the Employment Tribunal, and then been made bankrupt, Khan was permitted to limit the elements of his claim to the 'personal' aspects, so as to allow his claim to continue. It is difficult to see how that result was reached after the court had expressly recognised, following *Ord v Upton*, there was only one cause of action, a hybrid one, that vested in the trustee. The majority recognised that, in the absence of any assignment at all, the bankrupt himself could render the proceedings 'un-hybrid' simply by limiting the cause of action to the 'personal' aspects. This fails to recognise that the single cause of action was vested in the trustee.

17.44 In *Mulkerrins v Pricewaterhouse Coopers (A Firm)*[83] the dispute was whether the chose in action which represented Ms Mulkerrins' claim against PricewaterhouseCoopers was an asset which had vested in the trustee for the benefit of the creditors or remained vested in Ms Mulkerrins for her own benefit. At first instant the district judge held that the trustee had no interest in the claim. In the High Court the deputy judge considered that this referred to the beneficial interest and held that the effect of the district judge's order was that title to sue had vested in the trustee but that it he held it in trust for Ms Mulkerrins and not for the creditors.[84] This was rejected by the Court of Appeal[85] and Jonathan Parker LJ observed at para 61 that:

'... the district judge was not in any way concerned with accountability, or with the beneficial ownership of the cause of action. She was concerned only with the legal

82 The reference is to *Grady v HM Prison Service* [2003] EWCA Civ 527, [2003] BPIR 823, a claim based on unfair dismissal.

83 [2003] BPIR 1357.

84 [2000] BPIR 506.

85 [2001] BPIR 106.

ownership: with the question – who can sue PwC? The district judge was not contemplating that the Trustee would be accountable for anything. She was contemplating that it would be Mrs. Mulkerrins who would sue, not the Trustee.'

SAFEGUARDING ASSETS

17.45 The IA86 contains a variety of provisions to protect the bankrupt's assets and to permit the recovery of assets disposed of both before and after the presentation of a bankruptcy petition. As we have seen[86] when a petition is presented notice is sent to the Chief Land Registrar so that the petition can be registered as a pending action.[87] The purpose of registration is to prevent disposition of the debtor's property. Section 284, IA86 restricts dispositions of the debtor's property during the period following presentation of a petition and ending with the date on which a bankrupt's property vests in his trustee.[88] Any such disposition (or payment)[89] is void unless made with the consent of the court or subsequently ratified by the court. Note that subsection (4) provides protection to a *bona fide* purchaser for value without notice of the bankruptcy petition. The purpose of the statutory provisions is to ensure that the debtor's estate is not dissipated and that creditors are dealt with on a *pari passu* basis and in accordance with the statutory priorities. This is important because the provisions as to transactions at an undervalue[90] and preference[91] apply only to transactions entered into prior to the presentation of the bankruptcy petition. If a petition has been presented, then a disposition entered into by the debtor, but no bankruptcy order is made on that petition (whether by the petitioning creditor or someone else obtaining substitution or change of carriage) then the disposition is not void under s 284, IA86. The section does not apply.

What sort of 'dispositions' are void?

17.46 A disposition is regarded differently from a transaction. A transaction is usually regarded as requiring some bilateral agreement or understanding. However, a debtor can enter into a disposition against his will, or without his consent. Therefore, an order of the court making a property adjustment order against the debtor in respect of his interest in the matrimonial home will be treated as a disposition by him even if it is not by consent.[92] Similarly, an attempt to settle an existing ancillary relief claim outside of a court order will be void if made post-petition.[93] However, in the most part, the section will bite

---

86 See **chapter 7.**

87 IR86, r 6.13.

88 IA86, s 284(1) and (3).

89 As to what constitutes a payment see *Pettit v Novakovic* [2007] BCC 462, [2007] BPIR 1643.

90 Section 339, IA86, see chapter 16, from **16.14**.

91 Section 340, IA86, see chapter 16, from **16.6**.

92 *Treharne and Sand v Forrester* [2003] EWHC 2784 (Ch), [2004] BPIR 338, applying *Re Flint (a Bankrupt)* [1993] Ch 319, [1993] 1 FLR 763 and *Mountney v Treharne* [2002] EWCA Civ 1174, [2003] Ch 135, [2002] BPIR 1126.

93 *Warwick (formerly Yarwood) v The Trustee in Bankruptcy of Clive Graham Yarwood* [2010] EWHC 2272 (Ch), [2010] BPIR 1443. That case also considers the extent to which, if any, an agreement between spouses to compromise an ongoing ancillary relief claim outside of a court

on voluntary transactions entered into by the debtor with third parties, such as payments of debts or transfers of causes of action, property[94] or of money.[95] It applies to a payment (whether in cash or otherwise) as it applies to a disposition of property and where any payment is void by virtue of s 284(1), IA86, the person paid shall hold the sum paid for the bankrupt as part of his estate.[96] A disposition of property is void under s 284, IA86 notwithstanding that the property is not or would not be comprised in the bankrupt's estate.[97] But nothing in s 284, IA86 affects any disposition made by a person of property held by him on trust for any other person.[98]

How does the section 284 take effect?

17.47 Unlike with transactions 'at an undervalue', preferences, or transactions defrauding creditors (when relief is granted upon the exercise of the court's discretion) transactions that fall foul of s 284, IA86 are automatically void, unless ratified by the court. Therefore, third parties can rely upon the transaction being void; it does not depend upon proceedings issued by the trustee or the exercise of an option by him. So where, post-petition, a debtor assigned causes of action against various defendants to a company, and the company then re-assigned them back to the debtor after the bankruptcy order was made, the defendants were able to invoke the section when the debtor issued proceedings against them and argue that any rights in respect of the causes of action remained with the debtor's trustee.[99] A purchaser can argue that vacant possession of a property has not been given when a lease to the debtor tenant from the vendor was surrendered by the debtor tenant after a bankruptcy petition was presented against him.[100]

17.48 More commonly, the trustee will bring proceedings for a decoration that the particular disposition is void, and seek consequential relief. If a property has been transferred away, he will seek a declaration that it is vested in him. If money has been paid away, either as a gift, payment of a debt, then he will seek repayment of the money.[101]

---

order is enforceable. See also *Xydhias v Xydhias* [1999] 1 FLR 683, [1999] 2 All ER 386, explained in *Soulsbury v Soulsbury* [2007] EWCA Civ 969, [2008] Fam 1, [2008] 2 WLR 834, [2008] 1 FLR 90.

94 *Bateman and another v Hyde and others* [2009] EWHC 81 (Ch), [2009] BPIR 737.

95 *Warwick (formerly Yarwood) v The Trustee in Bankruptcy of Clive Graham Yarwood* [2010] EWHC 2272 (Ch), [2010] BPIR 1443.

96 IA86, s 284(2).

97 IA86, s 284(6).

98 IA86, s 284(6).

99 *Power v Brown and others* [2009] EWHC 9 (Ch), [2009] BPIR 340.

100 *Weir v Area Estates Ltd* [2010] BPIR 806, the subject of an unsuccessful appeal on other grounds in *Area Estates Ltd v Weir* [2010] EWCA Civ 801.

101 IA86, s 284(2).

What protection is available to third parties?

17.49 Section 284, IA86 does not give a remedy against any person

- in respect of any property or payment which he received before the commencement of the bankruptcy in good faith, for value and without notice that the petition had been presented;[102] or

- in respect of any interest in property which derives from an interest in respect of which there is, by virtue of this subsection, no remedy.[103]

Therefore, those who deal with the bankrupt in good faith, for value, and without notice of the petition (and anybody who acquires property from such a person) are protected under the express terms of the section. This is a question of fact. Obviously the closer that the recipient is to the bankrupt, the less likely that he will be able to show that he acted in good faith or without notice.[104]

17.50 In *Re Tain Construction Ltd; Rose v AIB Group (UK) Ltd*[105] (on the similar, though not identical provision in corporate insolvency under s 127, IA86) the court recognised that the allied remedy of seeking recovery of money or property, as a consequence of the disposition being void, is restitutionary in nature. Therefore, the standard restitutionary defence of change of position was available to the recipient. Whether the defence would succeed or not would depend upon the facts, and also to the extent that the recipient was acting in good faith and without notice of the true state of affairs.

Validation orders

What is a 'validation order' and how is one applied for?

17.51 A debtor or creditor may apply for relief from the effects of s 284, IA86 by means of an application for what is commonly called a 'validation order' (if applied for while the petition is pending) or a ratification order (if applied for after a bankruptcy order has been made).

17.52 Guidance as to the practice and procedure relating to such applications is given in the Practice Note titled: Validation Orders issued by the Chancellor in 2007,[106] para 10 onwards deals with applications in individual insolvency cases:

> '[10] A draft of the order sought should be attached to the application.

---

[102] IA86, s 284(4)(a).
[103] IA86, s 284(4)(a).
[104] *Sands and Treharne (Trustees in Bankruptcy of Mark Ward) v Wright* [2010] BPIR 6.
[105] [2003] 1 WLR 2791, [2004] BCC 11, [2003] BPIR 1188.
[106] Reported at [2007] BPIR 94.

Individuals

[11] Section 284, IA86 provides:

Where a person is adjudged bankrupt, any disposition of '(1) property made by that person in the period to which this section applies is void except to the extent that it is or was made with the consent of the court, or is or was subsequently ratified by the court.

Subsection (1) applies to a payment (whether in cash or (2) otherwise) as it applies to a disposition of property and, accordingly, where any payment is void by virtue of that subsection, the person shall hold the sum paid for the bankrupt as part of his estate.

This section applies to the period beginning with the day (3) of the presentation of the petition for the bankruptcy order and ending with the vesting, under Chapter IV of this Part [of the Act], of the bankrupt's estate in a trustee.'

[12] A person against whom a bankruptcy petition has been presented (the debtor) may apply to the court after presentation of the petition for relief from the effects of the foregoing provisions by seeking an order that any disposition of his assets or payment made out of his funds, including any bank account (whether it is in credit or overdrawn), shall not be void in the event of a bankruptcy order being made on the petition (a validation order).

[13] In accordance with the Practice Note on the Hearing of Insolvency Proceedings, an application for a validation order should be made to the registrar or district judge.

[14] Save in exceptional circumstances, notice of the making of the application should be given to: (a) the petitioning creditor(s) or other petitioner; (b) any creditor who has given notice to the petitioner of his intention to appear on the hearing of the petition pursuant to rule 6.23; (c) any creditor who has been substituted as petitioner pursuant to rule 6.30; and (d) any creditor who has carriage of the petition pursuant to rule 6.31.

[15] The application should be supported by written evidence in the form of an affidavit or witness statement which, save in exceptional circumstances, should be made by the debtor. If appropriate, supporting evidence in the form of an affidavit or witness statement from the debtor's accountant should also be produced.

[16] The extent and contents of the evidence will vary according to the circumstances and the nature of the relief sought, but in a case where the debtor is trading or carrying on business it should include, as a minimum, the following information:

(a) when and to whom notice has been given in accordance with para [14], above;
(b) brief details of the circumstances leading to presentation of the petition;
(c) how the debtor became aware of the presentation of the petition;
(d) whether the petition debt is admitted or disputed and, if the latter, brief details of the basis on which the debt is disputed;

(e) full details of the debtor's financial position including details of his assets (including details of any security and the amount(s) secured) and liabilities, which should be supported, as far as possible, by documentary evidence, eg accounts, draft accounts, management accounts or estimated statement of affairs;
(f) a cash flow forecast and profit and loss projection for the period for which the order is sought;
(g) details of the dispositions or payments in respect of which an order is sought;
(h) the reasons relied on in support of the need for such dispositions or payments to be made;
(i) any other information relevant to the exercise of the court's discretion;
(j) details of any consents obtained from the persons mentioned in para [14], above (supported by documentary evidence where appropriate).

[17] Where an application is made urgently to enable payments to be made which are essential to continued trading (eg wages) and it is not possible to assemble all the evidence listed above, the court may consider granting limited relief for a short period, but there should be sufficient evidence to satisfy the court that the interests of creditors are unlikely to be prejudiced.

[18] Where the, debtor is not trading or carrying on business and the application relates only to a proposed sale, mortgage or re-mortgage of the debtor's home evidence of the following will generally suffice:

(a) when and to whom notice has been given in accordance with para [14], above;
(b) whether the petition debt is admitted or disputed and, if the latter, brief details of the basis on which the debt is disputed;
(c) details of the property to be sold, mortgaged or re-mortgaged (including its title number);
(d) the value of the property and the proposed sale price, or details of the mortgage or re-mortgage;
(e) details of any existing mortgages or charges on the property and redemption figures;
(f) the costs of sale (eg solicitors' or agents' costs);
(g) how and by whom any net proceeds of sale (or sums coming into the debtor's hands as a result of any mortgage or re-mortgage) are to be held pending the final hearing of the petition;
(h) any other information relevant to the exercise of the court's discretion;
(i) details of any consents obtained from the persons mentioned in para [14], above (supported by documentary evidence where appropriate).

[19] Whether or not the debtor is trading or carrying on business, where the application involves a disposition of property the court will need to be satisfied that any proposed disposal will be at a proper value. Accordingly, an independent valuation should be obtained and exhibited to the evidence.

[20] The court will need to be satisfied by credible evidence that the debtor is solvent and able to pay his debts as they fall due or that a particular transaction or series of transactions in respect of which the order is sought will be beneficial to

or will not prejudice the interests of all the unsecured creditors as a class (Denney v John Hudson and Co Ltd; Re Fairway Graphics Ltd).

[21] A draft of the order sought should be attached to the application.

Ratification of transactions

[22] Similar considerations to those set out above are likely to apply to applications seeking ratification of a transaction or payment after the making of a winding up order or bankruptcy order.'

Onerous property and disclaimers

How is onerous property dealt with?

17.53 The trustee or the OR can disclaim onerous property in certain circumstances.[107] Before we analyse what this actually means it might first be prudent to have a recap on the meaning of property. Section 436 IA86 defines property. It notes:

> '"property" includes money, goods, things in action, land and every description of property wherever situated and also obligations and every description of interest, whether present or future or vested or contingent, arising out of, or incidental to, property.'

The general tenor of the exposition of property above (qualifying and exempt assets as property) and certainly in the next chapter, is that the property is valuable and hopefully of some use to the trustee in satisfying the creditors' demands. As we have shown some of the bankrupt's property is exempt due to employment and family reasons. Other property may not provide a positive asset to a bankrupt's estate but in fact be the very opposite, ie it could be onerous on the trustee to have to contend and deal with the property. Because of this fact the legislature has promulgated a number of provisions that enable the trustee to dispense with this property. Before we move to a consideration of the pertinent statutory provisions, it is first appropriate to define some of the key terms that arise in this part of the bankruptcy jurisdiction.

What is a disclaimer?

17.54 In terms of the word 'disclaimer' the Oxford English Dictionary notes that it is: '... an act of repudiating another's claim or renouncing one's own.' Penner goes further and provides some contextualization. He notes that a disclaimer is, 'a renunciation, denial, or refusal – of the refusal by the trustee in a bankruptcy to accept a burdensome lease or other onerous property of the bankrupt.' Curzon also cites a trustee as his authority for the term disclaimer when he notes that a disclaimer is a 'denial or disavowal of a claim;

---

[107] For background on this powerful tool see the Cork Report at chapter 27.

renunciation of title or interest – a trustee may disclaim unprofitable contracts, land burdened with very onerous covenants, etc'.

Why disclaim onerous property?

17.55 The immediate response is because it is a burden for the trustee to administer. One of the tasks of the trustee is to maximise recovery for the creditors. To do this they must be allowed to reduce the liabilities of the bankrupt. This is the effect of disclaiming onerous property. The action of disclaiming will save further costs and burdens on the estate by reducing the obligations that the estate owes.

What legislation covers the disclaimer process?

17.56 A trustee's and a liquidators' power of disclaimer are parallel. The pertinent provisions for personal insolvency cases are covered by s 315, IA86 and go on to s 321, IA86. Section 315, IA86 notes:

> '(1) Subject as follows, the trustee may, by the giving of the prescribed notice, disclaim any onerous property and may do so notwithstanding that he has taken possession of it, endeavoured to sell it or otherwise exercised rights of ownership in relation to it.
>
> …
>
> (3) A disclaimer under this section—
>
> (a) operates so as to determine, as from the date of the disclaimer, the rights, interests and liabilities of the bankrupt and his estate in or in respect of the property disclaimed, and
>
> (b) discharges the trustee from all personal liability in respect of that property as from the commencement of his trusteeship,
>
> but does not, except so far as is necessary for the purpose of releasing the bankrupt, the bankrupt's estate and the trustee from any liability, affect the rights or liabilities of any other person.
>
> …
>
> (5) Any person sustaining loss or damage in consequence of the operation of a disclaimer under this section is deemed to be a creditor of the bankrupt to the extent of the loss or damage and accordingly may prove for the loss or damage as a bankruptcy debt.'

What can be disclaimed?

17.57 Onerous property can be disclaimed. This is defined in s 315(2), IA86. The section notes:

'(2) The following is onerous property for the purposes of this section, that is to say—

(a) any unprofitable contract, and
(b) any other property comprised in the bankrupt's estate which is unsaleable or not readily saleable, or is such that it may give rise to a liability to pay money or perform any other onerous act.'

The trustee is allowed to disclaim property that is classified as onerous even though he has taken possession of it, has tried to sell it, or otherwise exercised rights of ownership over it.[108] The trustee cannot however disclaim property pursuant to s 307, IA86 that has been claimed for the estate as after-acquired property. In this regard s 315(1)(4), IA86 states:

'(4) A notice of disclaimer shall not be given under this section in respect of any property that has been claimed for the estate under section 307 (after-acquired property) or 308 (personal property of bankrupt exceeding reasonable replacement value) [or 308A], except with the leave of the court.'

17.58 Section 315(2), IA86[109] sets out a description of the type of property that can be disclaimed. These items are looked at in detail below.

What are the considerations for disclaiming a lease?

17.59 Section 317, IA86 specifically relates to the disclaimer of leaseholds by the trustee. A bankrupt will commonly be a tenant of premises at the date of the bankruptcy order. The disclaimer takes effect to relieve a trustee in the bankruptcy from all liability under the lease, not merely from liability as from the date of the disclaimer. It also operates as regards the entirety of the demised property, so where the bankrupt is the lessee of land and personal chattels, a disclaimer of the lease by the trustee operates as a surrender to the lessor of the chattels, as well as the land, with the effect of passing to the lessor the totality of the remainder of the demise in the lease.[110] The exercise of the power of disclaimer is particularly important as regards leases in respect of which the bankrupt is the tenant. Because the bankrupt's estate vests personally in the trustee, while he takes the benefit of the lease, he does so subject to the obligations under the lease. Therefore, the trustee becomes personally liable for the rent, and other obligations, under the lease.[111] Therefore, in most cases where a lease has vested in him, the trustee will seek to disclaim it as soon possible, unless it is readily realisable.

---

108 IA86, s 315(1).

109 See **17.33**.

110 *Ex parte Allen. Re Fussell* (1882) 20 ChD 341. The question of what cannot be disclaimed was examined in *City of London v Brown* [1990] 22 HLR 32. See also *Re Lee (a Bankrupt)* [1999] BPIR 926, [1998] 1 FLR 1018 and for a similar case on the corporate side see: *Re Park Air Services plc* [2000] 2 AC 172, which involved the disclaimer of a lease by a liquidator.

111 He has a right of indemnity against the bankrupt's estate, but the value of such indemnity is entirely dependent upon the value of the bankrupt's estate.

What are the considerations for disclaiming unprofitable contracts?

17.60 Section 315(2)(a), IA86 states that unprofitable contracts can be disclaimed. This is particularly useful to the trustee of a trader and this provision sits well within the current entrepreneurial driven statutory regulation. This may occur if the cost of maintaining the contract is greater than the benefit of maintenance. A contract is not unprofitable if the amount of profit is only small:[112] a contract is not an unprofitable contract merely because it is detrimental to the interests of the creditors of the bankrupt, financially disadvantageous or merely because the bankrupt could have made a better bargain. The critical feature is whether the performance of any future obligations contained in the contract would prejudice the trustee's obligations to realise the bankrupt's property and pay a dividend to creditors within a reasonable time.[113]

What rights do affected parties have?

17.61 Interested parties are given a power to require the trustee to decide whether to disclaim or not. A trustee shall not give a notice of disclaimer under s 315 IA86 in respect of any property if:

- a person interested in the property has applied in writing to the trustee or one of his predecessors as trustee requiring the trustee or that predecessor to decide whether he will disclaim or not;[114] and
- the period of 28 days beginning with the day on which that application was made has expired without a notice of disclaimer having been given under s 315 IA86 in respect of that property.[115]

How does an affected party give notice to elect to the trustee?

17.62 The application must be delivered to the trustee:

- personally;[116]
- by electronic means in accordance with Part 12A, IR86;[117] or
- by any other means of delivery which enables proof of receipt of the application by the trustee to be provided, if requested.[118]

---

[112] *Re Bastable* [1901] 2 KB 518.
[113] *Re SSSL Realisations (2002) Ltd (in Liquidation)* [2006] EWCA Civ 7, [2006] Ch 610, [2007] 1 BCLC 29, [2006] BCC 233, [2006] BPIR 457.
[114] IA86, s 316(1)(a).
[115] IA86, s 316(1)(b).
[116] IR86, r 6.183(2)(a).
[117] IR86, r 6.183(2)(b).
[118] IR86, r 6.183(2)(c).

These provisions apply where the property concerned cannot be disclaimed by the trustee without the permission of the court.[119] If within 28 days of the application the trustee applies to the court for permission to disclaim, the court shall extend the time allowed by that section for giving notice of disclaimer to a date not earlier than the date fixed for the hearing of the application.[120]

What is the position of the trustee?

17.63 So, the trustee is deemed to have adopted any contract which by virtue of this section he is not entitled to disclaim.[121] A trustee who has been given notice of election by an interested party cannot change his mind if he elects not to disclaim. The trustee is also given a power to require a potentially interested party to declare their interest in a potentially disclaimable property. If, in the case of property which the trustee has the right to disclaim, it appears to him that there is some person who claims, or may claim, to have an interest in the property, he may give notice to that person calling on him to declare within 14 days whether he claims any such interest and, if so, the nature and extent of it.[122] Failing compliance with the notice, the trustee is entitled to assume that the person concerned has no such interest in the property as will prevent or impede its disclaimer.[123]

What is the effect of disclaimer?

17.64 A disclaimer under s 315, IA86:

- operates so as to determine, as from the date of the disclaimer, the rights, interests and liabilities of the bankrupt and his estate in or in respect of the property disclaimed;[124] and

- discharges the trustee from all personal liability in respect of that property as from the commencement of his trusteeship;[125]

but does not, except so far as is necessary for the purpose of releasing the bankrupt, the bankrupt's estate and the trustee from any liability, affect the rights or liabilities of any other person.

Any person sustaining loss or damage in consequence of the operation of a disclaimer under this section is deemed to be a creditor of the bankrupt to the extent of the loss or damage and accordingly may prove for the loss or damage as a bankruptcy debt.[126]

---

119 IR86, r 6.183(3).
120 IR86, r 6.183(3).
121 IA86, s 316(2).
122 IR86, r 6.184(1).
123 IR86, r 6.184(2).
124 IA86, s 315(3)(a).
125 IA86, s 315(3)(b).
126 IA86, s 315(5).

17.65 The effect of a disclaimer of leasehold property has a complex effect, although matters have been made much simpler since the decision of the House of Lords in *Hindcastle Ltd v Barbara Attenborough Associates Ltd.*[127]

- Where the bankrupt was the original tenant and the trustee disclaims, the lease is determined for all purposes, including the obligation to pay rent, and the right to the reversion is accelerated to the bankrupt's immediate landlord. The bankrupt's immediate landlord is given a statutory claim for damages to compensate for the loss of future rent.

- Where the bankrupt's obligations as tenant are guaranteed by a third party surety, and the trustee disclaims, the disclaimer is of no effect on the guarantor, who remains liable under the terms of the guarantee as though the lease had continued.

- Where the bankrupt is an assignee of the lease from the original tenant, the disclaimer by the lease does not bring an end the assignor's liability to the landlord as original tenant.

- Where the bankrupt has sub-let the leased premises to a third party, the trustee's disclaimer has the same effect between the landlord and the bankrupt as if there had been no sub-tenant. Similarly, the disclaimer brings an end to the rights and obligations of each of the bankrupt and the tenant under the sub-lease. But, the sub-tenant, as against the landlord, is entitled to remain in occupation of the premises whilst he observes the terms of the headlease. The sub-tenant holds his estate on the same terms and subject to the same rights and obligations as would be applicable if the bankrupt tenant's interest had continued.

Note should be taken of the effect of the Landlord and Tenant (Covenants) Act 1995.[128]

What records must be maintained?

17.66 The trustee must keep a record of the parties to whom he sends the notice of disclaimer. The record must include details of:[129]

- the names of the recipients and the address that the notice was sent to;[130]

- the nature of the interest in the disclaimed property claimed by each recipient;[131]

---

127 [1997] AC 70.
128 *Shaw v Doleman* [2009] EWCA Civ 279, [2009] BPIR 945.
129 IR86, r 6.181A.
130 IR86, r 6.181A(a).
131 IR86, r 6.181A(a).

- the date on which the trustee sent the notice to each recipient;[132]
- the date on which a copy of the notice of disclaimer was filed with the court;[133] and
- in the case of the disclaimer of registered land, the date on which the trustee sent a copy of the notice to the Land Registry.[134]

A person with an interest in property can serve a notice to elect on a trustee in bankruptcy requesting the trustee to elect whether to disclaim the property.

How has the procedure for disclaimers changed since April 2010 and what are the differences between the two procedures?

17.67 The changes made in the amendment rules 2010[135] mean there is no longer any requirement for the court to seal the notice of disclaimer before it takes effect. The trustee prepares the notice of disclaimer in the new form (Form 6.61A). The notice must contain sufficient detail for the property being disclaimed to be easily identified. Rather than filing the notice at court and having to get it sealed prior to being able to serve the notices on the interested parties. Now the trustee simply authenticates and dates the notice which is effective from that date.[136] This process inevitably caused delay and the new procedure also amends the procedure in relation to notices to elect.

Vesting orders

What is a vesting order?

17.68 Once the disclaimer under s 315, IA86 has occurred, various interested parties may apply for vesting order for the vesting of the disclaimed property in, or its delivery to, them.

Who can apply for a vesting order?

17.69 An application may be made to the court under s 320, IA86 by:

- any person who claims an interest in the disclaimed property;[137]
- any person who is under any liability in respect of the disclaimed property, not being a liability discharged by the disclaimer;[138] or

---

132 IR86, r 6.181A(b).
133 IR86, r 6.181A(c).
134 IR86, r 6.181A(d).
135 SI 2010/686.
136 IR86, r 6.178(2).
137 IA86, s 320(2)(a).
138 IA86, s 320(2)(a).

- where the disclaimed property is property in a dwelling house, any person who at the time when the bankruptcy petition was presented was in occupation of or entitled to occupy the dwelling house.[139]

What is the procedure to apply for a vesting order?

17.70 The application must be made within 3 months of the applicant becoming aware of the disclaimer, or of his receiving a copy of the trustee's notice of disclaimer sent under r 6.179, IR86 whichever is the earlier.[140]

The applicant shall with his application file a witness statement:

- stating whether he applies under:[141]
  - section 320(2)(a), IA86 (claim of interest in the property);
  - section 320(2)(b), IA86 (liability not discharged); or
  - section 320(2)(c), IA86 (occupation of dwelling-house);
- specifying the date on which he received a copy of the trustee's notice of disclaimer, or otherwise became aware of the disclaimer;[142] and
- specifying the grounds of his application and the order which he desires the court to make.[143]

The court will fix a venue for the hearing of the application; and the applicant must, not later than 5 business days before the date fixed, give to the trustee notice of the venue, accompanied by copies of the application and the witness statement referred to above.[144] On the hearing of the application, the court may give directions as to other persons (if any) who should be sent or given notice of the application and the grounds on which it is made.[145] Sealed copies of any order made on the application shall be sent by the court to the applicant and the trustee.[146]

17.71 In a case where the property disclaimed is of a leasehold nature, or is property in a dwelling-house, and s 317 or s 318, IA86 apply to suspend the effect of the disclaimer, there shall be included in the court's order a direction giving effect to the disclaimer.[147] This does not apply if, at the time when the order is issued, other applications under s 320, IA86 are pending in respect of the same property.[148]

---

139 IA86, s 320(2)(c).
140 IR86, r 6.186(2).
141 IR86, r 6.186(3)(a).
142 IR86, r 6.186(3)(b).
143 IR86, r 6.186(3)(c).
144 IR86, r 6.186(4).
145 IR86, r 6.186(5).
146 IR86, r 6.186(6).
147 IR86, r 6.186(7).
148 IR86, r 6.186(7).

What powers does the court have to make a vesting order?

17.72 The court may, on an application under s 320, IA86, make an order on such terms as it thinks fit for the vesting of the disclaimed property in, or for its delivery to:

- a person entitled to it or a trustee for such a person;[149]
- a person who is under any liability in respect of the disclaimed property, not being a liability discharged by the disclaimer, or a trustee for such a person;[150] or
- where the disclaimed property is property in a dwelling house, any person who at the time when the bankruptcy petition was presented was in occupation of or entitled to occupy the dwelling house.[151]

The court shall not make an order to a person who is under any liability in respect of the disclaimed property, not being a liability discharged by the disclaimer, or a trustee for such a person except where it appears to the court that it would be just to do so for the purpose of compensating the person subject to the liability in respect of the disclaimer.[152]

The effect of any order under s 320, IA86 shall be taken into account in assessing for the purposes of s 315(5), IA86 the extent of any loss or damage sustained by any person in consequence of the disclaimer.[153]

An order under s 320, IA86 vesting property in any person need not be completed by any conveyance, assignment or transfer.[154]

Are there any special rules on leaseholds and vesting orders?

17.73 The court shall not make an order under s 320, IA86 vesting property of a leasehold nature in any person, except on terms making that person:

- subject to the same liabilities and obligations as the bankrupt was subject to under the lease on the day the bankruptcy petition was presented;[155] or
- if the court thinks fit, subject to the same liabilities and obligations as that person would be subject to if the lease had been assigned to him on that day.[156]

---

149 IA86, s 320(3)(a).
150 IA86, s 320(3)(b).
151 IA86, s 320(3)(c).
152 IA86, s 320(4).
153 IA86, s 320(5).
154 IA86, s 320(6).
155 IA86, s 321(1)(a).
156 IA86, s 321(1)(a).

For the purposes of an order under s 320 relating to only part of any property comprised in a lease, those requirements apply as if the lease comprised only the property to which the order relates.[157]

17.74 Where these provisions apply and no person is willing to accept an order under s 320, IA86 on the terms required the court may by order under s 320, IA86 vest the estate or interest of the bankrupt in the property in any person who is liable (whether personally or in a representative capacity and whether alone or jointly with the bankrupt) to perform the lessee's covenants in the lease.[158] The court may by virtue of this provision vest that estate and interest in such a person freed and discharged from all estates, encumbrances and interests created by the bankrupt.[159]

Where these provisions apply and a person declines to accept any order under s 320, IA86, that person shall be excluded from all interest in the property.[160]

---

[157] IA86, s 321(2).
[158] IA86, s 321(3).
[159] IA86, s 321(3).
[160] IA86, s 321(4).

Chapter 18

THE MATRIMONIAL HOME IN BANKRUPTCY

'Houses are like the human beings that inhabit them.'[1]

INTRODUCTION

18.1 This chapter will look exclusively at the treatment of the matrimonial home in bankruptcy and will look at the differing treatments depending the way in which the property is owned. It will also look at the differing ways in which ownership can be claimed, the effect of matrimonial proceedings and the effect of shared ownership in each of these circumstances. However, the chapter starts by looking at the circumstances in which the matrimonial home can cease to form part of the estate and the safeguards a trustee should ensure are in place to protect a potential asset.

What happens to the matrimonial home?

18.2 A house or similar property is generally the most valuable asset belongong to a brankrupt. The bankrupt's interest in any such property will have vested in his trustee in the same way as any other property.[2] Where the bankrupt owns the whole of the property he will be obliged to deliver it up to the trustee. If he fails to do so the trustee will have little difficulty in obtaining an order for possession compelling the bankrupt to do so. The position may, however, be more problematical where other parties enjoy a right of occupation or have an interest in the property.

What is the process for identifying and safeguarding a bankrupt's home as an asset?

18.3 Once a property has been identified by the trustee as being a bankrupt's dwelling-house which at the date of the bankruptcy was the sole or principal residence of the bankrupt;[3] the bankrupt's spouse or partner;[4] or a former spouse or partner,[5] the trustee only has a period of 3 years in which to realise any value.[6]

---

1 Victor Hugo (1802–1885)
2 See **17.3** in chapter 17.
3 IA86, s 283A(1)(a).
4 IA86, s 283A(1)(b).
5 IA86, s 283A(1)(c).
6 IA86, s 283A(2). The definition of realisation was discussed in *Lewis v Metropolitan Property Realisations Ltd* [2009] EWCA Civ 448.

In order for the 3 year period to be suspended the trustee must either realise any equity;[7] apply for an order for sale;[8] apply for an order of possession;[9] apply for a charging order[10] or make an agreement with the bankrupt to incur a liability to the estate (with or without additional interest from the date of the agreement).[11]

What actions are required by the trustee?

18.4 Once a property has been identified by the trustee as being a bankrupt's dwelling-house which at the date of the bankruptcy was the sole or principal residence of the bankrupt;[12] notices (Form 6.83) must be served as follows:

- on the bankrupt;
- on the bankrupts spouse or civil partner; or
- on any former spouse or former civil partner.

The trustee should also notify any lender or chargeholder (mortgagee) of his interest in the bankrupt's family home so that they are aware of any potential future enforcement action. This may have already been done by the OR but it is prudent to check that notice has been served. A trustee should also obtain confirmation of the title details by obtaining an official copy of the register entry at the Land Registry by submitting Form OC1. A restriction notice should also be placed on any solely owned property. The mortgagee of any property also has rights and can apply to court for the sale of the property.[13]

What are rights of occupation?

18.5 The Family Law Act 1996 (FLA96) protects the right of a spouse to occupy the matrimonial home. This right is not an overriding interest, but by virtue of s 31(2) and 31(5) is a charge on the matrimonial home. Section 336(1), IA86 provides that nothing occurring in the period between presentation of a bankruptcy petition and the date of vesting of the bankrupt's estate in the trustee is to be taken as having given rise to any matrimonial home rights. However, where the spouse of a bankrupt does acquire a right of occupation giving rise to a charge, the charge is effective against a trustee.[14] Where there is such a charge the trustee will need to apply to the court to terminate the right of occupation. Any application, which is made under s 33, FLA96, to have a

---

7 IA86, s 283A(3)(a).
8 IA86, s 283A(3)(b).
9 IA86, s 283A(3)(c).
10 IA86, s 283A(3)(d). This process is covered in detail at the end of this chapter.
11 IA86, s 283A(3)(e).
12 IA86, s 283A(1)(a).
13 See rr 6.197–6.199, IR86.
14 IA86, s 336(2)(a).

spouse evicted or to regain possession must be made to the court with jurisdiction in relation to the bankruptcy[15] and not that dealing with any other proceedings.

18.6 A bankrupt's spouse who is entitled to occupy a dwelling house by virtue of a beneficial estate or interest and any person under the age of 18 who has occupied the house has rights of occupation against the trustee in bankruptcy in the circumstances outlined in s 337, IA86. This applies whether or not the bankrupt's spouse has any rights of occupation under the FLA96 mentioned above.

What is a beneficial interest and how is this realised?

18.7 Where the bankrupt owns property in which another person has a beneficial interest the trustee may apply for an order for sale under s 14 Trusts of Land and Appointment of Trustees Act 1996 (TLA96).[16] Where such an application is made the court may make any order it thinks just and reasonable but must have regard to:

(a) the interests of the bankrupt's creditors;

(b) where the application is made in respect of land which includes a dwelling house which is or has been the home of the bankrupt or the bankrupt's spouse or civil partner or former spouse or former civil partner:

    (i) the conduct of the spouse, civil partner, former spouse or former civil partner, so far as contributing to the bankruptcy;
    (ii) the needs and financial resources of the spouse, civil partner, former spouse or former civil partner; and
    (iii) the needs of any children; and

    all the circumstances of the case other than the needs of the bankrupt.[17]

What is the time limit for dealing with the matrimonial home?

18.8 Where the property of the bankrupt is a dwelling-house which at the date of the bankruptcy was the sole or principal place of residence of:

- the bankrupt;
- the bankrupt's spouse or civil partner; or
- a former spouse or former civil partner of the bankrupt,

---

15 IA86, s 336(2)(b).
16 IA86, s 335A(1).
17 IA86, s 335A(2).

the bankrupt's (and hence the trustee's) interest ceases to be comprised in the bankruptcy estate and re-vests in the bankrupt after 3 years from the date of the bankruptcy order, unless the trustee during that period:

- realises his interest in the property;
- applies for an order for possession of the property;
- applies for an order for a charge on the property under s 313, IA86; or
- agrees with the bankrupt that the bankrupt will incur a liability to his estate in consideration for which the interest will cease to form part of the estate.[18]

18.9 If the trustee applies within the 3 year period and his application is dismissed, the bankrupt's interest in the property again re-vests in him.[19] If the bankrupt fails to inform the official receiver or trustee of his interest in a property within 3 months of the commencement of the bankruptcy, the 3 year period starts to run from the date on which the official receiver or trustee becomes aware of the bankrupt's interest.[20]

18.10 Where an application under s 335A, IA86 and s 14, TLA96[21] is made after the end of the period of one year beginning with the vesting of the bankrupt's estate in a trustee, the court must assume, unless the circumstances of the case are exceptional, that the interests of the bankrupt's creditors outweigh all other considerations.[22] It follows that in the majority of cases a prudent trustee will wait for the one year period to expire before issuing proceedings in order to benefit from the statutory presumption in favour of the interests of creditors. The scope of the exceptional circumstances referred to in s 335A(3), IA86 is considered below.

What is the minimum value that allows a trustee to apply for sale?

18.11 The court must dismiss an application for an order for sale of property of the bankrupt which is a dwelling-house which at the date of the bankruptcy was the sole or principal place of residence of:

- the bankrupt;
- the bankrupt's spouse or civil partner; or
- a former spouse or former civil partner of the bankrupt; and

---

18 IA86, s 283A(1)–(3).
19 IA86, s 283A(4).
20 IA86, s 283A(5).
21 Trusts of Land and Appointment of Trustees Act 1996.
22 IA86, s 335A(3).

- the value of the bankrupt's, and hence the trustee's, interest, is below the sum of £1,000.[23]

What can be considered an exceptional circumstance?

18.12 The courts have consistently refused to lay down in detail what constitutes exceptional circumstances within the meaning of s 335A(3), IA86. In *Harrington v Bennett*,[24] Lawrence Collins QC (as he then was) sitting as a deputy judge of the High Court, summarised the position as follows:

> 'The presence of exceptional circumstances is a necessary condition to displace the presumption that the interests of the creditors outweigh all other considerations, but the existence of exceptional circumstances does not prevent the court from making an order for sale.'[25]

18.13 Typically, exceptional circumstances in the modern cases relate to the personal circumstances of one of the joint owners of the property, such as medical or mental conditions.[26] The range of exceptional circumstances is not to be categorised or defined; the court makes a value judgment after looking at all the circumstances.[27] The circumstances must be exceptional. That expression is intended to apply the same test as existed before the Insolvency Act 1986, ie to refer to exceptional or special circumstances beyond the usual 'melancholy consequences of debt or improvidence'[28] or 'compelling reasons not found in the ordinary run of cases'.[29]

18.14 As to weighing the interest of creditors, the creditors have an interest in the order for sale being made even if the whole of the net proceeds will go towards the expenses of the bankruptcy. The fact that they will be swallowed up in paying those expenses is not an exceptional circumstance justifying the displacement of the presumption that the interest of the creditors outweigh all other considerations.[30]

18.15 For further examples of cases involving the consideration of exceptional circumstances see the following: *Re Holliday (a Bankrupt)*,[31] (providing a home for children); *Re Mott*,[32] (extreme hardship in old age); *Re Gorman (a Bankrupt)*,[33] (matrimonial division); *Re Ng (A Bankrupt)*,[34]

---

23 IA86, s 313A; Insolvency Proceedings (Monetary Limits) (Amendment) Order 2004, SI 2004/547.

24 [2000] BPIR 630.

25 *Re D R Raval* [1998] BPIR 389.

26 See also *Judd v Brown* [1997] BPIR 470, *Re D R Raval* [1998] BPIR 389, *Claughton v Charalambous* [1998] BPIR 558.

27 *Claughton v Charalambous* [1998] BPIR 558.

28 See *Re Citro* [1991] Ch 142) per Nourse LJ at p 157.

29 Per Bingham LJ at p 161.

30 *Trustee of the Estate of Eric Bowe (a Bankrupt) v Bowe* [1997] BPIR 747.

31 [1981] Ch 405, CA.

32 [1987] CLY 212.

33 [1990] 1 All ER 717.

34 [1997] BPIR 267.

(bankrupt forged wife's signature); *Re Bremner*,[35] (humanitarian need in old age with short life expectancy); *Foenander v Allan*,[36] (voting irregularity and insurance claim); *Barca v Mears*,[37] (educational needs); *Nicholls v Lan*[38] (chronic health condition) and *Martin-Sklan v White*[39] (balancing of creditor's and children's needs).

How is beneficial interest established?

18.16 Under s 14(2), TLA96 the court has power to declare the nature and extent of any share in property which is subject to a trust but not to vary the nature and extent of such share.

18.17 In the majority of cases the trusts on which property is held will be clear and will not give rise to any difficulty. An express declaration as to the trusts is conclusive as to the beneficial entitlement of the parties. For that reason the courts have emphasised the importance of express declarations as to beneficial entitlement.[40] An express trust will only rarely be set aside (eg in cases where there has been fraud, mistake or undue influence).

18.18 Since 1998 the Land Registry has operated a system to ensure that purchasers of land as joint proprietors execute a declaration of trust. Forms FR1 and TR1 prescribed by the Land Registration Rules 2003[41] now require intending proprietors to declare whether they are to hold the property on trust for themselves beneficially as (a) joint tenants, (b) as tenants in common in equal shares or (c) on such other trusts as are indicated. However, this does not assist as regards transactions which took place before the new forms came into use, nor do the forms require the proprietors to quantify their interests. Furthermore, as Baroness Hale noted in *Stack v Dowden*,[42]

> 'Unfortunately, however, the transfer will be valid whether or not this part of the form [TR1] is completed … So there may still be transfers of registered land where there is no express declaration of the beneficial interests.'

18.19 Where there is no express trust the court must determine whether there may be an implied trust which may take the form of either a resulting trust (the beneficial interests being based on the parties' relative contributions to the purchase price) or a constructive trust (arising out of an agreement or understanding as to the interests of the parties but which is not sufficiently formal to be enforceable as a contract). Trusts so arising are sometimes referred to as 'common intention trusts'.

---

35 [1999] BPIR 185.
36 [2006] BPIR 1392.
37 [2004] EWHC 2170, Ch, [2005] BPIR 15.
38 [2006] EWHC 1255, Ch, [2006] BPIR 1243.
39 [2006] EWHC 3313, Ch, [2007] BPIR 76.
40 See for example, *Carlton v Goodman* [2002] EWCA Civ 545, [2002] 2 FLR 259 at para 44.
41 SI 2003/1417.
42 [2007] UKHL 17, [2007] 2 AC 432.

18.20 In order to establish a common intention trust the courts will generally adopt a two stage approach.[43]

- The first stage is to ask whether there was a common intention that the beneficial ownership of the property would be shared, an agreement, understanding or arrangement based on 'express discussions, however imperfectly remembered and however imprecise the terms may be' that the property would be shared. Direct contributions to the purchase price of the property, initially or by payment of the mortgage may give rise to the necessary inference.

- The second stage is to ask whether the party seeking a share acted to his or her detriment in reliance on the common intention.

18.21 The courts have favoured a generous approach to finding a common intention, especially where one party gives a reason for taking the property in his sole name rather than in joint names and even where the reason given is a good one (see, for example, *Eves v Eves*,[44] where one of the parties was aged under twenty one, and Lord Walker's comment on *Lloyd's Bank v Rossett* in *Stack v Dowden* that 'the law has moved on').[45]

18.22 The conduct required by the second stage in Lord Bridge's approach must be 'referable to' the common intention 'and not conduct in which the applicant would have engaged anyway had there been no such intention'. It would appear to be sufficient if the understanding or promise relied on was not the sole cause of the action provided that it was a factor.[46] If the promise or understanding is established, the onus may be on the respondent to demonstrate that it was not acted on.[47]

18.23 In *Stack v Dowden*[48] the House of Lords set out the principles to be applied to determine the beneficial entitlement of individuals sharing a property and requires the courts to adopt a new approach to disputes in the domestic field. It asserted the need to ascertain 'the parties' shared intentions, actual, inferred or imputed, with respect to the property in the light of their whole course of conduct in relation to it'.[49] It laid down the following principles to be applied where there was no express declaration of trust (see the opinion of Baroness Hale):[50]

- The beneficial ownership of the property should follow the legal ownership (ie equity follows the law).

---

43 See *Lloyd's Bank v Rossett* [1991] 1 AC 107 per Lord Bridge at p 133.
44 [1975] 1 WLR 1338.
45 Paragraph 26.
46 *Wayling v Jones* [1995] 2 FLR 1029.
47 *Greasle v Cooke* [1980] 1 WLR 1306.
48 [2007] UKHL 17, [2007] 2 AC 432.
49 Paragraph 60.
50 Paragraph 51.

- If one party claims that the beneficial ownership is different from the legal ownership, he or she must substantiate such claim by reference to what the parties intended.
- It will be only in very unusual circumstances that the beneficial interests will be found to differ from the legal interests in the property.
- The court may consider a wide range of factors in determining the intention of the parties.

18.24 The House of Lords emphasised the primacy of the facts in ascertaining the intention of the parties:

> 'In law "context is everything" and the domestic context is very different from the commercial world. Each case will turn on its own facts. Many more factors than financial contributions may be relevant to divining the parties' true intentions.[51]

Baroness Hale went on to list the relevant factors:

- Any advice or discussions at the time of the transfer which cast light on the parties' intentions then.
- The reasons why the property was acquired in joint names.
- The reasons why (if it is the case) the survivor was authorised to give a good receipt for the capital moneys.
- The purpose for which the property was acquired.
- The nature of the parties' relationship.
- Whether they had children for whom they both had responsibility to provide a home.
- How the purchase was financed, both initially and subsequently.
- How the parties arranged their finances, whether separately or together or a mixture of both.
- How the parties discharged their outgoings on the property and their other household expenses.

18.25 Where the property was transferred into the sole name of one party the starting point was sole beneficial ownership, and the onus is on the party seeking to show that he or she has an interest and (if applicable) to establish the extent of any beneficial interest. The House of Lords emphasised that the

---

[51] Per Baroness Hall at para 69.

search was for the result that reflected the intention of the parties rather than a result which the court considered fair.[52]

18.26 *Stack v Dowden* concerned the affairs of a cohabiting couple. However, the approach of the court applies where any two people purchase a home together and fail to make an express declaration of their respective beneficial interests.[53]

How has the law moved on since Stack v Dowden?

18.27 The Supreme Court delivered a further layer of guidance regarding the division of assets held between co-habiting unmarried couples that separate in *Jones v Kernott*.[54] The case is to some extent a 're-visitation' of the beneficial interest determination issue that arose in *Stack v Dowden*[55] and another judicial examination of the financial consequences of relationship breakdown on co-habiting couples.[56]

18.28 The facts in *Jones v Kernott* are relatively straightforward. Mr Kernott, a sometime self-employed ice cream salesman, and Ms Jones, a mobile hairdresser, were an unmarried co-habiting couple who had two children from their relationship (born in June 1984 and September 1986 respectively). The relationship between Ms Jones and Mr Kernott began in 1980 and ended in October 1993.

A family home, 39 Badger Hall Avenue, Thundersley, Essex (hereafter Badger Hall), was purchased for £30,000 in 1984. The family moved to Badger Hall from a mobile home they had previously lived in. Ms Jones had owned the mobile home and the sale of that property provided the £6,000 deposit for Badger Hall. Legal title was vested in them equally as beneficial joint tenants. The balance of the purchase price was raised by way of mortgage in their joint names.

When their relationship ended and they separated in October 1993, Ms Jones remained in the property with the two children. Badger Hall was put on the market for £69,995 in October 1995. The property did not sell for 2 years. To enable Mr Kernott to obtain a property the family home was taken off the market and an insurance policy was realised. The proceeds were divided between the couple. The money from this policy allowed Mr Kernott to

---

52 Paragraph 61.

53 See *Fowler v Barron* [2008] EWCA Civ 377, *Abbott v Abbott* [2007] UKPC 53 and *Laskar v Laskar* [2008] EWCA Civ 347.

54 [2011] UKSC 53, [2011] BPIR 1653.

55 [2007] UKHL 17, [2007] 2 AC 432. For critical discussion of this decision see M Dixon 'The Never-Ending Story: Co-ownership After *Stack v Dowden*' [2007] Conv 456 and W Swadling 'The Common Intention Trust in the House of Lords: An Opportunity Missed' (2007) 123 LQR 511. See also S Gardner and K Davidson 'The Future of *Stack v Dowden*' (2011) 127 LQR 13, and E Cooke 'In the Wake of *Stack v Dowden*: the Tale of TR1' [2011] Fam Law 1142.

56 For recent reform work in this area see: Law Commission *Cohabitation: The Financial Consequences of Relationship Breakdown*, 2007, Law Com No 307.

purchase another property, 114 Stanley Road, Benfleet (hereafter Stanley Road). In terms of legal title, this second property was held in his sole name as legal owner.

In 2006, Mr Kernott initiated correspondence with a view to claiming his interest in Badger Hall. As a consequence Ms Jones began proceedings in 2007 to obtain a declaration under s 14 of the Trusts of Land and Appointment of Trustees Act 1996 that, *inter alia*, (1) she owned the entire beneficial interest in Badger Hall, (2) if Mr Kernott had any interest in Badger Hall she also had an interest in his new property, 114 Stanley Road.

18.29 At first instance and on appeal it was held that there was not enough evidence to rebut the presumption that beneficial interests followed legal title, ie Ms Jones and Mr Kernott were joint tenants in law and equity. It was argued by Ms Jones, and accepted by the judge at first instance and on appeal, that the intentions regarding the beneficial interests between the parties in Badger Hall had changed since the separation. This was based on the 'whole course of dealings between the parties' approach enunciated in *Stack v Dowden*. In essence the fact that Mr Kernott had not continued his contributions to the acquisition of Badger Hall, but instead invested in Stanley Road, meant his interest in Badger Hall could be limited, as, 'The parties could not have been taken to have intended that he [Mr Kernott] should have a significant part of the increased value of [Badger Hall] as well as the whole of the capital gain from [Stanley Road]'.[57] Mr Kernott appealed again.

18.30 At first instance and on appeal it was held that there was not enough evidence to rebut and the Court of Appeal allowed Mr Kernott's appeal and held that the parties owned the property as tenants in common in equal shares.[58] The majority of the Court of Appeal (Jacob, LJ dissenting) held that the evidence did not show that there was anything to indicate that the parties' intentions had changed since their separation. Essentially, the Court of Appeal (Rimer, LJ and Wall, P) were unable 'to find, by way of the imputation route, an intention were none was expressly uttered not inferentially formed'.[59] Ms Jones appealed to the Supreme Court.

Lord Walker and Lady Hale gave a composite judgment in the Supreme Court.[60] Their stated mission was to determine where parties already share beneficial interests, what their interests are and whether their interests have changed. In so doing the court will try to deduce what their actual intentions were at the relevant time. As the learned judges note the court, 'cannot impose a solution upon them which is contrary to what the evidence shows that they actually intended'.[61] However, if the court cannot deduce exactly what was intended, 'it may have no alternative but to ask what their intentions as

57 [2011] UKSC 53, [2011] BPIR 1653.
58 See [2011] EWCA Civ 578.
59 *Ibid*, at paras 57 and 58.
60 Lords Collins, Kerr and Wilson also gave judgments.
61 [2011] UKSC 53, at para 47.

reasonable and just people would have been had they thought about it at the time'.[62] As the judge at first instance found that the intentions of the parties had changed there was no need to impute an intention. Their original intention was to provide a home for the family. However separation then occurred. The family home was put on the market but failed to sell. As the Supreme Court judges observe, a new plan was formulated. The proceeds from the insurance life in policy and the investment in Stanley Road by Mr Kernott both indicated that Mr Kernott would no longer be able to invest in Badger Hall. This was not financially possible. Therefore, 'the logical inference is that they intended that his interest in [Badger Hall] should crystallise then. Just as he would have the sole benefit of any capital gain in his own home'.[63]

18.31 In terms of the application of this case to insolvency law a trustee in bankruptcy dealing with the estate of a co-habiting couple will need to be mindful of the perfection this case brings to the analysis in *Stack v Dowden* and to the guidance that the Supreme Court have provided in *Jones v Kernott* for dealing with a family home that is purchased in the joint names of a cohabiting couple where there is no expression declaration of their beneficial interests. The guidance is:

> '(1) The starting point is that equity follows the law and they are joint tenants in both law and equity.
>
> (2) That presumption can be displaced by showing (a) that the parties had a different common intention at the time when they acquired the home, or (b) that they later formed the common intention that their respective shares would change.
>
> (3) Their common intention is to be deduced objectively from their conduct …
>
> (4) In those cases where it is clear either (a) that the parties did not intend joint tenancy at the outset, or (b) had changed their original intention, but it is not possible to ascertain by direct evidence or by inference what their actual intention was as to the shares in which they would own property, "the answer is that each is entitled to that share which the court considers fair having regard to the whole course of dealing between them in relation to the property …
>
> (5) Each case will turn on its own facts. Financial contributions are relevant but there are many other factors which may enable the court to decide what shares were either intended or fair.'[64]

How are improvements to the property dealt with?

18.32 It is frequently suggested that making improvements to a property gives rise to an increased interest. Again, however, there must be a common intention to vary the beneficial ownership, and in the absence of express post-acquisition agreement the courts will be slow to infer from conduct alone that the parties

---

62 *Ibid.*

63 [2011] UKSC 53, at para 48.

64 [2011] UKSC 53, at para 51.

intended to vary existing beneficial interest established at the time of acquisition.[65] It is open to the court to infer, in the ordinary case of cohabitation, that there was no intention to account during the period of the relationship.[66]

EQUITABLE ACCOUNTING AND OCCUPATION RENT

18.33 The need to consider equitable accounting and a possible claim for an occupation rent arises most commonly where there is breakdown in a relationship and consideration has to be given to liability for the payment of mortgage instalments and other outgoings where only one party remains in occupation. An analogous situation arises in bankruptcy where the property rights of the bankrupt vest in the trustee who, however, does not benefit from an ability to occupy the property. The solution is often to give credit for a share of the capital part of the mortgage paid, treating the interest part as equivalent to an occupation rent. The aim of the court should be to do 'broad justice between the parties' (per Lawrence Collins, J in *Byford v Butler*,[67] in which the judge undertook a full review of the authorities to date).

ANCILLARY RELIEF PROCEEDINGS

What happens when matrimonial proceedings have been commenced prior to a bankruptcy order being made?

18.34 The bankruptcy regime commonly clashes with the matrimonial regime where a court has made a property transfer order and one of the parties to the matrimonial proceedings becomes bankrupt. In *Mountney v Treharne*[68] the Court of Appeal held that a transfer of property took effect on the making of the order which created an immediate equitable interest defeating the claim of the trustee. Trustee's should also be mindful of the outcome in *Jones v Kernott* in respect of cohabiting couples.[69]

18.35 In *Avis v Turner*[70] the Court of Appeal considered the effect of s 335A IA86 on a consent order in matrimonial proceedings in circumstances in which the trust for sale had been postponed until a number of events occurred and the order provided for liberty to apply. The court held that the trustee in bankruptcy was entitled to an order for sale since under the terms of the consent order the husband was able to make an application under s 14, TLA96. The trustee was similarly able to apply.

---

65 *James v Thomas* [2007] EWCA 1212 and *Morris v Morris* [2008] EWCA Civ 257.
66 *Wilcox v Tait* [2006] EWCA Civ 1867.
67 [2003] EWHC 1267 (Ch).
68 [2002] EWCA Civ 1174, [2003] Ch 135.
69 Refer to **18.25–18.29**.
70 [2007] EWCA Civ 748, [2008] 2 WLR 1.

18.36 In *Haines v Hill*[71] the Court of Appeal held that there was a need to strike a fair balance so as on the one hand to protect creditors against collusive orders in matrimonial proceedings whilst on the other hand protecting orders made justly and at arm's length. A collusive agreement arose where husband and wife sought to prefer one of them over creditors and thus dishonestly transfer more than an insolvent spouse's estate could truly bear if such spouse's debts were properly taken into account so as to make the transfer susceptible of attack under s 339, IA86. The court would not ordinarily go behind a consent order made in ancillary relief proceedings unless there was a vitiating factor:

> 'Finally, as to policy, it would be unfortunate in the extreme if a court approved, or even ... a court determined property adjustment order would be liable, in practice, to be undone for up to five years because the husband goes bankrupt within that period. That could even encourage such bankruptcy on the part of a dissatisfied husband. Although a collusive agreement by a divorcing husband and wife to prefer the wife and children over creditors and thus dishonestly to transfer to her more than his estate can truly bear, if his debts were properly taken into account, and thus more than her ancillary relief claim could really and knowingly be worth, is no doubt susceptible to section 339 relief despite the existence of a court order in her favour (see the decision in *Kumar*): nevertheless, in the ordinary case, where there is no dishonest collusion, and where a court approves or determines the sum or property to be transferred, it would be entirely foreign to the concept of a "clean break" if the husband's creditors could thereafter seek to recover, in bankruptcy, the property transferred or its value. However, in my judgment, it would require the overthrow of long established jurisprudence, the re-interpretation of section 39, the misunderstanding of the doctrine of consideration, and an assault on current views of the statutory entitlement to ancillary relief, to arrive at that unhappy and unnecessary situation'.[72]

As to the nature of a collusive agreement and vitiating factors, see *Re Jones (A Bankrupt)*.[73]

What is the equity of exoneration?

18.37

> 'If the property of a married woman is mortgaged or charged in order to raise money for the payment of her husband's debts or otherwise for his benefit, it is presumed, in the absence of evidence ... to the contrary, that she meant to charge her property merely by way of security. [...] [I]n such case she is in a position of surety and is entitled to be indemnified by her husband and to throw the debts on his estate to the exoneration of her own.'[74]

Thus, where a property is charged for the benefit of a business of one of the mortgagors the presumption is that any amount due to the mortgagee will be

---

71 [2007] EWCA Civ 1284, [2008] 2 WLR 1250.

72 Per Rix LJ at para 82.

73 [2008] BPIR 1051.

74 Per Scott J in *Re Pittortou (a Bankrupt)* [1985] 1 All ER 285.

marshalled against the share in the property of the person directly benefiting from the advance secured on the property.

18.38 The equity of exoneration does not apply where any money raised is used to discharge the obligations of or for the benefit of the non-bankrupt spouse or to maintain an extravagant lifestyle[75] or where the charge taken out replaces a prior charge so that the redemption of the first and creation of the second in effect constitute a single transaction.[76]

What is the impact of the Human Rights Act on the matrimonial home in bankruptcy proceedings?

18.39 Article 1 of the First Protocol to the Human Rights Act 1998 gives the right 'to the peaceful enjoyment of ... possessions' and not to 'deprived of ... possessions except in the public interest and subject to the conditions provided for by law'. Article 8 of Sch 1 gives a right to 'respect for ... private and family life', those rights are not absolute. Article 1 permits a state 'to control the use of property in accordance with the general interest', and art 8 allows a public authority to interfere with the right 'for the protection of the rights and freedoms of others'.

18.40 The need to balance human rights against other considerations was illuminated by the House of Lords in *Leeds City Council v Price*:[77]

> 'Subject to what I say below, I would hold that a defence which does not challenge the law under which the possession order is sought as being incompatible with the art 8 but is based only on the occupier's personal circumstances should be struck out. I do not think that *McPhail v Persons, Names Unknown* [1973] Ch 447 needs to be reconsidered in the light of Strasbourg case law. Where domestic law provides for personal circumstances to be taken into account, as in a case where the statutory test is whether it would be reasonable to make a possession order, then a fair opportunity must be given for the arguments in favour of the occupier to be presented. But if the requirements of the law have been established and the right to recover possession is unqualified, the only situations in which it would be open to the court to refrain from proceeding to summary judgment and making the possession order are these: (a) if a seriously arguable point is raised that the law which enables the court to make the possession order is incompatible with art 8, the county court in the exercise of its jurisdiction under the Human Rights Act 1998 should deal with the argument in one or other of two ways: (i) by giving effect to the law, so far as it is possible for it do so under s 3, in a way that is compatible with art 8, or (ii) by adjourning the proceedings to enable the compatibility issue to be dealt with in the High Court; (b) if the Defendant wishes to challenge the decision of a public authority to recover possession as an improper exercise of its powers at common law on the ground that it was a decision that no reasonable person would consider justifiable, he should be permitted to do this provided again that the point is seriously arguable:

---

75 *Gray v Dowman* [1858] 27 AJ Ch 702.

76 *Lewis v Nangle* [1752] Cox Eq Cas 240.

77 [2006] UKHL 10.

> *Wandsworth London Borough Council v Winder* [1985] AC 461. The common law as explained in that case is, of course, compatible with art 8. It provides an additional safeguard.'[78]

18.41 Similarly, s 335A, IA86 is domestic law to which the application of the Human Rights Act (and art 8 in particular) is limited, as is demonstrated by the judgment of Paul Morgan QC, (as he then was) in *Nicholls v Lan*:[79]

> '[43] In my judgment, the judicial discussion so far of the role of art 8 in connection with s 335A relates to the criterion of 'exceptional circumstances' in s 335A(3). That criterion does not cause Mrs Nicholls a difficulty in the present case because she meets that criterion. In these circumstances, the way in which s 335A operates in the present case is that the court is required to perform a balancing exercise and to decide what is 'just and reasonable' and amongst the circumstances which are to be taken into account are the interests of the creditors and the needs of someone like Mrs Nicholls. For my part, I do not see that the statutory test, leading to a balancing exercise, is inconsistent with the qualified nature of the rights enshrined in art 8 and in art 1 of the First Protocol. Indeed, it might be contended that s 335A precisely captures what is required by art 8 and art 1 of the First Protocol.
>
> [44] Article 8 speaks of respect for the home. However, the whole purpose of section 335A(2)(b) which refers to the home of the bankrupt's spouse is to identify the need to respect the home but, of course, not as an absolute objective to be guaranteed in every case but as a consideration in a balancing exercise. In this way, I have reached the conclusion that the submissions I have heard on the Human Rights Act 1998 do not take the matter any further.'

18.42 The same point was made in *Foyle v Turner*[80] by HH Judge Norris, as he then was:

> 'Parliament has struck the balance between the bankrupt and his creditors, and has provided for the court to undertake a consideration of the interests of the bankrupt's spouse and children. Parliament has also prioritised the interests of the creditors and of the spouse and children (which are not truly comparable ...) Provided that the provisions of section 335A are faithfully followed and applied there is no need to enter into any separate consideration of Article 8 rights.'

18.43 On the interaction between human rights and insolvency law considerations see also *Barca v Mears*,[81] *Re Karia* (A Bankrupt)[82] and *Holtham v Kelmanson*.[83]

---

78 Per Lord Bridge at para 110.
79 [2006] EWHC 1255, [2006] BPIR 1243.
80 [2007] BPIR 43.
81 [2004] EWHC 2170, Ch, [2005] BPIR 15.
82 [2006] BPIR 1226.
83 [2006] EWHC 2588, Ch, [2006] BPIR 1422.

CHARGING ORDERS

18.44 Charging orders were looked at in detail in chapter 4. In bankruptcy the court will generally decline to make a final charging order where the debtor becomes insolvent beforehand (*Roberts Petroleum Ltd v Bernard Kenny Ltd*;[84] although the case concerned a winding up order it would seem that the same approach would be taken where a bankruptcy order is made after an interim charging order).

What is the process for obtaining a charging order on a bankrupt's house?

18.45 Section 313, IA86 allows the trustee to apply to the court for a charge on a house occupied by the bankrupt or by his or her spouse, former spouse or civil partner where the trustee is unable to realise the property for the benefit of creditors. The application and the form of the charge are governed by rr 6.237D and 6.237E, IR86. Section 313(2), (2A) and (3), IA86 deal with the calculation of the bankrupt's interest for the purpose of creating the charge, the effect of which is that any increase in the value of the bankrupt's interest favours the bankrupt as opposed to the trustee and the creditors. Any interest of the bankrupt over and above that charged re-vests in the bankrupt.

18.46 As to the question of the limitation period applicable to the trustee's right to enforce a charge see *Doodes v Gotham*[85] and in relation to failure to register a charge see *Trustee in Bankruptcy of Louise St John Poulton v Ministry of Justice*.[86]

---

84 [1983] AC 192, HL.
85 [2006] EWCA Civ 1080, [2007] 1 WLR 86.
86 [2009] EWHC 2123, Ch, [2009] 159 NLJ 1362.

Chapter 19

COURT PROCEDURE IN BANKRUPTCY

'Bankruptcy is a legal proceeding in which you put your money in your pants pocket and give your coat to your creditors.'[1]

INTRODUCTION

19.1 This covers the various aspects of court procedure that apply in bankruptcy proceedings starting with the procedure rules and also covering the various practice statements that have been issued.

Where are details of the court's procedure to be found?

19.2 The IA86 and the IR86 provide a detailed code as to both substantive and procedural aspects of insolvency proceedings,[2] but they do not constitute a complete code. The Civil Procedure Rules (CPR) also play a part, whilst other legislation affecting personal insolvency, notably the Cross-Border Insolvency Regulations 2006,[3] contain their own procedural provisions. There are also practice directions issued by the court that relate to personal insolvency court proceedings. The most recent Practice Direction in respect of insolvency proceedings came into force on 23 February 2012 and replaced all previous Practice Directions, Practice Statements and Practice Notes relating to insolvency proceedings. The contents of this statement are set out below (a copy can be found at www.justice.gov.uk).

What matters are covered in the Practice Statement: Insolvency Proceedings?

19.3 The contents are as follows:

Part One: General provisions

1 Definitions
2 Coming into force
3 Distribution of business
4 Court documents
5 Evidence
6 Service of court documents in insolvency proceedings
7 Jurisdiction

---

1 Joey Adams, American Comedian and Author (1911–1999).

2 Defined by IR86, r 13.7 as 'any proceedings under the Act or the Rules'. See, however, in relation to proceedings under s 423 of the Insolvency Act 1986 *Jyske Bank (Gibraltar) Ltd v Spjeldnaes* [1999] 2 BCLC 101, [2000] BCC 16.

3 SI 2006/1030.

How are bankruptcy proceedings described and applications to court titled?

19.4 Bankruptcy proceedings (ie every proceeding under Parts IX to XI IA86) must be 'entitled' 'In Bankruptcy'.[4] This means that every petition or application should bear in the top left hand corner the name of the court in which the proceedings are brought (eg 'In the High Court of Justice' or 'In the x county court') with the words 'In Bankruptcy' immediately below.[5]

---

4 IR86, r 7.26 (substituted under 2010 rules amendments) or IRN91, r 7.026.

5 Paragraph 3.3, Practice Statement 2012.

What is the format for applications to court?

19.5 The Introductory Provisions of the IR86[6] contain definitions[7] but also provisions of substance, in particular governing the extent to which different parts of the IR86 apply. In addition section 1 of the *Practice Statement* (2012)[8] also contains the relevant references.

As set out in the previous chapters, the IR86 provide a number of prescribed forms for use in insolvency proceedings,[9] for example petitions for the commencement of bankruptcy proceedings and a prescribed form for use when applying to set aside a statutory demand. Save for a petition for a bankruptcy order,[10] all applications to court in relation to personal insolvency are now made by application.[11] Recent changes and in particular the 2010 Amendment Rules[12] introduced a move away from the use of prescribed forms and included instead details of the data that is required with each specific application to facilitate the use of different formats with the advent of electronic communication and data.

What should every application to court contain?

19.6 Any application must be made in writing and must contain the following:[13]

- that the application is made under the Act;
- the names of the parties;
- the name of the bankrupt, or the debtor, who is or the subject of the insolvency proceedings to which the application relates;
- the court (and where applicable, the division or district registry of that court) in which the application is made;
- where the court has previously allocated a number to the insolvency proceedings within which the application is made, that number;

---

6 IR86, rr 0.1–0.3.

7 IR86, r 0.2 or IRN91, r 0.002.

8 Paragraph 1.1, Practice Statement 2012.

9 Rule 12.7 Insolvency Rules provides that the forms in Sch 4 'shall be used'; see Appendix Four for a list of such forms and other prescribed forms.

10 IR86, r 7.1(c).

11 IR86, 7.3(1). Until the amendments introduced with effect from 6 April 2010, there were two types of insolvency application, an originating application (which meant an application to court which was not an application in pending proceedings before the court) or an ordinary application (which meant any other application to the court). Generally, in bankruptcy, applications were ordinary applications, because by the very nature of bankruptcy, there were already pending proceedings arising from the court file opened upon presentation of the bankruptcy petition.

12 SI 2010/686.

13 IR86, r 7.3(1).

- the nature of the remedy or order applied for or the directions sought;
- the names and addresses of the persons (if any) on whom it is intended to serve the application (or that no person is intended to be served);
- where the Act or Rules require that notice of the application is to be given to specified persons, the names and addresses of all those persons (so far as known to the applicant); and
- the applicant's address for service.

The application must be authenticated by the applicant if he is acting in person or, when he is not so acting, by or on behalf of his solicitor.[14]

What is the procedure for filing an application in court?

19.7 The application should be filed together with one copy and sufficient further copies for service on each person who is to receive notice of the application.[15] Unless the court otherwise directs the applicant should serve a sealed copy of the application endorsed with the venue for the hearing on each respondent to the application.[16] Service of documents in insolvency proceedings will be the responsibility of the parties and will not be undertaken by the court except where otherwise stipulated.[17]

What is the procedure and timing for service of documents?

19.8 Except where the Insolvency Rules otherwise provide, CPR Part 6 applies to the service of court documents both within and out of the jurisdiction as modified by the Practice Direction 2012 or as the court may otherwise direct.[18] Unless the Act or the Rules provide otherwise, the application should be served at least 14 days before the date fixed for the hearing;[19] note, however, that the court may direct service on persons other than those specified or may order that service be dispensed with or that notice be given other than in accordance with r 7.4(3), IR86.[20] However, the court may abridge or extend time.[21]

When is the application heard by the court?

19.9 Where the application is urgent the court may hear the application immediately either with or without the attendance of the other parties or authorise a shorter period of service[22] than that provided for by r 7.4(5), IR86.

---

14 IR86, r 7.3(3).
15 IR86, r 7.4(1) or IRN91, r 7.004(1).
16 IR86, r 7.4(3) or IRN91, r 7.004(3).
17 Paragraph 3.3, Practice Statement 2012.
18 Paragraph 6.1, Practice Statement 2012.
19 IR86, r 7.4(5) or IRN91, r 7.004(5).
20 IR86, r 7.4(4) or IRN91, r 7.004(4).
21 IR86, r 7.4(6) or IRN91, r 7.004(6).
22 IR86, r 7.4(6)(a) and (b) or IRN91, r 7.004(6)(a) and (b).

19.10 Where an application is properly made without notice[23] the court may hear it forthwith without notice or may fix a venue for the application to be heard.[24] In certain circumstances the court may make orders without any attendance.[25]

Who must hear an application to court: judge or registrar?

19.11 Rule 13.2(1), IR86 provides that:

> 'Anything to be done under or by virtue of the Insolvency Act 1986 or the Insolvency Rules 1986 by, to or before the court may be done by, to or before a judge or the registrar.'

Rule 13.2(3), IR86 defines the registrar (in relation to individual insolvency) as 'a Registrar in Bankruptcy of the High Court'.

19.12 As a general rule all petitions and applications should be listed for initial hearing before a Registrar (or a district judge in a county court) in accordance with r 7.6A(2) and (3).[26] The exceptions are listed below.

19.13 The following applications relating to insolvent individuals should always be listed before a judge:[27]

(1) applications for committal for contempt;

(2) applications for an injunction;

(3) interim applications and applications for directions or case management after any proceedings have been referred or adjourned to the judge (except where liberty to apply to the Registrar has been given).

19.14 When deciding whether to hear proceedings or to refer or adjourn them to the judge, the Registrar should have regard to the following factors:[28]

(1) the complexity of the proceedings;

(2) whether the proceedings raise new or controversial points of law;

(3) the likely date and length of the hearing;

(4) public interest in the proceedings.

---

23 See also IR86, r 0.2(2) and as to the obligations of a party seeking such relief to make full and frank disclosure see *Brink's Mat Ltd v Elcombe* [1988] 1 WLR 1350.

24 IR86, r 7.5.

25 As to which see para 16 of the Practice Direction: Insolvency Proceedings.

26 Paragraph 3.1, Practice Statement 2012.

27 Paragraph 3.3, Practice Statement 2012.

28 Paragraph 3.4, Practice Statement 2012.

In addition the availability in the court of relevant specialist expertise needs to be taken into account.[29]

19.15 Since 6 April 2010, unless otherwise directed by the court, the hearing of an application must be in open court.[30] Previously applications could be heard in chambers but these were not necessarily private.[31] In the county court, the jurisdiction of the court to hear and determine an application may be exercised by the district judge (to whom any application must be made in the first instance) unless:[32]

(a) a direction to the contrary has been given, or

(b) it is not within the district judge's power to make the order required.

19.16 In the High Court, the jurisdiction of the court to hear and determine an application may be exercised by the registrar (to whom the application must be made in the first instance) unless:[33]

(a) a direction to the contrary has been given, or

(b) it is not within the registrar's power to make the order required.

19.17 Where the application is made to the district judge in the county court or to the registrar in the High Court, the district judge or the registrar may refer to the judge any matter which the district judge or registrar thinks should properly be decided by the judge, and the judge may either dispose of the matter or refer it back to the district judge or the registrar with such directions as that judge thinks just.[34] This does not preclude an application being made directly to the judge in a proper case.[35]

What form does 'evidence' take when requested in personal insolvency proceedings?

19.18 Subject to the provisions of r 7.9, IR86 or any other provisions or directions as to the form in which evidence should be given, written evidence in insolvency proceedings must be given by witness statement.[36]

---

29 Cf the criteria mentioned in *Lewis v Secretary of State for Trade and Industry* [2001] BCLC 597 (although the case itself concerned proceedings under the Company Directors Disqualification Act 1986).

30 IR86, r 7.6A(1)

31 *Hodgson v Imperial Tobacco Ltd* [1998] 1 WLR 1056.

32 IR86, r 7.6A(2)

33 IR86, r 7.6A(3).

34 IR86, r 7.6A(4).

35 IR86, r 7.6A(5).

36 Paragraph 5.1, Practice Statement 2012.

When can a report be filed as evidence?

19.19 A report may be filed instead of witness statement in any case by the official receiver or a deputy official receiver and (unless the application involves other parties or the court orders otherwise) by:

- a trustee in bankruptcy;
- an interim receiver;
- a special manager;
- an insolvency practitioner appointed under s 273(2), IA86.[37]

Such a report is treated as a witness statement.[38]

What is the effect on the evidence when the witness or deponent does not attend the hearing and can the hearing be adjourned?

19.20 The court may, on the application of any party to the matter in question order the attendance for cross-examination of the person making the witness statement.[39] Where, after such an order has been made, the person in question does not attend, that person's witness statement must not be used in evidence without the leave of the court.[40] The modern tendency is, however, for the court to order specifically that the evidence of a witness cannot be read without permission if he fails to attend for cross-examination since it is not every case that requires oral evidence and cross-examination.

19.21 Minutes prepared in relation to any meeting in insolvency proceedings and signed by the chairman of that meeting are admissible without any further proof of content. The minutes are prima facie evidence of the conduct of the meeting including any resolutions passed.[41] Any document purporting to be or to contain any order, directions or certificate issued by the SoS must be received in evidence and deemed to contain the order, certificate or directions without further proof unless the contrary is shown.[42] A certificate signed by the SoS or an officer on his behalf confirming the making of any order, the issuing of any document or the exercise of any discretion, power or obligation arising or imposed under the IA86 or IR86 is conclusive evidence of the matters in the certificate.[43]

---

37 IR86, r 7.9.
38 IR86, r 7.9(2).
39 IR86, r 7.7A(2).
40 IR86, r 7.7A(3).
41 IR86, r 12.5.
42 IR86, r 12.6(1) and (2).
43 IR86, r 12.6(3).

19.22 Rule 12.13, IR86 allows for certain documents forming part of the court record to be treated as confidential and not be inspected without the permission of the court. However, the rule does not apply to the inspection of any proof or proxy.

19.23 The court may adjourn the hearing of any application on such terms as it thinks fit or it may give directions.[44]

How and when can proceedings be transferred between courts?

19.24 Where bankruptcy proceedings are pending in the High Court the court may transfer them to a specified county court (provided it has bankruptcy jurisdiction); similarly a county court may transfer proceedings to the High Court or another county court.[45] Note, however, that only a High Court judge (and not a registrar) may transfer proceedings to the High Court from a county court.[46]

19.25 Where proceedings are commenced in the wrong court the court may order them to be transferred to the correct court or may order them to be continued in the court in which they have been commenced; alternatively it may strike them out.[47]

19.26 Further detailed rules deal with the transfer of proceedings between different courts on the application of the official receiver.[48]

What records are the courts required to maintain of bankruptcy proceedings and who has right of access?

19.27 The court is obliged to keep records of all insolvency proceedings on which any step in the proceedings and the decision of the court are recorded.[49] The record is open to inspection, but if the registrar is not satisfied as to the propriety of the purpose for which inspection is required it may refuse to allow it. A party refused the right to inspect may appeal without notice to the judge who may refuse inspection or allow it on such terms as he thinks fit. There is no appeal from the judge to the court of appeal, the judge's decision being final.[50]

---

44 IR86, r 7.10.
45 IR86, r 7.11(1) and (2).
46 IR86, r 7.11(4).
47 IR86, r 7.12.
48 IR86, r 7.13ff.
49 IR86, r 7.27.
50 IR86, r 7.28; as to propriety of purpose and the restriction on the right to appeal see *Re an Application Pursuant to rule 7.28 of the Insolvency Rules 1986* [1994] BCC 369, in which inspection for purely commercial purposes was refused; on the same point and the right to appeal from the decision of the judge see *Re Austintel Ltd* [1997] 1 WLR 616. As to searching for bankruptcy petitions and the terms which the court may impose see *Re Haines Watts* [2004] EWHC 1970 Ch, [2005] BPIR 798.

19.28 The records retained by the court must be maintained on a court file (subject to any directions being given by the court).[51] The following have the right, at all reasonable times, to inspect the court's file of proceedings (including any person properly authorised[52]):

- the person who in relation to the proceedings is the responsible insolvency practitioner;
- any authorised officer of the Department;
- any person stating himself in writing to be a creditor of the individual to whom the proceedings relate;[53]
- the bankrupt;
- any person against whom or by whom a bankruptcy petition has been presented;
- any person who has been served with a statutory demand in accordance with chapter 1 of Part 6 of the IR86.[54]

19.29 In addition to the foregoing (who have a right to inspect the file) any other person may inspect the file 'by special leave of the court'.[55] However, such right does not extend to documents which the court has directed should not be open to inspection. The special leave of the court must be sought by formal application to the registrar who may refuse leave if he is not satisfied as to the propriety of the purpose of inspection. Again there is a right of appeal to the judge, but again the judge's decision is final and no appeal lies to the Court of Appeal.[56]

19.30 A person entitled to inspect the court file may require the court to provide an office copy of any document on the file.[57]

How is control of bankruptcy proceedings exercised by the court?

19.31 All bankruptcies are ultimately under the control of the court.[58] In fact it is a control that is rarely exercised. There is a good reason for that. As a general rule the person best equipped to make decisions about the conduct of a

---

51 IR86, r 7.30(1).
52 IR86, r 7.31(3).
53 IR86, r 7.31(1).
54 IR86, r 7.31(2).
55 IR86, r 7.31(4); for an example of consideration of special leave see *Mansell v Acton* [2005] EWHC 3048 (Ch), [2006] BPIR 778.
56 IR86, r 7.31(7) applying r 7.28.
57 Insolvency Rules 1986, SI 1925, r 7.61.
58 Insolvency Act 1986, s 363(1); see also s 303.

bankruptcy is the trustee and the courts have long recognised this. In *Re a Debtor (No 400 Of 1940) ex parte the Debtor v Dodwell*[59] Harman, J said:

> 'It seems to me clear that there must be circumstances in which the court can interfere at the instance of a bankrupt to control the actions of the trustee … I need not, I think, attempt to define what these circumstances are. They cannot, I think (in the absence of fraud) justify interference in the day-to-day administration of the estate, nor entitle the bankrupt to question the exercise by the trustee in good faith of his discretion, nor to hold him accountable for an error of judgment. Administration in bankruptcy would be impossible if the trustee must answer at every step to the bankrupt for the exercise of his powers and discretions in the management and realisation of the property.'

19.32 That is not to say that the court will not use its power under s 363, IA86. For examples of circumstances when it has done so see *Engel v Peri*[60] (the issue was annulment and the remuneration of the trustee) and *Donaldson v O'Sullivan and the Official Receiver* (the issue was the replacement of a trustee).[61]

What role do the Civil Procedure Rules play?

19.33 The provisions of the Civil Procedure Rules (CPR) in the first column of the table below (including any related practice direction) apply to insolvency proceedings with any necessary modifications, except so far as inconsistent with IR86.[62]

Provisions of CPR	Provisions of these Rules[63]
CPR Part 6 (except 6.30–6.51) (service of documents)	Chapter 3 of Part 12A
CPR Part 18 (further information)	Rules 7.60 and 9.2(3)(b)
CPR Part 31 (disclosure and inspection of documents)	Rules 7.60 and 9.2
CPR Part 37 (miscellaneous provisions about payments into court)	Rule 7.59
CPR Parts 44 and 47 (costs)	Chapter 6 of Part 7
CPR Part 52 (appeals)	Rule 7.49

The provisions of the CPR (including any related practice direction) not referred to in the table above apply to proceedings under the IA86 and IR86 with any necessary modifications, except so far as inconsistent with IR86 and

---

59 [1949] 1 Ch 236 at p 241.
60 [2002] BPIR 961 (where annulment and the remuneration of the trustee were in issue).
61 [2008] EWCA Civ 879, [2008] BPIR 288 (where the issue was the replacement of a trustee).
62 IR86, r 7.51A(1).
63 IR86, r 7.51A(1).

subject to r 7.51A(3).[64] All insolvency proceedings must be allocated to the multi-track for which CPR Part 29 makes provision, and accordingly those provisions of the CPR which provide for allocation questionnaires and track allocation do not apply.[65] CPR Part 32 applies to a false statement in a document verified by a statement of truth made under IR86 as it applies to a false statement in a document verified by a statement of truth made under CPR Part 22.[66]

What are the general rules on the service of documents?

19.34 In addition to specific rules governing service[67] the IR86 contain general rules as to service. Rule 12.10, IR86 contains provisions governing the manner and effect of service by post. A document served by post must be contained in an envelope addressed to the person on whom service is to be effected and pre-paid for first or second class post.[68] A document to be served by post may be sent to the last known address of the person to be served.[69] Where first class post is used the document is treated as served on the second business day after the date of posting, and where second class post is used on the fourth business day after posting unless the contrary is shown.[70] The date of posting is presumed, unless the contrary is shown, to be the date shown in the postmark on the envelope containing the document served.[71]

19.35 Subject to rr 12.10 and 12.10, IR86 (service out of the jurisdiction) CPR Part 6 applies as regards any matter relating to the service of documents and the giving of notice in insolvency proceedings.[72]

19.36 Where the rules provide for notice to be given or for document to be sent or served, the document may be sent by post unless personal service is expressly required by another rule. Any form of post may generally be used. Personal service is, however, always permissible.[73] Notice of the venue fixed for an application may be given by service of a sealed copy of the application.[74] Where a solicitor is acting and is authorised to accept service, notice may be given to such solicitor.[75]

---

64 IR86, r 7.51A(2).
65 IR86, r 7.51A(3).
66 IR86, r 7.51A(4).
67 For example r 6.18(1) governing the time that must elapse between service of a bankruptcy petition and the hearing, r 6.206(4) regarding annulment applications and r 7.4(5) regarding applications.
68 IR86, r 12.10(1).
69 IR86, r 12.10(1A).
70 IR86, r 12.10(2) and (3).
71 IR86, r 12.10(4).
72 IR86, r 12.11.
73 IR86, r 13.3(1)–(3).
74 IR86, r 13.3(4).
75 IR86, r 13.4.

19.37 Where there are joint office holders both acting as the responsible insolvency practitioner delivery of a document to one is treated as delivery to all.[76]

What rules govern service out of the jurisdiction?

19.38 Rule 12.12, IR86 used to govern service out of the jurisdiction, and disapplied CPR Part 6.17–6.35 in relation to insolvency proceedings. However, with effect from 6 April 2010, CPR Part 6 applies to the service of court documents outside the jurisdiction with such modifications as the court may direct.[77]

What time limits apply when serving documents?

19.39 Section 376, IA86 allows the court to extend time for doing anything where time is limited under Group of Parts either before or after it has expired on such terms as it thinks fit.[78]

What are the general rules on time limits?

19.40 The general law of limitations applies to insolvency proceedings as much as to other proceedings, save where special time limits apply.[79] The Limitation Act 1980 (LA 1980) provides for the ordinary time limits for bringing actions of the various classes more particularly set out in the Act and provides for the principles governing the extension and/or exclusion of those limits. Those of most general concern in relation to insolvency proceedings are set out below:

section 2	actions founded on tort	6 years
section 5	actions founded on simple contract	6 years
section 6	actions on loans	6 years from demand
section 8	actions on a specialty	12 years
section 9	actions on sums recoverable by statute	6 years
section 11	actions for personal injuries	3 years
section 11A	actions for defective products	3 or 10 years
section 15	actions to recover land	12 years
section 20	actions on mortgages	12 years
section 24	actions to enforce judgments	6 years

---

76 IR86, r 13.5.

77 IR86, r 12A.20.

78 See generally *Tager v Westpac Banking Corporation* [1998] BCC 73.

79 For example, the ability of trustees to sell the bankrupt's home is now subject to the 3 year time limit provided by IA86, s 283A (inserted by Enterprise Act 2002, s 261). Note the power to extend time (s 283A(6), IA86).

Particular considerations may apply in relation to claims for tax. Section 37, LA80 disapplies the normal limitation provisions to any proceedings by the Crown for tax or duty etc. However, this does not apply where the Crown has taken judgment and the doctrine of merger applies.

19.41 Limitation is generally a defence to a claim and not an absolute bar to a claim: it must generally be pleaded. However, the position in certain insolvency proceedings may be different. For example it has been held that a winding up petition may not be presented based on a debt which is statute-barred.[80] A statutory demand served on an individual may also be set aside where the debt is statute-barred.[81]

The LA80 does not affect the right of a creditor to petition for a winding up order (or by analogy a bankruptcy order) on a judgment debt when 6 years have elapsed from the date of the judgment, since a petition is not an action within the meaning of s 24(1), LA80.[82]

As to the time limit applicable to the enforcement of a charge under s 313, IA86 see *Gotham v Doodes*[83] to the effect that time began to run from the time when sale was possible and not from the date the charge was created.

An order for payment of costs to be taxed does not become enforceable for the purpose of s 24, LA80 until the costs are certified.[84]

19.42 The application of limitation periods to insolvency proceedings is not always straightforward. Note the following limitation periods which, prima facie, apply to various forms of relief available under the Insolvency Act 1986:

- section 339 (transactions at undervalue): 12 years (in relation to the recovery of property) or 6 years (in relation to the recovery of money);[85]

- section 340 (preference): 12 years (in relation to the recovery of property) or 6 years (in relation to the recovery of money);[86]

- section 343 (extortionate credit bargains): 12 years (in relation to the recovery of property) or 6 years (in relation to the recovery of money).[87]

---

80 *Re Karnos Property Co Ltd* (1989) 5 BCC 14.

81 *Re A Debtor (No 50A-SD-1995* [1997] Ch 310.

82 *Ridgeway Motors (Isleworth) Ltd v Alts Ltd* [2005] EWCA (Civ) 92, [2005] 2 BCLC 61.

83 [2006] EWCA Civ 1080, [2007] 1 WLR 86

84 *Times Newspapers Ltd v Chohan* [2001] BPIR 187.

85 Limitation Act 1980, s 9(1) and *Re Priory Garage (Walthamstow) Ltd* [2001] BPIR 144, *Re Yates (a bankrupt)* [2005] BPIR 476, *Re Nurkowski (a bankrupt); Hill v Spread Trustee Company Ltd and Warr* [2006] EWCA Civ 542, [2007] 1 WLR 2404, [2006] BPIR 789, [2007] 1 BCLC 450, [2007] 1 All ER 1106 and *Segal v Pasram and Pasram* [2007] BPIR 881.

86 Limitation Act 1980, s 9(1) and *Re Priory Garage (Walthamstow) Ltd* [2001] BPIR 144.

87 Limitation Act 1980, s 9(1) and *Nolan v Wright* [2009] EWHC 305 (Ch), [2009] BPIR 854.

The running of time may be postponed in cases of fraud until the fraud is discovered.[88] Again, however, this may not necessarily be relied on where the cause of action overlaps with other statutory claims.

19.43 Generally time begins to run from the date of the bankruptcy order. However, where the cause of action lies not with the trustee but with the bankrupt the office holder is fixed with the limitation period applicable to the bankrupt (eg in the case of an action for debt or damages).

What is the effect of any defects in the proceedings?

19.44 As regards the effect of defects in the proceedings r 7.55, IR86 is very clear:

> 'No insolvency proceedings shall be invalidated by any formal defect or by any irregularity, unless the court before which objection is made considers that substantial injustice has been caused by the defect or irregularity, and that the injustice cannot be remedied by any order of the court.'

The rule does not, however, provide an escape route for any kind of defect or irregularity:

- In *Re Awan*[89] it was held that it could not be used to excused failure to prove service of a bankruptcy petition.
- In *Re a Debtor (No 340 of 1992)*[90] it did not enable the creditor to overcome problems in the sheriff's return as to the levying of execution as a means of founding a petition.
- In *Re a Debtor (No 22 of 1993)*[91] it did enable a creditor to avoid the consequences of failing to state in a petition that there was an outstanding application to set aside the statutory demand.
- In *Times Newspapers v Chohan*[92] Anthony Mann QC as he then was expressed doubt that the existence of an application to set aside a statutory demand at the date of presentation of a petition was a waivable defect.

When can a writ of execution be used?

19.45 A writ of execution to enforce any order made in insolvency proceedings in the High Court may be issued on the authority of a registrar.[93]

---

88 Limitation Act 1980, s 32 and *Giles v Rhind* [2008] EWCA Civ 118, [2008] BPIR 342.
89 [2000] BPIR 241.
90 [1996] 2 All ER 211.
91 [1994] 1 WLR 46.
92 [2001] BPIR 187
93 Practice Direction: Insolvency Proceedings, para 1.5.

Permission is required to issue a writ of possession in insolvency proceedings,[94] and such permission will not be granted unless the court is shown that every person in actual occupation of the whole or any part of the land has received notice of the proceedings sufficient to enable him to apply to the court for any relief to which he may be entitled.[95]

A registrar has jurisdiction to make a third party debt order under CPR r 72.2 in relation to a debt arising from an order for costs made in insolvency proceedings in the High Court.[96]

What is the process for appealing a judgment?

19.46 Appeals in bankruptcy are governed by s 375, IA86. Detailed provisions regarding appeals are to be found in para 17 of the *Practice Direction: Insolvency Proceedings*. An appeal from a registrar of the High Court or any judge of the county court (a so-called 'first appeal') lies to a single judge of the Chancery Division of the High Court[97] Note that an appeal from a district judge never lies to a circuit judge.

19.47 The time limit for making an appeal is generally 21 days after the date of the decision of the lower court[98] but the court from which the appeal is to be made may direct a different period.[99]

19.48 Permission is required to appeal in insolvency proceedings. It should be asked for at the hearing on which the order to be appealed is made. In the High Court in London the registrar should be asked to complete a form indicating whether permission has been given or refused, giving brief reasons for the decision. Permission to appeal should only be given where the court considers that the appeal would have a real prospect of success or where there is some other compelling reason why the appeal should be heard.[100]

19.49 An appeal is made by filing a fee paid appellant's notice in Form PDIP 1 (which appears in the Practice Direction) together with a copy plus additional copies for each person to be served.[101] The appellant must also file a transcript of the judgment under appeal,[102] a copy of the order under appeal[103] and give a time estimate for the appeal.[104] If a respondent to the appeal files a respondent's notice that must also be in Form PDIP2 set out in the Practice Direction. If the appeal is from a decision of a registrar the appeal must be

94 RSC Order 45, r 3.
95 RSC Order 45, r 3(3): an affidavit or witness statement will generally be required.
96 *Thakerar v Lynch Hall and Hornby* [2005] EWHC 2752 (Ch), [2006] 1 WLR 1513.
97 Insolvency Act 1986, s 375(2).
98 Practice Direction, para 17.11(2)(b).
99 Practice Direction, para 17.11(2)(a).
100 CPR 52.3(5).
101 Practice Direction, para 17.22(1)(a).
102 Practice Direction, para 17.22(1)(aa).
103 Practice Direction, para 17.22(1)(b).
104 Practice Direction, para 7.22(1)(c).

filed in the Royal Courts of Justice;[105] if it is from a district judge or a county court judge it may be filed in either the Royal Courts of Justice or the designated District Registry.[106]

19.50 Unless the appeal court orders otherwise a notice of appeal must be served on each respondent 'as soon as practicable' and in any event not later than 7 days after it has been filed.[107] A respondent who wishes to serve a respondent's notice must file it 14 days after the date on which he is served with the appellant's notice unless the lower court has directed otherwise[108] and serve it as soon as practicable which in any event should not be later than 7 days after filing.[109] The appeal notice must be served on any other party affected by the appeal, eg the official receiver, liquidator or trustee.[110]

19.51 The procedure for a first appeal is the same as that applicable to an appeal to the Court of Appeal and is governed largely by CPR Part 32.[111] However, the Practice Direction itself contains much of the necessary guidance and imports some differences, the main difference being that the role of the registrar of appeals is taken by a registrar (if the appeal is filed in the Royal Courts of Justice) or a district judge (if the appeal is filed in a district registry).[112] Thus applications to extend time for filing a notice of appeal, for security for costs and other applications relating to the appeal (but not the appeal itself) will generally be heard by the registrar or the district judge.

19.52 Unless the appeal court or the lower court orders otherwise an appeal does not operate as a stay of any order or decision of the lower court.[113] An appeal in insolvency proceedings is (and always has been) a true appeal and not a re-hearing. Thus any appeal is limited to a review of the decision of the lower court.[114] It will be allowed, therefore, only where the decision of the lower court was wrong or unjust because of a serious procedural or other irregularity in the proceedings.[115] Oral evidence or evidence not adduced in the court below will not generally be received on the hearing of the appeal.[116]

An appeal from a High Court judge (a second appeal) lies to the Court of Appeal and requires permission.[117]

---

105 Practice Direction, para 17.10(1).
106 Practice Direction, para 17.10(2)–(3).
107 Practice Direction, para 7.11(3).
108 Practice Direction, para 17.12(3).
109 Practice Direction, para 17.11(4).
110 Practice Direction, para 17.22(4).
111 Practice Direction, para 17.1(2).
112 Practice Direction, para 17.8.
113 Practice Direction, para 17.4.
114 Practice Direction, para 17.18(1); see also *Re Gilmartin* [1989] 1 WLR 513, [1989] 2 All ER 835; and *Vadher v Weisgard* [1997] BCC 219, [1998] BPIR 295.
115 Practice Direction, para 17.18(3).
116 Practice Direction, para 17.18(2).
117 Insolvency Act 1986, s 375(2).

19.53 Proceedings in the bankruptcy court are issued in the bankruptcy issue and search room and are dealt with by the Registrars in Bankruptcy, not the Masters. Proceedings under Parts VIII to XI of the Insolvency Act 1986 should be entitled 'IN BANKRUPTCY'.

19.54 Certain matters, such as applications for injunctions or for committal for contempt, are heard by a judge. A judge is available to hear such matters each day in term time and applications may be listed for any such day. The judge will normally also be hearing the interim applications list for the day, but one or more other judges may be available to assist if necessary.

19.55 The Registrar may refer or adjourn proceedings to the judge, having regard to such matters as the complexity of the proceedings, whether the proceedings raise new or controversial points of law, the likely date and length of the hearing, public interest in the proceedings, and the availability of relevant specialist expertise. When proceedings have been referred or adjourned to the judge, interim applications and applications for directions or case management will be listed before a judge, except where liberty to apply to the Registrar has been given.

19.56 There are prescribed forms for use in connection with all types of statutory demand and of petitions for bankruptcy orders. Every other type of application is either an originating application in Form 7.1 (meaning an application to the court which is not an application in pending proceedings before the court) or an ordinary application in Form 7.2 (meaning any other application to the court).

Chapter 20

INTERNATIONAL CO-OPERATION AND RECOGNITION IN BANKRUPTCY PROCEEDINGS

'A bank is a place that will lend you money if you can prove that you don't need it.'[1]

INTRODUCTION

20.1 Whilst the insolvency law of England and Wales is sometimes represented and perceived as parochial this is far from the case. As Ian Fletcher has noted,[2] English law demonstrates a strong international tradition which can be traced back to the eighteenth and nineteenth centuries.[3] Jabez Henry, the judge who presided over the court which originally decided *Odwin v Forbes*,[4] went on to make two significant contributions to cross-border insolvency, first in the form of an account of the case,[5] the second in the form of a pamphlet, '*Outline of Plan of an International Bankruptcy Code for the Commercial States of Europe*', published at some time between 1823 and 1827.[6]

20.2 By the nineteenth century provisions for mutual aid were already in force.[7] However, the Cork Committee recommended that the provision in force when it reported in 1982[8] required improvement.[9] This resulted in the provision which remains s 426, IA86. Since 1986 there has been two major developments regarding international co-operation and recognition. These are the coming

---

1 Bob Hope (Leslie Townes Hope).

2 I F Fletcher *Insolvency in Private International Law* (Oxford University Press, 2nd edn, 2005).

3 Fletcher notes that in *Solomons v Ross* (1764) 1 Hy Bl 131n, 126 ER 76 the English court was prepared to rule that a foreign bankruptcy could have effect on the bankrupt's movable property within the jurisdiction of the court, whilst in *Odwin v Forbes* (1817) 1 Buck 57 (PC) the Privy Council confirmed the judgment of the Court of Demerara and Essequibo that an English discharge had no force by reason of Dutch law provisions in force when the colony came into British possession, thus fettering the generally held universalist principle and giving effect to comity.

4 [1817] 1 Buck 57.

5 [1823] The Judgment of the Court of Demerara in the case of *Odwin v Forbes.*

6 For an account and commentary see K H Nadelmann, *An International Bankruptcy Code: New Thoughts on an Old Idea* (1961) 10/1 ICLQ p 70 and David Graham, *Discovering Jabez Henry: Cross-Border Insolvency Law in the 19th Century* (2001) Int Insol Rev 10/2 p 153 and *In Search of Jabez Henry: the Readership of Foreign Law* (2005), International Insolvency Review 14, p 223.

7 Bankruptcy Act 1869, s 74.

8 Bankruptcy Act 1914, s 122.

9 See Chapter 49 of the Report entitled Extra-Territorial Aspects of Insolvency Law.

into force of the EC Regulation on Insolvency Proceedings 2000[10] and the Cross-Border Insolvency Regulations 2006.[11]

What are the statutory provisions relating to co-operation between courts?

20.3 Co-operation between courts exercising jurisdiction in relation to insolvency is covered in s 426, IA86 which provides as follows:

- An order made by a court in any part of the UK in the exercise of jurisdiction in relation to insolvency law shall be enforced in any other part of the UK as if it were made by a court exercising the corresponding jurisdiction in that other part.[12]

- However, nothing in s 426(1), IA86 requires a court in any part of the UK to enforce, in relation to property situated in that part, any order made by a court in any other part of the UK.[13]

- The SoS, with the concurrence in relation to property situated in England and Wales of the Lord Chancellor, may by order make provision for securing that a trustee or assignee under the insolvency law of any part of the UK has, with such modifications as may be specified in the order, the same rights in relation to any property situated in another part of the UK as he would have in the corresponding circumstances if he were a trustee or assignee under the insolvency law of that other part.[14]

- The courts having jurisdiction in relation to insolvency law in any part of the UK shall assist the courts having the corresponding jurisdiction in any other part of the UK or any relevant country or territory.[15]

- For the purposes of s 426(4), IA86 a request made to a court in any part of the UK by a court in any other part of the UK or in a relevant country or territory is authority for the court to which the request is made to apply, in relation to any matters specified in the request, the insolvency law which is applicable by either court in relation to comparable matters falling within its jurisdiction.[16]

- In exercising its discretion under s 426(4), IA86, a court must have regard in particular to the rules of private international law.

- Where a person who is a trustee or assignee under the insolvency law of any part of the United Kingdom claims property situated in any other part of the UK (whether by virtue of an order under s 426(3), IA86 or

10 Council Regulation (EC) No 1346/2000 of 29 May 2000 on insolvency proceedings.
11 SI 2006/1030.
12 IA86, s 426(1).
13 IA86, s 426(2).
14 IA86, s 426(3).
15 IA86, s 426(4).
16 IA86, s 426(5).

otherwise), the submission of that claim to the court exercising jurisdiction in relation to insolvency law in that other part shall be treated in the same manner as a request made by a court for the purpose of s 426(4), IA86.[17]

- Section 38 of the Criminal Law Act 1977 (execution of warrant of arrest throughout the UK) applies to a warrant which, in exercise of any jurisdiction in relation to insolvency law, is issued in any part of the UK for the arrest of a person as it applies to a warrant issued in that part of the UK for the arrest of a person charged with an offence.[18]

- Without prejudice to any power to make rules of court, any power to make provision by subordinate legislation for the purpose of giving effect in relation to companies or individuals to the insolvency law of any part of the UK includes power to make provision for the purpose of giving effect in that part to any provision made by or under the preceding provisions of s 426, IA86.[19]

- An order under s 426(3), IA86 must be made by statutory instrument subject to annulment in pursuance of a resolution of either House of Parliament.[20]

- In s 426, IA86 'insolvency law' means the following:[21]

  — in relation to England and Wales, provision extending to England and Wales and made by or under this Act or ss 1A, 6–10, 12–15, 19(c) and 20 (with Sch 1) of the Company Directors Disqualification Act 1986 and ss 1–17 of the Company Directors Disqualification Act 1986, as they apply for the purposes of those provisions of that Act;
  — in relation to Scotland, provision extending to Scotland and made by or under this Act, ss 1A, 6–10, 12–15, 19(c) and 20 (with Sch 1) of the Company Directors Disqualification Act 1986 and ss 1–17 of that Act as they apply for the purposes of those provisions of that Act, Part XVIII of the Companies Act or the Bankruptcy (Scotland) Act 1985;
  — in relation to Northern Ireland, provision made by or under the Insolvency (Northern Ireland) Order 1989 or Part II of the Companies (Northern Ireland) Order 1989;
  — in relation to any relevant country or territory, so much of the law of that country or territory as corresponds to provisions falling within any of the foregoing paragraphs;

---

17 IA86, s 426(6).
18 IA86, s 426(7).
19 IA86, s 426(8).
20 IA86, s 426(9).
21 IA86, s 426(10).

— and references in this subsection to any enactment include, in relation to any time before the coming into force of that enactment the corresponding enactment in force at that time.

- In this section 'relevant country or territory' means:[22]

— any of the Channel Islands or the Isle of Man, or
— any country or territory designated for the purposes of this section by the SoS by order made by statutory instrument.

What are the differences in Northern Ireland?

20.4 In the application of this section to Northern Ireland:[23]

- for any reference to the SoS there is substituted a reference to the Department of Economic Development in Northern Ireland;
- in s 426(3), IA86 for the words 'another part of the United Kingdom' and the words 'that other part' there is substituted the words 'Northern Ireland';
- for s 426(9), IA86 there is substituted the following subsection:

> '(9) An order made under subsection (3) by the Department of Economic Development in Northern Ireland shall be a statutory rule for the purposes of the Statutory Rules (Northern Ireland) Order 1979 and shall be subject to negative resolution within the meaning of section 41(6) of the Interpretation Act (Northern Ireland) 1954.'

- Section 129, Banking Act 2009 provides for provisions of that Act about bank insolvency to be 'insolvency law' for the purposes of s 426, IA86.
- Section 165, Banking Act 2009 provides for provisions of that Act about bank administration to be 'insolvency law' for the purposes of s 426, IA86.

What is the difference between inter court co-operation within the UK and with courts outside the UK?

20.5 It should first be noted that s 426, IA86 applies not only internationally but within the United Kingdom.[24] Thus courts in one part of the United Kingdom may seek the assistance of another. However, the provision should not be used simply to pass the work of one court on to another.[25] Sections 426(3) and (9), IA86 give the SoS power to make orders giving a trustee or liquidator the same rights with regard to property situated in another

---

22 IA86, s 426(11).
23 IA86, s 426(12).
24 IA86, s 426(1).
25 *Re Marquess of Huntley* [1917] 2 KB 729.

part of the UK as a trustee or assignee would have in such other part. Section 426, IA86 enables a trustee or liquidator to claim property situated in any other part of the UK by asking for assistance from the UK court with jurisdiction over the property. The section is, however, more usually used to promote corporation between the UK courts and the courts of other countries stop only countries or territories that are designated for the purpose of this section may apply to the UK court; such countries or territories are referred to as 'relevant countries or territories'.[26] The section applies to foreign proceedings in which an office holder seeks the assistance of the UK courts. A trustee in bankruptcy seeking the assistance of a foreign court will apply in the domestic bankruptcy for a letter of request or order in aid directed to the relevant foreign court which will deal with the matter in accordance with its commensurate legal provisions.

20.6 In spite of the fact that s 426(1) and (4), IA86 are expressed in mandatory terms the granting of an order (known as 'an order in aid') has always been a matter of discretion. This was most recently confirmed by the Court of Appeal in *Hughes v Hannover-Rückversicherungs AG*.[27] However, the general principle is to give assistance unless there is good reason not to.[28]

20.7 The effect of s 426(5), IA86 is to permit the court to which a request is made to apply the law which would be applicable in comparable matters in the country of the requesting court or domestic law. The discretion given must be exercised with regard to the rules of private international law. The impact of the choice of law provision will also go to the general exercise of the discretion to make an order.

How is s 426 affected by the common law?

20.8 Although like many decisions on international recognition and similar topics *Re HIH Casualty and General Insurance Ltd*[29] a corporate case that is of interest for the purpose of individual insolvency not only because it is a rare decision at such a high level on s 426, IA86 but because it deals with the question of international cooperation more widely. The case concerned four insurance companies incorporated in Australia but which carried on business in the UK. Joint provisional liquidators were appointed in England under letters of request sent by the Australian court. The question in the case was whether it

---

26 For the purposes of s 426(11), IA86 these are Anguilla, Australia, Bermuda, Botswana, Brunei, Canada, Cayman Islands, Falkland Islands, Gibraltar, Hong Kong, Ireland, Malaysia, Montserrat, New Zealand, St Helena, South Africa, Turks and Caicos Islands, Tuvalu and the Virgin Islands (see the Cooperation of Insolvency Courts (Designation of Relevant Countries and Territories) Order 1986, SI 1986/2123 (as amended by SI 1989/2409)).

27 [1997] BCC 921; see also *Re NJ TaylorPty Ltd* [1998] BPIR 347 and *England v Smith (Re Southern Equities Corp)* [2001] Ch 419, [2000] BPIR 28.

28 *Re BCCI Ltd (No 9)* [1994] 3 All ER 264 and *Re Focus Insurance Co Ltd* [1997] 1 BCLC 219

29 [2008] UKHL 21, [2008] Bus LR 905; for a full discussion see Gabriel Moss QC, 'Modified Universalism and the Quest for the Golden Thread', *Insolvency Intelligence* (2008), Volume 22/10, p 145.

was appropriate to send assets for distribution in Australia where the scheme for distribution differed substantially from that in the UK.

20.9 The House of Lords held that, Australia being a relevant country for the purposes of s 426(4), IA86, the English courts were obliged to assist the Australian courts and had discretion to order assets to be remitted to Australia even where the law differed from that obtaining in England. Lords Hoffmann and Walker also held that the discretion arose under the inherent powers of the court at common law pursuant to the principle that the English courts would cooperate with foreign courts where to do so did not conflict with the interests of justice or UK public policy. Lord Hoffmann traced the jurisdiction back to what he described (in para 6 of his judgment) as the

> 'general principle of private international law, namely that a bankruptcy (whether personal or corporate) should be unitary and universal. There should be a unitary bankruptcy proceeding in the court of the bankrupt's domicile which receives worldwide recognition and it should apply universally to all the bankrupt's assets.'

He pointed to nineteenth-century practice as based on the principle of universalism modified to allow the cooperation required in dealing with the foreign assets (so called 'modified universalism'). He made a clear distinction between the common law powers and those arising under s 426, IA86, the former based on 'principles of international comity'.[30]

20.10 As to the exercise of the discretion he referred to the:

> 'primary rule of private international law which seems to me to be applicable to this case [which] is the principle of "modified" universalism, which has been the golden thread running through English cross-border insolvency since the 18th century. That principle requires that English courts should, so far as is consistent with justice and UK policy, co-operate with the courts in the country of the principal liquidation …'[31]

Whilst Lord Hoffmann's view prevailed the dissenting reasoning of Lords Scott and Neuberger should be noted. It is submitted, however, that the decision lends force to the established practice of the bankruptcy courts in recognising foreign bankruptcies whether or not they are related to a relevant country within the scope of s 426, IA86.

20.11 The recent supreme court decision in *New Cap Reinsurance Corporation (In Liquidation) and another (Respondents/Cross Appellants) v A E Grant and others as Members of Lloyd's Syndicate 991 for the 1997 Year of Account and another (Appellants/Cross Respondents)*[32] (hereafter referred to as *Rubin*) adds a new perspective to cross-border insolvency cases. As Lord Collins noted in his

---

30 See para 10 of Lord Hoffmann's judgment, *Re HIH Casualty and General Insurance Ltd* [2008] UKHL 21, [2008] Bus LR 905.

31 See para 30 of Lord Hoffmann's judgment, R*e HIH Casualty and General Insurance Ltd* [2008] UKHL 21, [2008] Bus LR 905.

32 [2012] UKSC 46.

judgment the case involved a discussion of whether an order or judgment of a foreign court in proceedings to adjust or set aside prior transactions, eg preferences or transactions at an undervalue will be recognised and enforced in England. The Supreme Court by a majority allowed the appeal in *Rubin* holding that there should not be special rules for avoidance judgments. As the learned judges noted:[33]

> 'As a matter of policy, the Court did not agree that, in the interests of the universality of bankruptcy and similar procedures, there should be a more liberal rule for judgments given in foreign insolvency proceedings for the avoidance of transactions.'

20.12 As a general rule any application should be made to the registrar by originating application (unless it relates to an existing bankruptcy in England or Wales) and should be supported by an affidavit or witness statement. The application should generally be made on notice to the bankrupt.[34]

What is the effect of the EC Regulations on insolvency proceedings?

20.13 The EC Regulation on Insolvency Proceedings[35] came into force on 31 May 2002.[36] It applies only to proceedings after that date and has no retrospective effect.[37] It has direct application as domestic law. It applies to all EU member states except Denmark.

> 'Its purpose is to improve the efficiency and effectiveness of insolvency proceedings with a cross-border dimension by either simplifying or removing formalities previously associated with recognition and enforcement. It is not an attempt to harmonise the insolvency laws of member states but to provide a framework within which the different insolvency regimes can interact with more predictable outcomes.'[38]

The recitals refer to matters such as promoting judicial co-operation, assisting the proper functioning of the internal market, avoiding incentives for parties to transfer assets to obtain more favourable treatment, and avoiding forum shopping (see paras (2), (3) and (4) of the recitals). It applies to both corporate and individual insolvencies, but much of the language indicates that its drafters were more at home in the corporate than the individual realm (see fro example the definitions of centre of main interest and establishment which are harder to apply to people than companies).

---

33 Ibid at para 115.

34 *Re a Debtor (Order in Aid No 1 of 1979)* [1981] Ch 384, [1980] 3 All ER 665.

35 Council Regulation (EC) No 1346/2000 of 29 May 2000 on insolvency proceedings.

36 Council Regulation (EC) No 1346/2000, art 47.

37 Council Regulation (EC) No 1346/2000, art 43.

38 DTI Guidance Notes.

What does 'insolvency proceedings' mean in the EC Regulation?

20.14 The EC Regulation on Insolvency Proceedings applies to 'collective insolvency proceedings which entail the partial or total divestment of a debtor and the appointment of a liquidator'.[39]

The expression 'insolvency proceedings' means:

- winding up by or subject to court supervision;
- creditors' voluntary winding up (with court confirmation);
- administration;
- voluntary arrangements;
- bankruptcy or sequestration.[40]

Note that a CVL must be 'with confirmation of the court'.[41]

Who does 'liquidator' include?

20.15 The expression 'liquidator' means all of the following offices:

- a liquidator;
- a provisional liquidator;
- the supervisor of a voluntary arrangement;
- an administrator;
- the official receiver;
- a trustee in bankruptcy;
- a judicial factor.[42]

Note that the Regulation does not apply to administrative or Law of Property Act receiverships or to members' voluntary winding up; nor does it apply to schemes of arrangement under the Companies Acts, to winding up on the just and equitable ground or winding up in the public interest. There are also provisions excluding applicability to insurance undertakings, credit institutions and investment undertakings.[43]

---

39 Council Regulation (EC) No 1346/2000, art 1(1).
40 Council Regulation (EC) No 1346/2000, art 2(1), Ann A.
41 Council Regulation (EC) No 1346/2000, Ann A.
42 Council Regulation (EC) No 1346/2000, art 2(b), Ann C.
43 Council Regulation (EC) No 1346/2000, art 1(2).

What is the purpose and structure of the EU regulations?

20.16 The purpose of the Regulation is to apply a standard set of rules governing the law applicable to such proceedings (and their equivalents elsewhere). The regulation recognises two main kinds of proceedings:

- main proceedings, and
- territorial or secondary proceedings.

What are 'main proceedings'?

20.17 Main proceedings are proceedings brought in the place of the debtor's centre of main interests.[44] These are universal in scope.

What are 'territorial proceedings'?

20.18 These may be brought in the place where debtor has 'an establishment'[45] and are limited to assets in the relevant territory. Generally they can only be opened following the opening of main proceedings and cannot take place in isolation.[46] Where they are opened after main proceedings they are called secondary proceedings. They can only be for winding up (as defined in Annex B); they cannot be rescue or rehabilitation proceedings.[47]

What is the general rule on applicable law and what are the exceptions?

20.19 The place of the opening of proceedings determines applicable law[48] the *lex concursus*. Thus, the general rule is now that the national law of the state in which proceedings are opened will be the applicable law and will determine the conditions governing the 'opening, conduct and termination' of the proceedings.

20.20 There are exceptions to the general rule relating, broadly, to the following:

- rights in remuneration (especially security rights),
- set-off,
- retention of title,

---

[44] Council Regulation (EC) No 1346/2000, art 3(1).

[45] Council Regulation (EC) No 1346/2000, art 3(2).

[46] Council Regulation (EC) No 1346/2000, arts 3(4) and 29; see also chapter 3 generally.

[47] For a case where the application of local assets to the secondary proceedings, rather than the main proceedings, was important, see *Re Alitalia Linee Aeree Italiane Spa; Connock and Boyden (as the joint liquidators in England and Wales of Alitalia Linee Aeree Italiane Spa) v Professor Fantozzi (as the administrator in the Republic of Italy of Alitalia Linee Aeree Italiane Spa)* [2011] EWHC 15 (Ch) [2011] BPIR 308, ChD.

[48] Council Regulation (EC) No 1346/2000, art 4(1).

- contracts relating to immovable property,
- matters concerning payment systems and financial markets,
- employment contracts,
- rights subject to registration,
- EC patents and trade marks,
- certain rights of third party purchasers,
- certain application relating to the voidability of transactions, and
- applications as to the effect of insolvency on existing proceedings to which the *lex situs* or *lex fori* will apply.

20.21 There is power to apply to stay secondary proceedings[49] or to close them.[50] The law applicable to secondary proceedings is that of the territory in which they have been opened.[51]

What is 'recognition between states'?

20.22 The Regulation provides for automatic recognition within member states[52] without formality.[53] The judgment opening the main proceedings takes direct effect in other states, save as otherwise provided.[54] The same applies to other judgments.[55] Note, however the public policy exception.[56]

20.23 The term judgment has a wider meaning than the normal. A judgment may include a resolution for creditors' voluntary liquidation or the appointment of an administrator out of court.

How do main and secondary proceedings work together?

20.24 The Regulation is designed so that main and secondary proceedings work together; thus it provides for duties of co-operation and communication.[57] There are provisions for the protection of creditors' rights generally[58] designed to ensure *pari passu* distribution.

---

49 Council Regulation (EC) No 1346/2000, art 33.
50 Council Regulation (EC) No 1346/2000, art 34.
51 Council Regulation (EC) No 1346/2000, art 28.
52 Cross-Border Insolvency Regulations 2006, SI 2006/1030, art 16.
53 SI 2006/1030, art 17.
54 SI 2006/1030, art 17(1).
55 SI 2006/1030, art 25.
56 SI 2006/1030, art 26.
57 SI 2006/1030, art 31.
58 SI 2006/1030, arts 13 and 20: the 'hotchpot' provision.

20.25 Creditors (and the liquidator) may claim in main or secondary proceedings.[59] There is provision (in very broad terms) for the Regulation to apply to temporary administrators (provisional liquidators, interim receivers etc).[60]

What is the UNCITRAL Model law and what effect does it have?

20.26 The UNCITRAL Model Law on Cross-Border Insolvency took effect in Great Britain (England, Wales and Scotland but not Northern Ireland) on 4 April 2006. It was implemented by the Cross-Border Insolvency Regulations 2006[61] under power contained in s 14, Insolvency Act 2000 (IA 2000).

20.27 Its aim is to promote international co-operation in the conduct of insolvency proceedings by facilitating the recognition of insolvency office holders and providing access to the relevant courts. Broadly, it:

- enables a foreign court or foreign office holder ('foreign representative') to seek recognition of foreign proceedings in the UK;
- enables a foreign representative to seek direct access to the UK courts;
- enables creditors and other interested parties in a foreign state to request the commencement of or participate in British insolvency proceedings;
- provides a framework for international co-operation in international insolvency cases.

20.28 The Model Law does not regulate questions of jurisdiction or choice of law in the way the EC Regulation on Insolvency Proceedings seeks to do. The Regulation contains and enacts the Model Law;[62] regulates procedure in England and Wales[63] and Scotland;[64] deals with notices to be delivered to the registrar of companies;[65] and prescribes forms.[66]

Which courts have jurisdiction?

20.29 The 'competent court' for recognition and co-operation purposes is defined in art 4(1), Model Law (Sch 1). Jurisdiction is given to the High Court only (and specifically the Chancery Division) so any application must be dealt

---

59 SI 2006/1030, art 32.
60 SI 2006/1030, art 3.
61 SI 2006/1030.
62 SI 2006/1030, Sch 1.
63 SI 2006/1030, Sch 2.
64 SI 2006/1030, Sch 3.
65 SI 2006/1030, Sch 4.
66 SI 2006/1030, Sch 5.

with by the Royal Courts of Justice in London or a Chancery District Registry. Article 4(1) Model Law (Sch 1) in conjunction with para 1(3) of Sch 2 provides that:

> 'In proceedings under these Regulations, "Registrar" means:
>
> - a Registrar in Bankruptcy of the High Court; and
> - where the proceedings are in a district registry, the district judge.'

20.30 Subject to that the court having jurisdiction is further defined by art 4(2), Model Law (Sch 1). The court will:

> 'have jurisdiction if the debtor has
>
> - a place of business; or in the case of an individual, a place of residence; or assets situated in that part of Great Britain; or
> - the court in that part of Great Britain considers for any other reason that it is the appropriate forum in which to consider the question or provide the assistance requested.'

The 'part of Great Britain' referred to is England and Wales, not the jurisdiction of, say, a district registry.

20.31 Article 4(3) of the Model Law (Sch 1) provides:

> 'In considering whether it is the appropriate forum to hear an application for recognition of a foreign proceeding in relation to a debtor, the court shall take into account the location of any court in which a proceeding under British insolvency law is taking place in relation to the debtor and the likely location of any future proceedings under British insolvency law in relation to the debtor.'

It would seem, therefore, that one starts from the presumptions in art 4(2) (which relate to the location of business, residence and assets), but that flexibility is imported by art 4(3) (which refers to the location of other proceedings). The practical result is that the majority of applications are heard in the Royal Courts of Justice, but applications are made to the relevant Chancery district registries where the debtor has a connection of the kind specified with the relevant area or where there are existing or likely proceedings in that area.

20.32 There is no definition of 'debtor', but the term includes an individual or corporation as the law and the Regulations make references to companies and to the delivery of notices to the registrar of companies, and a whole range of provisions defining 'foreign representative' and 'foreign proceedings' are widely framed to provide for both individuals and corporations.

What entities are included or excluded?

20.33 The law does not apply to proceedings concerning a wide range of entities such as utility suppliers, railways and financial and public bodies.[67]

What are the key concepts?

20.34 A foreign proceeding is 'a collective judicial or administrative proceeding in a foreign state, including an interim proceeding, pursuant to a law relating to insolvency in which proceeding the assets and affairs of the debtor are subject to control or supervision by a foreign court, for the purpose of reorganisation or liquidation'.[68]

20.35 Proceedings are classified as 'foreign main proceedings' and 'foreign non-main proceedings'. A foreign main proceeding is one which takes place in the state where the debtor has his centre of main interests.[69] In the absence of proof to the contrary the debtor's registered office (in the case of a corporation) or habitual residence (in the case of an individual) is presumed to be his centre of main interests.[70] A foreign non-main proceeding is one which takes place in a state where the debtor has an establishment.[71] An establishment means any place of operations where the debtor carries out a non-transitory economic activity with human means and assets or services.[72]

20.36 The nature of the proceedings is important for two primary reasons:

- the foreign representative may only rely on the Model Law if he can establish that proceedings are main or non-main;
- a main proceeding gives rise to an automatic stay[73] whereas a non-main proceeding simply gives rise to the exercise of discretion to grant relief.[74]

What are the applications that can be made?

20.37 Article 9 provides generally (under the heading 'Right of direct access') that, 'A foreign representative is entitled to apply directly to a court in Great Britain'.

Schedule 2 deals with procedural matters in England and Wales relating to an application for recognition and a number of other applications.

---

67 SI 2006/1030, Sch 1, art 1(1) and (2).
68 SI 2006/1030, Sch 1, art 2(i).
69 SI 2006/1030, Sch 1, art 2(g).
70 As with the EC Regulation, a rebuttable presumption is created; Cross-Border Insolvency Regulations 2006, SI 2006/1030, Sch 1, art 16(3).
71 SI 2006/1030, Sch 1, art 2(h).
72 SI 2006/1030, Sch 1, art 2(e). See the provision in the EC Regulation.
73 SI 2006/1030, Sch 1, art 20.
74 SI 2006/1030, Sch 1, art 21.

What are recognition proceedings?

20.38 Recognition proceedings are dealt with in Chapter II of Sch 1 and Part 2 of Sch 2.

Article 15(1) provides specifically for an application for recognition. Part 2 of Sch 2 ('procedural matters') makes more detailed provisions as to procedure.

The application must be made in form ML1[75] and guides the applicant through what it must contain. Paragraph 3 of Sch 2 provides that the application must state the following:

- the name of the applicant and his address for service in England and Wales;
- the name of the debtor in respect of whom the foreign proceeding is taking place;
- the name or names in which the debtor carries on business in the country where the foreign proceeding is taking place and in this country, if other than the name previously given (see above);
- the principal; or last known place of business of the debtor in Great Britain (if any) and, in the case of an individual, his usual or last known place of residence in Great Britain (if any);
- any registered number allocated to the debtor under the Companies Act;[76]
- brief particulars of the foreign proceeding in respect of which recognition is applied for, including the country in which it is taking place and the nature of the proceeding;
- that the foreign proceeding is a proceeding within the meaning of art 2(i) of the Model Law;
- that the applicant is a foreign representative within the meaning of art 2(j) of the Model Law;
- the address of the debtor's centre of main interests and, if different, the address of its registered office or habitual residence, as appropriate;
- if the debtor does not have its centre of main interests in the country where the foreign proceeding is taking place, whether the debtor has an establishment within the meaning of art 2(e) of the Model Law in that country and, if so, its address.[77]

---

75 SI 2006/1030, Sch 2, para 2.

76 This provision and certain others clearly cannot apply in the case of an individual.

77 SI 2006/1030, Sch 3 para 3(a)–(j).

20.39 The court must first be satisfied that it has jurisdiction to deal with the application. Article 17(1)(d) provides for the application to be made to the court referred to in art 4, CBIR 2006, which as we have seen is the Chancery Division of the High Court. Article 4 provides that the High Court shall have jurisdiction if:

- the debtor has a place of business in England and Wales or (in the case of an individual) a place of residence in England and Wales;[78] or
- the debtor has assets in England and Wales;[79] or
- the court considers, for any other reason, that it is the appropriate forum to consider the question or provide the assistance required.[80]

20.40 Secondly, the court must be satisfied that the application relaters to a 'foreign proceeding' as defined by art 2(i), that is to say:

> 'a collective judicial or administrative proceeding in a foreign state, including an interim proceeding, pursuant to a law relating to insolvency in which proceeding the assets and affairs of the debtor are subject to control or supervision by a foreign court for the purpose of reorganisation or liquidation.'

20.41 The foreign proceeding in question must not be an excluded proceeding within the meaning of Sch 1, art 1.2, CBIR 2006 (which sets out the proceedings to which the Law does not apply).

20.42 Thirdly, the court must be satisfied that the applicant is a foreign representative as defined by art 2(j), CBIR 2006, that is to say,

> 'a person or body, including one appointed on an interim basis, authorised in a foreign proceeding to administer the reorganisation or the liquidation of the debtor's assets or affairs or to act as a representative of the foreign proceeding.'

What other documentation is required?

20.43 The application must be supported by an affidavit. Schedule 2, para 4, CBIR 2006 deals with the contents of the affidavit in support which must contain or exhibit the following:

- a certified copy of the decision commencing the foreign proceedings and appointing the foreign representative or a certificate from the foreign court affirming the existence of those proceedings; and the appointment of the foreign representative; or in the absence of such evidence any other evidence acceptable to the court of the existence of the foreign proceedings and the appointment of the foreign representative;

---

78 SI 2006/1030, Sch 1, art 4(2)(a)(i) and (ii).

79 SI 2006/1030, Sch 1, art 4(2)(a)(iii).

80 SI 2006/1030, Sch 1, art 4(2)(b).

- any other evidence which in the opinion of the applicant will assist the court in deciding whether the proceeding is a foreign proceeding and whether the applicant is a foreign representative within the meaning of art 2(j) of the Model Law;

- evidence that the debtor has his centre of main interests or an establishment within the country in which the foreign proceeding is taking place;

- any other matters which will assist the court in deciding whether to make a recognition order;

- the translations (into English) required by art 15(4) together with translations of any other foreign language documents relied on;[81] the translations must be certified.[82]

- The affidavit must also state whether in the applicant's opinion the EC Regulation on Insolvency Proceedings applies to any of the proceedings identified under art 15(3) Model Law and if so whether they are main, secondary or territorial.[83]

20.44 The application should generally be served[84] (although the court may direct otherwise) and service should be proved.[85] Further guidance as to the presentation of material to the court was given in *Re Rajapakse (Note)*.[86]

20.45 The Regulation is not part of the IA86 or the IR86. It may be assumed, therefore, that the CPR applies rather than the IR86 (save to the extent that Regulation makes its own procedural provisions or incorporates rules taken from the IR86, as it does). Query therefore whether in fact evidence can be given other than by affidavit (CPR 32.6, which provides that evidence at hearings other than trial may be given by witness statement unless the court, a practice direction or any enactment requires otherwise; cf. also the power of the court to control evidence under CPR 32.1).

20.46 The application will generally be heard and determined by the registrar or district judge, although there may be cases of sufficient weight and complexity to warrant referral to the judge (a High Court Chancery judge). Article 17(3) provides that the application 'shall be decided upon at the earliest possible time'.

20.47 Article 17(1) Model Law provides that:

---

81 SI 2006/1030, Sch 1, art 4(3).
82 SI 2006/1030, Sch 1, art 4(4).
83 SI 2006/1030, Sch 1, art 4(3).
84 SI 2006/1030, Sch 2, paras 21 and 22.
85 Schedule 2, para 23; there is a prescribed form, ML6.
86 [2007] BPIR 99.

'Subject to Article 6 [public policy exception] a foreign proceeding shall be recognised if the following apply:

- it is a foreign proceedings as defined;[87]
- the foreign representative applying is a person or body as defined;[88]
- the application meets the requirements of paragraphs 2 and 3 of Article 15; and
- the application has been submitted to the court referred to in Article 4.'

Article 17(2) provides that a foreign proceeding shall be recognised:

- as a foreign main proceeding if it is taking place where the debtor has the centre of its main interests; or
- as a foreign non-main proceeding if the debtor has an establishment within the meaning of para(e) of art 2 in the foreign State.

So in spite of the fact that Sch 2, para 5(1) (which deals with the hearing and the powers of the court) provides that the court may dismiss, adjourn (conditionally or unconditionally) or make any other order it thinks appropriate, the presumption must be that discretion is limited and that the court will as a general rule make the order as mandated by art 17(1).

20.48 It would appear, however, that an order may be refused on public policy grounds. Article 6 creates a public policy exception (which does not apply to revenue claims).

An important consideration will be the effect of recognition as provided by art 20 Model Law. Upon recognition of a foreign main proceeding:

- commencement or continuation of actions or proceedings is stayed;
- execution is stayed;
- the right to transfer, encumber or dispose of assets is stayed;
- as if a debtor had been adjudged bankrupt or a winding up order made (art 20(1) and (2)). Note, however, the exceptions relating to enforcing security, HP repossessions etc.

The effects of granting recognition are the same as the making of a bankruptcy order or a compulsory winding up order.[89]

20.49 There are strong indications that a purposive approach should be taken to giving effect to the Model Law. Paragraph 3 of the Regulation provides for

---

87 Council Regulation (EC) No 1346/2000, art 2(i).

88 Council Regulation (EC) No 1346/2000, art 2(j).

89 SI 2006/1030, Sch 1, art 20(2).

the modification of British insolvency law for the purpose of giving effect to the Model Law and for the Regulations to prevail where there is conflict. However, art 3 of the model law itself gives precedence to the EC Regulation on Insolvency Proceedings where there is conflict with it. Article 8 provides that the Law must be interpreted with regard to 'its international origin and the need to promote uniformity in its application and the observance of good faith'.

20.50 If an order is made it must be in the prescribed form, ML2. There is a form ML3 which provides for further information to be given to the court if required.

What applications for relief are available under the Model Law?

20.51 Article 19, Model Law allows the foreign representative to apply for interim relief 'from the time of filing an application for recognition … where relief is urgently needed to protect assets of the debtor or the interests of creditors'. It seems likely that the majority of these applications will be for injunctions, in which case they will have to go before a Chancery judge. The relevant procedural provisions are set out in Sch 2, paras 7–9 and contain no surprises.

20.52 Article 21 contains details of an array of other applications which may be made to protect assets or the interests of creditors including;

- staying the commencement or continuation of actions or proceedings;
- staying execution;
- suspending the right to transfer, encumber or dispose of assets;
- examination of witnesses or taking evidence or delivery of information about the debtor's assets, affairs, rights obligations or liabilities;
- entrusting the administration of assets in Great Britain to the foreign representative or some other person;
- extending relief granted under art 19(1) (urgent interim relief);
- granting additional relief that may be available to a British insolvency office holder under domestic law including any under para 43 of Sch B1, IA86.

Most of that will probably be dealt with at registrar/district judge level, but again some of that relief may well be in the exclusive domain of the judge (where it is in the nature of an injunction).

What is the process for replacing a foreign representative?

20.53 Schedule 2, paras 12–14 deal with the replacement of a foreign representative who has died or ceases to be the representative in the foreign proceedings.

20.54 Schedule 2, paras 15–17 deal with the power to review orders. There is power to review but there is a restriction relating to orders made by the court of its own motion. The court may not make a modification or termination order (ie an order made by the court under its powers under the Model Law modifying or terminating the recognition of a foreign proceeding, the stay and suspension referred to in art 20(1) (the automatic stay created by recognition) or any part of it or any relief granted under arts 19 or 21).[90]

What other applications can be made under the model law?

20.55 The category of available applications is not closed. Article 7 provides that nothing in the model law limits the power of a court or a British insolvency office holder to provide additional assistance to a foreign representative under other laws of Great Britain.

What other miscellaneous rules are applicable?

20.56 Schedule 2 ends with a set of miscellaneous rules which will be familiar as they have been largely lifted out of the IR86. However, proceedings under the Regulations are not primarily insolvency proceedings, the CPR apply, and the proceedings are multi-track.

---

[90] SI 2006/1030, Sch 2, para 1 (definitions). See also arts 22, 23 and 24 which deal with the protection of creditors and others, avoidance provisions and the intervention in proceedings by a foreign representative. There are also provisions as to cooperation with foreign courts and foreign representatives (arts 25, 26 and 27).

Chapter 21

INSOLVENT DECEASED ESTATES

'Will he pay all his debts before he leaves here? ... it seems to me hard that he should pay in life and money both?'[1]

INTRODUCTION

21.1 This chapter deals with the effect of death on a person who may be insolvent. There is a common misconception that a person's debts die with them. This is not the case. As with insolvent individuals that are alive there are both formal and informal solutions and these are set out below for England and Wales, Northern Ireland and Scotland. When the estate of a deceased person is insolvent the provisions of any will made relating to the beneficiaries no longer applies. This is a general rule which applies in all jurisdictions.

ENGLAND AND WALES

21.2 In England and Wales the right to appoint by will an executor to administer the personal estate and chattel interests in land of a testator, derives from the earliest period of English law which was later extended to include real estate. The appointment by the Ecclesiastical Courts of Administrators in cases of intestacy or failure to appoint an executor developed much later. The Chancery Division of the High Court now has jurisdiction in all matters concerning the administration and distribution of estates although the courts are rarely now involved.

21.3 In England and Wales an insolvent estate is normally administered under the provisions of the Administration of Insolvent Estates of Deceased Persons Order 1986 (IDP86) and s 421, IA86. This primary legislation was amended by The Administration of Insolvent Estates of Deceased Persons (Amendment) Order 2002.[2] In effect existing bankruptcy rules and regulations apply but with the modifications set out in these orders.

21.4 In all cases funeral and administration expenses are paid before any other debts.[3] The balance of the assets must then be distributed in accordance with the law of bankruptcy. There are several ways in which an insolvent estate of a deceased person can be formally administered depending on the timing of

---

1 Dickens, *Little Dorrit* (Penguin Books, 1994), Chapter 35.

2 SI 2002/1309.

3 Administration of Insolvent Estates of Deceased Persons Order 1986, SI 1986/1999, art 5(2) (as amended) and IA86, s 305 as amended by SI 1986/1999, Sch II para 20.

the death and any legal actions existing at that time including bankruptcy petitions, interim orders or other legal actions.

21.5 The following are some of the formal solutions:

- When a bankruptcy order has been made before death the trustee will continue to deal with the estate[4] with the modifications set out in Sch 2 of the IDP86.[5] These are set out below and relate to the submission of a Statement of Affairs and funeral expenses.

- After death, when an estate is insolvent, a petition (application) to the court for an insolvency administration order can be made by any creditor or the legal personal representatives. This is similar to a bankruptcy order on a creditor's petition.[6] The Insolvency Rules 1986 apply but as modified by Sch 1, Part II, IDP 1986.

- Alternatively a petition can be made by the personal representatives and this is equivalent to a debtor's own petition.[7] The IR86 apply but as modified by Sch 1, Part II, IDP 1986.

- Where an interim order has been for an IVA and the debtor dies before the s 257 meeting has approved the proposal, the interim order must be discharged.[8] The court must be notified of the death.[9]

- Where a debtor who is in an approved IVA dies, it is thought that the IVA then terminates[10]. There is uncertainty because IDP86 Sch 1, Part III, Para 4 provides that, among other things, upon the death of the debtor IA86, s 260 (which deals with the effect of approval of the proposal for the IVA) ceases to apply. The court must in any event be notified of the death.[11]

- Finally there can be administration by the Chancery Court which is rare. This involves Administration under a court order and requires an application for a grant of representation by the official solicitor under s 116 Supreme Court Act 1981 which is made on the direction of the Chancery Court.[12]

---

4 IDP86, art 5(1).
5 IDP86.
6 IDP86, Sch 3, Form 1.
7 IDP86, Sch 3, Form 6.
8 IDP86, Sch 1, Part III, para 1(1B).
9 IDP86, Sch 1, Part III, para 1(1A).
10 Because IDP86, Sch 1, Part III, Para 4 provides that, among other things, upon the death of the debtor IA86, s 260 (which deals with the effect of approval of the proposal for the IVA) ceases to apply.
11 IDP86, para 5(b).
12 See INS9548 on http://www.hmrc.gov.uk/manuals/insmanual/ins9548.htm.

21.6 The relevant date for the purposes of these processes is the date of death whether the estate is administered as a formal administration under IDP86[13] or an informal administration by a personal representative, a relative, accountant or solicitor.

Who are the key players in a deceased estate?

21.7 The key players in an insolvent deceased's estate include the following:

- Deceased person or testator (where the deceased person has left a valid will).
- The legal personal representative of the deceased person.
- The executor of the estate.
- The administrator of the estate.
- The OR (covered in detail in chapter 2).

Who is the personal representative and what are their duties?

21.8 The expression 'personal representative' is used to describe either an executor (whether they have proved the will or not) or an administrator of a deceased person. The personal representatives represent the deceased in regard to their real and personal estate and are deemed in law to be their heirs and assigns within the meaning of the law of trusts and powers.

21.9 On the application of a personal representative or of a beneficiary, the court has power to appoint a judicial trustee to act in the administration of a deceased person's property and, if sufficient cause is shown, to displace the personal representative. The court also has power to appoint a person to act as personal representative in place of the existing personal representative or representatives of them.

Who can be the executor and what are their duties?

21.10 An executor is the person appointed by the testator in their will to administer the testator's property and to carry into effect the provisions of the will. An executor may be appointed either:

- expressly by the testator in the body of their will;
- by the exercise of a power of nominating an executor conferred by the testator by their will;
- by implication from the testator's will or by virtue of statutory provisions.

---

[13] SI 1986/1999.

21.11 The executor may accept or reject the office as the title derives from the will. An executor can act before probate has been granted and is appointed for an indefinite period until all the provisions of the will or all of the testator's property has been dealt with. The acceptance of the office of executor is usually evidenced by the person appointed obtaining a grant of probate. However, acceptance can be inferred by acts by a nominated person which show intention to accept the office. A person appointed executor who has not acted to show an intention of accepting the office and who does not wish to act may renounce the office, either personally or by power of attorney. The renunciation is not final until it is lodged and recorded in the proper court. An executor who has acted to show an intention of accepting the office cannot later renounce the position. Only the court has discretion to replace any person who may no longer wish to act. An executorship cannot be assigned at common law because it is an office of personal trust. It can only devolve by operation of law.

21.12 An executor or administrator has the statutory power of a trustee to delegate by power of attorney the exercise of any trusts, powers or discretions vested in them as trustee for a period not exceeding 12 months. Any executor who has obtained probate or any administrator who has obtained letters of administration may, with the consent of the court, and after giving notice to the persons beneficially interested, transfer the estate to the Public Trustee for administration either solely or jointly with the continuing executors or administrators.

Who is the administrator and what are their duties?

21.13 An administrator is a person appointed by a court to administer the property of a deceased person usually where the deceased has died intestate. The administrator derives their title entirely from the grant of letters of administration, and the deceased's property does not vest in them until the grant is received. As a result the administrator cannot make any disposition before the grant. After the grant of administration the administrator has, subject to the limitations contained in the grant, the same rights and liabilities and is accountable in the same way as if they were the executor of the deceased. The administration of the property of a deceased person, whether they die testate or intestate, is a trust within the meaning of the Judicial Trustees Act 1896 so the court may appoint a judicial trustee either to act jointly with or in place of a personal representative.

What is a grant of probate and when is one required?

21.14 A grant of representation from the court (Probate Office) is required for a legal personal representative (executor or administrator) to administer a deceased estate, usually a grant of probate will be required when there is a will and one or more of the executors named in the will need to apply for the grant. Alternatively a grant of letters of administration (when there is no will) or 'letters of administration with will annexed' (issued when there is a will but no proving executor) must be obtained. The administrator's or executor's authority dates from the date of the grant. There are provisions for small estates to be administered without the need for a grant of representation. The executor's authority dates from the death of the deceased.

21.15 In certain cases small amounts of money may be disposed of by nomination or by payment to persons appearing to be entitled to them and no grant of probate or administration is required. In general however, a grant of probate or letters of administration in the United Kingdom is necessary to enable the personal representatives to make title to the deceased's property and thereafter to administer, collect and protect it for the benefit of the persons interested in the estate, whether as creditors, legatees or next of kin. In particular a grant is essential if the estate comprises real property or securities.

What informal solutions are available?

21.16 A legal personal representative may administer an insolvent deceased's estate on an informal basis (instead of going to the expense of applying for an order for the administration of a deceased insolvent estate). It should be administered in a similar way to a bankruptcy and normally the legal personal representative will have to confirm that they are happy to do this. In this case the trustee of the estate is not required to be a licensed insolvency practitioner.[14]

What formal solutions are available?

21.17 Most formal solutions are subject to the provisions of the IDP86[15] and s 421, IA86. In the case of any conflict between any provisions of the IR86[16] and any provision of the IDP86, the latter will always prevail.[17]

What is the statutory framework for a formal solution?

21.18 The amendments to the IA86 and IR86 are set out in the IDP86.[18] The main changes to the bankruptcy parts of the IA86 and IR86 are amendments to the terminology that is used. There are also amendments to the priority of expenses in that priority of reasonable funeral and testamentary expenses can be paid in priority to any preferential debts and administration expenses if there available funds.[19] In addition the preparation and submission of a statement of affairs have different requirements which are set out below.

---

14 IDP86, art 4(3).

15 SI 1986/1999.

16 SI 1986/1925.

17 IDP86, art 3.

18 SI 1986/1999.

19 In respect of an estate being administered outside the formal bankruptcy process see art 4(2); for cases where death occurs post petition see art 5(2); and for cases where an order is made post death see amendments made IDP86, Sch 1.

Who can present a petition for an insolvency administration order for a deceased person?

21.19 Where a person dies before a bankruptcy petition has been presented the following people are entitled to present a petition to court:

- a creditor or creditors jointly of the estate;
- the deceased's personal representative (the equivalent of a debtors petition but made on an amended form);
- a temporary administrator (within the meaning of Art 38 of the EC Regulation on Insolvency Proceedings);
- a liquidator appointed in proceedings by virtue of Art 3(1) of the EC Regulation on Insolvency Proceedings;
- where the deceased entered into a voluntary arrangement, the supervisor of that arrangement or a creditor bound by it;
- the official petitioner, where the deceased person was subject to a criminal bankruptcy order.

A petition for an insolvency administration order may not be presented where proceedings for the administration of the deceased debtor's estate have commenced in another court, for example, where a suit has been instituted in the Chancery Division for the administration of the deceased debtor's estate. Such proceedings may be transferred to the bankruptcy court where it appears that the estate is insolvent, thus enabling an insolvency administration order to be made.

What is the process for a creditor petition?

21.20 Similar rules apply as those set out for bankruptcy in chapter 7. The creditor or personal representative must be able to demonstrate to the court that the estate is insolvent before an order will be granted. The court can appoint the OR as interim receiver to protect the assets in the period between the presentation of that petition and the making of an insolvency administration order. The OR as interim receiver has all the powers and duties of a receiver and manager (see chapter 2) however the duties may be restricted and these restrictions must be observed. The personal representative has a duty to co-operate with the interim receiver and to provide full details of the assets. If the OR is appointed as interim receiver then the assets will be taken into immediate possession pending the hearing of the petition.

What happens if an insolvency administration order is made?

21.21 The OR becomes receiver and manager when the insolvency administration order is made, and control of the estate is removed from the personal representative on that date. Where the personal representative has notice of the petition, he/she is restrained from disposing of any of the assets of the estate. If the OR becomes aware that such a disposal has been made by the personal representative after notice of the petition, and it has not been subsequently ratified by the court, the person to whom the payment has been made or the asset been transferred must be notified immediately requiring them to hold the monies or property to the order of the OR for the benefit of the insolvent estate. Title to the assets of the estate will date back to the date of death as if the presentation of the petition, the insolvency administration order and the death all took place on the same day.[20]

21.22 If there are sufficient assets to warrant the appointment of an insolvency practitioner as trustee, the OR will call a meeting of creditors in the same way as for a bankruptcy appointment (see chapter 12 for appointment and chapter 14 for convening of meetings) however all correspondence and communication must make it clear that the meeting and the proceedings generally relate to an insolvency administration order and not to a bankruptcy order. The proof of debt forms must show the date of death as being the date to which claims should be made. In contrast to bankruptcy the OR has no statutory duty to investigate the affairs of a deceased debtor unless thought appropriate.[21]

21.23 The court can annul an insolvency administration order if the order should not have been made or if the debts and costs of the proceedings have been paid in full or secured to the satisfaction of the court.

21.24 One particular provision that is overlooked is that upon the making of the insolvency administration order IA86, ss 283–285 have effect as if the petition had been presented and the insolvency administration order made on the date of the death of the deceased. This means that all dispositions of the estate of the deceased from death (pre-insolvency administration order) and the appointment of a trustee in bankruptcy (post-insolvency administration order) are void under IA86, s 284, even though the death might have been many years before the insolvency administration order or dispositions entered into at a time when insolvency simply was not contemplated.[22]

What are the personal representative's duties in relation to the official receiver?

21.25 The personal representative has similar duties to that of a bankrupt in a bankruptcy (see chapter 9). The personal representative must do the following:

- provide a statement of affairs to the OR within 56 days of the order being made. The personal representative is required to complete this, or, in the

---

20 IDP86, Sch 1, Part II paras 12, 22, 27, 29, 31 and 35 which modify ss 283–285, 307, 341, 359, 382 and 387 of the IA86.

21 IDP86, Sch 1, Part II, para 16 which modifies s 289 of the IA86.

22 See Re *Vos; Dick v Kendall Freeman* [2006] BPIR 348, a decision of Chief Registrar Baister.

absence of a personal representative, such other person as the court may direct.[23] See below for more information on the content of the statement;

- in addition to the statement, notify the OR of any assets which can be claimed for the estate;
- provide a list of all the assets;
- attend on the OR as reasonably required;
- provide information regarding the assets, liabilities and affairs of the deceased debtor.

21.26 If a personal representative fails to comply with their obligations they can be found guilty of a contempt of court, and the OR can apply for a private examination (see chapter 9). Some protection is given to a personal representative regarding asset disposals made between the presentation of a petition for an insolvency administration order and the date of the order so long as the disposal was carried out in good faith. Good faith will normally be construed as meaning without notice of the petition or without awareness of the insolvency of the deceased debtor.

What information has to be provided in the statement of affairs?

21.27 The statement of affairs must include the financial position of the estate at the date of death and at the making of the insolvency administration order and evidence the transactions between the two dates. It is completed on the statutory form[24] and must be submitted together with a copy of the last will made by the deceased and a copy of the death certificate.

What is the priority of payments from a deceased estate?

21.28 Reasonable funeral and testamentary expenses can be paid in priority to any preferential debts and administration expenses if there are available funds.[25] In *Re Kitson Exp Thomas Sugden and Son Ltd*[26] the issue of priority of payments was discussed including the status of debts that had accrued after death such as rent. It was confirmed that these could not be creditors of the deceased's estate. There is also no opportunity for the administrator of a deceased estate to disclaim onerous property.

---

23 IDP86, Sch 1, Part II, para 15 which modifies s 288, IA86.

24 IDP86, Sch 3, Form 7.

25 In respect of an estate being administered outside the formal bankruptcy process see art 4(2); for cases where death occurs post petition see art 5(2); and for cases where an order is made post death see amendments made IDP86, Sch 1.

26 [1911] 2KB 109.

What are the official receivers duties in respect of an insolvency administration order?

21.29 The OR has the normal duties of a receiver and manager or trustee in bankruptcy. In addition, if the OR is trustee, he/she must have regard to any claim made by the personal representative in respect of reasonable funeral, testamentary and administrative expenses incurred. These claims have priority over the preferential debts, but are only payable from the estate balance if it is in credit after all administrative expenses of the insolvency administration order have been paid. The OR should take account of such a claim before making any distribution to creditors.

21.30 As trustee, the OR's title to the assets dates back to the date of death as if the presentation of the petition, the insolvency administration order and the death all took place on the same day. A deceased debtor's share in property held on a joint tenancy does not form part of his/her estate which passes under his/her will or intestacy; it passes by survivorship to the surviving joint tenant. Because of the right of survivorship when an insolvency administration order is made, the deceased debtor's interest in jointly held assets, such as a balance in a jointly held bank account, will pass to the surviving partner. The deceased debtor's interest in jointly held assets (other than those held under a tenancy in common – discussed below) will not fall within the estate.

What happens to property that was owned under a joint tenancy by the deceased debtor prior to his/her death?

21.31 Prior to the Insolvency Act 2000 (IA 2000)[27] the operation of the right of survivorship in relation to a jointly-owned property was not affected by a subsequent insolvency administration order against the deceased, with the effect that the deceased's former interest in the property was lost to the bankruptcy estate.[28] Now, the value[29] of the deceased's former interest in the property that would be lost (not the interest in the property itself) can be brought into the bankruptcy estate of the deceased.[30] The new cause of action amounts to a money claim against the surviving joint owner, or owners.[31] In determining whether to make an order under this section, and the terms of such an order, the court must have regard to all the circumstances of the case, including the interests of the deceased's creditors and of the survivor; but, unless the circumstances are exceptional, the court must assume that the

---

27 Insolvency Act 2000, s 12(1).

28 See *Re Palmer (Deceased) (A Debtor)* [1994] Ch 316.

29 For these purposes, 'value lost to the estate' means the amount which, if paid to the trustee, would in the court's opinion restore the position to what it would have been if the deceased had been adjudged bankrupt immediately before his death; IA86, s 421A(9).

30 IA86, s 421(A)(1).

31 For these purposes, 'survivor' means the person who, immediately before the death, was beneficially entitled as joint tenant with the deceased or, if the person who was so entitled dies after the making of the insolvency administration order, his personal representatives; IA86, s 421(7). If there is more than one survivor an order may be made against all or any of them, but no survivor shall be required to pay more than so much of the value lost to the estate as is properly attributable to him; IA86, s 421A(8).

interests of the deceased's creditors outweigh all other considerations.[32] Such an application requires an Insolvency Administration Order based on a petition presented after 2 April 2001 and made within 5 years of the date of death.[33]

21.32 An identical amendment was made in Northern Ireland by the Insolvency (Northern Ireland) Order 2002 which is covered in detail in the next section.

The table below is extracted from the impact assessment of the IA 2000.

Year	**1998**	**1999**	**2000**	**2001**	**2002**	**2003**	**2004**	**2005**
Bankruptcy Orders	19,647	21,611	21,550	23,477	24,292	28,021	35,898	47,287
Section 421A cases	1	6	9	11	8	12	7	3

Source: DTI Impact Assessment for IA 2000

What happens when a debtor dies after a bankruptcy petition is presented?

21.33 When a debtor dies after a bankruptcy petition is presented the bankruptcy proceedings will continue in the normal way, and if an order is made by the court it is a bankruptcy order and is administered accordingly, with some necessary modifications. The deceased debtor's personal representative or other appropriate person is required to complete a statement of affairs. The reasonable funeral and testamentary expenses have priority over the preferential debts, whether the deceased debtor dies before or after the making of the bankruptcy order.

21.34 Where a deceased debtor owned property under a joint tenancy and died after a bankruptcy petition was presented but before a bankruptcy order was made, the deceased debtor's interest in the property passes to the surviving tenant and does not form part of the estate. Section 421A, IA86 does not apply in this case, and the value lost to the estate cannot be recovered under this section.[34]

NORTHERN IRELAND

21.35 In Northern Ireland the legislative regime mirrors that in England and Wales and is governed by the Administration of Insolvent Estates of Deceased Persons Order (Northern Ireland) 1991[35] with subsequent changes made by

---

32 IA86, s 421A(3).

33 IA86, s 421A(1)(a).

34 However, the operation of the rule of survivorship might be regarded as an involuntary disposition by the debtor, such that it is void under IA86, s 284.

35 SR 1991/365.

Art 10 of Insolvency (Northern Ireland) Order 2002[36] together with the Administration of Insolvent Estates of Deceased Persons (Amendment) Order (Northern Ireland) 2003.[37]

21.36 Article 10 of Insolvency (Northern Ireland) Order 2002[38] inserted a new art 365A into the IO89 by addressing the effects of the Court of Appeal decision in the case of *Re Palmer Deceased (A Debtor)*.[39] In March 1994 the Court of Appeal attributed the ordinary, rather than the technical, meaning to 'the estate of a deceased person' used in the context of an order-making power in s 421, IA86.[40] This meant that the debtor's interest, on the day of his death, in property held on a joint tenancy (usually the matrimonial home) was no longer available to the trustee to distribute among the deceased's creditors. Article 365A, IO89 now allows the trustee of a deceased insolvent to apply to the High Court to recover the value of any interest the deceased had in a jointly-owned property from the survivor, for the benefit of the estate.[41]

SCOTLAND

21.37 When the estate of a deceased person is insolvent in Scotland the terms of any will made relating to the beneficiaries do **not** apply. Administration of the estate is usually governed by the Bankruptcy (Scotland) Act 1985.[42] Any executor, usually someone named in the will, who is aware or ought to be aware that the estate is insolvent and fails to petition the court for sequestration[43] or the appointment of a judicial factor may be held liable for some or all of the deceased's debts.

Judicial Factor

What is a Judicial Factor and what role do they play?

21.38 The appointment of a judicial factor is governed by the Judicial Factors Acts of 1849, 1880 and 1889 and the Children (Scotland) Act 1995. Judicial factors are appointed by the Court of Session, and supervised by the accountant of court, to manage and administer property in a range of different circumstances. The function of a judicial factor is to conserve and manage the estate under their charge but the estate does not vest in them.

21.39 A judicial factor is usually appointed to manage and administer estates in cases when it is necessary to afford protection against loss or injustice which cannot be prevented by means of any ordinary legal remedy. There is no limit

36 SI 2002/3152 (NI 6).
37 SR 2003/103.
38 SI 2002/3152 (NI 6).
39 1994 Ch 316.
40 In Northern Ireland, art 365.
41 Specific conditions need to be met.
42 Bankruptcy (Scotland) Act 1985, s 5(3).
43 BSA85, s 5(3)(a).

to the circumstances in which a judicial factor may be appointed but for this book the main concern is the administration of an insolvent deceased person's estate. To demonstrate the wide applicability of these powers some of the other uses are:

- intestate estates (on the application of a creditor or a person interested in the succession of the deceased estate);
- trust estates (for example, when there is a total failure of trustees or there has been misconduct on their part);
- partnership estates (either to carry on the business or to wind it up when, for example, there is a serious dispute as to the running of the business);
- estates of defaulting solicitors (for failure to comply with the Solicitor's Accounts Rules);
- estates of limited companies (to protect the interests of mortgage and debenture holders or on application by an aggrieved shareholder on allegations of illegal and dishonest conduct by controlling directors);
- *curator bonis* to minors (to manage any property until a minor reaches the age of majority);
- *curator bonis* to persons of unsound mind (to manage and protect the property of the person).

21.40 In addition to appointing a judicial factor where the deceased's estate is insolvent, the court may also sequestrate the estate and place the property in the custody of a neutral person accountable to the court for the preservation and management of the property for the benefit of creditors or other interested parties. The exact role will be set out by the court when making the order. The affairs under the control of a judicial factor are called a 'factory' however they are fairly rare and the role of the judicial factor is currently subject to review and a discussion paper was published in 2010. Currently a report and proposed new legislation is being drafted.

Sequestration

Who can sequestrate a deceased insolvent's estate in Scotland?

21.41 The estate of a deceased debtor may also be sequestrated. In sequestration the estate vests in the trustee and the following people are entitled to petition for sequestration:

- an executor;[44]

---

[44] BSA85, s 8(3)(a)(i).

- someone entitled to be appointed as executor;[45]
- a trustee acting under a trust deed granted by the deceased. An interim or permanent trustee will be appointed and the same procedures apply as for sequestration;[46]
- a temporary administrator;[47]
- the trustee of main proceedings opened in another EU state;[48]
- a qualified creditor with the following provisions:
  - in a case where the apparent insolvency of the debtor was constituted within 4 months before his death, at any time;
  - in any other case (whether or not apparent insolvency has been constituted), not earlier than 6 months after the debtor's death.

When can a sequestration order be recalled on a deceased estate?

21.42 The detailed procedural matters for sequestrations including the meaning of apparent insolvency are not covered in detail in this book but a brief outline of the initial process is included below. As with a BO if following a sequestration order an estate is subsequently found to be solvent, the trustee needs to apply to the court for a recall[49] and confirmation that the executor can continue to distribute the estate in the normal manner.

What is the process for an award of sequestration?

21.43 Sequestration is awarded by the issue of a warrant (the equivalent of a bankruptcy order). The warrant is issued by the relevant sheriff or the AiB (depending on the petitioner[50]).

21.44 After the date of the sequestration the sheriff's clerk or the AiB (or agent) must immediately register a certified copy of the order with the keeper of the register of inhibitions and adjudications for recording in the register.[51] If the trustee is still in office after 3 years have expired then this notice must be renewed in the register.[52]

21.45 The trustee must immediately publish in the *Edinburgh Gazette* a notice containing the following information:[53]

---

45 BSA85, s 8(3)(a)(ii).
46 BSA85, s 8(3)(a)(iii).
47 BSA85, s 8(3)(a)(iv).
48 BSA85, s 8(3)(a)(v).
49 BSA85, s 16.
50 BSA85, s 8(1).
51 BSA85, s 14(1)(a) and 1A.
52 BSA85, s 14(4).
53 BSA85, s 16(5).

(a) stating that sequestration of the debtor's estate has been awarded;

(b) inviting the submission of claims; and

(c) giving such other information as may be prescribed.

What matters are registered and where?

21.46 Awards of sequestration are registered in the Register of Inhibitions and Adjudications[54] in a similar manner as in England and Wales (see chapter 11). The trustee is also required to register the title to a debtor's heritable property with the Keeper of the Land Register. When a property is 'abandoned' by the trustee the notice of abandonment (Form 21) must also be registered in the Register of Inhibitions and Adjudications. The keeper of the register requires the notices to be sent to him at: Erskine House, 68 Queen Street, Edinburgh EH2 4NF (DX 550903 Edinburgh 9 or LP 51 Edinburgh 5).

54 BSA85, s 14(1)(a) and 1A.

Chapter 22

INSOLVENT PARTNERSHIPS

'The man who never has money enough to pay his debts has too much of something else.'[1]

INTRODUCTION

22.1 This chapter looks briefly at the solutions available for both creditors and debtors when a partnership is insolvent but will not cover the processes in any detail.[2] For these purposes the definition of a partnership plays a key role in looking at solutions especially when a trading partnership can be express or implied. The legal nature of a partnership is looked at very briefly and is then followed by a brief look at the solutions available for them. The number of available solutions for partnerships is many and varied but all involve the re-use of a combination of both bankruptcy and company legislation by treating the partnership as an unregistered company but still allowing a creditor the choice of pursuing one or more of the partners individually, or pursuing the partnership with or without proceeding against one or more of the individuals.

What is the statutory framework?

22.2 The original Insolvent Partnerships Order 1986 was revoked by the 1994 Order which came into effect 13 September 1994. The Insolvent Partnerships (Amendment) Order 2005[3] (IPA 2005) made substantial amendments to the Insolvent Partnerships Order 1994 (IPO 1994)[4] to reflect the changes in the law introduced by the Enterprise Act 2002 and these came into effect on 1 July 2005. The errors made in the IPA 2005 were subsequently corrected by the Insolvent Partnerships (Amendment) Order 2006,[5] which came into force on 6 April 2006.[6] A consultation on the current legislative framework is awaited but with no published timeframe.

22.3 Where a petition for an administration order was presented in relation to an insolvent partnership before 1 July 2005, the amendments to Part III and Schs 2 and 8 of the IPO 1994 do not apply.

---

1 James Lendall Basford.

2 For more detail on insolvent partnerships see Davis G, Glen, Steiner M, Cohen M (1996), *Insolvent Partnerships*, Jordan Publishing, Bristol.

3 SI 2005/1516.

4 SI 1994/2421.

5 SI 2006/622.

6 See Appendix 3 for details of the SI 1994/2421.

What solutions are available for a partnership and its members?

22.4 In summary the following solutions for insolvent partnerships are now available:

- Bankruptcy petitions can be filed against one or more of the individual members without proceedings being commenced against the partnership.
- To wind up the partnership as an unregistered company without presenting any concurrent bankruptcy petitions against any of the members.[7]
- To wind up the partnership and present one or more concurrent bankruptcy petitions against individual members.[8]
- A partner can petition for the partnership to be wound up without also bringing a petition against any of the members.[9]
- A partner can petition for the partnership to be wound up and also file bankruptcy petitions against all the members.[10]
- All the members can file a joint bankruptcy petition.[11]
- The members can propose a voluntary arrangement[12] (introduced by IPO 1994).
- The members can file a petition for administration[13] (introduced by IPO 1994).

What is the legal nature of a partnership?

22.5 The legal nature of partnerships has evolved during 200 years of case law mixed with concurrent legislation on contract, agency and trust issues. Partnerships are a simple solution for many business situations in that they require no registration and the partners can agree to their own terms and conditions if they so wish. In English law a partnership is not a separate legal entity whereas in Scotland a partnership does have a separate legal personality but in both jurisdictions the partners remain joint and severally liable for the partnership liabilities. The formal definition for a partnership in England and Wales is set out in s 1(1) Partnership Act 1890:

---

7 SI 1994/2421, art 7, Sch 3.
8 SI 1994/2421, art 8, Sch 4.
9 SI 1994/2421, art 9, Sch 5.
10 SI 1994/2421, art 10, Schs 4 and 6.
11 SI 1994/2421, art 11, Sch 7.
12 SI 1994/2421, Sch 1.
13 SI 1994/2421, Sch 2.

'Partnership is the relation which subsists between persons carrying on a business in common with a view of profit.'

In all jurisdictions every time there is a change in the membership of a partnership the old partnership ceases and a new partnership commences. However, for practical purposes a firm is often seen as enduring with the same name even though there have been changes in the members. The introduction of limited liability partnerships by the Limited Liability Partnerships Regulations 2001[14] allowed for the process of an enduring partnership to be formalised.

What type of 'relationship' constitutes a partnership agreement?

22.6 The relationship may be formally documented by way of a partnership deed but often there is no express agreement between the members, and the terms have to be implied from a course of conduct. In the absence of any express agreement the default provisions in the Partnership Act 1890 apply. The relationship between the members of the partnership is primarily contractual and there will be documentation evidencing issues such as internal decision making, profit shares, liability for losses etc. The Partnership Act 1890 sets out various rules to determine if a partnership exists as the mere joint ownership of property is not sufficient.[15] For instance a husband and wife jointly owning a property is not sufficient for them to be considered a partnership for these purposes.

22.7 The persons referred to above in the definition of a partnership can be individuals but can also be a company[16] or even another partnership or any combination of these. Minors can also legally become partners but in general cannot be liable for any debts.[17]

22.8 There is no definition of 'business' or 'profit' in the Partnership Act 1890 however case law has shown business to include every trade, occupation and profession which must include an element of commercial activity[18] whilst profit has been interpreted as implying any yearly gain[19] after deducting all expenses and losses including accrued items such as depreciation.[20]

---

14 SI 2001/1090.

15 Partnership Act 1890, s 2(1).

16 'A body of persons corporate or unincorporate'; Interpretation Act 1978, Sch 5 and Sch 1.

17 *Re A and M* [1926] Ch 274; *Lovell and Christmas v Beauchamp* [1894] AC 607; a minor can repudiate the partnership until the age of 18, or for a reasonable period after that date.

18 Using this test a railway society was found not to be a partnership see *Goddard v Mills* (1929) *The Times* 16 February.

19 Per Fletcher: Moulton LJ in *Re Spanish Prospecting Co Ltd* [1911] 1 Ch 92 at 98–99.

20 Per Atkinson J in *Rushden Hotel C Ltd v Keene* [1946], 2 All ER 141 at 144 See also *Gresham Life Assurance Society v Styles* [1892] AC 309; *Whimster v IRC* [1926] SC 20; *Beauchamp v F W Woolworth Plc* [1990] 1 AC 478.

What is the legislative framework for insolvent partnerships?

22.9 The Insolvent Partnerships Order 1994[21] sets out in a number of schedules the amendments required to the existing framework of insolvency legislation (IA86 and IR86) to allow it to be used for partnerships.

These are:

Schedule 1	Voluntary Arrangement for the partnership based on the CVA framework
Schedule 2	Administration for the partnership
Schedule 3	Compulsory liquidation for the partnership with no concurrent bankruptcy petitions
Schedule 4	Compulsory liquidation for the partnership with concurrent bankruptcy petitions
Schedule 5	Compulsory liquidation for the partnership with no concurrent bankruptcy petitions
Schedule 6	Compulsory liquidation for the partnership with concurrent bankruptcy petitions
Schedule 7	A joint bankruptcy debtor's petition for all the members without a compulsory petition against the partnership (members' petition only)

22.10 The forms currently in use for partnerships are listed in detail in Appendix 4.

CREDITORS' SOLUTIONS

What solutions are available to a creditor?

22.11 For a creditor there are several solutions available based mainly on petitioning for the liquidation of the partnership with or without bankruptcy petitions against the individual members of the partnership. These options should be considered carefully before embarking doggedly down one chosen route. The options available are covered below in more detail and the main consideration will often be determining which member has the most assets and the biggest incentive not to be made bankrupt. The partnership itself may or may not own sufficient assets to make it worthwhile taking recovery action against it directly.

22.12 The four courses open to a proposed petitioning creditor are:

- Winding up the insolvent partnership only.[22]

---

21 SI 1994/2421.
22 SI 1994/2421, art 7.

- Winding up the insolvent partnership, involving petitions against one or more of the insolvent members.[23]

- Insolvency proceedings against members of an insolvent partnership, not involving winding up of the partnership as an unregistered company.[24]

- Insolvency proceedings against one or more members of the partnership, without including the others and without presenting a petition for the winding up of the partnership as an unregistered company.[25]

What matters need to be considered before choosing an option?

22.13 The first step in the process will be the decision on who to sue and or enforce judgment against. For creditors the options are fairly limited. Similar rules apply here as for a bankruptcy petition and these are set out in detail in chapter 7. The main difference is the decision on whether or not to take action against the partnership or one of more of its members or both. There is a general principle that a winding-up or bankruptcy proceedings should not be used for debt collection however the fact remains that if there is an undisputed debt that is not being paid then quite often the issue of a statutory demand or petition will often result in the debt being settled or a composition being agreed.

22.14 As referred to above it is open to a creditor to make the choice of either suing the partnership as a firm or one or all of the individual partners. The advantage of obtaining a judgment against the partnership allows enforcement against either the partnership or one or more of the individual partners with the leave of the court. What action to take subsequently is a more difficult problem, as to take concurrent action against the partnership and all of the partners can be expensive[26] and these interrelated proceedings will invariably take longer to produce results especially where there is property involved.

22.15 Partnership leases are also a potential problem as frequently one or maybe two partners will contract on behalf of the partnership and as discussed above if the partnership membership has changed over time the landlord may not be sure who is bound by the agreement. It is usually good conveyancing practice to obtain separate covenants from all of the other partners but this is frequently overlooked and often the landlord will take proceedings against the individuals named on the lease as the cheapest method of enforcement.

---

23 SI 1994/2421, art 8, only one petition against a member is required: see also arts 8 and 13.

24 SI 1994/2421, art 13.

25 SI 1994/2421, art 1(3).

26 Although SI 1994/2421, art 13 provides that where concurrent petitions are used only one deposit is paid, the court fees and solicitors costs will be much more and if the petitions are being heard in the High Court the hearings will also be in different courts involving attendance on more than one occasion.

What is the procedure for the option chosen?

22.16 Statutory demands and bankruptcy petitions are discussed in detail in chapters 6 and 7. Winding-up petitions are not dealt with in detail in this book[27] but similar principles apply as to a bankruptcy petition.

MEMBERS' SOLUTIONS

What solutions are available to the members of a partnership?

22.17 For the partnership and the individual members there are a lot more options ranging from voluntary arrangements, administration to liquidation and bankruptcy with either the partnership or the individuals being involved depending on the circumstances of each case. Each of these options is discussed briefly below.

What matters need to be considered?

22.18 The process for considering the options are very similar to those set out in chapter 1 and in respect of bankruptcy requirements see also chapter 8 for procedural issues.

Voluntary arrangements

22.19 Article 4 and Sch 1, IPO 1994 introduced voluntary arrangements for partnerships based on the procedures prescribed for companies by Part I, IA86. They do not provide for the making of an interim order providing a moratorium which is available to individual debtors under s 253, IA86 while the arrangement is in preparation. A partnership voluntary arrangement may also be entered into in conjunction with interlocking individual arrangements entered into by each partner, but this procedure will confer no protection on the partnership assets. The law and procedure relating to individual voluntary arrangements under Part VIII IA86 is otherwise generally applicable with the modifications effected by Sch 1, IPO 2004.

Administration orders

22.20 Article 6 and Sch 2, IPO 1994 also introduced the administration order procedure for partnerships as set out in Part II, IA86. This has the advantage, over the voluntary arrangements procedure as the order is made and a moratorium is effected while the administrator examines the partnership's affairs and puts together a proposal for creditors.

---

27 See further P Loose and M Griffiths *Loose on liquidators* (Jordan Publishing, Bristol, 6th edn, 2010).

Winding-up of an insolvent partnership only

22.21 The petition may be presented by any of the following:

- the liquidator of a corporate partner; or
- the trustee of a bankrupt partner's estate; or
- by a creditor; or
- by the partnership itself; or
- any member of it.

In the case of a trustee or liquidator of a bankrupt member's estate, the object in taking this course is to get at the partnership assets. The petition must be in accordance with Form 1, Sch 3, IPO 1994 and the grounds for making the petition are set out in s 221(5), IA86. These are:

- dissolution or cessation of trading or business; or
- inability to pay debts; or
- 'just and equitable'.

A creditor must follow the normal procedure for the winding up of an unregistered company but using Form 5.

22.22 The assets of an individual partner of an insolvent partnership which is being wound up are not available to the partnership's creditors, unless and until the insolvency provisions have been applied to that member and those assets.[28] A petition can be presented by the partnership or by any member of it, if the partnership consisted of not less than eight members, or by a member if he presents, with the leave of the court, a petition, after serving a written demand in Form 2, IPO 1994[29] as follows:

(i) in respect of a joint debt or debts exceeding £750 unpaid by the partnership; and

(ii) subject to his satisfying the court, when granting leave to present the petition, that he has obtained a judgment, decree or order in respect of such sum as against the partnership, and that all reasonable steps have been taken by him to enforce that judgment, decree or order. Section 222, IA86 (inability to pay debts) was modified, so that a petition by a creditor or by the liquidator of a corporate partner, or by the trustee of a bankrupt partner, would have to be preceded by a 'written demand'.

---

28 See *Investment and Pensions Advisory Service v Gray* [1990] BCLC, (1989) 139 NLJ 1415.

29 Insolvent Partnerships Order 1994, SI 1994/2421, Sch 3.

Petition to wind-up a partnership together with insolvency petitions against two or more insolvent members

What are the requirements for this procedure?

22.23 Under IPO 1994 there was a requirement for there to be at least three petitions if this option was chosen ie one against the partnership and at least two against other members, whether corporate or individual members. The IPO 1994 reduced this requirement to two ie the partnership and at least one member.

22.24 In addition the partnership must have carried on business in England and Wales within a period of 3 years ending with the day on which the petition is presented.[30] The court having jurisdiction is the court of the district where the insolvent partnership has a principal place of business.[31]

22.25 The only ground for winding-up an insolvent partnership was that the partnership is unable to pay its debts.[32] The insolvent partnership is deemed unable to pay its debts, if a creditor, by assignment or otherwise, to whom the partnership owed a joint debt exceeding £750, had served on the partnership a written demand[33] together with members demands on any two or more insolvent members[34] and the partnership and its members, for three weeks after the service of the demands,[35] neglected to pay the sum or to secure or compound for it to the reasonable satisfaction of the creditor. Under IPO 1994 the alternative grounds for showing inability to pay debts as set out in ss 223 and 224, IA86 did not apply but have now been introduced by IPO 1994.

22.26 In the winding-up or bankruptcy of the two or more insolvent members, in conjunction with the winding-up of an insolvent partnership, all the provisions of IA86 apply as for the winding-up of a company with the modifications specified in Part II, Sch 2, IPO 1994 and in respect of bankruptcy of an individual members the IA86 applies with the modifications specified in Part III, Sch 2, IPO 1994.

---

30 IA86, s 117(7).

31 IA86, s 117(9).

32 IA86, s 221(5) (as amended by Insolvent Partnerships Order 1994 art 8(1)(c)).

33 In Form 3 as set out in Insolvent Partnerships Order 1994, Sch 3. In relation to the use of Form 3, a High Court Practice Note (Ch D: Bankruptcy: Statutory Demands) (No 2/88) [1988] 1 WLR 557, Practice Note (No 2/88), recommends its amendment by practitioners to make it clear that the demand is being served on the individual as a member of a particular partnership.

34 The member demands must be in accordance with SI 1994/2421, Sch 2, Part II, para 4, Part III, para 5.

35 The date runs from the last of the demands if they were served at different times.

Petition to wind-up a corporate partnership member

What are the requirements for this procedure?

22.27 Prior to the IPO 1994 a corporate member could only be wound up if it was unable to pay its debts[36] using the normal tests. Any corporate member of a partnership can be wound up[37] relying on this procedure by using the same procedure as for other members ie a written demand in Form 3.[38] However s 123, IA86 had a new subsection (4) inserted whereby a corporate member was deemed unable to pay its debts if the court had made a winding-up order against the partnership. The form of the petition in this case is Form 6, Sch 3, IPO 1994 which must be presented at the same time and to the same court as the petition for the winding-up of the insolvent partnership[39] and advertised in Form 5.[40]

Petition for the bankruptcy of an individual member

What are the requirements for this procedure?

22.28 The petition[41] must be presented at the same time, and to the same court, as the petition for the winding up of the partnership.[42] The petitioner might, at any time after presentation of the petition and with the leave of the court, add other partners as parties to the proceedings in relation to the insolvent partnership.[43] A bankruptcy petition can only be presented to the court under s 264, IA86, against the individual member, if the court has jurisdiction to wind-up the partnership.[44] In *Re Marr (Pauline) (A Bankrupt)*,[45] the Court of Appeal[46] resolved the conflict between s 271(1), IA86 and the inserted subsection (2A) by finding the provisions of s 271(1), IA86 must prevail.

---

36 IA86, s 122 (as amended).
37 SI 1994/2421, Sch 2, Part II.
38 SI 1994/2421, Sch 3.
39 IA86, s 124(2).
40 SI 1994/2421, Sch 3 and Insolvency Act 1986, s 123(4).
41 Using Form 7; SI 1994/2421, Sch 3.
42 IA86, s 264(1A).
43 IA86, s 264(1B).
44 See substituted s 265 of the Insolvency Act 1986.
45 [1990] Ch 773, CA.
46 Reversing Mervyn Davies J's finding, see *Re Marr (Pauline) (A Bankrupt)* [1989] 3 WLR 674, [1989] 3 WLR 674.

Insolvency proceedings against members of insolvent partnerships not involving the winding-up of the partnership as an unregistered company

What are the requirements for this procedure?

22.29 This option is designed for insolvent members who are 'individual members' only (excluding limited partners or companies).[47] The petition was previously in Form 8 but is now covered by Form 14 with amendments to IA86 set out in Sch 7, IPO 1994. This is a simple method by which all the individual members petition the court for bankruptcy orders to be made against themselves and the process includes the winding-up of the partnership business and property by the trustee without the need for a separate liquidator to be appointed.[48] As a result the members of the partnership are not treated as directors for the purposes of the Company Directors Disqualification Act 1986.

---

47 SI 1994/2421, art 11 and Sch 7.

48 Under art 13(3) of the SI 1994/2421, arts 3(b), 8(2) and 9–11 of the Order applied with necessary modifications to individual members.

Chapter 23

PROPOSING AN INDIVIDUAL VOLUNTARY ARRANGEMENT

'... I have a warranty
To unburden all my plots and purposes
How to get clear of all the debts I owe.'[1]

INTRODUCTION

23.1 Chapter 1 briefly covered each of the solutions available to insolvent individuals and this chapter sets out in more detail the process of entering into an IVA.[2] The next chapter covers the preparation of the proposal and statement of affairs and looks at the roles and duties of the nominee and supervisor (chapter 24). The communication with creditors is covered in chapter 25 and the monitoring and completion of an IVA in chapter 26. This chapter starts with some background and then provides a chronological overview by looking first at the initial contact with the debtor, when and if an interim order is required and if so how one is obtained. It then looks at the content of a proposal and compares a standard IVA with a 'fast-track' IVA together with the simplification of the process agreed using the IVA protocol which was updated in December 2012.

What is an IVA?

23.2 An individual voluntary arrangement ('IVA') is an agreement between a debtor and his creditors to receive less than payment in full in return for a binding agreement from the debtor in respect of his or her assets. Any assets to be excluded from the arrangement must be set out in the proposal. Assets to be included in the proposal can include contributions from future income either for a specified period or for a specific amount. The duration and amount of these contributions must be set out clearly in the proposal. An IVA is defined in s 253, IA86 as a composition in satisfaction of the debtor's debts or a scheme of arrangement of his affairs. The difference between these two alternatives is discussed below.

23.3 A 'composition' is generally an arrangement where the debtor retains title over and control of his assets and agrees to pay his creditors an agreed amount arising out of the proceeds of those assets (whether they derive from

---

1 Shakespeare, *Merchant of Venice,* Act 1, Scene 1, Bassanio.

2 An alternative treatment can be found in S Lawson, P French, G Frampton, and J Middleton *Individual Voluntary Arrangements* (looseleaf) Jordan Publishing, Bristol.

the sale of the assets or income produced by them). In a 'scheme of arrangement' the debtor usually transfers his assets to the supervisor who deals with them in accordance with the proposal.

23.4 The distinction between which option is being used is important in determining the date at which debts are discharged. This distinction was dealt with by Lightman, J in *March Estates plc v Gunmark Ltd*[3] and in this case the voluntary arrangement was held to be a scheme and not a composition. Whereas a composition clearly intends there to be a release of some part of the debt a scheme does not necessarily do the same.

What is the format and characteristics of a standard IVA?

23.5 A standard IVA proposal is usually written as a composition rather than a scheme of arrangement with the debtor retaining custody of the assets. An IVA is characterised by the following elements:

- In cases where there is an IO application it is subject to review by the court however the court relies on the nominee's report for guidance on efficacy.
- In the case of 'protocol' certified proposals they must comply with the agreed provisions.
- It is based on an agreement between the debtor and the debtor's creditors.
- It is binding on all creditors regardless of whether the individual creditor has agreed to the IVA or not (even contingent creditors).
- It is however a less formal and generally less expensive alternative to bankruptcy.
- If the debtor fails to comply with the agreed terms of the arrangement it may fail depending on the terms agreed for any revision. The debtor can then be made bankrupt depending on the terms of the arrangement. The definition and consequences of the acts that constitute failure must be set out clearly in the proposal. Usually if the terms of the agreed proposal are breached then the arrangement 'fails'.

What constitutes failure is discussed in more detail in the section on completion or termination in chapter 25.

How have current IVAs evolved?

23.6 Prior to 1861 the law merchant or '*lex mercatoria*' did not recognise the modern concept of 'consumer debt' and only 'traders' could seek the relief of

---

3 [1996] BPIR 439.

bankruptcy while other debtors were confined to prison until their debts were paid. The three basic principles of modern insolvency law were introduced as early as 1543.[4] These are:

- the collective participation of creditors in the solution;
- the concept of 'pari passu' ie assets are distributed in 'a portion rate and rate alike according to the quantity of their debts'; and
- the process of examining the debtor with prescribed penalties for non-disclosure or absconding.

23.7 The earliest compositions[5] of debt took place in the seventeenth century under the auspices of both the Privy Council and the Lord Chancellor.[6] The statute of 1697 gave compositions parliamentary authority. The 1861 Act finally extended the bankruptcy provisions to all persons whether traders or not and it also finally recognised the concept of rehabilitation with the end of debtor's prisons in 1869. The same act introduced arrangements with creditors by deed, outside of bankruptcy which was binding on all creditors if accepted by seventy five percent in value of them. The deed was presented to the bankruptcy court for registration and was also advertised in the *London Gazette*.

23.8 The 1883 Act laid down the basis for modern day insolvency legislation, and the role of the OR came into being. The Deeds of Arrangement Act 1887 was passed to ensure that the many private arrangements that had sprung up had to be registered at the Bills of Sale Office at the Supreme Courts, where they were available for search and inspection in much the same way as the personal insolvency register is available now. The Bankruptcy Act 1890 simplified the arrangements and allowed agreements where less than 37.5% was paid out to creditors. From this point annual accounts had to be submitted to the Board of Trade for each arrangement and these were open for inspection.

23.9 The 1913 Bankruptcy and Deeds of Arrangement Act were principally consolidating legislation but did reduce the assets available for distribution again, this time to 25%. In 1914, the Bankruptcy and Deeds of Arrangement legislation were separated but without modification, and then in 1925 the Deeds of Arrangement registration was transferred from the Supreme Courts to the Board of Trade. Little changed until the implementation of the

---

4 Professor Graham has suggested that the widely held view that this statute received Royal Assent in 1542 is incorrect. He observed, 'The statement in para 35 of the Cork Report that the Act was passed in 1542 (and repeated elsewhere) must now be regarded as erroneous'. See: D Graham 'The formative years of English Insolvency Law: 1543–1603' *Phoenix*, December 1995, Issue 21, pp 23–25. Regarding the Bill of Bankrupt 1532, see G Elton *Reform and Renewal: Thomas Cromwell and the Common Weal* (Cambridge, 1995), p 149.

5 An Act for relief of creditors, by making compositions with their debtors in cases where two thirds in number and value agreed. Royal Assent 1697.

6 J Tribe and D Graham Bacon in 'Debt – The Insolvency Judgments of Francis, Lord Verulam' *Insolvency Law & Practice* (2006) Vol. 22(1), 11–16, ISSN: 02670771.

Insolvency Act 1986 when these two procedures were effectively reunited with the latter becoming known as an IVA. The intention was to repeal the Deeds of Arrangement legislation after the introduction of the IA86 but this was never formalised. Despite this failure the procedure has fallen into disuse and 1998 was the last year in which a deed was registered. County court administration orders were introduced by the County Courts Act 1984 in an attempt to deal with debtors with small amounts of debt (less than £5,000) that were being enforced through the courts. The limits set for this procedure have never been increased and although improvements to this legislation were proposed in 1990 they were never implemented.

How are IVAs used today?

23.10 The IA86 was the first major reform in insolvency legislation for a hundred years. One of the major changes was the introduction of the modern IVA. The initial take-up of the IVA procedure in 1987 was slow (fewer than 100) with less than 1,000 IVAs in the first 2 years, increasing to around 10,000 by 2004 before rocketing to the current registrations which peaked at over 50,000 in 2010.[7] The take up in the late 1980's was championed by a few specialist firms who recognised a niche market they could fill. These firms discreetly marketed the IVA as a solution to debt problems for professions prohibiting bankruptcy of their members eg lawyers, accountants, police, politicians, and armed forces personnel. Many of these early IVAs involved a loan, providing a one off payment to creditors within a short period of time. These specialist firms were the forerunners of the large providers who currently mass market IVAs via the television and national newspapers and magazines.[8] The IVA in its current form was originally designed for trading individuals and partnerships and as a result the procedure is relatively cumbersome for simple consumer debt situations. The negotiated solution to this change of use resulted in an agreed protocol which was originally introduced in 2008 and an updated version was recently published in December 2012. This is discussed in more detail later in this chapter together with other solutions including the recent introduction of debt relief orders.

Who are the key players in an IVA?

23.11 An IVA can be proposed by an individual or partnership at various stages of indebtedness including both before and after a bankruptcy order has been made. The key players in the IVA process are the:

- Debtor or bankrupt.
- Creditors.

---

7 The Insolvency Service data is set out in **23.13**.

8 On IVA policy, background and use see J Tribe, *Personal Insolvency Law in England and Wales: Debtor Advice, Debtor Education, and the Credit Environment*, Volumes I and II, (July 2007), Kingston Business School Occasional Paper, No 62, and S Morgan, *Causes of Early Failures in Individual Voluntary Arrangements*, (2009) Kingston Business School Occasional Paper No 63.

- Insolvency Practitioner (IP) engaged as one or all of advisor, nominee and supervisor (see chapter 2 in respect of IPs generally and the various offices that can be held by an IP in personal insolvency cases).

- A unique feature of an IVA is that the IPs primary duty of care shifts with the role played as each stage of the process is reached. At the initial advice stage the IPs duty is to the debtor[9] but once the proposal has been produced and the IP becomes the nominee, the IPs role changes and he is required to report impartially on the efficacy of the proposal to court and creditors.[10] On appointment as supervisor the IPs role is to implement the terms of the proposal dispassionately, while maintaining regular contact with the debtor.[11] In the event of failure the supervisor should comply with whatever conditions were set out in the proposal.[12]

- Other organisations such as CAB, MAT or other debt management advisers[13] may have been approached for advice prior to a nominee being appointed.

- The court – county court or High Court.

- Registrar or district judge depending on jurisdiction.

THE IVA PROCESS

What is the IVA process?

23.12 The IVA process has a number of clear stages and these are listed in chronological order:

- An 'interim order' if applied for provides a moratorium on all other legal proceedings. It is no longer required in every case and is usually only requested for individuals who are trading and need protection while the proposals are drafted.[14]

- The 'proposal' sets out the terms of the arrangement proposed by the debtor or bankrupt and is usually drafted by the nominee based on information provided by them.[15]

- The 'nominees' report' is a statement made to the court by the nominee on the feasibility of the proposal.[16]

---

9 Paragraph SIP3, or para 15, SIP3A (NI) issued February 2007, with effect from 1 April 2007.
10 Paragraphs 3.4, 5–7, SIP3.
11 Paragraph 8, SIP3, 2003.
12 Paragraph 9, SIP3, 2003.
13 Citizens Advice Bureau; Money Advice Trust.
14 IR86, r 5.7 or IRN91, r 5.07.
15 IR86, r 5.3 or IRN91, r 5.03.
16 IR86, rr 5.11 and 5.14 or IRN91, rr 5.11 and 5.14.

- The 'creditor's meeting' is the forum at which the creditors vote on the contents of the proposal[17] which in simple terms require a 75% majority in value.[18] Other voting rules apply which are covered in more detail below.

- 'Creditor modifications' are changes to the proposal requested by creditors either before or during the meeting. Even if they are approved by the creditors they must also be agreed by the bankrupt / debtor.[19]

- The outcome (approval, approval with modifications or rejection) of the meeting must be reported to the court, all creditors[20] and the Secretary of State by the chairman of the meeting.[21]

- Any challenges to the outcome of the meeting must be made within 28 days.[22]

- On approval of an IVA an application for annulment for undischarged bankrupts.[23]

- The implementation of the proposal by the supervisor.[24]

- Every IVA is registered online and the details are available to the general public.[25]

What changes have occurred in the process since 1986?

23.13 In England and Wales, the initial take up of the procedure was slow and in most cases was used by professionals and businessmen who would lose their livelihood on bankruptcy. In 2000, a simplified version of the process was proposed as a response to the rapid increase in simple consumer debt cases but this suggestion has in part been superseded by a voluntary protocol scheme introduced in March 2008 and updated in December 2012. Creditor pressure has kept the number of arrangements being approved down by introducing hurdle rates[26] and other restrictions. However it should be noted that failure rates have increased slightly from around 30% to over 35% in more recent years. The data below should be read with caution as the completion data excludes

---

17 IR86, r 5.17 or IRN91, r 5.17.
18 IR86, r 5.23 or IRN91, r 5.23.
19 IR86, r 5.24 or IRN91, r 5.24.
20 IR86, r 5.27 or IRN91, r 5.27.
21 IR86, r 5.29 or IRN91, r 5.29.
22 IR86, rr 5.22(6) and 5.23(7) or IRN91, rr 5.22(6) and 5.23(7).
23 IA86, s 263D.
24 IR86, r 5.26 or IRN91, r 5.26.
25 From 1 April 2004, Dear IP Chapter 24, No 15 (previously IR86, r 5.28).
26 Hurdle rates are minimum rates of return expected by some financial institutions e g 30p in £ regardless of the circumstances of the debtor.

IVA registrations that were subsequently revoked or suspended and the number of ongoing arrangements in the last 5 years means that this data is constantly being revised.

	England & Wales	Northern Ireland	England & Wales				
	New Arrangements		Completed	% Total	Failed	% Total	IVAs ongoing
2012	**46,694**	**1,231**					
2011	**49,056**	**1,112**	**757**	1.5	**2,341**	4.8	**45,941**
2010	**50,693**	**1.002**	**1,499**	3.0	**6,543**	12.9	**42,612**
2009	**47,641**	**722**	**2,324**	4.9	**10,522**	22.1	**34,723**
2008	**39,116**	**559**	**2,675**	6.9	**12,398**	31.9	**23,781**
2007	**42,231**	**440**	**6,037**	14.4	**15,507**	37.0	**20,383**
2006	**44,331**	**774**	**15,996**	36.3	**16,168**	36.7	**11,920**
2005	**20,270**	**633**	**11,133**	55.0	**7,005**	34.6	**2,117**
2004	**10,751**	**449**	**6,550**	61.1	**3,833**	35.7	**342**
2003	**7,583**	**318**	**4,969**	85.6	**2,562**	33.8	**42**
2002	**6,295**	**207**	**4,402**	70.1	**1,873**	29.8	**6**
2001	**6,172**	**176**	**4,510**	71.9	**1,758**	28.0	**6**
2000	**7,729**	**267**	**5,646**	71.0	**2,304**	29.0	**2**
1999	**7,195**	**172**	**5,107**	71.1	**2,075**	28.9	**0**
1998	**4,902**		**3,378**	69.0	**1,510**	30.9	**5**
1997	**4,549**		**3,090**	68.6	**1,417**	31.4	**0**
1996	**4,466**		**3,082**	68.9	**1,387**	31.0	**1**
1995	**4,384**		**2,917**	66.8	**1,453**	33.2	**0**
1994	**5,103**		**3,442**	67.7	**1,639**	32.3	**0**
1993	**5,679**		**3,879**	68.8	**1,755**	31.2	**0**
1992	**4,686**		**3,326**	70.9	**1,364**	29.1	**0**
1991	**3,002**		**2,128**	69.4	**937**	30.6	**0**
1990	**1,928**		**1,379**	71.5	**549**	28.5	**0**
1989	**1,224**		**Data not available for earlier years**				
1988	**779**						
1987	**404**						

23.14 The first simplification process allowed a 'concertina procedure' to be used which combined the applications to court for the interim order and the nominees report on the proposal. Subsequently the Enterprise Act 2002 did away with the need to apply for an interim order on simple cases and the fast-track process was introduced for undischarged bankrupts. Post 2000 commercial debt management companies entered the IVA market as bulk providers offering a standard form of proposal with reduced costs based on providing a remote service from more cost effective locations. As a result the internet and telephone contact has in most cases replaced face to face advice; creditor representatives have become more robust in respect of terms of arrangements resulting in standard modifications being proposed and debtors have been discouraged from attending the creditors meeting with the majority of negotiations taking place before the meeting.

Proposals can be presented:

- to creditors prior to bankruptcy proceedings being commenced; or
- to creditors after a debtor has been made bankrupt. There is also a 'fast-track IVA' procedure for undischarged bankrupts which was introduced by the Enterprise Act 2002 and took effect from 1 April 2004. In these cases the nominee is the OR and there is no application for an interim order.

How is a fast-track IVA different from a standard IVA?

23.15 A fast-track IVA is one proposed by an undischarged bankrupt under s 263B, IA86. The OR acts as the nominee. The bankrupt is required to submit the proposal to the OR who will have 28 days to consider the contents.

What are the statutory provisions for fast-track IVAs?

23.16 The detailed rules are covered in Chapter 7, IR86. It should be noted that the best practice guidance in SIP 3 discussed below does not apply to fast-track IVA's.

What other general and specific guidance is there for other IVAs?

23.17 Each RPB and R3 issues these best practice statements on behalf of the Joint Insolvency Committee (JIC). These statements set out standards which Insolvency Practitioners must adhere to. SIP 3 relates specifically to voluntary arrangements both personal and corporate. It covers best practice issues during the whole process from the initial contact with the debtor through to completion. The following is a summary of the sections covered:

Statement of Insolvency Practice No 3 (SIP 3): Voluntary Arrangements

Section 1 – Introduction

Section 2 – Basis of the arrangement

Section 3 – Initial contact with the debtor

Section 4 – Statement of affairs and obtaining additional information

Section 5 – Consideration of the proposal

Section 6 – The Nominee's statement/report and comments

Section 7 – The meeting of creditors

Section 8 – Implementation following the creditors' meeting approval

Section 9 – Conclusion/termination of the arrangement

Section 10 – Version 4 implemented 1 April 2007 (Published version incorrectly states version 3)

Appendix – The contents of the proposal and R3 standard terms and conditions

INSOLVENCY SERVICE 'DEAR IP' GUIDANCE

23.18 The Insolvency Service also issues periodic guidance in 'Dear IP' newsletters which are available on their website and chapter 24 covers guidance on Voluntary Arrangements. All of the relevant provisions are included in Lawson's *Individual Voluntary Arrangements*[27] and below is a list of those that relate to IVAs. The missing numbered articles have either been withdrawn or relate to the CVA process.

CHAPTER 24: VOLUNTARY ARRANGEMENTS

1. The Role of the Nominee and Application of Professional Judgement (Mar-95)
2. Failed Individual Voluntary Arrangements (Mar-95)
3. IVAs – Notices to the Official Receiver and Secretary of State (Mar-95)
4. Modification of Court Jurisdiction (Oct-95)
5. Notification to Secretary of State Regarding IVA's (Oct-95)
6. Position of Preferential Creditors (Nov-92)
7. Receipts of Funds by Trustee Prior to an IVA (Apr-96)
8. Individual Voluntary Arrangements following Bankruptcy Order Rule 5.21 of The Insolvency Rules 1986 (Jul-99)
9. Individual Insolvency Register – Request for Searches (Oct-99)
10. IVA's reports to Court & SoS -Rules 5.22 and 5.24 IR 1986 (Oct-95)
11. Report of creditors' meeting (Feb-01)
12. Notification of completion/termination of the arrangement – Rule 5.29 May Edition (June-01)
14. IVA Registration of the arrangement April-02 Edition
15. Advertising of Individual Voluntary Arrangements (Sep-03)
16. Registration of Individual Voluntary Arrangements (IVAs) (Dec-03)
17. Fast Track Individual Voluntary Arrangements (Feb-04)
18. EC Provisions (Feb-04)
19. Individual Voluntary Arrangements – Termination (Mar-04)
21. Review of the Individual Voluntary Arrangement Process (Oct-04)
22. New Procedure for Acknowledgement of IVA Submissions (Dec-04)
23. IVA Submissions
24. IVA Details

---

[27] S Lawson, P French, G Frampton, and J Middleton *Individual Voluntary Arrangements* (looseleaf) Jordan Publishing, Bristol.

25. Review of the Individual Voluntary Arrangement Process
26. IVA registration, completion or failure
27. Review of the Individual Voluntary Arrangement Process (Dec-05)
28. Review of the Individual Voluntary Arrangement Process (April-06)
29. Authorisation of Voluntary Arrangements nominees and supervisors (Nov-06)
30. Joint or interlocking Individual Voluntary Arrangements (June-07)
31. Review of the Individual Voluntary Arrangement Process (June-07)
32. The IVA Forum and Plenary Session (June-07)
33. New e-mail registration facility (Sept-07)
34. IVA Forum:straightforward consumer IVA protocol (March-08)
35. Interim Order prior to proposal of voluntary arrangement:error in Statutory Form 5.2 (March-08)
37. Future publication of completion/failure rates of Individual Voluntary Arrangements (IVAs)
38. Registration of individual voluntary arrangements
39. Review of the IVA Protocol
40. Individual Voluntary Arrangements (IVAs) – Outcome Statistics
41. Rule 5.24(4) of the Insolvency Rules 1986 (Proceedings to obtain agreement on IVA proposal)
42. Operation of the IVA Regime
43. Charging of VAT in Individual Voluntary Arrangements
44. Report of a creditor's meeting
45. HMRC Voluntary Arrangements Service (VAS)
46. Notice of the result of a creditor's meeting

THE ASSOCIATION OF BUSINESS RECOVERY PROFESSIONALS (R3)

R3 standard terms and conditions

23.19 R3 issues standard terms and conditions which can be used by IPs as part of the debtor's proposals. The latest version was issued in January 2013. Details of the contents of a standard proposal are included in Appendix 5.

SIMPLE CONSUMER IVA 'PROTOCOL' – BACKGROUND

23.20 The large increase in consumer debt IVAs and the attendant high profile media interest highlighted the need to simplify the IVA process and reduce the costs for this type of arrangement. As legislative changes take time to implement, a protocol was put in place with agreement of the British Bankers' Association (BBA) and other organisations concerned with consumer with the purpose of facilitating the efficient handling of 'straightforward consumer IVAs'. The protocol is a voluntary code designed to provide transparency and consistency in the market by providing a standard framework for simple IVA proposals.

23.21 A consumer IVA is defined as one where the debtor has liabilities to a number of banks or other commercial financial organisations normally in respect of personal loans, finance agreements or credit card liabilities.[28] This agreement excludes any debtor who has trade debts and usually also owes HM Revenue and Customs for tax liabilities. This type of arrangement will also not normally involve the realisation of any assets other than the equity in a matrimonial home and would be expected to last for at least 5 years depending on the level of contributions being paid from income. The aim of the protocol initially was to fill the gap while the awaited for SIVA regime was implemented but this regime change has now been put on hold pending the outcome of the protocol.

What is the 'protocol' and what changes have been made to the agreement?

23.22 The initial IVA protocol introduced in March 2008 consisted of a number of documents which are available online from the Insolvency Service website. They include the following items which remain in force.

Annex 1 – BBA open letter to The Insolvency Service

Annex 2 – Regulatory Framework

Annex 3 – Terms of Reference of the Standing Committee

Annex 4 – Standard Terms and Conditions (STC)

Annex 5 – Standard front sheet setting out the terms of the IVA in an agreed format.

23.23 The 2013 updated version of the protocol has the same purpose[29] and scope of the original agreement but includes clarification on points raised by the Standing Committee. A copy can be obtained from the Insolvency Service website.[30] The scope of the protocol now includes the following:

- A protocol compliant arrangement must have a covering statement confirming that the proposal is protocol compliant.[31] (Previously Annex 5)

- The BBA open letter remains as confirmation that members support the protocol and will support any protocol compliant arrangement.[32] (Previously Annex 1)

---

28 Paragraph 3.1 The Straightforward Consumer IVA Protocol 2013 version.
29 Paragraph 3.1 The Straightforward Consumer IVA Protocol 2013 version.
30 http://www.insolvencydirect.bis.gov.uk/insolvencyprofessionandlegislation/policychange/foum2007/plenarymeeting.htm.
31 Paragraph 2.1 The Straightforward Consumer IVA Protocol 2013 version.
32 Paragraph 2.2 The Straightforward Consumer IVA Protocol 2013 version.

- It is recognised that an IVA is a regulated process under statute and that this results in certain work being undertaken which has a cost unconnected with the size of the estate.[33]

- Confirmation that the protocol does not override the regulatory framework.[34]

- Agreed definitions of IVA providers to include the IPs and the IVA provider firms; creditors to also include the agents of creditors who vote on their behalf.[35]

- Confirmation of the continuing role of the standing committee in the efficient monitoring and reviewing of the agreed terms of reference.[36] (Previously Annex 3)

23.24 The 2013 protocol also summarises the following requirements:

- Restates the characteristics of a straightforward consumer IVA including reference to the need for a debtor to have regular income and the number and type of creditors involved; the options for dealing with the matrimonial home together with potential issues that might make a protocol proposal unsuitable.[37]

- Restates the requirement for transparency and co-operation and the need to ensure compliance with SIP3 especially the detailed disclosure requirements. In addition each IP or firm must publish their processes for dealing with complaints and their relevant regulatory body.[38]

- Restates the requirement for co-operation with the standing committee including the provision of relevant non-sensitive information to allow them to determine the effectiveness of the protocol.[39]

- Clarifies the obligation on IPs and any related suppliers or referral agents to ensure that all advertising must comply with the OFT debt management guidance and other relevant codes of practice.[40]

- Provides a reminder that every individual must be given full information on all alternatives and copies of the guidance published on the IS website

---

33 Paragraph 2.3, The Straightforward Consumer IVA Protocol 2013 version.
34 Paragraph 2.4, The Straightforward Consumer IVA Protocol 2013 version.
35 Paragraph 2.5, The Straightforward Consumer IVA Protocol 2013 version.
36 Paragraph 2.6, The Straightforward Consumer IVA Protocol 2013 version.
37 Paragraphs 3.1–3.6, The Straightforward Consumer IVA Protocol 2013 version.
38 Paragraphs 4.1–4.4, The Straightforward Consumer IVA Protocol 2013 version.
39 Paragraphs 4.5–4.6, The Straightforward Consumer IVA Protocol 2013 version.
40 Paragraphs 5.1–5.3, The Straightforward Consumer IVA Protocol 2013 version.

as part of a best advice process. This is discussed in detail in chapter 1 and referred to below in relations to IVAs.[41]

- Clarifies the need to verify information provided in the proposal including the steps required to independently value assets; the verification of creditors and amounts from up to date documentation; the verification of income from a series of payslips, bank statements or suitable equivalents to ensure regularity.[42]

- Restates the requirement for allowable expenditure from income to be in line with the Step Change Debt Charity guidelines (formerly CCCS) with explanations being sought for any amounts that fall outside the parameters listed.[43]

- Clarifies the list of specific expenditure which must be formally verified including secured loan payments; rent; council tax; vehicle finance; pension payments and any other financial commitments.[44]

- Restates the requirement for the nominee's report to refer to this verification process being in accordance with the protocol.[45]

- Confirms acceptance of the use of standard documentation with a reminder that proposals must include the agreed standard conditions (Annex 4) and the summary sheet (Annex 5) as previously required. Copies of these documents need not be sent with every proposal but must be referred to and provided if requested. There is no agreed standard format for the proposal other than these documents.[46]

What additional 'protocol' requirements are there?

23.25 The 2013 protocol also deals with other matters that may arise during the ongoing administration of an IVA and these are set out briefly below:

- The protocol sets out the parameters for both calculating the net worth of the property and how that value can be realised into the estate.[47]

- Supervisor discretion is set out in detail in respect of the availability of evidence;[48] the variation of income.[49] There is a 10% allowance for understatement of creditor's claims by the debtor[50] and the reduction of

---

41 Paragraphs 6.1–6.2, The Straightforward Consumer IVA Protocol 2013 version.
42 Paragraphs 7.1–7.4, The Straightforward Consumer IVA Protocol 2013 version.
43 Paragraphs 7.5–7.6, The Straightforward Consumer IVA Protocol 2013 version.
44 Paragraphs 7.7–7.8, The Straightforward Consumer IVA Protocol 2013 version.
45 Paragraph 7.9, The Straightforward Consumer IVA Protocol 2013 version.
46 Paragraphs 8.1–8.3, The Straightforward Consumer IVA Protocol 2013 version.
47 Paragraphs 9.1–9.9, The Straightforward Consumer IVA Protocol 2013 version.
48 Paragraph 10.2, The Straightforward Consumer IVA Protocol 2013 version.
49 Paragraph 10.4, The Straightforward Consumer IVA Protocol 2013 version.
50 Paragraph 10.1, The Straightforward Consumer IVA Protocol 2013 version.

contributions by up to 15% to reflect changes in the debtor's circumstances[51] including informing the supervisor of any entitlement to redundancy.[52]

- Discretion in respect of non compliance includes the ability of the supervisor to allow payment breaks of up to 6 months and similarly extensions where additional income or assets have not been disclosed and come to light.[53] Where breaches cannot be remedied by using this flexibility the supervisor must report the circumstances to the creditors for agreement to: vary the proposal; issue a certificate of termination; or present a bankruptcy petition.[54]

- The annual progress reports to creditors must include up to date details of the debtor's income and expenditure.[55] Other obligations to creditors include full cooperation and as far as possible to prevent a debtor from getting themselves further into debt.[56]

- The use of agents for voting or data collection does not absolve any creditor from ensuring compliance with the protocol and the regulatory framework plus ensuring that the supervisor is aware of the relationship by providing the contact details.[57]

- Where a debt is sold before the proposal has been approved the creditor making the sale must ensure the buyer is a signatory to the banking/lending Code.[58]

- The requirement to provide an explanation to the IVA provider when a 'bound' creditor votes against a protocol compliant IVA proposal.[59]

INITIAL DEBTOR ADVICE AND SIP 3

23.26 Any advice given by an IP to an individual in debt is subject to the obligation of a duty of care. The changing role of the IP from adviser to nominee and then supervisor is discussed in more detail below and what constitutes 'best advice' is covered in chapter 1. Advice being provided by any other person must also follow this best advice process.

---

51 Paragraph 10.3, The Straightforward Consumer IVA Protocol 2013 version.
52 Paragraph 10.5, The Straightforward Consumer IVA Protocol 2013 version.
53 Paragraphs 10.6–10.7, The Straightforward Consumer IVA Protocol 2013 version.
54 Paragraph 10.8, The Straightforward Consumer IVA Protocol 2013 version.
55 Paragraph 11.1, The Straightforward Consumer IVA Protocol 2013 version.
56 Paragraphs 12.1–12.3, The Straightforward Consumer IVA Protocol 2013 version.
57 Paragraphs 15.1–15.2, The Straightforward Consumer IVA Protocol 2013 version.
58 Paragraph 16.1, The Straightforward Consumer IVA Protocol 2013 version.
59 A 'bound' creditor is one of the financial institutions covered by the BBA agreement. See para's 13.1–13.3, The Straightforward Consumer IVA Protocol 2013 version.

When are face-to-face meetings required?

23.27 An offer should always be made for a meeting to take place in person[60] and in complicated or cases of an individual who is or has traded then this is mandatory. Prior to 1 April 2007, the best practice guidance was that all debtors should have had a least one meeting in person before the creditors' meeting. This meeting also allowed the IP or one of his staff to check the identity of the individual and take copies of any photo identification provided.

23.28 If during any telephone interview, the interviewer forms the opinion that either the debtor does not fully understand any of the matters explained below or that the debtor has not adequately disclosed their financial circumstances, the adviser must insist that a meeting in person be conducted.[61] The initial meeting with a debtor (in whatever form) should always be with the IP or a suitably experienced member of his staff.[62] Unqualified and inexperienced staff should not be allowed to conduct interviews or give advice. In order for an IP to provide a debtor with the best advice the debtor must be able to provide all the necessary information about their assets and liabilities needed to complete a statement of his affairs. Details of the items and areas that need to be covered are set out below under 'Statement of Affairs & Proposal'[63] and the detail required has been split into sections looking at creditors and liabilities, and assets.

23.29 The following information must be explained to the debtor at the first meeting:

- The adviser must explain to the debtor the different roles he will perform during the conduct of the case and the different duties and responsibilities that they entail. The advisor (if an IP) must explain to the debtor the need for the nominee and supervisor to maintain independence.[64]

- The adviser must consider the need for separate representation of any third parties who intend to inject funds or who are otherwise affected by the IVA. Where there is a possibility that the IVA may adversely affect a spouse, partner, co-owner or other occupier of a dwelling house or other property, the potentially affected party should be advised to take independent advice.[65]

---

60 SIP3, para 3.1, version 4, issued 1 April 2007 or SIP3A (NI) issued February 2007 with effect from 1 April 2007.

61 SIP3, para 3.1, version 4, issued 1 April 2007 or SIP3A (NI) issued February 2007 with effect from 1 April 2007.

62 SIP3, para 3.1, version 4, issued 1 April 2007 or SIP3A (NI) issued February 2007 with effect from 1 April 2007.

63 SIP3, para 4.1, version 4 issued 1 April 2007 or SIP3A (NI) issued February 2007 with effect from 1 April 2007.

64 SIP3, para 3.2, version 4 issued 1 April 2007 or SIP3A (NI) issued February 2007 with effect from 1 April 2007.

65 SIP3, para 3.3, version 4 issued 1 April 2007 or SIP3A (NI) issued February 2007 with effect from 1 April 2007.

- The adviser must take all necessary steps to understand the debtor's financial circumstances and be satisfied that the debtor has received appropriate advice. He must also ensure that the debtor has been advised of all the options available together with their consequences so that any decision to propose an IVA has been properly considered and fully explained. The Association of Business Recovery Professionals (R3) has produced a booklet entitled *Is a Voluntary Arrangement Right for Me?* explaining the IVA procedure[66] and setting out the alternatives available to insolvent debtors and this booklet should be given to the debtor to read and if necessary raise questions on his circumstances.[67] Other advice booklets are available from the Insolvency Service and other organisations and these are discussed in detail in chapter 1.

- The adviser must explain the role of the nominee in relation to the debtor's proposal and of the duty of the nominee to perform an independent, objective review and assessment of the proposal for the purposes of reporting an opinion on the veracity of the proposal to the court while generally balancing the interests of the debtor and the creditors. This duty of independence and objectivity arises irrespective of the extent of any IP's involvement in drafting the debtor's proposals. The adviser must make it clear to the debtor that his duties as nominee cannot be fettered by any instructions of the debtor or any third party.[68]

- Before recommending an IVA to a debtor, the adviser must be reasonably satisfied, on the basis of an assessment of the debtor's income from all declared sources and his stated expenditure needs, that the debtor has sufficient income to sustain the payments proposed under the IVA.[69]

- The adviser must give consideration to the most appropriate entry route into the IVA having regard to the degree of protection which may be required in the circumstances of each case.[70]

- As part of the initial procedure the identity of the individual proposing the IVA must be confirmed.[71] This can be done in a number of ways including requesting sight of some form of photo ID (passport or driving licence) together with two other items that confirm the individuals address (utility bills or bank statements). Each of these documents must be

---

66 The booklet can be obtained from the R3 website at http://www.r3.org.uk/index.cfm?page=1204.

67 SIP3 para 3.4, version 4 issued 1 April 2007 or SIP3A (NI) issued February 2007 with effect from 1 April 2007.

68 SIP3, para 3.5, version 4 issued 1 April 2007 or SIP3A (NI) issued February 2007 with effect from 1 April 2007.

69 SIP3, para 3.7, version 4 issued 1 April 2007 or SIP3A (NI) issued February 2007 with effect from 1 April 2007.

70 SIP3, para 3.10, version 4 issued 1 April 2007 or SIP3A (NI) issued February 2007 with effect from 1 April 2007.

71 Regulation 4 of the Money Laundering Regulations 2003 (SI 2003/3075), 'Know your client' anti-money laundering verification.

photocopied (good quality required) and the copy signed and dated by the person interviewing the debtor. An alternative method is to use one of several electronic identification databases that are available and if one of these is used the individual must be told prior to the search taking place that this method is being used.

How should the best advice process be documented?

23.30 The adviser must keep a contemporaneous and full file note of all matters discussed with the debtor, including all the matters referred to above.[72] A copy of the file note must be sent to the debtor together with the Association of Business Recovery Professionals' (R3) booklet 'Is a Voluntary Arrangement Right for Me?' This is to provide the debtor with written information on the IVA procedure and the alternatives available, so that the debtor can raise with the IP any points or issues that are not understood. The debtor should confirm that he understands and accepts the course of action that is being proposed.[73]

23.31 Together with this note the IP should also send a letter of engagement to the debtor setting out in writing their respective duties and responsibilities in relation to the completion of the proposal in order to minimise the scope for misunderstandings.[74]

When is an interim order required?

23.32 Prior to 1 January 2003 an interim order was mandatory before an IVA was deemed to come into existence. However this is no longer a mandatory requirement. This change was made by the IA2000[75] which introduced a new s 256A into the IA86. However the necessity of the interim order in relevant circumstances was highlighted in *Fletcher v Vooght*[76] when it was confirmed that an interim order could not be obtained retrospectively.

23.33 An interim order is only now required if there are ongoing legal actions which need to be stayed while the proposal is drafted and put to creditors or where an individual who is already bankrupt is intending to propose an IVA (the 'fast-track voluntary arrangement' procedure was introduced 1 April 2004 to allow the OR to act as nominee and propose an IVA without the need for an interim order).

How is an interim order obtained?

23.34 In the few circumstances when an interim order is still required the debtor or nominee will usually make the application to court. Sections 252–255, IA86 sets out the purpose, effects and situations in which an interim can be

---

72 See chapter 1 from **1.4** on the best advice process.
73 Paragraph 3.8, SIP3, version 4 issued 1 April 2007 or SIP3A (NI) issued February 2007 with effect from 1 April 2007.
74 Paragraph 3.9, SIP3, version 4 issued 1 April 2007 or SIP3A (NI) issued February 2007 with effect from 1 April 2007.
75 Insolvency Act 2000, Sch 2, art 7.
76 [2000] BPIR 435, [2000] 97(12) LSG 39, [2000] 144 SJLB 135, ChD.

made. The main restriction being that only one interim order can be made in any 12 month period.[77] The procedure for making the application is set out in rr 5.7–5.10 and is summarised below. On receiving an application the court will fix a venue for the hearing giving the interested parties at least 2 days notice.[78]

What is the procedure for the application for an interim order and the hearing?

23.35 The application must include the following information:

- The reasons for the application.[79]
- Details of executions or other legal processes already commenced against the debtor.[80]
- Whether or not the individual is an undischarged bankrupt and if not, that he has grounds to file his own petition.[81]
- Confirmation that no previous application has been made in the last 12 months.[82]
- Confirmation that the named nominee is qualified to act and has agreed to do so.[83]
- If the debtor is an undischarged bankrupt, confirmation that the OR has not been requested to make an application under the 'fast-track' arrangements.[84]

23.36 Attached to the application (witness statement) should be an endorsed copy of the notice to the intended nominee under r 5.4, IA86 and a copy of the debtor's proposal:[85]

- the applicant must send copies to the interested parties who are,
- the OR where the debtor is an undischarged bankrupt,[86]
- any creditor who has presented a bankruptcy petition against the debtor,[87]

---

77 IA86, s 255(1)(c).
78 IR86, r 5.7(4) or IRN91, r 5.07(4).
78 IR86, r 5.7(1)(a) or IRN91, r 5.07.
79 IR86, r 5.7(1)(a) or IRN91, r 5.07(1)(a).
80 IR86, r 5.7(1)(b) or IRN91, r 5.07(1)(b).
81 IR86, r 5.7(1)(c) or IRN91, r 5.07(1)(c).
82 IR86, r 5.7(1)(d) or IRN91, r 5.07(1)(d).
83 IR86, r 5.7(1)(e) or IRN91, r 5.07(1)(e).
84 IR86, r 5.7(1)(f) or IRN91, r 5.07(1)(f).
85 IR86, r 5.7(2) or IRN91, r 5.07(2).
86 IR86, r 5.7(4)(a) or IRN91, r 5.07(4)(a).
87 IR86, r 5.7(4)(b) or IRN91, r 5.07(4)(b).

- the nominee who has agreed to act.[88]

23.37 The application must be made to the same court in which the debtor would be entitled to or already has filed a bankruptcy petition.[89] Any of the parties receiving notice may attend or be represented at the hearing.[90] If an interim order is granted then a date will be fixed for consideration of the nominees report and the interim order will be granted to cover the same period.[91]

88 IR86, r 5.7(4)(c) or IRN91, rule 5.07(4)(c).
89 IR86, r 5.8 or IRN91, r 5.08.
90 IR86, r 5.9(1) or IRN91, r 5.09(1).
91 IR86, r 5.9(3) or IRN91, r 5.09(3).

Chapter 24

THE PROPOSAL

'Methought you said you neither lend nor borrow ...'[1]

INTRODUCTION

24.1 Chapter 23 covered the initial advice process and provided an overview of the whole IVA process. This chapter looks at the completion of the Statement of Affairs (SoA) and proposal in detail and then goes on to look at the different roles and duties of the IP as potentially advisor, nominee and then supervisor. In the majority of situations this will almost certainly be the same person who will have also advised the individual in the period prior to agreeing to be the nominee. Chapter 25 looks at the creditor involvement in the process and chapter 26 goes on to discuss the agreement of claims and payment of dividends.

STATEMENT OF AFFAIRS AND PROPOSAL

24.2 The debtor's proposal is based on the information provided by the debtor produced in the SoA. Completing this document is the first step in determining the assets and liabilities that need to be accounted for in the proposal.

What information has to be included in the statement of affairs?

24.3 The SoA should detail the nature and amount of all the debtor's assets and liabilities. These are set out below in detail. A mis-statement of the amount of the assets and liabilities can constitute a 'material irregularity'[2] being a ground on which an approved IVA may be challenged by an aggrieved creditor. In addition, a debtor commits an offence if he makes any false representations or commits any other fraud for the purpose of obtaining the approval of the creditors to the proposed arrangement. The debtor must be informed of these dangers by the nominee.[3]

---

1 Shakespeare, *Merchant of Venice*, Act I, Scene III, Shylock.

2 Within the meaning of ss 6 and 262 and para 38, of Sch A1, IA86.

3 SIP3, para 4.1, version 4 issued 1 April 2007 or SIP3A (NI) issued February 2007 which also came into effect from 1 April 2007.

24.4 Where the debtor is an undischarged bankrupt and has already delivered a statement of affairs under s 272 or 288, IA86 a further statement is not usually required except on the request of the nominee.[4]

What 'creditor' information is the debtor required to provide?

24.5 The advising IP or a member of his staff will ask to the debtor to provide details of all known or possible liabilities including the following:[5]

- claims which are fully or partly secured: the status of the accounts and the existence of any arrears should be established;[6]
- preferential claims;[7]
- guarantee liabilities;[8]
- claims for breach of contract, including claims in respect of faulty and incomplete work and hire purchase and leasing agreements;[9]
- creditors who are 'associates' (as defined in s 435 IA86 and also see chapter 2);[10]
- guarantors of the debtor's debts, including connected persons or associates;[11]
- debts for an unliquidated amount or any debt whose value is unascertained, including particularly: contingent liabilities; the potential for liabilities arising under property leases (of both present and past tenancies).[12]

---

4 SIP3, para 4.2, version 4 issued 1 April 2007 or SIP3A (NI) issued February 2007 which also came into effect from 1 April 2007.

5 SIP3, para 4.3(a), version 4 issued 1 April 2007 or SIP3A (NI) issued February 2007 which also came into effect 1 April 2007.

6 SIP3, para 4.3(a)(i), version 4 issued 1 April 2007 or SIP3A (NI) issued February 2007 which also came into effect 1 April 2007.

7 SIP3, para 4.3(a)(ii), version 4 issued 1 April 2007 or SIP3A (NI) issued February 2007 which also came into effect 1 April 2007.

8 SIP3, para 4.3(a)(iii), version 4 issued 1 April 2007 or SIP3A (NI) issued February 2007 which also came into effect 1 April 2007.

9 SIP3, para 4.3(a)(iv), version 4 issued 1 April 2007 or SIP3A (NI) issued February 2007 which also came into effect 1 April 2007.

10 SIP3, para 4.3(a)(v), version 4 issued 1 April 2007 or SIP3A (NI) issued February 2007 which also came into effect from 1 April 2007.

11 SIP3, para 4.3(a)(vi), version 4 issued 1 April 2007 or SIP3A (NI) issued February 2007 which also came into effect from 1 April 2007.

12 SIP3, para 4.3(a)(vii), version 4 issued 1 April 2007 or SIP3A (NI) issued February 2007 which also came into effect from 1 April 2007.

24.6 The advising IP should also:

- identify any creditors who have commenced execution or any other legal process;[13]
- identify any creditors with special rights which may require special consideration in the proposal (for example insured claims or matrimonial debts);[14]
- consider the possibility of early informal discussions with the key creditors, including government departments, to establish their views;[15]
- obtain independent confirmation from any bank or other financial institution of their intention to continue to provide financial support to the debtor where this is necessary for the purpose of the arrangement;[16]
- establish whether connected persons/associates may consider withdrawing or deferring their claims.[17]

What 'asset' information is the debtor required to provide?

24.7 The advising IP should check to ensure that the value of the assets is appropriately reflected in the statement of affairs. Where the value of an asset is material to the outcome of the arrangement consideration should be given to obtaining corroborative evidence as to its value. The member must also ensure that a comprehensive schedule of non-trading assets in which the debtor has an interest has been prepared together with explanatory notes. If there is a business, the member should consider, in conjunction with the debtor, the manner in which that business is to be dealt with. If the business is to be continued by the debtor, a 'business plan' should be produced to justify this decision stating the assumptions on which it is based, and in appropriate detail having regard to the circumstances and size of the undertaking. The nominee must satisfy himself that the plan has a reasonable chance of success.[18]

---

13 SIP3, para 4.3(a)(viii), version 4 issued 1 April 2007 or SIP3A (NI) issued February 2007 which also came into effect from 1 April 2007.

14 SIP3, para 4.3(a)(ix), version 4 issued 1 April 2007 or SIP3A (NI) issued February 2007 which also came into effect from 1 April 2007.

15 SIP3, para 4.3(a)(x), version 4 issued 1 April 2007 or SIP3A (NI) issued February 2007 but came into effect from 1 April 2007.

16 SIP3, para 4.3(a)(xi), version 4 issued 1 April 2007 or SIP3A (NI) issued February 2007 which also came into effect from 1 April 2007.

17 SIP3, para 4.3(a)(xii), version 4 issued 1 April 2007 or SIP3A (NI) issued February 2007 which also came into effect from 1 April 2007.

18 SIP3, para 4.3(b), version 4 issued 1 April 2007 or SIP3A (NI) issued February 2007 which also came into effect from 1 April 2007.

What other information should be requested from the debtor?

24.8 The advising IP must also ask the debtor to provide details of any transactions that might fall into the following categories:[19]

- possible transactions at an undervalue;[20]
- payments which may be preferences;[21]
- liabilities which may be extortionate credit transactions, both those outstanding and paid.[22]

What other matters should be considered during the initial interview and what enquiries need to be made?

24.9 The advising IP should also consider the following:[23]

- whether the person making the proposal is credible and making a full disclosure. The advising IP should explain the consequences of making false representations;[24]
- whether (any of) the debtor has been involved in any previous business failure, either individually, in partnership or as a director or officer of a company, and if so the details of that failure and the person's responsibility for it;[25]
- the timetable for the IVA.[26]

24.10 The extent of the advising IP's or nominee's enquiries into issues raised is likely to vary according to the particular circumstances of each case but should be sufficient to ensure the proper discharge of the duty to report to the court as nominee.[27] This is discussed in more detail below.

---

19 SIP3, para 4.3(c), version 4 issued 1 April 2007 or SIP3A (NI) issued February 2007 which also came into effect from 1 April 2007.

20 IA86, ss 238, 339, and 423 and SIP3, para 4.3(c)(i) version 4 issued 1 April 2007 or SIP3A (NI) issued February 2007 which also came into effect from 1 April 2007.

21 IA86, ss 239 and 340 and SIP3, para 4.3(c)(ii), version 4 issued 1 April 2007 or SIP3A (NI) issued February 2007 which also came into effect from 1 April 2007.

22 IA86, ss 244 and 343 and SIP3, para 4.3(c)(v), version 4 issued 1 April 2007 or SIP3A (NI) issued February 2007 which also came into effect from 1 April 2007.

23 SIP3, para 4.3(d), version 4 issued 1 April 2007 or SIP3A (NI) issued February 2007 which also came into effect from 1 April 2007.

24 SIP3, para 4.3(d)(i), version 4 issued 1 April 2007 or SIP3A (NI) issued February 2007 which also came into effect from 1 April 2007.

25 SIP3, para 4.3(d)(ii), version 4 issued 1 April 2007 or SIP3A (NI) issued February 2007 which also came into effect from 1 April 2007.

26 SIP3, para 4.3(d)(iii), version 4 issued 1 April 2007 or SIP3A (NI) issued February 2007 which also came into effect from 1 April 2007.

27 SIP3, para 4.3(d), version 4 issued 1 April 2007 or SIP3A (NI) issued February 2007 which also came into effect from 1 April 2007.

Who prepares the debtor's proposal?

24.11 The original intention of the IVA process was for the debtor, having realised he was in financial difficulty, to approach an IP with a proposal[28] to be put to his creditors. In reality very few debtors are able to get to this stage before they seek out an IP or other adviser and the proposal is usually prepared by the adviser based on accepted standards (see both R3 standard terms and condition and in relevant cases the 'protocol' documents). Lawson in his IVA text[29] suggests other terms that may be useful in specific circumstances.

What are the duties of an advising IP when helping to draft a proposal?

24.12 The terms of the IVA will be contained in the proposal, which is approved by the creditors with or without modifications. A comprehensive and accurately drafted proposal is therefore fundamental to the arrangement. In view of the importance of the proposal the nominee should, where the circumstances are complex, consider whether it should be prepared or approved by a lawyer.[30] An IVA proposal should be a clear and concise document that sets out the proposed terms without any ambiguity or uncertainty.

24.13 In dealing with an IVA the IP as advising IP should bear in mind his overriding duty to ensure a fair balance between the interests of the debtor, the creditors and any other parties involved. In considering whether to accept appointment as either nominee or supervisor the IP should have regard to the ethical code of his authorising body.[31]

What needs to be included in the proposal?

24.14 The contents of a standard proposal are listed in r 5.3, IR86[32] and these are set out below together with the best practice guidelines however simply following this listing will not necessarily provide a clear statement of the proposals and may well result in duplication or ambiguity. The best written proposals are short, clear and concise with the detailed financial data provided in the appendices.[33]

(1) The nature of the arrangement: ie whether it is a composition in full and final settlement of debts, or a scheme of arrangement[34] see earlier guidance on the distinction.

---

[28] IR86, r 5.2 or IRN91, r 5.02.

[29] S Lawson, P French, G Frampton, and J Middleton *Individual Voluntary Arrangements* (looseleaf) Jordan Publishing, Bristol.

[30] SIP3, para 2.1, version 4 issued 1 April 2007 or SIP3A (NI) issued February 2007 which also came into effect from 1 April 2007.

[31] SIP3, para 2.2, version 4 issued 1 April 2007 or SIP3A (NI) issued February 2007 which also came into effect from 1 April 2007.

[32] IRN91, r 5.03.

[33] See an example at B1-1 to B1-11 in S Lawson, P French, G Frampton, and J Middleton *Individual Voluntary Arrangements* (looseleaf) Jordan Publishing, Bristol.

[34] IA86, s 253(1) and SIP3 Appendix (a).

(2) A statement setting out why, in the debtor's opinion, it is expected that the creditors will agree to the proposed arrangement[35] ('statement of reasons' are discussed in more detail below).[36]

(3) If the debtor is trading and whether there is any intention to continue trading.[37] The extent, if any, to which the supervisor intends to exercise control over the business. If the supervisor is not to exercise any degree of control, this should be specifically stated in the proposal. The purpose or aim of continued trading should be stated: have new opportunities been created that will generate profits to pay creditors; is the trade being wound down to generate funds from asset realisations or is the business being marketed (and if so, how) as a going concern? Consideration should be given to including a summary cash flow projection.[38]

(4) Details of any credit facilities that the debtor proposes to obtain or continue to use together with details of how these ongoing liabilities are to be met.[39]

(5) The statement of affairs, which should include full details of assets and liabilities (including both business and personal assets and liabilities).[40]

(6) Details of all of the debtor's assets including valuations and whether or not they are included or excluded for the purposes of the arrangement.[41]

(7) Details of all of the debtor's liabilities including amounts, security held, contingent and any amounts guaranteed and how they are to be met, modified, postponed or otherwise dealt with.[42]

(8) The position with regard to matrimonial or family orders or attachment of earnings orders, and with regard to fines.[43]

(9) Details of how any secured or preferential creditors are to be dealt with.[44]

(10) The attitude to be adopted with regard to any contingent creditors.[45]

---

35 IR86, r 5.3(1) or IRN91, r 5.03(1).
36 SIP3, Appendix (a), version 4, issued 1 April 2007 or SIP3A (NI) issued February 2007 which also came into effect from 1 April 2007.
37 IR86, r 5.3(2)(n) or IRN91, r 5.03(2)(n).
38 SIP3 Appendix (f), version 4 issued 1 April 2007 or SIP3A (NI) issued February 2007 which also came into effect from 1 April 2007.
39 IR86, r 5.3(2)(o) or IRN91, r 5.03(2)(o).
40 SIP3, Appendix (a), version 4 issued 1 April 2007 or SIP3A (NI) issued February 2007 which also came into effect from 1 April 2007.
41 IR86, r 5.3(2)(a) or IRN91, r 5.03(2)(a).
42 IR86, r 5.3(2)(c) or IRN91, r 5.03(2)(c).
43 SIP3, Appendix (p), version 4 issued 1 April 2007 or SIP3A (NI) issued February 2007 which also came into effect from 1 April 2007.
44 IR86, r 5.3(2)(c)(i) and (ii)) or IRN91, r 5.03(2)(c)(i) and (ii).
45 SIP3, Appendix (r), version 4 issued 1 April 2007 or SIP3A (NI) issued February 2007 which also came into effect from 1 April 2007.

(11) The situation with regard to any overseas creditors.[46]

(12) Details of any additional assets, property or guarantees that are to be included but which are not owned by the debtor.

(13) Details of how any associates are to be dealt with.[47]

(14) How un-notified creditors' claims are to be dealt with and how to deal with creditors who have not made claims.[48]

(15) Details of any potential actions that would be available in a bankruptcy including:

- possible preferences;[49]
- transactions at an undervalue;[50] or
- extortionate credit transactions.[51]

(15) The proposed duration of the arrangement.[52]

(16) The actual financial proposal to be put to the creditors.[53]
This section should include:

(a) details of assets to be realised for the benefit of creditors, and
(b) details of those which are to be excluded from the proposal, together with the reasons for the exclusion and whether alternatives are to be suggested;[54]
(c) proposals regarding after-acquired assets and windfall gains;[55]
(d) proposals regarding future profit/income over a specific period;[56]
(e) details of any contributions from the debtor (eg from future earnings) including the amounts (or the basis on which they are to be computed) and frequency;[57]

---

46 SIP3, Appendix (s), version 4 issued 1 April 2007 or SIP3A (NI) issued February 2007 which also came into effect from 1 April 2007.
47 IR86, r 5.3(2)(c)(i), and (ii) or IRN91, r 5.03(2)(c)(i) and (ii).
48 SIP3 Appendix (m), version 4 issued 1 April 2007 or SIP3A (NI) issued February 2007 which also came into effect from 1 April 2007.
49 IA86, s 340 or INO89, art 313.
50 IA86, s 339 or INO89, art 312.
51 IA86, s 343 and IR86, r 5.3(2)(c)(iii).
52 IR86, r 5.3(2)(e), or IRN91, r 5.03(2)(e).
53 SIP3, Appendix (e), version 4 issued 1 April 2007 or SIP3A (NI) issued February 2007 which also came into effect from 1 April 2007.
54 SIP3, Appendix (e)(i), version 4 issued 1 April 2007 or SIP3A (NI) issued February 2007 which also came into effect from 1 April 2007.
55 SIP3, Appendix (e)(ii), version 4 issued 1 April 2007 or SIP3A (NI) issued February 2007 which also came into effect from 1 April 2007.
56 SIP3, Appendix (e)(iii), version 4 issued 1 April 2007 or SIP3A (NI) issued February 2007 which also came into effect from 1 April 2007.
57 SIP3, Appendix (e)(iv), version 4 issued 1 April 2007 or SIP3A (NI) issued February 2007 which also came into effect from 1 April 2007.

(f) whether third party funds are to be injected;[58]
(g) the debtor's specific proposals with regard to any interest he may have in his dwelling house.[59]

(17) The expected dividend and proposed dates of payment;[60]

(18) A realistic comparison of the estimated outcomes of the IVA and bankruptcy including comparative costs.[61]

(19) How funds are to be collected, held and paid out during the administration of the arrangement including what is to happen to any potential surplus funds.[62]

(20) The quantum and payment of any nominee's fees and expenses.[63]

(21) The basis for charging and estimates of the supervisor's fees and expenses.[64]

(22) The supervisor's role and qualifications[65] including the powers, duties and responsibilities of the supervisor. This will need to deal with the question of admission or rejection of claims, the manner in which funds are to be distributed to creditors and the basis on which the supervisor is to report to creditors[66] plus other procedural issues such as meetings.

(23) The power of the supervisor to summon meetings of creditors for the purpose of obtaining their views and in particular for obtaining their approval to any modifications to the IVA.[67]

(24) The requisite majorities required to pass resolutions at any meetings convened.[68]

---

58 SIP3, Appendix (e)(v), version 4 issued 1 April 2007 or SIP3A (NI) issued February 2007 which also came into effect from 1 April 2007.
59 SIP3, Appendix (e)(vi), version 4 issued 1 April 2007 or SIP3A (NI) issued February 2007 which also came into effect from 1 April 2007.
60 IR86, r 5.3(2)(f) or IRN91, r 5.03(2)(f).
61 SIP3, Appendix (d), version 4 issued 1 April 2007 or SIP3A (NI) issued February 2007 which also came into effect from 1 April 2007.
62 IR86, r 5.3(2)(l) and (m) or IRN91, r 5.03(2)(l) and (m).
63 IR86, r 5.3(2)(h) or IRN91, r 5.03(2)(h).
64 IR86, r 5.3(2)(j) or IRN91, r 5.03(2)(j).
65 IR86, r 5.3(2)(p) and (q) or IRN91, r 5.03(2)(p) and (q).
66 SIP3, Appendix (g), version 4 issued 1 April 2007 or SIP3A (NI) issued February 2007 which also came into effect from 1 April 2007.
67 SIP3, Appendix (n), version 4 issued 1 April 2007 or SIP3A (NI) issued February 2007 which also came into effect from 1 April 2007.
68 SIP3, Appendix (o), version 4 issued 1 April 2007 or SIP3A (NI) issued February 2007 which also came into effect from 1 April 2007.

(25) The circumstances in which the supervisor is to present a petition for a bankruptcy order.[69]

(26) In view of the fact that the assets do not automatically vest in the supervisor it may be advisable for the proposal to provide for such vesting or for the supervisor to be granted a charge over assets, or to be given some other suitable form of security or for a declaration of trust or power of attorney to be executed.[70]

(27) The situation with regard to tax liabilities arising on disposal of the debtor's assets, or the future income of or gifts to the debtor from a third party, that are applied towards the payment of creditors' claims.[71]

(28) Whether a committee of creditors is to be appointed and if so what will be its powers, duties and responsibilities[72] and the inclusion of power for the supervisor or any creditor's committee to be able to determine that an IVA has no future and petition for bankruptcy and authority to retain and use funds for such costs.[73]

(29) What will happen to any surplus funds, for example, from more beneficial trading than was originally envisaged or funds from a windfall.[74]

(30) What will happen to unclaimed dividends or un-presented cheques when the IVA is concluded.[75]

(31) Whether the EC Regulation on Insolvency Proceedings will apply and, if so whether the proceedings will be main proceedings or territorial proceedings.[76]

(32) Confirmation that when the terms of the IVA have been successfully completed the creditors will no longer be entitled to pursue the debtor for the balance of their claim and that the IVA is in full and final settlement of their liabilities.[77]

---

69 SIP3, Appendix (t), version 4 issued 1 April 2007 or SIP3A (NI) issued February 2007 which also came into effect from 1 April 2007.

70 SIP3, Appendix (q), version 4 issued 1 April 2007 or SIP3A (NI) issued February 2007 which also came into effect from 1 April 2007.

71 SIP3, Appendix (u), version 4 issued 1 April 2007 or SIP3A (NI) issued February 2007 which also came into effect from 1 April 2007.

72 SIP3, Appendix (i), version 4 issued 1 April 2007 or SIP3A (NI) issued February 2007 which also came into effect from 1 April 2007.

73 SIP3, Appendix (v) ,version 4 issued 1 April 2007 or SIP3A (NI) issued February 2007 which also came into effect from 1 April 2007.

74 SIP3, Appendix (j), version 4 issued 1 April 2007 or SIP3A (NI) issued February 2007 which also came into effect from 1 April 2007.

75 SIP3, Appendix (l), version 4 issued 1 April 2007 or SIP3A (NI) issued February 2007 which also came into effect from 1 April 2007.

76 IR86, r 5.3(2)(r) or IRN91, r 5.03(2)(r).

77 SIP3, Appendix (k), version 4 issued 1 April 2007 or SIP3A (NI) issued February 2007 which also came into effect from 1 April 2007.

What is included in a fast-track IVA proposal and how is it different from a standard proposal?

24.15 The contents of a fast-track IVA proposal are listed in r 5.37, IR86. The contents of a fast-track and normal proposal are almost identical. The main difference being the details of the nominee and supervisor, which are not required for a fast-track arrangement as it must be supervised by the official receiver. The contents of a fastrack proposal are listed below for completeness:

1. A statement that the debtor is eligible to propose a voluntary arrangement.[78]

2. A short statement setting out why, in the debtor's opinion, it is expected that the creditors will agree to the proposed arrangement[79] ('statement of reasons').

3. A statement that the debtor is aware that he commits an offence under s 262A, IA86 if, for the purpose of obtaining the approval of his creditors to his proposal, he makes any false representation, or fraudulently does, or omits to do, anything.[80]

4. Particulars of any property, other than assets of the debtor himself, which is proposed to be included in the voluntary arrangement, the source of such property and the terms on which it is to be made available for inclusion.[81]

5. The nature and amount of the debtor's liabilities (so far as within his immediate knowledge), the manner in which they are proposed to be met, modified, postponed or otherwise dealt with by means of the voluntary arrangement and (in particular):[82]

   - how it is proposed to deal with preferential creditors[83] and creditors who are, or claim to be, secured;[84]
   - how associates of the debtor (being creditors of his) are proposed to be treated under the voluntary arrangement;[85] and
   - whether, to the debtor's knowledge, claims have been made under s 339, IA86 (transactions at an undervalue), s 340, IA86 (preferences), s 343, IA86 (extortionate credit transactions), or whether there are circumstances giving rise to the possibility of such claims, and, where any such circumstances are present, whether, and

---

78 IR86, r 5.37(1)(b)(i) or IRN91, r 5.37(2)(b)(i).
79 IR86, r 5.37(1)(b)(ii) or IRN91, r 5.37(2)(b)(ii).
80 IR86, r 5.37(1)(b)(iii) or IRN91, r 5.37(1)(b)(iii).
81 IR86, r 5.37(2)(b) or IRN91, r 5.37(2)(b).
82 IR86, r 5.37(2)(c) or IRN91, r 5.37(2)(c).
83 Defined in IA86, s 258(7).
84 IR86, r 5.37(2)(c)(i) or IRN91, r 5.37(2)(c)(i).
85 IR86, r 5.37(2)(c)(ii) or IRN91, r 5.37(2)(c)(ii).

if so how, it is proposed under the voluntary arrangement to make provision for wholly or partly indemnifying the insolvent estate in respect of such claims.[86]

6. Whether any, and if so what, guarantees have been given of the debtor's debts by other persons, specifying which (if any) of the guarantors are associates of his.[87]

7. The proposed duration of the voluntary arrangement.[88]

8. The proposed dates of distributions to creditors, with estimates of their amounts.[89]

9. How it is proposed to deal with the claims of any person who is bound by the arrangement by virtue of s 263D(2)(c), IA86.[90]

10. An estimate of the fees and expenses that will be incurred in connection with the approval and implementation of the voluntary arrangement.[91]

11. Whether, for the purposes of the voluntary arrangement, any guarantees are to be offered by any persons other than the debtor, and whether (if so) any security is to be given or sought.[92]

12. The manner in which funds held for the purpose of payment to creditors, and not so paid on the termination of the voluntary arrangement, are to be dealt with.[93]

13. The functions which are to be undertaken by the supervisor of the voluntary arrangement.[94]

14. An address of the OR to which correspondence with the OR is to be sent[95] which the OR will supply on demand.[96]

15. The names and addresses of all the debtor's creditors so far as within his immediate knowledge.[97]

---

86 IR86, r 5.37(2)(c)(iii) or IRN91, r 5.37(2)(c)(iii).
87 IR86, r 5.37(2)(d) or IRN91, r 5.37(2)(d).
88 IR86, r 5.37(2)(e) or IRN91, r 5.37(2)(e).
89 IR86, r 5.37(2)(f) or IRN91, r 5.37(2)(f).
90 IR86, r 5.37(2)(g) or IRN91, r 5.37(2)(g).
91 IR86, r 5.37(2)(h) or IRN91, r 5.37(2)(h).
92 IR86, r 5.37(2)(j) or IRN91, r 5.37(2)(j).
93 IR86, r 5.37(2)(k) or IRN91, r 5.37(2)(k).
94 IR86, r 5.37(2)(l) or IRN91, r 5.37(2)(l).
95 IR86, r 5.37(2)(m) or IRN91, r 5.37(2)(m).
96 IR86, r 5.37(3) or IRN91, r 5.37(3).
97 IR86, r 5.37(2)(n) or IRN91, r 5.37(2)(n).

16. Whether the EC Regulation on Insolvency Proceedings will apply and, if so, whether the proceedings will be main proceedings or territorial proceedings.

17. The proposal must be signed and dated by the debtor.[98]

What is the purpose of the debtor's 'statement of reasons' in the proposal?

24.16 The purpose of this statement is to allow the debtor the opportunity to provide some background to explain to the creditors how the debts have been incurred and why the creditors should therefore support the proposal. The reasons stated by the debtor should be frank and honest admissions of past indiscretions and should be included to demonstrate that the difficulties are being addressed honestly. Some creditors will almost certainly have already decided whether or not they intend to support the proposal and may be basing their decision on previous behaviour of the debtor. If some creditors have already expressed support or otherwise then this should also be reflected in the statement.

When can a proposal include a term which allows the arrangement to be varied later?

24.17 Current IVAs usually contain what is termed a 'variation clause' which sets out the terms on which a debtor can approach creditors to vary the terms if the conditions set out originally cannot be met. An example of a variation clause is set out in clause 81 in the R3 Standard Terms and Conditions. In the absence of a variation clause proposing amendments can be costly and difficult to enforce. Examples of problems caused by bad drafting and other drafting errors are covered in more detail in Lawson's text[99] on IVAs.

When can an arrangement be extended?

24.18 An arrangement can only be extended if the terms of the arrangement allowed for this to happen or a general clause allowing for variations has been included in the original proposal. Even with creditor agreement an arrangement cannot be extended and especially not retrospectively when it has already ceased to exist.[100]

What creditor information is required?

24.19 The details and status of every creditor is required together with how any security and how it is intended to be dealt with. A more detailed explanation of the various types of creditor and security can be found in

---

98 IR86, r 5.37(2)(o) or IRN91, r 5.37(2)(o).

99 S Lawson, P French, G Frampton, and J Middleton *Individual Voluntary Arrangements* (looseleaf) Jordan Publishing, Bristol. For further discussion on problems caused by bad drafting see *Raja v Rubin and Goodman* [1998] BPIR 647 Court of Appeal [1999] BPIR 575 OR 675; *Tanner v Everitt* [2004] EWHC 1130 (Ch), [2004] BPIR 1026; *Horrocks and Another v Broome* [1999] BPIR 66.

100 *Strongmaster Ltd v Kaye* [2002] BPIR 1259.

chapter 4. The status of every creditor includes the need to identify any creditor who is an associate of the debtor. The definition of an associate is explained at the end of chapter 2[101] and also dealt with in more detail in chapter 25 in respect of the restrictions on voting.

When are valuations required?

24.20 The nominee must check to ensure that the value of the assets is appropriately reflected in the statement of affairs and proposal. Where the value of an asset is material to the outcome of the arrangement consideration should be given to obtaining corroborative evidence as to its value. The debtor's advisor must also ensure that a comprehensive schedule of non-trading assets in which the debtor has an interest has been prepared together with explanatory notes.[102] Certain assets can be excluded from the arrangement and consideration needs to be given to any transactions that could be challenged as 'transactions at an undervalue' or 'preference' in bankruptcy proceedings. This is to ensure that creditors are not being disadvantaged by agreeing to an IVA when additional funds might be available in a bankruptcy.

What assets can be excluded from the proposal?

24.21 A debtor can propose exclusion for any asset but will need to demonstrate that creditors are getting some additional value in return for exclusion. For instance in the case of a debtor who is trading, stock and other assets would be excluded on the basis that ongoing profits raised from the use of the assets would exceed the loss from any immediate sale. Alternatively third party funds may be introduced to offset any realisations lost.

How are after-acquired assets dealt with in an IVA?

24.22 In bankruptcy, after-acquired assets must be declared to the trustee and can be claimed for the benefit of the creditors.[103] Therefore in most IVAs there will be a clause setting out the same requirements as in bankruptcy proceedings. Any transaction that can be challenged in a bankruptcy can equally be subject to scrutiny in an IVA. Each debtor is required to disclose any transaction that could be challenged as they may affect the support that creditors give to the arrangement.

---

101 See **2.57** and **2.58**.

102 Paragraph 4.3(b), SIP3, version 4 issued 1 April 2007 or SIP3A (NI) issued February 2007 which also came into effect from 1 April 2007.

103 IA86, s 307.

THE NOMINEE

What is a nominee and how does one get appointed?

24.23 An advising IP becomes the nominee when he accepts that role by signing the consent to act as nominee.[104] This request from the debtor should be accompanied by a draft proposal but in reality the advising IP will probably have assisted the debtor in getting to this stage in the process. However, once an IP has signed the notice[105] he becomes the nominee and as such his primary duty of care is no longer to the debtor but to the court (or creditors) however there is a continuing duty of care as long as there is no conflict for example when advising on proposed amendments.

What is the role of the nominee?

24.24 On cases where an interim order has been applied for the nominee's primary role is to report to the court (or creditors) on the efficacy of the proposed arrangement.[106] His duty is to advise the court (or creditors) on whether a meeting of creditors should be convened and the likelihood of whether the arrangement will be first approved and secondly successfully implemented.[107] In respect of cases where no interim order has been applied for and no application is pending then the report should be submitted to the debtor's creditors.[108]

What is the purpose of the nominees report?

24.25 The nominee is required to report to either the court[109] or the creditors[110] on the efficacy of the arrangement. The report is required to give clearly an opinion on whether:

- the voluntary arrangement which the debtor is proposing has a reasonable prospect of being approved and implemented;
- a meeting of the debtor's creditors should be summoned to consider the debtor's proposal; and
- if such a meeting should be summoned, the date, time and place at which, he proposes the meeting should be held.

---

104 IR86, r 5.4(3) or IRN91, r 5.05(3).
105 IR86, r 5.4(1) or IRN91, r 5.05(1).
106 IA86, s 256.
107 IR86, r 5.11(3) or IRN91, r 5.13(3).
108 IA86, s 256A(3).
109 IA86, s 256.
110 IA86, s 256A.

24.26 The courts in the cases of *Re A Debtor*[111] and *Greystoke v Hamilton-Smith and Others*[112] have set out three tests that should all be satisfied before the nominee can conclude that a meeting should be summoned:

(1) that the debtor's true position as to assets and liabilities is not materially different from that which it is represented to the creditors to be;

(2) that the debtor's proposal has a real prospect of being implemented in the way it is to be represented it will be;

(3) that there is no already manifest, yet unavoidable, prospective unfairness.

Test (2) is effectively the same as that which is now required by statute. If the nominee cannot satisfy himself that the other two conditions are met but still recommends that a meeting should be held, he should explain in his comments the basis on which he is making that recommendation and qualify his comments so that the fact that the conditions are not met is clearly stated for the court.

What guidance is there on the matters to be considered by the nominee?

24.27 Lawson's looseleaf[113] provides a suggested checklist which can be used in addition to SIP3 which provides guidance on matters which can be considered partially subjective but key when forming an opinion on the efficacy of the proposal. SIP3 lists the following matters for consideration[114]:

- The debtor's attitude.
- The likelihood of the debtor adhering to the terms of the proposal.
- The level of control the supervisor will have over the assets bearing in mind that assets do not automatically vest in the supervisor.
- The lack of restrictions that would otherwise be imposed by bankruptcy.

24.28 And more helpfully SIP3[115] then goes on to set out six key questions that should be answered during this process and covered in the report:

- Is the arrangement feasible?
- Is the arrangement fair to creditors?

---

[111] No 140 IO of 1995.

[112] [1996] 2 BCLC 429, [1997] BPIR 24.

[113] See B4-1 to B4-8 which combines and expands on these questions by topic area, S Lawson, P French, G Frampton, and J Middleton *Individual Voluntary Arrangements* (looseleaf) Jordan Publishing, Bristol.

[114] SIP3, para 5.1, version 4 issued 1 April 2007.

[115] SIP3, para 5.3.

- Is the arrangement an acceptable alternative to bankruptcy?
- Is the arrangement fit to be considered by the creditors?
- Where the debtor has previously put forward another proposal which has been rejected, are there good reasons why the creditors should be asked to consider the current proposal?

What does the nominees report comment on?

24.29 The matters upon which the nominee may wish to comment will vary from case to case but should normally include all of the following:[116]

- the extent to which the nominee has investigated the debtor's circumstances;[117]
- the basis upon which assets have been valued;[118]
- the extent to which the nominee considers that reliance can be placed upon the debtor's estimate of the liabilities to be included in the IVA;[119]
- information on the attitude adopted by the debtor with particular reference to instances of failure to co-operate with the nominee;[120]
- the result of any discussions between the nominee and secured creditors or other interested parties upon whose co-operation the performance of the IVA will depend;[121]
- information on the attitude of any major unsecured creditor which may affect the approval of the arrangement by creditors;[122]
- details of any previous history of failures in which the debtor has been involved, in so far as they are known to the nominee;[123]

---

116 SIP3, para 6.4, version 4 issued 1 April 2007 or SIP3A (NI) issued February 2007 which also came into effect from 1 April 2007.

117 SIP3, para 6.4(a), version 4 issued 1 April 2007 or SIP3A (NI) issued February 2007 which also came into effect from 1 April 2007.

118 SIP3, para 6.4(b), version 4 issued 1 April 2007 or SIP3A (NI) issued February 2007 which also came into effect from 1 April 2007.

119 SIP3, para 6.4(c), version 4 issued 1 April 2007 or SIP3A (NI) issued February 2007 which also came into effect from 1 April 2007.

120 SIP3, para 6.4(d), version 4 issued 1 April 2007 or SIP3A (NI) issued February 2007 which also came into effect from 1 April 2007.

121 SIP3, para 6.4(e) version 4 issued 1 April 2007 or SIP3A (NI) issued February 2007 which also came into effect from 1 April 2007.

122 SIP3, para 6.4(f) version 4 issued 1 April 2007 or SIP3A (NI) issued February 2007 which also came into effect from 1 April 2007.

123 SIP3 para 6.4(g) version 4 issued 1 April 2007 or SIP3A (NI) issued February 2007 which also came into effect from 1 April 2007.

- an estimate of the result for the creditors if the IVA is approved, explaining why it is more beneficial for creditors than any alternative insolvency proceeding;[124]
- the likely effect of the proposals rejection by the creditors;[125]
- details of any claims which have come to light which might be capable of being pursued by a trustee in bankruptcy if one were appointed;[126]
- the outcome of the three tests set out by the courts and if these have not been met then the basis for recommending that the meeting be held.[127]

24.30 In addition the following information must be provided, either in the proposal or in the nominee's comments:

- The source of any referrals to the nominee or his firm in relation to the proposed voluntary arrangement.[128]
- Any payments made, or proposed to be made, to the source of such referrals.[129]
- Any payments made, or proposed to be made, to the nominee or his firm by the debtor whether in connection with the proposed voluntary arrangement or otherwise.[130]
- An estimate of the total fee to be paid to the supervisor together with a statement of the assumptions made in producing the estimate.[131]

24.31 If the debtor has, within the previous 12 months, put forward a proposal that has been rejected, the nominee's comments should include a statement to that effect, and an explanation of why it is considered appropriate for the creditors to consider and vote on the current proposal.[132]

---

124 SIP3, para 6.4(h) version 4 issued 1 April 2007 or SIP3A (NI) issued February 2007 which also came into effect from 1 April 2007.

125 SIP3, para 6.4(i) version 4 issued 1 April 2007 or SIP3A (NI) issued February 2007 which also came into effect from 1 April 2007.

126 SIP3, para 6.4(j) version 4 issued 1 April 2007 or SIP3A (NI) issued February 2007 which also came into effect from 1 April 2007.

127 SIP3, para 6.4(k) version 4 issued 1 April 2007 or SIP3A (NI) issued February 2007 which also came into effect from 1 April 2007.

128 Paragraph 5.4 (bullet 1), version 4 issued 1 April 2007 or SIP3A (NI) issued February 2007 which also came into effect from 1 April 2007.

129 Paragraph 5.4 (bullet 2), version 4 issued 1 April 2007 or SIP3A (NI) issued February 2007 which also came into effect from 1 April 2007.

130 Paragraph 5.4 (bullet 3), version 4 issued 1 April 2007 or SIP3A (NI) issued February 2007 which also came into effect from 1 April 2007.

131 Paragraph 5.4 (bullet 4), version 4 issued 1 April 2007 or SIP3A (NI) issued February 2007 which also came into effect from 1 April 2007.

132 Paragraph 6.6, version 4 issued 1 April 2007 or SIP3A (NI) issued February 2007 which also came into effect from 1 April 2007.

24.32 If the report is being filed under s 256A, IA86 it should contain sufficient information to identify the correct court.[133] Examples of both positive and negative nominee's Report can be found in Lawson's looseleaf on *Individual Voluntary Arrangements*.[134]

What examples are there of potential issues?

24.33 Henderson, J's judgment in the *Miss Sixty* case[135] considered a company voluntary arrangement (CVA) and the potential liability of a parent company (Sixty SpA) to a landlord in relation to leases that the parent company had guaranteed following healthy incentive payments. The debtor company (Sixty), a fashion and retail concern that operated from 11 shops and concessions in department stores, entered into administration following liquidity problems. Part of the restructuring within the administration involved the proposal of a CVA, the effect of which was to release the parent company from its guarantee liability on the leases.[136] The parent company, an Italian plc, had agreed as part of the restructuring to pay compensation to the landlords of £300,000. The rest of the CVA would have the effect of paying the remaining creditors in full.

24.34 The landlords objected to the CVA on the grounds that it was unfairly prejudicial to their interests pursuant to s 6(1) of the Insolvency Act 1986. They applied to the court to have the CVA set aside on numerous grounds.

First, the CVA would leave the landlords in a worse position than on a liquidation of Sixty.

Secondly, the abrogation of the landlord's rights under the guarantees, particularly in the troubled rental market environment, was unfair.

Thirdly, £1.2 million, as opposed to £300,000, was a more accurate figure in terms of reflecting the loss of contractual rights.

Fourthly, independent adjudication would result in a more considered estimate of the compensation figure. This figure would also take account of post CVA factors.

Fifthly, the CVA differentiated between groups of creditors with no justification.

---

133 IA86, r 5.15(2).

134 See B2-1 to B2-6 and B3-1 to B3-6, S Lawson, P French, G Frampton, and J Middleton *Individual Voluntary Arrangements* (looseleaf) Jordan Publishing, Bristol.

135 [2010] EWHC 1890 (Ch), [2010] BCC 882. On this case see further S Deb 'Company Voluntary Arrangements: Recent Developments' (2011) Int CR, 8(2), 115–119.

136 This course of action had previously been approved in *Prudential Assurance Co Ltd v PRG Powerhouse Ltd* [2007] EWHC 1002 (Ch); (2007) BCC 500.

Finally, there was no enforceable obligation on Sixty SpA to make the compensation payments. The landlords could give up their guarantees and then have no redress.

24.35 Henderson J held that the *Powerhouse* case[137] countenanced 'guarantee stripping' in a CVA. However, he held that there was no line of authority that allowed a variation of the underlying contractual obligations that the debtor company and its guaranteeing parent owed to the landlord. He held that the effect of the CVA was to undermine the very purpose of the guarantees and to force the landlord to relinquish these rights was unfair and unreasonable. Furthermore, Henderson J held that the dispute over the £300,000 valuation was unanswerable according to expert evidence procured by the debtor company. The sum was simply too low and a figure of £1 million was more appropriate. In concluding Henderson J observed, 'This is, in my view, a CVA that should never have seen the light of day'.[138]

What is the role of the OR as nominee for a fast-track IVA?

24.36 The OR performs a similar role as nominee in a fast-track arrangement[139] in that on receipt of the proposal he must within 28 days of its receipt review the document and serve notice on the debtor stating one of the following:

- he agrees to act as nominee in relation to the proposal;[140]
- he declines to act as nominee in relation to the proposal and specifying reasons for his decision;[141] or
- on the basis of the information supplied to him he is unable to reach a decision as to whether to act and specifying what further information he requires.[142]

What documents are filed in court when an interim order has been made?

24.37 Where the nominee is reporting to the court under s 256, IA86 the following documents must be filed in court:[143]

- a copy of the debtor's proposal (with any amendments authorised under r 5.3(3), IR86; and
- a copy or summary of any statement of affairs provided by the debtor. The summary must include details of the creditors.

---

137 *Ibid.*
138 [2010] EWHC 1890 (Ch), [2010] BCC 882, at para 87.
139 IR86, r 5.38(1).
140 IR86, r 5.38(1)(a).
141 IR86, r 5.38(1)(b).
142 IR86, r 5.38(1)(c).
143 IR86, r 5.10(2) or IRN91, r 5.08(2).

24.38 On receipt the court will endorse one of the two copies submitted with the filing date and return it to the nominee.[144] Any creditor is entitled to inspect a copy of these documents at the court.[145] If the debtor is also an undischarged bankrupt the same documentation must also be sent to the OR who is trustee for the bankrupt[146] and to any petitioning creditors.[147]

24.39 The court will generally rely on the nominees report for guidance in deciding whether or not to approve the proposal for consideration by the creditors. There may be circumstances when the court requests additional information.

What happens to the nominees report where there is no interim order?

24.40 Where the nominee is reporting to the creditors under s 256A, IA86 the following documents must be sent to each of the debtor's creditors within 14 days:[148]

- a copy of the report;
- a copy of the nominee's comments attached to the report;
- a copy of the debtor's proposal (with amendments, if any, authorised under r 5.3(3));
- a copy or summary of the statement of affairs provided by the debtor;
- a copy of the notice endorsed by the nominee;[149] and
- a statement that no application for an interim order under s 253 is to be made.

What and why is duration of the arrangement important?

24.41 All parties need to know when the arrangement is expected to complete as unless the proposal includes provision to extend the arrangement there is no power under the legislation for the court to allow any extension.[150] The duration is flexible but should be set out clearly in the proposal.

What influence do the creditors have over the content of the proposal?

24.42 Creditors play a vital role in the approval of an IVA. They have the power to propose modifications or amendments and at least 75% in value must

---

144 IR86, r 5.3(4) or IRN91, r 5.04(3).
145 IR86, r 5.3(5) or IRN91, r 5.04(5).
146 IR86, r 5.3(6) or IRN91, r 5.04(6).
147 IR86r 5.3(7) or IRN91, r 5.04(7).
148 IR86, r 5.14A.
149 IR86, r 5.4(3).
150 *Strongmaster Ltd v Stephen Kaye* [2002] BPIR 1259.

vote for approval. Approval is obtained at the creditors'[151] meeting and the approved arrangement will take into account any proposed modifications subject to the debtor consenting to them in writing.

24.43 The meeting cannot approve any proposal or modification which affects the right of a secured creditor of the debtor to enforce his security, except with the concurrence of the creditor concerned. Also the meeting cannot approve any proposal or modification which allows:

(a) any preferential debt[152] of the debtor to be paid otherwise than in priority to such of his debts as are not preferential debts; or

(b) a preferential creditor of the debtor to be paid an amount in respect of a preferential debt that bears to that debt a smaller proportion than is borne to another preferential debt by the amount that is to be paid in respect of that other debt. However, the meeting may approve such a proposal or modification with the concurrence of the preferential creditor concerned.

THE SUPERVISOR

What are the supervisor's duties?

24.44 The supervisor's main duty is to ensure that the IVA proceeds in accordance with the terms of the agreed proposal. In order to do this he should maintain regular contact with the debtor, obtaining reports as may be appropriate to the case. If the supervisor or debtor consider that the terms of the arrangement may not be achieved then the supervisor should take steps to discuss the situation with the debtor. If actual events suggest a deviation from the terms of the arrangement, the supervisor should take appropriate action. Such action should correspond to further detailed provisions of the proposal. If he is authorised to exercise discretion in any area, and that discretion is exercised, the supervisor should explain the circumstances to creditors at the next available opportunity.[153] The supervisor also has the right to apply to the court for directions in relation to any matter.[154]

24.45 The supervisor is required to take possession of any assets included in the arrangement except as agreed in the proposal.[155] In addition if the debtor is an undischarged bankrupt the supervisor is required to discharge any balance due to the official receiver[156] or give a written undertaking to that effect.[157] The amounts due to the OR include:

---

151 IA86, s 258.

152 Defined by IA86, s 386.

153 SIP3 para 8.1, version 4 issued 2007 or SIP3A (NI) issued February 2007 which also came into effect from 1 April 2007.

154 IA86, s 263(4).

155 IR86, r 5.26(1) or IRN91, r 5.24(1).

156 IR86, r 5.26(2) or IRN91, r 5.24(2).

157 IR86, r 5.26(3) or IRN91, r 5.24(3).

- Pay fees, costs, charges and expenses properly incurred and payable under the IA86 and IR86; and
- any advances made in respect of the insolvent estate, together with interest on such advances at the rate specified in s 17 of the Judgments Act 1838 at the date of the bankruptcy order.

How and when does the supervisor keep creditors informed of the progress of the arrangement?

24.46 The supervisor is required to send creditors an annual update on the progress of the arrangement.[158] The same report also has to be sent to the court and the debtor. This progress report must include an abstract receipts and payments account which should show the amounts received and paid during the period plus the totals received and paid to date.[159]

24.47 This report together with the receipts and payment account must be sent out within 2 months of the end of each 12 month period, beginning with the date of the appointment.[160] There may be circumstances in which the supervisor needs to vary these reporting periods to coincide with other arrangements and the court has the power to vary these obligations.[161]

How are creditors' claims agreed for dividend purpose?

24.48 Creditor's claims will have been agreed for voting purposes by the chairman at the creditors' meeting but will need to be separately agreed by the supervisor for the purpose of receiving a dividend. Most claims will remain the same but any claim that was disputed or reduced will be looked at again and either agreed or rejected in part or in whole. In respect of creditors' meetings this process will be looked at in more detail in chapter 25 and for the purposes of paying a dividend this will be covered in chapter 26.

What are the debtor's duties to the supervisor?

24.49 The debtor is required to cooperate fully with the supervisor and provide any additional information as reasonably requested in order to comply with the terms of the arrangement.[162]

---

158 IR86, r 5.31(2).

159 IR86, r 5.31(2) and para 4, SIP7, version 2 issued September 1998.

160 IR86, r 5.31(3) or IRN91, r 5.29(3).

161 IR86, r 5.31(5) or IRN91, r 5.29(5).

162 SIP 3, para 8.1, version 4 issued 1 April 2007 or SIP3A (NI) issued February 2007 which also came into effect from 1 April 2007.

Chapter 25

CREDITOR INVOLVEMENT IN THE IVA PROCESS

'The unluckiest insolvent in the world is the man whose expenditure is too great for his income of ideas.'[1]

INTRODUCTION

25.1 This chapter covers all types of communication with the creditors including initial notices of the creditors meeting, the conduct and outcome of the meeting. This chapter also covers the agreement of claims for both voting purposes at the meeting and payment of dividends. The notices of the final outcome were dealt with in chapter 24 and completion and failure is dealt with in chapter 26. Communication with creditors is dealt with in chronological order under the following headings:

- Informal contact
- Formal notices.
- Proposing amendments to the proposal.
- Creditors meeting (formalities and agreement of claims).
- Creditors' committee.

INFORMAL CONTACT

25.2 Prior to sending out the initial meeting notices together with details of the proposed arrangement it is normal practice for key creditors to be contacted to gauge whether they are prepared to accept the proposed terms and avoid a series of adjournments while agreement is reached. Also in cases where an interim order has not been obtained it provides initial notice to them of the impending proposal and gives them time to provide the nominee with details of any outstanding debt.

---

1 C Morley *Inward Ho!, Aphorisms, Mainly on Literature* (William Heinemann, London, 1923).

FORMAL NOTICES

What formal information must be circulated to creditors?

25.3 Communication about an IVA is required as follows:

- Notice of the initial creditors meeting.[2]
- Notice of any adjournment.[3]
- Notice of the outcome of the meeting.[4]
- An annual report on the progress of the case.[5]
- Agreement of claim.
- Payment of dividend.
- Final outcome or default.[6]

What information is included in each of these notices?

25.4 The initial creditor's meetings[7] notice includes the following data:

- a notice explaining the effects of r 5.23(1), (3) and (4) IR86, the requisite majorities required for approving the arrangement;[8]
- a copy of the proposal;[9]
- a copy of the statement of affairs, or if appropriate a summary which must include a list of the creditors and amounts of their debts;[10]
- the nominee's comments on the efficacy of the proposals.[11]
- SIP 9 Guidance note in respect of fee approvals or details of where a copy of the guidance can be obtained.[12]

---

2 IR86, r 5.17(2) or IRN91, r 5.16(2).
3 IR86, r 5.24(4) or IRN91, r 5.22(4).
4 IR86, r 5.27(4) or IRN91, r 5.25(4).
5 IR86, r 5.31(2)(c) or IRN91, r 5.29(2)(c).
6 IR86, r 5.34(1) or IRN91, r 5.32(1).
7 IR86, r 5.17(3) or IRN91, r 5.16(3).
8 IR86, r 5.17(2) or IRN91, r 5.16(2).
9 IR86, r 5.17(3)(a) or IRN91, r 5.16(3)(a).
10 IR86, r 5.17(3)(b) (or IRN91, r 5.16(3)(b).
11 IR86, r 5.17(3)(c) or IRN91, r 5.16(3)(c).
12 SIP9, para 3.1, version 5 published 1 April 2007.

25.5 The notice of the outcome of the meeting[13] must include the following data:

- whether the proposal was accepted or rejected;[14]
- the resolutions taken at the meeting and the outcome on each one;[15]
- a list of the creditors present or represented and the value of their votes;[16]
- whether the EU regulations applied and if so whether these were main or territorial proceedings;[17]
- any other information that chairman considers appropriate to include.[18]

Plus any notice of adjournment[19] must provide the details of the date and venue of the reconvened meeting.

25.6 The annual report on the progress of the case[20] must include the following data:

- report on the progress of the arrangement during the period and the efficacy of the arrangement being completed in accordance with the agreed proposal;
- receipts and payments account for the period.

PROPOSING AMENDMENTS

What is the process for a creditor to propose amendments before the arrangement is approved?

25.7 The proposal can be amended at any time up to the delivery of the nominee's report to the court.[21] Amendments can also be proposed at the creditors meeting[22] provided that the debtor agrees to them.[23] The debtor must specifically agree to each amendment or modification and the consequences of

---

13 IR86, r 5.27(2) or IRN91, r 5.25(2).
14 IR86, r 5.27(2)(a) or IRN91, r 5.25(2)(a).
15 IR86, r 5.27(2)(b) or IRN91, r 5.25(2)(b).
16 IR86, r 5.27(2)(c) or IRN91, r 5.25(2)(c).
17 IR86, r 5.27(2)(d) or IRN91, r 5.25(2)(d).
18 IR86, r 5.27(2)(e) or IRN91, r 5.25(2)(e).
19 IR86, r 5.24(4) or IRN91, r 5.22(4).
20 IR86, r 5.31(2)(c) or IRN91, r 5.29(2)(c).
21 IA86, s 256 or s 256A.
22 Paragraphs 7.8 and 7.9, version 5 (published incorrectly as version 4) which came into effect 1 April 2007.
23 Paragraph 7.6, version 5 (published incorrectly as version 4) which came into effect 1 April 2007.

each alteration must be explained to the debtor by the nominee and it is good practice for this to be formally documented. This process may require an adjournment if the debtor is not present in person at the meeting. If a nominee agrees to any modifications in the absence of the debtor the creditors are entitled to assume that the nominee has the debtor's authority to make the proposed changes. Often the debtor will appear to have no choice except to agree but the debtor must be provided with clear information on all the consequences in order to be able to make an informed decision. Challenges to the outcome of a meeting are dealt with in more detail below.

25.8 Lists of standard modifications are frequently used and these need to be included individually and agreed only with care as they may contradict or duplicate in some way other terms already included in the proposal. Amendments should always be incorporated into the original document for this reason and not simply added as an addendum. Modifications are not allowed for fast-track proposals.

MEETINGS

What is the purpose and procedure for convening a meeting of creditors?

25.9 The purpose of the creditors' meeting is to consider the contents of the debtor's proposal[24] and either approve the proposal, propose amendments or reject it in its entirety. The nominee's report will have included a date on which the meeting should be held.[25] Depending on whether an interim order is in place the meeting must be convened for a date in accordance with the following:

- Where there is no interim order: not less than 14 days and not more than 28 days from the date on which the nominee's report has been delivered to the creditors under r 5.14A, IR86.[26]
- Where an interim order is in place: not less than 14 days from the date on which the nominee's report is filed in court and not more than 28 days from the date on which the nominee's report is considered by the court.[27]

Notices must be sent to every creditor listed in the SoA and any other known creditors at least 14 days before the meeting date.[28] See further comment below on meetings that can be attended remotely.

---

24 IA86, s 258.
25 IR86, r 5.17(1) or IRN91, r 5.16(1).
26 IR86, r 5.17(1)(a) or IRN91, r 5.16(1)(a).
27 IR86, r 5.17(1)(b) or IRN91, r 5.16(1)(b).
28 IR86, r 5.17(2) or IRN91, r 5.16(2).

What information does the meeting notice contain?

25.10 The meeting notice must contain:[29]

- The date, time and place of the meeting.

- A time and date, not more than 4 days before the date fixed for the meeting, by which proofs must be lodged and (if applicable) proxies, in order to be entitled to vote at the meeting.

- Voting: requisite majorities[30] (the majority required to approve an IVA is explained in para **25.38**).

25.11 The meeting has to be located at a venue that is convenient for the creditors[31] and must be held between 10.00 and 16.00 unless the court otherwise directs.[32] Creditors can object if the location chosen makes it difficult for them to attend in person.

When can meetings be held remotely?

25.12 Where the person summoning a meeting considers it appropriate that the meeting can be held in such a way that those who are not present can attend the meeting remotely then the same rules apply.[33] The convenor must ensure that any creditor attending remotely can exercise the same rights to speak and vote and be able to recognise all the other parties also attending. There must also be sufficient security to ensure that only those people entitled to attend can do so.[34]

In addition creditors can request to attend a meeting remotely.[35] The request to the convenor must be made within 7 business days of receiving a notice of the meeting in question[36] and accompanied by a list of creditors making or concurring with the request together with written confirmation from each creditor confirming their concurrence.[37]

What happens when a request for remote attendance or a location for a meeting needs to be actioned?

25.13 Where the convenor of a meeting considers that a creditors request has been properly made by at least 10% of the creditors in value,[38] either to attend remotely or to have a location to attend in person, the convenor must:

---

29 IR86, r 5.17(3) or IRN91, r 5.16(3).
30 IR86, r 5.17(3) or IRN91, r 5.16(3).
31 IR86, r 5.18(1) or IRN91, r 5.17(1).
32 IR86, r 5.18(2) or IRN91, r 5.17(2).
33 IA86, s 379A.
34 IA86, s 379A(5), (7).
35 IR86, r 12A.22(1).
36 IR86, r 12A.22(3).
37 IR86, r 12A.22(2)(d).
38 IA86, s 379A(8).

- give notice to all those previously given notice as to whether there is any change in the date and time of the proposed meeting,[39] giving at least 14 days notice of the meeting date;[40]

- set a venue (including specification of a place if required) for the meeting, the date of which must not be later than 28 days after the original meeting;[41]

- where a place has been specified the chairman of the meeting must attend the meeting in person at that place.[42]

Meeting formalities

What happens at the creditors meeting?

25.14 Before the formal business of the meeting commences the chairman of the meeting will ask all attendees to sign an attendance register[43] or otherwise identify themselves if they are attending as a proxy holder for one or more of the creditors or attending remotely. The formal business of a meeting will usually include a presentation of the proposal followed by the voting. The voting process is set out in more detail below.

When is a creditors' meeting validly constituted?

25.15 A meeting is validly constituted as long as there is at least one creditor who is entitled to vote in attendance. Attendance can be in person, remotely or by proxy.[44] The chairman must allow 15 minutes for known creditors to arrive or attend a meeting before declaring a meeting inquorate.[45]

Who can act as chairman of the creditors' meeting and what are his duties?

25.16 The chairman of the meeting should be the nominee[46] or another IP or experienced member of the nominee's staff.[47] The chairman has the following duties:

- Ensure the meeting has been validly convened by checking that notices, advertisements and gazetting have all been completed in accordance with the relevant rules.

---

39 IR 86, r 12.4A(4)(a).
40 IR 86, r 12.4A(4)(c).
41 IR 86, r 12.4A(4)(b).
42 IR86, r 12A.22(6).
43 IR86, r 5.22(1).
44 IR 86, r 12A.21(2).
45 IR86, r 12A.21(4).
46 IR86, r 5.19(1) or IRN91, r 5.18(1).
47 IR86, r 5.19(2) (or IRN91, r 5.18(2).

- Inspect and adjudicate on all proxies and proofs in accordance with the detailed rules set out below before the meeting commences.
- Take control of the proceedings and present a report on the purpose of the meeting.
- Ensure that a register is kept of all attendees.[48]
- Conduct all voting in accordance with the rules set out below.
- Prepare minutes of the meeting.[49]
- Prepare a report of the outcome of the meeting.[50]

When a meeting is summoned under s 257, IA86 a copy of the report must be filed in court within 4 days of the meeting being held.[51] This additional filing is not required when a meeting is convened under s 256A, IA86

25.17 The chairman's decision on the adjudication of claims and proxies is subject to appeal to the court by any creditor or by the debtor. If the chairman has any doubts the claim can be marked as objected to and the vote allowed subject to any subsequent declaration on invalidity if the objection is sustained. Any appeal must be made within 28 days beginning with the first day on which the report required by s 259, IA86 is made to the court.

25.18 If on an appeal the chairman's decision is reversed or varied, or votes are declared invalid, the court may order another meeting to be summoned, or make such order as it thinks just. The court's power to make an order can only be exercised if it considers that the circumstances giving rise to the appeal are such as give rise to unfair prejudice or material irregularity. The chairman is not personally liable for any costs incurred by any person in respect of an appeal.

Voting formalities

How do creditors vote at a meeting?

25.19 Creditors can either attend the meeting in person, attend remotely[52] or they can give a proxy to another person to vote on their behalf. Every notice summoning a creditors' meeting must have a proxy [Form 8.1][53] attached. The person nominated on the proxy form can be any person authorised by the creditor to attend the meeting or alternatively the proxy can be given to the

48 IR86, r 5.27(2)(c) or IRN91, r 5.25(2)(c).
49 IR86, r 12.5.
50 IR86, r 5.27 or IRN91, r 5.25.
51 IR86, r 5.27(3) or IRN91, r 5.25(3).
52 IA86, s 379A.
53 IR86, r 5.18(3) or IRN91, r 5.17(3).

chairman of the meeting to vote on the creditors behalf, or to any other person who intends to attend the meeting in person.

What is a proxy?

25.20 'A proxy' is an authority given by a person ('the principal') to another person ('the proxy-holder') to attend a meeting and speak and vote as his representative.[54] A proxy can be either 'general' or 'special'. A general proxy allows the proxy holder to vote in whatever manner they want on the creditor's behalf whereas a special proxy includes details on how the proxy holder must vote on specific resolutions. A special proxy can be used as a general proxy when voting on resolutions not specified on the proxy form. For an IVA the proxy must contain resolutions regarding the following:

- To vote for or against the terms of the proposal.
- To vote for or against the constitution of a committee (the proposal will set out the terms under which any nominated committee can function).
- To vote for or against the nominee's and supervisors remuneration as set out in the proposal.

25.21 Only one proxy may be given by a person for any one meeting at which he desires to be represented; and it may only be given to one person, being an individual aged 18 or over. But the principal may specify one or more other such individuals to be alternative proxy-holders, in the order in which they are named on the proxy.[55]

Who provides the proxy form and how can it be used?

25.22 Proxies are issued with the notice of the meeting.[56] The proxy form should not be pre-completed with any name or description of proxy holder.[57] The proxy form must be signed by the principal, or by some person authorised by him (either generally or with reference to a particular meeting). If the form is signed by a person other than the principal, the nature of the person's authority must be stated clearly.[58]

25.23 Proxies given for a meeting can be used at any subsequent adjournment.[59] When a proxy is given to the chairman of the meeting, the chairman cannot decline to be proxy holder[60] and it can be used by any person

---

54 IR86, r 8.1(1).
55 IR86, r 8.1(3).
56 IR86, r 8.2(1).
57 IR86, r 8.2(1).
58 IR86, r 8.2(3).
59 IR86, r 8.3(1).
60 IR86, r 8.1(4) and (5).

authorised to chair the meeting.[61] Proxies must not be sent out pre-completed except for the title of the proceedings and the date and time of the meeting.

What documentation needs to be retained for inspection?

25.24 Proxies used for voting at any meeting must be retained by the chairman[62] and passed to the supervisor after the meeting if he is not the supervisor himself.[63] Any person attending the meeting is entitled, immediately before or in the course of the meeting, to inspect proxies and associated documents (including proofs) sent or given for the purpose of that meeting.[64] Any advice given in respect of the provision of proxies should be put in writing. The chairman must also make the proxies available for inspection by the following at all reasonable times on any business day:

- any creditor who has submitted a proof of debt[65] that has not been rejected.[66]
- for the purposes of r 8.5(1) (right of inspection of proxies) a member state liquidator appointed in main proceedings is deemed to be a creditor.[67]
- the debtor.[68]

An office holder does have the power to treat any document as confidential if disclosing that information could be prejudicial to the conduct of the proceedings or disclosure would put a person at risk of violence.[69] However, this can be overruled by the court on application by the creditor wishing to inspect the document,[70] or in the case of a person at risk of violence an application must be made to the court by any of the debtor, the supervisor, the official receiver or the Secretary of State.[71]

How does a company give a proxy?

25.25 The authority to sign a proxy on behalf of a principal which is a corporation does not have to be in the form of a resolution[72] but can be signed by any appropriately designated employee. However, if no proxy has been submitted any person wishing to attend a meeting of creditors or contributories and represent the company then they must produce to the chairman of the

---

61 IR86, r 8.3(2) and (3).
62 IR86, r 8.4(2).
63 IR86, r 8.4(2).
64 IR86, r 8.5(4).
65 IR86, r 8.5(1)(a).
66 IR86, r 8.5(2)(b).
67 IR86, r 8.8(2).
68 IR86, r 8.5(3)(b).
69 IR86, r 5.67(1).
70 IR86, r 12A.51.
71 IR86, r 5.67(3).
72 IR86, r 8.7(3).

meeting a copy of the resolution from which authority is derived.[73] The copy resolution must be under the seal of the corporation, or certified by the secretary or a director of the corporation to be a true copy.[74]

What are the restrictions for a proxy holder with a financial interest?

25.26 A proxy-holder must not vote in favour of any resolution which would directly or indirectly place him, or any associate of his, in a position to receive any remuneration out of the insolvent estate, unless the proxy specifically directs him to vote in that way.[75]

25.27 Where a proxy-holder has signed the proxy as being authorised to do so by his principal and the proxy specifically directs him to vote in the way mentioned above, he shall nevertheless not vote in that way unless he produces to the chairman of the meeting written authorisation from his principal sufficient to show that the proxy-holder was entitled so to sign the proxy.[76]

What is the meaning of 'associate' for proxy holders?

25.28 When any person who is acting as chairman of a meeting and uses proxies in that capacity under r 8.3, IR86 (where the responsible insolvency practitioner delegates chairmanship to some other person), the proxy-holder is deemed an associate of his.[77]

What can the chairman do as proxy holder?

25.29 As proxy holder the chairman may vote as follows:

- Where the proxy requires him to vote for a particular resolution, and no other person proposes that resolution:
  - he shall himself propose it, unless he considers that there is good reason for not doing so, and
  - if he does not propose it, after the meeting he must notify his principal of the reason why not.
- Where the proxy gives him general discretion he may vote as he thinks fit.[78]
- A proxy-holder must not vote in favour of any resolution which would directly or indirectly place him, or any associate of his, in a position to

---

73 IR86, r 8.7(1).
74 IR86, r 8.7(2).
75 IR86, r 8.6(1).
76 IR86, r 8.6(1A).
77 IR86, r 8.6(2).
78 IR86, r 8.1(6).

receive any remuneration out of the insolvent estate, unless the proxy specifically directs him to vote in that way.[79]

- Where a proxy-holder has signed the proxy as being authorised to do so by his principal and the proxy specifically directs him to vote in the way mentioned in para (1), he shall nevertheless not vote in that way unless he produces to the chairman of the meeting written authorisation from his principal sufficient to show that the proxy-holder was entitled so to sign the proxy.[80]

- Rule 8.6, IR86 applies to any person acting as chairman of a meeting and using proxies in that capacity;[81] and in its application to him, the proxy-holder is deemed an associate of his.[82]

What documentation needs to be lodged to entitle a creditor to vote?

25.30 A proof of debt needs to be lodged by the time and date specified on the meeting notice together with a proxy issued specifically for that meeting.[83] A proxy is only valid if the creditor has also submitted a claim which has been admitted for voting purposes.

25.31 A person claiming to be a creditor needs to confirm the amount outstanding so that the chairman of the meeting can agree the amount to be used for voting purposes at the creditors' meeting. This is usually done by a completing a proof of debt form or notice of claim. The following information is required on a proof of debt form:[84]

- Full name of the creditor.

- Full address of the creditor.

- Details of the amount outstanding.

- Details of any documents attached evidencing the amount stated.

- Details of any interest included in the claim.

- Details of how and when the debt was incurred.

- Details of any security held.

- Details of any reservation of title claim being made.

---

79 IR86, r 8.6(1).
80 IR86, r 8.6(1A).
81 IR86, r 8.6.
82 IR86, r 8.6(2).
83 IR86, r 8.2(2).
84 Form 8.1.

- Full name and position of the person making the claim.

Agreement of claims

How are claims agreed?

25.32 A creditor's entitlement to vote is calculated with reference to the following date:

- where the debtor is not an undischarged bankrupt and an interim order is in force, by reference to the amount of the debt owed to him as at the date of the interim order;
- where the debtor is not an undischarged bankrupt and an interim order is not in force, by reference to the amount of the debt owed to him at the date of the meeting;
- where the debtor is an undischarged bankrupt, by reference to the amount of the debt owed to him as at the date of the bankruptcy order;
- a creditor may vote in respect of a debt for an unliquidated amount or any debt whose value is not ascertained, and for the purposes of voting (but not otherwise) the debt will be valued at £1 unless the chairman agrees to a higher value.

The chairman of the meeting will check every creditor's entitlement to vote as above and admit or reject their claims accordingly[85] taking into account any double claims, guarantees or security.

How are liens and charges dealt with?

25.33 Liens were discussed generally in chapter 4. In an IVA proposal this type of liability needs to be identified and quantified especially if it purports to grant some sort of security. Land charge and land registry searches should be completed to identify any charges on property.

How are negligence and other claims dealt with?

25.34 Anyone with a claim must be notified of the proposed IVA. Any claims should be quantified if possible and details of the claims discussed with any insurance company as regards the nature and scope of the claim. Future claims cannot be bound by an IVA even if they relate to prior actions or dealings.

How are subrogated and contingent claims dealt with?

25.35 Subrogated claims are when one person assumes the liability for another party. For instance a debt may be guaranteed and if the guarantor pays the liability they will then stand in the shoes of the original creditor. Until any

---

[85] IR86, r 5.22(2) or IRN91, r 5.20.

guarantor actually pays the liability they remain as a contingent creditor. Any contingent creditors therefore need to be notified of any arrangement but will only be allowed to vote for a nominal £1 for the purposes of the meeting.

How are student loans dealt with?

25.36 Student loans were also covered in detail in chapter 4 and the position will be similar to bankruptcy proceedings.

How are secured creditors' claims calculated?

25.37 A secured creditor's claim is calculated in the same manner as bankruptcy by calculating the value of the security and only allowing a claim for the shortfall. As in bankruptcy a secured creditor can forego their security and claim for the full amount of the debt.

How are votes counted?

25.38 Votes are counted by value and not number.[86] Every creditor who has had notice of the meeting is entitled to vote for the amount agreed in the claim submitted. The percentage required for approval is explained in detail below.

Approval or rejection of the proposal

What percentages of votes are required for approval?

25.39 Approval is obtained if the following voting procedures are followed:

- to approve the proposal or any modifications proposed there must be a majority of three-quarters or more in value of the creditors present in person, remotely or by proxy and voting on the resolution;[87]

- to approve any other resolution proposed at the meeting, one-half in value of the creditors present in person, remotely or by proxy and voting on the resolution is required.[88]

25.40 However, any resolution is invalid if those voting against it include more than half in value of the creditors, counting in these latter only those:

- who have had notice of the meeting;[89]

- secured or part secured creditors;[90] and

---

86 IR86, r 5.23(1) or IRN91, r 5.21(1).
87 IR86, r 5.23(2).
88 IR86, r 5.23(1).
89 IR86, r 5.23(4)(a).
90 IR86, r 5.23(4)(b).

- who are not, to the best of the chairman's belief, associates of the debtor.[91]

25.41 In addition, the following creditor's votes in respect of any claim or part of a claim must be excluded:

- where written notice of the claim was not given, either at the meeting or before it, to the chairman or the nominee;[92]

- where the claim or part is secured;[93]

- where the claim is in respect of a debt wholly or partly secured, unless the creditor is willing:[94]

  — to treat the liability as secured;
  — to estimate the value of the security and to deduct it from the claim; and
  — to vote with the remaining value.

25.42 It is for the chairman of the meeting to decide whether a vote is to be left out of account, or a person is an associate of the debtor for these purposes. In relation to determining associates the chairman is entitled to rely on the information provided by the debtor's statement of affairs or from other information provided in accordance with the rules.[95]

25.43 If the chairman uses a proxy contrary to r 5.20, IR86, his vote with that proxy does not count towards any majority needed. The chairman's decision on any voting matter under r 5.20, IR86 is subject to appeal to the court by any creditor or by the debtor.[96]

What other resolutions will be put to the creditors' meeting?

25.44 Once agreement has been reached on the terms of the proposal the following additional resolutions must be put to the meeting:

1. for the appointment of a supervisor which may include more than one person;

and if so, then

2. whether acts to be done in connection with the arrangement may be done by any one of them, or must be done by both or all.[97]

---

91 IR86, r 5.23(4)(c).
92 IR86, r 5.23(3)(a).
93 IR86, r 5.23(3)(b).
94 IR86, r 5.23(3)(c).
95 IR86, r 5.23(5).
96 IR86, r 5.23(6) or IRN91, r 5.21(6).
97 IR86, r 5.25(1) or IRN91, r 5.23(1).

If the chairman of the meeting is not the nominated supervisor then he must have presented to him:

- that person's written consent to act; and
- his written confirmation that he is qualified to act as an insolvency practitioner in relation to the debtor or is an authorised person in relation to the debtor.[98]

How is voting conducted for approval of the supervisor's remuneration?

25.45 In most cases the details of the supervisor's fees will be agreed as part of the proposal but should be separately agreed to avoid the need for a creditor to vote against a proposal when it is the level of proposed Supervisor's fees that is an issue.

What are the rules governing meeting adjournments?

25.46 To facilitate the agreement of a proposal the meeting can be adjourned on the day of the meeting from time to time to allow for further negotiation to take place.[99] If agreement cannot be reached the chairman can adjourn for a period of up to 14 days.[100] If further adjournments are required this is permissible as long as the final adjournment is not later than 14 days after the date of the original meeting.[101] Notice of each adjournment must be given to the creditors and the court.[102]

In respect of meetings held with remote attendance additional rules apply in the event that creditors are excluded in part or in whole from attendance. These rules and circumstances are covered in more detail below.

What is an excluded person in relation to remote attendance at a meeting and what actions can be taken by the chairman?

25.47 An excluded person relation to remote attendance a creditors' meeting is someone who has taken all the necessary steps to attend or take part in a meeting and where arrangements have prevented them from attending that meeting in part or in whole.[103]

25.48 Where the chairman of the meeting becomes aware that there are one or more excluded persons he has the following options:

- continue the meeting;[104]

98 IR86, r 5.25(2) or IRN91, r 5.23(1).
99 IR86, r 5.24(1) or IRN91, r 5.22(1).
100 IR86, r 5.24(2) or IRN91, r 5.22(2).
101 IR86, r 5.24(3) or IRN91, r 5.22(3).
102 IR86, r 5.24(4) or IRN91, r 5.22(4).
103 IR86, r 12A.23(1).
104 IR86, r 12A.23(2)(a).

- declare the meeting void and convene the meeting again;[105]
- declare the meeting valid up to the point of exclusion and adjourn the meeting;[106]
- suspend the meeting for up to an hour.[107]

Where the chairman continues the meeting, the meeting is valid unless the chairman of that meeting receives a complaint which he upholds or the court otherwise directs.[108]

What information can an excluded person request from the chairman?

25.49 An excluded person can request an indication of what happened during a meeting from the chairman. The request must be made as follows:

- as soon as reasonably practicable (during or after the meeting has concluded), or at least by 1600 hours on the first business day following the meeting;[109]
- to the chairman of the meeting or the supervisor if made after the business of the meeting has been concluded.[110]

The chairman or supervisor having satisfied themselves that the applicant is an excluded person must provide the 'indication' requested as soon as reasonably practicable or at least by 1600 hours on the first business day following the receipt of the request.[111]

How is the outcome of the meeting recorded?

25.50 The chairman of the meeting is required to report on the outcome of the meeting[112] and minutes should also be prepared.[113] In cases where the meeting has been under s 256, IA86 (interim order in place) a copy must be sent to the court within 4 business days of the meeting being held.[114] In all cases the creditors must also receive a copy of the report of the outcome[115] and where the debtor is an undischarged bankrupt the OR must also be sent a copy.[116]

---

105 IR86, r 12A.23(2)(b).
106 IR86, r 12A.23(2)(c).
107 IR86, r 12A.23(4).
108 IR86, r 12A.23(3).
109 IR86, r 12A.24(3)(a).
110 IR86, r 12A.24(3)(b).
111 IR86, r 12A.24(4).
112 IR86, r 5.27(1) or IRN91, r 5.25(1).
113 IR86, r 12.5.
114 IR86, r 5.27(4A).
115 IR86, r 5.27(4).
116 IR86, r 5.27(4).

Who can challenge the outcome of the meeting and what grounds are available?

25.51 The following parties can challenge the outcome of a meeting by applying to court:[117]

- The debtor can challenge in the following circumstances:

  - if the arrangement was refused; or
  - if the arrangement was modified without his consent; or
  - if creditors were allowed to vote for too large an amount so effectively altering the voting power.

- Any creditor can challenge in the following circumstances:

  - if a proof was rejected in part or whole;[118] or
  - if unfair prejudice was alleged;[119] or
  - if material irregularity was alleged.[120]

- The nominee can challenge in the following circumstances:

  - if he was voted in as supervisor; or
  - if the proposal was refused and other irregularities came to light; or
  - if the debtor failed to agree to a modification.
  - an excluded person (meeting attended remotely) or any other attendee at a meeting (either in person or by proxy) can make a complaint that they have been adversely affected by a person's actual apparent or claimed exclusion.[121]

What remedies can the court offer and what is the time limit for challenging the outcome of the meeting?

25.52 The court can order one or any of the following:[122]

- revoke, or suspend any approval given by the meeting;[123]

- give directions that a further meeting be held to reconsider the proposal.[124]

---

117 IA86, s 262 or INO89, art 236.
118 IR86, r 5.22(2).
119 IA86, s 262(1)(a) or INO89, art 236(1)(a).
120 IA86, s 262(1)(b) or INO89, art 236(1)(a).
121 IR86, r 12A.25(1).
122 IA86, s 262(4) or INO89, art 236(4).
123 IA86, s 262(4)(a) or INO89, art 236(4)(a).
124 IA86, s 262(4)(b) or INO89, art 236(4)(b).

25.53 An application must be made to court within 28 days of knowledge of the meeting for any creditor who was not given notice[125] and within 28 days of the report being filed in court for all other creditors,[126] the debtor.[127]

CREDITORS' COMMITTEE

What is the purpose of a creditors' committee?

25.54 The purpose of a creditors' committee is to protect and promote the interests of the general body of creditors and to exercise control over the costs and expenses being incurred. IVA proposals usually include reference to the bankruptcy rules in the event that any committee is constituted by the creditors at the creditors' meeting. This is not a mandatory requirement and creditors should be advised that these requirements may give rise to additional costs as the reporting requirements can be onerous. In addition, creditors should be advised that unless the case is complicated with likely variations or additional agreement of fees are required then the costs involved will almost certainly outweigh any benefits from additional control. For more detailed information on committees see chapter 14.

---

[125] IA86, s 262(3)(b) or INO89, art 236(3)(b).
[126] IA86, s 262(3)(a) or INO89, art 236(3)(a).
[127] IA86, s 262(2)(b) or INO89, art 236(2)(b).

Chapter 26

MONITORING AND COMPLETION OF AN IVA (INCLUDING DISTRIBUTION OF FUNDS)

'Small debts are like small shot; they are rattling on every side, and can scarcely be escaped without a wound; great debts are like cannon; of loud noise, but little danger.'[1]

INTRODUCTION

26.1 This chapter looks at the ongoing monitoring of an IVA including proposing amendments when circumstances change and making distributions. It then looks at completion and what happens when an IVA completes successfully, or fails. Finally, there is a section on the registration process which sets out details of the information that is recorded and published and the process for errors to be corrected.

MONITORING

How is an IVA monitored by the supervisor?

26.2 The terms of the IVA are vital to the monitoring process and it is the duty of the supervisor to ensure that the terms are complied with. In straighforward arrangements the role may simply require an annual review of the debtor's income and circumstances but in more complicated cases this may involve the review of accounts or other circumstances if the debtor is trading or engaged in other business activities. If the terms of the arrangement are breached or the debtor advises the supervisor that circumstances have changed and the terms can no longer be adhered to the supervisor may ask creditors to vary the terms of the arrangement.

26.3 Creditors must be provided with annual updates[2] on the arrangement and may be invited to a further meeting in the event that any modification is required. Any modification will rely on the original proposal providing for potential problems. If the IVA did not include a term allowing for modification and setting the process required then a modification cannot be proposed.

---

1 Dr Johnson, *The Great Cham of Literature*.

2 IR86, r 5.31(2)(c) or IRN91, r 5.29(2)(c).

What is the usual process for agreeing a modification?

26.4 Details of the process should be set in the proposal and there will usually be a requirement to either hold a creditors' meeting or postal vote on any material modification to the original proposal. The voting procedure must be clearly set out in the proposal and will usually use the same majority and exclusions as for the original approval. For protocol approved IVAs a certain amount of leeway is given to the supervisor to vary the terms in order to keep costs low including unexpected variations in creditor's claims and or the debtor's income and expenditure.[3]

Costs, fees and expenses

26.5 Costs, fees and expenses of the estate must be paid in advance of distributions to the creditors. The distribution process is discussed later in this chapter however the basis and agreement of the supervisor's fees are dealt with first.

How are the supervisor's fees calculated and agreed?

26.6 The basis for calculating the supervisor's fees must be set out in the proposal together with an estimate of the final cost. If it becomes clear to the supervisor that the fee payable to him will exceed the estimate provided in the proposal[4] he must, in his next report to creditors:[5]

- notify the creditors of that fact; and
- explain why the estimate has been exceeded; and
- provide a revised estimate.

Additional fees should not be taken until creditors have approved the variation. For more information on remuneration generally see also chapter 13.

What is the procedure for challenging the supervisor's fees?

26.7 A supervisor is only entitled to fees agreed in the proposal. This usually comprises of the basis together with an estimate of the amounts to be billed. The proposal should contain a realistic estimate of the quantum of fees to be charged and any material increase must be reported to creditors before the fees are taken. If creditors wish to challenge the quantum of fees taken then this should be done as soon as the matter is reported by the supervisor and not at the end of the case. Section 263(3), IA86[6] allows the debtor, creditor or any

---

3 The Straightforward Consumer IVA Protocol 2013 version, Section 10.

4 SIP3 para 5.4, version 4 issued 1 April 2007 or SIP3A (NI) issued February 2007 with effect from 1 April 2007.

5 SIP3 para 8.2, version 4 issued 1 April 2007 or SIP3A (NI) issued February 2007 with effect from 1 April 2007.

6 IA86, s 263(3) or INO89, art 237(3).

other interested party to apply to court if they are dissatisfied with the supervisor's actions. In addition s 263(4) gives the supervisor a similar right to apply to court for directions in relation to any particular matter.

Distributions to creditors

What is the procedure for making a distribution?

26.8 The proposal will usually set out the expected timing and level of distribution to be paid and any specific process to be followed. Any material difference in outcome should be advised to creditors as soon as possible. The acceptance and rejection of claims for the purposes of voting at the creditors' meeting was dealt with in chapter 25 however for distribution purposes some areas require additional attention.

How are multiple claims for the same debt dealt with?

26.9 The basic principal here is the rule against double proofs,[7] that is a dividend can only be paid once in respect of the same debt so that the principle of pari passu is maintained. This issue can arise when liabilities are subject to guarantees or are sold on either before or during the administration of the IVA. So in the case of competing claims for the same debt each claim must be reviewed in detail to determine who has the valid claim to the distribution. In order to ensure that all creditors are bound by the arrangement contingent claims (guarantors) are usually allowed to vote for £1 as being a claim for an unascertained amount.

Who has the valid claim in respect of guarantee claims?

26.10 A creditor who has obtained an additional guarantor to a debt can pursue both the guarantor and the debtor for the debt and can effectively request the full amount from both parties with the proviso that he can only receive 100% of the debt owed. If a creditor obtains some funds from the guarantor prior to making a claim in the estate he is still entitled to submit a proof for the full amount of the debt until the guarantor has paid off the debt in full.[8] A guarantor can only stand in the shoes of the creditor once full payment has been made.

In some circumstances both the debtor and the guarantor are both insolvent and in this case the creditor can equally prove for the full amount in both estates in what is known as a 'double dip'. Again the creditor can only receive 100% of the debt owed but has effectively increased his chances of being paid in full.[9]

---

7 For definitions see *Re Oriental Commercial Bank* (1871) 7 Ch App 99 and *Barclays Bank Ltd v TOSG Trust Fund* [1984] AC 626.

8 See *Re Amalgamated Investment and Property Co Ltd* [1984] 3 All ER 272.

9 For example see *Re Polly Peck International Plc* [1996] 2 All ER 433.

TERMINATION: COMPLETION OR FAILURE

How and when are the debts discharged?

26.11 An IVA can either complete satisfactorily or fail. Both outcomes result in termination. However, the debts included in an IVA involving a composition are only discharged on satisfactory completion. In the event of a failure in these cases the creditors continue to have the right to pursue any outstanding debt against the individual. An IVA involving a scheme can be satisfactorily concluded without a release of any outstanding debts.

What happens on completion of the arrangement?

26.12 On completion of the arrangement the final notices are sent to each of the creditors, the debtor, the SoS and the court (only where the creditors' meeting was summoned under s 257, IA86) within 28 days.[10] The court can extend the 28 day period on application of the supervisor.[11] The notice circulated must include the following information:

- A report setting out the difference between expected and actual outcome and whether the arrangement has completed satisfactorily or been terminated.[12]
- A detailed receipts and payments account.[13]

The supervisor must not vacate office until the notice has been sent to the SoS.[14]

26.13 The date of completion will usually be set out in the approved proposal or will have been amended during any modification process. This is normally a fixed time period but with allowances for some minor extensions depending on any modification or other terms that may allow the term to be extended. For instance, the proposal may state that sixty contributions are required over a 5 year period and if one or more instalments are missed the proposal may allow the end date to be extended until the required instalments have been paid.

What happens on failure?

26.14 The terms of failure will be set out in the arrangement and these should be adhered to unless the creditors have approved an amendment to the agreed proposal. Failure can be linked specifically to outcome or may be linked to other specific conditions especially in respect of trading cases.

---

10 IR86, r 5.34(1) & (3A).

11 IR86, r 5.34(4). On this area see further J Tribe The IVA time extensions under the Insolvency Act 1986: uncertainty or necessity? *Insolvency Law & Practice*, Volume 18, No 6 [2002], pp 190–192.

12 IR86, r 5.34(1).

13 IR86, r 5.34(2).

14 IR86, r 5.34(3).

What are the consequences of failure for the debtor and the creditors?

26.15 The consequences of failure for a debtor are very serious as this effectively puts the debtor back into the same position as before the IVA was approved. The choices for the debtor will be to file for bankruptcy, propose a new IVA or simply deal with creditors piecemeal. Equally for creditors, their position also reverts to the pre approval status with the need to recommence recovery procedures.

REGISTRATION

What information is recorded in the Electronic Individual Insolvency Register of an IVA?

26.16 The Electronic Individual Insolvency Register (EIIR) is open to the public and has been available online since 2004.[15] It contains entries in respect of all current IVAs together with current bankruptcies, debt relief orders, all restriction orders and agreements. Historical data is not available online but may be made available on request to financial or other institutions.

What information is recorded in the register about an IVA?

26.17 The following data is recorded on the register:[16]

- the name of the debtor;[17]
- any other name by which the debtor has been known;[18]
- the debtor's address;[19]
- the gender of the debtor;[20]
- the date of birth of the debtor;[21]
- the date the arrangement was approved;[22]
- the court reference number;[23]

---

15 IR86, r 6A.1(4) The register can be found at: http://www.insolvency.gov.uk/bankruptcy/bankruptcysearch.htm.
16 IR86, r 6A.2.
17 IR86, rr 6A.2(1)(b)(i) and 5.29(1)(a).
18 IR86, r 6A.2(1)(c).
19 IR86, r 5.29(1)(a).
20 IR86, r 6A.2(1)(c).
21 IR86, r 6A.2(1)(c).
22 IR86, r 6A.2(1)(b)(ii).
23 IR86, r 6A.2(1)(b)(iii).

- the name of the court in which the chairman's report was filed;[24]
- the name of the supervisor;[25]
- the address of the supervisor;[26]
- details of any change in supervisor;[27]
- details of completion or termination of the arrangement.[28]

When can entries in the register be corrected?

26.18 If the SoS becomes aware of any inaccuracy in any information contained in the register it must be corrected as soon as reasonably practicable.[29] In addition when the SoS receives notification of the date of death of any person whose details are held on the register that information will be added.[30]

---

24 IR86, r 5.29(1)(d) or IRN91, r 5.27(1)(d).
25 IR86, r 5.29(1)(c) or IRN91, r 5.27(1)(c).
26 IR86, r 5.29(1)(c) or IRN91, r 5.27(1)(c).
27 IR86, r 5.29(2) or IRN91, r 5.27(2).
28 IR86, rr 5.34(3) and 6A.3 or IRN91, r 5.32(3).
29 IR86, r 6A.8(1).
30 IR86, r 6A.8(2).

Chapter 27

LOW INCOME SOLUTIONS IN THE UK

Neither have I money nor commodity
To raise a present sum. Therefore go forth,
Try what my credit can in Venice do—[1]

INTRODUCTION

27.1 Chapter 2 provided an overview of the various solutions available (formal and informal) across the whole of the UK but this chapter concentrates on individuals with low incomes and few assets who have debt problems. Chapter 5 looked at the different enforcement procedures and how these impact on the options available to individuals in financial difficulty. This chapter compares a number of different low-income debt solutions available across the UK:

- the debt relief order (DRO) (England and Wales/Northern Ireland);
- sequestration (Low Income Low Asset) (LILA) (Scotland);
- the straightforward IVA Protocol[2] (England and Wales);
- the Protected Trust Deed (Scotland);
- the county court administration order (CCAO) (England and Wales);
- a deed of arrangement (DoA) (England and Wales/Northern Ireland);
- the Debt Arrangement Scheme (DAS) (Scotland).

At least one commentator has discussed the superabundance of personal insolvency debt solutions and the possible confusion that this plethora of mechanisms gives rise to as regards debtor entry into each of the procedures.[3] This chapter does go someway to support this point, namely, that there are numerous (perhaps confusing) avenues into debt solutions at the lower end of debt relief (see also chapter 1). It is correct to note that both CCAO and DoA

---

1 Shakespeare, *Merchant of Venice*, Act I, Scene I, Antonio.
2 Latest version came into effect January 2013.
3 P Joyce 'A simple solution to debt? Cork revisited' *Insolvency Intelligence* (2009) 22(5), pp 71–73.

are rarely used,[4] but they do still exist on the statute book, serving to provide further debt solutions for the low-income debtor. Broadly speaking it can be argued that most of the personal insolvency mechanisms are similar in terms of procedural substance and that the key difference relates to entry levels and costs. These issues and the various mechanisms are discussed in more detail below.

DEBT RELIEF ORDERS

How have DROs developed?

27.2 The background to the DRO procedure has been looked at briefly in chapter 1 but is revisited here in more detail. There are two documents that can be looked to in relation to the development of the DRO procedure. The first, *A Choice of Paths: better options to manage over-indebtedness and multiple debt*[5] emanated from the Department for Constitutional Affairs (as it then was, now the Ministry of Justice). The second, *Relief for the Indebted – An Alternative to Bankruptcy*[6] was produced by the Insolvency Service. It could be argued that this potential crossover between the Ministry of Justice's remit and the Insolvency Service's remit could be problematic. The DRO implementation process has not however highlighted a conflict between the two Government departments dealing with very similar debt related issues. From a public perception point of view however, it must seem strange to the lay-person that the Insolvency Service is not the only department with responsibility for dealing with insolvency issues.

27.3 Once these DRO proposals were formulated and consulted upon, by the Ministry of Justice and the Insolvency Service, the process then moved to the legislative stage. A particularly illuminating submission was made to the House of Commons by Mr Oliver Heald MP in relation to the DRO procedure on the 5 March 2007. He observed:

> 'Part 5 of the Bill covers helping people deal with over-indebtedness and multiple debts through debt management. Over-indebtedness is an issue of vital concern in our society. With the number of individual insolvencies reaching a record 107,000 in 2006, and with the amount people owe on credit cards, loans and mortgages now more than £1 trillion, this is clearly an area where help is needed. Over-indebtedness can be caused by low levels of financial literacy and awareness, and we would like more effort to be made in that regard. The Citizens Advice Bureaux state that:

---

4 On this point see: J Ziegel *Comparative Consumer Insolvency Regimes: a Canadian Perspective*, (Hart Publishing, Oxford, 2003).

5 A Choice of Paths: better options to manage over-indebtedness and multiple debt, Department for Constitutional Affairs. Consultation Paper, CP 23/04, 2004.

6 *Relief for the Indebted – An Alternative to Bankruptcy*, Insolvency Service, March 2005. See also: *Relief for the Indebted–An Alternative to Bankruptcy: Summary of Responses and Government Reply*, Insolvency Service, November 2005. For a summary of these reforms see: Ed. *Proposals for New Debt Relief Scheme*, Insolvency Service (2005) Comp. Law, 26(7), 215.

> "in particular, the Debt Relief Order proposals have the potential to help a substantial proportion of CAB clients, many of whom are vulnerable and on low incomes."

> The debt relief orders will enable many people who were unable to access any of the debt solutions currently available to plan their debt repayments, and will help them in respect of the question of application fees.

> We therefore cautiously welcome the intention behind the envisaged debt relief orders. As with much of the Bill, secondary legislation will be needed. For debt relief orders, it will cover the criteria specifying liabilities, and the levels of assets and of surplus income. The debt relief orders will also reduce some of the pressure on the courts, because to maintain the lowest application fee possible, applicants will need not to apply to them but to use the internet. With the court system currently in crisis, anything that can reduce the burdens is an important benefit.'[7]

27.4 In the context of an answer on enforcement restriction orders (ERO), Ms Bridget Prentice MP noted 'This package includes the new debt relief order, which took effect from 6 April, and is intended to assist those who will never be able to pay their debts and who have minimal assets.'[8] Taken together these two statements in the House of Commons are particularly enlightening, not least because of the focus on a low cost low income alternative to bankruptcy.

What are the entry criteria for a DRO?

27.5 The eligibility criterion for a DRO brings the new procedure squarely below the bankruptcy entry point. In this respect the DRO can be seen as a kind of *bankruptcy-lite*, as in many respects the DRO procedure and bankruptcy are similar, save for the eligibility criteria. The eligibility criteria must be satisfied by any individual who is unable to pay his 'qualifying' debts who wishes to apply for a DRO.[9] In outline the conditions for entry into a DRO are that:

(1) the debtor's total liabilities (not including unliquidated or excluded debts) must not exceed £15,000;[10]

(2) the debtor's gross assets must be less than £300;[11] if the debtor owns any motor vehicles which are valued under £1000 these will not be included in the calculation of total assets; and finally

(3) any surplus income must be less than £50 a month.[12]

27.6 There are also a number of criteria that any prospective DRO user has to be aware of which will affect possible access to the procedure. The gatekeepers

---

7 Hansard, House of Commons, 5 Mar 2007: Column 1318.

8 Hansard, House of Commons, 29 April 2009: Column 1328W.

9 IA86, s 251A.

10 IA86, Sch 4ZA, para (6). Limit on debtor's overall indebtedness.

11 IA86, Sch 4ZA, para (2). Limit on value of debtor's property.

12 IA86, Sch 4ZA, para (7). Limit on debtor's monthly surplus income.

of this access are the Approved Intermediaries (AI). A debtor cannot gain access to a DRO if they have already had the benefit of a DRO in the last 6 years. Similarly an undischarged bankrupt or a debtor who is in a current IVA, or a debtor who is subject to a BRO or DRO, cannot gain access to the procedure.[13] It may be an obvious qualification, but it must nevertheless be stated that the debtor must be unable to pay their debts.[14] Finally, any aspiring DRO user must be domiciled in England and Wales, or be resident or have carried on business in England and Wales in last 3 years.[15] There can be no existing bankruptcy petition left outstanding whilst the DRO application is being processed. This procedure has subsequently been extended to Northern Ireland with effect from 30 June 2011.[16]

What is the application process?

27.7 The DRO application is made to the OR through an AI.[17] The application must include:

- A list of the debts to which the debtor is subject at the date of the application, (specifying the amount of each debt including any interest, penalty or other sum that has become payable in relation to that debt on or before that date) and the creditor to whom it is owed.[18]

- There must also be included in the application details of any security held in respect of any of those debts.[19]

What role does the official receiver play?

27.8 Decisions as to the DRO application and its acceptance are made by the OR.[20] Section 251C, IA86 contains a lengthy set of conditions that the OR can take into consideration when deciding to refuse or accept a DRO proposal.[21] Consideration need not be rushed. The OR may stay consideration of the application until he has received answers to any queries raised with the debtor in relation to anything connected with the application.[22] The application can be refused if the OR considers that the application does not meet all the

---

13 IA86, Sch 4ZA, para (2). Debtor's previous insolvency history.

14 IA86, s 251A.

15 IA86, Sch 4ZA, para (1).

16 The detailed rules were introduced by the Insolvency (Amendment) Rules (Northern Ireland) 2011, SR 2011/151. See also art 360 of SI 1989/2405 (NI 19), art 359 of which was amended by the Insolvency (Northern Ireland) Order 1989 (Amendment) Regulations (Northern Ireland) 2002 (SR 2002/223), s 15 of and para 81 of Sch 5 to the Constitutional Reform Act 2005, and by art 15(5) of and para 142 of Sch 18 to the Northern Ireland Act 1998 (Devolution of Policing and Justice Functions) Order 2010 (SI 2010/976).

17 IA86, s 251B.

18 IA86, s 251B(2).

19 IA86, s 251B(2)(b).

20 IA86, s 251C.

21 Each of the conditions set out in Part 1 of Sch 4ZA must also be met and the OR may refuse the application if he is not satisfied that each condition specified in Part 2 of Sch 4ZA is met (s 251C (5)(c) and (6) IA86).

22 IA86, s 251C(2).

requirements imposed by or under s 251B, IA86 (making an application)[23] or where any queries raised with the debtor have not been answered to the satisfaction of the OR.[24] Perhaps most seriously, the OR can refuse an application where the debtor has made any false representation or omission in making the application or on supplying any information or documents in support of it.[25] There is also a statutory duty on the OR to refuse the DRO application if he is not satisfied that the debtor is an individual who is unable to pay his debts.[26]

27.9 Any decision, whether positive or negative, will be notified to the prospective DRO debtor by email and postal notification with reasons for any refusal.[27] The IS circulated a sample letter containing the proposed contents. Once the DRO application has been determined, pursuant to s 251C, IA86, the OR must make the order in the proscribed form.[28] The order must include a list of the debts which the OR is satisfied were qualifying debts of the debtor at the application date, specifying the amount of the debt at that time and the creditor to whom it was then owed.[29] A copy of the order must then be given to the debtor by the OR[30] and an entry must be made on the individual insolvency register containing the prescribed information about the order or the debtor.[31]

27.10 Sceptics may think that the DRO regime is an easy way for debtors to escape their debts. This might be a particular concern of the credit community for example.[32] The Insolvency Service (IS) have ensured that a number of conditions exist that will safeguard the integrity of the system and make certain (as far as is possible) that the DRO procedure is not open to abuse.[33] The

---

23 IA86, s 251C(4)(a).

24 IA86, s 251C(4)(b).

25 IA86, s 251C(4)(c).

26 IA86, s 251C(5)(a).

27 IA86, s 251C(7).

28 IA86, s 251E(2).

29 IA86, s 251E(3).

30 IA86, s 251E(4)(a).

31 IA86, s 251E(4)(b).

32 Indeed, the IS ran a session at their Bloomsbury Street headquarters which was specifically aimed at this stakeholder group. The event was entitled the: Insolvency Service (IS) DRO Creditor Conference. It was held to discuss the DRO regime and its implementation. Approximately 70 people attended the conference on 10 March 2009 that was held at the Insolvency Service, 21 Bloomsbury St, London. The conference began with an introduction from Mr Jon McGurk who is the Plymouth Official Receiver and the person who is heading up the DRO unit. Mr Nick Howard, Director of Policy, then followed and gave a presentation on the background to the DRO and a summary of the principal policy points regarding the DRO regime. Mr Roger Weatherley (DRO Project Manager) and Mr Rob Woolley (Assistant Official Receiver and DRO Unit Manager) then followed with a detailed presentation on the DRO. A whole range of matters relating to DROs were discussed.

33 For example, s 251O, IA86, relates to false representations and omissions during the DRO process. Subsection 1 notes: '(1) A person who makes an application for a debt relief order is guilty of an offence if he knowingly or recklessly makes any false representation or omission in making the application or providing any information or documents to the official receiver in support of the application.' See also, s 251Q, IA86 – Fraudulent disposal of property, and, s 251R, IA86 – Fraudulent dealing with property obtained on credit.

provisions are wide ranging and include debtor focused mechanisms that borrow from the law of bankruptcy and also provisions that are OR focused in terms of oversight and control. A debtor may be subject to restrictions during the duration of the DRO. There is a direct parallel here with the BRO.[34] The OR is also empowered to revoke the DRO if circumstances change.[35] There are also various sanctions against those who are guilty of misconduct. But how would this possibly miscreant behaviour be discovered? Section 251K, IA86 relates to objections to DROs and investigations. Objections can be made during the moratorium period to the OR.[36] The OR may, as part of his consideration of an objection, or on his own initiative, carry out an investigation of any matter that appears to the OR to be relevant.[37]

27.11 There is a statutory duty on the debtor to co-operate with the OR[38] and the debtor who successfully applies for a DRO will have their name recorded on the Individual Insolvency Register.[39] As with bankruptcy, the DRO process culminates in discharge from qualifying debts.[40] The debtor is discharged from all the qualifying debts specified in the DRO. This includes all interest, penalties and other sums which may have become payable in relation to those debts since the application date.[41]

Who are the key players in a DRO?

27.12 The DRO regime is in essence a partnership between the IS and the skilled debt advice sector that harnesses an automated web based system. The IS says that the 'fee will be kept to a minimum and the regime will be largely self financing'.[42] The effectiveness of the DRO procedure in obtaining these laudable low cost aims is therefore of the utmost importance. The governing procedure is contained in, *prima facie*, two separate sources; first, the provisions of the Tribunals, Courts and Enforcement Act 2007, and secondly, the Insolvency (Amendment) Rules 2009.[43] This statutory instrument introduces, *inter alia*, the rules for the DRO procedure. The key functionaries who administer the DRO regime are the Competent Authorities and the Approved Intermediaries.[44] These agents in the process are discussed below.

---

34 Bankruptcy Restrictions Order, see chapter 10 for more detail.
35 IA86, s 251L.
36 IA86, s 251K(2)(b).
37 IA86, s 251(4).
38 IA86, s 251J.
39 IA86, s 251E(4)(b).
40 IA86, s 251.
41 IA86, s 251L(1).
42 IS PowerPoint slides presented 10 March DRO Creditor Consultation Day.
43 Insolvency (Amendment) Rules 2009, SI 2009/642.
44 IA86, s 251B.

Who are the competent authorities?

27.13 The competent authorities (CA)[45] who administer the DRO regime are currently:

(1) The National Association of Citizens Advice Bureau (CAB) who may only authorise its own staff;[46]

(2) The Foundation of Credit Counselling Service now called Step Change (CCCS) who also may only authorise its own staff;[47]

(3) Totemic Ltd trading as Payplan may only authorise its own staff;[48]

(4) Baines & Ernst Ltd also known as Paymex who may only authorise its own staff;[49]

(5) Money Advice Trust trading as National Debtline may only authorise its own staff;[50]

(6) The Institute of Money Advisors who may only authorise its own staff;[51]

(7) The Insolvency Practitioners' Association (IPA).[52]

These bodies are monitored closely. The CAs have to complete a detailed and rigorous application process before being accredited. The CAs have to ensure that the Approved Intermediaries meet all the pertinent criteria, ie clear demonstration of experience and expertise in provision of debt advice as well as the more specific criteria as follows:

- the AI must have no convictions;
- the AI cannot be an insolvent or be subject to any insolvency restrictions (such as BROs);
- the AI must exhibit independence and integrity (how this is to be measured is not quite clear);
- the AI must have a consumer credit licence and indemnity insurance.

---

45 See chapter 2 and on the regulation of Competent Authorities see also the Debt Relief Orders (Designation of Competent Authorities) Regulations 2009, SI 2009/457.
46 http://www.citizensadvice.org.uk/.
47 http://www.cccs.co.uk/.
48 http://www.payplan.com/.
49 http://www.paymex.co.uk/.
50 http://www.nationaldebtline.co.uk/.
51 http://www.i-m-a.org.uk/.
52 http://www.insolvency-practitioners.org.uk/.

27.14 The CAs themselves have to provide the information to support their application to become a CA. They must describe the type of organisation that they are as well as providing an exposition of their operations and purpose. The DRO function must also be compatible with purpose and this accord's with the current list of CAs.[53] As with AIs, the CA must be solvent and have a source of income. Perhaps the most important function that the CA has to perform relates to the educational programme for the AIs. This includes both initial training courses and continuing professional development (CPD) courses. The second most important function of the CAs relates to their ongoing obligation to monitor their AIs and ensure their continued quality and competence. If an AI is deficient there may be complaints and the CAs must therefore ensure that they have an appropriate complaints procedure in place.[54]

How have DROs been digitised?

27.15 We can now move to the most innovative part of the DRO procedure, namely, the total computerisation of the whole DRO process. Some commentators will see the digitisation of the process as a necessary quality in this modern, computer driven age. Other commentators will of course lament that this method of entry into this debt forgiveness procedure will be damaging, not least because it may remove some form of personal responsibility from the decision process, but also because it makes the process of debt write-off that much easier. The internet based application process for a DRO is now in place. The speed and simplicity of the process is not in doubt and on this basis alone the new procedure should be a very valuable option for the debtor and AI users.

What is the process to enter a DRO?

27.16 The process for the DRO is relatively straightforward. The AI interviews the debtor. The AI then fills in the web-based forms if the appropriate criteria and tests have been met in relation to entry into a DRO. Documentary evidence must support the finding of suitability by the AI. Once the £90 fee has been received from the debtor (this can be paid in instalments, but the application will not progress until full payment has been made) then the AI submits the DRO application via the website to the IS. IS acceptance is evidenced either via an email to the debtor or by post if the debtor does not provide an email address. Creditors then have 30 days to lodge objections to the DRO which has been accepted by the IS.

---

53 See chapter 2.

54 For a recent exposition of complaints handling in relation to IPs see Walters, Ad & Seneviratne, M (2008) *Complaints Handling in the UK Insolvency Practitioner Profession* (January 23, 2008). Available at SSRN: http://ssrn.com/abstract=1094757, and: Seneviratne, M & Walters, A (2009) *Complaints Handling by the Regulators of Insolvency Practitioners: A Comparative Study* (January 2009). Available at SSRN: http://ssrn.com/abstract=1310791.

How popular has the DRO been?

27.17 The DRO procedure came into force on the 6 April 2009 in England and Wales and 30 June 2011 for Northern Ireland. The reported number of DROs for England and Wales exceeded 31,000 for 2012 which was almost on par with bankruptcy orders for 2012, however these have dropped substantially since 2009 from nearly 75,000 to nearly 32,000.[55] The IS reported data for England and Wales is as follows:

Year	Total England & Wales	Bank-ruptcy Orders	Debt Relief Orders	% BO + DRO	Individual Voluntary Arrangements
2009	134,142	74,670	11,831	14	47,641
2010	135,045	59,173	25,179	30	50,693
2011	119,941	41,876	29,009	41	49,056
2012	109,477	31,756	31,027	49	46,694

In June 2009, CCCS chairman Malcolm Hurlston said:

> 'As the DRO gathers pace we expect it to outstrip traditional bankruptcy by up to 2:1, … As a result total bankruptcies may soar. But that will be good news rather than bad, since many more people in serious debt will have found the right solution. In the past, stigma and cost have put people off going bankrupt, in circumstances when it would have been best for them and neutral for their lenders.'

As can be seen from the most recent data in England and Wales this has not happened with bankruptcy numbers falling and the DRO effectively becoming around 50% of the total orders made. Even IVA numbers have levelled off and have fallen back to just under the 2009 figures. However as can be seen below the numbers for Northern Ireland are still rising as this relief was only introduced in June 2011.

Year	Total Northern Ireland	Bank-ruptcy Orders	Debt Relief Orders	% BO + DRO	Individual Voluntary Arrangements
2011	2,839	1,615	112	10	1,112
2012	3,190	1,453	506	26	1,231

What is the outcome for the key players?

27.18 There is no doubt that the practical effect of the DRO procedure on the wider personal insolvency landscape will be to relieve the burden on the courts and OR in relation to the administration of the bankruptcy jurisdiction. DROs will take some of the burden of the more costly procedure. It will be interesting to see how the DRO procedure works in practice. In the interim a number of

[55] See the Insolvency Service at http://www.bis.gov.uk/insolvency, for further information.

comments can be made at this stage on the DRO procedure. The first main issue relates to quantification of the sum owed by the debtor. If a debtor thinks they owe £3,000 and the creditor thinks they owe £5,000, only £3,000 is caught in the DRO and the creditor can continue to chase for the remaining £2,000. This seems a strange anomaly that certainly differentiates a DRO from bankruptcy. It will be interesting to see how this aspect is going to work. It is respectfully submitted that it would have been better if the whole debt was caught.

27.19 The second main issue relates to debt collection charges. How will this affect the above situation, particularly in circumstances when creditors add on additional debt collection charges? The DRO area has the potential to be a minefield especially when the over-indebtedness is nearing the £15,000 limit. The third issue relates to charges for the DRO procedure. There will be a £90.00 charge to enter a DRO. This can be paid at the Post Office or through Payzone. This figure still appears to be quite high. The respondents to the bankruptcy courts survey[56] certainly had some issues with the entry costs of bankruptcy. The £90 can be paid over a 6 month time period. This may go some way to alleviate the burden of entry. It is only once this sum has been paid that the AI can submit the DRO application.

LILA (SEQUESTRATION)

What is a LILA?

27.20 A LILA is a low income low asset sequestration which is the Scottish version of bankruptcy. The LILA[57] procedure in Scotland is very similar in terms of substance to the DRO and was introduced in April 2008.[58] The picture in Scotland was initially a heavy take up of the LILA procedure and a dramatic increase in sequestration across the board. Figures released by the accountant in bankruptcy (AiB)[59] reveal a sharp increase in redress to the bankruptcy laws in Scotland. The AiB has been reported as saying, 'new laws making it easier for people with low income to apply for bankruptcy had contributed to the leap … the new Low Income, Low Asset (LILA) route into bankruptcy, introduced on 1 April 2008, accounted for 2,284 of these cases'.[60] There have also been speculative suggestions in the broad sheets that DRO will lead to an

---

[56] J Tribe (2006) *Bankruptcy Courts Survey 2005 – A Pilot Study: Final Report* – January 2006. Kingston Business School Occasional Paper No 59, January 2006. Available at SSRN: http://ssrn.com/abstract=1329109.

[57] A LILA is an alternate route into sequestration in Scotland and is administered by the AiB. The statutory framework is set out in the Bankruptcy (Scotland) Act 1985 (Low Income, Low Asset Debtors etc.) Regulations 2008 (LILA08) which came into force on 1 April 2008.

[58] For more details on the LILA procedure see chapter 28.

[59] http://www.aib.gov.uk/.

[60] BBC news story – Bankruptcies up after law change – 24 April 2009 http://news.bbc.co.uk/1/hi/scotland/8016133.stm24th.

increase in debtor numbers.[61] The predictions could be seen as quite bleak, especially when one considers what the likely increase represents, ie a huge un-catered for group of debtors who until now have had no sensible route out of their over indebtedness. One commentator has noted that:

> 'Accountants and debt agencies expect tens of thousands of indebted consumers on low incomes to declare themselves bankrupt using the new low-cost debt relief orders ....'[62]

The most recent IS statistics[63] reveal that in a similar way to bankruptcy in England and Wales the take up has actually fallen both in real numbers and as a percentage of total sequestration awards.

Year	Total	Sequestrations (No of LILA)		% Sequestrations	Protected Trust Deeds
2008	19,991	12,449	(7,133)	57	7,542
2009	23,541	14,415	(8,775)	61	9,126
2010	20,344	11,906	(6,801)	57	8,438
2011	19,650	11,128	(4,812)	43	8,522
2012	18,392	9,620	(3,883)	40	8,772

What are the requirements to enter a LILA?

27.21 To qualify to enter sequestration under the LILA route a debtor must:

- currently live in Scotland or have lived there during the past year;[64]
- have total debt of at least £1,500;[65]
- not own land, a home, or other property either jointly or individually;[66]
- not have total assets worth more than £10,000 with no single asset worth more than £1,000;[67]
- not have been in sequestration during the previous 5 years;[68]
- not have income that exceeds the current standard national minimum wage established for a 40-hour workimg week, which currently equals

61 This suggestion was made in: Moore, E. *Bankruptcies to grow in online scheme. Financial Times*, 10 April 2009.

62 See E Moore 'Bankruptcies to grow in online scheme' *Financial Times*, 10 April 2009.

63 See: www.insolvency.gov.uk/otherinformation/statistics/statisticsmenu.htm.

64 BSA85, s 9.

65 BSA85, s 5(2B)(a).

66 BSA85, s 5A(3).

67 BSA85, s 5A(4).

68 BSA85, s 5(2B)(b).

£243.20 per week. Anyone in receipt of income support, income-based jobseekers allowance, or working tax credits, automatically meet this income-based criteria.[69]

Who are the key players in a LILA and how much does it cost?

27.22 The key players in a LILA are the AiB and the debtor. The various roles of the AiB are covered in detail in chapter 2.

The cost of the application is £200 payable to the AiB.

What is a certificate for sequestration?

27.23 The Bankruptcy (Certificate for Sequestration) (Scotland) Regulations 2010[70] came into force on 15th November 2010. The certificate provides those people who would normally not qualify for sequestration or a LILA with access to sequestration as a debt solution.[71] Previously an individual was required to wait for a creditor to start legal action for debt recovery if they did fall into the low income, low asset restrictions required by LILA. The certificate serves as written proof of the individual's insolvency and therefore qualification for sequestration. The certificate can be provided by a local authority, Citizens Advice Bureau Money Adviser or an Insolvency Practitioner[72] after reviewing the individual's documentation. The best advice process must be followed including the provision of a Debt Advice and Information package.[73] Once a certificate has been issued[74] the individual has 30 days to submit it with an application for sequestration.[75]

What are the restrictions on an individual in sequestration?

27.24 In a similar way to bankruptcy (see chapter 10) any individual in sequestration is subject to the following restrictions:

- may not serve as company director;
- must receive court permission to participate in formation, management, or promotion of a limited company;
- may not engage in business trade under another name without first notifying all parties involved in sequestration;

---

69 Bankruptcy (Scotland) Act 1985 (Low Income, Low Asset Debtors etc) Regulations 2008, SI 2008/81, reg 2.

70 SSI 2010/397.

71 BSA85, s 5(2B)(ic).

72 Regulation 3 of the Bankruptcy (Certificate for Sequestration) (Scotland) Regulations 2010, SSI 2010/397.

73 BSA85, s 5(2D).

74 Regulations 5 and 6 of SSI 2010/397. The certificate must be signed and dated and no charge can be made.

75 Regulation 7 of SSI 2010/397.

- cannot serve as governor of a school;
- may not act as a justice of the peace;
- some occupations feature limitations regarding sequestration (see chapter 10[76]).

What are the advantages and disadvantages of a LILA?

27.25 The advantages are:

- low cost designed specifically for low income individuals with few assets;
- moratorium on creditor action;
- no contributions required unless affordable;
- release from liabilities after 12 months.

27.26 The disadvantages are:

- can lose and any vehicle or assets if worth more than £1,000;
- any assets must be sold however total assets must not exceed £10,000 and no single asset should be worth more than £1,000. Any asset that does not vest in the trustee can be disregarded;
- details are publicly available;
- cannot incur credit exceeding £250 without informing the lender of the sequestration;
- credit rating negatively affected for 6 years.

PROTOCOL COMPLIANT IVA

What is a Protocol Compliant IVA (PCIVA)?

27.27 A straight forward consumer IVA protocol has been in place since 2008. An updated protocol was issued with effect from January 2013. These are covered in detail in chapter 23.[77] The purpose of the protocol:

> '... is to facilitate the efficient handling of straightforward consumer individual voluntary arrangements (IVAs) (as described below). The protocol recognises that the IVA supports a valid public policy objective by providing debt relief for

---

76 Some occupational restrictions were lifted in England and Wales in the Enterprise Act 2002.

77 Paragraph 20 onwards.

individuals in financial distress. It also recognises that at the centre of this process there is a person, who needs to understand the process and the associated paperwork and the impact that the IVA will have on their lives.'

What is the scope of the 2013 protocol?

27.28 The scope of the 2013 protocol is set out at the beginning of the issued guidance (see below) and it also includes detailed instructions on the process including confirmation of income and expenditure as well as the valuation of any assets. These issues are all discussed in detail in chapters 23–26:

- The protocol is a voluntary agreement, which provides an agreed standard framework for dealing with straightforward consumer IVAs and applies to both IVA providers and creditors. By accepting the content of the protocol, IVA providers and creditors agree to follow the processes and agreed documentation that forms part of the protocol. IVA providers indicate their acceptance of the content of the protocol by drawing up a proposal based on the standard documentation, and which states that it follows the protocol. Creditors are expected to abide by the terms of the protocol in relation to proposals drawn up on that basis.

- Creditors who are members of the British Bankers' Association have indicated their support for the protocol process in a letter attached at Annex 1. A list of BBA members can be found at www.bba.org.uk

- It is accepted that an IVA is a regulated process under statute, which requires certain work to be undertaken, which may have a cost unconnected with the size of the IVA.

- The protocol does not override the regulatory framework relevant to each party (Annex 2).

- For the avoidance of doubt, IVA provider means both insolvency practitioners and IVA provider firms employing insolvency practitioners. References to creditor in this protocol refer to both creditors and the agents who vote on their behalf and act in accordance with their instructions in relation to an IVA.

- The efficient operation of the protocol will be monitored and reviewed by a standing committee. The standing committee is a representative group, its membership reflecting the participants in the IVA process (debtor, creditor, IP, regulatory bodies and government). The terms of reference of the standing committee and details of its current membership are attached at (Annex 3). The committee's role will include communication and consultation, where necessary, on future developments on the IVA protocol.

TRUST DEED

What is a trust deed?

27.29 A trust deed[78] is a voluntary agreement between a debtor and his creditors to repay part of what they are owed. A trust deed usually includes a contribution from income for a specified period. This is normally 3 years but does vary and is not usually longer than 5 years. The trustee must also be an IP (see chapter 3 for more detail). An ordinary trust deed is not binding on creditors unless they agree to its terms including the level of fees to be charged but a trust deed can become protected. This was explained in detail in chapter 1[79] together with a list of key players. Chapter 2 provided an explanation of the voluntary trust deed as a solution and discussed the advantages and disadvantages to the debtor. Chapter 4 provided a summary of the statutory provisions with the detail listed in Appendix 3. This chapter will look at the process in more detail covering the following aspects:

- Debtor requirements and consequences.
- Trust deed and protected status.
- Creditor communication.
- The role of the trustee.
- Costs, fees and remuneration.

Debtor requirements and consequences

Who can sign a trust deed as a debtor?

27.30 A debtor can grant a trust deed for a single estate and the debtor must be one of the following:[80]

- A living individual;[81]
- A partnership;[82]
- A limited partnership within the meaning of the limited partnership Act 1907;[83]

---

78 BSA85, s 72, Sch 5.
79 Paragraph 174 onwards.
80 PTDR08, reg 4(1).
81 PTDR08, reg 4(1)(a).
82 PTDR08, reg 4(1)(b).
83 PTDR08, reg 4(1)(c).

- A trust;[84] or
- A corporate body or unincorporated body.[85]

What are the disqualifications from signing a trust deed?

27.31 The debtor cannot be subject to sequestration, an approved debt payment programme under the Debt Arrangement Scheme or an entity referred to in s 6(2), BSA85 (a company registered under the Companies Act 1985).[86]

What advice must be provided to a debtor prior to the signing of a trust deed?

27.32 The trustee must provide the debtor with a copy of a debt advice and information package[87] referred to in s 10(5) of the Debt Arrangement and Attachment (Scotland) Act 2002. Both the trustee and the debtor must also sign a statement to the effect that the trustee has fulfilled the duties set out below. These duties include advising the debtor of the following consequences[88] of signing a trust deed:

- that the debtor's estate may be sequestrated;
- that the debtor may be refused creditor both before and after discharge;
- that the debtor may have to move home;
- that the debtor may have to allow the sale of certain assets;
- that the debtor may be required to make contributions to the estate from income;
- that the debtor's business interests and employment prospects may be damaged; and
- that the trust deed will be public knowledge.

What are the advantages and disadvantages of a trust deed?

27.33 The advantages are:

- There is a moratorium.
- Contributions are calculated on ability to pay.
- Liabilities are discharged on successful completion.

---

84 PTDR08, reg 4(1)(d).
85 PTDR08, reg 4(1)(e).
86 PTDR08, reg 4(2).
87 PTDR08, reg 6(2)(b).
88 PTDR08, reg 6(2)(a).

- Avoids the stigma of sequestration.

27.34 The disadvantages are:

- details are publicly available.
- credit rating negatively affected for 6 years.

Trust deeds and protected status

What property does a trust deed include?

27.35 The trust deed must include all of the debtor's estate except property listed in s 33(1) of the BSA85 or any other property which would be excluded from vesting in a trustee of a sequestrated estate.[89]

What is the process for creditors to agree to the terms of the trust deed?

27.36 A trust deed must be agreed (acceded to) by the creditors[90] and this is done by giving them the opportunity to formally object in writing.[91] The process requires creditors to be notified of the trust deed immediately after it has been advertised in the *Edinburgh Gazette*.[92] If more than one third in value object in writing within 'the relevant period' then this will prevent the trust deed from becoming protected.[93] 'The relevant period' means the period of five weeks beginning with the date of publication in the *Edinburgh Gazette*.[94]

How does a trust deed become protected?

27.37 A trust deed will be given protected status from the date that the trust deed is recorded in the register of insolvencies[95] if the following conditions[96] are met by providing the AiB with the following information:

- a copy of the trust deed;[97]
- a copy of the *Edinburgh Gazette* notice[98] referred to in reg 7;
- a statement by the trustee that any creditors who have objected in writing to the trust deed during the relevant period do not constitute either;[99]

---

89 PTDR08, reg 6(1).
90 PTDR08, reg 9(1).
91 PTDR08, reg 9(2).
92 PTDR08, regs 7 and 8.
93 PTDR08, reg 9(2).
94 PTDR08, reg 2.
95 PTDR08, reg 3.
96 PTDR08, regs 4–10.
97 PTDR08, reg 10(1)(a).
98 PTDR08, reg 10(1)(b).
99 PTDR08, reg 10(1)(c).

(i) a majority in number of the creditors; or
(ii) one third or greater in value of the creditors;

- a copy of the signed statement confirming that all the debtor's property has been accounted for and the debtor has been provided with all the relevant information[100] referred to in reg 6;
- a copy of the statement of the debtor's affairs[101] mentioned in reg 8(c);
- a statement setting out anticipated realisations from the protected trust deed[102] as set out in Form 3 of Sch 1 to the PTDR08.

What is the effect of the protected status?

27.38 The effect of protected status means that all creditors will be bound by the deed regardless of whether they received notice[103] with the proviso that they may have the right to petition for sequestration instead. While in a protected trust deed the debtor cannot file his own petition for sequestration.[104] Creditors will no longer be deemed to have acceded to a trust deed in terms of reg 9(2) if the trustee issues a determination that the debtor is not discharged from the debtor's liabilities in terms of reg 19(5).[105]

How can a creditor challenge the implementation of a trust deed?

27.39 A qualified creditor who has not been sent the documents mentioned in reg 8, PTDR08 or who has notified the trustee of objection to the trust deed within the relevant period may present a petition to the sheriff for sequestration of the debtor's estate:[106]

- not later than 5 weeks after the date of publication of the notice under reg 7;[107] or
- subject to s 8(1)(b), PTDR08, at any time if the creditor avers that the provision for distribution of the estate is or is likely to be unduly prejudicial to a creditor or class of creditors.[108]

The sheriff may award sequestration if it can be demonstrated to be in the best interests of the creditors.[109] The sheriff will award sequestration if it is demonstrated that the creditor's said averment is correct.[110]

---

100 PTDR08, reg 10(1)(d).
101 PTDR08, reg 10(1)(e).
102 PTDR08, reg 10(1)(f).
103 PTDR08, reg 11(1)(a).
104 PTDR08, reg 11(1)(b).
105 PTDR08, reg 11(2).
106 PTDR08, reg 12(1).
107 PTDR08, reg 12(1)(a).
108 PTDR08, reg 12(1)(b).
109 PTDR08, reg 12(2).
110 PTDR08, reg 12(3).

When and how are the debts discharged?

27.40 The following conditions need to be met before debtor can be discharged from their debts:

- the trustee must make a statement that the debtor has met the their obligations under the trust deed;[111] and

- any notice of inhibition under para 2 of Sch 5 to the Act has been recalled or expired.[112]

Only debts that were included in the trust deed can be discharged. Any liability arising after the date on which the trust deed was signed is excluded from discharge under s 55(2), BSA85. Discharge does not affect the rights of any secured creditor.[113]

27.41 The trustee must send the debtor a letter of discharge[114] with a copy being sent to the AiB.[115] The AiB is required to record details of the discharge[116] and if the trustee decides not to grant the discharge he must also inform him setting out the reasons.[117]

Creditor involvement

How are creditors notified of a trust deed?

27.42 The trustee must advertise details of the trust deed in the *Edinburgh Gazette* immediately after the signing of the deed. The format of the gazette notice is prescribed (Form 1).[118]

What documents have to be sent to creditors?

27.43 The following documents must be sent to creditors within 7 days of the publication of the notice in the *Edinburgh Gazette*:[119]

- a copy of the trust deed;[120]

- a copy of the *Edinburgh Gazette* notice;[121]

---

111 PTDR08, reg 19(1)(a).
112 PTDR08, reg 19(1)(b).
113 PTDR08, reg 19(2).
114 PTDR08, reg 19(3), Form 5.
115 PTDR08, reg 19(3).
116 PTDR08, reg 19(4).
117 PTDR08, reg 19(5).
118 PTDR08, reg 7.
119 PTDR08, reg 7.
120 RPTDR08, reg 8(a).
121 RPTDR08, reg 8(b).

- a statement by the trustee setting out the details of the debtor's affairs;[122]

- a statement explaining:[123]

  — the conditions which must be fulfilled before the trust deed will become a protected trust deed; and
  — the consequences of the deed becoming a protected trust deed; together with

  a copy of Form 2 on which the creditor can make a statement of their claim.[124]

What is included in the trustee's statement of the debtor's affairs?

27.44 The following information must be included:[125]

- a list of the debtor's assets and liabilities;

- a list of income and expenditure as at the date the trust deed was signed;

- a statement as to the extent to which those assets and income will not vest in the trustee;

- a statement as to any contribution from income which the debtor is expected to make;

- a statement whether, and on what basis, the EU Regulation applies or does not apply to the trust deed and, if it applies, whether the proceedings are main proceedings or territorial proceedings;

- a statement by the trustee about the likelihood of a dividend being paid based on the information available;

- a statement that the trustee on request must provide a copy of:

  — any valuation held by the trustee which has been made by a third party and which relates to an asset of the debtor;
  — any statement showing the amount due by the debtor under a security; and
  — any document showing the present income of the debtor.

How are student's loans treated?

27.45 Any student loan that was made under the Education (Student Loans) Act 1990 or by virtue of regulations made under para (f) of s 73 of the

---

122 RPTDR08, reg 8(c).
123 RPTDR08, reg 8(c)(viii).
124 RPTDR08, reg 8(d).
125 RPTDR08, reg 8(c).

Education (Scotland) Act 1980 cannot be discharged by a trust deed. Student loans are covered generally in chapter 5.

COUNTY COURT ADMINISTRATION ORDERS

What is a county court administration order?

27.46 A county court administration order (CCAO) is a court led personal insolvency debt repayment and forgiveness process. The current statutory framework for CCAOs is set out in the County Courts Act 1984 (CCA 1984).[126] A CCAO is only currently[127] available to individuals if at least one of their debts is subject to a county court or High Court judgment and the total amount of their debts is less than £5,000. This procedure requires the debtor to make regular payments for the benefit of his creditors. In that sense or quality the CCAO procedure is not wholly removed from the IVA procedure.[128] It is the destination and manner of payment that differs. The CCAO is then, like an IVA, an alternative to bankruptcy. The court administers the order after the relevant forms on income are completed. Regular income is therefore required. The court collects the agreed monthly payments and distributes the funds to the creditors. There is no fee payable by the individuals but the court retains a small percentage to cover its costs. There is a moratorium (legal action is suspended and no further interest is charged) on the debts included on the order. In some circumstances part of the debt can be written off. This procedure is designed to assist insolvent individuals with few, if any, assets but who have an income from which small levels of debt can be repaid over a period of time. It is a useful procedure but only appropriate in smaller cases. It is cheaper than bankruptcy and does not have the disabilities which are attached to a debtor presenting his own bankruptcy petition or a DRO.

What is the statutory framework for county court administration orders?

27.47 The CCAO regime is currently governed by Part VI, CCA 1984 (ss 112–117). Improvements were proposed in the Courts and Legal Services Act 1990 but were never implemented. The Tribunals, Courts and Enforcement Act 2007 has also affected the CCAO procedure. These reforms are likely to take effect in 2010. Section 106 substitutes Part 6 of the CCA 1984 with a new Part 6 entitled 'Administration orders'. The changes include an increase to the limits and to limit the period of a CCAO to a maximum of 5 years.[129] There will be a requirement to list all debts whether they are due or not, with only

---

[126] CCA1984, ss 112–117 contains the framework and the procedures are governed by the Civil Procedure Rules 1998 (CPR 1998), Sch 2, CCR Order. The CCAO must not be confused with the corporate procedure of the same name, i e administration pursuant to Sch B1 of the Insolvency Act 1986.

[127] March 2009. The CCAO has been subject to a period of reform. This is discussed below.

[128] On IVAs see chapters 23 to 26.

[129] Tribunal Courts and Enforcement Act 2007, s 106 inserts a new s 112K(5) into the CCA 1984.

'declared' qualifying debts being subject to the order.[130] The new criteria will only allow debtors with at least two declared non-business debts to participate, (subject to limits on their total debts and income)[131] and for the first time will allow one off payments from assets rather than being restricted to regular payments from income only. county court judgments will no longer be required.[132]

27.48 Section 112E(4) is an interesting new feature of the latest reforms. Its insertion into the CCA 1984 arguably allows the concept of pari passu to be abandoned for the first time when dealing with insolvency debts. The section allows different debts to be repaid to different extents. New ss 112D and 112E are inserted into the CCA 1984 which give the court power to order that new debt (incurred during the CCAO) is not paid until after the agreed repayments due on declared debts have been made. This may be a new feature to discourage both irresponsible lending and borrowing. The CCAO procedure will be explained as if the new provisions are in force, indeed, the statute has received Royal Assent. The implementation date has however not yet been published (at the time of writing). There is also a brief summary of existing arrangements.

How does a debtor apply for an order?

27.49 If a debtor is unable to pay the amount of a judgment which has been made against him immediately, and he alleges that his total indebtedness does not exceed the county court limit (currently £5,000) inclusive of the debt for which the judgment was obtained, he may request the court to make an administration order.[133]

27.50 The procedures may be initiated by the debtor who files a request for an order in the county court for the district in which he resides or carries on business. Alternatively, where a debtor furnishes to the court a list of creditors and particulars of his means, either in his oral examination or by some other means, the court may proceed as if the debtor had filed a request for an administration order.[134] The debtor is required to verify the statements he makes on oath.[135]

Which debts are included?

27.51 At present administration orders work by aggregating debts which must not exceed £5,000. However, the s 112, CCA 1984 does not define or clarify the nature of a debt for the purposes of an administration order. Consequently, there is little consistency about the types of debts included in, or excluded

---

130 Tribunal Courts and Enforcement Act 2007, s 106 inserts a new s 112C and D into the CCA 1984.

131 Limits to be prescribed; Tribunal Courts and Enforcement Act 2007, s 106 inserts a new s 112B(6) and (7) into CCA 1984.

132 Tribunal Courts and Enforcement Act 2007, s 106 inserts a new s 112B(2) into CCA 1984.

133 CCA 1984, s 112 on Form N92.

134 CPR 1998, Sch 2, CCR Order 39, r 2.

135 CPR 1998, Sch 2, CCR Order 39, r 3.

from, administration orders particularly where they relate to mortgages, other secured debts, consumer credit debts, maintenance payments and community charges.[136] There are also diverging views regarding the inclusion of arrears, either that the entire sum is the debt or that only the arrears should be included.

What rights do creditors have?

27.52 Before an administration order is made, the court must notify each of the creditors on the list provided by the debtor[137] and any creditor, whether or not he is on the debtor's list, has a right to prove his debt and to object to any debt included in the list. The court may appoint a day on which the application for the administration order is to be heard, and give at least 14 days notice to the debtor and the creditors mentioned in the list to attend and present their views. In general, it is undesirable for administration actions to take place without the participation of all the interested parties.

27.53 A creditor on the list may object to any other debt on the list or to the manner in which payments are to be made but must give not less than 7 days notice of any objection,[138] stating the grounds, to the court, the debtor and to the creditor to whose debt he objects. If a creditor does not give such notice, he will require the leave of the court prior to making his objection at a later time.[139]

27.54 After an administration order is made, a creditor who did not receive notice under rule 5 and who wishes to object to a debt scheduled to the order or to the manner in which payment is to be made by instalments, should give notice to the court of his objection and its grounds.[140] The court will then consider the objection and may allow it, dismiss it or adjourn it for hearing.

27.55 If a person becomes a creditor after the date of the order, he may apply to be scheduled as a creditor but will only rank for a dividend after the 'original' creditors have been paid.[141] There is no provision in an administration order for preferential creditors.

What are the contents of a county court administration order?

27.56 An administration order may provide for the payment of debts by instalments to the court either in full or to such extent as appears practicable to the court in view of the circumstances of the case and subject to any conditions the court may think just relating to the debtor's future earnings or income. The court may make an attachment of earnings order to secure the payments required by the administration order. The court may exercise this power at any

---

[136] *Re Preston Borough Council v Riley and another* (1995) *The Times* 19 April, CA.

[137] CCA 1984, s 112(3), CPR 1998, Sch 2, CCR Order 39, r 5(2)(b).

[138] CCA 1984, s 112(3), CPR 1998, Sch 2, CCR Order 39, r 5(2)(b).

[139] CPR 1998, Sch 2, CCR Order 39, r 10.

[140] On notice see: County Courts Act 1984, s 113 and CPR 1998, Sch 2, CCR Order 39, r 6.

[141] CPR 1998, Sch 2, CCR Order 39, r 11, County Courts Act 1984, s 113(d).

time whilst an administration order is in force, if it appears to the court that the debtor has failed to make a payment.[142]

What are the effects of a county court administration order on a creditor?

27.57 Whilst an administration order is in force, a creditor whose name is included in the schedule to the order cannot, without leave of the court, present a bankruptcy petition, unless his name was notified by the debtor to the court as a creditor, his debt exceeds £1,500 and notice of the administration order was received within 28 days preceding the date of the presentation of the bankruptcy petition. Any county court proceedings in respect of a scheduled debt which are pending shall be stayed on receipt of notice of the administration order. Costs incurred by a creditor in respect of those proceedings may, on application, be added to the debt. However, there is no requirement that a county court should stay any pending bankruptcy proceedings.[143]

What are the effects of a county court administration order on the debtor?

27.58 A CCAO is an order that schedules debt and requires the debtor to undertake certain activities in relation to that schedule of debt.[144] The jurisdiction to make the CCAO resides with the County Court.[145] A CCAO may only be made in respect of individual debtors (ie not companies) who have 'qualifying' debts.[146] This individual debtor cannot seek redress to the CCAO if the nature of the debt is business debt[147] and must be unable to pay one or more of his qualifying debts.[148] The first step in a CCAO is to apply to the court. Information on how to do this can be obtained from the court website.[149] In essence the following occurs. Form N270 needs to be completed. The court will make a CCAO based on what the debtor can afford. The CCAO will state how much the debtor has to pay each month and how long the CCAO will last. Often the court will state that the debtor must go on paying until their debts are cleared in full, although some CCAO ask the debtor to repay only a percentage of debts. The CCAO may also state that the amount the debtor pays must be reviewed from time to time. The debtor will make monthly payments to the court and the court distributes the money to the creditors. There is a charge for this service. The fee may be up to ten percent of the total debt. The court takes a percentage of the court fee every time it pays a share to the creditors.[150]

---

[142] See Attachment of Earnings Act 1971, s 5.
[143] CCA 1984, s 114(3).
[144] CCA 1984, s 112A.
[145] CCA 1984, s 112B(1).
[146] CCA 1984, s 112B(2). See the discussion below of *Preston Borough Council v Riley & Anor* [1995] BCC 700, where the Court of Appeal considered whether the community charge constituted a debt for the purposes of a CCAO.
[147] CCA 1984, s 112B(3).
[148] CCA 1984, s 112B(5) while CCA 1984, s 112AC defines the tests for Inability to pay debts.
[149] At www.hmcourts-service.gov.uk.
[150] This is one of the central problems with the CCAO, especially in relation to the involvement of the court. It could be argued that the proper function of the court is not to administer an insolvency regime and repayment process, but to preside as a dispute resolution forum.

27.59 There is an upper limit to the CCAO maximum sum of indebtedness. Prior to the Tribunals, Courts and Enforcement Act 2007 reforms this level was set at £5,000. According to Ziegel this sum was set too low for modern levels of over-indebtedness.[151] The prescribed maximum was so low in fact that it precluded use of the procedure, almost to the extent that the CCAO became a redundant mechanism. The following extract from the Ministry of Justice's Judicial and Court Statistics report 2007 (Chapter Four – County Courts) is illuminating in this regard:

> 'In certain circumstances a debtor may apply to county court to combine debts into an administration order. The debtor must have a judgment debt and at least one other that he is unable to pay with the total indebtedness not exceeding £5,000. Once the debts have been examined and found to be correctly calculated a District Judge can make an order for the debtor to make regular payments to the court. The court will then distribute the money in the appropriate proportions to the creditors listed by the debtor. There were 4,000 administration orders made in 2007, 18% less than in 2006 and 51% less than in 2000.'[152]

The report goes on to note that, 'Provisions in Chapter 1 of Part 5 of the Tribunals, Courts and Enforcement Act 2007 significantly amend the administration order, amongst other matters, removing the need for a judgment. These provisions have still not been commenced although they were due to commence in 2010'.[153] The new upper limit is to be set at a higher level.[154] This may have some positive effect on take up. The following table sets out take up over the last 12 years and the number of orders has continued to fall and more markedly since 2009 when DROs were introduced:[155]

Year	**County Court Administration Orders**		**Orders to obtain information from judgment debtors**
	Applications	Orders made	
2000	6,352	7,183	61,247
2001	5,549	6,398	68,148
2002	5,294	5,964	58,173
2003	3,471	4,342	43,322
2004	2,722	3,739	34,758
2005	2,939	3,662	31,512
2006	2,945	4,377	28,462
2007	2,219	3,587	27,148
2008	1,883	2,686	30,261

151 J Ziegel *Comparative Consumer Insolvency Regimes: a Canadian Perspective* (Hart Publishing, Oxford, 2003).

152 Judicial and Court Statistics report 2007 (Chapter Four – County Courts), Ministry of Justice, 2007. Available at: http://www.justice.gov.uk.

153 Judicial and Court Statistics report 2007 (Chapter Four – County Courts), Ministry of Justice, 2007. Available at: http://www.justice.gov.uk.

154 County Courts Act 1984, s 112B(6).

155 Source: Judicial and Court Statistics report 2007 (Chapter Four – County Courts), Ministry of Justice, 2007. Available at: http://www.justice.gov.uk.

2009	1,230	1,894	29,672
2010	694	1,023	22,811
2011	437	577	22,693

27.60 Individuals who are so minded may make representations to the county court in relation to any CCAO. The court must have regard to these representations from any person about why the order should not be made, or by a creditor about why the debt should not be taken into account in calculating the total amount of the debtor's qualifying debts.[156] This issue arose in *Preston Borough Council v Riley & Anor*.[157] The Court of Appeal was asked to consider whether or not the liability for unpaid community charge was a 'debt' for the purposes of a CCAO. It was held that this species of debt did fall within the CCAO definition of a debt. In his judgment, Hobhouse, LJ, makes a number of interesting observations that help to shine a light on both the qualities of the CCAO and on the nature of a debt.[158] In relation to the former he notes:

> 'Part VI therefore contains a simplified scheme for dealing with insolvent debtors in the county court. It has some of the features of the provisions of the Bankruptcy Act 1914, now superseded by the Insolvency Act 1986, and in a simplified way deals with the same problems as those Acts. In my judgment it is the bankruptcy legislation which provides the context in which the provisions of Pt. VI have to be construed.'[159]

27.61 Once made the CCAO imposes a number of requirements on the debtor, specifically in relation to repayment. An administration order must, during the currency of the order, impose a repayment requirement on the debtor.[160] This repayment can be very specific. For example, the repayment requirement may provide for the debtor to repay a particular scheduled debt in full or to some other extent,[161] or, the repayment requirement may provide for the debtor to repay different scheduled debts to different extents.[162] The repayment requirement must provide that the due repayments are to be made by instalments.[163]

27.62 The CCAO can only be made by a county court on the application of the debtor.[164] Once made the county court may, at the time it makes an administration order, specify a day on which the order will cease to have

---

156 CCA 1984, s 112B(8).
157 [1995] BCC 700.
158 On the nature of debt for the purpose of the Bankruptcy Act 1914 see *Re McGreavy* [1950] Ch 269 and *Re Pascoe* [1944] Ch 310.
159 [1995] BCC 700.
160 CCA 1984, s 112E(2).
161 CCA 1984, s 112E(3).
162 CCA 1984, s 112E(4).
163 CCA 1984, s 112E(6).
164 CCA 1984, s 112J(1).

effect.[165] In terms of duration the maximum permitted period is the period of 5 years beginning with the day on which the order is made.[166]

27.63 The debtor has a duty to provide the county court with particulars of his: (a) earnings, (b) income, (c) assets, and (d) outgoings.[167] It is an offence if information is provided incorrectly.[168] A person who commits an offence may be ordered to pay a fine of not more than £250 or to be imprisoned for not more than 14 days.[169] As with bankruptcy, DRO and IVA the CCAO provides for a form of discharge from debts. If the debtor repays a scheduled debt to the extent provided for by the administration order, the county court must order that the debtor is discharged from the debt.[170]

How often are county court administration orders used?

27.64 As noted above, CCAO[171] are seldom used in practice in the modern climate compared to the other personal insolvency procedures; although they have had a long history of providing a solution to personal over-indebtedness originally being introduced in 1883.[172] The lack of use of the CCAO is perhaps a driver behind the fairly recent[173] considerations for reform of the procedure by the Department for Constitutional Affairs (now Ministry of Justice).[174] The procedure was singled out for reform by the Insolvency Service in their White Paper, *Productivity and Enterprise; Insolvency – A Second Chance*.[175] These movements have been considered in chapter 1. There are a number of advantages and also disadvantages to the CCAO. The new CCAO reforms have

---

165 CCA 1984, s 112K(1).

166 CCA 1984, s 112K(5).

167 CCA 1984, s 112M.

168 CCA 1984, s 112N.

169 CCA 1984, s 112N.

170 CCA 1984, s 112Q.

171 On CCAOs see: Ed. (2006) *Administration Orders: Remedy 'Against Person or Property of the Debtor' – Effect of Existing Council Tax Attachment Order*, Adviser, 118, 40–41; Ed. (2005) *A Path out of Debt, Business Law Review* 26(5), 130–131; Gibbons, D (1997) *Magistrates' Fines and Administration Orders*, Legal Action, Jun, 16–17; Boyle, B (1997) *Administration Orders: Council Tax Attachments of Earnings and Direct Deductions from Income Support must Stop*, M. Advice, 49, 12–13; Ed. (1997) *Administration Orders*, M. Advice 1997, 46, 17; Ed. *Adding Debts to an Administration Order* (1997) M. Advice, 44, 26; P Torsney (1997) *Adding Debts to an Existing Administration Order* Q.A, 45 (Autumn), 4–6; P Madge (1996) *Did you know …?* Adviser, 54, 33; A Lane (1996) *Administration Orders* Q.A, 42 (Win), 8–10; J Gibson 'Administration Orders: County Court' (1991) *Insolvency Intelligence*, 4(1), 7.

172 D Gibbons (1997) *The History of Administration Orders*, Q.A, 44(Sum), 4–5. In this regard see also: H Impey (1910) *Administration Orders by the County Court – A Practical Guide for Debtor and Creditor*. For an early case on CCAO see: *Pearson v Wilcock* [1906] 2 KB 440.

173 Reform has of course been mooted in the past. See for example: Ed. (1996) *Reform of Administration Orders*, M. Advice, 43, 30–31.

174 E Kempson (2004) *Managing Multiple Debts: Experiences of County Court Administration Orders among Debtors, Creditors and Advisors*, Department for Constitutional Affairs, London. See also: J Tribe & D Graham 'Diffusing the debt "time bomb"' (2004) 154 NLJ 1328.

175 White Paper, Cm 5234. One this reform document see: D Milman (2001) *Insolvency Reform, Insolvency Law* 4 (Sep), 153–154.

yet to come into force.[176] If or when they do it will be interesting to observe to what extent the procedure will experience a renaissance. In terms of a low income alternative to the DRO procedure there may be some further issues with competition, ie the DRO procedure may be preferred.

What are the advantages and disadvantages of the CCAO?

27.65 The advantages are:

- Only one monthly payment has to be made to the court.
- The payment is based on what the debtor can afford.
- Once the order is in place, there is a moratorium in place and creditors cannot take any further legal action without leave of the court.

27.66 The disadvantages are:

- The CCAO may fail if payment is missed.
- The maximum level of debt owned must be less than £5,000 and the individual must have at least one county court judgment (currently).
- CCAO are registered in the Register of County Court judgments and this will affect the individual's ability to get credit. When the order is paid in full the entry on the register will be marked as 'satisfied'. A certificate can be requested to prove payment has been made. A fee is charged for this document.

What happens when an existing administration order is satisfied?

27.67 When an existing administration order has been paid in full, the court will notify Registry Trust Ltd (RTL) so that the Register can be amended. The debtor can also apply to the court for a certificate of satisfaction.[177] Any county court judgments included in the order can only be marked as satisfied if the judgment is paid in full and, if required, a separate fee must be paid for any certificate of satisfaction.

How is an existing administration order revoked?

27.68 If the debtor does not make the regular payment ordered by the court, the arrangement under the administration order may be withdrawn and the order is then revoked. This releases creditors from the restrictions imposed and enables them to take further legal action by either obtaining a judgment where one does not already exist or filing a bankruptcy petition. The court will notify RTL of the revocation so that the register can be amended.

---

176 At the time of writing in December 2009.

177 Available for a court fee of £15 and the cheque/postal order should be payable to HMCS.

How and why can an existing administration order set aside?

27.69 When an administration order is set aside by the court, or repaid within one calendar month, RTL will be notified so that the order can be removed from the register. If full payment is made within one month, the debtor can also apply to the court for a Certificate of Cancellation.[178] The cancellation or setting aside of an Administration Order does not affect any county court judgments included in that order.

How and why is an existing administration suspended?

27.70 This occurs when the debtor is unable to continue payments for a period and where the reason for this is acceptable to the court. Registry Trust Ltd is not notified of this change. Details of administration orders and any subsequent amendments are passed to the credit reference agencies for inclusion in their records, to be notified to lenders on receipt of a credit application.

DEEDS OF ARRANGEMENT

What is a deed of arrangement?

27.71 In England and Wales deeds of arrangement (DoA) are regulated by the Deeds of Arrangement Act 1914. Section 1 Deeds of Arrangement Act 1914 notes that a DoA shall include any instrument, whether under seal or not, made by, for or in respect of the affairs of a debtor for the benefit of his creditors generally, or made by, for or in respect of the affairs of a debtor who was insolvent at the date of the execution of the instrument for the benefit of any three or more of his creditors.[179] A DoA can take the form of, inter alia: (a) an assignment of property;[180] (b) a deed of or agreement for a composition; and in cases where creditors of the debtor obtain any control over his property or business.[181] In Northern Ireland deeds of arrangement are covered by arts 209–225 of the Insolvency (Northern Ireland) Order 1989[182] and the Deeds of Arrangement Regulation (Northern Ireland) 1996.[183] The provisions are very similar and cover the registration and execution of any deed of arrangement that might otherwise fail to be registered together with the circulation of accounts to the relevant creditors.

When and how are deeds of arrangement used?

27.72 As with CCAOs, DoAs[184] are also more notable by their almost complete absence, rather than use, as well as their long history.[185] Despite the

---

178 Available for a court fee of £15 (cheque/postal order payable to HMCS).

179 Deeds of Arrangement Act 1914, s 1.

180 See for example *Cole and Another v Lynn* [1942] 1 KB 142.

181 See for example *Cole and Another v Lynn* [1942] 1 KB 142.

182 The Insolvency (Northern Ireland) Order 1989, SI 1989/2405 (NI 19)

183 SR 1996/575.

184 On deeds of arrangement see: K Pond 'Putting a Cork in it: an Appreciation of the May 2007

dearth of use some commentators have extolled the virtues of the procedure,[186] and there is plenty of early (as well as some modern)[187] case law on the subject.[188] Lundy's rallying cry did not cause a notable uptake in the procedure as the table at Appendix 1 from the Insolvency Service demonstrates.[189] Perhaps one reason for the continued low up take is that the DoA has been in essence superseded by subsequent statutory developments in the realm of compositions and arrangements, ie the advent of the IVA has made them superfluous. In this regard the following comments by Chadwick, LJ are interesting:

> '... voluntary arrangements should be treated as – and have the same consequences as – consensual deeds of arrangement, and not be regarded as a substitute for compositions or arrangements in bankruptcy proceedings. It is, perhaps, significant, in this context, that the recommendations of the Cork Committee (Report of the Review Committee on Insolvency Law and Practice, 1982, Cmnd. 8558) which led to the introduction of individual voluntary arrangements were based on the need to provide an alternative to bankruptcy proceedings, a need then not met in practice by consensual deeds of arrangement: see in particular, at paragraph 359: "a satisfactory form of proceedings for dealing with the insolvent debtor otherwise than directly through the machinery of the Bankruptcy Court ... would fulfil an important social need."'[190]

IVA Consultation Document' *Insolvency Intelligence* (2007) 20(9), 2007, 136–138; Ed. (1998) Bankruptcy: Objection to Release of Trustee – Deed of Arrangement Grants Permanent Protection to Debtor – Funds after Release, M.L.B, 30, 36–37.

185 From an historical perspective see: *The Bankruptcy and Deeds of Arrangement Act*, 1913 [3 & 4 Geo. V. c. 34.] See also: DP Davies (1907) *Deeds of Arrangement. A Practical Manual Intended Principally for the use of Trustees.* Gee & Co, London; Ollason, GC (1929) *Bankruptcy and Deeds of Arrangement*, Gee & Co, London; Mackenzie, MJM & Clarke, FA (1913) *The Bankruptcy and Deeds of Arrangement Act*, Forming a supplement to Chalmers and Hough's *Commentary on the Bankruptcy Acts* (sixth edition) ... Second edition (1914) Waterlow & Sons: London; Ball, WV (1921) *Bankruptcy, Deeds of Arrangement and Bills of Sale*, 4th edn, Pitman, London; Benn, DW (1958) *Bankruptcy in a Nutshell including Deeds of Arrangement and Bills of Sale*, Sweet & Maxwell, London.

186 S Lundy 'Deeds of Arrangement: A Better Way Forward' (1987) *Accountancy* 100(1128), 92–93.

187 The following cases feature discussion of DoA to varying degrees: *Somji v Cadbury Schweppes Plc* [2000] BPIR 950; *R v P (A Bankrupt)* [2000] 1 WLR 1568; *Upton v Taylor* [1999] BPIR 168.

188 See for example: In *Re Fenton, Ex parte Fenton Textile Association, Limited* [1931] 1 Ch 85; *Green Ex p. Parker*, Re [1917] 1 KB 183; In *Re A Debtor, Ex parte the Debtor v the Petitioning Creditors and the Official Receiver* [1939] Ch 145; *In Re C S Wilson and G M Wilson, Ex parte F T D, Wilson v the Trustee of A Deed of Arrangement* [1937] Ch 675; *Re E J Casse* [1937] Ch 405; *Re A Debtor (No 11 of 1935)* [1936] Ch 165; *Re Rissik* [1936] Ch 68; *Re Shenton* [1935] Ch 651; *Re A Debtor* [1927] 1 Ch 97; *Re Ellis* (9 of 1924) [1925] Ch 564; *Re A Bankruptcy Notice (62 of 1924)* [1924] 2 Ch 76; *B. Lipton, Limited v Bell* (1922 B 1129) [1924] 1 KB 701; *Re Lee* [1920] 2 KB 200.

189 Source: Insolvency Service, 2009, available at: http://www.insolvency.gov.uk/otherinformation/statistics/historicdata/HDmenu.htm.

190 *Johnson v Davies* [1999] Ch 117, at page 131G. On the historical background to IVAs see: see *Re a Debtor (No 140 IO of 1995)* [1996] 2 BCLC 429.

This dearth of uptake is perhaps no bad thing, especially for trustees of DoA as one old authority demonstrates. In *Re Allen*[191] Clauson, J observed:

> 'This is a bad case. I will make an order for committal forthwith. I have power by virtue of s 105, sub-s. 5, of the Bankruptcy Act 1914, to make an immediate order for his committal and I do so. It may be that, the order having been made, the respondent will either before or after his arrest comply with the directions contained in the orders of the Board of Trade. But even if he should comply with those directions and apply for his release, I should not myself, if the application came before me, be disposed to release him until he had been in prison for a period sufficient to mark the Court's serious view of his default.'[192]

Clauson J had the power of prison committal, pursuant to s 105(5) of the Bankruptcy Act 1914, if the trustee of a DoA failed to transmit accounts, pursuant to s 13, Deeds of Arrangement Act 1914, to the Board of Trade (as it then was) in relation to the DoA.

What is the majority for agreeing a deed of arrangement?

27.73 One of the principle drivers of dissatisfaction with the DoA process is that a majority of creditors is required for it to pass.[193] This may have accounted for the low up take, especially as the procedure does not have a moratorium like the competitor IVA procedure. This has undoubtedly contributed to the low up take in recent years. DoAs are seldom used, despite the fact that they are an incredibly powerful tool in terms of variety and application. Similarly in Northern Ireland both a majority of creditors in value and number are required for execution except for creditors with a value of less than £100 when they are counted in the majority by value but not in the majority by number.[194]

As with other sequential processes in the event that bankruptcy follows an earlier uncompleted deed of arrangement any expenses properly incurred in the deed of arrangement are allowed as a first charge on the subsequent estate.[195]

Where is financial advice available in Scotland?

27.74 The best advice process was covered generally in chapter 1. What is best for the individual will depend on a number of things including their personal circumstances and whether they have any property or assets. In Scotland free impartial advice is available from Money Advice Scotland or Citizens Advice Scotland. The Scottish Government publishes a booklet called Debt and the consequences. The accountant in bankruptcy also publishes information in a

---

[191] *(1106 of 1932)* [1935] Ch 74.

[192] *(1106 of 1932)* [1935] Ch 74, the quoted paragraph is the entirety of the judgment.

[193] Deeds of Arrangement Act 1914, s 3. For an example of where a debtor failed to garner the requisite majority see: *Re Zakon, Ex parte the Trustee v Bushell* [1940] Ch 253.

[194] Article 215(5), The Insolvency (Northern Ireland) Order 1989, SI 1989/2405 (NI 19).

[195] Article 220, The Insolvency (Northern Ireland) Order 1989, SI 1989/2405 (NI 19).

booklet called Debtor's Guide.[196] The Scottish Government also publishes a range of booklets which sets out details of agencies throughout Scotland that give free, independent, impartial and confidential money advice:

Dealing with debt: South Strathclyde, Dumfries & Galloway

Dealing with debt: Tayside, Central & Fife

Dealing with debt: Lothian & Borders

Dealing with debt: North Strathclyde

Dealing with debt: Grampian, Highland & Islands

Dealing with debt: Glasgow & Strathkelvin

The Debt Arrangement Scheme

27.75 As a formal solution the requirements of a Debt Arrangement Scheme (DAS) were looked at in Chapter 2 and the key players in chapter 3. A DAS freezes interest, fees and charges on all debts from the date the payment programme is approved. Debts will be written off if the programme is completed successfully. The scheme is delivered free by approved money advisers[197] at local authority money advice units or Citizens Advice Scotland. The scheme protects debtor's assets, including their home (as long as they keep up their mortgage payments).

How does a debt arrangement scheme work?

27.76 The first requirement is to locate a money adviser by using the search facilities on one of the Money Advice Agencies. Their advice is often free, but some money advisers may charge for their services. The money adviser will talk through the individual's debt problems and suggest the different paths available for dealing with the problem and a DAS will usually be one of the options suggested.

What is 'debt' for the purposes of a DAS?

27.77 Debt for the purposes of the Debt Arrangement Scheme Regulations 2004[198] includes any sum due by a debtor constituted by:

- decree or document of debt;[199]

---

196 Both publications can be found on the AiB website or can be requested in hard copy by e-mailing AIB@aib.gsi.gov.uk or by telephoning them on 0845 612 6171.

197 Regulations 7–11 of the Debt Arrangement Scheme Regulations 2004, SSI 2004/468.

198 Regulation 3 of the Debt Arrangement Scheme Regulations 2004, SSI 2004/468.

199 Regulation 3(a)(i)(aa) of the Debt Arrangement Scheme Regulations 2004, SSI 2004/468.

- judicial or contractual interest;[200]
- charges or penalties due under a contract on any default in respect, or breach of, that contract;[201]
- lease or tenancy agreement;[202]
- enactment;[203]
- any sum secured by a standard security to the extent that the sum is arrears of a periodic payment that is overdue;[204]
- any sum due as an enforcement expense[205] except any amount due in respect of legal aid expenses.[206]

What is the process for entering a DAS?

27.78 If a DAS is the preferred option the money adviser will refer the individual to a DAS approved money adviser who can apply for a debt payment programme (DPP). Under a DAS, a single regular payment is made to an approved payments distributor.[207] If the agreed payments are made the creditors cannot carry out any enforcement action. Creditors are barred from taking any enforcement action if the debtor has registered an intention to apply for a debt payment programme, or has an application awaiting approval. DAS also freezes interest, fees and charges from the date the DAS the payment plan is approved.

Eligibility for the scheme

27.79 Eligibility for a DPP under a DAS has the following conditions:

- the debtor must live in Scotland (it does not matter where the creditors are based);[208]
- the debtor must have more than one debt (if there are two or more debts to a single creditor, such as 2 years arrears of council tax, this counts as multiple debt);[209]

---

[200] Regulation 3(a)(i)(bb) of the Debt Arrangement Scheme Regulations 2004, SSI 2004/468.
[201] Regulation 3(a)(i)(cc) of the Debt Arrangement Scheme Regulations 2004, SSI 2004/468.
[202] Regulation 3(a)(i)(dd) of the Debt Arrangement Scheme Regulations 2004, SSI 2004/468.
[203] Regulation 3(a)(i)(ee) of the Debt Arrangement Scheme Regulations 2004, SSI 2004/468.
[204] Regulation 3(a)(ii) of the Debt Arrangement Scheme Regulations 2004, SSI 2004/468.
[205] Regulation 3(a)(iii) of the Debt Arrangement Scheme Regulations 2004, SSI 2004/468.
[206] Section 17(2)(b), Legal Aid (Scotland) Act 1986. Section 2B was inserted by the Law Reform (Miscellaneous Provisions) (Scotland) Act 1990, Sch 8, para 36.
[207] Regulation 2 of the Debt Arrangement Scheme Regulations 2004, SSI 2004/468.
[208] Regulation 20(1) of the Debt Arrangement Scheme Regulations 2004, SSI 2004/468.
[209] Regulation 21(1) of the Debt Arrangement Scheme Regulations 2004, SSI 2004/468.

- the debtor must not already be in a trust deed or protected trust deed;[210]
- the debtor must not be sequestrated, bankrupt or subject to a bankruptcy restrictions order.[211]

Who are the key players in a debt arrangement scheme?

27.80 Chapter 3 looked at each of these key players in detail however listed below is a recap of the various parties involved in a DAS.

- The debtor: someone who has personal debts and has agreed to a debt payment programme (DPP) with a DAS approved money adviser.
- The creditor: someone who is owed money and has agreed or is obliged to accept payments under a debt payment programme (DPP).
- The DAS administrator is the Scottish Minister or any person or body who is authorised to perform the function.[212] This role has been given to The AiB who is responsible for maintaining the DAS register which contains details of debt payment programmes, the approval of money advisers and payments distributors, and the approval of a debt payment programme (DPP).
- The payments distributor: they distribute sums received to creditors in accordance with the debt payment programme (DPP).
- The DAS approved money adviser who provides debt management advice to the debtor. There are two types of money advisers in relation to debt management. There are routine money adviser's who are trained to offer advice on debt and can help negotiate informal repayment plans and these should be differentiated from DAS approved money advisers. These are money advisers who have received additional training and can negotiate a formal debt payment programme between a debtor and their creditors. These advisers have to be approved by the DAS administrator, a civil servant appointed by Scottish Ministers.

What is a 'debt payment programme'?

27.81 A debt payment programme (DPP) is an agreement that allows an individual to pay off their debts over an extended period of time. The programme can be for any amount of money or for any reasonable length of time. If creditors all agree or are deemed to have agreed (because they do not respond) the debt payment programme under DAS is agreed automatically. Creditors will then be bound by this DPP as long as the payments are made in accordance with the plan. If creditors do not consent then the DAS

---

210 Regulation 21(2)(b) of the Debt Arrangement Scheme Regulations 2004, SSI 2004/468.

211 Regulation 21(2)(c), (d) and (e) of the Debt Arrangement Scheme Regulations 2004, SSI 2004/468.

212 Regulation 2 of the Debt Arrangement Scheme Regulations 2004, SSI 2004/468.

administrator can still approve the debt payment programme if it is fair and reasonable to do so. If the individual's circumstances change, the programme can be varied to take account of this as long as all the creditors agree or if the DAS administrator decides it is fair and reasonable.

What updates have been made to the programme?

27.82 Since June 2007, there has been a register of DAS approved schemes and the following changes have also been implemented:[213]

- The DAS administrator will be able to revoke programmes where the debtor has failed to make payments for a continuous period of 6 months.
- The approval period for money advisers now lasts for 3 years instead of 2.
- A money adviser is now required to review a debt payment programme once every 12 months instead of once every 6 months.
- A money adviser is no longer required to seek revocation of a programme where the debtor has failed to make payments.
- A fee charging money adviser will not be required to tell the debtor about any 'free' alternative service, for example a local authority money advice service.
- Creditors will no longer be entitled to object to programmes on the grounds that a debtor has too much equity in land, or should be sequestrated; however, the DAS administrator will be able to take information about land and buildings into account when deciding whether or not to approve an application for a debt payment programme.
- The sheriff will no longer determine any application for approval of a debt payment programme.
- There will be a final right of appeal to the sheriff alone, and not to either the sheriff or the sheriff principal.
- When a DPP is approved, whether automatically or decided by the DAS administrator, that approval takes effect immediately (ie removal of the 'two day delay').
- If a debtor informs the DAS administrator, in writing, that they intend to apply for the approval of a debt payment programme, this intimation will be entered on the DAS register. No creditor will be able to take enforcement action against the debtor for a period of six weeks following the date of the entry on the DAS register. However the debtor can only make one such intimation in any 12-month period.

---

[213] Regulations 17 and 18 of the Debt Arrangement Scheme Regulations 2004, SSI 2004/468.

- No creditor will be able to take enforcement action against the debtor while an application for approval of a debt payment programme is being considered by the DAS administrator.

- Only interest, fees and charges which are already owed at the date the application for a DPP is approved are payable; no further interest, fees and charges can be added during the period of the DPP. However, if the DPP is revoked, or otherwise not completed, then all interest, fees and charges become payable.

- Similarly, for DPP cases which were in place prior to the implementation of these changes, it is open to money advisers to apply for a variation seeking the freezing of interest and charges. This 'freezing' would come into effect on the date the variation is approved. However, if the DPP is revoked, or otherwise not completed, then all interest, fees and charges become payable.

- Where there is disagreement about the amount of a debt, the DAS administrator can be asked to determine the debt.

Appendix 1

GLOSSARY

A

ACCA	Association of Certified Chartered Accountants	The Association of Certified Chartered Accountants is one of the seven RPBs that license and regulate insolvency practitioners in the UK.
AiB	Accountant in Bankruptcy (Scotland)	The Accountant in Bankruptcy is the Scottish equivalent of the Insolvency Service. The significant difference between the two organisations is that the AiB does not administer corporate insolvency. The AiB does however record corporate insolvency activity in Scotland. The AiB is therefore mainly concerned with the administration of personal insolvency law and policy in Scotland.
	Apparent insolvency (Scotland)	A legal term that means you are unable to pay your debts and that at least one of your creditors has taken legal action against you.
AI	Approved Intermediary (England & Wales)	An individual approved by a competent authority to act as intermediary for the purposes of applying for a Debt Relief Order
	Approved money adviser (Scotland)	An approved money adviser is a Scottish based debt advisor who operates under the auspices of the Debt Arrangement Scheme.
AS2008	Act of Sederunt (Sheriff Court Bankruptcy Rules) 2008	SSI 2008/119 Introduced BRO and BRU into BSA85 and amended the period of discharge from 3 years to 1 year.

B

BAD07	Bankruptcy and Diligence (Scotland) Act 2007	2007 (asp 3) as amended including changes made to 31 December 2012.
	Bankruptcy	Bankruptcy is a formal court process which transfers the bankrupts' property to a trustee. This process is also known as vesting.
	Bankrupt	An individual who is undischarged from bankruptcy proceedings
BIS	Department for Business Innovation and Skills	The Department for Business, Innovation and Skills (BIS) is the ministerial department of state that has ultimate responsibility for insolvency law and policy. The Insolvency Service is an executive agency of BIS. The current Secretary of State in charge of BIS is Dr Vince Cable MP.
BO	Bankruptcy Order	The order made by the court on either a debtor or creditor's petition.
BRO	Bankruptcy Restriction Order	A Bankruptcy Restriction Order is an order made against an undischarged bankrupt extending the period during which bankruptcy restrictions remain in place. They are designed to protect the public and as a deterrent. Orders can be made for any period between 2 and 15 years. The court is notified and the order registered.
BRU	Bankruptcy Restriction Undertaking	A Bankruptcy Restriction Undertaking is similar to an order but is less formal and is entered into voluntarily by an undischarged bankrupt. It acts in the same way as an order and is also notified to court and registered. They last for similar periods between 2 and 15 years.
BPIR	Bankruptcy and Personal Insolvency Reports	Case summaries issued by Jordan Publishing

BSA85	Bankruptcy Scotland Act 1985	1985 (c 66) as amended including changes made to 31 December 2012.
C		
CA	Competent authority	A competent authority is the term given to the organisations that are designated by the Secretary of State (SoS) as being able to authorise intermediaries as part of the Debt Relief Order (DRO) regime. For these purposes the CAs are currently: the National Association of Citizens' Advice Bureaux (CAB); The Foundation of Credit Counselling; Baines & Ernst Ltd; Institution of Money Advisers (IMA); National Debtline; Payplan; Insolvency Practitioners Association; Advice UK; Shelter; Christians Against Poverty; and, Think Money.
	Charge for payment (Scotland)	The formal demand for payment following a decree. A Sheriff Officer usually serves it on you and you have to pay the debt within 14 days.
CAB	Citizens Advice Bureau	The Citizens' Advice Bureau (CAB) is a not for profit charitable organisation that advises citizens on a number of different issues, including debt, from over 3,500 locations across the country and is also a competent authority for the purposes of the DRO regime.

CCAO	County Court Administration Order (England & Wales and Northern Ireland)	The County Court Administration Order is a personal insolvency solution that is available to debtors in England and Wales and Northern Ireland. Administered through the County Courts, the procedure is in essence a debt repayment scheme. There is a very low debt level for this procedure – £5,000. If the debtor satisfies the conditions for the CCAO the indebtedness can be repaid to creditors through the County Court (which takes an administration fee). The procedure is seldom used, particularly since the advent of the DRO. The CCAO has the advantage of being binding on creditors.
CCA 1974	Consumer Credit Act 1974	1974 (c39) as amended including changes made to 31 December 2012
CCA84	County Courts Act 1984	1984 (c28) as amended including changes made to 31 December 2012
CCCS	The Consumer Credit Counselling Service	The Consumer Credit Counselling Service has recently changed its name to Step Change Debt Charity. In both incarnations the organisation provides free debt advice to consumer debtors. The organisation has debt advice expertise in all the major procedures, i.e. bankruptcy, IVAs, DRO, etc.
CPD	Continuing Professional Development	Continuing Professional Development is the process whereby practitioners engage in a continued series of education throughout their careers. In a number of professions this is a strict requirement of continued license holding. It was previously referred to as Continuing professional Education.

CPR	Civil Procedure Rules	The civil procedure rules are published by the Ministry of Justice and make up a detailed procedural code whose overriding aim is to enable the courts to deal with cases fairly and efficiently.
	Creditor	Any person, business or organisation that is owed money.
CTAER92	The Council Tax (Administration and Enforcement) Regulations 1992	SI 1992/613 as amended including changes made to 31 December 2012
D		
DAS	Debt Arrangement Scheme (Scotland)	A free debt management tool introduced by the Scottish Executive accessed through an approved money adviser.
DAS04	The Debt Arrangement Scheme Regulations 2004 (Scotland)	SSI 2004/468 as amended including changes made to 31 December 2012
DAAS02	Debt Arrangement and Attachment (Scotland) Act 2002	2002 asp 17 as amended including changes made to 31 December 2012
DAA 1914	Deeds of Arrangement Act 1914	1914 (c 47) as amended including changes made to 31 December 2012
	Deeds of Arrangement Rules 1925	SI 1925/210 as amended including changes made to 31 December 2012
DETI	Department of Enterprise Trade and Investment (Northern Ireland)	The Department of Enterprise Trade and Investment is the equivalent of BIS in England & Wales and is responsible for NI Insolvency Service.
	Disclaimer	For the purposes of bankruptcy the trustee of the estate has the power to 'disclaim' any onerous property / asset so that the burden of dealing with that property does not fall onto the already insolvent estate and become an additional expense for the creditors.

DMP	Debt Management Plan	A debt management plan in England and Wales is an informal agreement with creditors. A DMP can be proposed by the debtor but is usually proposed through the agency of a professional accountant or other advisors from organisations such as the CAB. No moratorium is available to stop any non-assenting creditor from pursuing their debts.
DPP	Debt Payment Programme (Scotland)	The Debt Payment Programme (DPP) is a personal insolvency solution that is used in Scotland as part of the DAS. The debtor makes a single payment to one functionary instead of multiple creditors pursuant to the DPP.
	Debtor	A debtor is any person who owes money, usually used to refer to someone who is insolvent.
	Decree (Scotland)	A formal order of court which says the debtor must pay money to a creditor.
	Decree of adjudication (Scotland)	Adjudication is an action in the Court of Session (Scotland's Supreme Civil Court) where property you own which can be inherited, usually a house or similar, is transferred to a creditor to pay a debt.
DRO	Debt Relief Order	A Debt Relief Order is in essence a bankruptcy-lite. Introduced by the Tribunals, Courts and Enforcement Act 2007, the procedure provides the bankruptcy process for debtors who have minimal assets. A debtor must have debts of less than £15,000 and restriction on available income and assets.
DSA87	Debtors (Scotland) Act 1987	1987 (c18) as amended including changes made to 31 December 2012

DoA	Deed of Arrangement	Deeds of Arrangement are compositions between a debtor and creditors much in the same vein as IVA. The Deeds of Arrangement Act 1914 regulates this procedure. DoAs have fallen into almost total disuse mainly due to the fact that the 1914 statute does not include provision for a moratorium.
E		
EA02	Enterprise Act 2002	This statute affected both personal and corporate insolvency law. In relation to personal insolvency the most important change related to the reduction in automatic discharge from three years to one year and the introduction of Bankruptcy Restrictions Orders.
EAIPS	Estate Accounts and Insolvency Practitioner Services	The Estate Accounts and Insolvency Practitioner Services (EAIPS) is a newly combined unit that merged the Insolvency Practitioner Unit (IPU) and the Estate Accounts Directorate (EAD).
EAS	The Estate Accounts Services	The Insolvency Service's Estate Accounts Services (EAS) and administers the Insolvency Services Account (ISA) for Insolvency Practitioners and the Official Receiver (OR).
EAT	Employment Appeal Tribunal	The main function of the Employment Appeal Tribunal (EAT) is to hear appeals from decisions made by Employment Tribunals.
EIIR	The Electronic Individual Insolvency Register	The Electronic Individual Insolvency Register is open to the public and has been available online since 2004. It contains searchable details of all current orders including bankruptcies, IVAs, DROs, BROs and BRUs.

ERO	Enforcement Restriction Order	An Enforcement Restriction Order is a personal insolvency procedure that was introduced in the Tribunals, Courts and Enforcement Act 2007. The procedure is designed to stay enforcement actions by creditors where the debtor has suffered from a sudden and unforeseen deterioration in financial circumstances. There however must also be a realistic prospect that the debtor's financial circumstances will improve within the period of six months beginning when the order is made.
	Estate	An estate is literally everything of value owned by an individual, including any rights they may have to receive money or goods from anyone else.
	European Communities (Recognition of Professional Qualifications) Regulations 2007	SI 2007/2781 as amended including changes made to 31 December 2012
	Exempt property	Exempt property is the list of items that fall outside the estate in bankruptcy and include items that are considered to provide the basic needs to live and obtain employment.
F		
FSA	The Financial Services Authority	The Financial Services Authority (FSA) is an independent non-governmental body, given statutory powers by the Financial Services and Markets Act 2000. From 1 April 2013 the FSA will no longer exist as one body and will be split into two regulators, the Prudential Regulatory Authority (PRA) and the Financial Conduct Authority (FCA).

FCA	The Financial Conduct Authority	The Financial Conduct Authority will focus separately on the bigger risk issues and policies. As a result some organisations will be monitored by both of these new organizations.
H		
HMRC	Her Majesty's Revenue and Customs	Her Majesty's Revenue and Customs are the national government agency with responsibility for administering the tax system in England and Wales and Northern Ireland. They are a major creditor in personal insolvency, particularly in the London region and courts.
HRA98	Human Rights Act 1998	1998 (c 42) as amended including changes made to 31 December 2012.
I		
IA2000	Insolvency Act 2000	2000 (c 39) as amended including changes made to 31 December 2012. It introduced among other things key changes to the IVA process by allowing the process to commence without an interim order.
IA86	Insolvency Act 1986	1986 (c 45) as amended including changes made to 31 December 2012
ICAEW	The Institute of Chartered Accountants in England and Wales	The Institute of Chartered Accountants in England and Wales is one of the seven RPBs that license and regulate insolvency practitioners.
	Insolvency Practitioners (Recognised Professional Bodies) Order 1986	SI 1986/1764 as amended including changes made to 31 December 2012

IG	Inspector General	The Inspector General of the Insolvency Service (currently Dr Richard Judge) reports to the responsible Minister who then reports to the SoS. The Secretary of State for BIS therefore has ultimate legislative and policy responsibility for the activity of the Insolvency Service and the regulation of insolvency issues in England and Wales.
IMA	Institute of Money Advisers	The Institute of Money Advisers is a money advice charity. The IMA was previously known as the Money Advice Association and has been in existence since 1984. The primary role of the IMA is to act as a professional body to approximately 1700 money advisers. A key function of the IMA is to raise professional standards and provide support for members on money advice issues and is also a competent authority for the purposes of the DRO regime.
INO89	Insolvency (Northern Ireland) Order 1989	SI 1989/2405 (NI 19) as amended including changes made to 31 December 2012
IP	Insolvency Practitioner	A person licensed to act as an office holder in relation to formal insolvency processes set out in the Insolvency Act 1986.
IPA	Insolvency Practitioners Association	The Insolvency Practitioners Association (IPA) is one of the seven RPBs. Like the other RPBs it is a membership body that licenses its members to practice as insolvency practitioners. However, it is the only dedicated insolvency RPB, as opposed to the other RPBs that also have other regulatory functions for other types of accountancy or legal work. It is also a competent authority for the purposes of the DRO regime.

IPA	Income Payments Agreement	An agreement made by a debtor to contribute a regular sum of money from his surplus income into his insolvent estate.
IPC	The Insolvency Practices Council	The Insolvency Practices Council (IPC) was a public interest body set up to monitor and influence the professional and ethical standards of IPs but has now been disbanded. This abolition is to be lamented as the organisation provided a valuable watchdog function which has now been largely lost. The organisation's yearly reports provided a valuable insight from its lay and professional Council members regarding the insolvency profession and its ongoing development and progression. The IPC worked closely with the Joint Insolvency Committee (JIC) which has now largely taken over the IPC's previous functions and role.
IPO	Income payments Order	An order made or sanctioned by the court to ensure a debtor or undischarged bankrupt contributes a regular sum of money from any surplus income into his insolvent estate.
IPRN06	Insolvency Practitioner Regulations (Northern Ireland) 2006	SR 2006/33 as amended including changes made to 31 December 2012
IPR05	Insolvency Practitioners Regulations 2005	SI 2005/524 as amended including changes made to 31 December 2012
IR94	Insolvency Regulations 1994	SI 1994/2507 as amended including changes made to 31 December 2012
IRN91	Insolvency Rules (Northern Ireland) 1991	SR 1991/364 as amended including changes made to 31 December 2012
IR86	Insolvency Rules 1986	SI 1986/1925 as amended including changes made to 31 December 2012

IS	Insolvency Service	The Insolvency Service is an executive agency of the Department for Business, Innovation and Skills (BIS). In Northern Ireland the NI Insolvency Service is part of the Department of Enterprise Trade and Investment (DETI).
ISA	Insolvency Services Account	The Insolvency Service's Estate Accounts Services (EAS), which is part of the Estate Accounts and Insolvency Practitioner Services (EAIPS), administers the ISA using the Government Banking Service (GBS). The EAS provides the banking and investment service to Insolvency Practitioners (IPs) and Official Receivers (ORs) in respect of bankruptcy estates.
	Interim trustee	Someone appointed by the court to handle the estate of an insolvent individual until a permanent trustee is appointed.
IVA	Individual Voluntary Arrangement (England & Wales and Northern Ireland)	The Individual Voluntary Arrangement is a personal insolvency statutory procedure that exists for debtors in England & Wales and Northern Ireland.
J		
JIEB	Joint Insolvency Examination Board	The Joint Insolvency Examination Board (JIEB) is the organisation which sets and administers the Joint Insolvency Examinations. Any person who wishes to become a licensed insolvency practitioner (IP) must pass these examinations as a matter of statutory requirement.

JIC	Joint Insolvency Committee	The Joint Insolvency Committee is a body which is made up of representatives from the RPBs and the Insolvency Service which was created in December 1999. R3 has observer status as does the Northern Irish Insolvency Service. The function of the JIC is to provide an arena in which issues relevant to the insolvency profession can be discussed and debated leading to a common and unified solution in both professional and ethical standards.
L		
LGFA92	Local Government Finance Act 1992	1992 (c14) as amended including changes made to 31 December 2012
LILA	Low income low assets	The low income low assets procedure is a relatively new introduction into Scottish personal insolvency law. Essentially the procedure allows for entry into bankruptcy where the debtor has low assets, i.e. no single asset worth more than £1,000. The debtor's total assets cannot equate to more than £10,000.
M		
Matrix	Money Advice Training, Resources, Information and Consultancy Service	
MAS	Money Advice Scotland	Money Advice Scotland is a registered charity set up in 1989 by the Scottish Consumer Council. It is an umbrella organisation set up to promote and encourage the development of free, confidential and impartial debt advice.

	Moratorium	A moratorium is a temporary stay on creditor enforcement activity. In common parlance it is sometimes referred to as a breathing space. The effect of a moratorium is to suspend the ability of all creditors to enforce whatever rights they have against the debtor for a specified period of time. Moratoriums do not affect the underlying rights of creditors, the procedure merely suspends the creditors ability to enforce whilst a reorganisation occurs.
N		
	Nominee	The nominee is an officeholder in an Individual Voluntary Arrangement (IVA). The role encompasses the duties of the provisional officeholder in the sense that they are responsible for organising the IVA and the approval of its terms.
O		
OFT	Office of Fair Trading	The OFT is a non-ministerial government department established by statute in 1973. The OFT is the UK's consumer and competition authority and has recently launched an investigation into the UK corporate insolvency Market. Its purpose is to ensure markets work well for consumers.
OR	Official Receiver (England & Wales)	The Official Receiver (often referred to as the OR) is the oldest insolvency officeholder in English law after Commissioners in Bankruptcy. The post of OR was created by the Bankruptcy Act 1883 (46 & 47 Vict c 52). The OR is the key Government functionary for dealing with insolvent estates and is an officer of the court.

P

	Permanent trustee (Scotland)	Someone appointed by the court to take possession of an insolvent individual's estate; sell any property owned by the insolvent individual; and pay that individual's creditors as much as possible from the realisation of the assets.
	Petition	A formal application to the court usually for an order to be made
PRA	The Prudential Regulatory Authority	The Prudential Regulatory Authority is one of the two new regulators that will come into operation from 1 April 2013 on the demise of the Financial Services Authority. Its role will be to continue the day to day supervision of businesses.
	Prescribed Forms	These are forms whose content have been laid out in the various statutory instruments to ensure that the correct information is provided in a standard format.
PTDR08	The Protected Trust Deeds (Scotland) Regulation 2008	SSI 2008/143 as amended including changes made to 31 December 2012.

Q

	Qualified creditor or creditors (Scotland)	In Scotland this is a creditor to whom you owe at least £1500 (or a number of creditors to whom you owe at least £1500 in total).

R

R3	The Association of Business Recovery Professionals – Rescue Renewal Recovery	The Association of Business Recovery Professionals – Rescue Renewal Recovery or R3, as it is colloquially known. It was formerly known as the Society of Practitioners of Insolvency (SPI).

RPB	Recognised Professional Body	The RPBs regulate, authorise and punish officeholders in insolvency matters. They perform an annual monitoring function to ensure that officeholders are properly scrutinised and appropriately regulated. It is a statutory requirement that all officeholders are licensed by one of the RPBs. The name was changed to reflect the core functions of its officeholder membership, namely, Rescue, Renewal, and Recovery. R3 is not an RPB. It is however a key component in the regulatory structure of insolvency practitioners as the organisation provides a key role in education, networking and research in the area of insolvency. The vast majority of officeholders are members of R3.
RTL	Registry Trust (Trust Online)	The Registry Trust is a not-for-profit company which operates the Register of Judgments, Orders and Fines for England and Wales on behalf of the Ministry of Justice, as well as similar registers for Scotland, Republic of Ireland, Northern Ireland, the Isle of Man and Jersey.
S		
SERPS	State Earnings Related Pension Scheme	
SIP	Statement of Insolvency Practice	The Statements of Insolvency Practice (SIPs) are a set of extra-statutory guidance documents that are issued under the auspices of the Joint Insolvency Committee. The SIPs regulate and affect the activity of all officeholders.

SoS	Secretary of State	The Secretary of State for Business, Innovation and Skills (BIS) is a member of the cabinet and is currently Dr Vince Cable MP. Ms Jo Swinson MP is the Minister with responsibility for the Insolvency Service and she reports to the SoS.
	Sequestration (Scotland)	Sequestration is the Scottish legal term for bankruptcy.
	Sequestration for rent (Scotland)	A court process that can be raised by a landlord for outstanding rent in Scotland. This is not the same as bankruptcy or formal sequestration.
	Statutory demand (all jurisdictions)	A formal demand by a creditor which allows the debtor 21 days to repay the amount demanded. The demand must be on the proper form and in Scotland be served by a sheriff officer.
	Summary Warrant (Scotland)	An order granted by the court to local or public authorities giving the creditor authority to recover amounts outstanding in Scotland. This procedure is generally used to recover unpaid rates, taxes, community charge and so on.
	Supervisor (England & Wales and Northern Ireland)	This is the title of the office holder who is appointed to administer an insolvent estate for an individual in a voluntary arrangement. Once an IVA has been formally approved the nominee can convert into being the supervisor of the IVA. In some circumstances a different office holder can be appointed.

T

TCEA 2007	Tribunals Courts and Enforcement Act 2007	This statute received Royal assent on 19 July 2007. The statute introduced a number of new procedures and perfected some older provisions that affect personal insolvency law. The statute affected or introduced: Debt Relief Orders (DROs), Enforcement Restriction Orders, Administration and Debt Management schemes as have been shown in this book.
THEA98	The Teaching and Higher Education Act 1998	1998 (c30) as amended including changes made to 31 December 2012.
	Trust Deed and Protected Trust Deed	A trust deed transfers all of an individual's estate to a trustee. The trust deed becomes protected if no objections are made by the majority of the creditors. It requires at least one-third of the individual's creditors to stop the trust deed from becoming protected. The trust deed becomes binding on all the creditors, that is, 'protected'. None of the creditors may then apply to have the individual sequestrated. If protection is not obtained the individual can continue with the arrangement but creditors are not bound and may take alternative legal action to collect their debts.
	Trustee	This is the title of the office holder who is appointed to administer an insolvent estate for an individual. This term is used for all types of bankruptcy proceedings including sequestration, trust deeds, deeds of arrangement and debt relief orders.
TUV	Transaction at an undervalue	A 'transaction at an undervalue' is where a bankrupt enters into a transaction to dispose of an asset at less than its real value. See section 339 IA86 and chapter 16 for a detailed exposition.

U

UNCITRAL	United Nations Commission on International Trade Law	The United Nations Commission on International Trade Law (UNCITRAL) was established by the General Assembly in 1966 (Resolution 2205(XXI) of 17 December 1966). The General Assembly recognized that disparities in national laws governing international trade was creating obstacles to the flow of trade, and it regarded the Commission as the vehicle by which the United Nations could play a more active role in reducing or removing these obstacles.

V

	Vesting	Vesting is the process whereby the assets of the bankrupt are transferred to the Trustee in Bankruptcy. The property of the bankrupt is upon the making of the bankruptcy order said to vest in the Trustee in Bankruptcy.

Appendix 2
JURISDICTION

COURTS WITH BANKRUPTCY JURISDICTION

England & Wales

County Courts

Court	**Post code**	**Official Receiver**
Aberdare	CF44 0NW	Cardiff
Aberystwyth	SY23 2LP	Swansea
Altrincham	M33 7WX	Manchester
Aylesbury	HP20 2NQ	St Albans
Banbury	OX16 2AW	Northampton
Barnsley	S70 2EW	Sheffield
Barnstaple	EX31 1DY	Exeter
Barrow-in-Furness	LA14 5QX	Blackpool
Bath	BA1 1DJ	Bristol
Bedford	MK40 3NN	Northampton
Birkenhead	CH41 5EN	Liverpool
Birmingham	B4 6DS	Birmingham
Blackburn	BB1 6DJ	Blackpool
Blackpool	FY1 5RJ	Blackpool
Blackwood	HP12 1NY	Cardiff
Bolton	BL1 1SU	Manchester
Boston	PE21 6PE	Nottingham
Bournemouth	BH7 7DS	Bournemouth
Bradford	BD1 1JA	Leeds
Bridgend	CF31 4AJ	Cardiff
Brighton	BN2 0RF	Brighton
Bristol	BS1 2NR	Bristol
Burnley	BB11 1XD	Blackpool
Burton-on-Trent	DE14 1BP	Leicester

Court	Post code	Official Receiver
Bury St Edmunds	IP33 1TR	Ipswich
Caernarfon	LL55 2DF	Chester
Cambridge	CB1 1BA	Cambridge
Canterbury	CT1 1ZA	Canterbury
Cardiff	CF10 1ET	Cardiff
Carlisle	CA1 1DJ	Blackpool
Carmarthen	SA31 1BJ	Swansea
Chelmsford	CM2 0QR	Southend
Cheltenham	GL1 2DE	Gloucester
Chester	CH1 1SN	Chester
Chesterfield	S41 7TD	Sheffield
Colchester	CO3 3EG	Ipswich
Coventry	CV1 2SN	Birmingham
Crewe	CW1 2DP	Stoke-on-Trent
Croydon	CR9 5AB	Croydon
Darlington	DL3 7RL	Stockton
Derby	DE1 2XE	Leicester
Dewsbury	WF13 2PE	Leeds
Doncaster	DN1 3BT	Sheffield
Dudley	DY5 1LN	Birmingham
Durham	DH1 3RG	Stockton
Eastbourne	BN21 4UN	Brighton
Exeter	EX1 1UH	Exeter
Gloucester	GL1 2DE	Gloucester
Great Grimsby	DN31 1HX	Hull
Guildford	GU1 4PS	Croydon
Halifax	HX1 2JJ	Leeds
Harrogate	HG1 1EL	Leeds
Hastings	TN34 1QX	Canterbury
Haverfordwest	SA61 2AX	Swansea
Hereford	HR4 9BA	Gloucester
Hertford	SG13 8DY	Cambridge
Huddersfield	HD1 2RR	Leeds
Ipswich	IP1 1EJ	Ipswich
Kendal	LA9 4NF	Blackpool

Court	Post code	Official Receiver
Kidderminster	DY10 1QR	Birmingham
Kings Lynn	PE30 1ES	Norwich
Kingston-upon-Hull	HU1 2EZ	Hull
Kingston-upon-Thames	KT1 2AD	Croydon
Lancaster	LA1 1UZ	Blackpool
Leeds	LS1 3BG	Leeds
Leicester	LE1 6HG	Leicester
Lincoln	LN5 7PS	Nottingham
Liverpool	L2 2BX	Liverpool
Llangefni	LL77 7EN	Chester
Luton	LU1 2PU	St Albans
Macclesfield	SK11 7NA	Stoke-on-Trent
Maidstone	ME16 8EQ	Medway
Manchester	M60 9DJ	Manchester
Medway	ME4 4DW	Medway
Merthyr Tydfil	CF47 8BH	Cardiff
Middlesborough	TS1 2AE	Stockton
Milton Keynes	MK9 2DT	Northampton
Mold	CH7 1AE	Chester
Neath & Port Talbot	SA11 3BN	Swansea
Newbury	RG14 5QS	Reading
Newcastle-upon-Tyne	NE1 3LA	Newcastle
Newport (Gwent)	NP20 1PQ	Cardiff
Newport (IoW)	PO30 5YT	Southampton
Northampton	NN1 3HQ	Northampton
Norwich	NR3 1UR	Norwich
Nottingham	NG1 7EJ	Nottingham
Oldham	OL1 1NL	Manchester
Oxford	OX1 1TL	Reading
Peterborough	PE1 1EJ	Cambridge
Plymouth	PL1 2ER	Plymouth
Pontypridd	CF37 1JR	Cardiff
Portsmouth	PO1 2EB	Southampton
Preston	PR1 2LL	Blackpool
Reading	RG1 1HE	Reading

Court	Post code	Official Receiver
Rhyl	LL18 3LA	Chester
Romford	RM1 4DP	Southend
Salford	M5 4RR	Manchester
Salisbury	SP1 2PN	Bournemouth
Scarborough	YO11 2JS	Hull
Scunthorpe	DN15 6QB	Hull
Sheffield	S3 8PH	Sheffield
Shrewsbury	SY1 1NA	Chester
Slough	SL1 2HE	Reading
Southampton	SO15 2XQ	Southampton
Southend	SS1 2AW	Southend
St Albans	AL1 3TJ	St Albans
Stafford	ST16 2QQ	Stoke-on-Trent
Stockport	SK1 3DJ	Manchester
Stoke-on-Trent	ST1 3BP	Stoke-on-Trent
Stourbridge	DY8 1QL	Birmingham
Sunderland	SR1 1RB	Newcastle
Swansea	SA1 1SP	Swansea
Swindon	SN1 2HG	Gloucester
Tameside	OL6 7TP	Manchester
Taunton	TA1 4EU	Bristol
Torquay & Newton Abbott	TQ2 7AZ	Exeter / Plymouth
Truro	TR1 2PB	Plymouth
Tunbridge	TN1 1DP	Medway
Wakefield	WF1 1JW	Leeds
Walsall	WS1 1JQ	Stoke-on-Trent
Warrington & Runcorn	WA1 1UR	Chester
Warwick	CV34 4RB	Birmingham
Welshpool & Newtown	SY21 7UX	Chester
Weymouth & Dorchester	DT4 8TE	Bournemouth
Whitehaven	CA28 7NU	Blackpool
Wigan	WN1 1NG	Liverpool
Winchester	SO23 9EL	Southampton
Wolverhampton	WV1 3LQ	Birmingham
Worcester	WR1 1EQ	Gloucester

Court	Post code	Official Receiver
Wrexham	LL13 8XN	Chester
Yeovil	BA20 2QD	Exeter
York	YO1 9WL	Hull

High Court & District Registry

Court	Post code	Official Receiver
High Court	EC4A 1NL	
District Registry – Manchester	M60 9DJ	
District Registry – Liverpool	L2 2BX	

Northern Ireland

High Court & District Registry

Court	Post code	Official Receiver
High Court – Belfast	BT1 3JF	OR Northern Ireland

Scotland

Sheriffs Courts

Court	Post code	Accountant in Bankruptcy
Aberdeen Sheriff Court	AB10 1WP	LP 4 – Kilwinning
Aberdeen Sheriff Court Annex & High Court	AB11 5BB	LP 4 – Kilwinning
Airdrie Sheriff Court	ML6 6EE	LP 4 – Kilwinning
Alloa Sheriff	FK10 1HR	LP 4 – Kilwinning
Arbroath Sheriff Court	D11 1HL	LP 4 – Kilwinning
Ayr Sheriff Court	KA7 1EE	LP 4 – Kilwinning
Banff Sheriff Court	AB45 1AU	LP 4 – Kilwinning
Campbeltown Sheriff Court	PA28 6AN	LP 4 – Kilwinning
Court of Session Edinburgh	EH1 1RQ	LP 4 – Kilwinning
Cupar Sheriff Court	KY15 4LX	LP 4 – Kilwinning
Dingwall Sheriff Court	IV15 9QX	LP 4 – Kilwinning
Dornoch Sheriff Court	IV25 3FD	LP 4 – Kilwinning
Dumbarton Sheriff Court	G82 1LL	LP 4 – Kilwinning
Dumfries Sheriff Court	DG1 2AN	LP 4 – Kilwinning
Dundee Sheriff Court	DD1 9AD	LP 4 – Kilwinning
Dunfermline Sheriff Court	KY12 7HJ	LP 4 – Kilwinning
Dunoon Sheriff Court	PA23 8BQ	LP 4 – Kilwinning
Duns Sheriff Court	TD11 3DU	LP 4 – Kilwinning

Court	Post code	Accountant in Bankruptcy
Edinburgh High Court	EH1 1RQ	LP 4 – Kilwinning
Edinburgh Sheriff Court	EH1 1LB	LP 4 – Kilwinning
Hamilton Sheriff Court Civil Department	ML3 0AL	LP 4 – Kilwinning
Inverness Sheriff Court	IV2 3EG,	LP 4 – Kilwinning
Jedburgh Sheriff Court	TD8 6AR	LP 4 – Kilwinning
Kilmarnock Sheriff Court	KA1 1ED	LP 4 – Kilwinning
Kirkcaldy Sheriff Court	KY1 1XQ	LP 4 – Kilwinning
Kirkcudbright Sheriff Cour	DG6 4JW	LP 4 – Kilwinning
Kirkwall Sheriff Court	KW15 1PD	LP 4 – Kilwinning
Lanark Sheriff Court	ML11 7NE	LP 4 – Kilwinning
Lerwick Sheriff Court	ZE1 0HD	LP 4 – Kilwinning
Livingston Sheriff & Justice of the Peace Court	EH54 6FF	LP 4 – Kilwinning
Lochmaddy Sheriff Court	HS6 5AE	LP 4 – Kilwinning
Oban Sheriff Court	PA34 4AL	LP 4 – Kilwinning
Paisley Sheriff Court	PA3 2AW	LP 4 – Kilwinning
Peebles Sheriff Court Peeblesshire	EH45 8HH	LP 4 – Kilwinning
Perth Sheriff Court	PH2 8NL	LP 4 – Kilwinning
Peterhead Sheriff Court	AB42 1TP	LP 4 – Kilwinning
Portree Sheriff Court	IV51 9EH	LP 4 – Kilwinning
Rothesay Sheriff Court	PA20 9HQ	LP 4 – Kilwinning
Scottish Court Service Headquarters	EH11 3XD	LP 4 – Kilwinning
Selkirk Sheriff Court	TD7 4LE	LP 4 – Kilwinning
Stirling Sheriff Court	FK8 1NH	LP 4 – Kilwinning
Stonehaven Sheriff Court	AB39 2JH	LP 4 – Kilwinning
Stornoway Sheriff Court	HS1 2JF	LP 4 – Kilwinning
Stranraer Sheriff Court	DG9 7AA	LP 4 – Kilwinning
Tain Sheriff Court	IV19 1AB	LP 4 – Kilwinning
Wick Sheriff Court Caithness	KW1 4AJ	LP 4 – Kilwinning

Appendix 3

STATUTORY PROVISIONS FOR PERSONAL INSOLVENCY PROCEDURES

ENGLAND & WALES AND NORTHERN IRELAND

Bankruptcy

Insolvency Act 1986 (as amended) (IA86)

The Insolvency (Northern Ireland) Order 1989 (as amended) (IO89)

Part IX Bankruptcy

IA86 Section	**IO89 Article**	
CHAPTER 1		**BANKRUPTCY PETITIONS; BANKRUPTCY ORDERS**
		Preliminary
264	238	Who may present a bankruptcy petition
265	239	Conditions to be satisfied in respect of debtor
266	240	Other preliminary conditions
		Creditor's petition
267	241	Ground's of a creditor's petition
268	242	Definition of 'inability to pay', etc the statutory demand
269	243	Creditor with security
270	244	Expedited petition
271	245	Proceedings on creditor's petition
		Debtor's petition
272	246	Ground's of a debtor's petition
273	247	Appointment of insolvency practitioner by court
274	248	Action on report of insolvency practitioner
274A		Debtor who meets conditions for debt relief order
275	249	*Repealed by Enterprise Act 2002*
		Other cases for special consideration

IA86 Section	IO89 Article	
276	250	Default in connection with voluntary arrangement
277	251	*Repealed by Criminal Justice Act 1988*
		Commencement and duration of bankruptcy; discharge
278	252	Commencement and continuance
279	253	Duration
280	254	Discharge by order of the court
281	255	Effect of discharge
281A	255A	Post-discharge restrictions
282	256	Court's power to annul bankruptcy order/ Power of High Court to annul bankruptcy order
CHAPTER II		**PROTECTION OF BANKRUPT'S ESTATE & INVESTIGATION OF HIS AFFAIRS**
283	11	Definition of bankrupt's estate
283A	256A	Bankrupt's home ceasing to form part of the estate
284	257	Restrictions on dispositions of property
285	258	Restrictions on proceedings and remedies
286	259	Power to appoint interim receiver
287	260	Receivership pending appointment of trustee
288	261	Statement of affairs
289	262	Investigatory duties of official receiver
290	263	Public examination of bankrupt
291	264	Duties of bankrupt in relation to official receiver
CHAPTER III		**TRUSTEES IN BANKRUPTCY**
		Tenure of office as trustee
292	265	Power to make appointments
293	266	Summoning of meeting to appoint first trustee
294	267	Power of creditors to requisition meeting
295	268	Failure of meeting to appoint trustee
296	269	Appointment of trustee by Secretary of State
297	270	Special cases
298	271	Removal of trustee; vacation of office
299	272	Release of trustee
300	273	Vacancy in office of trustee
		Control of trustee
301	274	Creditors' committee

IA86 Section	**IO89 Article**	
302	275	Exercise by Secretary of State of functions of creditors' committee
303	276	General control of the trustee by the court
304	277	Liability of trustee
CHAPTER IV		**ADMINISTRATION BY TRUSTEE**
		Preliminary
305	278	General functions of trustee
		Acquisition, control and realisation of bankrupt's estate
306	279	Vesting of bankrupt's estate in trustee
306A	279A	Property subject to restraint order
306B	279B	Property in respect of which receivership or administration order is made
306C	279C	Property subject to certain orders where confiscation order discharged or quashed
307	280	After-acquired property
308	281	Vesting in trustee of certain items of excess value
308A		Vesting in trustee of certain tenancies
309	282	Time-limit for notice under section 307 or Article 308
310	283	Income payments orders
310A	283A	Income payments agreement
311	284	Acquisition by trustee of control
312	285	Obligation to surrender control to trustees
313	286	Charge on bankrupt's home
313	286A	Low value home: application for sale, possession or charge
314	287	Powers of trustee
		Disclaimer of onerous property
315	288	Disclaimer (general power)
316	289	Notice requiring trustee's decision
317	290	Disclaimer of leaseholds
318	291	Disclaimer of dwelling house
319	292	Disclaimer of land subject to rent charge
320	293	Court order vesting disclaimed property
321	294	Order under section 320 in respect of leaseholds

IA86 Section	IO89 Article	
		Distribution of bankrupt's estate
322	295	Proof of debts
323	296	Mutual credit and set-off
324	297	Distribution by means of dividend
325	298	Claims by unsatisfied creditors
326	299	Distribution of property in specie
327	300	Distribution in criminal bankruptcy
328	301	Priority of debts
329	302	Debts to spouse or civil partner
330	303	Final distribution
331	304	Final meeting
332	305	Saving for bankrupt's home
		Supplemental
333	306	Duties of bankrupt in relation to trustee
334	307	Stay of distribution in case of second bankruptcy
335	308	Adjustment between earlier and later bankruptcy estate
CHAPTER V		**EFFECT OF BANKRUPTCY ON CERTAIN RIGHTS, TRANSACTIONS ETC.**
		Rights under trusts of land
335A		Rights under trusts of land
		Rights of occupation
336	309	Rights of occupation, etc., of bankrupt's spouse or civil partner
337	310	Rights of occupation of bankrupt
338	311	Payments in respect of premises occupied by bankrupt
		Adjustment of prior transactions, etc
339	312	Transactions at an undervalue
340	313	Preferences
341	314	'Relevant time' under Sections 339, 340 / Articles 312, 313
342	315	Orders under Sections 339, 340 / Articles 312, 313
342A	315A	Recovery of excessive pension contributions
342B	315B	Orders under Section 342A/ Orders under Article 315A.

IA86 Section	**IO89 Article**	
342C	315C	Orders under Section 342A: supplementary/ Orders under Article 315A: supplementary.
342D	315D	Recovery of excessive pension contributions in pension-sharing cases
342E	315E	Orders under Sections 339 or 340 in respect of pension-sharing transactions/ Orders under Article 312 or 313 in respect of pension-sharing transactions.
342F	315F	Orders under Sections 339 or 340 in pension-sharing cases: supplementary/ Orders under Article 312 or 313 in pension-sharing cases: supplementary.
343	316	Extortionate credit transactions
344	317	Avoidance of general assignment of book debts
345	318	Contracts to which bankrupt is a party
346		Enforcement procedures (NI see rule 6.031)[1]
347		Distress, etc
348	319	Apprenticeships, etc
349	320	Unenforceability of liens on books, etc
349A	320A	Arbitration agreements to which bankrupt is party
CHAPTER VI		**BANKRUPTCY OFFENCES**
		Preliminary
350	321	Scheme of this chapter
351	322	Definitions for the purposes of this chapter
352	323	Defence of innocent intention
		Wrongdoing by the bankrupt before and after bankruptcy
353	324	Non-disclosure
354	325	Concealment of property
355	326	Concealment of books and papers; falsification
356	327	False statements
357	328	Fraudulent disposal of property
358	329	Absconding
359	330	Fraudulent dealing with property obtained on credit

[1] In Northern Ireland Article 14 Judgments Enforcement (Northern Ireland) Order 1981 gives the Enforcement Office the power to stay enforcement on the grounds that the estate ought to be administered for the benefit of all the creditors. This effectively provides a 6 week moratorium in which action is stayed until either an IVA is agreed a BO is made.

IA86 Section	IO89 Article	
360	331	Obtaining credit; engaging in business
361	332	Revoked
362	333	Revoked
CHAPTER VII		**POWERS OF COURT (IA86)** POWERS OF HIGH COURT IN BANKRUPTCY (IO89)
363	334	General control of court
364	335	Power of arrest
365	336	Seizure of bankrupt's property
366	337	Inquiry into bankrupt's dealings and property
367	338	Court's enforcement powers under Section 366 / High Court's enforcement powers under Article 337
368	339	Provision corresponding to Section 366 or Article 337, where interim receiver appointed
369	340	Order for production of documents by Inland Revenue
370	341	Power to appoint special manager
371	342	Re-direction of bankrupt's letters, etc.

Part X INDIVIDUAL INSOLVENCY: GENERAL PROVISIONS

Part XI INTERPRETATION FOR SECOND GROUP OF PARTS

Part XIV PROVISIONS AGAINST DEBT AVOIDANCE

IA86 Section	IO89 Article	
PART X		**INDIVIDUAL INSOLVENCY: GENERAL PROVISIONS**
372	343	Supplies of gas, water, electricity, etc
373		Jurisdiction in relation to insolvent individuals
374		Insolvency districts
375		Appeals etc from courts exercising insolvency jurisdiction
376	344	Time-limits
377	345	Formal defects
378	377	Exemption from stamp duty
379	372	Annual report

IA86 Section	IO89 Article	
379A		Remote attendance at meetings
379B		Use of websites
PART XI		**INTERPRETATION FOR SECOND GROUP OF PARTS**
380		Introductory
381	9	'Bankrupt' and associated terminology
382	9	'Bankruptcy debt', etc
383	9	'Creditor', 'security', etc
384		'Prescribed' and the 'the rules'
385	2	Miscellaneous definitions / General Interpretation
PART XVI		**PROVISIONS AGAINST DEBT AVOIDANCE**
423	367	Transactions defrauding creditors
424	368	Those who may apply for an order under section 423 / Article 367
425	369	Provisions which may be made by order under section 423 / Article 367

Bankruptcy Restrictions Order And Undertaking

Schedules

Sch 4A	**Sch 2A**	**BANKRUPTCY RESTRICTION ORDERS AND UNDERTAKINGS**
		Bankruptcy restriction order
1	1	Application for order
		Grounds for making an order
2	2	Conduct of the debtor
		Timing of application for order
3	3	Period for application
		Duration of order
4	4	Minimum and maximum duration
		Bankruptcy restrictions order
5	5	Grounds for making the order
6	6	Application of the order
		Bankruptcy restrictions undertaking
7	7	Parties to the undertaking

8	8	Effect of interim order
9	9	Enactment and duration
		Effect of annulment of bankruptcy order
10	10	Annulment under section 282(1)(a) or (2) / Article 256(1)(a)
10	10	Annulment under section 261, 263D or 282(1)(b) / Article 235, 237D, or 256(1)(b)
		Registration
12	12	Registration

Insolvency Rules 1986 (as amended) (IR86)

The Insolvency (Northern Ireland) Rules 1991 (as amended) (IRN91)

Part 6 Bankruptcy

IR86	IRN91	
CHAPTER I		**STATUTORY DEMAND**
6.1	6.001	Form and content of statutory demand
6.2	6.002	Information to be given in statutory demand
6.3	6.003	Requirements as to service
6.4	6.004	Applications to set aside statutory demand
6.5	6.005	Hearing of application to set aside
CHAPTER 2		**BANKRUPTCY PETITION (CREDITOR'S)**
6.6	6.006	Preliminary
6.7	6.007	Identification of debtor
6.8	6.008	Identification of debt
6.9		Revoked
6.9A		Court in which petition to be presented
6.10	6.009	Procedure for presentation and filing
6.11	6.010	Proof of service of statutory demand
6.12	6.011	Verification of petition
6.13	6.012	Notice to Chief Land Registrar
6.14	6.013	Service of petition
6.15	6.014	Revoked
6.15A		Proof of service
6.16	6.015	Death of debtor before service
6.17	6.016	Security for costs (section 268(2) only)
6.18	6.017	Hearing of petition

IR86	IRN91	
6.19		Revoked
6.20		Revoked
6.21	6.018	Petition opposed by debtor
6.22	6.019	Amendment of petition
6.23	6.020	Notice by persons intending to appear
6.24	6.021	List of appearances
6.25	6.022	Decision on the hearing
6.26	6.023	Non-appearance of creditor
6.27	6.024	Vacating registration on dismissal of petition
6.28	6.025	Extension of time for hearing
6.29	6.026	Adjournment
6.30	6.027	Substitution of petitioner
6.31	6.028	Change of carriage of petition
6.32	6.029	Petitioner seeking dismissal or permission to withdraw
6.33	6.030	Settlement and content of bankruptcy order
6.34	6.031	Action to follow making of order
6.35	6.032	Amendment of title proceedings
6.36	6.033	Revoked
CHAPTER 3		**BANKRUPTCY PETITION (DEBTOR'S)**
6.37	6.034	Preliminary
6.38	6.035	Identification of debtor
6.39	6.036	Admission of insolvency
6.40		Replaced by rule 6.40A
6.40A		Court in which petition to be presented
6.41	6.037	Statement of affairs
6.42	6.038	Procedure for presenting and filing
6.43	6.039	Notice to Chief Land Registrar
	6.040	Dismissal or withdrawal of petition or stay of proceedings
6.44	6.041	Report of insolvency practitioner
6.45	6.042	Settlement and content of bankruptcy order
6.46	6.043	Action to follow making of order
6.46A	6.044	Expenses of Voluntary arrangement
6.47	6.045	Amendment of title proceedings

IR86	IRN91	
6.48	6.046	Revoked
6.49	6.047	Revoked
6.50	6.048	Revoked
CHAPTER 4		**THE INTERIM RECEIVER**
6.51	6.049	Application for appointment of interim receiver
6.52	6.050	Order of appointment
6.53	6.051	Deposit
6.54	6.052	Security
6.55	6.053	Failure to give or keep up security
6.56	6.054	Remuneration
6.57	6.055	Termination of appointment
CHAPTER 5		**DISCLOSURE BY BANKRUPT WITH RESPECT TO THE STATE OF HIS AFFAIRS**
Section A:		Creditor's Petition
6.58	6.056	Preliminary
6.59	6.057	The statement of affairs
6.60	6.058	Verification and filing
6.61	6.059	Limited disclosure
6.62	6.060	Release from duty to submit statement of affairs; extension of time
6.63	6.061	Expenses of statement of affairs
6.64	6.062	Requirement to submit accounts
6.65	6.063	Submission and filing of accounts
6.66	6.064	Further disclosure
Section B:		Debtor's Petition
6.67	6.065	Preliminary
6.68	6.066	Contents of statement
6.69	6.067	Requirement to submit accounts
6.70	6.068	Submission and filing of accounts
6.71	6.069	Expenses of preparing accounts
6.72	6.070	Further disclosure
CHAPTER 6		**INFORMATION TO CREDITORS**
6.73	6.071	General duty of official receiver
6.74	6.072	Those entitled to be informed
6.75	6.073	Report where statement of affairs lodged

IR86	IRN91	
6.76	6.074	Statement of affairs dispensed with
6.77	6.075	General rule as to reporting
6.78	6.076	Bankruptcy order annulled
6.78A		Reports to creditors
6.78B		Final report to creditors and bankrupt
6.78C		Creditors' request for further information
6.78D		Distribution of property in specie
CHAPTER 7		**CREDITORS' MEETING**
6.79	6.077	First meeting of creditors
6.80	6.078	Business at first meeting
6.81	6.079	General power to call meetings
6.82	6.080	The chairman at a meeting
6.83	6.081	Requisitioned meetings
6.84	6.082	Attendance at meetings of bankrupt, etc
6.85	6.083	Notice of meetings by advertisement only
6.86	6.084	Venus of meetings
6.87	6.085	Expenses of summoning meetings
6.88	6.086	Resolutions
6.88A		Resolutions by correspondence
6.89	6.087	Chairman of meeting as proxy-holder
6.90	6.088	Suspension of meeting
6.91	6.089	Adjournment
6.92	6.090	Revoked
6.93	6.091	Entitlement to vote
6.93A		Chairman's discretion to allow vote
6.94	6.092	Admission and rejection of proof
6.95	6.093	Record of proceedings
CHAPTER 8		**PROOF OF BANKRUPTCY DEBTS**
Section A:		Procedure for proving
6.96	6.094	Meaning of "prove"
6.97	6.095	Supply of forms
6.98	6.096	Contents of proof
6.99	6.097	Revoked
6.100	6.098	Cost of proving
6.101	6.099	Trustee to allow inspection of proofs

IR86	IRN91	
6.102		Revoked
6.103	6.100	Transmission of proofs to trustee
6.103A		New trustee appointed
6.104	6.101	Admission and rejection of proofs for dividend
6.105	6.102	Appeal against decision on proof
6.106	6.103	Withdrawal or variation of proof
6.107	6.104	Expunging of proof by court
Section B:		Quantification of Claim
6.108	6.105	Negotiable instruments etc
6.109	6.106	Secured creditors
6.110	6.107	Discounts
6.111	6.108	Debt in foreign currency
6.112	6.109	Payments of a periodical nature
6.113	6.110	Interest
6.114	6.111	Debt payable at a future date
CHAPTER 9		**SECURED CREDITORS**
6.115	6.112	Value of security
6.116	6.113	Surrender for non-disclosure
6.117	6.114	Redemption by trustee
6.118	6.115	Test of security's value
6.119	6.116	Realisation of security by creditor
CHAPTER 10		**TRUSTEE**
Section A:		Appointment and Associated Formalities
6.120	6.117	Appointment by creditors' meeting
6.120A		Official receiver not to be appointed trustee
6.121	6.118	Appointment by the court
6.122	6.119	Appointment by Secretary of State
6.123	6.120	Authentication of trustee's appointment
6.124	6.121	Advertisement of appointment
6.125	6.122	Hand-over of estate to trustee
Section B:		Resignation and Removal; Vacation of Office
6.126	6.123	Creditors' meeting to receive trustee's resignation
6.126A		Resignation (application under Rule 6.142)
6.127	6.124	Action following acceptance of resignation
6.128	6.125	Permission to resign granted by court

IR86	IRN91	
6.129	6.126	Meeting of creditors to remove trustee
6.130	6.127	Court's power to regulate meeting under Rule 6.129
6.131	6.128	Procedure on removal
6.132	6.129	Removal of trustee by the court
6.133	6.130	Removal of trustee by the Secretary of State
6.134	6.131	Notice of resignation or removal
6.135	6.132	Release of resigning or removed trustee
Section C:		Release on Completion of Administration
6.136	6.133	Release of official receiver
6.137	6.134	Final meeting of creditors
6.137A	6.134A	Rule as to reporting
Section D:		Remuneration
6.138	6.135	Fixing of remuneration
6.138A	6.135A	Trustee's remuneration where it is not fixed in accordance with Rule 6.138 / Rule 6.135 (NI)
6.139	6.136	Other matters affecting remuneration
6.140	6.137	Replaced by rule 6.140A
6.140A		Recourse of trustee to meeting of creditors
6.141	6.138	Recourse to the court
6.142	6.139	Creditor's claim that remuneration is or other expenses are excessive
6.142A		Review of remuneration
6.142B		Remuneration of new trustee
6.142C		Apportionment of set fee remuneration
Section E:		Supplementary Provisions
6.143	6.140	Trustee deceased
6.144	6.141	Loss of qualification as insolvency practitioner
6.145	6.142	Notice to official receiver of intention to vacate office
6.146	6.143	Trustee's duties on vacating office
6.147	6.144	Power of court to set aside certain transactions
6.148	6.145	Rule against solicitation
6.149	6.146	Enforcement of trustee's obligations to official receiver
CHAPTER 11		**CREDITORS COMMITTEE**

IR86	IRN91	
6.150	6.147	Membership of creditors' committee
6.151	6.148	Formalities of establishment
6.152	6.149	Obligations of trustee to committee
6.153	6.150	Meetings of the committee
6.154	6.151	The chairman at meetings
6.155	6.152	Quorum
6.156	6.153	Committee-members' representatives
6.157	6.154	Resignation
6.158	6.155	Termination of membership
6.159	6.156	Removal
6.160	6.157	Vacancies
6.161	6.158	Voting rights and resolutions
6.162	6.159	Resolutions otherwise than at a meeting
6.163	6.160	Trustee's reports
6.164	6.161	Expenses of members etc
6.165	6.162	Dealings by committee-members and others
6.166	6.163	Committee's functions vested in Secretary of State
CHAPTER 12		**SPECIAL MANAGER**
6.167	6.164	Appointment and remuneration
6.168	6.165	Security
6.169	6.166	Failure to give or keep up security
6.170	6.167	Accounting
6.171	6.168	Termination of appointment
CHAPTER 13		**PUBLIC EXAMINATION OF BANKRUPT**
6.172	6.169	Order for public examination
6.173	6.170	Order on request by creditors
6.174	6.171	Bankrupt unfit for examination
6.175	6.172	Procedure at hearing
6.176	6.173	Adjournment
6.177	6.174	Expenses of examination
CHAPTER 14		**DISCLAIMER**
6.178	6.175	Trustee's notice of disclaimer
6.179	6.176	Communication of disclaimer to persons interested
6.180	6.177	Additional notices

IR86	IRN91	
6.181	6.178	Revoked[2]
6.181A		Records (of disclaimers)
6.182	6.179	Application for permission to disclaim
6.183	6.180	Application by interested party under section 316
6.184	6.181	Interest in property to be declared on request
6.185	6.182	Disclaimer presumed valid and effective
6.186	6.183	Application for exercise of court's power under section 320
CHAPTER 15		**REPLACEMENT OF EXEMPT PROPERTY**
6.187	6.184	Purchase of replacement property
6.188	6.185	Money provided in lieu of sale
CHAPTER 16		**INCOME PAYMENTS ORDER**
6.189	6.186	Application for order
6.190	6.187	Action to follow making of order
6.191	6.188	Variation of order
6.192	6.189	Order to payor of income: administration
6.193	6.190	Review of order
CHAPTER 16A		**INCOME PAYMENTS AGREEMENTS**
6.193A	6.190A	Approval of income payments agreements
6.193B	6.190B	Acceptance of income payments agreements
6.193C	6.190C	Variation of income payments agreements
CHAPTER 17		**ACTION BY COURT UNDER SECTION 369; ORDER TO INLAND REVENUE OFFICIAL**
6.194	6.191	Application for order
6.195	6.192	Making and service of the order
6.196	6.193	Custody of documents
CHAPTER 18		**MORTGAGED PROPERTY**
6.197	6.194	Claim by mortgagee
6.198	6.195	Power of court to order sale
6.199	6.196	Proceeds of sale
CHAPTER 19		**AFTER-ACQUIRED PROPERTY**
6.200	6.197	Duties of bankrupt in respect of after-acquired property
6.201	6.198	Trustee's recourse to disponee of property

2 Duty to keep court informed was revoked by SI 2010/686 when the court was removed from an active role in the disclaimer process

IR86	IRN91	
6.202	6.199	Expenses of getting in property for the estate
CHAPTER 20		**PERMISSION TO ACT AS A DIRECTOR, ETC**
6.202A	6.199A	
6.203	6.200	Application for permission
6.204	6.201	Report of official receiver
6.205	6.202	Court's order on application
CHAPTER 21		**ANNULMENT OF BANKRUPTCY ORDER**
6.206	6.203	Application for annulment
6.207	6.204	Report by trustee
6.207A		Applicant's claim that remuneration is or expenses are excessive
6.208	6.205	Power of court to stay proceedings
6.209	6.206	Notice to creditors who have not proved
6.210	6.207	The hearing
6.211	6.208	Matters to be proved under section 282(1)(b)
6.212	6.209	Notice to creditors
6.212A		Revoked
6.213	6.211	Other matters arising on annulment
6.214	6.212	Trustee's final account
CHAPTER 21A		**NOTICE UNDER SECTION 279(2)**
6.214A	6.212A	Notice under section 279(2) that an investigation of the conduct and affairs of a bankrupt is unnecessary or concluded
CHAPTER 22		**DISCHARGE**
6.215	6.213	Application for suspension of discharge
6.216	6.214	Lifting of suspension of discharge
6.217	6.215	Application by bankrupt for discharge
6.218	6.216	Report of official receiver
6.219	6.217	Order of discharge on application
6.220	6.218	Certificate of discharge
6.221	6.219	Deferment of issue of order pending appeal
6.222	6.220	Costs under this Chapter
6.223	6.221	Bankrupt's debts surviving discharge
CHAPTER 23		**ORDER OF PAYMENT OF COSTS, ETC, OUT OF ESTATE**
6.224	6.222	General rule as to priority

IR86	IRN91	
CHAPTER 24		**SECOND BANKRUPTCY**
6.225	6.223	Scope of this Chapter
6.226	6.224	General duty of existing trustee
6.227	6.225	Delivery up to later trustee
6.228	6.226	Existing trustee's expenses
CHAPTER 25		**CRIMINAL BANKRUPTCY**
		Revoked
CHAPTER 26		**MISCELLANEOUS RULES IN BANKRUPTCY**
6.235	6.227	Revoked
6.235A	6.227A	Application for redirection order
6.235B		Persons at risk of violence
6.236	6.228	Consolidation of petitions
6.237	6.229	Bankrupt's Home-Notification of property falling within section 283A
6.237A	6.229A	Application in respect of the vesting of an interest in a dwelling-house (registered land)
6.237B	6.229B	Vesting of bankrupt's interest (unregistered land)
6.237C	6.229C	Substituted period
6.237CA	6.229D	Vesting of bankrupt's estate-substituted period
6.237D	6.229E	Charging Order
6.237E	6.229F	Interpretation
CHAPTER 27		**EC REGULATION-MEMBER STATE LIQUIDATOR**
6.238	6.231	Interpretation of creditor and notice to member State liquidator
6.239	6.232	Interpretation of creditor and notice to member State liquidator appointed in main proceedings
CHAPTER 28		**BANKRUPTCY RESTRICTIONS ORDER**
6.240	6.233	Bankruptcy restrictions order
6.241	6.234	Application for bankruptcy restrictions order
6.242	6.235	Service on the defendant
6.243	6.236	The bankrupt's evidence
6.244	6.237	Making a bankruptcy restrictions order
CHAPTER 29		**INTERIM BANKRUPTCY RESTRICTIONS ORDER**
6.245	6.238	Application for interim bankruptcy restrictions order

IR86	IRN91	
6.246	6.239	The case against the defendant
6.247	6.240	Making an interim bankruptcy restrictions order
6.248	6.241	Application to set aside an interim bankruptcy restrictions order
CHAPTER 30		BANKRUPTCY RESTRICTIONS UNDERTAKING
6.249	6.242	Acceptance of the bankruptcy restrictions undertaking
6.250	6.243	Notification to the court
6.251	6.244	Application under paragraph 9(3) of Schedule 4A to the Act to annul a bankruptcy restrictions undertaking

Part 6A

IR86	**IR(NI)89**	
CHAPTER 1		**GENERAL**
6A.1	6A.1	The individual insolvency register; the bankruptcy restrictions register
CHAPTER 2		**INDIVIDUAL INSOLVENCY REGISTER**
6A.4	6A.4	Entry of information onto the individual insolvency register -bankruptcy orders
6A.5	6A.5	Deletion of information from the individual insolvency register – bankruptcy orders
CHAPTER 3		**BANKRUPTCY RESTRICTIONS REGISTER**
6A.6	6A.6	Bankruptcy restrictions orders and undertakings – entry of information onto the bankruptcy restrictions register
6A.7	6A.7	Deletion of information from the bankruptcy restrictions register – bankruptcy restrictions orders and undertakings
CHAPTER 4		**RECTIFICATION OF REGISTERS**
6A.8	6A.8	Rectification of the registers

Debt Relief Orders

Insolvency Act 1986 (as amended) (IA86)

The Insolvency (Northern Ireland) Order 1989 (as amended) (IO89)

Part 7A and Schedule 4ZA & B / Schedule 2ZA & B [3]

IA86 Section	IO89 Article	
		Preliminary
251A	208A	Debt relief orders
		Applications for a debt relief order
251B	208B	Making of application
251C	208C	Duty of official receiver to consider and determine application
251D	208D	Presumptions applicable to the determination of an application
		Making and effect of debt relief order
251E	208E	Making of debt relief orders
251F	208F	Effect of debt relief order on other debt management arrangements
251G	208G	Moratorium from qualifying debts
251H	208H	The moratorium period
251I	208I	Discharge from qualifying debts
		Duties of debtor
251J	208J	Providing assistance to official receiver, etc.
		Objections, investigations and revocation
251K	208K	Objections and investigations
251L	208L	Power of official receiver to revoke or amend a debt relief order
		Role of the court
251M	208M	Powers of court in relation to debt relief orders / Powers of High Court in relation to debt relief orders
251N	208N	Inquiry into debtor's dealings and property
		Offences
251O	208O	False representations and omissions

---

3 For Northern Ireland debt relief orders were introduced by the Debt Relief Act (Northern Ireland) 2010 (c16).

IA86 Section	IO89 Article	
251P	208P	Concealment or falsification of documents
251Q	208Q	Fraudulent disposal of property
251R	208R	Fraudulent dealing with property obtained on credit
251S	208S	Obtaining credit or engaging in business
251T	208T	Offences: supplementary
		Supplementary
251U	208U	Approved intermediaries
251V	208V	Debt relief restrictions orders and undertakings
251W	208W	Register of debt relief orders etc
251X	208X	Interpretation

Schedule 4ZA & B / Schedule 2ZA & B

Sch 4ZA	**Sch 2ZA**	**CONDITIONS FOR MAKING A DEBT RELIEF ORDER**
PART 1		**CONDITIONS WHICH MUST BE MET**
		Connections with England and Wales / Northern Ireland
1	1	Debtors domicile & business address
		Debtor's previous insolvency history
2	2	Previous insolvency
3	3	Debtors' petitions
4	4	Creditors' petitions
5	5	Previous debt relief orders
		Limit on the debtor's overall indebtedness
6	6	Total debts
		Limit on the debtor's monthly surplus income
7	7	Surplus income
		Limit on value of debtor's property
8	8	Value of property
PART 2		**OTHER CONDITIONS**
9	9	Transactions at an undervalue
10	10	Preferences
Sch 4ZB	**Sch 2ZB**	**DEBT RELIEF RESTRICTION ORDERS AND UNDERTAKINGS**
		Debt relief restriction order

Deeds of Arrangements

The Insolvency Regulations (Northern Ireland) 1996 (IRN96)

IR94 Reg

Part 6	**DEEDS OF ARRANGEMENT**
38	Introductory
	Registration of Deeds etc
39	Endorsement on copy of a deed of arrangement for filing
40	Execution of assignment by prior trustee to registration
41	Certificate of registration on original deed of arrangement
42	Notice by new trustee of appointment
43	Notice to registrar of order declaring deed of arrangement to be void
	Statements, Accounts and Records
44	Financial records
45	Trustee carrying on business
46	Audit of trustee's accounts
47	Dividends
48	Production and inspection of records
	Forms
49	Forms

Individual Voluntary Arrangements

Insolvency Act 1986 (IA86) and The Insolvency (Northern Ireland) Order 1989 (IO89)

Part VI Individual Voluntary Arrangements

Chapter 2 Individual Voluntary Arrangements

IA86	**IO89**	
CHAPTER 2		
		Moratorium for insolvent debtor
252	226	Interim order of court
253	227	Application for interim order
254	228	Effect of application
255	229	Cases in which interim order can be made
256	230	Nominee's report on debtor's proposal
		Procedure where no interim order made

IA86	**IO89**	
256A	230A	Debtor's proposal and nominee's report
		Creditors' meeting
257	231	Summoning of creditors' meeting
258	232	Decisions of creditors' meeting
259	233	Report of decisions to court/Report of decisions to High Court.
260	234	Effect of approval
261	235	Additional effect on undischarged bankrupt
262	236	Challenge of meeting's decision
262A	236A	False representation etc
262B	236B	Prosecution of delinquent debtors
262C	236C	Arrangements coming to an end prematurely
263	237	Implementation and supervision of approved voluntary arrangement
		Fast-track voluntary arrangement
263A	237A	Availability
263B	237B	Decision
263C	237C	Result
263D	237D	Approval of voluntary arrangement
263E	237E	Implementation
263F	237F	Revocation
263G	237G	Offences

Insolvency Rules 1986 (as amended) (IR86)

The Insolvency (Northern Ireland) Rules 1991 (as amended)[4] *(IRN91)*

Part 5 Individual Voluntary Arrangements

Chapter 1 Individual Voluntary Arrangements

IR86	**IRN91**	
	5.01	Service of application under Articles 221(3) or 224
CHAPTER 1	**CHAPTER 2**	**PRELIMINARY**
5.1	5.02	Introductory

4 New Chapter inserted by Insolvency Amendment Rules (Northern Ireland) 2003 SR 2003/549

IR86	IRN91	
CHAPTER 2	**CHAPTER 3**	**PREPARATION OF THE DEBTOR'S PROPOSAL**
5.2	5.03	Preparation of proposal
5.3	5.04	Contents of proposal
5.4	5.05	Notice to the intended nominee
5.5	5.06	Statement of Affairs
5.6	5.07	Additional disclosure for assistance of nominee
CHAPTER 3	**CHAPTER 4**	**CASES IN WHICH AN APPLICATION FOR AN INTERIM ORDER IS MADE**
5.7	5.08	Application for interim order
5.8		Court in which application to be made
5.9	5.09	Hearing of the application
5.10	5.10	Action to follow making of order
5.11	5.11	Nominee's report on the proposal
5.12	5.12	Replacement of nominee
5.13	5.13	Consideration of nominee's report
CHAPTER 4	**CHAPTER 5**	**CASES WHERE NO INTERIM ORDER IS TO BE OBTAINED**
	5.14	Nominee's report to the court
5.14A		Nominee's report
5.14B	5.15	Applications to the court
5.15		Revoked
5.16		Revoked
CHAPTER 5	**CHAPTER 6**	**CREDITORS' MEETINGS**
5.17	5.16	Summoning of creditor' meeting
5.18	5.17	Creditor's meeting: supplementary
5.19	5.18	The chairman at the meeting
5.20	5.19	The chairman as proxy-holder
5.21	5.20	Entitlement to vote
5.22	5.21	Procedure for admission of creditors' claims for voting purposes
5.23	5.22	Requisite majorities
5.24	5.23	Proceedings to obtain agreement on the proposal
CHAPTER 6	**CHAPTER 7**	**IMPLEMENTATION OF THE ARRANGEMENT**

IR86	IRN91	
5.25	5.24	Resolutions to follow approval
5.26	5.25	Hand-over of property, etc to supervisor
5.27	5.26	Report of creditors' meeting
5.28	5.27	Revoked
5.29	5.28	Reports to the Secretary of State / Department
5.30	5.29	Revocation or suspension of the arrangement
5.31		Revoked
3.21A	5.30	Supervisor's accounts and reports
5.32	5.31	Production of accounts and records to the Secretary of State
5.33	5.32	Fees, costs, charges and expenses / Costs
5.34	5.33	Completion or termination of the arrangement
CHAPTER 7	**CHAPTER 8**	**FAST-TRACK VOLUNTARY ARRANGEMENT**
5.35	5.34	Application of Chapter
5.36	5.35	Interpretation
5.37	5.36	Contents of proposal
5.38	5.37	Requirement for the official receiver's decision
5.39	5.38	Arrangements for approval of fast-track voluntary arrangement
5.40	5.39	Approval by creditor
5.41	5.40	Entitlement to vote
5.42	5.41	Procedure for admission of creditors' claims for voting purposes
5.43	5.42	Requisite majorities
5.44	5.43	Revoked / Notifications to the court
5.45	5.44	Notice of appointment as supervisor etc
5.46	5.45	Revocation of the fast-track voluntary arrangement
5.47		Revoked
5.47A	5.46	Supervisor's accounts and reports
5.48	5.47	Fees, costs and expenses in respect of the performance of the functions of the official receiver

IR86	IRN91	
5.49	5.48	Employment of agents by the supervisor
5.50	5.49	Completion or termination of the fast-track voluntary arrangement
CHAPTER 8	**CHAPTER 9**	**APPLICATION BY A BANKRUPT TO ANNUL A BANKRUPTCY ORDER UNDER SECTION 261(2)(A) / ARTICLE 235(2)(A)**
5.51	5.50	Application of this Chapter
5.52	5.51	Application to court
5.53	5.52	Notice to creditors
CHAPTER 9	**CHAPTER 10**	**APPLICATION BY A BANKRUPT TO ANNUL A BANKRUPTCY ORDER UNDER SECTION 261(2)(B) / ARTICLE 235(2)(B)**
5.54	5.53	Application of this Chapter
5.55	5.54	Application to court
5.56	5.55	Notice to creditors
CHAPTER 10	**CHAPTER 11**	**APPLICATION BY A BANKRUPT TO ANNUL A BANKRUPTCY ORDER UNDER SECTION 263D(3)**
5.57	5.56	Application of this Chapter
5.58	5.57	Application to court
5.59	5.58	Notice to creditors
CHAPTER 11	**CHAPTER 12**	**OTHER MATTERS ARISING ON ANNULMENTS UNDER SECTION 261(2)(A),261(2)(B) OR 263D(3) / ARTICLES**
5.60	5.59	Notices
5.61	5.60	Trustee's final account
CHAPTER 12	**CHAPTER 13**	**EC REGULATION: CONVERSION OF VA INTO BANKRUPTCY**
5.62	5.61	Application for conversion of voluntary arrangement into bankruptcy
5.63	5.62	Contents of witness statement
5.64	5.63	Power of court
5.65	5.64	Notices to be given to member State liquidator

Part 6A

IR86	IR(NI)89	
CHAPTER 1		**GENERAL**
6A.1	6A.1	The individual insolvency register; the bankruptcy restrictions register
CHAPTER 2		**INDIVIDUAL INSOLVENCY REGISTER**
6A.2A	6A.2	Entry of information onto the individual insolvency register – individual voluntary arrangements
6A.3	6A.3	Deletion of information from the individual insolvency register – individual voluntary arrangements

Partnerships

Insolvency Act 1986 (as amended) (IA86)

Insolvent Partnerships Order 1994 SI 1994/2421 (IPO94)

The Insolvent Partnerships Order (Northern Ireland) 1995 (IPON95)

IPO94	IPON95	
PART I		**GENERAL**
1	1	Citation, commencement and extent
2	2	Interpretation: definitions
3	3	Interpretation: expressions appropriate to companies
PART II		**VOLUNTARY ARRANGEMENTS**
4	4	Voluntary arrangement of insolvent partnership
5	5	Voluntary arrangements of members of insolvent partnership
PART III		**ADMINISTRATION**
6	6	Administration in relation to insolvent partnership
PART IV		**CREDITORS' ETC WINDING-UP PETITIONS**
7	7	Winding up of insolvent partnership as unregistered company on petition of creditor etc where no concurrent petition presented against member
8	8	Winding up of insolvent partnership as unregistered company on the petition of creditor etc where concurrent petitions presented against one or more members
PART V		**MEMBERS' PETITIONS**

IPO94	IPON95	
9	9	Winding up of insolvent partnership as unregistered company on member's petition where no concurrent petition presented against member
10	10	Winding up of insolvent partnership as unregistered company on member's petition where concurrent petitions presented against all members
11	11	Insolvency proceedings not involving winding up of insolvent partnership as unregistered company where individual members present joint bankruptcy petition
PART VI		**PROVISIONS APPLYING IN INSOLVENCY PROCEEDINGS IN RELATION TO INSOLVENT PARTNERSHIPS**
12	12	Winding up of unregistered company which is a member of insolvent partnership being wound up by virtue of this Order
13	13	Deposit on petitions
14	14	Supplemental powers of court
15	15	Meaning of "act as insolvency practitioner
PART VII		**DISQUALIFICATION**
17	17	Forms
PART VIII		**MISCELLANEOUS**
17	17	Forms
18	18	Application of subordinate legislation
19	19	Supplemental and transitional provisions
20	20	Revocation
		SCHEDULES
Sch 1		Modified provisions of Part I of, and Schedule A1 to, the Act (Company Voluntary Arrangements) as applied by article 4
Part I		Modified provisions of sections 1 to 7B of the Act
Part II		Modified provisions of Schedule A1 to the Act
Sch 2		Modified provisions of Part II of, and Schedule B1 to, the Act (administration) as applied by article 6
	Sch 2	Provisions of the Order which apply with modifications for the purposes of article 6 to administration orders in relation to insolvent partnerships

IPO94	**IPON95**	
	Part I	Modified provisions of Part III of the Order
	Part II	Modified provisions of Schedule 7 to the Order
	Part III	Other modified provisions of the Order about administration orders
Sch 3	Sch 3	Provisions of the Act / Order which apply with modifications for the purposes of article 7 to winding up of insolvent partnerships on petition of creditor etc. where no concurrent petition presented against member.
Part I		Modified provisions of Part V of the Act
	Part I	Modified provisions of Part VI of the Order
Part II		Other modified provisions of the Act about winding up by the court
	Part II	Other modified provisions of the Order about winding up by the High Court
Sch 4	Sch 4	Provisions of the Act / Order which apply with modifications for the purposes of article 8 to winding up of insolvent partnerships on creditor's petitions where concurrent petitions are presented against one or more members.
Part I	Part I	Modified provisions of Part V of the Act /Order
Part II	Part II	Other modified provisions of the Order about winding up by the court / High Court and bankruptcy of individuals
Sch 5	Sch 5	Provisions of the Act / Order which apply with modifications for the purposes of article 9 to winding up of insolvent partnership on member's petition where no concurrent petitions are presented against member.
Sch 6	Sch 6	Provisions of the Act / Order which apply with modifications for the purposes of article 10 to winding up of insolvent partnership on member's petition where concurrent petitions are presented against all the members.
Sch 7	Sch 7	Provisions of the Act / Order which apply with modifications for the purposes of article 11 where joint bankruptcy petition presented by individual members without winding up partnership as unregistered company.
Sch 8		Modified provisions of Company Directors Disqualification Act 1986 for the purposes of article 16

IPO94	IPON95	
	Sch 8	Provisions of Part II of the Companies (Northern Ireland) Order 1989 which apply with modifications for the purposes of Article 16
Sch 9	Sch 9	Forms
Sch 10	Sch 10	Subordinate legislation applied

SCOTLAND

Sequestration

Bankruptcy (Scotland) Act 1985 (BSA85)

BSA85 Section	
	Administration of bankruptcy
1	Accountant in Bankruptcy
1A	Supervisory functions of the Accountant in Bankruptcy
1B	Performance of certain functions of the Accountant in Bankruptcy
1C	Directions
2	Appointment and functions of the trustee in the sequestration
3	Functions of the trustee
4	Commissioners
	Petitions for sequestration
5	Sequestration of the estate of living or deceased debtors
5A	Debtor applications by low income, low asset debtors
5B	Certificate for sequestration
6	Sequestration of other estates
6A	Petition for sequestration of estate: provision of information
6B	Debtor application: provision of information.
7	Meaning of apparent insolvency
8	Further provisions relating to presentation of petitions
8A	Further provisions relating to debtor applications
9	Jurisdiction
10	Duty to notify existence of concurrent proceedings for sequestration or analogous remedy
10A	Powers in relation to concurrent proceedings for sequestration or analogous remedy

BSA85 Section	
11	Creditor's oath
	Award of sequestration and appointment and resignation of interim trustee
12	When sequestration is awarded
13	Resignation, removal etc of interim trustee
13A	Termination of interim trustee's functions where not appointed as trustee
13B	Termination of Accountant in Bankruptcy's functions as interim trustee where not appointed as trustee
14	Registration of warrant or determination of debtor application
15	Further provisions relating to award of sequestration
16	Petitions for recall of sequestration
17	Recall of sequestration
	Initial stages of sequestration
18	Interim preservation of estate
19	Statement of assets and liabilities etc
20	Trustee's duties on receipt of list of assets and liabilities
	Statutory meeting of creditors and confirmation of permanent trustee
20A	Statutory meeting
21	Revoked
21A	Calling of statutory meeting
21B	Procedure where no statutory meeting called
22	Submission of claims for voting purposes at statutory meeting
23	Proceedings at statutory meeting before trustee vote
23A	Revoked
24	Trustee vote
25	Appointment of replacement trustee
25A	Revoked
26	Provisions relating to termination of original trustee's functions
26A	Accountant in Bankruptcy to account for intromissions
27	Discharge of original trustee
	Replacement of permanent trustee
28	Resignation and death of trustee
28A	Replacement of trustee acting in more than one sequestration

BSA85 Section	
29	Removal of trustee and trustee not acting
	Election, resignation and removal of commissioners
30	Election, resignation and removal of commissioners
	Vesting of estate in permanent trustee
31	Vesting of estate at date of sequestration
31ZA	Proceedings under EC Regulation: modified definition of "estate"
31A	Property subject to restraint order
31AA	Property released from detention
31B	Property in respect of which receivership or administration order is made
31BA	Property in respect of which realisation order made
31C	Property subject to certain orders where confiscation order discharged or quashed
32	Vesting of estate, and dealings of debtor, after sequestration
33	Limitations on vesting
	Safeguarding of interests of creditors of insolvent persons
34	Gratuitous alienations
35	Recalling of order for payment of capital sum on divorce
36	Unfair preferences
36A	Recovery of excessive pension contributions
36B	Orders under section 36A
36C	Orders under section 36A: supplementary
36D	Recovery of excessive contributions in pension-sharing cases
36E	Recovery orders
36F	Recovery orders: supplementary
	Effect of sequestration on diligence
37	Effect of sequestration on diligence
	Administration of estate by trustee
38	Taking possession of estate by trustee
39	Management and realisation of estate
39A	Debtor's home ceasing to form part of sequestrated estate
40	Power of trustee in relation to the debtor's family home
41	Protection of rights of spouse against arrangements intended to defeat them

BSA85 Section

41A	Protection of rights of civil partner against arrangements intended to defeat them
42	Contractual powers of trustee
43	Money received by trustee
43A	Debtor's requirement to give account of state of affairs
	Examination of debtor
44	Private examination
45	Public examination
46	Provisions ancillary to sections 44 and 45
47	Conduct of examination
	Submission and adjudication of claims
48	Submission of claims to trustee
49	Adjudication of claims
	Entitlement to vote and draw dividend
50	Entitlement to vote and draw dividend
	Distribution of debtor's estate
51	Order of priority in distribution
52	Estate to be distributed in respect of accounting periods
53	Procedure after end of accounting period
53A	Modification of procedure under section 53 where Accountant in Bankruptcy is trustee
	Discharge of debtor
54	Automatic discharge of debtor
55	Effect of discharge under section 54
56	Discharge on composition
	Bankruptcy restrictions orders and undertakings[5]
56A	Bankruptcy restrictions order
56B	Grounds for making order
56C	Application of section 67(9)
56D	Timing of application for order
56E	Duration of order and application for annulment
56F	Interim bankruptcy restrictions order
56G	Bankruptcy restrictions undertaking

---

[5] Bankruptcy and Diligence etc. (Scotland) Act 2007 (asp 3)

BSA85 Section	
56H	Bankruptcy restrictions undertakings: application of section 67(9)
56J	Effect of recall of sequestration
56K	Effect of discharge on approval of offer of composition
	Discharge of trustee
57	Discharge of trustee
58	Unclaimed dividends
58A	Discharge of Accountant in Bankruptcy
	Voluntary trust deeds for creditors
59	Voluntary trust deeds for creditors
59A	Petition for conversion into sequestration
59B	Contents of affidavit
59C	Power of sheriff
	Miscellaneous and supplementary
60	Liabilities and rights of co-obligants
60A	Member State liquidator deemed creditor
60B	Trustee's duties concerning notices and copies of documents
61	Extortionate credit transactions
62	Sederunt books and other documents
63	Power to cure defects in procedure
64	Debtor to co-operate with trustee
65	Arbitration and compromise
66	Meetings of creditors and commissioners
67	General offences by debtor etc
68	Summary proceedings
69	Outlays of insolvency practitioner in actings as interim trustee or trustee
69A	Fees for the Accountant in Bankruptcy
70	Supplies by utilities
71	Edinburgh Gazette
71A	Further duty of Accountant in Bankruptcy
71B	Disqualification provisions: power to make orders[6]
72	Regulations

[6] Bankruptcy and Diligence etc. (Scotland) Act 2007 (asp 3)

SCBR08

1	Citation and interpretation
2	Forms of petition
3	Petitions for sequestration
4	Intimation of appointment of trustee
5	Applications
5A	Service of sequestration petitions
6	Application to determine amount for aliment and obligations, etc
7	Appeals to the sheriff
8	Appeals to the sheriff principal and the Court of Session
9	Forms and register of insolvencies
10	Reports
11	Holding of sederunt book by Accountant in Bankruptcy
12	Approved debt payment programmes
13	UNCITRAL Model Law on Cross-Border Insolvency
14	Vulnerable witnesses
15	Representation
16	Expenses
Appendix 1	Forms
Appendix 2	Information to be contained in the register of insolvencies

Voluntary Trust Deeds

Bankruptcy (Scotland) Act 1985 (BSA85)

BSA85
Section

	Voluntary trust deeds for creditors
59	Voluntary trust deeds for creditors
59A	Petition for conversion into sequestration
59B	Contents of affidavit
59C	Power of sheriff
Schedule 5	Voluntary trust deeds for creditors

The Protected Trust Deeds (Scotland) Regulations 2008 (PTDR08)

PTDR08
Regulation

Debt Arrangement Schemes

The Debt Arrangement Scheme (Scotland) Regulations 2011

DAS Regulation	
Part 1	**GENERAL**
1	Citation and commencement
2	Interpretation: general
3	Interpretation: debt
4	Dispensing power
5	Fees
6	Consequential amendments
Part 2	**MONEY ADVISERS**
7	Debtor to have an approved money adviser
8	Approval categories of money adviser
9	Approval of a money adviser
10	Persons who are not and may not be approved
11	Revocation, or suspension, of approval of a money adviser
12	Functions and duty of a money adviser
Part 3	**PAYMENTS DISTRIBUTORS**
13	Payments distributors for a debt payment programme
14	Approval of a payments distributor
15	Revocation of approval of a payments distributor
16	Functions and duty of a payments distributor / Charges by a payments distributor
17	Charges by a payments distributor
Part 4	**DEBT ARRANGEMENT SCHEME REGISTER**
18	Debt Arrangement Scheme Register
19	Information on the DAS Register
Part 5	**APPROVAL OF DEBT PAYMENT PROGRAMMES**
20	Application for approval
21	Debtors who may apply for approval
22	Joint debt payment programme
23	Consent of creditors
24	Approval of agreed programmes
25	Approval by the DAS administrator
26	Notice of intention to approve, and approval of, a programme

DAS Regulation	
27	Standard conditions
28	Discretionary conditions
29	Notification of approval or rejection
30	Diligence or sequestration in the period before a debt payment programme is approved
Part 6	**DEBT PAYMENT PROGRAMMES**
31	Methods of payment
32	Payment instruction to employer
33	Effect on a creditor
34	Diligence: further provision as regards effect of debt payment programme
35	Effect on trust deeds which are not protected
Part 7	**VARIATION OF DEBT PAYMENT PROGRAMMES**
36	Application for variation
37	Grounds for variation
38	Approval of a variation
39	Notification of approval or rejection of a variation
Part 8	**REVOCATION OF DEBT PAYMENT PROGRAMMES**
40	Revocation on sequestration or protected trust deed
41	Application for revocation
42	Grounds for revocation
43	Determination of a revocation
44	Notification of revocation
45	Apparent insolvency
Part 9	**COMPLETION OF A DEBT PAYMENT PROGRAMME**
46	Notice of completion
Part 10	**APPEALS**
47	Appeals
Part 11	**Revocations, Saving and Transitional Arrangements**
48	Notices by a money adviser: completion
	Savings and transitional arrangements
49	Status of money adviser / administrator
49A	Interest, fees, penalties or other charges
50	Previous debt payment programmes
51	Consent of creditors

DAS Regulation	
Sch 1	Arrangement of forms
Sch 2	Consequential amendments
Sch 3	Money adviser training
Sch 4	Payments distributors
Sch 5	Revocations

ENGLAND & WALES AND NORTHERN IRELAND

General Provisions

Insolvency Regulations 1994 (IR94)

The Insolvency Regulations (Northern Ireland) 1996 (IRN96)

IR94 Reg	**IR94 Reg**	
PART 1		**GENERAL**
1	1	Citation and commencement
2	2	Revocation
3	3	Interpretation and application
PART 3		**BANKRUPTCY**
19	19	Introductory
		Payments into and out of the Insolvency Services Account
20	20	Payments into the Insolvency Services Account
21	21	Local bank account and handling of funds forming part of the bankrupt's estate
22	22	Payment of disbursements etc out of the Insolvency Services Account
		Dividends to creditors
23	23	Payment
23A		Investment or otherwise handling of funds in bankruptcy and payment of interest
	24	Interest
		Records to be maintained by trustees and the provision of information
24	25	Financial records

IR94 Reg	IR94 Reg	
25	26	Provision of information by trustee
26	27	Trustee carrying on business
27	28	Retention and delivery of records
28	29	Provision of accounts by trustee and audit of accounts
29	30	Production and inspection of records
30	31	Disposal of bankrupt's books, papers and other records
31	32	Payment of unclaimed or undistributed assets, dividends or other money
PART 4		**CLAIMING MONEY PAID INTO THE INSOLVENCY SERVICES ACCOUNT**
32	33	Claiming money paid into the Insolvency Services Account
PART 5		**REMUNERATION OF OFFICIAL RECEIVER**
33	34	Official receiver's remuneration while acting as liquidator or trustee calculated as a percentage of the value of assets realised or distributed
34	35	Limits on official receiver's remuneration as trustee
35	36	Official receiver's general remuneration while acting as interim receiver, provisional liquidator, liquidator or trustee
36	37	Official receiver's remuneration while acting as liquidator or provisional liquidator in respect of the realisation of property charged
PART 6		**INFORMATION ABOUT TIME SPENT ON A CASE TO BE PROVIDED BY INSOLVENCY PRACTITIONER TO CREDITORS ETC**
36A		
SCHEDULES		
2		Forms
3		Transitional and Saving Provisions

ENGLAND & WALES, SCOTLAND AND NORTHERN IRELAND

General Provisions

Insolvency Practitioners Regulations 2005 (IPR2005)

Insolvency Practitioners Regulations (Northern Ireland) 2006 (IPRN2006)

IPR2005 Reg	**IPRN2006 Reg**	
PART 1		**INTRODUCTORY**
1	1	Citation and commencement
2	2	Interpretation: general
3	3	Interpretation-meaning of initial and subsequent capacity
4	4	Revocations and transitional and saving provisions
PART 2		**AUTHORISATION OF INSOLVENCY PRACTITIONERS BY CONNMPETENT AUTHORITIES**
5	5	Interpretation of Part
6	6	Matters for determining whether an applicant for an authorisation is a fit and proper person
7	7	Requirements as to education and training – applicants who have never previously been authorised to act as insolvency practitioners
8	8	Requirements relating to education and training etc – applicants previously authorised to act as insolvency practitioners
8A	8A	Requirements relating to education and training etc – further authorisation to act as insolvency practitioners
9	9	Records of continuing professional development activities
10	10	Maximum period of authorisation
11	11	Returns by insolvency practitioners authorised by the Secretary of State
PART 3		**THE REQUIREMENTS FRO SECURITY AND CAUTION FOR THE PROPER PERFORMANCE OF THE FUNCTIONS OF AN INSOLVENCY PRACTITIONER ETC**
12	12	

IPR2005 Reg	IPRN2006 Reg	
PART 4		**RECORDS TO BE MAINTAINED BY INSOLVENCY PRACTITIONERS: INSPECTION OF RECORD**
13	13	Records to be maintained by insolvency practitioners
14	14	Notification of whereabouts of records
15	15	Inspection of records
16	16	Inspection of practice records
17	17	Inspection of records in administration and administrative receivership
		SCHEDULES
2	2	Requirements for Security or Caution and Related Matters
3	3	Records to be Maintained – Minimum Requirements

Appendix 4

STATUTORY FORMS

ENGLAND & WALES AND NORTHERN IRELAND

Bankruptcy

These forms are listed in Schedule 4, Part 6: Bankruptcy, Insolvency Rules 1986 and Insolvency Rules (Northern Ireland) 1989 and copies can be obtained from the Insolvency Service website:

IR86 Form No	**IRNI89 Form No**	
6.1	6.01	Statutory demand under section 268(1)(a) of IA86 or Article 242(1)(a) I989 – Debt for liquidated sum payable immediately
6.2	6.02	Statutory demand under section 268(1)(a) of IA86 or Article 242(1)(a) I989 – Debt for liquidated sum payable immediately following a judgment or order of the court
6.3	6.03	Statutory demand under section 268(2) of IA 1986 or Article 242(2) Debt payable at future date
6.4	6.04	Application to set aside a statutory demand
6.5	6.05	Witness statement in support of application to set aside statutory demand or Affidavit in support of Application to set aside a Statutory Demand
6.6		Order setting aside statutory demand
6.7	6.07	Creditor's bankruptcy petition on failure to comply with a statutory demand for a liquidated sum payable immediately
6.8	6.08	Creditor's bankruptcy petition on failure to comply with a statutory demand for a liquidated sum payable at a future date
6.9	6.09	Bankruptcy petition where execution or other process on a judgment has been returned in whole or part or Creditor's Bankruptcy Petition On Certificate of Unenforceability of a Judgment

IR86 Form No	IRNI89 Form No	
6.10		Bankruptcy petition for default in connection with voluntary arrangement
6.11		Certificate of personal service of statutory demand
	6.13	Affidavit of personal service of statutory demand where service not acknowledged in writing
6.12	6.14	Certificate of substituted service of statutory demand where service not acknowledged in writing or Affidavit of Substituted Service of Statutory Demand Where Service Not Acknowledged in Writing
6.13A		Statement of truth of statements in bankruptcy petition
	6.15	Affidavit of truth of statements in bankruptcy petition
6.14		Application for registration of petition in bankruptcy against an individual under Land Charges Act 1972
6.15A		Order for substituted service of a bankruptcy petition
6.16		Substituted service of bankruptcy petition – notice in Gazette
	6.18	Affidavit of personal service of bankruptcy petition
	6.19	Affidavit of substituted service of bankruptcy petition
6.17A		Certificate of personal service of bankruptcy petition
6.18		Affidavit of substituted service of bankruptcy petition
6.18A		Certificate of substituted service of bankruptcy petition
6.19	6.20	Notice by debtor of Intention to oppose bankruptcy petition
6.20	6.21	Notice of Intention to appear on bankruptcy petition
6.21	6.23	List of creditors intending to appear on the hearing of the bankruptcy petition
6.22		Dismissal [or withdrawal] of bankruptcy petition

IR86 Form No	IRNI89 Form No	
6.23		Order of adjournment of bankruptcy petition
6.24		Notice to debtor [and creditors] of order of adjournment of bankruptcy petition
6.24A		Order for substitution of petitioner on creditor's petition
6.24B		Change of carriage order
6.25		Bankruptcy order on [creditor's] petition other than debtor's
6.26		Application for registration of a bankruptcy order against an individual under Land Charges Act 1972
6.27	6.30	Debtor's bankruptcy petition
6.28	6.31	Statement of affairs (debtor's petition)
6.29		Order of appointment of insolvency practitioner to prepare a report under section 274(1) IA86 or Article 248(1) INO89
6.30		Bankruptcy order on debtor's petition
6.31 (*Revoked*)		Revocation of certificate for summary administration
6.32		Order of appointment of interim receiver
6.33A	6.36	Statement of affairs (creditor's petition) [petition other than debtors] or Statement of Affairs (Petition other than Debtor's)
6.34		Request by creditor(s) for a meeting of the bankrupt's creditors
6.35		Notice to creditors of meeting of creditors
6.36		Notice to bankrupt of meeting of creditors
6.37	6.40	Proof of debt – general form or Proof of Debt – General form – Bankruptcy
6.38		Proof by existing trustee as a claim in later bankruptcy
6.39 (*Revoked*)		Affidavit of debt
6.40		Certificate of appointment of trustee by creditors' meeting
6.41		Certificate of appointment of two or more trustees by creditors' meeting
6.42		Order of court appointing trustee

IR86 Form No	IRNI89 Form No	
6.43		Order of court appointing two or more trustees
6.44		Notice to court of resignation of trustee following meeting of creditors
6.45		Order of court giving trustee permission to resign
6.46		Notice to court of resignation of trustee following permission of the court
6.47		Certificate of removal of trustee
6.48		Order of court removing trustee or directing trustee to summon a meeting of creditors for the purpose of his removal
6.49		Trustee's application to the Secretary of State for his release
6.50	6.53	Notice to court of final meeting of creditors or Notice to Court of Final Meeting of Creditors – Bankruptcy
6.51		Notice of official receiver by trustee on loss of qualification as insolvency practitioner
6.52		Certificate of constitution [amended certificate] of creditors' committee
6.53 (*Revoked*)		Report by trustee of any change in membership of creditors' committee
6.54		Order of appointment of special manager
6.55		Order for public examination of bankrupt
6.56		Request by creditor(s) for the holding of a public examination of the bankrupt
6.57		Order as to examination of bankrupt who lacks capacity to manage and administer his property and affairs or is suffering from a physical affliction or disability
6.58		Statement of truth verifying record of the public examination of the bankrupt
6.59		Order of adjournment of public examination of bankrupt
6.60		Order appointing time for proceeding with public examination of bankrupt adjourned
6.61A		Notice of disclaimer under section 315 IA86 or Article 288 INO89
6.62		Notice to elect

IR86 Form No	IRNI89 Form No	
6.63		Notice of intended disclaimer to interested party
6.64		Notice to bankrupt of application under section 310 IA86 for income payments order or Article 283
6.65		Order for income claimed under section 310(3)(a) IA86 or Article 283(3)(a)
6.66		Order for income claimed under section 310(3)(b) IA86 or Article 283(3)(b)
6.67		Order converting income payments order made under section 310(1)(a) to an order under section 310(3)(b) IA86 or Article 283(3)(b)
6.68		Discharge or variation of order for income claimed under section 310 IA86 or Article 283
6.69		Order under section 369(1) IA86 or Article 340(1)
6.70		Order under section 369(2) IA86 or Article 340(2)
6.71		Order of annulment under section 282 IA86 or Article 256
6.72		Order of suspension of discharge under section 279(3) IA86 or Article 253(3)
6.73		Order of court lifting suspension of discharge
6.74		Certificate that order suspending discharge has been lifted
6.75		Notice to court by bankrupt that he intends to dispute statements made by official receiver in his report under section 289(2) IA86 or Article 262(2)
6.76		Order granting absolute/suspended discharge under section 280(2)(b) or (c) IA86 or Article 254(2)(b)
6.77		Certificate of discharge
6.78		Notice to existing trustee of the presentation of a petition for a later bankruptcy
6.79		Criminal bankruptcy petition
6.79A		Charging order under section 313 IA86 or Article 286
6.80		Order to postal operator under section 371 IA86 or Article 342
6.81		Variation of income payments agreement under section 310A IA86
6.82		Notice under section 279(2) IA86

IR86 Form No	IRNI89 Form No	
6.83		Notice to interested parties of a dwelling-house falling within section 283A IA86
6.84		Certificate issued pursuant to rule 6.237B(1) IR86

Court Procedure and Practice

These forms are found in Schedule 4, Part 7: Court Procedure, Insolvency Rules 1986 and Insolvency Rules (Northern Ireland) 1989:

IR86 Form No	**IRNI89 Form No**	
7.1A		Application Notice
7.3 (*Revoked*)		Order to post office under section 371 IA86 or
7.4 (*Revoked*)		Variation of income payments agreement under section 310A IA86 or
7.5 (*Revoked*)		Notice under section 279(2) IA86 or
7.6 (*Revoked*)		Notice to interested parties of a dwelling-house falling within section 283A IA86 or
7.7 (*Revoked*)		Certificate issued pursuant to Rule 6.237B(1) IR86
7.8 (*Revoked*)		Warrant of arrest etc. under section 364 IA86
7.9 (*Revoked*)		Warrant of arrest etc. under section 236 or 366 IA86
7.10 (*Revoked*)		Order for production of person arrested under warrant issued under sections 134, 236, 364 or 366 IA86 or
7.11 (*Revoked*)		Warrant to registrar of court in whose
7.12 (*Revoked*)		Endorsement of warrant of arrest issued by a court to which the same has been sent for execution by the court which originally issued it
7.13 (*Revoked*)		Warrant of seizure of property under section 365 IA86 or
7.14 (*Revoked*)		Search warrant under section 365 IA86 or
7.15 (*Revoked*)		Order of discharge from custody under the IA86 [General]
7.16 (*Revoked*)		Affidavit in support of application for committal for contempt of court
7.17 (*Revoked*)		Warrant of committal for contempt

IR86 Form No	**IRNI89 Form No**	
7.18 (*Revoked*)		Order of discharge from custody on contempt
7.19 (*Revoked*)		Order Appointing Person to Act for Incapacitated Person
7.20A		Confirmation by Court of Creditors' Voluntary Winding Up Applicaton and Order

Individual Voluntary Arrangements

These forms are found in Schedule 4, Part 5: Individual Voluntary Arrangements, Insolvency Rules 1986:

IR86 Form No	**IRNI89 Form No**	
5.1		Order for stay pending hearing of application for interim order
5.2		Interim order of court under section 252 IA86 or Article 226 INO89
5.3		Order extending effect of interim order
5.4		Alternative orders to be made at hearing to consider chairman's report
5.5 (*Revoked*)		Documents to be submitted to court under rule 5.14
5.6		Voting form in relation to a proposal for a voluntary arrangement under section 263A IA86
5.7		Order of annulment under section 261 IA86
5.8		Order of annulment under section 263D IA86

SCOTLAND

Sequestration

Bankruptcy (Scotland) Act 1985 c 66 (BSA85)

Act of Sederunt (Sheriff Court Bankruptcy Rules) 2008, SSI 2008/119(AS(SCBR)08)

AS(SCBR)08

Form 1	Form of Petition by Qualified Creditor(s) Under s 5(2)(b)(i) of the Bankruptcy (Scotland) Act 1985
Form 2	Form of Petition by a Temporary Administrator, a Member State Liquidator in Main Proceedings or a Foreign Representative (r 3(2))
Form 3	Form of Petition by a Trustee Under a Trust Deed in Terms of S 5(2)(b)(iv) of the Bankruptcy (Scotland) Act 1985 (r 3(3))
Form 4	Form of Undertaking Required by Section 2(3)(c) of the Bankruptcy (Scotland) Act 1985 (r 3(4))
Form 5	Form of Application Under the Bankruptcy (Scotland) Act 1985 (r 5(1))
Form 5A	Form of Citation
Form 5B	Form of Certificate of Citation
Form 6	Form of Note of Appeal to Sheriff Under the Bankruptcy (Scotland) Act 1985 (r 7(1))
Form 7	Form of Memorandum by Trustee to be Recorded in the Register of Inhibitions and Adjudications Under Section 14(4) of the Bankruptcy (Scotland) Act 1985 (r 9(1))
Form 8	Form of Notice of Inhibition by Trustee Under Trust Deed to be Recorded in the Register of Inhibition and Adjudications Under Paragraph 2(1) of Schedule 5 to the Bankruptcy (Scotland) Act 1985 (r 9(2))
Form 9	Form of Notice of Recall of Inhibition in the Register of Inhibitions and Adjudications Under Paragraph 2(2) of Schedule 5 to the Bankruptcy (Scotland) Act 1985 (r 9(3))
Form 10	Form of Report by the Accountant in Bankruptcy Under Section 24(3A) of the Bankruptcy (Scotland) Act 1985 (r 10(1))
Form 11	Form of Report by the Original Trustee Under s 24(4)(b) of the Bankruptcy (Scotland) Act 1985 (r 10(2))

AS(SCBR)08

Form 12 Form of Statement to be Lodged by Creditor in Petitioning for Sequestration (r 12(3))

Trust Deeds

Bankruptcy (Scotland) Act 1985 c 66 (BSA85)

The Protected Trust Deeds (Scotland) Regulations 2008 (PTDR08)

PTDR08

A1	Consents required for exclusion of a secured creditor from a Protected Trust Deed (reg 5A)
1	Notice in Edinburgh Gazette by Trustee Under a Trust Deed for the Benefit of Creditors (reg 7)
2	Statement of Claim by Creditor in Trust Deed (reg 8(d))
3	Trustee's Statement of Anticipated Realisations from a Protected Trust Deed (reg 10(1)(f))
4	Trustee's statement of anticipated realisations from a protected trust deed (reg 17(3))
5	Letter of Discharge for Debtor (reg 19(3)(a))
6	Application to Creditors for Discharge of the Trustee of a Protected Trust Deed (reg 21(1))
7	Trustee's Statement of Realisation and Distribution of Estate Under a Protected Trust Deed (reg 22(b))

Debt Arrangement Schemes

The Debt Arrangement Scheme (Scotland) Regulations 2011, SSI 2011/141 (DAS)

DAS

1	Application for Approval of a Debt Payment Programme (reg 20(2))
2	Notification to Creditors of Approval of a Debt Payment Programme (reg 29(4)(a))
3	Payment Instruction to Employer (reg 32(1))
4	Application for Variation of a Debt Payment Programme (36(3)(b))
5	Application for revocation of a Debt Programme (reg 41(2)(b))

Appendix 5

STANDARD CONDITIONS FOR INDIVIDUAL VOLUNTARY ARRANGEMENTS

Produced by the Association of Business Recovery Professionals

TABLE OF CONTENTS FOR STANDARD CONDITIONS INDIVIDUAL VOLUNTARY ARRANGEMENTS

PART IV: DEBTOR'S WARRANTY, DUTIES & OBLIGATIONS

PART V: ARRANGEMENT ASSETS

PART VI: CLAIMS

PART VII: CREDITORS WHO DO NOT HAVE NOTICE

PART VIII: PAYMENT OF DIVIDENDS

PART IX: PRIORITY OF PAYMENTS AND DISTRIBUTIONS

57 Costs and Expenses of the Arrangement
58 Priority of Debts and application of surplus

PART X: THE CREDITORS COMMITTEE & MEETINGS OF CREDITORS

59 The Creditors' Committee
60 Power to call/requisition meetings of Creditors
61 Calling Creditors' meetings
62 Cost of summoning meetings
62A Remote attendance at meetings
62B Use of websites
63 Entitlement to vote
64 Admission and rejection of claim
65 Majorities required to pass resolutions
66 Chairman of meeting as proxy-holder
67 Suspension/adjournment of meeting
68 Record of proceedings
69 Postal resolutions

PART XI: PROVISIONS FOLLOWING BREACH OF THE ARRANGEMENT

70 Breach by the Debtor of the terms of the Arrangement
71 Procedure following breach
72 Retention of funds by Supervisor

PART XII: CONDITIONS WHERE TAX AUTHORITIES ARE CREDITORS

73 Claims by HM Revenue and Customs
74 Income commencing after approval
75 Post approval statutory returns and payments
76 Overdue accounts and returns
77 Funds to be paid to Supervisor
78 Restriction on payment of dividend
79 Set-off of repayments

PART XIII: MISCELLANEOUS PROVISIONS

80 Third Party obligations
81 Variation of the Arrangement
82 Tax liabilities arising on realisations
83 Invalidity and/or illegality

PART I: INTERPRETATION

1 Miscellaneous definitions

1(1) In the Arrangement, except where the context otherwise demands:

(a) **"the Act"** means the Insolvency Act 1986 as amended;

(b) **"the Arrangement"** means the Proposal and the Conditions read together;

(c) **"Associate"** shall have the meaning given to it in section 435 of the Act;

(d) **"the Conditions"** are these Conditions;

(e) **"the Court"** means any court having jurisdiction in respect of the Arrangement;

(f) **"Creditor"** is a person bound by the Arrangement to whom a Debt is owed;

(g) **"Debt"** has the meaning given to it in section 382 of the Act with the modifications necessary to refer to a voluntary arrangement;

(h) **"the Debtor"** means the person who makes the Proposal;

(i) **"Dividend"** means a distribution to Creditors;

(j) **"Excluded Assets"** are those assets identified in the Proposal as being excluded from the Arrangement;

(k) **"Paragraphs"** are Paragraphs of these Conditions; and Sub-paragraph shall be construed accordingly;

(l) **"Preferential Creditor"** is a Creditor with a Debt falling within section 386 of the Act and "Preferential Debt" shall be construed accordingly;

(m) **"Property"** has the meaning given to it in section 436 of the Act;

(n) **"the Proposal"** is the document annexed hereto together with modifications and documents incorporated thereto, being a proposal under Part VIII of the Act;

(o) **"the Rules"** means the Insolvency Rules 1986 as amended;

(p) **"Security"** has the meaning given to it in section 383 of the Act; and "Secured Creditor" shall be construed accordingly;

(q) **"the Secretary of State"** means the Secretary of State for Business Innovation and Skills or any successor office;

(r) **"the Supervisor"** is the person or persons for the time being appointed to supervise the implementation of the Arrangement;

1(2) References in the Arrangement to any statutory provision shall include a reference to any modification or re-enactment thereof for the time being in force.

2 The Conditions

2 The Conditions are an integral part of the Arrangement. In the event of any ambiguity or conflict between the Conditions and the Proposal and any modifications to it, the Proposal as modified shall prevail.

PART II: COMMENCEMENT, EFFECT, AND DURATION OF ARRANGEMENT

3 Commencement of Arrangement

3 The Arrangement shall come into effect upon the approval thereof by the Creditors pursuant to the provisions of the Act and Rules.

4 Nature and effect of the Arrangement

4(1) [Nature of Arrangement] The Arrangement is a proposal under Part VIII of the Act for a scheme of arrangement of the Debtor's affairs or a composition in full and final satisfaction of the Debtor's Debts.

4(2) [Claims against third parties] Unless the Proposal indicates to the contrary, nothing in the Arrangement shall be construed as effecting a composition or satisfaction of any Debt owed by a person other than the Debtor, whether that Debt is owed jointly by the Debtor or otherwise.

4(3) [Restriction on Creditors' rights] After the commencement of the Arrangement, no Creditor shall, in respect of any Debt which is subject to the Arrangement:

(a) have any remedy against the property or person of the Debtor;

(b) commence or continue any action or other legal proceeding against the Debtor.

4(4) [Saving for certain rights] Nothing in this Paragraph or elsewhere in the Conditions shall be construed as affecting the following rights:

(a) the right of any Secured Creditor to enforce his Security, except with the Secured Creditor's consent;

(b) the right of the Supervisor or any Creditor to present a bankruptcy petition under section 264(1)(c) of the Act for default in connection with the Arrangement

(c) the right of any Creditor to bring or continue legal proceedings against the Debtor and to obtain a judgment against the Debtor in the full amount of its Debt for the sole purpose of making a claim against an insurer of the Debtor by virtue of the Third Party (Rights Against Insurers) Act 1930.

5 Existing proceedings against Debtor

5(1) [Discontinuance of existing proceedings] Legal proceedings against the Debtor in existence at the commencement of the Arrangement in respect of Debts which are subject to the Arrangement shall, unless they are of a type contemplated by Paragraph 4(4) or the Supervisor otherwise directs, be discontinued by the Creditor with no order as to costs as soon after the commencement of the Arrangement as is practicable.

5(2) [Costs of existing proceedings] Legal costs of a Creditor in proceedings other than bankruptcy referred to in Sub-paragraph (1) shall be a Debt falling within the Arrangement.

5(3) [Costs of bankruptcy proceedings] Petition costs of a Creditor who presented a bankruptcy petition against the Debtor prior to the commencement of the Arrangement shall be treated as an expense of the Arrangement to rank after the costs of the Nominee but before those of the Supervisor.

5(4) [Prior distress] Where any person has distrained on the goods or effects of the Debtor in the period of three months prior to the making of the interim order, those goods or effects, or the proceeds of their sale, shall be charged with the Preferential Debts of the Debtor to the extent that the assets of the Arrangement are insufficient for meeting those debts.

6 Existing execution against Debtor's assets

6(1) [Partly-completed execution] A Creditor who, before the commencement of the Arrangement, has issued execution against the goods or land of the Debtor in respect of a Debt which is subject to the Arrangement, or has attached a Debt due to the Debtor from another person in respect of such a Debt shall, unless the execution or attachment was completed before the commencement of the Arrangement, discontinue the execution or attachment as soon after the commencement of the Arrangement as is practicable.

6(2) [Completion of execution or attachment] For the purposes of Sub-paragraph (1):

(a) an execution against goods is completed by seizure and sale or by the making of a charging order absolute under section 1 of the Charging Orders Act 1979;

(b) an execution against land is completed by seizure, by the appointment of a receiver or by the making of a charging order absolute under section 1 of the Charging Orders Act 1979;

(c) an attachment of a Debt is completed by the receipt of the Debt.

7 Mutual credit and set-off

7(1) [Application] This Paragraph applies where before the commencement of the Arrangement there have been mutual credits, mutual Debts or other mutual dealings between the Debtor and any Creditor other than in the circumstances to which Paragraph 79 of these Conditions apply.

7(2) [Account to be taken] An account shall be taken of what is due from each party to the other in respect of the mutual dealings and the sums due from one party shall be set-off against the sums due from the other.

7(3) [No account where Creditor has notice] Sums due from the Debtor to another party shall not be included in the account taken under Sub-paragraph (2) if that other party had notice at the time they became due that a bankruptcy petition relating to the Debtor was pending or that an interim order was made in relation to the Debtor.

7(4) [Restriction on post-commencement set-off] Other than as provided for in this Paragraph, set-off shall not be available in respect of any Debt or item of Property.

7(5) [Balance provable or to be paid] Only the balance (if any) of the account taken under Sub-paragraph (2) is provable in the Arrangement or, as the case may be, to be paid to the Debtor or, if the Proposal so provides, to the Supervisor.

8 Duration of Arrangement

8(1) [General rule] Unless extended under the provisions of these Conditions, the Arrangement shall continue until the end of the period stated in the Proposal.

8(2) [Extension of duration by Supervisor] The Supervisor may, if he thinks fit, extend the duration of the Arrangement by sending a notice to this effect ("an Extension Notice") to the Debtor and all Creditors. This may be done on up to 2 occasions: for a period of up to 6 months in the first instance and for a period of up to 3 months in the second instance.

8(3) [Extension Notice] An Extension Notice shall be sent not less than 7 days prior to the date upon which the Arrangement is otherwise due to complete and must state the reason or reasons for the extension.

8(4) [Effect of extension] In the event of an Extension Notice being sent, the Arrangement shall continue for the period specified therein, or for the maximum allowable period for that extension (being 6 months for a first extension and 3 months for a second extension) commencing on the date immediately after that on which the Arrangement would otherwise have been completed, whichever is sooner.

8(5) [Supervening notice calling a meeting of Creditors] In the event that a meeting of Creditors has been called by the Supervisor for a time after the Arrangement would otherwise have expired, the duration of the Arrangement shall be extended to the date of that meeting and of any adjournment thereof.

8(6) [Further extension] Any extension for a period longer than that provided for under Paragraph 8(2) shall require approval as a variation in accordance with Paragraph 81.

9 Completion of Arrangement

9(1) [The Completion Certificate] Upon the expiration of the Arrangement, the Supervisor shall, if the Debtor has complied with his obligations under the Arrangement, issue a certificate ("the Completion Certificate") stating that the Proposal has been fully implemented.

9(2) [Effect of Completion Certificate] Save to the extent provided in Paragraph 4(4), upon the issue by the Supervisor of a Completion Certificate, the Debtor shall be released from all Debts which are subject to the Arrangement.

9(3) [Notification of issue of Completion Certificate] Copies of the Completion Certificate issued under this Paragraph shall be sent by the Supervisor to the Debtor, the Creditors, the Secretary of State and the Court together with the Supervisor's report under Rule 5.34 (completion or termination of Arrangement).

10 Substantial Compliance

10(1) [Issue of certificate where substantial compliance] The Supervisor may, if he thinks fit, issue a Completion Certificate notwithstanding the fact that the Debtor has not complied with all of his obligations under the Arrangement provided that the Debtor has:

(a) made all payments required of him under the terms of the Arrangement;

(b) provided a full explanation of any breach of the terms of the Arrangement required by the Supervisor;

(c) paid to the Supervisor such sum (if any) as the Supervisor shall reasonably have required to compensate the Creditors for any reduction in Dividend caused by the Debtor's breach of the terms of the Arrangement.

10(2) [Notification to creditors] Where the Supervisor proposes to issue a Completion Certificate under Sub-paragraph 1 he shall notify the Creditors accordingly and invite them to submit any comments within 21 days from the date of notification.

10(3) [Treatment as full implementation] If the Supervisor issues a Completion Certificate under Sub-paragraph (1), the Arrangement shall be treated as fully implemented for the purposes of Rule 5.34.

11 Termination of Arrangement

11(1) [Termination in certain circumstances] The Arrangement shall terminate

upon:

(a) the Supervisor issuing a Certificate of Termination under Paragraph 71;

(b) the making of a bankruptcy order against the Debtor;

(c) the Debtor's death, none of which circumstances shall affect the trusts created under Paragraph 28.

11(2) [Notice of termination] The Supervisor shall, on discovering the occurrence of a terminating event, but in any event not more than 28 days after such discovery, give notice of such termination and the reason therefor to the Debtor (or, if the Debtor has died, his representative) and Creditors.

PART III: SUPERVISOR'S FUNCTIONS, POWERS ETC

12 Supervisor's functions

12(1) [Primary function] The Supervisor's primary function is to supervise the Debtor's performance of his obligations under the Arrangement and to administer the Arrangement.

12(2) [Other functions] The Supervisor shall also undertake such functions as are given to him in the Proposal, Act and Rules.

13 Supervisor's powers

13(1) Subject to those powers more particularly given to him in the Arrangement, Act and Rules, the Supervisor shall have the following powers:

(1) [*Getting in assets*] power to take possession of, collect, get in and hold any or all of the assets which, under the terms of the Arrangement, he is to hold as trustee;

(2) [*Realisation of assets*] power to sell or otherwise dispose of any asset referred to in Sub-paragraph (1) in such manner as may seem to him expedient;

(3) [*Putting funds on deposit*] power to place money coming into his hands during
the course of the Arrangement on deposit with any established United Kingdom clearing bank or building society;

(4) [*Appointing agents*] power to engage legal representatives, managers, agents and other persons to assist the Supervisor in the performance of his functions under the Arrangement;

(5) [*Delegation*] power to delegate to his firm and any appropriate partner, employee or agent thereof any or all of his duties and functions under the Arrangement save those which by law he is required to perform personally;

(6) [*Insurance*] power to effect and maintain insurances in respect of any asset subject to the Arrangement;

(7) [*Power to claim*] power to prove, rank, claim and draw a Dividend in respect of such Debts owed to the Debtor as fall within the Arrangement;

(8) [*Power to direct Debtor*] power, in the event that the Supervisor is unable or it is impracticable for him to do any act or thing which he is empowered to do himself, to direct the Debtor to do that act or thing on his behalf;

(9) [*Ancillary power*] power to do any other act or thing which is necessary or expedient for the purposes of exercising the above powers or for carrying out his functions under the Arrangement.

13(2) Where more than person is appointed as Supervisor, any act required or authorised to be done under any enactment or otherwise may be done by all or any one or more of the persons for the time being holding office.

14 Supervisor's powers upon completion/termination

14(1) [Exercise of powers after completion/termination] Completion and/or termination of the Arrangement shall not affect the Supervisor's power to carry out such of his functions and to exercise such of his powers as are necessary for him to fully carry out his duties, obligations and responsibilities under the Arrangement, Act and Rules and to resolve such matters as may have arisen during the course of the Arrangement.

14(2) [Retention of funds by Supervisor] Upon completion and/or termination of the arrangement, the Supervisor shall be entitled to retain for such period as he reasonably deems necessary from any funds under his control such moneys as he reasonably thinks fit on account of his fees, costs, charges, liabilities and expenses, and shall advise Creditors and the Debtor in writing of the quantum of the funds so retained and the reasons why.

15 Exercise of Supervisor's functions and powers

15(1) [Application of bankruptcy provisions] In the event that the Arrangement does not provide guidance to the Supervisor as to what action he should take in any given situation, the Supervisor shall apply the provisions of the Act and Rules in so far as they relate to bankruptcy with necessary modifications.

15(2) [Consultation of Creditors] If the Supervisor is uncertain as to what action he should take in any situation, or wishes to ascertain the wishes of Creditors on a matter concerning the Arrangement, he may seek the advice and/or direction of the Creditors' Committee and/or the majority or most material of the Creditors and he may act upon such advice and/or direction.

15(3) [Directions from the Court] This Paragraph is without prejudice to the Supervisor's right to refer matters concerning the Arrangement to the Court for guidance and/or directions if, in his discretion, he shall think fit.

16 Restriction upon Supervisor's duty and liability

16(1) [Supervisor's duty] The Supervisor shall be under no obligation to perform any act or carry out any function save for those expressly provided for in the Arrangement, the Act or Rules.

16(2) [Supervisor's liability] Neither the Supervisor, his firm or any of his agents or employees shall incur any personal liability in negligence or otherwise for any act or omission carried out by him or any of them in connection with the Arrangement, unless such act or omission constitutes one of dishonesty or a breach of the Supervisor's obligations under the Act, Rules or the Arrangement.

17 Supervisor's fees, costs and expenses

17(1) [Amount of fees] The Supervisor shall be entitled to charge fees for his services (whether as trustee or otherwise) in accordance with the time actually and reasonably expended by him and his staff in carrying out the Supervisor's functions under the Arrangement by reference to the ordinary hourly rates of the Supervisor and his staff as shall apply from time to time.

17(2) [Payment of fees, costs and expenses] The fees, costs, charges and expenses of the Supervisor shall be paid out of the assets of the Arrangement from time to time as the Supervisor thinks fit. The Supervisor shall provide such information to any Creditors' committee appointed in relation to the Arrangement as is reasonably necessary to explain how the fees, costs, charges and expenses were determined or incurred, as the case may be.

17(3) [Supervisor's right of recourse to Court] If the Supervisor is dissatisfied with a determination of the Creditors Committee or a meeting of Creditors on a matter involving his fees, costs, charges and/or expenses, he shall have the right to refer the matter to the Court, whose decision on the matter shall bind all parties.

18 Supervisor's resignation

18(1) [Methods of resignation] A Supervisor may resign from office with the approval of a meeting of Creditors or with the leave of the Court.

18(2) [Grounds of Supervisor's resignation] The Supervisor may only resign from office on one or more of the following grounds:

(a) ill health;

(b) cessation of practice as an insolvency practitioner;

(c) change of circumstances rendering it impracticable for him to continue in office;

(d) impracticability to have the present number of persons acting as Supervisor to the Arrangement.

18(3) [Report of Supervisor's administration] The notice to Creditors convening a meeting for the purpose of receiving his resignation shall specify the grounds upon which the Supervisor wishes to resign and shall be accompanied by a report of the Supervisor's administration of the Arrangement which includes an up to date summary of his receipts and payments.

19 Removal of Supervisor from office

19(1) [Methods of removal] On cause being shown, the Supervisor may be removed from office by the Court or by a resolution of a meeting of Creditors.

19(2) [Notice of requisitioned meeting] Any notice served by a Creditor upon the Supervisor under Paragraph 60(2) (notice requisitioning meeting) for the purpose of convening a meeting of Creditors to remove the Supervisor from office must set out the grounds upon which his removal is sought.

19(3) [Report of Supervisor's administration] The notice sent out by the Supervisor to Creditors convening such a requisitioned meeting shall specify the grounds upon which his removal is sought and shall be accompanied by a report of the Supervisor's administration of the Arrangement including an up to date summary of his receipts and payments.

20 Vacation of Office by Supervisor

20(1) [Resignation/removal of Supervisor where more than one acting] If the Creditors resolve to accept the resignation of a Supervisor, or to remove a Supervisor from office, and there will be another person in the office of Supervisor for the time being, the Supervisor who is resigning or being removed shall vacate office immediately.

20(2) [Resignation/removal of Supervisor where no other acting] If the Creditors resolve to accept a Supervisor's resignation or to remove a Supervisor from office, and there is no other person in the office of Supervisor for the time being, that resignation and/or removal shall not take effect and the Supervisor shall not vacate office unless and until a meeting of Creditors or the Court appoints a replacement Supervisor.

20(3) [Loss of qualification] The Supervisor shall vacate office immediately if he ceases to be a person who is for the time being qualified to act as Supervisor.

20(4) [Notice of vacation of office] A Supervisor who, for any reason, vacates office shall forthwith give notice of that fact to the Court, the Debtor the Creditors and the Secretary of State.

20(5) [Duties of Supervisor upon vacation of office] A Supervisor who, for any reason, vacates office shall, as soon as practicable, deliver up to his successor Supervisor or Supervisors all books, records and papers relating to the Arrangement and his administration thereof together with all assets of which he is a trustee under the terms of the Arrangement.

20(6) [Continuing duty of former Supervisor] Former Supervisors shall be obliged to give such assistance to the Supervisor of the Arrangement from time to time as he may reasonably require for ascertaining what transpired during the tenure of office by the former Supervisor.

21 Vacancy in the office of Supervisor

21(1) [Meeting of Creditors to fill vacancy] If, for any reason, there is a vacancy in the office of Supervisor, that vacancy may be filled by a meeting of Creditors or by the Court.

21(2) [Convening a meeting where no Supervisor acting] If no Supervisor is in office, such a meeting of Creditors may be convened by the Debtor, any Creditor, any person who was in partnership with the Supervisor immediately before the vacancy occurred, the former Supervisor's authorising body, or by any other interested party.

21(3) [Chairman where no Supervisor acting] In the event that a meeting of Creditors is called when no Supervisor is in office, the person who convened the meeting shall act as chairman of that meeting.

PART IV: DEBTOR'S WARRANTY, DUTIES & OBLIGATIONS

22 Debtor's warranty

22(1) [Disclosure in Proposal] The Debtor warrants that he has disclosed in the Proposal full and complete particulars of all matters required of him under the Act and Rules including (without prejudice to the generality of the foregoing) particulars of all of his assets, Debts and liabilities, whether actual, contingent or prospective.

22(2) [Accuracy of Proposal] The Debtor warrants that the contents of the Proposal are true and accurate in all material respects as at the date of the commencement of the Arrangement, subject only to those qualifications that may be disclosed by the Debtor at the meeting of Creditors held to approve the arrangement, which qualifications shall be recorded by the Supervisor in his report to the Court under Rule 5.27 (report of Creditors' meeting).

22(3) [Disclosure of third party information] The Debtor authorises any creditor to disclose to the Supervisor such information relating to the Debtor, his dealings or property as may reasonably be required to assist in the implementation of the Arrangement.

23 Debtor's duties in relation to Supervisor

23(1) [Duty to co-operate with Supervisor] The Debtor undertakes and agrees that during the subsistence of the Arrangement he will:

(a) give to the Supervisor such information as to his assets, liabilities and other affairs;

(b) attend on the Supervisor, his agents, representatives or nominees at such times; and

(c) do all such other things;

as the Supervisor shall reasonably require for the purpose of carrying out his functions and duties under the Arrangement.

23(2) [Duty to submit accounts] The Debtor undertakes and agrees to furnish the Supervisor with accounts relating to his affairs of such nature, as at such date and for such period as the Supervisor may reasonably require.

23(3) [Notice of after-acquired assets and increased income] Where at any time during the subsistence of the Arrangement After-Acquired Property of a description falling within Paragraph 27 is acquired by or devolves upon the Debtor, or there is an increase in the Debtor's income if the Debtor is under an obligation to make contributions out of income, the Debtor shall forthwith give the Supervisor notice of the property or, as the case may be, of the increase.

24 Further Documents

24 Without prejudice to the generality of the Debtor's other duties under the Arrangement, the Debtor shall, at the request of the Supervisor, execute such Mortgages, Charges, Deeds, Transfers, Trusts, Powers of Attorney or other documents as may reasonably be required by the Supervisor for the protection and/or realisation of assets, to secure the Debtor's compliance with his obligations under the Arrangement, or otherwise to facilitate the implementation of the Arrangement.

25 Debtor's acknowledgement

25(1) [Agreement to be bound] The Debtor undertakes to carry out the obligations imposed upon him under the Arrangement in full and at the times provided for.

25(2) [Consequences of breach] The Debtor acknowledges that the likely consequence of his failure to comply with his obligations hereunder in full and at the times provided for is that the Arrangement will fail and he will be adjudged bankrupt on a petition presented by the Supervisor.

25(3) [Section 262A] The Debtor acknowledges that he commits an offence if he makes any false representation or commits any other fraud for the purpose of obtaining the approval of his Creditors to the Arrangement.

PART V: ARRANGEMENT ASSETS

26 Arrangement assets

26 Property other than Excluded Assets belonging to or vested in the Debtor at the date of commencement of the Arrangement which would form part of the Debtor's estate in a bankruptcy shall be subject to the Arrangement and be an asset thereof.

27 After-acquired assets

27(1) [After-acquired property subject to Arrangement] The Supervisor may claim as an asset of the Arrangement any Property acquired by the Debtor between the commencement date of the Arrangement and the date of its completion and/or termination which would have been an asset of the Arrangement if it had belonged to or was vested in the Debtor at the date of commencement of the Arrangement ("After- Acquired Assets"). Any such asset shall be subject to the Arrangement and be an asset thereof.

27(2) [Proviso for excess assets] After-Acquired Assets shall only be sold or realised to the extent necessary to repay the Creditors in full together with interest, if any, to which Creditors are entitled pursuant to the Arrangement.

28 Trust of Arrangement assets

28(1) [Assets in the possession of the Debtor] Property constituting an asset of the Arrangement in the possession, custody or control of the Debtor shall be held by the Debtor upon trust for the purposes of the Arrangement until realisation thereof (if so provided) in accordance with the Arrangement.

28(2) [Assets in the possession of the Supervisor] Property constituting an asset of the Arrangement in the possession, custody or control of the Supervisor shall be held by the Supervisor upon trust for the purposes of the Arrangement.

28(3) [Trusts to survive termination of Arrangement] The trusts referred to in Subparagraphs (1) and (2) shall not come to an end upon termination of the Arrangement. Instead those assets shall be got in and realised by the Supervisor, and any proceeds applied and distributed in accordance with the terms of the Arrangement.

29 Restriction on dispositions

29(1) The Debtor shall not sell, charge or otherwise dispose of any interest he may have in any asset subject to the Arrangement without the Supervisor's written consent.

29(2) The Debtor hereby consents, agrees to procure that any co-owner also consents, and hereby requests the Chief Land Registrar to register a restriction on the Proprietorship Register of any registered land which is subject to the Arrangement in the following form: "No disposition of the registered estate by the proprietor of the registered estate or by the proprietor of any registered charge is to be registered without a written consent signed by [name of Supervisor] of [address] (or his conveyancer)."

PART VI: CLAIMS

30 Notice to submit claims

30 As soon as practicable after the commencement of the Arrangement, and provided no application under Section 262 of the Act (challenge of meeting's decision) or an appeal under Rule 5.22(3) (appeal from chairman's decision) is pending, the Supervisor shall send a notice ("a Notice to Submit Claims") to every Creditor and other person to whom the Debtor may be indebted of whom he has notice requiring them to provide such details of their claims as the Supervisor thinks fit.

31 Submission of claims

31 Creditors shall submit their claims in writing to the Supervisor in the form, if any, required by the Supervisor, or one which is substantially similar.

32 Variation of claims

32 A Creditor's claim may at any time be withdrawn or varied.

33 Production of documents

33 The Supervisor may call for any document or other evidence to be produced to him, where he thinks it necessary, for the purpose of substantiating the whole or any part of the claim.

34 Witness statement substantiating claim

34 The Supervisor may, if he thinks it necessary, require a claim to be verified by witness statement with a statement of truth.

35 Supervisor to allow inspection of claims

35 The Supervisor shall, so long as claims lodged with him are in his hands, allow them to be inspected, at all reasonable times on any business day, by: 16

(a) any Creditor who has submitted his claim (unless that claim has been wholly rejected for the purposes of Dividend or otherwise); and

(b) the Debtor.

36 Admission and rejection of claims for Dividend

36(1) [Admission] A claim may be admitted for Dividend either for the whole of the amount claimed by the Creditor, or for part of that amount.

36(2) [Rejection] If the Supervisor rejects a claim in whole or in part, he shall prepare a written statement of his reasons for so doing and send it to the Creditor.

37 Appeal against decision on claim

37(1) [Application by Creditor] If a Creditor is dissatisfied with the Supervisor's decision with respect to his claim or its ranking he may apply to the Court, within 21 days (or such longer period as the Court shall, in the special circumstances, allow) of receiving the statement sent under Paragraph 36(2) for the decision to be reversed or varied.

37(2) [Application by Debtor or other Creditor] The Debtor or any other Creditor may, if dissatisfied with the Supervisor's decision admitting or rejecting the whole or any part of a claim, make such an application within 21 days (or such longer period as the Court shall, in the special circumstances, allow) of becoming aware of the Supervisor's decision.

37(3) [Costs of appeal] The Supervisor is not personally liable for the costs incurred by any person in respect of an appeal under this Paragraph unless the Court so orders.

38 Debts of uncertain value

38(1) [Estimation of Debt or liability] The Supervisor shall estimate the value of any Debt which, by reason of its being subject to a contingency or for any other reason, does not bear a certain value.

38(2) [Notification to Creditor] The Supervisor shall notify the Creditor in writing of any such estimate. If the Creditor is dissatisfied with the Supervisor's decision he may exercise his rights under paragraph 37.

38(3) [Claim of Debts of uncertain value] Where the value of any Debt is estimated by the Supervisor under Sub-paragraph (1), the amount provable in the Arrangement shall be the amount of the estimate.

39 Secured Creditors

39(1) [Proving for balance of Debt] A Secured Creditor may claim for the balance of his Debt (if any), after deducting the value of his Security.

39(2) [Voluntary surrender of Security] If a Secured Creditor voluntarily surrenders his Security for the general benefit of the Creditors, he may claim for his whole Debt, as if it were unsecured.

39(3) [Altering value of Security] A Secured Creditor may, with the agreement of the Supervisor or the leave of the Court, at any time alter the value which he has, in his claim, put upon his Security.

39(4) [Test of Security's value] If the Supervisor is dissatisfied with the value which a Secured Creditor puts on his Security (whether in his claim or by way of revaluation), he may require the Security to be professionally valued by a person agreed as between the Creditor and the Supervisor, or in default of such agreement by the Court.

39(5) [Professional valuation treated as amended valuation] Where a professional valuation has been carried out under the previous Sub-paragraph, that valuation shall be treated as an amended valuation of the Creditor.

39(6) [Realisation of Security] If a Creditor who has valued his Security subsequently realises it:

(a) the Creditor shall forthwith notify the Supervisor and shall give the Supervisor such information relating thereto as he may reasonably require;

(b) the net amount realised shall be substituted for the value previously put by the Creditor on the Security, and

(c) that amount shall be treated in all respects as an amended valuation by him.

40 Foreign currency Debts

40(1) [Conversion into sterling] For the purpose of claiming for a Debt incurred or payable in a currency other than sterling, the amount of the Debt shall be converted into sterling at the official exchange rate prevailing on the date of the commencement of the Arrangement.

40(2) [The official exchange rate] The official exchange rate is the middle exchange rate on the London Foreign Exchange Market at the close of business, as published for the date in question. In the absence of any such published rate, it is such rate as the Supervisor and Creditor agree or, in default of such agreement, the Court determines.

41 Debts payable at future time

41 Subject to Paragraph 55 (adjustment of Dividend where payment made before time) a Creditor may claim for a Debt of which payment was not yet due at the date of commencement of the Arrangement.

42 Interest on Debts

42 Where a Debt bears interest, that interest may be claimed as part of the Debt except in so far as it is payable in respect of any period after the commencement of the Arrangement.

43 Cost of submitting claims

43(1) [Creditor bears cost of submitting claim] Every Creditor bears the cost of submitting his own claim, including such cost as may be incurred in obtaining valuations, providing documents, witness statements or other evidence to the Supervisor.

43(2) [Supervisor's costs] Costs incurred by the Supervisor in estimating the value of a Debt of uncertain value shall be an expense of the Arrangement.

PART VII: CREDITORS WHO DO NOT HAVE NOTICE

44 Claims arising where funds available

44 If at the time the claim is notified to the Supervisor the arrangement is still in force and the Supervisor is holding sufficient funds to pay a Dividend to such Creditor or Creditors, then the Supervisor will, subject to agreement of the claim, forthwith pay to the Creditor a Dividend or distribution of an amount which is on the same basis as the Dividends and distributions already paid. Such payments will be made before any further payments to any other Creditors and will be paid so as to bring about an equalisation in Dividends or distributions between Creditors who fall within section 260 (2) (b) (i) on the one hand and section 260 (2) (b) (ii) on the other hand.

45 Claims arising where no funds available

45 If the claims are notified to the Supervisor at a time when he is holding no funds available for payment of a Dividend then as and when any funds are received the Supervisor will subject to agreement of the claim, out of such funds, first make such payment to such Creditors so as to bring about an equalisation as aforesaid.

46 Effect of claims on debtor

46(1) [Claim not to constitute default] The notification to the Supervisor of any such claim or claims shall not constitute an act of default unless the failure to give notice to such Creditor was a deliberate act on the part of the Debtor.

46(2) [Obligation to provide further funds] Unless the Proposal otherwise provides there shall be no obligation upon the Debtor to pay to the Supervisor any further sums of money or make any further assets available (other than already provided for in the Proposal) so as to meet the claim falling to be dealt with under Rule 5.3 (2) (g) unless the Proposal as agreed provides for a minimum Dividend to be paid to Creditors.

47 Notification of claims to Creditors

47 On receipt of any such claim the Supervisor will notify all Creditors bound of such receipt, the name of the Creditor, the amount claimed, and will provide such other information as may be relevant including particulars as to the Debtor's explanation why the Creditor was not given notice, and also the impact which such claim is likely to have on the outcome of the Arrangement. Such notification may, if the Supervisor considers it appropriate, be included in the progress report to Creditors provided that such report is due to be circulated within a period of 3 months from the date on which the claim is notified. Where, in the opinion of the Supervisor, the claim, whether taken alone or in conjunction with other such claims, will not materially reduce the amount of the estimated Dividend, he may defer notification and include it in his next progress report.

48 Claims arising after termination

48 If the claim is notified to the Supervisor after the date on which the Arrangement ceases to have effect, then the Creditor shall be entitled to rely upon section 260 (2A) of the Act and shall be entitled to recover from the Debtor such sum as the Creditor would have received had the claim been notified to the Supervisor prior to the date on which the Arrangement ceased to have effect and the Supervisor had been able to include the claim in the Arrangement for the purpose of payment of Dividends or distributions. The Supervisor shall be under no obligation to agree any such claim or take any action in respect thereof other than to furnish the Creditor who relies on section 260 (2A) with a certificate as to the Dividend or distribution the Creditor would have received had the claim been included in the Arrangement for Dividend or distribution purposes and on the assumption that the claim would have been agreed in the sum claimed.

PART VIII: PAYMENT OF DIVIDENDS

49 Distribution by Dividend

49(1) [Duty to declare and distribute Dividends] At the time or times specified in the Proposal or, if none, whenever the Supervisor has sufficient funds in hand for the purpose, the Supervisor shall, subject to the retention of such sums as he considers necessary for payment of the expenses of the Arrangement, declare and distribute Dividends among the Creditors in respect of those of their claims which have been admitted.

49(2) [Calculation and distribution of Dividend] In the calculation and distribution of a Dividend the Supervisor shall make provision:

(a) for any Debts which are the subject of claims which have not yet been determined; and

(b) for disputed claims.

50 Notice of intended Dividend

50(1) [Notice to Creditors who have not claimed] No more than three months before declaring a Dividend to non-preferential Creditors, the Supervisor shall give notice of his intention to do so to all such Creditors whose addresses are known to him and who have not submitted their claims.

50(2) [Last date for submitting claims] Any notice sent out to Creditors under Subparagraph (1) shall specify a date ("the Last Date for Submitting Claims") up to which claims may be lodged. The Last date for Submitting Claims shall be the same for all Creditors, and not less than 21 days from the date of the notice.

51 Notice of declaration

51(1) [Notice to Creditors who have claimed] The Supervisor shall give notice of the Dividend to all Creditors who have submitted their claims.

51(2) [Particulars in notice] The notice shall include the following particulars:

(a) amounts realised from the sale of assets subject to the Arrangement and/or amounts paid by the Debtor to the Supervisor under the Arrangement;

(b) payments made by the Supervisor during the course of the Arrangement;

(c) provision (if any) made for unsettled claims, and funds (if any) retained for particular purposes;

(d) the total amount to be distributed, and the rate of Dividend;

(e) whether, and if so when, any further Dividend is expected to be declared.

51(3) [Simultaneous distribution] The Dividend may be distributed simultaneously with the notice declaring it.

51(4) [Method of payment] Payment of Dividend may be made by post, or arrangements may be made with any Creditor for it to be paid in another way, or held for his collection.

51(5) [Endorsement in negotiable instrument] Where a Dividend is paid on a bill of exchange or other negotiable instrument, the amount of the Dividend shall be endorsed on the instrument, or on a certified copy of it, if required to be produced by the holder for that purpose.

52 Claim altered after payment of Dividend

52(1) [Amount claimed increased] If, after payment of Dividend, the amount claimed by a Creditor is increased, the Creditor is not entitled to disturb the distribution of the Dividend; but he is entitled to be paid, out of any money for the time being available for the payment of any further Dividend, any Dividend or Dividends which he has failed to receive before that money is applied to the payment of any such further Dividend.

52(2) [Claim withdrawn, disallowed, reduced] If, after a Creditor's claim has been admitted, the claim is withdrawn or disallowed, or the amount of it is reduced, the Creditor shall repay to the Supervisor any amount overpaid by way of Dividend.

53 Secured Creditors

53(1) [Application of Paragraph] The following applies where a Creditor re-values his Security at a time when a Dividend has been declared.

53(2) [Reduction in unsecured claim] If the re-valuation results in a reduction of his unsecured claim ranking for Dividend, the Creditor shall, as soon as practicable, repay to the Supervisor any amount received by him as Dividend in excess of that to which he would be entitled having regard to the re-valuation of the Security.

53(3) [Increase of unsecured claim] If the re-valuation results in an increase of his unsecured claim, the Creditor is entitled to receive from the Supervisor, out of any money for the time being available for the payment of a further Dividend, before any such Dividend is paid, any Dividend or Dividends which he has failed to receive, having regard to the re-valuation of the Security. However, the Creditor is not entitled to disturb any Dividend declared (whether or not distributed) before the date of the revaluation.

54 Assignment of Debts or rights to Dividend

54(1) [Notice of assignment] If a person entitled to a Dividend gives notice to the Supervisor that he wishes the Dividend to be paid to another person, or that he has assigned his entitlement or Debt to another person, the Supervisor shall pay the Dividend to that other person accordingly.

54(2) [Contents of notice] A notice given under this Paragraph must specify the name and address of the person to whom payment is to be made.

55 Debts payable at future time

55(1) [Entitlement to Dividend] Where a Creditor has claimed for a Debt of which payment is not due at the date of the declaration of Dividend, he is entitled to Dividend equally with other Creditors, but subject as follows.

55(2) [Calculation of amount of reduction] For the purpose of Dividend (and for no other purpose), the amount of the Creditor's admitted claim (or, if a distribution has previously been made to him, the amount remaining outstanding in respect of his admitted claim) shall be reduced by a percentage calculated as follows:

$I \times M/_{12}$

where I is 5 per cent and M is the number of months (expressed, if need be, as or as including, fractions of months) between the declaration of Dividend and the date when payment of the Creditor's Debt would otherwise be due.

56 Debts of unpaid Creditors

56(1) [Creditors not entitled to Dividend] Creditors who do not claim in the Arrangement shall not be entitled to receive any Dividend.

56(2) [Unclaimed Dividends paid to Debtor] Dividends due to Creditors who have claimed in the Arrangement but whom the Supervisor has been unable to pay shall, at the end of the Arrangement, be paid to the Debtor or, if there is one, his trustee in bankruptcy.

56(3) [Debtor liable for unclaimed Dividends] Once a Dividend has been paid to the Debtor or his trustee in bankruptcy under the previous Sub-paragraph, the Creditor must claim it from the Debtor or, as the case may be, his trustee in bankruptcy and no other person.

PART IX: PRIORITY OF PAYMENTS AND DISTRIBUTIONS

57 Costs and Expenses of the Arrangement

57(1) [Expenses to be paid first] Subject to Paragraphs 5(3) and 72 the fees, costs, charges, expenses and liabilities properly charged or incurred by or on behalf of the Nominee or the Supervisor are expenses of the Arrangement and shall be paid in priority to all other charges, expenses, liabilities and Debts.

57(2) [Charge in relation to expenses] The Supervisor shall have a charge on the assets subject to the Arrangement in respect of the expenses of the Arrangement.

58 Priority of Debts and application of surplus

58(1) [Priority of preferential Debts] In the distribution of sums due to be paid to Creditors under the terms of the Arrangement, Preferential Debts shall be paid in priority to other Debts.

58(2) [Ranking of preferential Debts] Preferential Debts rank equally between themselves after the expenses of the Arrangement.

58(3) [Ranking of ordinary Debts] Debts other than Preferential Debts rank equally between themselves and, after the Preferential Debts, shall be paid in full unless the sums due to be paid to Creditors are insufficient for meeting them, in which case they abate in equal proportions between themselves.

58(4) [Surplus after payment] Any surplus remaining after the payment of the Preferential and other Debts shall first be applied in paying interest on those Debts in respect of the periods during which they have been outstanding since the commencement of the Arrangement (for this purpose interest on Preferential Debts ranks equally with interest on Debts other than Preferential Debts) and thereafter returned to the Debtor.

58(5) [Interest rate on surplus] The rate of interest payable under Sub-paragraph (4) in respect of any Debt is whichever is the greater of the following:

(a) the rate specified in section 17 of the Judgments Act 1838 at the commencement of the Arrangement; and

(b) the rate applicable to that Debt apart from the Arrangement.

PART X: THE CREDITORS COMMITTEE & MEETINGS OF CREDITORS

59 The Creditors' Committee

59(1) [Establishment] Any meeting of Creditors may establish a committee ("the Creditors' Committee"), consisting of not less than 3 and not more than 5 members to represent the interests of the Creditors and to provide such assistance and guidance to the Supervisor as he may reasonably require.

59(2) [Eligibility] All the members of the Creditors' Committee must be Creditors of the Debtor; and any Creditor (other than one who is fully secured) may be a member, so long as:

(a) he has lodged a claim, and

(b) his claim has neither been wholly disallowed for voting purposes, nor wholly rejected for the purposes of distribution or Dividend.

59(3) [Application of Rules] The Rules relating to the Creditors' Committee in a bankruptcy contained in Rules 6.151 to 6.163 shall apply to the Arrangement with the modifications necessary to apply those rules to a voluntary arrangement.

59(4) [Expenses of members] The reasonable travelling expenses directly incurred by any member of the Creditors' Committee or their representatives in respect of their attendance at the meetings of the Creditors' Committee, or otherwise on the Creditors' Committee's business, shall rank as an expense of the Arrangement.

60 Power to call/requisition meetings of Creditors

60(1) [Supervisor's power to call meetings] The Supervisor may, if he thinks it desirable, summon and conduct meetings of Creditors for any purpose connected with the Arrangement.

60(2) [Power to requisition a meeting] If requested in writing by the Debtor, or by Creditors with not less than one-quarter in value of the total amount of Debts subject to the Arrangement, the Supervisor shall, unless relieved by the Court from so doing, convene a meeting of Creditors within 21 days from the receipt of such request.

60(3) [Content of notice requisitioning meeting] A notice served upon the Supervisor under Sub-paragraph (2) shall state the purpose for which the meeting is to be held.

61 Calling Creditors' meetings

61(1) [Notice of meeting] Notice of a Creditor's meeting shall be given by the person convening the meeting to the Debtor and every Creditor whose address is known to him or identified in the Proposal at least 14 days before the date fixed for the meeting, or such shorter period as the Court may allow.

61(2) [Contents of notice] The notice to Creditors shall specify the purpose for which the meeting is convened and a time and date (not earlier than 4.00 p.m. on the business day before the meeting) by which Creditors must lodge proxies and those who have not already lodged claims must do so, in order to be entitled to vote at the meeting.

61(3) [Forms of proxy] With every notice convening a Creditors' meeting there shall be sent out forms of proxy.

61(4) [Venue of meeting] In fixing the venue for a meeting of Creditors, the person convening it shall have regard to the convenience of the parties who may wish to attend.

61(5) [Time of meeting] Meetings of Creditors shall be convened for commencement between the hours of 10.00 and 16.00 on a business day, unless the Court otherwise directs.

61(6) [Chairman of meeting] Unless Paragraph 21(3) (chairman where no Supervisor acting) applies, the Supervisor, or a person experienced in insolvency matters and nominated by him, shall be chairman of the meeting.

62 Cost of summoning meetings

62(1) [Security for payment of expenses] Subject to Sub-paragraph (3) below, the cost of summoning and holding a meeting of Creditors at the instance of the Debtor or Creditors under Paragraph 60(2) shall be paid by that person or persons, who shall deposit security for their payment with the Supervisor.

62(2) [Appropriate security] The sum to be deposited shall be such as the Supervisor determines to be appropriate; and the Supervisor shall be under no obligation to act without the deposit having been paid.

62(3) [Vote for cost to be an expense of arrangement] Where a meeting is so summoned, it may vote that the expenses of convening and holding it shall rank as an expense of the Arrangement.

62(4) [Repayment of deposit] To the extent that any deposit made under this Paragraph is not required for the payment of expenses of convening and holding the meeting, it shall be repaid to the person who made it.

62A Remote attendance at meetings

62A(1) [Attendance at meeting by persons not present together] Where a person convening a meeting considers it appropriate, the meeting may be conducted and held in such a way that persons who are not present together at the same place may attend it.

62A(2) [Attendance at meeting by exercise of right to speak and vote] Where a meeting is conducted and held in the manner referred to in Sub-paragraph (1), a person attends the meeting if that person is able to exercise any rights which that person may have to speak and vote at the meeting.

62A(3) [Application of Act and Rules] The provisions of Section 379A(4)-(8) and Rules 12A.22-23 relating to remote attendance shall apply to the Arrangement with any necessary modifications.

62B Use of websites

62B(1) [Contents of notice re website] A Supervisor who wishes to give, deliver or send a document to any person may satisfy that requirement by sending that person a notice:

(a) stating that the document is available for viewing on a website;

(b) specifying the address of that website together with any password necessary to view and download the document from that site; and

(c) containing a statement that the person to whom the notice is given, delivered or sent may request a hard copy of the document and specifying a telephone number, e-mail address and postal address which may be used to request a hard copy.

62B(2) [Application of Rules] The provisions of Rules 12A.12-23 relating to use of websites shall apply to the Arrangement with any necessary modifications.

63 Entitlement to vote

63(1) [Conditions for voting] Subject as follows, at a meeting of Creditors a person is entitled to vote as a Creditor only if:

(a) he has duly lodged his claim by the time and date stated in the notice of the meeting, and

(b) the claim has been admitted under the next Paragraph for the purpose of entitlement to vote, and there has been lodged, by that time and date, any proxy requisite for that entitlement.

63(2) [Unliquidated and unascertained claims] A Creditor shall not vote in respect of a Debt for an unliquidated amount, or any Debt whose value is not ascertained, except where the Chairman agrees to put upon the Debt an estimated minimum value for the purpose of entitlement to vote.

63(3) [Secured Creditors] A Secured Creditor is entitled to vote only in respect of the balance (if any) of his Debt after deducting the value of his Security as estimated by him.

64 Admission and rejection of claim

64(1) [Chairman's discretion] The chairman has power to admit or reject a Creditor's claim for the purpose of his entitlement to vote. The power is exercisable with respect to the whole or any part of the claim, and whether the claim is secured or unsecured.

64(2) [Appeal from chairman's decision] The chairman's decision on entitlement to vote is subject to appeal to the Court by any Creditor, or by the Debtor, within 21 days of the meeting of Creditors at which the decision was made, or such longer period as the Court shall, in the special circumstances, allow.

64(3) [Voting subject to objection] If the chairman is in doubt whether a claim should be admitted or rejected, he shall mark it objected to and allow the Creditor to vote, subject to his vote being subsequently declared invalid if the objection to the claim is sustained.

64(4) [Where chairman's decision reversed] If, on an appeal, the chairman's decision is reversed or varied, or a Creditor's vote is declared invalid, the Court may order another meeting to be summoned, or make such other order as it thinks fit, provided that the Court considers the matter is such as to give rise to unfair prejudice or a material irregularity.

64(5) [Costs of appeal] The chairman is not personally liable for the costs incurred by any person in respect of an appeal under this Paragraph unless the Court so orders.

65 Majorities required to pass resolutions

65(1) [Resolutions by majority in value] Subject as follows, at a meeting of Creditors a resolution is passed when a majority in value of Creditors present and voting, in person or by proxy, have voted in favour of the resolution.

65(2) [Resolutions varying terms of Arrangement] In the case of a resolution varying the terms of the Arrangement, a majority of three-quarters or more in value of those present and voting, in person or by proxy, is required to pass the resolution.

65(3) [Votes rendering resolution invalid] Any resolution is invalid if those voting against it include more than half in value of the Creditors who are not, to the best of the chairman's belief, Associates of the Debtor.

65(4) [Resolution for the appointment of Supervisor] In the case of a resolution for the appointment of a Supervisor:

(a) if on any vote there are 2 nominees for appointment, the person who obtains the most support is appointed, provided that such support represents a majority in value of all those present (in person or by proxy) at the meeting and entitled to vote; and

(b) if there are 3 or more nominees, and one of them has a clear majority over both or all of the others together, that one is appointed; and

(c) in any other case, the chairman shall continue to take votes (disregarding at each vote any nominee who has withdrawn and, if no nominee has withdrawn, the nominee who obtained the least support last time), until a clear majority is obtained for any one nominee.

65(5) [Resolution for joint appointment] The chairman may at any time put to the meeting a resolution for the joint appointment of any 2 or more nominees if he thinks it appropriate.

66 Chairman of meeting as proxy-holder

66 Where the chairman at a meeting holds a proxy for a Creditor which requires him to vote for a particular resolution, and no other person proposes that resolution, he shall himself propose it

67 Suspension/adjournment of meeting

67(1) [Suspension] Once only in the course of any meeting, the chairman may, in his discretion and without an adjournment, declare the meeting suspended for any period up to one hour.

67(2) [Adjournment] The chairman at any meeting may, in his discretion, and shall, if the meeting so resolves, adjourn it to such time and place as seems to him to be appropriate in the circumstances; provided that if the chairman is the Supervisor and a resolution has been proposed for his removal, the chairman shall not adjourn the meeting without the consent of at least one half in value of the Creditors present (in person or by proxy) and entitled to vote.

67(3) [Period of adjournment] An adjournment under this Paragraph shall not be for a period of more than 21 days, or such longer period as the Court may allow.

67(4) [Use of claims and proxies at adjourned meeting] Where a meeting is adjourned under this Paragraph, claims and proxies may be used if lodged at any time up to 4.00 p.m. on the business day immediately before the adjourned meeting.

68 Record of proceedings

68(1) [Minutes of proceedings] The chairman of any Creditors' meeting shall cause minutes of the proceedings at the meeting, signed by him, to be retained as part of the records of the Arrangement.

68(2) [List of Creditors attending] The chairman shall also cause to be made and kept a list of all the Creditors who attended the meeting either in person or by proxy and the amount of their claims for voting purposes.

68(3) [Record of resolutions] The minutes of the meeting shall include a record of the resolutions which were taken at the meeting and the decision on each one.

68(4) [List of creditors to be circulated] The list of Creditors referred to in Subparagraph (2) shall be sent with the chairman's report to Creditors, the Debtor and the Court.

69 Postal resolutions

69(1) [Application of procedure] The following procedure may be utilised by the Supervisor, if he thinks fit, for the purposes of ascertaining the wishes of Creditors on any matter concerning the Arrangement other than the removal of the Supervisor.

69(2) [Notice of proposed resolution] The Supervisor may send to the Debtor and every Creditor whose address is known to him or identified in the Proposal a notice containing a copy of any proposed resolution on which a decision is sought, which shall be set out in a such a way that agreement with or dissent from each separate resolution may be indicated by the recipient on the copy so sent.

69(3) [Contents of notice] The notice must specify a date ("the Last Date for Voting"), not less that 21 days after the date of sending thereof, by which Creditors must lodge their votes with the Supervisor and those who have not already lodged claims must do so, in order to be entitled to vote.

69(4) [Creditors requiring meeting] Creditors with one-quarter in value of the total amount of Debts subject to the Arrangement may, within 14 days from the date upon which the Supervisor sent out the resolution, request the Supervisor in writing to summon a meeting of Creditors to consider the matters raised by the resolution and, if they so request, the Supervisor shall call a meeting of Creditors for that purpose.

69(5) [Deemed passing of resolution] In the absence such a request, the resolution is deemed to have been carried at a duly convened meeting of Creditors, if, of the written votes received by the Supervisor by the end of the Last Date for Voting, a sufficient majority of Creditors as defined in Paragraph 61 entitled to vote on the resolution have indicated their consent to the resolution in writing.

69(6) [Application of voting rights and majorities] The provisions of Paragraphs 63(entitlement to vote), 64 (admission and rejection of claims) and 65 (majorities required to pass resolutions) shall apply to postal votes as they do to votes at meetings of Creditors.

69(7) [Copy of resolutions] A copy of every resolution taken under this Paragraph, together with copies of the votes of Creditors received by the Supervisor endorsed by the Supervisor with the date upon which the vote was received by him, shall be kept with the records of the Arrangement.

PART XI: PROVISIONS FOLLOWING BREACH OF THE ARRANGEMENT

70 Breach by the Debtor of the terms of the Arrangement

70 The Debtor shall be regarded as in breach of the Arrangement if:

(a) he fails to comply with any of his obligations under the Arrangement;

(b) information which was false or misleading in any material particular or contains any material omissions:

- (i) was contained in any statement of affairs or other document supplied by the Debtor under Part VIII under the Act to any person, or
- (ii) was otherwise made available by the Debtor to his Creditors at or in connection with any meeting of Creditors held, or any postal resolution taken, in connection with the Arrangement, or

(c) the Debtor fails to do all such things as may for the purposes of the Arrangement have been reasonably required of him by the Supervisor.

71 Procedure following breach

71(1) [Notice of Breach] If, at any time, it appears to the Supervisor that the Debtor is in breach of the Arrangement, then, unless such breach is remedied forthwith or the Supervisor has already presented a petition for the Debtor's bankruptcy, he shall as soon as practicable issue to the Debtor a notice ("Notice of Breach") identifying the breach and requiring the Debtor within one month of sending the notice:

(a) to remedy the breach if it is capable of being remedied, and, if he thinks fit

(b) to give a full explanation of the breach.

71(2) [Remedy of breach] If, within the one month period referred to in Subparagraph (1), or such longer period not exceeding a further one month as the Supervisor shall reasonably allow, the Debtor:

(a) remedies his breach of the Arrangement;

(b) if so required in the Notice of Breach, provides a full explanation of the breach, and

(c) pays to the Supervisor such sum (if any) as the Supervisor may reasonably require to compensate the Creditors for any reduction in Dividend caused by the Debtor's breach, no further action shall be taken against the Debtor save that the Supervisor shall report the breach to the Creditors when he next sends his comments to Creditors on the progress and efficacy of the Arrangement under Rule 5.31A (Supervisor's accounts and reports), or on the next convenient occasion, if earlier.

71(3) [Certificate of Termination/bankruptcy petition] If the Debtor has not done those things specified in Sub-paragraph (2) by the time specified or allowed, the Supervisor shall as soon as practicable convene a meeting of Creditors to resolve whether or not to do the following things:

(i) issue a certificate ("Certificate of Termination") terminating the Arrangement by reason of the Debtor's breach;

(ii) present a petition for the Debtor's bankruptcy;

(iii) vary the terms of the arrangement under Paragraph 81;

(iv) take no action.

71(4) [Supervisor's duty] If the Creditors resolve to issue a Certificate of Termination and/or to present a bankruptcy petition against the Debtor, the Supervisor shall do so as soon as practicable.

71(5) [Copies of Certificate of Termination] A copy of any Certificate of Termination issued by the Supervisor shall be sent to the Debtor and Creditors together with the notice under Paragraph 11.

72 Retention of funds by Supervisor

72 The Supervisor shall, at all times during the course of the Arrangement, retain sufficient of the funds coming into his hands as represents his best estimate of the costs of petitioning for the Debtor's bankruptcy should the Creditors so direct under the previous Paragraph hereof. Such costs shall be provided for in priority to any other costs of the Arrangement.

PART XII: CONDITIONS WHERE TAX AUTHORITIES ARE CREDITORS

73 Claims by HM Revenue and Customs

73(1) HM Revenue and Customs' provisional claim in the Arrangement will include (i) any tax credit overpayment and (ii) Self-Assessment payments on account due for the tax year which the Arrangement is approved, PAYE/SC/NIC deductions due to the date of approval, plus any other earlier unpaid liabilities

73(2) HM Revenue and Customs' final claim in the Arrangement will additionally include the Self-Assessment balancing adjustment for the tax year in which the Arrangement is approved due with the Self-Assessment Return on the 31 January of the following year.

74 Income commencing after approval

74 The debtor shall be responsible for payment of Self-Assessment/NIC on any source of income that commences after the date of approval of the Arrangement.

75 Post approval statutory returns and payments

75 All statutory returns and payments due to HM Revenue and Customs post approval shall be provided on or before the date they fall due.

76 Overdue accounts and returns

76 All statutory accounts and returns overdue at the date of the creditors' meeting must be provided to HM Revenue and Customs within 3 months of the approval date together with any other information or explanations required.

77 Funds to be paid to Supervisor

77 The debtor's monthly provision for income tax/NIC as it appears in the income and expenditure statement shall, from the date of approval of the Arrangement to the 5 April ending the tax year in which the Arrangement is approved, be paid to the Supervisor for the benefit of the arrangement.

78 Restriction on payment of dividend

78 No non preferential Dividend will be made until (i) the HM Revenue and Customs Self-Assessment return for the tax year in which the Arrangement is approved (ii) a VAT or other levy or duty return due to HM Revenue and Customs to the date of the meeting, has been filed or (iii) an HM Revenue and Customs Determination and/or a Customs assessment has been made and the Supervisor has admitted their final claims.

79 Set-off of repayments

79 During the currency of the Arrangement, any tax/excise/VAT or other repayments that become due to the Debtor by HM Revenue and Customs for periods for which claims may arise under the Arrangement, shall be offset against either department's claims in the Arrangement. Any remaining surplus shall be similarly applied to the claims of other government departments before being offered to the Supervisor for the benefit of the Arrangement. Any repayments for any later periods shall be offset against any post approval debts due to HM Revenue and Customs. Any remaining surplus will then be treated as a windfall and offered to the Supervisor for the benefit of the Arrangement.

PART XIII: MISCELLANEOUS PROVISIONS

80 Third Party obligations

80(1) [Application of Paragraph] This Paragraph applies where the Proposal includes any obligation on the part of a person other than the Supervisor or Debtor to pay moneys, transfer assets or do any other thing.

80(2) [Evidence of agreement] The third party shall sign the Proposal or such other document evidencing his agreement to be bound by the obligation as the Supervisor shall reasonably require.

80(3) [Enforcement of obligation] The obligations of the third party shall be enforceable by the Supervisor, or by the Debtor at the direction of the Supervisor.

80(4) [Failure a default of arrangement] The failure by the third party to carry out the obligation when due shall constitute a breach of the arrangement.

81 Variation of the Arrangement

81(1) [Variation with Creditors' approval] The provisions of this Arrangement may be amended with the approval of a meeting of Creditors.

81(2) [Consent of Debtor/third party to variation required] No variation of the terms of the Arrangement shall be of any effect unless made with the consent of the Debtor and any third party affected thereby.

81(3) [Saving for certain rights] No variation which restricts the following rights shall be of effect:

(a) the right of any Secured Creditor to enforce his Security, except with the Secured Creditor's consent;

(b) the right of any Creditor to present a bankruptcy petition under section 264(1)(c) of the Act for default in connection with Arrangement;

(c) the right of a Preferential Creditor to be paid in priority to other Creditors, except with that Creditor's consent;

(d) the right of a Preferential Creditor to be paid pro rata with other Preferential Creditors, except with that Creditor's consent.

81(4) [Unfair prejudice and material irregularity] No variation shall be of effect if it unfairly prejudices the rights of any Creditor or if there has been any material irregularity in the operation of the provisions of this Paragraph.

81(5) [Restriction on variation] No variation shall be of effect if it causes the Arrangement to cease to be a voluntary arrangement within Part VIII of the Act.

82 Tax liabilities arising on realisations

82(1) [Tax to be paid out of proceeds] Taxation liabilities of the Debtor arising on the sale or other realisation of any asset subject to the Arrangement shall, in so far as those proceeds are sufficient, be discharged out of the sale proceeds of the asset in question.

83 Invalidity and/or illegality

83 If any provision or part of the Arrangement is found to be contrary to the Act or Rules, illegal, invalid or contrary to public policy, that will not affect the validity of the remainder of the Arrangement and the provision or part of the Arrangement in question shall be construed accordingly.

VERSION 3
JANUARY 2013

INDEX

References are to paragraph numbers.